RELIGION IN
AMERICAN HISTORY

RELIGION IN
AMERICAN HISTORY
A Reader

JON BUTLER AND HARRY S. STOUT

New York   Oxford
OXFORD UNIVERSITY PRESS
1998

Oxford University Press

Oxford   New York
Athens   Auckland   Bangkok   Bombay   Buenos Aires
Calcutta   Cape Town   Dar es Salaam   Delhi   Florence   Hong Kong
Istanbul   Karachi   Kuala Lumpur   Madras   Madrid   Melbourne
Mexico City   Nairobi   Paris   Singapore   Taipei   Tokyo   Toronto   Warsaw

and associated companies in
Berlin   Ibadan

Copyright © 1998 by Oxford University Press, Inc.

Published by Oxford University Press, Inc.
198 Madison Avenue, New York, New York 10016

Oxford is a registered trademark of Oxford University Press

Library of Congress Cataloging-in-Publication Data
Religion in American History : a reader / [edited by] Jon Butler and Harry S. Stout.
p.   cm.
Includes index
ISBN 0–19–509776–9
1. United States—Religion—History.   I. Butler, Jon, 1940–
II. Stout, Harry S.
BL2525.A535   1997   96–39446
200'.973—DC21   CIP

3 5 7 9 8 6 4 2

Printed in the United States of America
on acid-free paper

Contents

Contents

Contents

RELIGION IN
AMERICAN HISTORY

INTRODUCTION

One of the more interesting commentaries on the age in which we live is that no field of American history has enjoyed a greater renaissance over the past three decades than religion. From a cottage industry that was once limited to seminaries and denominational colleges, the field has grown exponentially, and now major books and articles are emerging from history departments and religious studies departments located in major research universities. Ambitious doctoral programs are turning out new scholars at a prodigious rate, and major university presses have inaugurated series devoted exclusively to the study of religion in American life and history.

As editors, we have prepared this Reader with this efflorescence of religious history-writing in mind. Having participated in this renaissance over the past three decades, our concern is to introduce the themes and methods of recent scholarship. Even more important, we are concerned to introduce the sheer excitement and satisfaction of exploring religion as a means of better understanding our times. We want readers to know something about the substance of religious history, but also about how historians do their work and conduct their debates. What is a primary source? How is it that reasonable scholars can come up with vastly different interpretations of the same event? These and many other related questions are the burden of the present volume.

As the numbers of religious volumes have grown, so have the definitions and places where religion is discovered. The study of "religion" in the traditional sense of the word, as the religion of the major denominations and their major intellectual spokespersons, continues to appear. But alongside this scholarship are substantial studies of "religious outsiders" who were generally ignored (or ridiculed) in the older "mainline" denominational histories. Even more important, religion is turning up in many studies of "secular" life. Increasingly, studies of American political behavior, economic acquisitiveness, women and the family, racism, or social reform are all discovering that religion was a major "independent variable" explaining differences and rationales for behavior. Nowhere has this become more apparent than in the explosion of books and articles that trace virtually all of the major events and movements throughout American history—good *and* bad—to "evangelicalism."

In selecting the readings for this volume we are particularly sensitive to the most recent scholarship in all periods of American religious history from colonial origins through the twentieth century. The coverage is not—cannot be—comprehensive. But it illustrates the diversity and eclecticism that have come to characterize the best in contemporary scholarship on religion in American history.

American religious history, like all history, is the record of change over time. In thinking about both the labor of history and this Reader, it is convenient to distinguish two basic categories: history and historiography. "History," the inert record *of* the past, is typically recovered through documents professional historians call "primary sources." Primary sources are the "stuff" of which all history is made. These include, but are not limited to, public and private writings recorded by participant–subjects at the time, oral interviews of more recent subjects, artifacts and objects that constitute the "material culture" of a given time period or event, official records of organizations, and "vital records" of large populations. From these various primary sources, historians build their analyses and narratives. Historiography, the writing *about* the past, is sometimes called a "secondary" source. It represents the books and articles written by historians in consultation with their primary sources and with one another in the professional guild. Every time period and event, of course, has its own history. And almost every time period and event in American history has its own historiography, or body of literature that represents the interpretations historians have collectively made over the ages. Thus, for example, we can talk about the history of religious revivals in America, or we can talk about the historiography of revivalism, that is, the way that historians have described this revivalism. In practice the two go together as cause and effect of one another. Take away one and to all intents and purposes the other ceases to be real.

It is this symbiotic relation of history and historiography that we hope to reproduce in this Reader. In each chronological period we include documents illustrative of religious experience in that era. In no sense are these primary sources "inclusive" or "representative" of all American religious history; in fact they are a minuscule drop in the documentary bucket that constitutes American religious history. But they illustrate the actual evidence that historians encounter in their research. The number of primary sources is intentionally small to encourage students to study them intensively, and all of them deliberately center on a crucial topic: the role religion can or should play in shaping American society, from eighteenth-century Maryland to late twentieth-century politics.

It is not enough simply to read these primary sources from a distant past as one reads a novel. One must work hard to read them through the eyes of imagination. Every word, every image, every paragraph contains clues that the attentive historian picks up in telling his or her story. In reading the selected primary sources, the reader is encouraged to enter the world from which they originated. What was it like to be a colonial woman speaking publicly? a slave preacher? an abolitionist? What clues can *you* discover in the language, emotion, or rhetorical strategy of the primary text? What book or article would *you* write using this source as your foundation? In asking questions like these, the student becomes his or her own historian.

Besides primary sources, each chronological section includes a broad sampling of secondary writings produced by American religious historians. Some of these are "classics" written by professional historians twenty, thirty, or forty years ago. Even more are recent histories that represent new subjects and new modes of analysis. By juxtaposing the classical and recent, students will readily see how the field has changed. A great historiographical transition has occurred over the past generation—the transition from the "intellectual history" of major philosophers and theologians and a history of "public events" in churches and denominations that dominated early scholarship, to the "social history" of "ordinary people" that characterizes recent historiography. Neither of these traditions is "right" or "wrong," rather, they complement each other; when they are taken together, they greatly enrich and deepen our understanding of religion in American life.

Differences in subject matter and subjects are not the only differences registered in this Reader. Insofar as historiography is about interpretation it is about differences in interpretation. Every scholar brings his or her own preoccupations and presuppositions to their work, investing the field with vibrant diversity and debate. Insofar as possible, we have tried to group selected readings around issues of historiographical debate. The editors have even included their own conflicting interpretations as a case in point. Through comparing these paired essays, readers will see that scholars can and do differ even as they remain part of a common enterprise. Readers of these selections will also differ in their assessments, and through talking and debating with one another gain a clearer understanding of what it means to be a historian.

Above everything else, we hope these selections will awaken students to the importance of religion in American society. We have tried to give voice to the largest possible range of participants: women as well as men; African Americans as well as European Americans; "ordinary people" as well as more "elite" public figures. One can praise these participants or religion generally for social achievements, or blame them for social ills, or, more accurately, probably do both. But in all cases one emerges from the literature with a renewed sense of how intimately this continent has been visited by the gods, from Native Americans, to enchained slaves, to immigrant newcomers. Collectively, Americans are peoples of faith who find in their spirituality standards for judgment and achievement every bit as binding as language, ideology, or geographic region. In exploring these selections we hope to launch students on a voyage of discovery into the rich and exciting terrain of American religious history.

The readings are divided into three major sections representing the colonial era, the nineteenth century, and the twentieth century. The editors have provided a general introduction to each section, together with a more focused preface that is designed to foster reflection, debate, and classroom discussion. Insofar as possible the texts have been unedited and include all the footnotes, which reveal much about each author's sources and methods.

THE COLONIAL PERIOD

Stereotypically, the colonial period seems most synonymous with the prosperity of American religion. It is the setting of the Puritans in the seventeenth century and the rise of religious pluralism and evangelical revivalism in the eighteenth century.

In fact, the reality of religion in the colonial era was much more complex and, inevitably, much more interesting. For American Indians, the European arrival challenged not only Native Americans' religious and political identity but their spiritual understanding of nature and the world. Puritans soon discovered that their "errand," seemingly so straightforward, produced antagonisms with others and divisions among themselves. Quakers demonstrated both the complexity of the English religious heritage and the opportunities and difficulties that would stem from the colony's unusual ethnic and religious pluralism. Slavery demanded real moral choices in managing human interrelationships, with fateful consequences for the captured, their owners, and society. And revivalism thrust up potential implications for culture and even politics over which historians still argue.

By the time of the American Revolution, then, the American religious experience had assumed a complexity and richness the Puritans never imagined and helped create only in part.

CHAPTER

1

The Spiritual Crisis of
European Colonization

This essay by Calvin Martin, always controversial, argues that the ecological crisis experienced by Native Americans precipitated by European settlement in North America took root in profoundly different attitudes among Native Americans and Europeans toward the animal and natural worlds. What was the relationship between faith and nature in Algonquian religion? How did European Christianity challenge this traditional faith? Would Native Americans have accepted the division between "religious" and "secular" that we moderns seem to accept? And finally, in a secular vein, to what extent do the seeds of the modern environmental crisis lie in the seventeenth century?

Additional Reading: The past two decades have produced an unusual number of uncommonly good studies of Native American religion and culture in the colonial era. Peter H. Wood, "The Changing Population of the Colonial South: An Overview by Race and Region, 1685–1790," in *Powhatan's Mantle: Indians in the Colonial Southeast,* edited by Peter H. Wood, Gregory A. Waselkov, and M. Thomas Hatley (Lincoln, 1989), 35–103, outlines population change in the colonial South that had immense significance for the fate of Native American religious systems. James H. Merrell, *The Indians' New World: Catawbas and Their Neighbors from European Contact through the Era of Removal* (Chapel Hill, 1989) describes a remarkable story of the Catawbas and their creation of a new culture and new religious sensibilities in the face of European conquest. Gregory E. Dowd, *A Spirited Resistance: The North American Indian Struggle for Unity, 1745–1815* (Baltimore, 1992) and Joel W. Martin, *Sacred Revolt: The Muskogees' Struggle for a New World* (Boston, 1991) explain the differing results of two attempts to use religion to preserve traditional culture in the late eighteenth century.

Calvin Martin[1]

The European Impact on the Culture of a Northeastern Algonquian Tribe: An Ecological Interpretation

As the drive for furs, known prosaically as the fur trade, expanded and became more intense in seventeenth-century Canada, complaints of beaver extermination became more frequent and alarming. By 1635, for example, the Huron had reduced their stock of beaver to the point where the Jesuit Father Paul Le Jeune could declare that they had none.[2] In 1684 Baron Lahontan recorded a speech made before the French governor-general by an Iroquois spokesman, who explained that his people had made war on the Illinois and Miami because these Algonquians had trespassed on Iroquois territory and overkilled their beaver, "and contrary to the Custom of all the Savages, have carried off whole Stocks, both Male and Female."[3] This exploitation of beaver and other furbearers seems to have been most intense in the vicinity of major trading posts and among the native tribes most affected by the trade (the Montagnais, Huron, League Iroquois, Micmac, and others[4]), while those tribes which remained beyond European influence and the trade, such as the Bersimis of northeastern Quebec, enjoyed an abundance of beaver in their territories.[5]

Even before the establishment of trading posts, the Micmac of the extreme eastern tip of Canada were engaged in lively trade with European fishermen. Thus areas that were important in the fishing industry, such as Prince Edward Island, the Gaspé Peninsula, and Cape Breton Island, were cleaned out of moose and other furbearers by the mid-seventeenth century.[6] Reviewing this grim situation, Nicolas Denys observed that game was less abundant in his time than formerly; as for the beaver, "few in a house are saved; they [the Micmac] would take all. The disposition of the Indians is not to spare the little ones any more than the big ones. They killed all of each kind of animal that there was when they could capture it."[7]

In short, the game which by all accounts had been so plentiful was now being systematically overkilled by the Indians themselves. A traditional explanation for this ecological catastrophe is neatly summarized by Peter Farb, who conceives of it in mechanistic terms: "If the Northern Athabaskan and Northern Algonkian Indians husbanded the land and its wildlife in primeval times, it was only because they lacked both the technology to kill very many animals and the market for so many furs. But once white traders entered the picture, supplying the Indians with efficient guns and an apparently limitless market for furs beyond the seas, the Indians went on an orgy of destruction." The Indian, in other words, was "economically seduced" to exploit the wildlife requisite to the fur trade.[8]

First published in the *William and Mary Quarterly* 31 (1974), 3–26; reprinted by permission of the author.

Such a cavalier dismissal of northeastern Algonquian culture, especially its spiritual component, renders this explanation superficial and inadequate. One can argue that economic determinism was crucial to the course of Algonquian cultural development (including religious perception) over a long period of time. Yet from this perspective European contact was but a moment in the cultural history of the Indians, and it is difficult to imagine that ideals and a life-style that had taken centuries to evolve would have been so easily and quickly discarded merely for the sake of improved technological convenience. As we shall see, the entire Indian-land relationship was suffused with religious considerations which profoundly influenced the economic (subsistence) activities and beliefs of these people. The subsistence cycle was regulated by centuries of spiritual tradition which, if it had been in a healthy state, would have countered the revolutionizing impact of European influence. Tradition would doubtless have succumbed eventually, but why did the end come so soon? Why did the traditional safeguards of the northeastern Algonquian economic system offer such weak resistance to its replacement by the exploitive, European-induced regime?

When the problem is posed in these more comprehensive terms, the usual economic explanation seems misdirected, for which reason the present article will seek to offer an alternative interpretation. The methodology of cultural ecology will be brought to bear on the protohistoric and early contact phases of Micmac cultural history in order to examine the Indian-land relationship under aboriginal and postcontact conditions and to probe for an explanation to the problem of wildlife overkill.[9]

Cultural ecology seeks to explain the interaction of environment and culture, taking the ecosystem and the local human population as the basic units of analysis.[10] An ecosystem is a discrete community of plants and animals, together with the nonliving environment, occupying a certain space and time, having a flow-through of energy and raw materials in its operation, and composed of subsystems.[11] For convenience of analysis, an ecosystem can be separated into its physical and biological components, although one should bear in mind that in nature the two are completely intermeshed in complex interactions. And from the standpoint of cultural ecology, there is a third component: the metaphysical or spiritual.

The ecosystem model of plant and animal ecologists is somewaht strained when applied to a human population, although, as Roy A. Rappaport has demonstrated in his *Pigs for the Ancestors,* the attempt can be very useful.[12] The difficulties encountered include the assignment of definite territorial limits to the area under consideration (resulting in a fairly arbitrary delimitation of an ecosystem), the quantification of the system's energy budget and the carrying capacity of the land, and the identification of subsystem interrelations. Assigning values to variables becomes, in many instances, quite impossible.

The transposition of the ecosystem approach from cultural anthropology to historical inquiry complicates these problems even further, for the relationships between a human population and its environment are seldom amenable to rigorous quantitative analysis using historical documents as sources. Yet this is certainly not always so. In the case of the fur trade, for example, one may in fact be able to measure some of its effects on the environment from merchants' records—showing numbers of pelts obtained from a region over a certain time period—and also from lists of goods given to the Indians at trading posts and by treaties. Even when available, such records are too incomplete to satisfy the rigorous demands of the ecologist, but to say that they are of limited value is not to say that they are useless.

Few historians have used the ecological model in their work.[13] Recognizing the need for the environmental perspective in historiography, Wilbur R. Jacobs recently observed that "those who hope to write about such significant historical events [as the despoiling of the American west] . . . will need a sort of knowledge not ordinarily possessed by historians. To study the impact of the fur trade upon America and her native people, for instance, there must be more than a beginning acquaintance with ethnology, plant and animal ecology, paleoecology, and indeed much of the physical sciences."[14]

In the case of the northeastern Algonquian, and the Micmac in particular, the fur trade was but one factor—albeit an important one—in the process of acculturation. Long before they felt the lure of European technology, these littoral Indians must have been infected with Old World diseases carried by European fishermen, with catastrophic effects. Later, the Christian missionaries exerted a disintegrative influence on the Indians' view of and relation to their environment. All three of these factors—disease, Christianity, and technology—which may be labeled "trigger" factors, must be assessed in terms of their impact on the Indians' ecosystem.[15]

Among the first North American Indians to be encountered by Europeans were the Micmacs who occupied present-day Nova Scotia, northern New Brunswick and the Gaspé Peninsula, Prince Edward Island, and Cape Breton Island. According to the Sieur de Dièreville, they also lived along the lower St. John River with the Malecites, who outnumbered them.[16] For our present purposes, the Micmac territory will be considered an ecosystem, and the Micmac occupying it will be regarded as a local population. These designations are not entirely arbitrary, for the Micmac occupied and exploited the area in a systematic way; they had a certain psychological unity or similarity in their ideas about the cosmos; they spoke a language distinct from those of their neighbors; and they generally married within their own population. There were, as might be expected, many external factors impinging on the ecosystem which should also be evaluated, although space permits them only to be mentioned here. Some of these "supralocal" relations involved trade and hostilities with other tribes; the exchange of genetic material and personnel with neighboring tribes through intermarriage and adoption; the exchange of folklore and customs; and the movements of such migratory game as moose and woodland caribou. The Micmac ecosystem thus participated in a regional system, and the Micmac population was part of a regional population.[17]

The hunting, gathering, and fishing Micmac who lived within this Acadian forest, especially along its rivers and by the sea, were omnivores (so to speak) in the trophic system of the community. At the first trophic level, the plants eaten were wild potato tubers, wild fruits and berries, acorns and nuts, and the like.

Trees and shrubs provided a wealth of materials used in the fashioning of tools, utensils, and other equipment.[18] At the time of contact, none of the Indians living north of the Saco River cultivated food crops. Although legend credits the Micmac with having grown maize and tobacco "for the space of several years,"[19] these cultigens, as well as beans, pumpkins, and wampum (which they greatly prized), were obtained from the New England Algonquians of the Saco River area (Abnakis) and perhaps from other tribes to the south.[20]

Herbivores and carnivores occupy the second and third trophic levels respectively, with top carnivores in the fourth level. The Micmac hunter tapped all three levels in his seasonal hunting and fishing activities, and these sources of food were "to them like fixed rations assigned to every moon."[21] In January, seals were hunted when they bred on islands off the coast; the fat was reduced to oil for food and body grease, and the women made clothing from the fur.[22] The principal hunting season lasted from February till mid-March, since there were enough marine resources, especially fish and mollusks, available during the other three seasons to satisfy most of the Micmacs' dietary needs. For a month and a half, then, the Indians withdrew from the seashore to the banks of rivers and lakes and into the woods to hunt the caribou, moose, black bear, and small furbearers. At no other time of the year were they so dependent on the caprice of the weather: a feast was as likely as a famine. A heavy rain could ruin the beaver and caribou hunt, and a deep, crustless snow would doom the moose hunt.[23]

Since beaver were easier to hunt on the ice than in the water, and since their fur was better during the winter, this was the chief season for taking them.[24] Hunters would work in teams or groups, demolishing the lodge or cutting the dam with stone axes. Dogs were sometimes used to track the beaver which took refuge in air pockets along the edge of the pond, or the beaver might be harpooned at air holes. In the summer hunt, beaver were shot with the bow or trapped in deadfalls using poplar as bait, but the commonest way to take them was to cut the dam in the middle and drain the pond, killing the animals with bows and spears.[25]

Next to fish, moose was the most important item in the Micmac diet, and it was their staple during the winter months when these large mammals were hunted with dogs on the hard-crusted snow. In the summer and spring, moose were tracked, stalked, and shot with the bow; in the fall, during the rutting season, the bull was enticed by a clever imitation of the sound of a female urinating. Another technique was to ensnare the animal with a noose.[26]

Moose was the Micmacs' favorite meat. The entrails, which were considered a great delicacy, and the "most delicious fat" were carried by the triumphant hunter to the campsite, and the women were sent after the carcass. The mistress of the wigwam decided what was to be done with each portion of the body, every part of which was used. Grease was boiled out of the bones and either drunk pure (with "much gusto") or stored as loaves of moose-butter;[27] the leg and thigh bones were crushed and the marrow eaten; the hides were used for robes, leggings, moccasins, and tent coverings;[28] tools, ornaments, and game pieces were made from antlers, teeth, and toe bones, respectively.[29] According to contemporary French observers, the Micmac usually consumed the moose meat immediately, without storing any, although the fact that some of the meat was preserved rather effectively by smoking it on racks, so that it would even last the year, demonstrates that Micmac existence was not as hand-to-mouth as is commonly believed of the northeastern Algonquian.[30] Black bear were also taken during the season from February till mid-March, but such hunting was merely coincidental. If a hunter stumbled upon a hibernating bear, he could count himself lucky.[31]

As the lean months of winter passed into the abundance of spring, the fish began to spawn, swimming up rivers and streams, in such numbers that "everything swarms with them."[32] In mid-March came the smelt, and at the end of April the herring. Soon there were sturgeon and salmon, and numerous waterfowl made nests out on the islands—which meant there were eggs to be gathered. Mute evidence from seashore middens and early written testimony reveal that these Indians also relied heavily on various mollusks, which they harvested in great quantity.[33] Fish was a staple for the Micmac, who knew the spawning habits of each type of fish and where it was to be found. Weirs were erected across streams to trap the fish on their way downstream on a falling tide, while larger fish, such as sturgeon and salmon, might be speared or trapped.[34]

The salmon run marked the beginning of summer, when the wild geese shed their plumage. Most wildfowl were hunted at their island rookeries; waterfowl were often hunted by canoe and struck down as they took to flight; others, such as the Canadian geese which grazed in the meadows, were shot with the bow.[35]

In autumn, when the waterfowl migrated southward, the eels spawned up the many small rivers along the coast. From mid-September to October the Micmac left the ocean and followed the eels, "of which they lay in a supply; they are good and fat." Caribou and beaver were hunted during October and November, and with December came the "tom cod" (which were said to have spawned under the ice) and turtles bearing their young.[36] In January the subsistence cycle began again with the seal hunt.

As he surveyed the seasonal cycle of these Indians, Father Pierre Biard was impressed by nature's bounty and Micmac resourcefulness: "These then, but in a still greater number, are the revenues and incomes of our Savages; such, their table and living, all prepared and assigned, everything to its proper place and quarter."[37] Although we have omitted mention of many other types of forest, marine, and aquatic life which were also exploited by the Micmac, those listed above were certainly the most significant in the Micmacs' food quest and ecosystem.[38]

Frank G. Speck, perhaps the foremost student of northeastern Algonquian culture, has emphasized that hunting to the Micmacs was not a "war upon the animals, not a slaughter for food or profit."[39] Denys's observations confirm Speck's point: "Their greatest task was to feed well and to go a hunting. They did not lack animals, which they killed only in proportion as they had need of them."[40] From this, and the above description of their effective hunting techniques, it would appear that the Micmac were not limited by their hunting technology in the taking of game. As Denys pointed out, "the hunting by the Indians in old times was easy for them. . . . When they were tired of eating one sort, they killed some of another. If they did not wish longer to eat meat, they caught some fish. They never made an accumulation of skins of Moose, Beaver, Otter, or others, but only so far as they needed them for personal use. They left the remainder [of the carcass] where the animals had been killed, not taking the trouble to bring them to their camps."[41] Need, not technology, was the ruling factor, and need was determined by the great primal necessities of life and regulated by spiritual considerations. Hunting, as Speck remarks, was "a *holy occupation*";[42] it was conducted and controlled by spiritual rules.

The bond which united these physical and biological components of the Micmac ecosystem, and indeed gave them definition and comprehensibility, was the world view of the Indian. The foregoing discussion has dealt mainly with the empirical, objective, physical ("operational") environmental model of the observer; what it lacks is the "cognized" model of the Micmac.[43]

Anthropologists regard the pre-Columbian North American Indian as a sensitive member of his environment, who merged sympathetically with its living and nonliving components.[44] The Indian's world was filled with superhuman and magical powers which controlled man's destiny and nature's course of events.[45] Murray Wax explains:

> To those who inhabit it, the magical world is a "society," not a "mechanism," that is, it is composed of "beings" rather than "objects." Whether human or nonhuman, these beings are associated with and related to one another socially and sociably, that is, in the same ways as human beings to one another. These patterns of association and relationship may be structured in terms of kinship, empathy, sympathy, reciprocity, sexuality, dependency, or any other of the ways that human beings interact with and affect or afflict one another. Plants, animals, rocks, and stars are thus seen not as "objects" governed by laws of nature, but as "fellows" with whom the individual or band may have a more or less advantageous relationship.[46]

For the Micmac, together with all the other eastern subarctic Algonquians, the power of these mysterious forces was apprehended as "manitou"—translated "magic power"—much in the same way that we might use the slang word "vibrations" to register the emotional feelings emanating (so we say) from an object, person, or situation.[47]

The world of the Micmac was thus filled with superhuman forces and beings (such as dwarfs, giants, and magicians), and animals that could talk to man and had spirits akin to his own, and the magic of mystical and medicinal herbs—a world where even inanimate objects possessed spirits.[48] Micmac subsistence activities were inextricably bound up within this spiritual matrix, which, we are suggesting, acted as a kind of control mechanism on Micmac land-use, maintaining the environment within an optimum range of conditions.

In order to understand the role of the Micmac in the fur-trading enterprise of the colonial period, it is useful to investigate the role of the Micmac hunter in the spiritual world of precontact times. Hunting was governed by spiritual rules and considerations which were manifest to the early French observers in the form of seemingly innumerable taboos. These taboos connoted a sense of cautious reverence for a conscious fellow member of the same ecosystem who, in the view of the Indian, allowed itself to be taken for food and clothing. The Indian felt that "both he and his victim understood the roles which they played in the hunt; the animal was resigned to its fate."[49]

That such a resignation on the part of the game was not to be interpreted as an unlimited license to kill should be evident from an examination of some of the more prominent taboos. Beaver, for example, were greatly admired by the Micmac for their industry and "abounding genius"; for them, the beaver had "sense" and formed a "separate nation."[50] Hence there were various regulations associated with the disposal of their remains: trapped beaver were drawn in public and made into soup, extreme care being taken to prevent the soup from spilling into the fire; beaver bones were carefully preserved, never being given to the dogs—lest they lose their sense of smell for the animal—or thrown into the fire—lest misfortune come upon "all the nation"—or thrown into rivers—"because the Indians fear lest the spirit of the bones . . . would promptly carry the news to the other beavers, which would desert the country in order to escape the same misfortune." Likewise, menstruating women were forbidden to eat beaver, "for the Indians are convinced, they say, that the beaver, which has sense, would no longer allow itself to be taken by the Indians if it had been eaten by their unclean daughters." The fetus of the beaver, as well as that of the bear, moose, otter, and porcupine, was reserved for the old men, since it was believed that a youth who ate such food would experience intense foot pains while hunting.[51]

Taboos similarly governed the disposal of the remains of the moose—what few there were. The bones of a moose fawn (and of the marten) were never given to the dogs nor were they burned, "for they [the Micmac] would not be able any longer to capture any of these animals in hunting if the spirits of the martens and of the fawns of the moose were to inform their own kind of the bad treatment they had received among the Indians."[52] Fear of such reprisal also prohibited menstruating women from drinking out of the common kettles or bark dishes.[53] Such regulations imply cautious respect for the animal hunted. The moose not only provided food and clothing, but was firmly tied up with the Micmac spirit-world—as were the other game animals.

Bear ceremonialism was also practiced by the Micmac. Esteem for the bear is in fact common among boreal hunting peoples of northern Eurasia and North America, and has the following characteristics: the beast is typically hunted in the early spring, while still in hibernation. It is addressed, when either dead or alive, with honorific names; a conciliatory speech is made to the animal, either before or after killing it, by which the hunter apologizes for his act and perhaps explains why it is necessary; and the carcass is respectfully treated, those parts not used (especially the skull) being ceremonially disposed of and the flesh consumed in accordance with taboos. Such rituals are intended to propitiate the spiritual controller of the bears so that he will continue to furnish game to the hunter.[54] Among the Micmac the bear's heart was not eaten by young men lest they get out of breath while traveling and lose courage in danger. The bear carcass could be brought into the wigwam only through a special door made specifically for that purpose, either in the left or right side of the structure. This ritual was based on the Micmac belief that their women did not "deserve" to enter the wigwam through the same door as the animal. In fact, we are told that childless women actually left the wigwam at the approach of the body and did not return until it had been entirely consumed.[55] By means of such rituals the hunter satisfied the soul-spirit of the slain animal. Of the present-day Mistassini (Montagnais) hunter, Speck writes that "should he fail to observe these formalities an unfavorable reaction would also ensue with his own soul-spirit, his 'great man' . . . as it is called. In such a case the 'great man' would fail to advise him when and where he would find his game. Incidentally the hunter resorts to drinking bear's grease to nourish his 'great man.'"[56] Perhaps it was for a similar reason that the Micmac customarily forced newborn infants to swallow bear or seal oil before eating anything else.[57]

If taboo was associated with fishing, we have little record of it; the only explicit evidence is a prohibition against the roasting of eels, which, if violated, would prevent the Indians from catching others. From this and from the fact that the Restigouche division of the Micmac wore the figure of a salmon as a totem around their necks, we may surmise that fish, too, shared in the sacred and symbolic world of the Indian.[58]

Control over these supernatural forces and communication with them were the principal functions of the shaman, who served in Micmac society as an intermediary between the spirit realm and the physical. The lives and destinies of the natives were profoundly affected by the ability of the shaman to supplicate, cajole, and otherwise manipulate the magical beings and powers. The seventeenth-century French, who typically labeled the shamans (or *buowin*) frauds and jugglers in league with the devil, were repeatedly amazed at the respect accorded them by the natives.[59] By working himself into a dreamlike state, the shaman would invoke the manitou of his animal helper and so predict future events.[60] He also healed by means of conjuring. The Micmac availed themselves of a rather large pharmacopia of roots and herbs and other plant parts, but when these failed they would summon the healing arts of the most noted shaman in the district. The illness was often diagnosed by the *buowin* as a failure on the patient's part to perform a prescribed ritual; hence an offended supernatural power had visited the offender with sickness. At such times the shaman functioned as a psychotherapist, diagnosing the illness and symbolically (at least) removing its immediate cause from the patient's body.[61]

It is important to understand that an ecosystem is holocoenotic in nature: there are no "walls" between the components of the system, for "the ecosystem reacts as a whole."[62] Such was the case in the Micmac ecosystem of precontact times, where the spiritual served as a link connecting man with all the various subsystems of the environment. Largely through the mediation of the shaman, these spiritual obligations and restrictions acted as a kind of control device to maintain the ecosystem in a well-balanced condition.[63] Under these circumstances the exploitation of game for subsistence appears to have been regulated by the hunter's respect for the continued welfare of his prey—both living and dead—as is evident from the numerous taboos associated with the proper disposal of animal remains. Violation of taboo desecrated the remains of the slain animal and offended its soul-spirit. The offended spirit would then retaliate in either of several ways, depending on the nature of the broken taboo: it could render the guilty hunter's (or the entire band's) means of hunting ineffective, or it could encourage its living fellows to remove themselves from the vicinity. In both cases the end result was the same—the hunt was rendered unsuccessful—and in both it was mediated by the same power—the spirit of the slain animal. Either of these catastrophes could usually be reversed through the magical arts of the shaman. In the Micmac cosmology, the overkill of wildlife would have been resented by the animal kingdom as an act comparable to genocide, and would have been resisted by means of the sanctions outlined above. The threat of retaliation thus had the effect of placing an upper limit on the number of animals slain, while the practical result was the conservation of wildlife.

The injection of European civilization into this balanced system initiated a series of chain reactions which, within a little over a century, resulted in the replacement of the aboriginal ecosystem by another. From at least the beginning of the sixteenth century, and perhaps well before that date, fishing fleets from England, France, and Portugal visited the Grand Banks off Newfoundland every spring for the cod, and hunted whale and walrus in the Gulf of St. Lawrence.[64] Year after year, while other, more flamboyant men were advancing the geopolitical ambitions of their emerging dynastic states as they searched for precious minerals or a passage to the Orient, these unassuming fishermen visited Canada's east coast and made the first effective European contact with the Indians there. For the natives' furs they bartered knives, beads, brass kettles, assorted ship fittings, and the like,[65] thus initiating the subversion and replacement of Micmac material culture by European technology. Far more important, the fishermen unwittingly infected the Indians with European diseases, against which the natives had no immunity. Commenting on what may be called the microbial phase of European conquest, John Witthoft has written:

> All of the microscopic parasites of humans, which had been collected together from all parts of the known world into Europe, were brought to these [American] shores, and new diseases stalked faster than man could walk into the interior of the continent. Typhoid, diphtheria, colds, influenza, measles, chicken pox, whooping cough, tuberculosis, yellow fever, scarlet fever and other strep infections, gonorrhea, pox (syphilis), and smallpox were diseases that had never been in the New World before. They were new among populations which had no immunity to them. . . . Great epidemics and pandemics of these diseases are believed to have destroyed whole communities, depopulated whole regions, and vastly decreased the native population everywhere in the yet unexplored interior of the continent. The early pandemics are believed to have run their course prior to 1600 A.D.[66]

Disease did more than decimate the native population; it effectively prepared the way for subsequent phases of European contact by breaking native morale and, perhaps even more significantly, by cracking their spiritual edifice. It is reasonable to suggest that European disease rendered the Indian's (particularly the shaman's) ability to control and otherwise influence the supernatural realm dysfunctional—because his magic and other traditional cures were now ineffective—thereby causing the Indian to apostatize (in effect), which in turn subverted the "retaliation" principle of taboo and opened the way to a corruption of the Indian-land relationship under the influence of the fur trade.

Much of this microbial phase was of course protohistoric, although it continued well into and no doubt beyond the seventeenth century—the time period covered by the earliest French sources. Recognizing the limitations of tradition as it conveys historical fact, it may nevertheless be instructive to examine a myth concerning the Cross-bearing Micmac of the Miramichi River which, as recorded by Father Chrestien Le Clercq, seems to illustrate the demoralizing effect of disease. According to tradition, there was once a time when these Indians were gravely threatened by a severe sickness; as was their custom, they looked to the sun for help. In their extreme need a "beautiful" man, holding a cross, appeared before several of them in a dream. He instructed them to make similar crosses, for, as he told them, in this symbol lay their protecion. For a time thereafter these Indians, who believed in dreams "even to the extent of superstition," were very religious and devoted in their veneration of this symbol. Later, however, they apostatized:

> Since the Gaspesian [Micmac] nation of the Cross-bearers has been almost wholly destroyed, as much by the war which they have waged with the Iroquois as by the maladies which have infected this land, and which, in three or four visitations, have caused the deaths of a very great number, these Indians have gradually relapsed from this first devotion of their ancestors. So true is it, that even the holiest and most religious practices, by a certain fatality attending human affairs, suffer always much alteration if they are not animated and conserved by the same spirit which gave them birth. In brief, when I went into their country to commence my mission, I found some persons who had preserved only the shadow of the customs of their ancestors.[67]

Their rituals had failed to save these Indians when threatened by European diseases and intergroup hostilities; hence their old religious practices were abandoned, no doubt because of their ineffectiveness.

Several other observers also commented on the new diseases that afflicted the Micmac. In precontact times, declared Denys, "they were not subject to diseases, and knew nothing of fevers."[68] By about 1700, however, Dièreville noted that the Micmac population was in sharp decline.[69] The Indians themselves frequently complained to Father Biard and other Frenchmen that, since contact with the French, they had been dying off in great numbers. "For they assert that, before this association and intercourse [with the French], all their countries were very populous, and they tell how one by one the different coasts, according as they have begun to traffic with us, have been more reduced by disease." The Indians accused the French of trying to poison them or charged that the food supplied by the French was somehow adulterated. Whatever the reasons for the catastrophe, warned Biard, the Indians were very angry about it and "upon the point of breaking with us, and making war upon us."[70]

To the Jesuit fathers, the solution to this sorry state of affairs lay in the civilizing power of the Gospel. To Biard, his mission was clear:

> For, if our Souriquois [Micmac] are few, they may become numerous; if they are savages, it is to domesticate and civilize them that we have come here; if they are rude, that is no reason that we should be idle; if they have until now profited little, it is no wonder, for it would be too much to expect fruit from this grafting, and to demand reason and maturity from a child.
>
> In conclusion, we hope in time to make them susceptible of receiving the doctrines of the faith and of the christian and catholic religion, and later, to penetrate further into the regions beyond.[71]

The message was simple and straightforward: the black-robes would enlighten the Indians by ridiculing their animism and related taboos, discrediting their shamans, and urging them to accept the Christian gospel. But to their chagrin the Indians proved stubborn in their ancient ways, no matter how unsuited to changing circumstances.[72]

Since the advent of European diseases and the consequent disillusionment with native spiritual beliefs and customs, some Indians appear to have repudiated their traditional world view altogether, while others clung desperately to what had become a moribund body of ritual. We would suppose that the Christian message was more readily accepted by the former, while the latter group, which included the shamans and those too old to change, would have fought bitterly against the missionary teachings.[73] But they resisted in vain for, with time, old people died and shamans whose magic was less potent than that of the missionaries were discredited.[74] The missionary was successful only to the degree that his power exceeded that of the shaman. The nonliterate Indian, for example, was awed by the magic of handwriting as a means of communication.[75] Even more significant was the fact that Christianity was the religion of the white man, who, with his superior technology and greater success at manipulating life to his advantage, was believed to have recourse to a greater power (manitou) than did the Indian. Material goods, such as the trading articles offered the Indians by the French, were believed by the native to have a spirit within, in accord with their belief that all animate and inanimate objects housed such a spirit or power.[76] Furthermore, there were degrees of power in such objects, which were determined and calibrated in the Indian mind by the degree of functionalism associated with a particular object.[77] For example, the Micmac believed that there was a spirit of his canoe, of his snowshoes, of his bow, and so on. It was for this reason that a man's material goods were either buried with him or burned, so that their spirits would accompany his to the spirit world, where he would have need of them. Just as he had hunted game in this physical world, so his spirit would again hunt the game spirits with the spirits of his weapons in the land of the dead.[78] Denys described an incident which emphasized the fact that even European trading goods had spirits, when he related how the brass kettle was known to have lost its spirit (or died) when it no longer rang when tapped.[79] Thus Christianity, which to the Indians was the ritual harnessing all of this power, was a potent force among them. Nevertheless, the priests who worked among the Indians frequently complained of their relapsing into paganism, largely because the Micmac came to associate Christianity and civilization in general with their numerous misfortunes, together with the fact that they never clearly understood the Christian message anyway, but always saw it in terms of their own cosmology.[80]

As all religious systems reflect their cultural milieux, so did seventeenth-century Christianity. Polygamy was condemned by the French missionaries as immoral, the consultation of shamans was discouraged, the custom of interring material goods was criticized, eat-all feasts were denounced as gluttonous and shortsighted, and the Indians were disabused of many of their so-called superstitions (taboos).[81] The priests attacked the Micmac culture with a marvelous fervor and some success.[82] Although they could not have appreciated it, they were aided in this endeavor by an obsolescent system of taboo and spiritual awareness; Christianity merely delivered the coup de grace.

The result of this Christian onslaught on a decaying Micmac cosmology was, of course, the despiritualization of the material world. Commenting on the process of despiritualization, Denys (who was a spectator to this transformation in the mid-seventeenth century) remarked that it was accomplished with "much difficulty"; for some of the Indians it was achieved by religious means, while others were influenced by the French customs, but nearly all were affected "by the need for the things which come from us, the use of which has become to them an indispensable necessity. They have abandoned all their own utensils, whether because of the trouble they had as well to make as to use them, or because of the facility of obtaining from us, in exchange for skins which cost them almost nothing, the things which seemed to them invaluable, not so much for their novelty as for the convenience they derived therefrom."[83]

In the early years of the fur trade, before the establishment of permanent posts among the natives, trading was done with the coast-wise fishermen from May to early fall.[84] In return for skins of beaver, otter, marten, moose, and other furbearers, the Indians received a variety of fairly cheap commodities, principally tobacco, liquor, powder and shot (in later years), biscuit, peas, beans, flour, assorted clothing, wampum, kettles, and hunting tools.[85] The success of this trade in economic terms must be attributed to pressure exerted on a relatively simple society by a complex civilization and, perhaps even more importantly, by the tremendous pull of this simple social organization on the resources of Europe.[86] To the Micmac, who like other Indians measured the worth of a tool or object by the ease of its construction and use, the technology of Europe became indispensable. But as has already been shown, this was not simply an economic issue for the Indian; the Indian was more than just "economically seduced" by the European's trading goods.[87] One must also consider the metaphysical implications of Indian acceptance of the European material culture.

European technology of the sixteenth and seventeenth centuries was largely incompatible with the spiritual beliefs of the eastern woodland Indians, despite the observation made above that the Micmacs readily invested trading goods with spiritual power akin to that possessed by their own implements. As Denys pointed out, the trade goods which the Micmac so eagerly accepted were accompanied by Christian religious teachings and French custom, both of which gave definition to these alien objects. In accepting the European material culture, the natives were impelled to accept the European abstract culture, especially religion, and so, in effect, their own spiritual beliefs were subverted as they abandoned their implements for those of the white man. Native religion lost not only its practical effectiveness, in part owing to the replacement of the traditional magical and animistic view of nature by the exploitive European view, but it was no longer necessary as a source of definition and theoretical support for the new Europe-derived material culture. Western technology made more "sense" if it was accompanied by Western religion.

Under these circumstances in the early contact period, the Micmac's role within his ecosystem changed radically. No longer was he the sensitive fellow-member of a symbolic world; under pressure from disease, European trade, and Christianity, he had apostatized—he had repudiated his role within the ecosystem. Former attitudes were replaced by a kind of mongrel outlook which combined some native traditions and beliefs with a European rationale and motivation. Our concern here is less to document this transformation than to assess its impact on the Indian-land relationship. In these terms, then, what effect did the trade have on the Micmac ecosystem?

The most obvious change was the unrestrained slaughter of certain game. Lured by European commodities, equipped with European technology, urged by European traders,[88] deprived of a sense of responsibility and accountability for the land, and no longer inhibited by taboo, the Micmac began to overkill systematically those very wildlife which had now become so profitable and even indispensable to his new way of life. The pathos of this transformation of attitude and behavior is illustrated by an incident recorded by Le Clercq. The Indians, who still believed that the beaver had "sense" and formed a "separate nation," maintained that they "would cease to make war upon these animals if these would speak, howsoever little, in order that they might learn whether the Beavers are among their friends or their enemies."[89] Unfortunately for the beaver, they never communicated their friendliness. The natural world of the Indian was becoming inarticulate.

It is interesting to note that Dièreville, who observed the Micmac culture at the beginning of the eighteenth century, was the only witness to record the native superstition which compelled them to tear out the eyes of all slain animals. Somehow, perhaps by some sort of symbolic transference, the spirits of surviving animals of the same species were thereby blinded to the irreverent treatment accorded the victim; otherwise, through the mediation of the outraged spirits, the living would no longer have allowed themselves to be taken by the Indians.[90] The failure of the earlier writers to mention this particular superstition suggests that it was of fairly recent origin, a result of the overexploitation of game for the trade. To the Micmac mind, haunted by memories of a former time, the practice may have been intended to hide his guilt and insure his continued success.

Together with this depletion of wildlife went a reduction of dependency on the resources of the local ecosystem. The use of improved hunting equipment, such as fishing line and hooks, axes, knives, muskets, and iron-tipped arrows, spears, and harpoons,[91] exerted heavier pressure on the resources of the area, while the availability of French foodstuffs shifted the position of the Micmac in the trophic system, somewhat reducing his dependency on local food sources as it placed him partly outside of the system. To be sure, a decreasing native population relieved this pressure to a degree, but, according to evidence cited above, not enough to prevent the abuse of the land.

Other less obvious results of the fur trade were the increased incidence of feuding and the modification of the Micmac settlement patterns to meet the demands of the trade. Liquor, in particular brandy, was a favorite item of the trade—one for which the Indians "would go a long way."[92] Its effects were devastating. Both Jean Saint-Vallier (François Laval's successor as bishop of Quebec) and Biard blamed liquor as a cause for the increased death rate of the natives. Moreover, it was observed that drunkenness resulted in social disintegration as the Indians became debauched and violent among themselves, and, at times, spilled over into the French community which they would rob, ravage, and burn. Drunkenness also provided a legitimate excuse to commit crimes, such as murdering their enemies, for which they would otherwise be held accountable.[93]

European contact should thus be viewed as a trigger factor, that is, something which was not present in the Micmac ecosystem before and which initiated a concatenation of reactions leading to the replacement of the aboriginal ecosystem by another.[94] European disease, Christianity, and the fur trade with its accompanying technology—the three often intermeshed—were responsible for the corruption of the Indian-land relationship, in which the native had merged sympathetically with his environment. By a lockstep process European disease rendered the Indian's control over the supernatural and spiritual realm inoperative, and the disillusioned Micmac apostatized, debilitating taboo and preparing the way for the destruction of wildlife which was soon to occur under the stimulation of the fur trade. For those who believed in it, Christianity furnished a new, dualistic world view, which placed man above nature, as well as spiritual support for the fur trade, and as a result the Micmac became dependent on the European marketplace both spiritually and economically. Within his ecosystem the Indian changed from conservator to exploiter. All of this resulted in the intense exploitation of some game animals and the virtual extermination of others. Unfortunately for the Indian and the land, this grim tale was to be repeated many times along the moving Indian-white frontier. Life for the Micmac had indeed become more convenient, but convenience cost dearly in much material and abstract culture loss or modification.

The historiography of Indian-white relations is rendered more comprehensible when the Indian and the land are considered together: "So intimately is all of Indian life tied up with the land and its utilization that to think of Indians is to think of land. The two are inseparable."[95] American Indian history can be seen, then, as a type of environmental history, and perhaps it is from this perspective that the early period of Indian-white relations can best be understood.

NOTES

1. Mr. Martin was a graduate student at the University of California at Santa Barbara when he wrote this essay. He is now Professor of History at Rutgers University. He thanked Professors Wilbur R. Jacobs, Roderick Nash, and Albert C. Spaulding for their helpful comments and criticisms of this article.

2. Reuben Gold Thwaites, ed., *The Jesuit Relations and Allied Documents: Travels and Explorations of the Jesuit Missionaries in New France, 1610–1791* (New York, 1959 [orig. publ. Cleveland, Ohio, 1896–1901]), VIII, 57.

3. Baron Lahontan, *New Voyages to North-America . . . An Account of the Several Nations of that vast Continent . . .* , ed. Reuben Gold Thwaites (Chicago, 1905), I, 82.

4. Thwaites, ed., *Jesuit Relations,* V, 25; VI, 297–299; VIII, 57; XL, 151; LXVIII, 47, 109–111; LXIX, 95, 99–113.

5. *Ibid.,* VIII, 41.

6. Nicolas Denys, *The Description and Natural History of the Coasts of North America (Acadia),* ed. and trans. William F. Ganong, II (Toronto, 1908), I, 187, 199, 209, 219–220, hereafter cited as Denys, *Description of North America.*

7. *Ibid.,* 432, 450.

8. Peter Farb, *Man's Rise to Civilization as Shown by the Indians of North America from Primeval Times to the Coming of the Industrial State* (New York, 1968), 82–83.

9. See Wilson D. Wallis and Ruth Sawtell Wallis, *The Micmac Indians of Eastern Canada* (Minneapolis, Minn., 1955), for a thorough ethnographic study of the Micmac. Jacques and Maryvonne Crevel, *Honguedo ou l'Histoire des Premiers Gaspesiens* (Quebec, 1970), give a fairly good general history of the Micmac during the 17th century, together with a description of the fishing industry.

10. Julian H. Steward, "The Concept and Method of Cultural Ecology," in his *Theory of Culture Change: The Methodology of Multilinear Evolution* (Urbana, Ill., 1955), 30–42, and Andrew P. Vayda and Roy A. Rappaport, "Ecology, Cultural and Noncultural," in James A. Clifton, ed., *Introduction to Cultural Anthropology: Essays in the Scope and Methods of the Science of Man* (Boston, 1968), 494.

11. W. D. Billings, *Plants, Man, and the Ecosystem,* 2d ed. (Belmont, Calif., 1970), 4.

12. Roy A. Rappaport, *Pigs for the Ancestors: Ritual in the Ecology of a New Guinea People* (New Haven, Conn., 1968).

13. Among the few who have are William Christie MacLeod, "Conservation Among Primitive Hunting Peoples," *Scientific Monthly,* XLIII (1936), 562–566, and Alfred Goldsworthy Bailey in his little-known book, *The Conflict of European and Eastern Algonkian Cultures, 1504–1700,* 2d ed. (Toronto, 1969).

14. Wilbur R. Jacobs, *Dispossessing the American Indian: Indians and Whites on the Colonial Frontier* (New York, 1972), 25.

15. Billings, *Plants, Man, Ecosystem,* 37–38.

16. Sieur de Dièreville, *Relation of the Voyage to Port Royal in Acadia or New France,* trans. Mrs. Clarence Webster and ed. John Clarence Webster (Toronto, 1933), 184, hereafter cited as Dièreville, *Voyage to Port Royal.* According to the editor, 216, the Malecites later replaced the Micmacs living along the St. John, the latter withdrawing to Nova Scotia. See also Diamond Jenness, *The Indians of Canada,* 3d ed. (Ottawa, 1955), 267.

17. See Rappaport, *Pigs for the Ancestors,* 225–226. If the present article were intended as a more rigorous analysis of the Micmac ecosystem, we would report on the topography of this region, on the soil types, the hydrological characteristics, the climate, the influence of the ocean, and the effects of fires caused by lightning. But since neither the Micmac nor the first Europeans had any appreciable effect on these physical variables—except perhaps

that of water relations—we shall pass over the physical environment and go on to the biological. Suffice it to say that the water of numerous rivers and streams was regulated in its flow by beaver dams throughout much of this region, and Indian beaver-hunting and trapping certainly upset this control.

18. For a thorough discussion of Micmac plant and animal use see Frank G. Speck and Ralph W. Dexter, "Utilization of Animals and Plants by the Micmac Indians of New Brunswick," *Journal of the Washington Academy of Sciences*, XLI (1951), 250–259.

19. Father Chrestien Le Clercq, *New Relation of Gaspesia, with the Customs and Religion of the Gaspesian Indians*, ed. and trans. William F. Ganong (Toronto, 1910), 212–213, hereafter cited as Le Clercq, *Relation of Gaspesia*. Thwaites, ed., *Jesuit Relations*, III, 77; Marc Lescarbot, *The History of New France*, trans. W. L. Grant (Toronto, 1907), III, 93, 194–195, hereafter cited as Lescarbot, *History of New France*. Lescarbot asserts that the Micmac definitely grew tobacco, most likely the so-called wild tobacco (*Nicotiana rustica*): *ibid.*, 252–253.

20. Lescarbot, *History of New France*, II, 323–325; III, 158.

21. Thwaites, ed., *Jesuit Relations*, III, 77–83.

22. *Ibid.*; Denys, *Description of North America*, II, 403; Lescarbot, *History of New France*, III, 80; Le Clercq, *Relation of Gaspesia*, 88–89, 93; Dièreville, *Voyage to Port Royal*, 146.

23. Lescarbot, *History of New France*, III, 219–220, and Thwaites, ed., *Jesuit Relations*, III, 77–79.

24. Lescarbot, *History of New France*, III, 222–224. See Horace T. Martin, *Castorologia, or the History and Traditions of the Canadian Beaver* (Montreal, 1892), for a good treatise on the beaver.

25. Le Clercq, *Relation of Gaspesia*, 276–280; Dièreville, *Voyage to Port Royal*, 133–134; Denys, *Description of North America*, II, 429–433; Lescarbot, *History of New France*, III, 222–224.

26. Lescarbot, *History of New France*, III, 220–222; Denys, *Description of North America*, II, 426–429; Le Clercq, *Relation of Gaspesia*, 274–276. Speck and Dexter place caribou before moose in order of importance, but they cite no evidence for such ranking. Speck and Dexter, "Utilization of Animals and Plants by Micmacs," *Jour. Wash. Acad. Sci.*, XLI (1951), 255.

27. Le Clercq, *Relation of Gaspesia*, 118–119.

28. *Ibid.*, 93–94; Denys, *Description of North America*, II, 412; Lescarbot, *History of New France*, III, 133; Speck and Dexter, "Utilization of Animals and Plants by Micmacs," *Jour. Wash. Acad. Sci.*, XLI (1951), 255.

29. Speck and Dexter, "Utilization of Animals and Plants by Micmacs," *Jour. Wash. Acad. Sci.*, XLI (1951), 255.

30. Le Clercq, *Relation of Gaspesia*, 116, 119; Dièreville, *Voyage to Port Royal*, 131; Thwaites, ed., *Jesuit Relations*, III, 107–109.

31. Denys, *Description of North America*, II, 433–434.

32. Thwaites, ed., *Jesuit Relations*, III, 79.

33. *Ibid.*, 81, and Speck and Dexter, "Utilization of Animals and Plants by Micmacs," *Jour. Wash. Acad. Sci.*, XLI (1951), 251–254.

34. Lescarbot, *History of New France*, III, 236–237, and Denys, *Description of North America*, II, 436–437.

35. Le Clercq, *Relation of Gaspesia*, 92, 137; Lescarbot, *History of New France*, III, 230–231; Denys, *Description of North America*, II, 435–436.

36. Thwaites, ed., *Jesuit Relations*, III, 83.

37. *Ibid.*

38. Le Clercq, *Relation of Gaspesia*, 109–110, 283, and Denys, *Description of North America*, II, 389, 434.

39. Frank G. Speck, "Aboriginal Conservators," *Audubon Magazine,* XL (1938), 260.

40. Denys, *Description of North America,* II, 402–403.

41. *Ibid.,* 426.

42. Speck, "Aboriginal Conservators," *Audubon Magazine,* XL (1938), 260. Italics in original.

43. Rappaport, *Pigs for the Ancestors,* 237–238, and Vayda and Rappaport, "Ecology, Cultural and Noncultural," in Clifton, ed., *Cultural Anthropology,* 491.

44. See, for example, the writings of Speck, esp. "Aboriginal Conservators," *Audubon Magazine,* XL (1938), 258–261; John Witthoft, "The American Indian as Hunter," *Pennsylvania Game News,* XXIX (Feb.–Apr. 1953); George S. Snyderman, "Concepts of Land Ownership among the Iroquois and their Neighbors," *Bureau of American Ethnology Bulletin 149,* ed. William N. Fenton (Washington, D.C., 1951), 15–34. Robert F. Heizer, "Primitive Man as an Ecological Factor," Kroeber Anthropological Society, *Papers,* XIII (1955), 1–31. See also William A. Ritchie, "The Indian and His Environment," *Conservationist* (Dec.–Jan. 1955–1956), 23–27; Gordon Day, "The Indian as an Ecological Factor in the Northeastern Forest," *Ecology,* XXIV (1953), 329–346; MacLeod, "Conservation," *Scientific Monthly,* XLIII (1936), 562–566.

45. Witthoft, "American Indian," *Pa. Game News* (Mar. 1953), 17.

46. Murray Wax, "Religion and Magic," in Clifton, ed., *Cultural Anthropology,* 235.

47. See William Jones, "The Algonkin Manitou," *Journal of American Folk-Lore,* XVIII (1905), 183–190, and Frederick Johnson, "Notes on Micmac Shamanism," *Primitive Man,* XVI (1943), 58–59.

48. See Stansbury Hagar, "Micmac Magic and Medicine," *Jour. Am. Folk-Lore,* IX (1896), 170–177, and Johnson, "Shamanism," *Primitive Man,* XVI (1943), 54, 56–57, who report that such beliefs in the supernatural and spiritual survive even in modern times, although in suppressed and attenuated form. Le Clercq, *Relation of Gaspesia,* 187, 209, 212–214, and Denys, *Description of North America,* II, 117, 442.

49. Witthoft, "American Indian," *Pa. Game News* (Feb. 1953), 16.

50. Dièreville, *Voyage to Port Royal,* 139, and Le Clercq, *Relation of Gaspesia,* 225–229, 276–277.

51. Le Clercq, *Relation of Gaspesia,* 225–229.

52. *Ibid.,* 226.

53. *Ibid.,* 227–229.

54. Witthoft, "American Indian," *Pa. Game News* (Mar. 1953), 16–22; A. Irving Hallowell, "Bear Ceremonialism in the Northern Hemisphere," *American Anthropologist,* N.S., XXVIII (1926), 1–175.

55. Le Clercq, *Relation of Gaspesia,* 227.

56. Frank G. Speck, "Mistassini Hunting Territories in the Labrador Peninsula," *Am. Anthropologist,* XXV (1923), 464. Johnson, "Shamanism," *Primitive Man,* XVI (1943), 70–72, distinguishes between the Montagnais, Wabanaki, and Micmac ideas of the "soul."

57. Le Clercq, *Relation of Gaspesia,* 88–89; Dièreville, *Voyage to Port Royal,* 146; Lescarbot, *History of New France,* III, 80.

58. Denys, *Description of North America,* II, 430, 442, and Le Clercq, *Relation of Gaspesia,* 192–193.

59. Denys, *Description of North America,* II, 417–418, and Le Clercq, *Relation of Gaspesia,* 215–218.

60. Thwaites, ed., *Jesuit Relations,* II, 75; Le Clercq, *Relation of Gaspesia,* 215–216; George H. Daugherty, Jr., "Reflections of Environment in North American Indian Literature" (Ph.D. diss., University of Chicago, 1925), 31; Johnson, "Shamanism," *Primitive Man,* XVI (1943), 71–72.

61. Le Clercq, *Relation of Gaspesia*, 215–218, 296–299; Denys, *Description of North America*, II, 415, 417–418; Hagar, "Micmac Magic," *Jour. Am. Folk-Lore*, IX (1896), 170–177. Denys, *Description of North America*, II, 418, observed that most of these ailments were (what we would call today) psychosomatic in origin.

62. Billings, *Plants, Man, Ecosystem*, 36.

63. Thwaites, ed., *Jesuit Relations*, II, 75.

64. H. P. Biggar, *The Early Trading Companies of New France: A Contribution to the History of Commerce and Discovery in North America* (New York, 1965 [orig. publ. Toronto, 1901]), 18–37.

65. John Witthoft, "Archaeology as a Key to the Colonial Fur Trade," *Minnesota History*, XL (1966), 204–205.

66. John Witthoft, *Indian Prehistory of Pennsylvania* (Harrisburg, Pa., 1965), 26–29.

67. Le Clercq, *Relation of Gaspesia*, 146–152. The Recollet fathers, especially Father Emanuel Jumeau, were able to cause a renaissance of the old traditional religion by encouraging these people to look to the cross once more for their salvation, although, of course, this time it was the Christian cross. We should bear in mind that the cross was an art motif common among non-Christian people, and of independent origin from that of the Christian cross. Whether the cross mentioned in this particular tradition was of Christian or aboriginal origin should make little difference, for the story still serves to illustrate the process of apostatization.

68. Denys, *Description of North America*, II, 415. Estimates of the aboriginal population of North America at the time of European contact are constantly being revised upward. Henry F. Dobyns, "Estimating Aboriginal American Population: An Appraisal of Techniques with a New Hemispheric Estimate," *Current Anthropology*, VII (1966), 395–416, has recently placed the figure at a controversial and fantastically high total of 9,800,000 natives.

69. Dièreville, *Voyage to Port Royal*, 116. See Thwaites, ed., *Jesuit Relations*, I, 177–179.

70. Thwaites, ed., *Jesuit Relations*, III, 105–107.

71. *Ibid.*, I, 183.

72. *Ibid.*, II, 75–77; III, 123; and Le Clercq, *Relation of Gaspesia*, 193, 220, 224–225, 227, 239, 253. See also Denys, *Description of North America*, II, 117, 430, 442.

73. Notice that when a custom in any society becomes a mere formality and loses its practical meaning, it is easily discarded when challenged by detractors, who may or may not replace it with something more meaningful. See Le Clercq, *Relation of Gaspesia*, 206, 227, and Lescarbot, *History of New France*, III, 94–95.

74. Jean Baptiste de la Croix Chevrières de Saint-Vallier, *Estat Présent de l'Eglise et de la Colonie Françoise dans la Nouvelle France, par M. l'Evêque de Québec* (Paris, 1688), 36–37, and Thwaites, ed., *Jesuit Relations*, II, 75–77. See Le Clercq, *Relation of Gaspesia*, 220–221, where he speaks of converting a noted shaman to Christianity. André Vachon, "L'Eau-de-Vie dans la Société Indienne," Canadian Historical Association, *Report of the Annual Meeting* (1960), 22–32, has observed that the priest replaced the shaman and sorcerer in Indian society by virtue of his superior powers. By discrediting his Indian counterparts (and rivals), the priest became the shaman-sorcerer (i.e., a source of both good and evil power).

75. Lescarbot, *History of New France*, III, 128, and Le Clercq, *Relation of Gaspesia*, 133–135.

76. Le Clercq, *Relation of Gaspesia*, 209, 213–214, and Bailey, *Conflict of Cultures*, 47.

77. Denys, *Description of North America*, II, 439.

78. Le Clercq, *Relation of Gaspesia*, 187, 209, 212–214, 238–239, 303; Lescarbot, *History of New France*, III, 279, 285; Thwaites, ed., *Jesuit Relations*, I, 169; Denys, *Description of North America*, II, 437–439; Dièreville, *Voyage to Port Royal*, 161.

79. Denys, *Description of North America*, II, 439–441.

80. Le Clercq, *Relation of Gaspesia*, 125, 193, and Thwaites, ed., *Jesuit Relations*, I, 165. See *ibid.*, II, 89, where baptism was understood by the Micmac (of Port Royal, at least) "as a sort of sacred pledge of friendship and alliance with the French."

81. Lescarbot, *History of New France*, III 53–54; Denys, *Description of North America*, II, 117, 430, 442; Le Clercq, *Relation of Gaspesia*, 116; Dièreville, *Voyage to Port Royal*, 161; Thwaites, ed., *Jesuit Relations*, III, 131–135. See *Ibid.*, II, 75–77, where the shamans complain of having lost much of their power since the coming of the French.

82. Le Clercq observed that since the introduction of Christianity and especially baptism the manitou had not afflicted them to the degree that he did formerly. See Le Clercq, *Relation of Gaspesia*, 225. See also *ibid.*, 229–233, where cases are recorded of native men and women who seemed to feel a divine call and ordination, representing themselves as priests among their fellows.

83. Denys, *Description of North America*, II, 440–441.

84. Samuel de Champlain, *The Voyages of the Sieur de Champlain of Saintoge* . . . in H. P. Biggar, ed. and trans., *The Works of Samuel de Champlain*, I (Toronto, 1922), *passim*, and Thwaites, ed., *Jesuit Relations*, III, 81.

85. Lescarbot, *History of New France*, II, 281–282, 323–324; III, 158, 168, 250; Thwaites, ed., *Jesuit Relations*, III, 75–77; Le Clercq, *Relation of Gaspesia*, 93–94, 109; Dièreville, *Voyage to Port Royal*, 132–133, 139–141.

86. Harold A. Innis, *The Fur Trade in Canada: An Introduction to Canadian Economic History*, rev. ed. (Toronto, 1956), 15–17.

87. Farb, *Man's Rise to Civilization*, 82–83.

88. See Thwaites, ed., *Jesuit Relations*, I, 175–177, and Denys, *Description of North America*, II, 439, for mention of the French lust for furs.

89. Le Clercq, *Relation of Gaspesia*, 276–277. See also Dièreville, *Voyage to Port Royal*, 139.

90. Dièreville, *Voyage to Port Royal*, 161.

91. Lescarbot, *History of New France*, III, 191–192, and Denys, *Description of North America*, II, 399, 442–443.

92. Dièreville, *Voyage to Port Royal*, 174, and Denys, *Description of North America*, II, 172, 443–452. If we are to believe Craig MacAndrew and Robert B. Edgerton, *Drunken Comportment: A Social Explanation* (Chicago, 1969), 111, the Micmac encountered by Jacques Cartier along the shores of Chaleur Bay in 1534 were the first historically documented North American tribe to receive European liquor.

93. Saint-Vallier, *Estat Présent*, 36–37, 42; Thwaites, ed., *Jesuit Relations*, III, 105–109; Denys, *Description of North America*, II, 443–452; Dièreville, *Voyage to Port Royal*, 166; Le Clercq, *Relation of Gaspesia*, 244–245, 254–257. The subject of North American Indian drinking patterns and problems has been the topic of much debate from the 17th century to the present. The best current scholarship on the subject, which has by no means been exhausted, is contained in MacAndrew and Edgerton, *Drunken Comportment;* Vachon, "L'Eau-de-Vie," Can. Hist. Assn., *Report* (1960), 22–32; Nancy Oestreich Lurie, "The World's Oldest On-Going Protest Demonstration: North American Indian Drinking Patterns," *Pacific Historical Review*, XL (1971), 311–332.

94. Billings, *Plants, Man, Ecosystem*, 37–38.

95. See John Collier's report on Indian affairs, 1938, in the *Annual Report of the Secretary of the Interior* (Washington, D.C., 1938), 209–211, as quoted by Wilcomb Washburn, ed., *The Indian and the White Man* (Garden City, N.Y., 1964), 394.

CHAPTER
2

Did the Puritans Start It All?

This classic essay by Perry Miller is one of the most influential articles ever written in American history, perhaps exceeded only by Frederick Jackson Turner's famous thesis on the frontier in American history. It provides an account of Puritan motivations for colonization that still stands as a benchmark for all subsequent interpretations of the Puritans' immigration, religion, and culture. Miller revolutionized Puritan studies in two ways. First, together with historians Clifford K. Shipton and Samuel Eliot Morrison, Miller treated the Puritans as serious intellectuals rather than bigoted prudes, as commentators like H. L. Mencken had done for decades. Second, by explaining just what the word "errand" meant to the Puritans, Miller recast the understanding of what the Puritans intended to do in America. Seldom has the analysis of a single word so profoundly reshaped historians' understanding of an entire people and culture.

According to Professor Miller, what was the Puritans' sense of errand when they left England, and how did it change on the American shores? How do we know that the Puritan ideas Miller describes were broadly representative of all Puritans, much less of colonists everywhere? Do the ideas of an elite clergy reflect the values and aspirations of the laity? If so, how do we know?

Additional Reading: The literature on Puritanism is mammoth. A good guide to the many available books on the subject can be found in David L. Ammerman and Philip D. Morgan, eds., *Books about Early America: 2001 Titles* (Williamsburg, 1989). Michael McGiffert, *God's Plot: Puritan Spirituality in Thomas Shepard's Cambridge,* revised ed. (Amherst, 1994) offers a superb collection of Puritan conversion narratives from the notebooks of one of the movement's most distinguished clergymen. Edmund S. Morgan, *The Puritan Dilemma: The Story of John Winthrop* (Boston, 1958) remains a classic biography. David D. Hall, *World of Wonder, Days of Judgment: Popular Religious Belief in Early New England* (New York, 1989) studies lay understandings of the Puritan religious experience, and Harry S. Stout, *The New*

England Soul: Preaching and Religious Culture in Colonial New England (New York, 1986) follows the evolution of the sermon from the mid-seventeenth century to the American Revolution.

Perry Miller

Errand Into the Wilderness

[The title of an election sermon preached in 1670 provided the fitting title for an exhibition of New England imprints at the John Carter Brown Library in Brown University, where I delivered this address on May 16, 1952. Only thereafter did I discover that the Reverend Samuel Danforth had also given me a title.

In his own language, Danforth was trying to do what I too am attempting: to make out some deeper configuration in the story than a mere modification, by obvious and natural necessity, of an imported European culture in adjustment to a frontier. He recognized, as do I, that a basic conditioning factor was the frontier—the wilderness. Even so, the achievement of a personality is not so much the presence of this or that environmental element—no matter how pressing, how terrifying—as the way in which a given personality responds. The real theme is so complex that any simplification does it injustice, though for the sake of communication simplifications are manufactured. Danforth made his simplification by stressing the "errand" more than the "wilderness." So I follow him, and in my context, as in his, "errand" is not a formal thesis but a metaphor.

A metaphor is a vastly different thing from Frederick Jackson Turner's "thesis" that democracy came out of the forest. Happily we no longer are obliged to believe this, although we are ready to recognize, thanks to Turner, that unless we acknowledge the existence of the forest the character of American history is obscure. A newer generation, confessing the importance of Turner's speculations, is concerned with an inherent cultural conflict, in relation to which the forest was, so to speak, as external as the Atlantic Ocean. This ostentatiously simple and monolithic America is in fact a congeries of inner tensions. It has been so from the beginning; it is more so now than at the beginning—as is proved by the frenetic insistence of many Americans that this statement is untrue. Confronted with so gigantic a riddle, the analyst becomes wary of generalizations, though incessantly he strives to comprehend.

In this address, then, I am not thinking, nor in any paper of this volume am I thinking, within the framework of interpretation—the "frontier hypothesis"— that Turner bequeathed us. Immense as is the debt that all seekers after national self-knowledge owe to Turner, we have to insist—at least I do—that he did as much to confuse as to clarify the deepest issue. He worked on the premise—which any Puritan logician (being in this regard a scholastic) could have corrected—that the subject matter of a liberal art determines the form, that the content of a discipline automatically supplies the angle of vision. I might even argue that, by remote implication, the struggle of a Protestant culture in America against its weakening hold on the Puritan insight into this law of the mind, namely, that form controls matter, constitutes one theme of the collection. From Turner's conception of the ruling and compulsive power of the frontier no further avenue could be projected to any cultural synthesis. Ideally, this volume might include a study of Turner as being himself an exemplification—I might more accurately say the foremost victim—of his fallacy, rather than the master of it. However, by now it has become rather the mode to point out the romantic prepossessions of Turner; I mention him not only to salute a great name but also, by calling attention to my dissent from him, to underscore my use of the two concepts, both "errand" and "wilderness," as figures of speech.]

It was a happy inspiration that led the staff of the John Carter Brown Library to choose as the title of its New England exhibition of 1952 a phrase from Samuel Danforth's election sermon, delivered on May 11, 1670: *A Brief Recognition of New England's Errand into the Wilderness.* It was of course an inspiration, if not of genius at least of talent, for Danforth to invent his title in the first place. But all the election sermons of this period—that is to say, the major expressions of the second generation, which, delivered on these forensic occasions, were in the fullest sense community expression—have interesting titles; a mere listing tells the story of what was happening to the minds and emotions of the New England people: John Higginson's *The Cause of God and His People In New-England* in 1663, William Stoughton's *New England's True Interest, Not to Lie* in 1668, Thomas Shepard's *Eye-Salve* in 1672, Urian Oakes's *New England Pleaded With* in 1673, and, climactically and most explicitly, Increase Mather's *A Discourse Concerning the Danger of Apostasy* in 1677.

All of these show by their title pages alone—and, as those who have looked into them know, infinitely more by their contents—a deep disquietude. They are troubled utterances, worried, fearful. Something has gone wrong. As in 1662 Wigglesworth already was saying in verse, God has a controversy with New England; He has cause to be angry and to punish it because of its innumerable defections. They say, unanimously, that New England was sent on an errand, and that it has failed.

To our ears these lamentations of the second generation sound strange indeed. We think of the founders as heroic men—of the towering stature of Bradford, Winthrop, and Thomas Hooker—who braved the ocean and the wilderness, who conquered both, and left to their children a goodly heritage. Why then this whimpering?

Some historians suggest that the second and third generations suffered a failure of nerve; they weren't the men their fathers had been, and they knew it. Where the founders could range over the vast body of theology and ecclesiastical polity and produce profound works like the treatises of John Cotton or the subtle psychological analyses of Hooker, or even such a gusty though wrongheaded book as Nathaniel Ward's *Simple Cobler,* let alone such lofty and righteaded pleas as Roger Williams' *Bloudy Tenent,* all these children could do was tell each other that they were on probation and that their chances of making good did not seem very promising.

Since Puritan intellectuals were thoroughly grounded in grammar and rhetoric, we may be certain that Danforth was fully aware of the ambiguity concealed in his word "errand." It already had taken on the double meaning which it still carries with us. Originally, as the word first took form in English, it meant exclusively a short journey on which an inferior is sent to convey a message or to perform a service for his superior. In that sense we today speak of an "errand boy"; or the husband says that while in town on his lunch hour, he must run an errand for his wife. But by the end of the Middle Ages, errand developed another connotation: it came to mean the actual business on which the actor goes, the purpose itself, the conscious intention in his mind. In this signification, the runner of the errand is working for himself, is his own boss; the wife, while the husband is away at the office, runs her own errands. Now in the 1660's the problem was this: which had New England originally been—an errand boy or a doer of errands? In which sense had it failed? Had it been despatched for a further purpose, or was it an end in itself? Or had it fallen short not only in one or the other, but in both of the meanings? If so, it was indeed a tragedy, in the primitive sense of a fall from a mighty designation.

If the children were in grave doubt about which had been the original errand—if, in fact, those of the founders who lived into the later period and who might have set their progeny to rights found themselves wondering and confused—there is little chance of our answering clearly. Of course, there is no problem about Plymouth Colony. That is the charm about Plymouth: its clarity. The Pilgrims, as we have learned to call them, were reluctant voyagers; they had never wanted to leave England, but had been obliged to depart because the authorities made life impossible for Separatists. They could, naturally, have stayed at home had they given up being Separatists, but that idea simply did not occur to them. Yet they did not go to Holland as though on an errand; neither can we extract the notion of a mission out of the reasons which, as Bradford tells us, persuaded them to leave Leyden for "Virginia." The war with Spain was about to be resumed, and the economic threat was ominous; their migration was not so much an errand as a shrewd forecast, a plan to get out while the getting was good, lest, should they stay, they would be "intrapped or surrounded by their enemies, so as they should neither be able to fight nor flie." True, once the decision was taken, they congratulated themselves that they might become a means for propagating the gospel in remote parts of the world, and thus of serving as steppingstones to others in the performance of this great work; nevertheless, the substance of their decision was that they "thought it better to dislodge betimes to some place of better advantage and less danger, if any such could be found." The great hymn that Bradford, looking back in his old age, chanted about the landfall is one of the greatest passages, if not the very greatest, in all New England's literature; yet it does not resound with the sense of a mission accomplished—instead, it vibrates with the sorrow and exultation of suffering, the sheer endurance, the pain and the anguish, with the somberness of death faced unflinchingly:

> May not and ought not the children of these fathers rightly say: Our fathers were Englishmen which came over this great ocean, and were ready to perish in this wilderness; but they cried unto the Lord, and he heard their voyce, and looked on their adversitie. . . .

We are bound, I think, to see in Bradford's account the prototype of the vast majority of subsequent immigrants—of those Oscar Handlin calls "the Uprooted": they came for better advantage and for less danger, and to give their posterity the opportunity of success.

The Great Migration of 1630 is an entirely other story. True, among the reasons John Winthrop drew up in 1629 to persuade himself and his colleagues that they should commit themselves to the enterprise, the economic motive frankly figures. Wise men thought that England was overpopulated and that the poor would have a better chance in the new land. But Massachusetts Bay was not just an organization of immigrants seeking advantage and opportunity. It had a positive sense of mission—either it was sent on an errand or it had its own intention, but in either case the deed was deliberate. It was an act of will, perhaps of willfulness. These Puritans were not driven out of England (thousands of their fellows stayed and fought the Cavaliers)—they went of their own accord.

So, concerning them, we ask the question, why? If we are not altogether clear about precisely how we should phrase the answer, this is not because they themselves were reticent. They spoke as fully as they knew how, and none more magnificently or cogently than John Winthrop in the midst of the passage itself, when he delivered a lay sermon aboard the flagship *Arbella* and called it "A Modell of Christian Charity." It distinguishes the motives of this great enterprise from those of Bradford's forlorn retreat, and especially from those of the masses who later have come in quest of advancement. Hence, for the student of New England and of America, it is a fact demanding incessant brooding that John Winthrop selected as the "doctrine" of his discourse, and so as the basic proposition to which, it then seemed to him, the errand was committed, the thesis that God had disposed mankind in a hierarchy of social classes, so that "in all times some must be rich, some poor, some highe and eminent in power and dignitie; others mean and in subjeccion." It is as though, preternaturally sensing what the promise of America might come to signify for the rank and file, Winthrop took the precaution to drive out of their heads any notion that in the wilderness the poor and the mean were ever so to improve themselves as to mount above the rich or the eminent in dignity. Were there any who had signed up under the mistaken impression that such was the purpose of their errand, Winthrop told them that, although other peoples, lesser breeds, might come for wealth or pelf, this migration was specifically dedicated to an avowed end that had nothing to do with incomes. We have entered into an explicit covenant with God, "We haue professed to enterprise these Accions vpon these and these ends"; we have drawn up indentures with the Almighty, wherefore if we succeed and do not let ourselves get diverted into making money, He will reward us. Whereas if we fail, if we "fall to embrace this present world and prosecute our carnall intencions, seekeing greate things for our selves and our posterity, the Lord will surely breake out in wrathe against us be revenged of such a periured people and make us knowe the price of the breache of such a Covenant."

Well, what terms were agreed upon in this covenant? Winthrop could say precisely—"It is by a mutuall consent through a specially overruleing providence, and a more than ordinary approbation of the Churches of Christ to seeke out a place of Cohabitation and Consorteshipp under a due forme of Government both civill and ecclesiasticall." If it could be said thus concretely, why should there be any ambiguity? There was no doubt whatsoever about what Winthrop meant by a due form of ecclesiastical government: he meant the pure Biblical polity set forth in full detail by the New Testament, that method which later generations, in the days of increasing confusion, would settle down to calling Congregational, but which for Winthrop was no denominational peculiarity but the very essence of organized Christianity. What a due form of civil government meant, therefore, became crystal clear: a political regime, possessing power, which would consider its main function to be the erecting, protecting, and preserving of this form of polity. This due form would have, at the very beginning of its list of responsibilities, the duty of suppressing heresy, of subduing or somehow getting rid of dissenters—of being, in short, deliberately, vigorously, and consistently intolerant.

Regarded in this light, the Massachusetts Bay Company came on an errand in the second and later sense of the word: it was, so to speak, on its own business. What it set out to do was the sufficient reason for its setting out. About this Winthrop seems to be perfectly certain, as he declares specifically what the due forms will be attempting: the end is to improve our lives to do more service to the Lord, to increase the body of Christ, and to preserve our posterity from the corruptions of this evil world, so that they in turn shall work out their salvation under the purity and power of Biblical ordinances. Because the errand was so definable in advance, certain conclusions about the method of conducting it were equally evident: one, obviously, was that those sworn to the covenant should not be allowed to turn aside in a lust for mere physical rewards; but another was, in Winthrop's simple but splendid words, "we must be knit togeher in this worke as one man, wee must entertaine each other in brotherly affection." We must actually delight in each other, "always having before your eyes our Commission and community in the worke, our community as members of the same body." This was to say, were the great purpose kept steadily in mind, if all gazed only at it and strove only for it, then social solidarity (within a scheme of fixed and unalterable class distinctions) would be an automatic consequence. A society despatched upon an errand that is its own reward would want no other rewards; it could go forth to possess a land without ever becoming possessed by it; social gradations would remain eternally what God had originally appointed; there would be no internal contention among groups or interests; and though there would be hard work for everybody, prosperity would be bestowed not as a consequence of labor but as a sign of approval upon the mission itself. For once in the history of humanity (with all its sins), there would be a society so dedicated to a holy cause that success would prove innocent and triumph not raise up sinful pride or arrogant dissension.

Or, at least, this would come about if the people did not deal falsely with God, if they would live up to the articles of their bond. If we do not perform these terms, Winthrop warned, we may expect immediate manifestations of divine wrath; we shall perish out of the land we are crossing the sea to possess. And here in the 1660's and 1670's, all the jeremiads (of which Danforth's is one of the most poignant) are castigations of the people for having defaulted on precisely these articles. They recite the long list of afflictions an angry God had rained upon them, surely enough to prove how abysmally they had deserted the covenant: crop failures, epidemics, grasshoppers, caterpillars, torrid summers, arctic winters, Indian wars, hurricanes, shipwrecks, accidents, and (most grievous of all) unsatisfactory children. The solemn work of the election day, said Stoughton in 1668, is "Foundation-work"—not, that is, to lay a new one, "but to continue, and strengthen, and beautifie, and build upon that which has been laid." It had been laid in the covenant before even a foot was set ashore, and thereon New England should rest. Hence the terms of survival, let alone of prosperity, remained what had first been propounded:

> If we should so frustrate and deceive the Lords Expectations, that his Covenant-interest in us, and the Workings of his Salvation be made to cease, then All were lost indeed; Ruine upon Ruine, Destruction upon Destruction would come, until one stone were not left upon another.

Since so much of the literature after 1660—in fact, just about all of it—dwells on this theme of declension and apostasy, would not the story of New England seem to be simply that of the failure of a mission? Winthrop's dread was realized: posterity had not found their salvation amid pure ordinances but had, despite the ordinances, yielded to the seductions of the good land. Hence distresses were being piled upon them, the slaughter of King Philip's War and now the attack of a profligate king upon the sacred charter. By about 1680, it did in truth seem that shortly no stone would be left upon another, that history would record of New England that the founders had been great men, but that their children and grandchildren progressively deteriorated.

This would certainly seem to be the impression conveyed by the assembled clergy and lay elders who, in 1679, met at Boston in a formal synod, under the leadership of Increase Mather, and there prepared a report on why the land suffered. The result of their deliberation, published under the title *The Necessity of Reformation,* was the first in what has proved to be a distressingly long succession of investigations into the civic health of Americans, and it is probably the most pessimistic. The land was afflicted, it said, because corruption had proceeded apace; assuredly, if the people did not quickly reform, the last blow would fall and nothing but desolation be left. Into what a moral quagmire this dedicated community had sunk, the synod did not leave to imagination; it published a long and detailed inventory of sins, crimes, misdemeanors, and nasty habits, which makes, to say the least, interesting reading.

We hear much talk nowadays about corruption, most of it couched in generalized terms. If we ask our current Jeremiahs to descend to particulars, they tell us that the republic is going on the rocks, or to the dogs, because the wives of politicians aspire to wear mink coats and their husbands take a moderate five per cent cut on certain deals to pay for the garments. The Puritans were devotees of logic, and the verb "methodize" ruled their thinking. When the synod went to work, it had before it a succession of sermons, such as that of Danforth and the other election-day or fast-day orators, as well as such works as Increase Mather's *A Brief History of the Warr With the Indians,* wherein the decimating conflict with Philip was presented as a revenge upon the people for their transgressions. When the synod felt obliged to enumerate the enormities of the land so that the people could recognize just how far short of their errand they had fallen, it did not, in the modern manner, assume that regeneration would be accomplished at the next election by turning the rascals out, but it digested this body of literature; it reduced the contents to method. The result is a staggering compendium of iniquity, organized into twelve headings.

First, there was a great and visible decay of godliness. Second, there were several manifestations of pride—contention in the churches, insubordination of inferiors toward superiors, particularly of those inferiors who had, unaccountably, acquired more wealth than their betters, and, astonishingly, a shocking extravagance in attire, especially on the part of these of the meaner sort, who persisted in dressing beyond their means. Third, there were heretics, especially Quakers and Anabaptists. Fourth, a notable increase in swearing and a spreading disposition to sleep at sermons (these two phenomena seemed basically connected). Fifth, the Sabbath was wantonly violated. Sixth, family government had decayed, and fathers no longer kept their sons and daughters from prowling at night. Seventh, instead of people being knit together as one man in mutual love, they were full of contention, so that lawsuits were on the increase and lawyers were thriving. Under the eighth head, the synod described the sins of sex and alcohol, thus producing some of the juiciest prose of the period: militia days had become orgies, taverns were crowded; women threw temptation in the way of befuddled men by wearing false locks and displaying naked necks and arms "or, which is more abominable, naked Breasts"; there were "mixed Dancings," along with light behavior and "Company-keeping" with vain persons, wherefore the bastardy rate was rising. In 1672, there was actually an attempt to supply Boston with a brothel (it was suppressed, but the synod was bearish about the future). Ninth, New Englanders were betraying a marked disposition to tell lies, especially when selling anything. In the tenth place, the business morality of even the most righteous left everything to be desired: the wealthy speculated in land and raised prices excessively; "Day-Labourers and Mechanicks are unreasonable in their demands." In the eleventh place, the people showed no disposition to reform, and in the twelfth, they seemed utterly destitute of civic spirit.

"The things here insisted on," said the synod, "have been oftentimes mentioned and inculcated by those whom the Lord hath set as Watchmen to the house of Israel." Indeed they had been, and thereafter they continued to be even more inculcated. At the end of the century, the synod's report was serving as a kind of handbook for preachers: they would take some verse of Isaiah or Jeremiah, set up the doctrine that God avenges the iniquities of a chosen people, and then run down the twelve heads, merely bringing the list up to date by inserting the new and still more depraved practices an ingenious people kept on devising. I suppose that in the whole literature of the world, including the satirists of imperial Rome, there is hardly such another uninhibited and unrelenting documentation of a people's descent into corruption.

I have elsewhere endeavored to argue[1] that, while the social or economic historian may read this literature for its contents—and so construct from the expanding catalogue of denunciations a record of social progress—the cultural anthropologist will look slightly askance at these jeremiads; he will exercise a methodological caution about taking them at face value. If you read them all through, the total effect, curiously enough, is not at all depressing: you come to the paradoxical realization that they do not bespeak a despairing frame of mind. There is something of a ritualistic incantation about them; whatever they may signify in the realm of theology, in that of psychology they are purgations of soul; they do not discourage but actually encourage the community to persist in its heinous conduct. The exhortation to a reformation which never materializes serves as a token payment upon the obligation, and so liberates the debtors. Changes there had to be: adaptations to environment, expansion of the frontier, mansions constructed, commercial adventures undertaken. These activities were not specifically nominated in the bond Winthrop had framed. They were thrust upon the society by American experience; because they were not only works of necessity but of excitement, they proved irresistible—whether making money, haunting taverns, or committing fornication. Land speculation meant not only wealth but dispersion of the people, and what was to stop the march of settlement? The covenant doctrine preached on the *Arbella* had been formulated in England, where land was not to be had for the taking; its adherents had been utterly oblivious of what the fact of a frontier would do for an imported order, let alone for a European mentality. Hence I suggest that under the guise of this mounting wail of sinfulness, this incessant and never successful cry for repentance, the Puritans launched themselves upon the process of Americanization.

However, there are still more pertinent or more analytical things to be said of this body of expression. If you compare it with the great productions of the founders, you will be struck by the fact that the second and third generations had become oriented toward the social, and only the social, problem; herein they were deeply and profoundly different from their fathers. The finest creations of the founders—the disquisitions of Hooker, Shepard, and Cotton—were written in Europe, or else, if actually penned in the colonies, proceeded from a thoroughly European mentality, upon which the American scene made no impression whatsoever. The most striking example of this imperviousness is the poetry of Anne Bradstreet: she came to Massachusetts at the age of eighteen, already two years married to Simon Bradstreet; there, she says, "I found a new world and new manners, at which my heart rose" in rebellion, but soon convincing herself that it was the way of God, she submitted and joined the church. She bore Simon eight children, and loved him sincerely, as her most charming poem, addressed to him, reveals:

If ever two were one, then surely we;
If ever man were loved by wife, then thee.

After the house burned, she wrote a lament about how her pleasant things in ashes lay and how no more the merriment of guests would sound in the hall; but there is nothing in the poem to suggest that the house stood in North Andover or that the things so tragically consumed were doubly precious because they had been transported across the ocean and were utterly irreplaceable in the wilderness. In between rearing children and keeping house she wrote her poetry; her brother-in-law carried the manuscript to London, and there published it in 1650 under the ambitious title, *The Tenth Muse Lately Sprung Up in America*. But the title is the only thing about the volume which shows any sense of America, and that little merely in order to prove that the plantations had something in the way of European wit and learning, that they had not receded into barbarism. Anne's flowers are English flowers, the birds, English birds, and the landscape is Lincolnshire. So also with the productions of immigrant scholarship: such a learned and acute work as Hooker's *Survey of the Summe of Church Discipline,* which is specifically about the regime set up in America, is written entirely within the logical patterns, and out of the religious experience, of Europe; it makes no concession to new and peculiar circumstances.

The titles alone of productions in the next generation show how concentrated have become emotion and attention upon the interest of New England, and none is more revealing than Samuel Danforth's conception of an errand into the wilderness. Instead of being able to compose abstract treatises like those of Hooker upon the soul's preparation, humiliation, or exultation, or such a collection of wisdom and theology as John Cotton's *The Way of Life* or Shepard's *The Sound Believer,* these later saints must, over and over again, dwell upon the specific sins of New England, and the more they denounce, the more they must narrow their focus to the provincial problem. If they write upon anything else, it must be about the halfway covenant and its manifold consequences—a development enacted wholly in this country—or else upon their wars with the Indians. Their range is sadly constricted, but every effort, no matter how brief, is addressed to the persistent question: what is the meaning of this society in the wilderness? If it does not mean what Winthrop said it must mean, what under Heaven is it? Who, they are forever asking themselves, who are we?—and sometimes they are on the verge of saying, who the Devil are we, anyway?

This brings us back to the fundamental ambiguity concealed in the word "errand," that *double entente* of which I am certain Danforth was aware when he published the words that give point to the exhibition. While it was true that in 1630, the covenant philosophy of a special and peculiar bond lifted the migration out of the ordinary realm of nature, provided it with a definite mission which might in the secondary sense be called its errand, there was always present in Puritan thinking the suspicion that God's saints are at best inferiors, despatched by their Superior upon particular assignments. Anyone who has run errands for other people, particularly for people of great importance with many things on their minds, such as army commanders, knows how real is the peril that, by the time he returns with the report of a message delivered or a bridge blown up, the Superior may be interested in something else; the situation at headquarters may be entirely changed, and the gallant errand boy, or the husband who desperately remembered to buy the ribbon, may be told that he is too late. This tragic pattern appears again and again in modern warfare: an agent is dropped by parachute and, after immense hardships, comes back to find that, in the shifting tactical or strategic situations, his contribution is no longer of value. If he gets home in time and his service proves useful, he receives a medal; otherwise, no matter what prodigies he has performed, he may not even be thanked. He has been sent, as the devastating phrase has it, upon a fool's errand, than which there can be a no more shattering blow to self-esteem.

The Great Migration of 1630 felt insured against such treatment from on high by the covenant; nevertheless, the God of the covenant always remained an unpredictable Jehovah, a *Deus Absconditus*. When God promises to abide by stated terms, His word, of course, is to be trusted; but then, what is man that he dare accuse Omnipotence of tergiversation? But if any such apprehension was in Winthrop's mind as he spoke on the *Arbella,* or in the minds of other apologists for the enterprise, they kept it far back and allowed it no utterance. They could stifle the thought, not only because Winthrop and his colleagues believed fully in the covenant, but because they could see in the pattern of history that their errand was not a mere scouting expedition: it was an essential maneuver in the drama of Christendom. The Bay Company was not a battered remnant of suffering Separatists thrown up on a rocky shore; it was an organized task force of Christians, executing a flank attack on the corruptions of Christendom. These Puritans did not flee to America; they went in order to work out that complete reformation which was not yet accomplished in England and Europe, but which would quickly be accomplished if only the saints back there had a working model to guide them. It is impossible to say that any who sailed from Southampton really expected to lay his bones in the new world; were it to come about—as all in their heart of hearts anticipated—that the forces of righteousness should prevail against Laud and Wentworth, that England after all should turn toward reformation, where else would the distracted country look for leadership except to those who in New England had perfected the ideal polity and who would know how to administer it? This was the large unspoken assumption in the errand of 1630: if the conscious intention were realized, not only would a federated Jehovah bless the new land, but He would bring back these temporary colonials to govern England.

In this respect, therefore, we may say that the migration was running an errand in the earlier and more primitive sense of the word—performing a job not so much for Jehovah as for history, which was the wisdom of Jehovah expressed through time. Winthrop was aware of this aspect of the mission—fully conscious of it. "For wee must Consider that wee shall be as a Citty upon a Hill, the eies of all people are uppon us." More was at stake than just one little colony. If we deal falsely with God, not only will He descend upon us in wrath, but even more terribly, He will make us "a story and a by-word through the world, wee shall open the mouthes of enemies to speake evill of the wayes of god and all professours for

Gods sake." No less than John Milton was New England to justify God's ways to man, though not, like him, in the agony and confusion of defeat but in the confidence of approaching triumph. This errand was being run for the sake of Reformed Christianity; and while the first aim was indeed to realize in America the due form of government, both civil and ecclesiastical, the aim behind that aim was to vindicate the most rigorous ideal of the Reformation, so that ultimately all Europe would imitate New England. If we succeed, Winthrop told his audience, men will say of later plantations, "the lord make it like that of New England." There was an elementary prudence to be observed: Winthrop said that the prayer would arise from subsequent plantations, yet what was England itself but one of God's plantations? In America, he promised, we shall see, or may see, more of God's wisdom, power, and truth "then formerly wee have beene acquainted with." The situation was such that, for the moment, the model had no chance to be exhibited in England; Puritans could talk about it, theorize upon it, but they could not display it, could not prove that it would actually work. But if they had it set up in America—in a bare land, devoid of already established (and corrupt) institutions, empty of bishops and courtiers, where they could start *de novo,* and the eyes of the world were upon it—and if then it performed just as the saints had predicted of it, the Calvinist internationale would know exactly how to go about completing the already begun but temporarily stalled revolution in Europe.[2]

When we look upon the enterprise from this point of view, the psychology of the second and third generations becomes more comprehensible. We realize that the migration was not sent upon its errand in order to found the United States of America, nor even the New England conscience. Actually, it would not perform its errand even when the colonists did erect a due form of government in church and state: what was further required in order for this mission to be a success was that the eyes of the world be kept fixed upon it in rapt attention. If the rest of the world, or at least of Protestantism, looked elsewhere, or turned to another model, or simply got distracted and forgot about New England, if the new land was left with a polity nobody in the great world of Europe wanted—then every success in fulfilling the terms of the covenant would become a diabolical measure of failure. If the due form of government were not everywhere to be saluted, what would New England have upon its hands? How give it a name, this victory nobody could utilize? How provide an identity for something conceived under misapprehensions? How could a universal which turned out to be nothing but a provincial particular be called anything but a blunder or an abortion?

If an actor, playing the leading role in the greatest dramatic spectacle of the century, were to attire himself and put on his make-up, rehearse his lines, take a deep breath, and stride onto the stage, only to find the theater dark and empty, no spotlight working, and himself entirely alone, he would feel as did New England around 1650 or 1660. For in the 1640's, during the Civil Wars, the colonies, so to speak, lost their audience. First of all, there proved to be, deep in the Puritan movement, an irreconcilable split between the Presbyterian and Independent wings, wherefore no one system could be imposed upon England, and so the

New England model was unserviceable. Secondly—most horrible to relate—the Independents, who in polity were carrying New England's banner and were supposed, in the schedule of history, to lead England into imitation of the colonial order, betrayed the sacred cause by yielding to the heresy of toleration. They actually welcomed Roger Williams, whom the leaders of the model had kicked out of Massachusetts so that his nonsense about liberty of conscience would not spoil the administrations of charity.

In other words, New England did not lie, did not falter; it made good everything Winthrop demanded—wonderfully good—and then found that its lesson was rejected by those choice spirits for whom the exertion had been made. By casting out Williams, Anne Hutchinson, and the Antinomians, along with an assortment of Gortonists and Anabaptists, into that cesspool then becoming known as Rhode Island, Winthrop, Dudley, and the clerical leaders showed Oliver Cromwell how he should go about governing England. Instead, he developed the utterly absurd theory that so long as a man made a good soldier in the New Model Army, it did not matter whether he was a Calvinist, an Antinomian, an Arminian, an Anabaptist or even—horror of horrors—a Socinian! Year after year, as the circus tours this country, crowds howl with laughter, no matter how many times they have seen the stunt, at the bustle that walks by itself: the clown comes out dressed in a large skirt with a bustle behind; he turns sharply to the left, and the bustle continues blindly and obstinately straight ahead, on the original course. It is funny in a circus, but not in history. There is nothing but tragedy in the realization that one was in the main path of events, and now is sidetracked and disregarded. One is always able, of course, to stand firm on his first resolution, and to condemn the clown of history for taking the wrong turning: yet this is a desolating sort of stoicism, because it always carries with it the recognition that history will never come back to the predicted path, and that with one's own demise, righteousness must die out of the world.

The most humiliating element in the experience was the way the English brethren turned upon the colonials for precisely their greatest achievement. It must have seemed, for those who came with Winthrop in 1630 and who remembered the clarity and brilliance with which he set forth the conditions of their errand, that the world was turned upside down and inside out when, in June 1645, thirteen leading Independent divines—such men as Goodwin, Owen, Nye, Burroughs, formerly friends and allies of Hooker and Davenport, men who might easily have come to New England and helped extirpate heretics—wrote the General Court that the colony's law banishing Anabaptists was an embarrassment to the Independent cause in England. Opponents were declaring, said these worthies, "that persons of our way, principall and spirit cannot beare with Dissentors from them, but Doe correct, fine, imprison and banish them wherever they have power soe to Doe." There were indeed people in England who admired the severities of Massachusetts, but we assure you, said the Independents, these "are utterly your enemyes and Doe seeke your extirpation from the face of the earth: those who now in power are your friends are quite otherwise minded, and doe professe they are much offended with your proceedings." Thus early commenced that chronic weakness in the foreign policy of Americans, an inability to recognize who in truth constitute their best friends abroad.

We have lately accustomed ourselves to the fact that there does exist a mentality which will take advantage of the liberties allowed by society in order to conspire for the ultimate suppression of those same privileges. The government of Charles I and Archbishop Laud had not, where that danger was concerned, been liberal, but it had been conspicuously inefficient; hence, it did not liquidate the Puritans (although it made halfhearted efforts), nor did it herd them into prison camps. Instead, it generously, even lavishly, gave a group of them a charter to Massachusetts Bay, and obligingly left out the standard clause requiring that the document remain in London, that the grantees keep their office within reach of Whitehall. Winthrop's revolutionaries availed themselves of this liberty to get the charter overseas, and thus to set up a regime dedicated to the worship of God in the manner they desired—which meant allowing nobody else to worship any other way, especially adherents of Laud and King Charles. All this was perfectly logical and consistent. But what happened to the thought processes of their fellows in England made no sense whatsoever. Out of the New Model Army came the fantastic notion that a party struggling for power should proclaim that, once it captured the state, it would recognize the right of dissenters to disagree and to have their own worship, to hold their own opinions. Oliver Cromwell was so far gone in this idiocy as to become a dictator, in order to impose toleration by force! Amid this shambles, the errand of New England collapsed. There was nobody left at headquarters to whom reports could be sent.

Many a man has done a brave deed, been hailed as a public hero, had honors and ticker tape heaped upon him—and then had to live, day after day, in the ordinary routine, eating breakfast and brushing his teeth, in what seems protracted anticlimax. A couple may win their way to each other across insuperable obstacles, elope in a blaze of passion and glory—and then have to learn that life is a matter of buying the groceries and getting the laundry done. This sense of the meaning having gone out of life, that all adventures are over, that no great days and no heroism lie ahead, is particularly galling when it falls upon a son whose father once was the public hero or the great lover. He has to put up with the daily routine without ever having known at first hand the thrill of danger or the ecstasy of passion. True, he has his own hardships—clearing rocky pastures, hauling in the cod during a storm, fighting Indians in a swamp—but what are these compared with the magnificence of leading an exodus of saints to found a city on a hill, for the eyes of all the world to behold? He might wage a stout fight against the Indians, and one out of ten of his fellows might perish in the struggle, but the world was no longer interested. He would be reduced to writing accounts of himself and scheming to get a publisher in London, in a desperate effort to tell a heedless world, "Look, I exist!"

His greatest difficulty would be not the stones, storms, and Indians, but the problem of his identity. In something of this sort, I should like to suggest, consists the anxiety and torment that inform productions of the late seventeenth and early eighteenth centuries—and should I say, some thereafter? It appears most clearly in *Magnalia Christi Americana*, the work of that soul most tortured by the problem,

Cotton Mather: "I write the Wonders of the Christian Religion, flying from the Depravations of Europe, to the American Strand." Thus he proudly begins, and at once trips over the acknowledgment that the founders had not simply fled from depraved Europe but had intended to redeem it. And so the book is full of lamentations over the declension of the children, who appear, page after page, in contrast to their mighty progenitors, about as profligate a lot as ever squandered a great inheritance.

And yet, the *Magnalia* is not an abject book; neither are the election sermons abject, nor is the inventory of sins offered by the synod of 1679. There is bewilderment, confusion, chagrin, but there is no surrender. A task has been assigned upon which the populace are in fact intensely engaged. But they are not sure anymore for just whom they are working; they know they are moving, but they do not know where they are going. They seem still to be on an errand, but if they are no longer inferiors sent by the superior forces of the Reformation, to whom they should report, then their errand must be wholly of the second sort, something with a purpose and an intention sufficient unto itself. If so, what is it? If it be not the due form of government, civil and ecclesiastical, that they brought into being, how otherwise can it be described?

The literature of self-condemnation must be read for meanings far below the surface, for meanings of which, we may be so rash as to surmise, the authors were not fully conscious, but by which they were troubled and goaded. They looked in vain to history for an explanation of themselves; more and more it appeared that the meaning was not to be found in theology, even with the help of the covenantal dialectic. Thereupon, these citizens found that they had no other place to search but within themselves—even though, at first sight, that repository appeared to be nothing but a sink of iniquity. Their errand having failed in the first sense of the term, they were left with the second, and required to fill it with meaning by themselves and out of themselves. Having failed to rivet the eyes of the world upon their city on the hill, they were left alone with America.

NOTES

1. See *The New England Mind: From Colony to Province* (1952), Chapter II.

2. See the perceptive analysis of Alan Heimert (*The New England Quarterly*, XXVI, September, 1953) of the ingredients that ultimately went into the Puritans' metaphor of the "wilderness," all the more striking a concoction because they attached no significance a priori to their wilderness destination. To begin with, it was simply a void.

CHAPTER 3

William Penn and the English Origins of American Religious Pluralism

Like the Puritans, the Society of Friends, or "Quakers" as their enemies labeled them, emerged as a dissenting, "nonconformist" movement in seventeenth-century England. But beyond their common status as dissenters, Puritans and Quakers could not have offered a more striking contrast. Where Puritans considered themselves to be the preeminent "people of war" in the New World, the Quakers were pacifist, opposed to all wars and capital punishment; where Puritans were led by an educated clergy, the Quakers were led by the Spirit and accorded all members of the congregation or "meeting" the right to speak in worship; perhaps most significantly, where Puritans created a "theocracy," or state church, the Quakers believed in religious toleration and the separation of church and state. It was this last conviction that lent Quakers a sense of mission no less compelling than the Puritan "errand" to be a "City Upon a Hill." As articulated by their New World leader, William Penn, the Quakers would inaugurate a "Holy Experiment," whose legacy would be religious toleration and pluralism.

In the essay that follows, Edmund S. Morgan offers a superb biographical account of one of the best-known and least-understood religious figures of the colonial period. What was the central dilemma of Penn's life? How was the distinctive "pluralism" (ethnic and religious diversity) of the "Middle Colonies" fixed by one of the smallest American religious traditions? What is the difference between complete religious liberty and the religious toleration espoused by Penn?

Additional Reading: Frederick B. Tolles, *Meeting House and Counting House: The Quaker Merchants of Colonial Philadelphia, 1682–1763* (Chapel Hill, 1948) offers a still-unsurpassed view of Quakerism and Pennsylvania culture from the founding of the colony to the end of the colonial period. Gary B. Nash, *Quakers and Politics, Pennsylvania, 1681–1726* (Princeton, 1968) and Barry Levy, *Quakers and the American Family: British Settlement in the Delaware Valley* (New York, 1988) describe politics, social life, and religion in Penn's early colony. Gillian Lindt Gollin,

Moravians in Two Worlds: A Study of Changing Communities (New York, 1967) and Stephanie Grauman Wolf, *Urban Village: Population, Community, and Family Structure in Germantown, Pennsylvania, 1683–1800* (Princeton, 1976) describe the different experiences of Pennsylvania's important German groups.

Edmund S. Morgan   The World and William Penn

Christ said that his kingdom was not of this world and embodied the message in his other teachings. His followers have nevertheless had to live in the world, trying in spite of his warning to bring it under his dominion or else bending his precepts almost beyond recognition in order to fit them to the ways of the world. Over the centuries Christianity has vibrated uneasily between what its founder prescribed and what the world demands. When the church becomes too fat and comfortable with the world, the contrast between the medium and the message will always prompt some prophet to summon true believers out of so unchristian an institution and into a way of life and worship that will more closely resemble Christ's. We may call them protesters, but in the course of time they become Protestants, with a capital P, against whom new prophets must in turn raise the flag of protest.

When William Penn was born in 1644, England was filled with prophets, each with his own version of what the Christian life entailed. The Church of England, which had been Protestant with a capital P from its inception, was under challenge not only by Presbyterians and Congregationalists but by a host of more radical visionaries, many of whom thought that Christ's kingdom was shortly to commence, not by subduing the world, but by putting an end to it: Antinomians, Muggletonians, Fifth-monarchy men, Anabaptists, Seekers, and so on. Penn's father and mother were none of these. They were genteel Protestants, good Church of England folk, but perhaps with some sympathy for Presbyterianism or Congregationalism. The father, also named William, certainly had no scruples about working for a government run by a Congregationalist, for he made a brilliant career in Oliver Cromwell's navy, before bringing himself to disgrace in an unsuccessful expedition against the Spanish in the Caribbean. But he also had no scruples about working for Charles II. When Charles returned to the throne in 1660, he restored Penn to his command as admiral and to a handsome living from lands in Ireland that had been confiscated from their Catholic owners. The elder Penn had reason to be content with a world that had served him well.[1]

His son was cut from another cloth. From an early age, at least from his early teens, William Penn was preoccupied with religion to an extent that his parents found disconcerting in a young gentleman with a career in the highest places before him. They wanted him to have all the advantages that his father's position

First published in the *Proceedings of the American Philosophical Society* 127 (1983), 291–315; reprinted by permission of the author.

entitled him to. They saw to it that he met all the right people, that he learned all the social graces. And indeed it all came easy to him. He was lively, energetic, and quickwitted. People liked him, and he liked them, including apparently a lot of pretty girls. But he had this unseemly bent for religion and for pursuing accepted religious beliefs to unacceptable conclusions.

When he was sixteen, they packed him off to Oxford, where the learned clergymen with which the place abounded might be able to keep him on the track. But he proved too hot to handle. In less than two years the learned clergy sent him back, expelled for his outspoken contempt for them and their church. In desperation his parents sent him on the grand tour of the Continent with other young gentlemen, in hopes that there he would get the spirit and the flesh sorted out into the right proportions. And though he spent some of his time in France studying theology, when he returned to London in 1664, not quite twenty, his religious zeal had momentarily abated. He was full of fashionable continental mannerisms, and he showed a proper appreciation for the sensual pleasures awaiting a young gentleman in Restoration London.

In London he attended Lincoln's Inn to learn the smattering of law appropriate to a gentleman of property; and he also attended at the King's Court, where his father was in high favor, especially with the Duke of York, the king's brother. The duke was in charge of naval affairs, with Sir William Penn, now knighted, as his leading admiral. The elder Penn, who could not have been more pleased with the way his son had seemingly turned out, introduced him to the duke, and the two quickly became friends. In 1666 Sir William sent the boy to Ireland to look after the family estates, and young William at once made friends among the Anglo-Irish nobility. But his career as a proper young gentleman was shortlived. At Cork he met up with Thomas Loe, a Quaker preacher who had entranced him as a teenager ten years before. By the end of 1667, after a brief spell in an Irish jail, he was back in London, where Samuel Pepys, a clerk in the Navy office, made that classic entry in his diary: "Mr. Will Pen, who is lately come over from Ireland, is a Quaker again, or some very melancholy thing."[2]

THE PROPHET

He was indeed a Quaker, and for his father and mother it was indeed a melancholy thing. Quakerism appeared to be another of those visionary, fringe movements that the 1640s and 1650s had continued to spawn, and of them all it may have seemed the most offensive. Its members were not content to depart from established institutions; they seemed to enjoy dramatic confrontations with authority, in which they defied not only the established church and all its ways but also the customary forms of good behavior. They wore their hats in the presence of their superiors, right up to the king himself. They refused to address people by their proper titles: they would not even vouchsafe a Mr. before the names of their betters. Some of them appeared naked at local church services. And instead of meeting in secret, where the authorities could ignore their violation of the laws against dissenting religions, they insisted on making their meetings public, in effect daring the sheriffs and constables to arrest them, a dare that was often taken.[3]

Their beliefs were as offensive as their conduct. They claimed what amounted to direct revelation from God—the inner light they called it—of the same kind that the apostles had had from Christ himself. The Holy Scriptures, therefore, on which the whole Protestant movement rested, were no more to them than an imperfect record of past revelations of people like themselves. They denied that Christ's sacifice was sufficient in itself to bring redemption, but they thought that all men were capable of redemption, if they followed the inner light. Thus they denied the central Christian doctrines of atonement and predestination. They rejected not only all other churches and ministers, refusing to pay their tithes to the established church, but also all sacraments and sermons. Their only preaching came from those who claimed to be enunciating messages from on high via the inner light. And they rejected original sin too, in its usual sense, for they claimed that with the assistance of the inner light they could completely free themselves from sin in their daily lives.

In espousing such beliefs William Penn appeared to be repudiating his heritage, repudiating the society in which he had grown, repudiating his education, repudiating his class, repudiating his parents. And there can be no doubt that he thought he was doing so. His first important tract, *No Cross No Crown,* written while he was imprisoned in the Tower of London, had as its theme the conflict between the world and the cross, the import of its title being that no crown of eternal glory could be won without taking up the cross and undergoing the suffering and humiliation ever inflicted by the world on those who reject its ways.[4]

There may have been something of adolescent, youthful rebellion in Penn's stance, but it persisted throughout his life in a posture of no compromise with the world. In counseling other adherents to the cause, he continually admonished them that they should "Keep out of base Bargainings or Conniving at fleshly Evasions of the Cross," that they should avoid "Reasonings with Opposers," lest the purity of their commitment be sullied.[5]

This last piece of advice was one that Penn was never able to follow himself, for Penn, in spite of being a likeable person, had a contentious streak that impelled him not only to reason with opposers but to denounce them. Although the Quakers officially professed an aversion to controversy, Penn took upon himself (with the blessing of other Quaker leaders) to defend them against all comers and especially against the Church of England and the more respectable dissenters of Presbyterian or Congregational persuasion. Nearly all his voluminous writings are polemical. In a three-year span alone, from 1672 to 1674, he published twenty-two tracts, several of them lengthy, in which he went on the attack with no holds barred.[6]

When one critic disclosed in a preface that he was sixty years of age, Penn, then at the ripe age of twenty-seven, mocked the man's "decrepit" reasoning and rang the changes on the fact "that any Man should live so long, and to so little Purpose." To Richard Baxter, perhaps the foremost dissenting divine of the Restoration period, he announced that "Scurvy of the minde is thy distemper; I feare its Incurable." He was fond of proclaiming his own moderate spirit as enjoined by his faith, but even in doing so he could not resist a jab at his opponents, as when in an answer to one critic he began by saying "I would give the Worst of Men their Due," and then added, "I justly esteem him of that Number."[7]

In a running controversy with John Faldo, an anglican minister, he addressed Faldo successively as Whistling Priest, Busie Priest, ungodly Priest, cavilling Priest, rude priest, ignorant priest, and told his readers:

> . . . in the Earth there is not any Thing so Fantastical, Conceited, Proud, Railing, Busie-Body, and sometimes Ignorant, as a sort of Priests to me not unknown (among whom our *Adversary* is not the least) who think their Coat will bear out their worst Expressions for Religion, and Practice an haughty Reviling for Christ, as one of the greatest Demonstrations of their Zeal; an ill-bred and Pedantick Crew, the *Bane of Reason, and Pest of the World;* the old Incendiaries to Mischief, and the best to be *spar'd of Mankind;* against whom the boiling Vengeance of an irritated God is ready to be poured out to the Destruction of such, if they repent not, *and turn from their Abominable Deceits.*[8]

This diatribe was not mere youthful exuberance. In one of his last tracts, written when he was fifty-four, he described his opponent as a "snake-in-the-grass" and then specified what kind, a rattlesnake.[9]

Penn coupled his unrelenting hostility to conventional Christians with an anti-intellectualism that attributed the whole apparatus of Christian theology and ecclesiastical institutions, both Catholic and Protestant, to the pursuit of forbidden knowledge which had caused the expulsion from paradise.[10] It was one of the marks of purity in the early followers of Christ, Penn thought, that "for the first Hundred Years, scarce an Eminent Scholar was to be found amongst the *Christians.*"[11]

In his first publication he warned against "Extollers of Humane Learning," and throughout his life in offering advice to the godly he warned them against "that Thirsting Spirit after much Head-Knowledge," which would only clog the passages to truth that lay within them. "My Friends," he would write, "disquiet not your Selves to comprehend Divine Things, for they that do so are of the Flesh."[12]

Those who claim direct access to divinity, whether they call it the inner light or the over-soul or by any other name, have always discounted the learning to be had from books, though they often, like Penn, couch their anti-book message in books of their own (Penn's bibliography runs to over 130 titles). Penn from the time of his conversion professed to be wary of books. Solitude and silence, not books, he thought, were the way to reach the Spirit. In his final testimony of advice to his children he cautioned them that "reading many Books is but a taking off the Mind too much from Meditation. . . . much reading is an Oppression of the Mind, and extinguishes the natural Candle; which is the Reason of so many senseless Scholars in the World."[13]

The senseless scholars he had encountered personally in his stay at Oxford, and his impatience with human learning rose to a crescendo whenever he considered what went on in universities, those places of "Folly, Ignorance, and Impiety" which "infect the whole Land with Debauchery, and at best Persecution, and anti-Christian clumsy-witted Pedants, and useless pragmaticks."[14] The universities were simply the last stop in the long line of degeneration from the simple truth of Christ and the prophets. God's message had been lost in "the obscure, unintelligible and unprofitable *Metaphysicks* of the *Heathen,* too greedily received and mischievously increased by *Fathers, Councils, School-Men* and our modern *Universities,* to the corrupting of Christian Doctrine, and disputing away the Benefit of Christian life."[15] He was not against secular learning that devoted itself to secular things, to "Building, Improvement of Land, Medicine, Chirurgery, Traffick, Navigation, History, Government."[16] But when brought to bear on religion, human learning was only a block to the true knowledge that came from within.

Penn's hostility to universities extended to the ministers trained there. Their objective, he claimed, was only to make a living out of religion, and their ministry was unavailing because they relied on book learning instead of the inner light.[17] Penn thought of himself as a minister, unpaid and unordained but called, like all true ministers, directly by God. He advised others like him that

> We are not to *Study* nor speak our *own Words.* . . . We are to minister, *as the Oracles of God;* if so, then must we receive *from Christ,* God's Great Oracle, what we are to minister. And if we are to minister what we receive, then not what we Study, Collect, and beat out of our own Brains, for that is not the Mind of Christ, but our own Imaginations, and this will not profit the People.[18]

True Christian doctrine, Penn insisted, did not need to be "prov'd by *Aristotle* and his Philosophy."[19] The Scriptures themselves needed no interpretation. Indeed it was ridiculous to suppose that God had made the Scriptures so obscure that they required a privileged race of scholar-priests to explain. They were "suited to the Capacity of the Young, the Ignorant, and the Poor."[20] And that was how Penn liked to think of the Quakers. To him they were always a "poor, despised people," poor not only in their ignorance and in the bad treatment they received, but poor in lacking the good things of the world on which false Christians prided themselves. They were, he assured himself, mostly mechanics.[21] And he gladly assimilated their humility to himself, gladly shared their sufferings, for he was convinced that in doing so he was opening the way for the spirit, which could scarcely penetrate the antichristian world of fleshly delights and scholarly philosophy that had been his heritage.

In his professed affinity for the poor, Penn touched a dynamic element of the Christian tradition that has sparked more than one rebel against the ways of the world. There is an egalitarian leaven in Christianity, subdued by the institutions that Christianity fosters, but ever ready to breed prophets in sackcloth to denounce the churches that forget it. "Christ," Penn observed in *No Cross No Crown,* "came Poor into the World, and so lived in it."[22] Did he call his disciples from among the learned? "I would fain know," asked Penn,

> how many *Rabbies, Greek* and *Latin Philosophers,* yielded themselves Proselytes to the Christian Religion, though they had his *Presence, Ministry, Death and Ressurection amongst them,* who was and is the Author and Master of it? If such Learning be so great a Friend to Truth, how comes it that the greatest Things have fallen to the Share of Poor and Illiterate Men; And that such have been

most apt to receive, and boldest to suffer for it? Why not *Rabbies* rather than *Fishermen. . . . ?*"[23]

True Christians now as then, Penn believed, were most likely to be found among "Handicraft, Labouring, and Husband-men, Persons inexpert in the Scholastick Adages, Disputations and Opinions of the Heathenish Philosophical World."[24] George Fox, the founder of Quakerism, whom Penn revered, had been a simple and untutored man, "not of *High Degree,*" Penn recalled, "or *Elegant Speech* or *Learned* after the Way of this World."[25] To be a Christian was to be humble, meek, of low degree. Penn never tired of citing the first epistle to the Corinthians that "not many wise men after the flesh, not many mighty, not many noble, are called." And he continued to identify the Quakers with "the *Weary* and *Heavy Laden,* the *Hungry* and *Thirsty,* the *Poor* and *Needy,* the *Mournful* and Sick."[26]

Quaker doctrine, moreover, spelled out for him some of the egalitarian implications of Christian teaching. Quakers, as we have seen, made it a matter of principle to ignore and flatten social distinctions. Penn found refreshing their insistence on simplicity, their drab clothing, their refusal to doff their hats or to use customary forms of address. The world's addiction to these empty forms was simply another sign of its apostasy. With his usual air of defiance Penn dismissed the objections that his own sort of people made to this seeming uncouthness: if, as they claimed, it would "overthrow all Manner of Distinctions among Men," then so be it. "I can't help it," he said, "the Apostle *James* must answer for it, who has given us this Doctrine for Christian and Apostolical," and he cited the second chapter of James, where the apostle warns against respect of persons.[27]

After joining the Quakers and assuming, however proudly, the mantle of meekness, Penn welcomed unmeek confrontations with the authorities of Restoration England, representatives of the world he had left behind. With his acid tongue and sharp wit he was more than a match for the judges before whom he and his Friends appeared. The incarceration he nevertheless suffered at Newgate Prison and the Tower of London only gave him the leisure to grind out more books and pamphlets denouncing the ways of the world he had known and justifying the ways of the Quakers.

We have, then, a man who made his life a testimony against the world he grew up in, a world that called itself Christian and allowed, indeed enjoined, its people to study and do what Christ had taught, but which seemed to a sharp young mind to deny his teachings in all its institutions, not least in all the churches save one that claimed the name of Christ. Why, then, may we ask, have we ever heard of William Penn? The world is pretty good at sending into oblivion those who defy or deny it. The meek may inherit it later on, but they don't get far in the here and now. If we have heard of William Penn before this, it is because he was not meek. He was not humble. And being neither meek nor humble, he did not in fact reject as much of the world as he seemed to. The man who sassed his judges and filled the presses from his cell in Newgate was not content to inherit the world later on or to leave it as he found it. He wanted to change it now, and he did in fact leave his mark on it.

He left his mark, because what he wanted and argued for, pleaded for, almost fought for was not quite outside the possible. He left his mark because he knew how the world worked and was prepared, in spite of his denunciations, to work within its terms.

We may find a first clue to his capacity for coming to terms with the world in his relationship to his parents. He was obviously fond of them, proud of his father's success in a career that he himself must eschew. In recounting the sacrifices he had to make for his faith, he always dwelt on the displeasure of his parents. And his father's displeasure was real. Penn spoke of "The bitter usage" he underwent when sent down from Oxford in 1662, "whipping, beating, and turning out of Dores."[28] And when he returned from Ireland a full-fledged Quaker in 1667, it must have gone just as badly, though by this time whipping and beating were out of the question. But the Penns, after trying to talk their son out of his queer beliefs, became reconciled to them and to him. By the time the admiral died in 1670 (not yet forty-nine years old), he had entrusted his son with many of his business affairs and made him his principal heir and executor of his considerable estate. Indeed, according to Penn, both his parents "that once disown'd me for this blessed Testimonys sake . . . have come to love me above all, thinking they could never do and leave enough for me."[29] He showed no hesitation in accepting that share of the world which his father had accumulated, nor did he ever think of disowning his parents, as they for a time had thought of disowning him.

Admiral Penn had raised his son as a Protestant, as a gentleman, and as an Englishman. Penn was proud to be all of these. His understanding of what each entailed might differ from his father's and from many other Englishmen's, but not to the point of disavowal. Rather he thought that if Protestants were true to their principles they ought to become Quakers as he had. If gentlemen were true to their principles they ought to give up the vices that he had given up. And if Englishmen were true to their principles, they ought to prevent their government from meddling in religion and threatening the liberty and property of Englishmen like him, who did not conform to the dictates of a set of bigoted priests. As a Protestant, a gentleman, and an Englsihman, Penn presented his case, in terms designed to appeal to Protestants, to gentlemen, and to Englishmen.

THE PROTESTANT

Penn insisted throughout his life that he was a Protestant. In a speech before a committee of Parliament in 1678, supporting a bill for religious toleration, he told the members:

> I was bred a Protestant, and that strictly too. . . . reading, travail and observation made the Religion of my education the Religion of my judgement. . . . I do tell you again, and here solemnly declare in the presence of Almighty God, and before you all, that the Profession I now make, and the society I now adhere to, have been so far from altering that Protestant judgment I had, that I am not conscious to myself of having receded from an Iota of any one principle maintained by those first Protestants and Reformers in Germany, and our own Martyrs at home against the Pope or See of Rome.[30]

Protestantism, as Penn saw it, was Christianity rescued from the apostasy that had befallen it under Roman Catholicism. And Quakerism was Protestantism rescued from the apostasy that had befallen it after the passing of the great Reformers of the sixteenth century. Almost all his voluminous writings were designed to demonstrate this proposition and to defend Quakerism from denials of it by Anglicans, Presbyterians, Congregationalists, Socinians, Anabaptists, and Catholics. His first tract, in 1668, like so many seventeenth-century tracts, tried to get the whole argument on the title page: *Truth Exalted; In a Short, But Sure Testimony against all those Religions, Faiths, and Worships, That have been formed and followed in the Darkness of Apostacy: And For that Glorious Light which is now Risen, and Shines forth, in the Life and Doctrine of the Despised Quakers, as the Alone Good Old Way of Life and Salvation. Presented to Princes, Priests, and People, That they may Repent, Believe, and Obey. By William Penn, whom Divine Love constrains in an Holy Contempt, to trample on Egypt's Glory, not fearing the King's Wrath, having beheld the Majesty of Him who is Invisible.*[31] The same intent is apparent in his other tracts, such as, (without the subtitles), *Quakerism a New Nick-name for Old Christianity* and *Primitive Christianity Revived in the Faith and Practice of the People called Quakers.*[32]

Quakerism as Protestantism required a good deal of defending, because its distinctive doctrines seemed clearly heretical, in direct defiance, as we have seen, of central Protestant Christian dogmas. Protestant heresies generally went in one of two directions: either on the one hand toward Antinomianism, in which the true believer was thought to be freed from adherence to the Law by the presence of Christ within him, or on the other hand toward Arminianism, in which the believer was thought to be capable of achieving his own salvation by escaping from original sin and obeying the Law. Antinomianism entailed a belief in direct revelation, which was supposed by the orthodox to have ceased with the writing of the Bible. Arminianism amounted to a denial of justification by faith and thus a return to the repudiated Catholic doctrine of justification by works. Quakerism, it seemed, embraced not one of these heresies but both at once. In the doctrine of an inner light Quakers claimed a direct revelation from God. At the same time they affirmed that everyone possessed this inner voice of God and could achieve salvation by obedience to it. They thus rejected predestination and affirmed or seemed to affirm justification by works.

This combination of heresies appeared to subordinate the Scriptures to some fancied inner voice, and to eliminate Christ's atonement for human sin. The recovery of the Scriptures had been central to the Reformation, which had also restored Christ as the sole savior of man, freeing the church from reliance on any kind of human merit. But the Quakers, as if to emphasize that they had no need of Christ, eliminated the sacraments that memorialized him. And to top off their heresies, they denied the conventional doctrine of resurrection of the dead at the last day.

In defending Quaker heresies as Protestant and Christian, Penn had one advantage. Protestants prided themselves on eliminating idolatry and superstition from their worship. They emphasized the holy spirit, which brought unmerited grace to those whom God would save. They destroyed graven images and denounced the materialism of the Roman church. Quakers too emphasized the spirit and explicitly affirmed God to be an infinite spirit, affirmed it far more unequivocally than orthodox Protestants did.[33] It was thus possible for Penn to turn some accepted Protestant doctrines and institutions against his opponents in the Church of England, which still harbored many of the sensual accompaniments of worship inherited from Rome. English churches, despite the Puritans, still contained paintings and statuary, still contained some ceremonies and trappings that betrayed, in Penn's and the Quakers' view, the Protestant repudiation of graven images. It was, as Penn put it in his devastating fashion, as though "God was an *old Man*, indeed, and Christ a *little Boy*, to be treated with a kind of *Religious Mask* [i.e. drama], for so they picture him in their Temples; and too many in their Minds."[34]

The sacraments of baptism and the Lord's Supper, in spite of the Protestant denial of transubstantiation, Penn dismissed as relics of superstition. Water baptism was only slightly less offensive than the Old Testament circumcision that it replaced, and the Lord's Supper was "a Kind of Protestant Extream Unction."[35] Both sacraments were departures from true Christian and Protestant freedom from formalistic, external devices that encouraged sinners to think they could be saved without an inner transformation. Circumcision of the heart, baptism by fire was what Christ demanded of those who believed in him. "Where Ceremonies, or Shadowy Services [Penn's term for traditional rituals] are continued, People rest upon the Observance of them, and *Indulge* themselves in the Neglect of the *Doctrine of the Cross of our Lord Jesus Christ*."[36] The ceremonies by which other Protestants memorialized Christ were in fact ways of escaping the burden that he laid on his followers.

The orthodox doctrine of resurrection of the dead similarly departed from Christ's insistence on the spirit. Penn did not deny that the dead would be raised, but he regarded as grossly materialistic the notion that men would recover their earthly bodies. It betrayed a continuing sensual element in the orthodox view, as though heaven would be incomplete without a resumption of the earthly pleasures enjoyed in this world. "It makes the Soul," said Penn, "uncapable of Compleat Happiness without a Fleshly Body, as if Heaven were an Earthly Place to see, walk in, and for all our Outward Senses to be enjoyed and exercised, as in this World, though in an higher degree." This, Penn maintained, was neither Christian nor Protestant but Mohammedan. And he went on to heap scorn on the notion: if the dead were supposed to rise "so strictly . . . as they Dyed, then every Man is to rise *Married*, [*single*], *Low, High, Fat, Lean, Young, Old, Homely, Handsome*, and according to former Complexion and Sex. . . ." The idea was too ridiculous to contemplate.[37]

The central Quaker doctrine of an inner light, the voice of God in every man, was nothing if not spiritual. To Penn, it was no novelty but the essence of Christianity and especially Protestant Christianity. Nor was it difficult to find passages in the writings of Christians from St. Paul onward that could be interpreted to support it, a task to which Penn gladly devoted himself. Almost all explanations of saving grace, of God's calling of his saints to salvation, could be read as expositions of the Quaker doctrine. Orthodox divines, to be sure, took pains to indicate that saving grace did not involve direct revelation; but the line between the two had always been difficult to maintain, and Quakers relieved themselves of the difficulty by erasing it. The inner light and saving grace, Penn maintained, were one and the same. They were the voice of Christ, who was God within man, enabling man to sin no more, to be made pure and thus acceptable to God.

In answer to the charge that Quakers denied Christ's atonement for sin, Penn developed a distinction made by other Quakers, between past and present sin. Christ's sacrifice, he maintained, was necessary to atone for the sins that every man committed before he submitted to the inner light. Christ justified man before God for these past sins, but this did not excuse future sins. And it was sacrilege to suggest that God would welcome to his bosom men who continued to sin. The inner light, Christ within man, enabled believers to stop sinning. Christ not only atoned for past sins but prevented future ones, and he did so for all men and women who heeded his voice within them.[38] Such a view precluded predestination and robbed original sin of its power. And Penn went on the offensive against both these dogmas. Predestination he derided as the work of narrow, pinched-up souls who made "the Eternal God, as partial as themselves, like some Ancients, That because they could not Resemble God, they would make such Gods as might Resemble them."[39]

But it was unnecessary to waste much argument on predestination, for it was out of favor in the Church of England anyhow. Penn reserved his greatest scorn for the doctrine of original sin as something that debilitated men and prevented them while in the flesh from ever fully complying with the will of God. Penn dubbed this a "lazy" doctrine for "sin-pleasing times." It was simply, in his view, an excuse for sinning, and he mocked the orthodox ministers who preached it. "Methinks," he wrote,

> these Hireling Ministers are like some Mercenary Souldiers . . . that cannot bear to think of the Enemy's being totally routed, lest their War end, and their Pay with it. . . . They had rather the Devil were unsubdued, than they disbanded, that his being unconquered might be a Pretence for keeping such Mercenaries always on foot.[40]

For all his wit, Penn was hard pressed to defend as Protestant a doctrine that resembled so closely the Catholic one of justification by works, but he could cite a good many Protestant divines, as well as Scripture, to show that the presence of saving faith was normally evidenced by good works. And he argued that making good works necessary to salvation was not the same as making them merit salvation. Good works, he said, were

> not strictly meritorious; only they have an inducing, procuring, and obtaining Power and Virtue in them. That is Merit where there is an Equality betwixt the Work and Wages; but all those Temporary [i.e. temporal] Acts of Righteousness, can never equal Everlasting Life, Joy, and Happiness (being of Grace, and not of Debt) and therefore strictly no Merit.[41]

This may seem a distinction without much difference, but Penn was convinced that "Preferring Opinion before Piety hath filled the World with Perplexing

Controversies," and this was one of them.[42] The Puritan's tendency to separate saving grace from morality seemed to him monstrous. Indeed "This Distinction betwixt moral and Christian," he thought, was *"a deadly Poyson these latter Ages have been infected with* to the Destruction of Godly Living, and *Apostatizing* of those Churches [Presbyterian and Congregational] in whom there might once have been begotten some *Earnest, Living Thirst* after the Inward Life of Righteousness." It was God who had joined grace and virtue, and it was human "stinginess of spirit," not Protestantism, that separated them.[43]

In demonstrating the Christian and Protestant character of Quakerism, Penn knew that he had to meet other Protestants on their own ground. They would not listen to an argument that defended the inner light and other Quaker doctrines by means of the inner light itself. Erudition was what it would take, and in spite of his hostility to learning, Penn was prepared to supply erudition, probably better equipped to do so than any other Quaker. He knew Latin. He knew French. He knew enough Greek to discusss Greek texts of the New Testament. He could even put on a display of linguistic pyrotechnics (discussing the ninth chapter of First John) that included translations into French, Italian, German, Dutch, Anglo-Saxon, Hebrew, Syriac, and Chaldee (though it is clear that he did not know all these).[44] Although he was no theologian and thought that theologians were in large measure responsible for the apostasy of Christianity from its primitive purity, he had studied the church fathers and the scholastic and Protestant divines enough to mine their writings for arguments. Similarly, although he held fast to the Quaker insistence that the inner light was a more direct and reliable avenue to God's will than the Scriptures, he knew the Scriptures backwards and forwards and could always summon up appropriate passages to serve his cause.

Penn's usual method of attack was to refute his opponents by appeals to reason and to Scripture and then to offer voluminous passages from past authorities. For example, in arguing that the inner light was present and recognized in all men before Christ's appearance as well as after, he quoted, among others, passages from Orpheus, Hesiod, Thales, Sybilla, Pythagoras, Heraclitus, Anaxagoras, Socrates, Timaeus Locrus, Antisthenes, Plato, Parmenides Magnus, Zeno, Chrysippus, Antipater, Hieron, Sophocles, Menander, Philo, Cleanthes, Plutarch, Epictetus, Seneca, Diogenes, Xenocrates, Virgil, Justin Martyr, Clemens Alexandrinus, Tertullian, Origen, Lactantius, Athanasius, Chrysostom, and Augustine.[45] In defending the Quaker refusal to take oaths, he dredged up no less than 122 authorities from ancient times to the seventeenth century.[46]

When Penn was not occupied in defending the Quaker movement, he was often busy keeping it defensible. He recognized how vulnerable it was to the charge that reliance on the inner light could be used to justify any kind of conduct, say "Murder, Adultery, Treason, Theft, *or any such like Wickedness."* In answer he could only say, in effect, that it did not, that "God's Spirit makes People free from Sin, and *not to commit Sin."*[47] Which was to say that Quaker morality was for the most part conventional Protestant morality: the inner light did not call Quakers to immoral actions. But Quakers had broken with convention at several points: in their mode of address, in refusing to take oaths, in wearing their hats before their betters. Penn was aware that some members, having broken convention at one point, might throw it to the winds. Such had been the case with another group, the so-called Ranters, antinomians who defined their actions, whatever they might be, as righteous by attributing them to the spirit of Christ within them. This was dangerously close to Quaker doctrine, and if Quakers were to gain the acceptance Penn thought they deserved, it was necessary to keep the movement free from such anarchistic tendencies.

Accordingly Penn took a strong stand, along with George Fox, in support of a church discipline that could restrain eccentricity and eccentrics. There was, for example, the case of William Mucklow, who carried his attachment to his hat to a stage that violated the whole purpose of Quaker practice. Quakers refused to take off their hats to human superiors in order to testify against worldly honors, and they could thereby distinguish their reverence for God by taking off their hats in worship. But Mucklow insisted on wearing his hat in prayer. When admonished for it, he fell back on the inner light and denied the right of the church to command his conscience. Others took up the same cry, challenging the right of the weekly, monthly, or yearly meetings of Quakers to supervise the conduct of members, including the right which the meetings had begun to exercise, of determining the appropriateness of members' marriages.[48]

In these controversies Penn was always on the side of authority, affirming the right of the church to rid itself of "Wrong Spirits under never such right Appearances."[49] His commitment was not simply to the doctrines of Quakerism but to the movement. He was ready to use arguments that he would have scorned in a Church of England man, maintaining that the majority in a church were more likely to be right than any individual, and advising anyone who dissented to "wait upon God in Silence and Patience . . . and as thou abidest in the *Simplicity of the* TRUTH, thou wilt receive an Understanding with the rest of thy Brethren." And if this failed, "since the Spirit of the Lord is one in all, it ought to be obey'd through another, as well as in one's self."[50] If anyone persisted in mistaking his own idiosyncrasies for the Spirit of the Lord, the only recourse was to expel him from the movement.

With Penn's assistance, though it required adjusting principles a little, the Quakers avoided the errors of the Ranters. Though Quakers remained at the outer edge of Protestantism, they became, thanks in no small measure to Penn, a recognized church, a force in the world, unlike the ephemeral groups around them. And Penn, fervently a Quaker, could continue to think of himself as a Protestant.

THE GENTLEMAN

That Penn was a gentleman and remained a gentleman is apparent both in his behavior and in his beliefs. His social position gave him an access to power that no other Quaker enjoyed. At the same time, his gentility affected his understanding of Quakerisms' most controversial doctrine and helped to shape that doctrine in ways that presented a special challenge to men of his class.

The most radical departure of Quakerism from orthodox Protestantism was its insistence on the possibility of perfection in this world, the possibility of living entirely as God would have us live, pure and sinless. When Penn called on Christians to take up Christ's cross in opposition to the ways of the world, he did not think he was asking the impossible. True Christians could imitate Christ, for Christ would enable them to make the imitation, to become pure and sinless. But what did purity and sinlessness require?

Since Penn continually emphasized the affinity of Christ for the poor and humble and of the poor and humble for Christ, it would be plausible to suppose that he thought the imitation of Christ required poverty, that those of his own class who gave up the ways of the world must give up the privileges and perquisities that went with wealth and rank. And the Quaker refusal to recognize worldly honors in forms of address and behavior would seem to support such a supposition. But Penn took pains to assure everyone that this was not his meaning.

We get our first hint of his position in *No Cross No Crown,* immediately after his defiant statement that if Quaker doctrine will overthrow all distinctions among men, so be it, the apostle James must bear the blame, not the Quakers.[51] This ringing declaration is followed by a statement that sounds odd to modern ears, beginning with a derision of worldly honors and closing with an affirmation of the obligations that Christianity imposes on the different ranks of men: "The World's Respect," he says, "is an Empty Ceremony, no Soul or Substance in it. The Christian's is a solid Thing, whether by Obedience to Superiors, Love to Equals, or *Help* and *Countenance* to Inferiors."[52] Superiors, inferiors, equals—to an age that associates human progress with equality, Christian perfection would seem to have little to do with the duties of inferiors toward superiors or of superiors toward inferiors.

What this passage tells us is that Penn's world was not ours. It was a world that, for all its faults, still bore the mark of its Creator. Most of the people who lived in it violated the Creator's intention in many ways but not in the orderly, hierarchical structure of their societies. That kind of order, for Penn (and for virtually everyone else at the time) was part of the original plan. "Divine Right," Penn believed, "runs through more Things of the World, and Acts of our Lives, than we are aware of; and Sacrilege may be committed against more than the Church."[53] It could be committed, one gathers, by ignoring social order as much as by following the empty ceremonies that proffered unfelt or exaggerated honor. "Envy none," Penn told his children, for "it is God that maketh Rich and Poor, Great and Small, High and Low."[54]

In taking up a strange religious belief, Penn seemed to many of his contemporaries to be himself committing a kind of sacrilege against the divine right embedded in the social order: gentlemen ought not to depart from the religion established by law and thus set a bad example for lesser folk. When his Quakerism got him in trouble again on a visit to Ireland in 1670, an Irish friend, Lord O'Brien, thought it sheer stubbornness for Penn to persevere in so strange a religious belief when it would have been perfectly easy for him to stick to the standard Anglican one. Penn, he said, was rejecting "not what you cant but what you wont believe, . . . it is certainly possible for you to believe our faith, for it is reasonable."[55] Nevertheless, Lord O'Brien and Penn's other noble friends in Ireland were clear that queer and stubborn religious beliefs were not sufficient in themselves to deprive a gentleman of his rank. His friends intervened for him against the mayor of Cork, because as one of them said, wrong religious opinions "certainly cannot make any man degenerate from being a Gentleman who was borne so."[56]

Penn's priorities differed from his friends'. If religion and social position were at odds, religion must prevail. But Penn saw no good reason why they should be at odds. Although he thought religion demanded of gentlemen a standard of virtue that few attained or even attempted, it did not follow that a man's religious beliefs, whether strict or loose, should affect his place or power in society. That his friends should pull rank to help one of their own kind was perfectly proper, and he in turn used his own rank and influence to help himself and his Quaker friends in their encounters with authority.

Penn's knowledge of the law, gained during his brief period of studies at Lincoln's Inn, may have been superficial, but he had learned enough to be a troublesome defendant. When brought before the courts he assumed not merely the defiant stance of the self-righteous, but also the assurance of the cultivated gentleman in dealing with officials whom he evidently regarded as not quite his equals either socially or intellectually. When arrested for preaching at a Quaker meeting in 1670, he lectured the judges on the law and taunted them into statements that left the jury totally committed to him. He demanded to know what law he had broken, and when he was told it was the Common Law, he asked what that was, as if he didn't know. There then followed this exchange:

> Court: You must not think that I am able to run up so many Years, and over so many adjudged Cases, which we call Common-Law to answer your Curiosity.
> Penn: This answer I am sure is very short of my Question; for if it be Common, it should not be so hard to produce.

This evoked an apoplectic response and more exchanges, in which Penn seemed to be interrogating the Court instead of vice versa. When the judge told him, "If I should suffer you to ask Questions till to Morrow-Morning, you would be never the wiser," Penn could not resist the opening thus given him, and replied that whether he was wiser or not would depend on the answers he got.[57]

The jury, in spite of browbeating by the bench, refused to convict this Quaker who talked back to his judges with such aplomb.[58] A few months later the constables caught Penn preaching again and hauled him before the court, this time for violating the so-called five-mile act, which required no jury trial. Even without a jury to play up to, Penn maintained his posture of superiority and contempt. Asked at the outset of the hearing if his name was Penn, he answered, "Dost thou not know me? Hast thou forgotten me?" to which the judge replied, "I don't know you, I don't desire to know such as you are."

> "If not," said Penn, "why dost thou send for me hither?"
> "Is that your Name Sir?"
> "Yes, yes, my Name is Penn, thou knowst it is, I am not ashamed of my name."

After he had reduced the court to fury with a number of diatribes, the judges called for a corporal with musketeers to escort him to Newgate Prison, to which Penn gave his final sneer: "No, no send thy Lacky, I know the Way to Newgate."[59]

Although he served his terms in Newgate and the Tower of London, as other gentlemen had done before, Penn was able to retain or recover the place at the king's court that his father had won for him, and he was able to do it without sacrificing his religious convictions. In 1681 he got the king to give him Pennsylvania as a refuge for Quakers, presumably in payment of a debt owed his father.[60] After the Duke of York came to the throne as James II in 1685, Penn enjoyed even greater opportunities for influence, and he took them. His father, on his deathbed, had adjured the duke to help young Penn out of the difficulties that his religion would surely get him into, and the duke honored the request as king. From 1685 until revolution ousted James from the throne in 1688, Penn was in daily and effective attendance at Whitehall, pulling strings for better treatment of Quakers and of other religious dissenters.[61]

Penn's rejection of the world, then, was not a rejection of the existing social order or of the allocation of power within it. "I would not be thought," he said, "to set the Churl upon the present Gentleman's Shoulder."[62] And at every opportunity he advertised the submission and obedience of Quakers to civil authority, excepting always when civil authority required a violation of their special beliefs.

In keeping with this acceptance of the existing social order, Penn's appeals for the Quaker cause were directed upward, to those in power, not downward to the mass of mechanics and laborers whom he liked to think the cause embraced. The direction of his efforts is apparent even in the record of his extended missionary tour, along with other leading Quakers, through the Rhineland and the low countries in 1677. His journal of the tour is studded with the names of potentates and of highly placed merchants and gentlemen and gentlewomen whom he sought to convert, if not to the cause, at least to toleration of it. Wherever he and his friends arrived, their first inquiry was to find out who were the most "worthy" local people, and it quickly becomes apparent that by "worthy" he meant the people who were worth something in wealth and power.[63] He spent hours and days with Elizabeth, the Princess Palatine of the Rhine, and with her companion, the Countess van Hoorn, and later urged them to the faith in lengthy, almost passionate letters. The faith did not require, he was careful to assure them, that they give up their power and possessions. "I speak not," he said, "of deserting or flinging away all outward substance."[64]

If Penn did not think the imitation of Christ required flinging away all outward substance, we may fairly ask what he did think it required. If perfect obedience to God was possible in this world and it did not mean a change in the social or political order, what precisely did it mean? Penn gives us the answer in numerous admonitions, denunciations, and apostrophes. Here is one written in 1677, and intended, he says, for "all Ranks and Qualities, from the Highest to the Lowest, that walk not after the Spirit, but after the Flesh":

Arise, O God, for thy Name's Sake! O what tremendous Oaths and Lyes! What Revenge and Murders, with Drunkenness and Gluttony! What Pride and Luxury! What Chamberings and Wantonness! What Fornications, Rapes, and Adulteries! What Masks and Revels! What Lustful Ornaments, and Enchanting Attires! What Proud Customs, and Vain Complements! What Sports and Pleasures! Again, what Falseness and Treachery! What Avarice and Oppression! What Flattery and Hypocrisie! What Malice and Slander! What Contention and Law-Suits! What Wars and Bloodshed! What Plunders, Fires and Desolations![65]

These are supposedly the sins of the age, and there are a number of them like lying and swearing and fornication that were available to all classes, but hardly anyone outside the higher ranks of society and outside the corridors of power would have had the resources to indulge in most of them. Similarly, *No Cross No Crown*, Penn's longest diatribe against self-indulgence, was aimed primarily at men and women who took pleasure in "curious Trims, Rich and changeable Apparel, Nicety of Dress, Invention and Imitation of Fashions, Costly Attire, Mincing Gates, Wanton Looks, Romances, Plays, Treats, Balls, Feasts, and the like. . . ."[66] In yet another catalog of the five great crying sins of the time, in 1679, Penn included: first, drunkenness; second, whoredom and fornication; third, luxury; fourth, gaming; and fifth, oaths, cursing, blasphemy, and profaneness. All but luxury would presumably be possible for the general run of people, but in discussing the prevalence of these sins Penn showed that he had in mind the people of his own class. Drunkenness was exemplified by having several different wines at one meal, whoredom and fornication resulted from following French fashions, gaming was bad because it resulted in the careless loss of great estates, cursing was most reprehensible in persons of quality, and so on.[67]

In other words, Penn identified sin with the failings of his own class. He had been brought up among the gentry and nobility and reached his young manhood at a time when gentlemen were cutting loose from the restrictions of Puritan England. He was just sixteen when Charles II returned to the throne and set an example of licentiousness that had been missing in England for two decades. For a time Penn followed the example. He knew the vices of the gentry at first hand, as he often reminded his readers, and it was these vices he had in mind in his denunciations of the ways of the world; they were the ways of his world. His insistence that perfect obedience to God was possible for Christians meant that it was possible to do without the vices of gentlemen, the vices that he had learned at the court of the king and on the grand tour in France. Perfection was a matter of not doing what he had formerly done, and taking satisfaction instead in the pleasures of the spirit.

Thus the sinless perfection that Penn called for consisted largely in giving up those extravagant pleasures that only the few could afford anyhow. He sometimes defended this kind of abstention as socially beneficial. If gentlemen would deny themselves extravagant food, drink, and other fleshly pleasures, they could give more to the poor. He even recommended forming a public stock for the purpose, derived from "the Money which is expended in every Parish in such vain Fashions, as wearing of Laces, Jewels, Embroideries, Unnecessary Ribbons, Trimming, Costly Furniture and Attendance, together with what is commonly consumed in Taverns, Feasts, Gaming etc." The funds could be used to provide "Work-Houses for the Able, and Alms Houses for the Aged and Impotent."[68] He never doubted that there would always be a supply of poor both able and impotent, to be thus relieved, as there would always be a supply of gentlemen to deny themselves in order to relieve the poor.[69]

But relief of the poor was not the main objective of self-denial. Self-denial was an end in itself, pleasing to God, the essence of virtue. By suppressing the self men not only avoided sin, but opened the way to spiritual communion with the part of God that lay within them, the inner light. For some Quakers the inner light demanded specific actions. And it was standard Quaker doctrine, which Penn defended at length, that the inner light rather than Scripture was the guide by which to determine the rightness or wrongness of any particular action. Penn also, as we have seen, thought that ministers should be no more than mouthpieces for the inner light, passing on to their hearers what the inner light revealed to them. Yet Penn seems to have thought of the highest communion with the spirit as something that could not be put into words, as a feeling unconnected with the thoughts that words conveyed. Indeed thoughts were to be banished from the mind, lest they get in its way. Not words, not speech, not even works, but silence, solitude, passivity were its usual accompaniment: "wait in the Stilness upon the God of all Families of the Earth, and then shall you have a true *Feeling* of him."[70]

Nowhere did Penn argue that this feeling, this silent, wordless, thoughtless reception of the spirit must eventuate in positive actions. He continually insisted on the good works that Christ would enable the believer to perform and that would justify him in the sight of God. But precisely what these works must be, apart from avoidance of the sins he cataloged, remained nebulous. It was good to give to the poor, and especially to widows and orphans, but the objective to be sought in self-denial seems to have consisted mainly in the feeling of bliss that came to the soul when it was freed from the distractions of earthly pleasures.

What Penn demanded of Christians, then, was not beyond their reach: self-denial and passive reception of the spirit. It was no wonder that Christians were to be found most often among the humble, for the humble could reach these goals with less effort than the mighty. Penn directed his appeals upward, because it was the high and mighty who most needed them, and even for them the goals were not impossible. In order to make way for the spirit, his noble friends need only do out of choice what the humble did out of necessity. If it seemed to them like a pretty dull life to do without their accustomed pleasures of the flesh, Penn asked them to consider how they expected to amuse themselves throughout eternity. Better begin learning to appreciate spiritual joys now!

Few of the gentry and nobility to whom Penn addressed his demand were ready to comply with it, and his own austerity, he tells us, brought him a good deal of derision from his former boon companions. But if self-denial was not in fashion among the gentlemen of Restoration England, the demand for it was not something to disgrace a gentleman. Indeed it was part of the traditional ideal of what a gentleman was supposed to be.

Penn did not compile a list of authorities to prove that gentlemen should be Quakers, as he did to prove that Protestants should be, but it would not have been impossible for him to do so. In handbooks that told seventeenth-century Englishmen how to behave, there are passages strikingly similar to the injunctions that Penn urged on them. The most popular handbook, Richard Brathwait's *The English Gentleman*,[71] could almost have been written as an introduction to *No Cross No Crown*. Brathwait argued, as did Penn, that virtue, not wealth, was what conferred nobility, and that the essence of virtue lay in self-restraint. Brathwait even urged something like the Quaker simplicity of dress. "Gorgeous attire," he said, "is to be especially restrained, because it makes us dote upon a vessell of corruption, strutting upon earth, as if we had our eternall mansion on earth."[72] Virtue was something internal: "she seeketh nothing that is without her." And Brathwait went on to praise the Levites who "were to have no possessions: *for the Lord was their inheritance.*"[73] Brathwait can scarcely have expected English gentlemen to follow that example literally, but neither did Penn. And like Penn, Brathwait believed "there is no *Patterne* which we ought sooner to imitate than Christ himself."[74] Penn could even have found in Brathwait a rationale for directing his efforts so exclusively to those at the top. Self-restraint, temperance, was particularly important for gentlemen, Brathwait told them, because "You are the *Moulds* wherein meaner men are casten; labour then by your example to stampe impressions of vertue in others, but principally *Temperance,* seeing *no* vertue can subsist without it."[75]

In urging temperance, Brathwait probably did not have in mind quite the degree of restraint that Penn required. But Penn, in comparing such admonitions with the conduct of his noble friends on the one hand and of the Quakers on the other, could easily conclude that the Quakers were closer to the ideal of what a gentlemen should be. As to be a Quaker meant, for him, to be truly a Protestant, to be a Quaker could also mean to be truly a gentleman.

THE ENGLISHMAN

Penn grew up in England at a time when it was not altogether clear what an Englishman was supposed to be, as the country swung from monarchy to republic and back to monarchy, from the Church of England to Presbyterianism, Congregationalism, and back to the Church of England. In spite of these transformations, perhaps because of them, most Englishmen who thought about the matter tried to locate themselves in relation to a more distant past. The national identity of any people generally rests, if not on their history as it actually happened, at least on a shared popular opinion about that history. Since the sixteenth century, Englishmen had seen themselves at the end of two great chains of past events: those comprised in the rise, fall, and recovery of the Christian church and those that gave their country its special form of civil government. In the minds of Englishmen the two were intertwined at many points, and there was a tendency for every group to identify itself and its own time as the proper culmination of developments inherent in both.

It was agreed by all except Catholics that the Christian church, beginning in purity, had quickly fallen prey to evil and worldly ways, indeed had fallen into the hands of Antichrist in Rome. John Foxe, in his *Book of Martyrs*, had shown how the spark of true faith had been kept alive in England, had been blown into flame by Wycliffe and the Lollards in the fourteenth century, who spread it to Hus in Bohemia, who spread it to Martin Luther. England had thus been the spearhead of the Reformation. The English were an elect nation, replacing the Jews as God's chosen people, and the English must therefore lead the way in recovering primitive Christianity.[76] There were many variations on this theme in the seventeenth century, as Englishmen disagreed over what primitive Christianity might be, what it required of true believers, and what the organization of England's exemplary churches should be. By the time Penn came of age a certain weariness had set in, as the high expectations of the preceding decades faded.

There was no weariness among the Quakers. They took a somewhat less provincial view of church history than other Englishmen, but they saw themselves nevertheless as the culmination of the Reformation. Penn believed that the apostasy of Christians "began immediately after the Death of the Apostles" with the development of ceremonial worship. It continued with the conversion of kings and emperors, who tried to enforce Christianity on all and thus change the kingdom of Christ into a kingdom of this world, "and so they became *Worldly*, and not true Christians."[77]

Penn dwelt less on the rise of the papacy than he did on the general degeneration of Christians, and he saw the beginnings of recovery in the French Waldensians and Albigensians of the twelfth and thirteenth centuries.[78] But he also gave more immediate credit to the English martyrs of the sixteenth century and to the Presbyterians and Congregationalists of his father's day. The difficulty was that the Presbyterians and Congregationalists too had succumbed to worldliness, and by his own time he thought they were no better than the Church of England, especially in the Presbyterians' continuing wish to force their own way on the whole nation. Quakers, he said, honored all true worshippers, especially the Waldensians and Albigensians, but it was the Quakers themselves who represented the highest point of the recovery that began with the Reformation. "We do confess," he said, "it is our Faith, that so glorious a Vision, since the Primitive Days, has not happened to any, as to us in this our Day."[79] Not all England, but a small group of Englishmen at least, remained at the forefront of the history of redemption, making their way, not through force, not through any kind of coercion, but by their words and their example. In their own way, Christ's way, they might eventually bring the whole country, nay the whole world, back to primitive Christianity and forward into the kingdom of God.

In thus placing the Quakers within a position that Englishmen had long assigned to themselves, Penn was following the path that might have been expected of any English spokesman for a holy cause. But Penn was also concerned, probably more than any other leading Quaker, to place the Quakers in the center of the English political tradition, at the end of the other chain of past events by which Englishmen identified themselves.

That chain of events, like the sacred one, had begun to take shape in the minds of Englishmen during the sixteenth century and had been fully articulated in the ferment of the contest between king and Parliament in the seventeenth century.[80] It rested on the assumption that the people of a country are the ultimate source of the powers exercised by their government and the determiners of the form their government should take, the doctrine that has come to be known as popular sovereignty. The people of England, as Saxons, were supposed to have begun the exercise of these powers in the forests of Germany. When they migrated to England, it was held, they established a constitution of government to which they had adhered ever since and which their chosen governors could not rightfully alter. That constitution provided for a mixed government in which a hereditary king was limited by an assembly of his subjects. True, England had been invaded more than once by conquering hosts, most notably by William the Conqueror in 1066. But the conquests were not, in this view, truly conquests, for the conquerors had agreed to abide by the ancient constitution of the Saxons and had obtained the consent of the people to their authority only on that condition.

The kings and queens of England over the centuries had occasionally defied the ancient constitution and attempted to rule the land by arbitrary power, but the people had each time brought them back to the mark and obliged them to recognize the limits that the constitution set on them. The result was a set of landmarks in which the details of the constitution and of the rights of Englishmen had been set down in black and white, most notably in Magna Carta in 1215 and in the Petition of Right in 1628. The years since 1628 had seen more varied assaults on the constitution, first by Charles I attempting to rule without Parliament, then by Parliament attempting to rule without the king, and finally by Oliver Cromwell establishing a government without a king. But the English people, after suffering these usurpations had restored the ancient constitution and the monarch in 1660.

What the contest between Charles I and Parliament had demonstrated most significantly for Penn was that not only kings but Parliaments too could violate the constitution. The Long Parliament that began in 1640 had attempted to perpetuate itself without recourse to the people who chose it. It had tried to alter the form of government, thus destroying its own foundation. Hitherto it had been Parliament that repaired breaches made in the constitution by the king. But how to repair breaches made by Parliament itself, by the very persons whom the people chose to protect their constitution? Englishmen had thought long and hard about this question without finding a satisfactory answer, though Oliver Cromwell had effected an unsatisfactory one. Yet one thing was clear: the representatives of the people in Parliament ought not to have powers that their constituents did not vest in them.

Such was the political tradition into which Penn was born, such was the history of England into which he must fit the Quaker cause. Penn was no more successful than other Englishmen in finding a solution to the problem of how the people could prevent their own representatives from exceeding their powers, but he was squarely in the center of tradition, as the recent past had shaped that tradition, in affirming that those representatives could not rightly alter the ancient constitution on which their very existence rested. There were two kinds of law, as Penn saw it. First, there were fundamental laws that obtained their authority from the direct consent of the people. Such was the constitution itself, the structure of the government inherited from the immemorial past, which neither king nor Parliament could legally change. Second, there were superficial laws, made for convenience. These were the proper business of Parliament, which could alter them or make new ones whenever circumstances demanded. For Parliament to meddle with fundamental laws was to betray its trust: "The Fundamental makes the People Free, this Free People makes a Representative; Can this Creature unqualify it's Creator? What Spring ever rose higher than it's Head?"[81]

From this premise, for which he cited a multitude of authorities, especially Chief Justice Edward Coke, Penn argued that Parliament had no business at all to meddle with religion. Quakers did not ask that their religion be supported by government. Their political ideal was to have no religion supported by government. And this, Penn maintained, was precisely what fundamental law required, because the ancient constitution, the most fundamental of fundamental laws, gave Parliament no authority to prescribe religion. "Religion," he insisted, had been "no Part of the Old *English* Government."[82] Indeed how could the ancient constitution have made adherence to the Church of England a requirement for the enjoyment of the rights of Englishmen when the Church of England did not even exist at the time when the constitution was formed: "Our Claim to these *English* privileges, rising higher than the Date of Protestancy, can never justly be invalidated for Non-Conformity to any Form of it."[83] Yet the Restoration Parliament did require conformity to the Church of England, required everyone to pay tithes to support the church, virtually forbade other religions to exist at all, and thus deprived Englishmen of their fundamental rights in direct violation of Magna Carta. That great charter, Penn said, "considers us not, as of this or that perswasion in matters of Religion, in order to the obtaining of our antient Rights and Priviledges, but as English men."[84] And being English did not mean being of the Church of England: "A Man may be a very good *Englishman,* and yet a very indifferent *Churchman.*"[85]

Penn's position, that the English government was purely secular, was not a novel one. It had been adumbrated by radical religious groups in the 1640s and 1650s. But Penn was able to attach his argument to English political tradition in a variety of ways designed to win support even from the most ardent conservatives of his day. Given the propensity of men in all ages to justify revolution or rebellion on religious grounds, there is an inherent paradoxical conservatism in denying government any religious function or sanction.[86] Penn, like Roger Williams before him, could denounce the monarchomachs, whether Catholic or Protestant, who called for the overthrow of kings whom they thought heretical. The Puritans who persecuted Quakers in Massachusetts were of a piece with the Puritans who brought Charles I to the block in England. Both, in Penn's view, were enemies to civil peace and freedom. And he never lost an opportunity to denounce the arch-Puritan and monarchomach, Oliver Cromwell, and the "Oppression & Persecution which Reign'd during his Usurpation," a position well designed to win the approval of the restored monarchy.[87]

Although the new monarch himself was unwilling to forego his position as head of the Church of England, Penn continually suggested to him that in attaching his regimen to any church, he was actually subjecting himself to ecclesiastical control, allowing "the *State* . . . to be Rid by the *Church.*"[88] Charles II was content to be rid by the Church of England if that was the price of his throne, but he probably did not enjoy it. Penn's good relations with him and his brother and Penn's influence at Court may have been owing in part at least to the fact that Penn did not regard the king's religion as having any proper connection with his authority. Charles and James were both Catholics, Charles secretly, James openly; their subjects were not, and ultimately they ousted James from the throne because of his Catholicism, but not with any help from Penn.

Although Penn's close ties with James resulted in accusations that he was himself a Catholic, accusations that jeopardized his campaign to prove that Quakers were Protestants, he considered his position to be the ultimate and true Protestant one. Religion, he maintained, was something that did not affect authority. The allegiance of subjects to their king was based on the fulfillment of his civil and political duties; his religion was his own business.

By the same token, according to Penn (though not according to Charles or James), a subject's religion was his own business, not the king's. It was probably on this ground that Penn and his father had finally become reconciled. Penn gives us a hint at least that his father shared his feelings about mixing religion and politics. At the beginning of the war with the Dutch in 1665, Charles asked the elder Penn for a list of the ablest naval officers to serve in the war. The admiral, according to his son,

> pickt them by their Ability, not their [religious] Opinions; and he was in the Right; for that was the best Way of doing the King's Business. And of my own Knowledge, *Conformity robb'd the King at that Time of Ten Men, whose greater Knowledge and Valour* . . . [would] *have saved a Battel, or perfected a Victory.*[89]

Father and son agreed at least in making religious opinion irrelevant to the functions of government; and if Admiral Penn felt that way, probably a good many other Englishmen did.

But Penn's strongest appeal against government interference in religion rested on the threat it posed, not to the monarch's power but to the subject's property. In the apostrophes that Englishmen regularly addressed to the ancient constitution, the protection it offered to property had always been paramount. Penn pointed out to them that bringing religion into the picture could impair this fundamental protection. The "plain *English* of publick Severity for *Nonconformity,*" he said, could be reduced to a simple maxim: "no Property out of the Church."[90] This was not only unconstitutional, it was a ridiculous intrusion of the church into a sphere where religion had no place, an attempt to make the security of property depend on religious opinion. Accordingly when Penn proposed to Parliament in 1678 two bills for toleration of religious dissent, he entitled the first one "An Act for the Preserving of the Subjects Properties, and for the repealing of Several penal Laws, by which the lives and properties of the subjects were subject to be forfeited for things not in their power to be avoyded." The second one he called "An other Form of bill for the better Preserving, and maintaining English Property, being the true Fundation of English Government." In the preambles to both bills, Penn recited the evils that the penal laws (against nonconformity in religion) had brought upon England, especially in inducing sober and industrious men to leave the country and in preventing others from coming there.[91]

Penn did not get either of his bills passed, and three years after they failed, he took the step that made him famous, in establishing a refuge where sober and industrious people could enjoy the security of property that England continued to deny to people of his persuasion. Pennsylvania was not designed as an alternative to the ancient constitution of England, but as the fulfillment of it in an age that had betrayed it.

PENNSYLVANIA

If his colony had turned out as he wished, it would have been appropriate to call William Penn finally a Pennsylvanian. As he dreamt his dreams of the New World, he envisioned "a blessed government, and a vertuous ingenious and industrious society, so as people may Live well and have more time to serve the Lord, then in this Crowded land." In Pennsylvania Penn expected Quakers to set an example of Christian, Protestant virtue. Quaker gentlemen would prove to be truly gentlemen, and with the willing consent of the people their paternal government would revive the ancient constitution of England, free from domineering prelates. Penn even rose to millennial hopes for his colony. "God," he wrote, "will plant Americha and it shall have its day: the 5th kingdom or Gloryous day of [Jesus?] Christ . . . may have the last parte of the world, the setting of the son or western world to shine in."[92]

The prospect of a millennial kingdom in the New World brought out the prophet in Penn. While he was engaged in defending the Protestantism of Quakers and the rights of Englishmen, while he had George Fox by his side, fighting to keep the Quaker movement from splintering, Penn was dealing with a world where he knew his limits, a world in which one contended with hostile authority to achieve whatever approximation of right one could. In a new world, where he himself would hold the reins of authority, there seemed no limits to what might be achieved. If men were capable of perfection, Pennsylvania was the place where they could begin to show it, unhampered by the corruption that had overtaken England. Unfortunately Pennsylvania and the Pennsylvanians proved less than perfect.

And so did Penn. In escaping from the restraints of the world that had hitherto bound him he expected too much both of himself and of those whom he persuaded to settle in his colony. If perfection meant self-denial, he was not ready to deny himself privileges and rights that he thought his position as founder of the colony entitled him to. And his colonists seemed unwilling to deny themselves anything.

Penn's unfounded optimism became apparent even before the founding, as he planned and replanned a constitution for the colony. He had had some experience at planning already as one of the proprietors of West New Jersey, where he and his colleagues proposed a government in which virtually all power was placed in a representative assembly of the colony's freemen.[93] In his initial plans for Pennsylvania Penn again envisaged a government close to the people, with power centered in their representatives, who would be unable to act at all except under the instruction of their constituents. Though he provided for a bicameral legislature, the upper house was to be chosen by the representative lower house, which would have the initiative in proposing legislation (approved in advance by constituents). In assigning so much power to the people and their immediate representatives, Penn seems to have assumed that the settlers of Pennsylvania would align themselves willingly with his wishes for them or that they would spontaneously want for themselves what he wanted for them. It was symptomatic of his thinking about the colony that he did not specify his own power, except to place limits on it by providing for meetings of the assembly without summons from a governor and by providing for laws to take effect automatically if not assented to by the governor within fourteen days. He simply took for granted that there would be a governor—either himself or his substitute—and that the governor would normally give his assent to legislation.[94]

As Penn thought about this scheme and discussed it with others, he evidently became concerned that the settlers might include some of the wrong sort of people and that the government should therefore be placed more firmly in the hands of the right sort, of which he must be one. In his final "Frame of Government," he provided for an upper house of the legislature, to be elected from "Persons of most Note for their Wisdom, Virtue and Ability" ("ability" in the seventeenth century carried the connotation of wealth) and for a governor who should sit with this "Council" and have a treble vote in its proceedings. He now assigned to the council virtually all governmental powers, with the sole authority to initiate legislation, which the representative assembly, no longer bound by instruction of their constituents, was empowered only to accept or reject without amendment. Again Penn left unspecified most of his own powers as governor (beyond the treble vote in the council), but provided that laws should be enacted "by the Governour, with the Assent and Approbation of the Freemen in Provincial Council and General Assembly." He may have intended this to mean that laws would now require his assent. And he implied that his powers (whatever they might be) were to descend to his children, for in one clause he referred to "the governour, his Heirs or Assigns," and he made provision for a commission to serve in case the governor should be a minor.[95]

What Penn wanted was a popular government in which a grateful people would gladly accept the measures which he and other men of "Wisdom, Virtue and Ability" devised for them. He disclosed his manner of thinking when he sent an agent to West New Jersey to take charge of the town of Salem there, which he had acquired as one of the proprietors. He had bought the title, but he wanted the people to sign some sort of agreement (the text is now lost) asking him to assume government over them. The agent went to Salem and reported the reaction: "some said if the Government belonged to thee, thou might assume it without our petitioning thee thereto, I replyed, thou wouldst rather have it by Consent of the people also; for William called the Conqueror acknowledged, he was chosen King, by the consent of the people."[96]

That was perhaps how Penn saw himself, a Quaker king by consent, William the First of Pennsylvania. Besides deciding on a proper government for Pennsylvania, he decided on a set of laws for the people of the colony to consent to at the outset. Here again he revealed his high hopes—and wishful thinking—for a society that was not to be troubled by the self-indulgent gentlemen, misguided statesmen, and corrupt prelates whom he contended against in England. Pennsylvania would be a place where his laws favored the industrious and penalized the idle (all children would be taught a skilled trade), where he would make all persons free to worship God as they chose, where he would allow no one to engage in "Stage-Plays, Cards, Dice, May-Games, Gamesters, Masques, Revels, Bull-baitings, Cock-fightings, Bear-baitings, and the like, which excite the People to Rudeness, Cruelty, Looseness and Irreligion," and where he would restrain the litigious by requiring every litigant to declare in court, before beginning a suit, "That he believes in his Conscience, his Cause is Just."[97]

In his plans for Pennsylvania Penn showed none of the realism that marked his dealings with the English world. Instead of consulting his own past experience, he studied the scheme of government that James Harrington had concocted for an imaginary England in *Oceana*.[98] This was the source of his notion of a representative assembly whose supine members would be content with saying "yea" or "nay" to laws proposed by their superiors. Anyone who thought twice about the behavior of England's actual House of Commons should have known better. Quaker representatives might practice self-denial, but they were no more ready than other Englishmen for this kind of self-denial.

To be sure, some of Penn's troubles with his colony came from the presence there and nearby of non-Quakers. After learning a little of the geography of Pennsylvania he thought that he must have, in addition to his original grant, the area now comprised in the state of Delaware. Otherwise his settlers would not have proper access to the sea. He succeeded, through his friend the Duke of York, in wresting this area from Lord Baltimore, who claimed it as part of Maryland. But it was already inhabited by Swedish, Finnish, Dutch, and English settlers who showed no sympathy with Quaker principles. And Baltimore, though frustrated here, entered into a lengthy dispute with Penn over Pennsylvania's southern boundary, a dispute that kept Penn in England, after a brief stay in his colony (1682–84), during most of the rest of his life.[99]

But it was neither Baltimore in England nor the outsiders on the Delaware who turned the early history of Pennsylvania into a contest between Penn and his settlers. The settlers at first accepted most of the Frame of Government he devised for them and elected leading Quakers, men of "ability" if not of wisdom and virtue, to the powerful Council. They even accepted, however grudgingly, the gubernatorial veto power over legislation that Penn made explicit once the colony was founded. But they saw Pennsylvania as their colony, and Penn saw it as his. In moving from England to the New World, both Penn and his settlers thought of themselves as moving from a position of opposition to a position of control. In England Penn was their spokesman and defender against a hostile government—and he continued to fill that role in England before and after the overthrow of his friend James II—but within Pennsylvania the settlers did not need him. Within Pennsylvania he became the authority against which they would themselves contend, assisted by new home-grown leaders: the very men of ability who sat on the Council.[100]

What they contended about mostly was property and the power that accompanied property. Penn, as proprietor of the colony, felt that it should bring him some revenue. He had never thought of it as a way of flinging away all outward substance. Though he had sold and continued to sell large amounts of Pennsylvania land, he had spent more than he gained in getting the colony started, and he expected some return on his investment, at the very least a small quitrent, such as the king collected in royal colonies, on lands in private hands. Moreover, the political power he claimed as governor seemed to him small indeed for one who still owned most of the colony. But the settlers did not see it that way. They had invested their savings and committed their lives in an enterprise that was supposed to make them free as they had never before been free, free not only in their religion but in their property and government. They wanted to pay no quitrents and they wanted no directions from Penn or from the governors and agents he sent to represent him.

The settlers won. Though they were divided among themselves, they united in resisting Penn in almost every measure he proposed. The story is familiar and need not be repeated here. Penn's settlers, led by large Quaker landowners and merchants, paid him no quitrents, or none to speak of; they defied his governors; they ignored his messages. In the end, though he retained his formal veto power, it was of little use. He continued to plead for his rights, both against the settlers and against attempts by the English government to bring the colony under royal control, but the settlers were less willing than the king to recognize his rights (though for two years, 1692–94, King William assumed control of the government). In Pennsylvania, it seemed, everyone's rights were secure except Penn's. After two decades of strife the colony wound up with a popularly elected unicameral legislative assembly that dominated the government and continued throughout the colonial period to quarrel with Penn and his heirs.

And yet Pennsylvania must be counted a success, a success not for Penn himself but for the principles he fought for all his life. He had contended that Quakers were Protestants, in the mainstream of Christianity and not wild enthusiasts who threatened the social order. In Pennsylvania, despite internal quarrels, they proved it. Though the settlers defied Penn, they established on a small scale the same sort of social order that prevailed in England, with small men deferring to those who had made their way in the world. And in Pennsylvania enterprising men made their way very rapidly indeed. Penn had contended that religion should be no concern of government, that making it so was a threat to the security of property and the rights of Englishmen. In Pennsylvania, although Penn compromised his principles by limiting public office to Christians (of whatever persuasion), all religions were tolerated, and the colony flourished economically beyond any other. The rapid growth of Philadelphia, outpacing all other colonial cities, the ships loading and unloading at its docks, the lush farms of the interior, all testified to the viability of a society where government was not entangled with the church.

Penn was not part of it. While his colony flourished, he languished in an English debtor's prison (an institution he had tried to eliminate in Pennsylvania). But

Pennsylvania could not have happened without him. There, in spite of himself, he left his mark on the world. If it was not as deep a mark as he might have wished, that was because, when it came to Pennsylvania, he wished for too much. But a prophet may be forgiven for sometimes asking more of himself and others than they can give. Without Penn's prophetic vision, his colony would not have offered to the world the example that it did of religious freedom coupled with economic prosperity. And without his acceptance of so much of the world, he would not have had the opportunity to found a colony at all. Though he never became a Pennsylvanian, Pennsylvania became the testimony of William Penn—his mark on the world and at the same time a mark of his accommodation with the world.

NOTES

1. The most convenient account of Penn's life and background is Catherine O. Peare, *William Penn* (Philadelphia, 1957). More important for the present study are several monographs on various aspects of Penn's career. Three have been especially useful: Mary Maples Dunn, *William Penn: Politics and Conscience* (Princeton, 1967); Melvin B. Endy, Jr., *William Penn and Early Quakerism* (Princeton, 1973); and Gary B. Nash, *Quakers and Politics: Pennsylvania, 1681–1726* (Princeton, 1968).

2. Samuel Pepys, *Diary*, Robert Latham, William Matthews, et al., eds. (Berkeley and Los Angeles, 1970–76), 8: 395. (Dec. 29, 1667).

3. The best account of early Quaker beliefs and practices is Endy, *Penn and Early Quakerism.*

4. Reprinted in [Joseph Besse, ed.], *A Collection of the Works of William Penn, in Two Volumes* (London, 1726) (hereafter *Works*), 1: 272–439. All references to Penn's published writings are to this edition.

5. *Works*, 1: 161, 230, 441.

6. See Mary Maples Dunn, Richard S. Dunn, et al., eds., *The Papers of William Penn* (Philadelphia, 1981–), 1: 249 (hereafter *Papers*).

7. *Works*, 2: 34, 39, 44, 498; *Papers*, 1: 350.

8. *Works*, 2: 285.

9. *Works*, 2: 876.

10. *Works*, 1: 211, 306 ff.

11. *Works*, 2: 56.

12. *Works*, 1: 212, 243; II, 257.

13. *Works*, 1: 899.

14. *Works*, 2: 56; cf. *Works*, 1, 243.

15. *Works*, 2: 494.

16. *Works*, 2: 495.

17. *Works*, 2: 369, 494. Penn's position on the essential qualification of a minister was remarkably similar to that of another anti-intellectual intellectual fifty years later, Gilbert Tennent of Penn's colony of New Jersey. Penn, like Tennent after him, flatly denied "that they are fit to teach others what *Regeneration* and the way to Heaven are, *that have never been Born Again Themselves.*" *Works*, 2: 782.

18. *Works*, 2: 872.

19. *Works*, 1: 749.

20. *Works,* 1: 749, 790–96.

21. *Works,* 2: 151; cf. *Works,* 2: 463. Penn may have been wrong. A scholarly study of early Quaker social origins in a single English county finds a larger proportion of gentry and merchants in the sect than in the population at large. See Richard Vann, *The Social Development of English Quakerism 1655–1755* (Cambridge, Mass., 1969).

22. *Works,* 1: 407.

23. *Works,* 2: 494.

24. *Works,* 2: 17.

25. *Works,* 1: 881.

26. *Works,* 1: 865.

27. *Works,* 1: 324.

28. *Papers,* 1: 476.

29. *Papers,* 1: 462; cf. *Works,* 2: 590.

30. *Papers,* 1: 535.

31. *Works,* 1: 238–48.

32. *Works,* 2: 227–313, 863–75. On Penn's theology see again Endy, *Penn and Early Quakerism.*

33. *Works,* 2: 153–56.

34. *Works,* 1: 292.

35. *Works,* 2: 910.

36. *Works,* 2: 910; cf. *Works,* 2, 535.

37. *Works,* 2: 545.

38. *Works,* 1: 567; 2: 281–83, 409–14, 522–32. Cf. Endy, *Penn and Early Quakerism,* 166–68.

39. *Works,* 1: 526.

40. *Works,* 2: 10, 68, 634.

41. *Works,* 2: 68.

42. *Works,* 2: 617.

43. *Works,* 2: 231, 617.

44. *Works,* 2: 113–20.

45. *Works,* 1: 542–64.

46. *Works,* 1: 612–72.

47. *Works,* 2: 781.

48. *Papers,* 1: 249–59 and passim; *Works,* 2: 189–227.

49. *Works,* 2: 204.

50. *Works,* 2: 208, 696.

51. See above, note 27.

52. *Works,* 1: 524.

53. *Works,* 2: 729.

54. *Works,* 1: 900.

55. *Papers,* 1: 155.

56. *Papers,* 1: 154.

57. *Works,* 1: 7–18.

58. The case eventuated in a more important one after the court fined the jurors for their

refusal. One of the jurors, Edward Bushell, appealed to the Court of Common Pleas and won a judgment that has served as a precedent against the punishment of jurors for their verdicts. *Papers*, 1: 171–72; Dunn, *William Penn*, 15–18.

59. *Papers*, 1: 197–201. Penn's manner in addressing those he considered his social superiors was quite different. See, for example, *Papers*, 2: 26–29; *Works*, 1: 435–39.

60. *Papers*, 2: 30–31.

61. *Works*, 1: 136.

62. *Works*, 1: 333.

63. *Papers*, 1: 425–508. See, for examples, pp. 447, 466, 472.

64. *Papers*, 1: 497.

65. *Works*, 1: 195.

66. *Works*, 1: 362.

67. *Works*, 1: 722–32.

68. *Works*, 1: 373.

69. Even in Pennsylvania Penn anticipated a need for workhouses. *Papers*, 2: 175, 206, 222.

70. *Works*, 1: 212. Emphasis added.

71. References are to the second edition, London, 1633.

72. P. 324.

73. P. 113.

74. P. 426.

75. P. 315. Cf. Henry Peacham, *The Compleat Gentleman* (London, 1627), 9–10.

76. William Haller, *The Elect Nation: The Meaning and Relevance of Foxe's Book of Martyrs* (New York, 1963).

77. *Works*, 1: 861; 2: 52.

78. *Works*, 1: 412–18, 858–62; 2: 516.

79. *Works*, 2: 53.

80. This paragraph and the next depend heavily on J. G. A. Pocock, *The Ancient Constitution and the Feudal Law* (Cambridge, 1957).

81. *Works*, 1: 674–75, 683; *Papers*, 1: 280.

82. *Works*, 1: 688; *Papers*, 1: 223–24.

83. *Works*, 1: 455–56, 688.

84. *Papers*, 1: 175.

85. *Works*, 1: 688.

86. Cf. my *Roger Williams: The Church and the State* (New York, 1967), 125–26.

87. *Works*, 2: 86.

88. *Works*, 1: 689.

89. *Works*, 2: 737.

90. *Works*, 1: 689.

91. *Papers*, 1: 537–39.

92. *Papers*, 2: 106.

93. *Papers*, 1: 387–410.

94. *Papers*, 2: 140–56.

95. *Papers*, 2: 211–20. Penn's unspecified powers are examined at length in a letter to him from Jasper Batt in 1683. *Papers*, 2: 462–66.

96. *Papers*, 2: 355.

97. *Papers*, 2: 220–27.

98. On Harrington's influence: Dunn, *William Penn*, 81–88.

99. Ibid., 100–103 and *Papers*, 2: passim. He returned to the colony for an equally brief period in 1699–1701.

100. The best discussion of Penn's contests with his settlers and of the divisions among them is Nash, *Quakers and Politics*.

CHAPTER
4

Document: Christianity Shapes American Slavery

Before the Anglican (Church of England) minister at St. Paul's Parish in Maryland, Thomas Bacon, published two sermons for slaves in 1749 (followed by the publication of four sermons to owners), no writer in the British mainland settlements, clergy member, jurist, or slaveholder, had ever before set out a comprehensive view of slaves' duties and responsibilities for a mainland colony audience.

Although the rudiments of slavery had been established by 1660, the distinctive slaveholding system of the British mainland colonies came into being slowly between 1680 and 1760, as 250,000 captured Africans were forcibly transported to the colonies, and as slavery became a commonplace experience in the lives of settlers in all colonies, rather than a rarity, as it was even in the 1660s, 1670s, and 1680s. Bacon's sermons to captured Africans and slaveholders have been the subject of little scholarship, but they summarized many developments in the emerging British–American slave system and advanced others, and they were reprinted several times from the time of their original publication to the 1810s.

Bacon sought to "Christianize" the developing slaveholding system of mid-eighteenth-century America. In doing so, Bacon coined a term, "God's overseers," to describe the Africans' owners, a term that would later become infamous to nineteenth-century abolitionists but proved extremely useful to slave owners in the interim. Bacon came close to advocating a system of absolute obedience, something never required of English servants, apprentices, or even "villeins" of the medieval period. Slaves had to obey "if any of your OWNERS should prove WICKED OVERSEERS, and use you, who are his under Servants here, as they ought not to do." Disobedience even in these circumstances still constituted "faults done against God himself." Finally, Bacon induced owners to think of themselves in self-pitying paternalistic terms. He suggested that the owners were constantly caring for slaves—powerful images by the nineteenth century—when he castigated slaves for stealing: "Do not your masters, under God, provide for you?" Bacon asked.

How does Bacon justify slavery? What would slaveholders have heard in these sermons that would have made Bacon's argument very attractive to them? Who do you think would have listened more attentively to Bacon's sermon to slaves, the slaves themselves or their owners? Does "race" figure strongly in Bacon's justification for slavery and in his views about what slavery should mean, or does Bacon highlight traditional English views about social hierarchy to rationalize slavery's existence and character? How does Bacon's view of slavery compare with the views of Rev. George D. Armstrong written in 1857 and printed later in this Reader? Finally, thinking of Bacon's sermon explicitly, how would you describe religion as a social force in eighteenth-century Maryland?

Additonal Reading: Surprisingly, the scholarship on religion and seventeenth- and eighteenth-century slaveholding is not large. Frank J. Klingberg, *The Carolina Chronicle of Dr. Francis Le Jau 1706–1717* (Berkeley, 1956) offers a fascinating glimpse of a Church of England minister who attempted to minister to both slaves and owners in early South Carolina. Thomas N. Ingersoll, "'Releese us out of this Cruel Bondegg': An Appeal from Virginia in 1723," *William and Mary Quarterly,* 3d ser., 51 (1994): 777–782, prints an extraordinary petition for freedom from an anonymous Virginia slave using explicitly religious language. James David Essig, *The Bonds of Wickedness: American Evangelicals against Slavery, 1770–1808* (Philadelphia, 1982) and Jean R. Soderlund, *Quakers and Slavery: A Divided Spirit* (Princeton, 1985) describe the often limited results of antislavery efforts by evangelicals and Quakers in the mid and late eighteenth century. Winthrop D. Jordan, *White Over Black: American Attitudes toward the Negro, 1550–1812* (Chapel Hill, 1968) remains the most comprehensive single study of its topic in which religion often figures importantly.

Thomas Bacon

A Sermon to Maryland Slaves, 1749

> Knowing that whatsoever good Thing any
> Man doth, the same shall be receive of the LORD,
> whether he be Bond or Free
>
> EPHES. VI 8

When I consider the Station in which the Divine Providence hath been pleased to place me, and to how weighty an Office and Charge I am called, as Minister of this Parish,—that I am appointed a *Messenger, Watchman,* and *Steward* of the great LORD of Heaven and Earth, to teach, and to premonish, to feed and provide for the LORD'S Family;—to seek for CHRIST'S Sheep that are dispersed Abroad, and for his Children that are in the midst of this wicked World, that they may be saved

Reprinted from Thomas Bacon, *Two Sermons, Preached to a Congregation of Black Slaves, at the Parish Church of S[aint] P[eter's], in the Province of Maryland* (London, 1749), 7–38.

through CHRIST for ever;—When I call to mind how great a Treasure is committed to my Charge, even those Sheep which CHRIST brought with his Death, and for whom he shed his most precious Blood;—and that I am to *watch¹ for their Souls as* one *that must give Account,* I am struck with an awful Dread, and my Heart trembles within me, lest any one of these precious Souls, for which our Savior died, should be left through my Carelessness;—knowing, that if the Church of CHRIST, or any the least or poorest Member thereof, should take any Hurt or Hindrance by reason of my Negligence, how great a Crime I should have to answer for at the Judgment Seat of Almighty GOD,—and how horrible a Punishment would fall upon my guilty Head, when not only my own Sins, which are many, but also the Blood of those unhappy Souls, which perished through my Fault, should be required at my Hands.

These Considerations, my dear Christian Brethren, have long employed my serious Thoughts, and put me upon various Methods of performing this great and important Duty, which I owe to the *poorest Slave,* as well as the *richest* and most *powerful* among my Parishioners. And indeed, in this Province, the Clergy are under a particular temporal Tie, as we are Supported by a *Poll Tax,* in which every Slave, above Sixteen Years of Age is rated as high, and pays as much as the master he or she belongs to, and, consequently, have an equal Right to Instruction with their Owners. But through the common Duties of Christianity, as Godliness, Righteousness, and Temperance, do belong to them, as much as to those of a higher Rank;—and though these, with their several Branches, are explained every LORD's Day at Church, whither they may, with their Masters Leave, resort for Instruction; yet there are other Duties, peculiar to their State of Life, which need a particular Explanation,—Besides their Ignorance of the first Principles of Religion is generally such, that Discourses, suited to those who are but indifferently acquainted with the Ground of Christianity, and know but a little of the holy Scriptures, are no way suited to their Capacities and Understandings;—And most of them, from their Want of Skill in our Tongues, are not able to reap such Instruction from what they hear, as they would from Discourses framed on Purpose, wherein the Language is lowered as near as possible to their own Level, and the Christian Doctrine stoops, as it were, to meet them.—This I have attempted in *Exhortations* as Opportunity offered, at their *Funerals* (several of which I have attended) and to such small Congregations as their *Marriages* have brought together, as well as at my own House, on Sunday, and other Evenings, when those in their Neighborhood come in.—But these occasional Instructions can reach but to a very few and much the greatest Number, either from their Distance, which keeps them most Sundays from Chruch, or their understanding but little of what is said or done when they come there, are deprived of a great Part of the Benefit they might otherwise receive.—These Hindrances might, indeed, be in a great Measure removed, if their *Masters* and *Mistresses* would but take a little Pains with them at Home, by Reading, or causing some early Portions of the holy Scriptures, particularly the Gospels, to be read to them in an Evening, together with such plain short Tracts, upon the Principles of Christianity, as are easily procured, and of which, Numbers have been distributed in the Parish since my coming into it.—Some few Heads of Families do, from a Principle of Conscience, take pious Care in these

Matters; and it is to be hoped, that by the Blessing of God, their Number will increase:—But till that is the Case, other Methods must be taken, and particular Days be now and then appointed for the Instruction of these poor People, as this hath been:—In which, may Almighty GOD, of his great Mercy, assist me, his poor unworthy Servant, in the faithful Performance of my Part; and open their Hearts and Minds, that they may gladly receive, and truly understand the Things which belong to their Peace, through our Lord and Savior JESUS CHRIST. *Amen*

And now, *my dear* BLACK *Brethren and Sisters,* I beg that you will listen seriously to what I shall say.—You all know what Love and Affection I have for you, and I do believe that most of you have always found me ready to serve you, when you wanted my Help.—I doubt not therefore, that you will readily hearken to the good Advice I shall now give you, (as you know me to be your Friend and Well-wisher) and hope you will remember it hereafter, and think upon it at Home, and talk of it to your Fellow Servants that are not here, that they may receive Advantage by it, as well as you, that hear it from my own Mouth.

I have chosen a Text of Scripture, which I could wish you all had by Heart, and would all remember;—because it shews you what a *Great Friend* you may have in Heaven, if you will but take any Pains to gain Favour.—For St. *Paul,* who wrote by the Direction of the Holy Spirit of GOD, assures you, that *whatsoever good Thing a Man* or Woman *doth,* they *shall receive the same,* that is, be rewarded for it by *the LORD, whether* they *be Bond or Free.*—And this cannot be assured, that whatever good Thing you do, though you be Slaves, bound to serve Masters and Mistresses, here upon Earth, for the Sake of a bare Maintenance;—yet, while you are doing what is right and good, you are, at the same Time, working for a just Master in Heaven, who will pay you good Wages for it, and will make no Difference between you, and the richest Freeman, upon the Face of the Earth.—For GOD is no Respecter of Persons.—He values no Man for his Riches and Power, neither does he despise or overlook any one for his Rags and Poverty.—He loves none but those that are Good, and hates none but those that are Bad.—And our LORD and Saviour JESUS CHRIST hath given us an Account, from his own Mouth, of a certain great Man, who had Riches and Pleasures and Will, while he lived in this World, that was thrown into Hell at his Death, because he was not Good:—While a poor despised Beggar, all overrun with Sores and Filth, who died for Want at this great Man's Gate, was carried by Angels into Heaven, because he had been a good Man, and had served GOD, his heavenly Master, so far as he had Knowledge and Opportunity.

That you may easier understand, and better carry away in your Memory what you shall hear, I shall endeavour, by GOD'S Help to lay before you, in the plainest Words,

    I. Why you ought to serve GOD
    II. What Service, or what good Things GOD expects from you.
    III. What kind of Reward you may expect to receive from him.

    I. And the first Reason why you ought to serve GOD, is, BECAUSE THAT GOD MADE YOU;—and he *made* you, and all Men, to *serve* him.—You know that, when you were born, you did not come into the World by any Power or Help of your own:—Nay, you were so far from knowing any Thing about it, or how you came here;—whether you were found in the Woods, or grew out of the Ground,—that it was some Years before you could help yourselves, or had so much Sense as to know your right Hand from your left.—It was Almighty GOD, therefore, who made you, and all the World, that sent you here, as he had sent your Fathers and Mothers, your masters and Mistresses before you, to take Care of you, and provide for you, while you could take no Care of, or help, or provide for yourselves.—And can you think that Almighty GOD, who is so wise and good himself, would send you into the World for any bad Purposes?—Can you be so silly as to fancy, that He, who made every Thing so good and useful in its Kind, sent you here to be Idle, to be Wicked, or to make a bad Use of any good Thing he hath made?—No, my Brethren, the most ignorant among you has more Sense than to think any such Thing:—And there is none of you but knows, that you ought to be good;—and whosoever is good, let him be ever so Poor and Mean, is serving GOD.—For this whole World is but one large Family, of which Almighty GOD is the Head and Master:—He takes Care of all, by causing the *Sun to shine,* the *Rains to fall,* the *Waters to Spring,* the *Winds to blow,* the *Grass,* the *Trees, and the Herbs to Spring, and the Corn, the Plants, and the Fruits to come in their due Season;* thus providing Food and Shelter for all living Creatures.—And to Mankind in particular, he hath given *Reason* and *Knowledge,* to teach them how to make use of, and turn all these Things to their own Comfort and Support, giving more or less of them to every one, according as he thinks fit, and as he knows to be best for them.—And this general Provision which GOD makes of all Things, and this particular Disposal of them, in giving *more* to some, and *less* to others,—together with his own secret Ways of bringing it about, is what we call, his DIVINE PROVIDENCE.

Now, for carrying on these great and wonderful Ends, GOD hath appointed several *Offices* and *Degrees* in his Family, as they are dispersed and scattered all over the Face of the Earth.—Some he hath made *Masters* and *Mistresses,* for taking Care of their Children, and others that belong to them:—Some he hath made *Merchants* and *Seafaring Men,* for supplying distant Countries with what they want from other Places: Some he hath made *Tradesmen* and *Husbandmen, Planters* and *Labouring-Men,* to work for their own Living, and help to supply others with the Produce of their Trades and Crops:—Some he hath made *Servants* and *Slaves,* to assist and work for the *Masters* and *Mistresses* that provide for them;—and others he hath made *Ministers* and *Teachers,* to instruct the rest to shew them what they ought to do, and put them in mind of their several Duties.—And as Almighty GOD hath sent each of us into the World for some or other of these Purposes;—so, from the King, who is his head Servant in a Country, to the poorest Slave, we are all obliged to do the Business he hath set us about, in that State of Life to which he hath been pleased to call us.—And while you, whom he hath made Slaves, are honestly and quietly doing your Business, and living as poor Christians ought to do, you are serving GOD, in your low Station, as much as the greatest Prince alive, and will be as much Favour shewn you at the last Day.

2. A second Reason why you ought to serve GOD, is—BECAUSE YOU HAVE SOULS TO BE SAVED—If you have nothing in this World but hard

Labour, with your coarse Food and Clothing, you have a Place provided for you in Heaven, when you die, and go into the next World, if you will but be at the Pains of seeking for it while you stay here.—And there is no other Way of getting to Heaven, but by serving GOD upon Earth.—Besides, when People die, we know but of two Places they have to go to, and that is *Heaven* or *Hell:*—so that whoever misses the one, must go to the other.—Now *Heaven* is a Place of great Happiness, which GOD hath prepared for all that are good, where they shall enjoy Rest from their Labours, and a Blessedness which will never have an End:—And *Hell* is a Place of great Torment and Misery, where all wicked People will be shut up with the *Devil,* and *other evil Spirits,* and be punished for ever, because they will not serve GOD in this World.—It was to save you, and all Men, from that dreadful Punishment, that our blessed LORD JESUS CHRIST came down from Heaven,—was made a Man like us, and suffered a most shameful and bitter Death, his Hands and Feet being riveted with great Nails to a *cross Piece of Timber,* and his Side pierced through with a Spear, as he hung upon it in all that Pain and Agony.—And if he so loved our Souls, that he gave himself up to so cruel a Death to redeem them from Hell, ought not we to have as much Regard for ourselves as he had, and take some Pains to save our own souls?—Believe me, *my black Brethren and Sisters,* there was not a single Drop of his precious Blood spilled, in which the poorest and meanest of you hath not as great a Share, as the richest and most powerful Person upon the earth.—And think, O think, what a sad Thing it must be, to lose any Soul which cost Almighty GOD so dear as the Life of his own well beloved Son!—But you must always remember, that though our Saviour dies for the Sins of all Men, yet none shall have the Benefit of what he did for us, but such as will *serve* GOD:—For he made that the Condition of our Salvation, through him, that we should *love and fear GOD, and keep his Commandments.*—If, therefore, we would have our Souls saved by Christ, if we would escape *Hell,* and obtain *Heaven,* we must set about doing what he requires of us, and that is, to *serve* GOD.—Your own poor Circumstances in this Life ought to put you particularly [UNREADABLE], and taking Care of your souls:—For you cannot have the Pleasures and Enjoyments of this Life, like rich free People, who have Estates, and Money to lay out as they think fit.—If others will run the Hazard of their Souls, they have a Chance of getting wealth and Power,—of heaping up Riches, and enjoying all the Ease, Luxury, and Pleasure, their Hearts should long after:—but you can have none of these Things,—So that if you sell your Souls for the Sake of what poor Masters you can get in this World, you have made a very foolish Bargain indeed.—Almighty GOD hath been pleased to make you Slaves here, and to give you nothing but Labour and Poverty in this World, which you are obliged to submit to, as it is his Will it should be so.—And think within yourselves what a terrible Thing it would be, after all your Labours and Sufferings in this Life, to be turned into Hell in the next Life;—and after wearing out your Bodies in Service here, to go into a far worse Slavery when this is over, and your poor Souls be delivered over into the Possession of the Devil, to become his Slaves for ever in Hell, without any Hope of ever getting free from it.—If therefore, you would be GOD'S *Free men* in Heaven, you must strive to be good, and serve him here on Earth.

Your Bodies, you know, are not your own, they are at the Disposal of those you belong to:—But your precious souls are still your own, which nothing can take from you if it be not your own Fault. Consider well then, that if you lose your souls by leading idle, wicked Lives here, you have got nothing by it in this World, and you have lost your All in the next.—For your Idleness and Wickedness is generally found out, and your Bodies suffer for it here, and, what is far worse, if you do not repent and amend, your unhappy Souls will suffer for it hereafter.—And our blessed Saviour, who well knew the Value of a soul, and paid so dear for putting them in the Way leading to Heaven, hath assured us in his holy Word, *that if a Man was to gain the whole World by it, it could not make him amends for the Loss of his Soul.*—You see, then, how necessary it is for you to be *good,* and *serve* GOD, since that is the only Way by which your souls can be saved, the only Means by which you can secure the Favour and Friendship of Almighty GOD, who, upon that Condition, will make you great Amends in the next World, for whatever you want, and whatever you suffer in this for his Sake.

3. Another reason why you ought to serve GOD, is—That *far the greatest Part of you* HAVE BEEN BAPTIZED, and do profess yourselves to be *Christians.*—Many of you were baptized my coming into the Parish, and since that Time, I have myself baptized, of Young and Old, near TWO HUNDRED.

—Now, as many as call themselves Christians, do profess to serve the LORD CHRIST:—And as many as have been baptized, have made a solemn Promise and Vow,—*That they will obediently keep GOD'S Commandments, and walk in the same all the Days of their Life.*—Such of you, therefore as have been baptized, ought to consider that you are bound by a Promise and a vow, made before GOD and the Congregation, to *serve him;*—and that if you neglect it, you shall severely answer for it at the Judgment Seat of GOD; when your own Promise shall be brought to witness against you; and your Punishment in Hell will be the greater, because you mocked GOD, in making him a Promise, which you took no Care to perform, and because you knew your Duty and would not do it.

Having thus laid before you some Reasons why you ought to *serve* GOD,—I shall, in the next Place, endeavour to shew you,

II. *What Service, or what good Things, GOD expects from you* And here, you must not think that you can be of any Advantage or Benefit to Almighty GOD by *serving* him.—He that hath Millions of glorious and powerful Angels waiting continually round his Throne in Heaven, and ready every Moment to perform his Commands, cannot want, or stand in need of any *Help* or *Service,* from the Hands of such poor mean Creatures as we are.—But when GOD made us, he intended that we should all be happy with him in Heaven, when we leave this World, if we would live in such a Manner *here,* as to be fit Company for his blessed Saints and Angels *hereafter*—For he delights in the Happiness of all his Creatures, and his Holy Spirit is grieved when they, by their Wickedness, make themselves miserable.—To this great end, he hath given us Rules to walk by;—which, if we follow, will prepare us for that happy State he hath provided for us in the next Life.—And whosoever observes these Rules, and ordereth his Behaviour according to their Directions, is said to *serve* GOD, though, in reality, he is then *serving himself* in the highest Degree.

Now these rules of Behaviour relate to three Things; namely, how we ought to behave—*towards* GOD,—*towards Mankind,*—and *towards Ourselves;*—and these I shall endeavour to explain to you under the following Heads:

1. Your Duty or Behaviour towards GOD.
2. Your Duty or Behaviour towards your Masters and Mistresses.
3. Your Duty or Behaviour towards your Fellow Servants, and others.
4. Your Duty towards Yourselves.

1. And in the First Place, Your Duty towards GOD is to look upon him as *your Great and chief Master,* to whom you are accountable for all your Behaviour, either in Private or Publick; both towards Himself, and to all Mankind.—You are to remember, that you can do nothing so secretly but he will know it, and that no Place is so dark and private, but his all-piercing Eye can see what you are doing in it: *For the Darkness and the Light are both alike to him.*—You are farther to consider, that his Eyes are continually upon you, and that it is impossible for you to conceal yourself a single Moment out of his Sight:—That he is *pleased* when he sees you doing what is right, and *angry* with you when he sees you doing any Thing that is bad.—And this will surely be a mighty Check upon you, when you are inclined to do any bad Thing, to think that Almighty GOD is that very Moment looking upon you, and taking an Account of your Behaviour.—So that if it should be done so secretly and artfully as never to be known in this World, yet your heavenly Master sees it, and knows it, and will not fail to punish you for it in the next World, for doing what he hath forbidden you to do.—This Consideration will also be of great Comfort and Encouragement to you, in doing what is Right and Good;—for if no Body else was to take Notice of it, you are sure that He will:—And if you meet with no Recompense for it here, you know that Almighty GOD, who is the best of Masters, will reward you for it hereafter.—For you are assured in the Text, That *whatsoever good Thing any Man doth, the same shall he receive of the Lord, whether he be Bond or Free.*

2. Another Duty you owe to GOD Almighty, is,—*To love him with all your Heart with all your Mind, with all your Soul, and with all your Strength.*—In short, you must love GOD above all Things.

And indeed, if you do but seriously think what GOD hath done, is every Day doing, and will do for you hereafter, if it be not your own Fault,—you cannot chuse but love him beyond the whole World.—Hath not GOD made you?—Hath he not given you all the Comforts you have enjoyed in Life?—Hath he not given you, along with the rest of Mankind, *Sense* and *Reason* beyond all other Sorts of earthly Creatures?—Hath he not preserved and supported you to this very Hour?—And do not your very Lives this Moment depend upon his Goodness and Mercy?—These are great Obligations to Love and Thankfulness;—but what he hath done for your Souls is of far greater Value.—Hath he not given you *Souls to be saved?*—Hath he not brought you out of a Land of Darkness and Ignorance, where your Forefathers knew nothing of Him, to a Country where you may come to the Knowledge of the only true GOD, and learn a sure Way to Heaven?—Hath he not shewn such wonderful Love and Kindness for your Souls, as to send his only *Son, our Saviour* JESUS CHRIST, to suffer Death for your Sakes, and to leave

Rules and *Directions* behind him, which, if you follow, will bring you to everlasting Happiness?—And hath he not so ordered it in his Providence, that you should be taught those Rules this Holy Day of his own appointing, and at other Times?—And will He not bestow Heaven itself upon you, if you will make good Use of the Opportunities he hath given you of learning his Laws, and living accordingly?—You see that Almighty GOD hath thought nothing too good for you, and surely, you cannot think any Love too great for Him.—Take good Heed therefore, that you do not let *Idleness* and *Vanity, Lust,* and *Sin,* run away with those Hearts and Affections which you ought to bestow intirely upon so kind and good a GOD.—For while you desire to do any Thing which is not lawful and good, you love that Thing, whatever it is, better than you love GOD; and therefore, he will not love you:—and the Loss of GOD'S Love is the dreadfulest Loss that can happen to you.

3. Another Duty you owe to GOD, is FEAR.—Now there are two Sorts of *Fear,*—the one proceeding from *Love,*—and the other from *Terror.*—If we sincerely love any one, we are afraid of doing any Thing that will make him uneasy:—And if we love GOD sincerely, we shall be afraid of doing any ill Thing, because we know that his Holy Spirit is grieved at our Wickedness.—But if our *Love* to GOD be not strong enough to make us *afraid of grieving his Holy Spirit,* the *Dread of his terrible Judgments* will surely keep us in Awe.—When any of you have done something that deserves Correction, and you find that your Masters have come to the Knowledge of it, does not the Fear of a Whipping make you tremble?—Do not your Hearts fail you, and the Terror of the Lash make you wish you never had done it?—And while that *Fear,* and the *Thoughts of Correction* hang over you, does it not keep you from doing what may bring upon you such severe Punishments?—Alas, my Brethren, all this is a meer trifle!—If Men for your Faults should be provoked to lash you immoderately,—if your Correction should be so severe that you die under it,—there would be an End of that Suffering, and you could feel no more, if they were to cut your Body into Pieces, or throw it into Fire.—But if you lead wicked Lives, and provoke GOD to Anger, he can not only, if he thinks proper, strike you dead upon the Spot, or cause you to die of some lingering, painful Distemper, but can also plunge your Souls into Hell fire, there to remain in Pain and Torment for ever.—Let this Thought be strongly fixed in your Hearts,—and when sinful Desires arise in your Minds, and evil Inclinations begin to get the better, then remember that the great GOD is looking at you, and say within yourselves as *Joseph* said, when he was tempted to sin by his wicked Mistress—*How can I do this great Wickedness against GOD?*—Now *Joseph,* like you, was a *Slave* in a strange Land, and was sold by his wicked Brethren, as many of you, or your Forefathers, have been sold to Masters of Ships, by your Parents or Relations:—His Temptation was very great: He was a *Young Man* and a *Slave;*—But his *Fear* of GOD was such, that he rather chose to suffer the Consequences of his Mistress's Rage, and to go to Prison, where he remained several Years, than to displease GOD by committing Sin.—Our blessed Saviour, speaking of this holy *Fear* and *Dread* of offending Almighty GOD, saith—*Fear not [those things] which kill the Body, but are not able to kill the Soul: but rather fear him, which is able to destroy both Body and Soul in Hell.*

4. Another Duty, you owe to Almighty GOD, is—WORSHIP;—and this is of

two Sorts,—PUBLICK and PRIVATE.—PUBLICK WORSHIP is that Devotion we pay to GOD at *Church,* in SUNDAYS and other *Holy Days;*—and PRIVATE WORSHIP, is that Duty of *Prayer* and *Thanksgiving* which we offer up to GOD at Home.—It gives me great Satisfaction, and I bless GOD for it, that I see so many of you come here on Sundays:—It looks well, and seems as if your Inclinations were good, and I hope many of you will receive great Benefit by it.—But I cannot help saying, that Many more might come if they would, who spend their Sundays in *Idling* and *Visiting, Drinking, Hunting,* and *Fishing,* and spending the *best* of Days to the *worst* of Purposes.—It is certain you cannot all be spared, and that some are at a great Distance from Church.—But such of you as can be spared, to visit, trifle away your Time, and ride about, might spend this Time much better at Chruch, and do their Masters Horses less Harm.—Others of you work on Sundays, which is a great Sin:—For those that will labour on the LORD'S own Day, which he hath ordered to be set apart for his Worhsip, GOD will most certainly punish them either in this World or the next.

PRIVATE PRAYER is a Duty which GOD expects from you, as much as from People of a higher Rank.—It were indeed much to be wished, that we had more *praying Families* among us, where Servants would have an Opportunity of praying regularly every Day:—But there are few of you but can say the *Lord's Prayer,* and that, said over devoutly Morning and Evening upon your Knees, would bring down a Blessing upon you and the Family you belong to.—If you were to consider what PRAYER is,—that it is speaking to Almighty GOD, and asking freely from him a Supply of every Thing that is needful for you, you surely would be very fond of Praying.—For if you want any Favour from your *Masters* and *Mistresses,* you can find Words plain enough to ask it from them.—Now Almighty GOD invites you to come to him, and tells you, that you need but *ask* of him, *and you shall have, seek and you shall find, knock and it shall be opened unto you.*—If therefore, you will not ask a Blessing from him in Prayer, you cannot expect to have it;—if you will not seek for his Favour, you cannot expect to find it;—and if you will not take the Trouble of knocking at the Gate of Heaven, you cannot hope to have it opened to let you in.—It is not long Prayers, not a Set of fine Words, that GOD requires.—But if the *Heart* be desirous of obtaining any Request, the *Tongue* will find out Words to express it in;—and GOD, who looks upon the *Heart* more than the *Tongue,* will grant whatever you ask of Him, if it be for your Good.—It is no matter how short your Prayer is, if your Heart go along with it:—And any of you have Sense enough to pray in this Manner.—*"Lord have Mercy upon me, I am a great Sinner: I have done such a Thing which I ought not to have done, and I am sorry for it—Spare me, good Lord, pardon me this once, for the Sake of my Saviour Jesus Christ, and, by the Blessing of GOD, I will do so no more.—Lord, give me Grace, and make me a good Man!—Lord, bless my Master and Mistress, and prosper the House I live in!—GOD bless me, and keep me from Sin and Danger!—Lord, make me truly thankful for thy great Goodness to me!—Lord, make me your Servant while I live, that when I die, I may remain in your House for ever!"*

You can never want *Time* for Prayers of this Sort:—You can think of your Souls, and pray thus, either in the *House* or the *Field,* whether you are *Up* or in *Bed,* or *Walking,* or *Waking;* at the *Plough,* the *Axe,* the *House,* or the *Spade.*—And GOD is always ready to hear you.—But remember this, that whenever you pray to GOD from *Grace,* you must strive *to be* what you pray for.—If you desire of GOD to make you good, or sober, or honest, or diligent, you must first of all strive to be that *good,* that *sober,* that *honest,* that *diligent* Servant you desire to be, and then GOD will help you with his Grace in making you so.

5. Another Duty you owe to GOD is REVERENCE and HONOUR.—But many of you are so far from shewing any *Honour* or *Respect* to GOD Almighty, that you will *curse* and *swear,* and *blaspheme* his Name upon every little Fit of Passion, at any silly Thing that crosses your Humor,—and sometimes out of meer Wantonness, when nothing disturbs you at all.—Take Care, my Brethren, it is very dangerous sporting with *the great and fearful Name of the Lord our GOD:* And he hath threatened that he *will not hold that Person guiltless that taketh his Name in vain;*—that is, that whosoever makes an irreverent Use of his holy Name by *vain Oaths,* and *Cursing* and *Swearing,* shall certainly be punished for it, either in this World, or in the World to come.

6. Another Duty you owe Almighty GOD, is TRUTH.—For GOD is a GOD of Truth, and hates all *Lies* and *Liars.*—The HOLY SCRIPTURES are full of Texts to this Purpose, of which, I shall repeat a few, to shew you what a sad Thing it is to tell Lies.—In one Place we are told by King *Solomon,* that *Lying Lips are an Abomination to the Lord.*—Our Saviour himself tells us in another Place, that *the Devil is a Liar, and the Father of it.*—And St *John* tells us, that *all Liars shall have their Part in the Lake that burneth with Fire and Brimstone;* that is in Hell.—Now many of you think there is little Harm in a Lie;—but you see what a sad Mistake it is.—For you see, by what has been said, that if you have a Mind to make yourselves hateful and abominable to GOD,—if you have a mind to become the Devil's own Children,—if you want to plunge yourselves headlong into Hell, and wallow to all Eternity in Fire and Brimstone, you need but get an Habit of Lying, and it will surely destroy your Souls, as Murder, Fornication, Adultery, or any other Sin.

II. Having thus shewn you the chief Duties you owe to your great Master in Heaven, I now come to lay before you the Duties you owe to your *Masters* and *Mistresses* here upon Earth.

And for this, you have one general Rule, that you ought always to carry in your Minds;—and that is,—*to do all Service for THEM, as if you did it for GOD himself.*—Poor Creatures! you little consider, when you are idle and neglectful of your Master's Business,—when you *steal,* and *waste,* and *hurt* any of their Substance,—when you are *saucy* and *impudent,*—when you are telling them *Lies,* and deceiving them,—or when you prove *stubborn* or *sullen,* and will not do the Work you are set about without Stripes and Vexation;—you do not consider, I say, that what Faults you are guilty of towards your Masters and Mistresses, are Faults done against GOD himself, who hath set your Masters and Mistresses over you, in his own Stead, and expects that you will do for them, just as you would do for Him.—And pray, do not think that I want to deceive you, when I tell you, that your *Masters* and *Mistresses* are GOD'S OVERSEERS,—and that if you are faulty towards them, GOD himself will punish you severely for it in the next World, unless you repent of it, and strive to make amends, by your *Faithfulness* and *Diligence* for the Time to come;—for GOD himself hath declared the same.—And you have, at the same

Time, this Comfort, that if any of your OWNERS should prove WICKED OVER-SEERS, and use you, who are his under Servants here, as they ought not to do;—though you must submit to it, and can have no Remedy in this World, yet, when GOD calls you and them together Face to Face before him in the next World, and examines into these Matters, He will do you strict Justice, and punish those that have been bad Stewards and Overseers over you with greater Severity, as they had more of this World entrusted to their Care:–and that whatever you have suffered *unjustly* here, GOD will make you amends for it in Heaven.—I will now read over to you the Rules which GOD hath given you, in his own Words, that you may see what I say is Truth.—*Servants, be obedient to them that are your Masters according to the Flesh, with Fear and Trembling, in Singleness of your Heart, as unto Christ:—Not with Eye-service, as Men-pleasers, but as the Servants of Christ, doing the Will of GOD from the Heart.—With good Will doing Service as to the Lord and not to Men—Knowing, that whatsoever good Thing any Man doeth, the same shall he receive of the Lord, whether he be bond or Free.—And ye masters, do the same Things unto them, forbearing* (or moderating) *Threatening; knowing that your master also is in Heaven; neither is there Respect of Persons with him.*

Now, from this great general Rule, namely, that you are to *do all Service for your Masters and Mistresses, as if you did it for GOD himself,* there arise several other Rules of Duty towards your *Masters* and *Mistresses,* which I shall endeavour to lay in order before you.

1. And in the First Place, *You are to be obedient and subject to your Masters in all Things*—For the Rules which GOD hath left us in the Scriptures are these—[2]*Servants, obey in all Things your Masters according to the Flesh, not with Eye-service as Men-pleasers, but in Singleness of Heart, fearing GOD:—And whatsoever ye do, do it heartily, as to the Lord, and not unto Men; knowing, that of the Lord ye shall receive the Reward of Inheritance, for ye serve the Lord Christ.—But he that doeth Wrong shall receive for the Wrong he hath done; and there is no Respect of Persons.—[3]Servants, be subject to your Masters, with all Fear, not only to the good and gentle, but also to the froward* [sic]—And Christian Ministers are commanded to[4] *exhort Servants to be obedient unto their own Masters, and to please them well in all Things, not answering again,* or murmuring, or gainsaying.—You see how strictly GOD requires this of you, that whatever your *Masters and Mistresses* order you to do, you must set about it immediately, and faithfully perform it, without any disputing or grumbling,—and take care to please him well in all Things.—And, for your Encouragement, he tells you, that he will reward you for it in heaven, because, while you are honestly and faithfully doing your Master's business here, you are serving your Lord and Master in Heaven. You see also, that you are not to take any Exceptions to the Behaviour of your Masters and Mistresses, and that you are to be subject and obedient, not only to such as are *good*, and *gentle*, and *mild* towards you, but also to such as may be *froward* [sic], *peevish*, and *hard*.—For you are not at liberty to chuse your own Masters, but into whatever Hands GOD hath been pleased to put you, you must do your Duty, and GOD will reward you for it.—And if they neglect to do theirs, GOD will punish them for it:—For there is no Respect of Persons with him.—There is only *one Case*, in which you may refuse Obedience to your Owners,—and that is, if they should command you to do any *sinful* Thing.—As *Joseph*

would not hearken to his Mistress, when she tempted him to lie with her.—So that if any Master could be so wicked as to command you to *steal*, to *murder*, to *set a Neighbour's House on Fire*, to *do Harm to any Body's Goods, or Cattle*, or to get *drunk*, or to *curse and swear*, or to *work on Sundays*, (unless it should be in a case of great Necessity)—or to do any Thing that GOD hath forbidden there it is your duty to refuse them;—because GOD is your HEAD MASTER, and you must not do a Thing which you know is contrary to his Will.—But in every Thing else, you must obey your Owners; and GOD requires it of you,

2. You are *not* to be *Eye-Servants*.—Now *Eye-Servants* are such as will *work hard,* and seem mighty diligent, while they think that any body is taking notice of them; but when their Masters and Mistresses Backs are turned, they are idle, and neglect their Business.—I am afraid that there are a great many such *Eye-Servants* among you,—and that you do not consider how great a Sin it is to be so, and how severely GOD will punish you for it.—You may easily deceive your Owners, and make them have an opinion of you that you do not deserve, and get the Praise of Men by it.—But remember, that you cannot deceive Almighty GOD, who sees your Wickedness and Deceit, and will punish you accordingly.—For the Rule is, that you must *obey your Masters in all Things,* and do the work they set you about *with Fear and Trembling, in Singleness of Heart, as unto Christ, not with Eye-Service, as Men-pleasers, but as the Servants of Christ, doing the Will of God from the Heart: With good Will doing Service, as to the Lord, and not as to Men.*—If then, you would but think, and say within yourselves,—"My Master hath set me about this Work, and his Back is turned, so that I may loiter and idle if I please, for he does not see me.—but there is my GREAT MASTER in Heaven, whose Overseer my other Master is,—and his Eyes are always upon me, and taking Notice of me, and I cannot get any where out of his Sight, nor be idle without his knowing it, and what will become of me if I lose his good Will and make his angry with me."—If, I say, you would once get the Way of thinking and saying thus, upon all Occasions, you then would do what GOD commands you, and serve your Masters with SINGLENESS OF HEART,—that is, with *Honesty and Sincerity;* you would do the Work you are set about *with Fear and Trembling,* not for Fear of your Masters and Mistresses upon Earth (for you may easily cheat them, and make them believe you are doing their Business when you do not)—but *with Fear and Trembling,* lest GOD, your HEAVENLY MASTER, whom you cannot deceive, should call you to Account, and punish you in the next World, for your *Deceitfulness* and *Eye-Service* in this.

3. You are to be *faithful and honest to your Masters and Mistresses,—not purloining*[5] (or wasting their Goods or Substance) *but shewing all good Fidelity in all Things.*

If you were to *rob* or *steal* from others, you know that it would be a very bad Thing, and how severely the Law would punish you for it.—But if your Master is robb'd of what belongs to him by your Wastefulness or Negligence, do not you think that it is as wicked and as bad as if you were to *steal* his Goods and *give* them to other People?—For, pray, what is the Difference to me, when my Substance is gone, whether a Thief took it away from me, or whether I am robbed of it by my Servant's Negligence?—The Loss is the same, and they will have it equally to answer for.—How then, can many of you be so careless about your Master's

Business?—How can you be so unfaithful and wicked, as to see their Substance perish and be lost, when a little of your timely Care would prevent the Loss?—Is not this a very common Case among you?—And do not most Masters complain, with great Justice, that unless they happen to see unto every Thing themselves, their Servants will take no Care?—Nay, even when they are told of it, and ordered to do it, they will still neglect, and let the Goods perish?—Do not your Masters, under GOD, provide for you?—And how shall they be able to do this, to *feed* and to *cloath* you, unless you take honest Care of every Thing that belongs to them?— Remember that GOD requires this of you, and if you are not afraid of suffering for it here, you cannot escape the Vengeance of Almighty GOD, who will judge between you and your Masters, and make you pay severely in *the next World* for all the Injustice you do them *here*—And tho' you could manage so cunningly as to escape the Eyes and Hands of Man, yet think what a dreadful Thing it is, to fall *into the Hands of the living GOD, who is able to cast both Soul and Body into Heaven.*

4. You are to *serve your Masters with Chearfulness, and Reverence, and Humility.*—You are to do your Masters Service *with good Will,* doing it as *the Will of GOD, from the Heart,* without any Sauciness or answering again.—How many of you do Things quite otherwise and instead of going about your Work with a good Will and a good Heart, *dispute,* and *grumble,* give saucy Answers, and behave in a surly Manner?—There is somethng so becoming and ingaging in a modest, chearful, good natur'd Behaviour, that a little Work, done in that Manner, seems better done, and gives far more Satisfaction, than a great deal more, that must be done with Fretting, Vexation, and the Lash always held over you.—It also gains the good Will and Love of those you belong to, and makes your own Life pass with more Ease and Pleasure.—Besides, you are to consider, that this *Grumbling* and *ill Will* does not affect your *Masters* and *Mistresses* only:—They have Ways and Means in their Hands of forcing you to do your Work, whether you are willing or not.—But your *Murmuring* and *Grumbling* is against GOD, who hath placed you in that Service, who will punish you severely in the next World for despising his Commands.

Thus I have endeavoured to shew you, why you ought to serve GOD, and what Duty in particular you owe to him:—I have also shewn you, that while you are serving your Masters and Mistresses, or doing any Thing that GOD hath commanded, you are, at the same Time, *serving* him; and have endeavoured to shew you what Duty or Service you owe to your Owners, in Obedience to GOD, and that in so plain a Manner, as, I hope, the greatest Part of you did well understand.—The other Parts of your Duty and the Rewards which GOD hath promised to you (if you will honestly set about doing it) I shall endeavour to lay before you at our next Meeting here for that Purpose.—In the mean Time, consider well what hath been said.—Think upon it, and talk about it with one another, and strive to fix it on your Memories.—And may GOD, of his infinite Mercy, grant, that it may sink deep into your Hearts, and, taking Root there, may bring forth in you the fruit of good Living, to the Honour and Praise of his holy Name, the Spreading abroad of his Gospel, and the eternal Salvation of your precious Souls, through our Lord and Saviour JESUS CHRIST, to whom, with the Father, and the Holy Spirit, be all Honour and Glory, World without End. *Amen.*

NOTES

1. Heb. xiii.7.
2. Col. iii. 22, 23, 24, 25.
3. I Pet. 18.
4. Tit ii 9.
5. Tit. ii 10.

CHAPTER
5

Debate: "The Great Awakening"— Fact or Fiction?

In the period between first colonial settlements and the American Revolution, no event has received more attention from religious historians than the mid-eighteenth-century religious revivals labeled "The Great Awakening." In these articles by the editors of this Reader, Harry S. Stout and Jon Butler, the Great Awakening is surveyed from diametrically opposed vantage points. What is the central thesis of each article? How can historians come to such opposite conclusions over a common body of evidence? Is it possible that both authors are "right"? If so, what does this say about the nature of historical research and writing or about historical events themselves?

Additional Reading: The literature on "The Great Awakening" and eighteenth-century revivalism is very large and much of it is mentioned in the notes to the essays by Butler and Stout. Among additional readings, W. R. Ward, *The Protestant Evangelical Awakening* (Cambridge, 1992) and Leigh Eric Schmidt, *Holy Fairs: Scottish Communions and American Revivals in the Early Modern Period* (Princeton, 1989) offer superb surveys of the complexities and interrelationships in eighteenth-century German, English, Scottish, and colonial American revivalism. Edwin S. Gaustad, *The Great Awakening in New England* (New York, 1957) remains one of the best local studies of eighteenth-century colonial revivalism, and Harry S. Stout, *The Divine Dramatist: George Whitefield and the Rise of Modern Evangelicalism* (Grand Rapids, 1991) describes the public career of the century's best-known evangelist.

Harry S. Stout

Religion, Communications, and the Ideological Origins of the American Revolution

. . . I saw before me a Cloud or fogg rising; I first thought it came from the great River, but as I came nearer the Road, I heard a noise something like a low rumbling thunder and presently found it was the noise of Horses feet coming down the Road and this Cloud was a Cloud of dust made by the Horses feet; it arose some Rods into the air over the tops of Hills and trees and when I came within about 20 rods of the Road, I could see men and horses Sliping along in the Cloud like shadows and as I drew nearer it seemed like a steady Stream of horses and their riders, scarcely a horse more than his length behind another, all of a Lather and foam with sweat, their breath rolling out of their nostrils every Jump; every horse seemed to go with all his might to carry his rider to hear news from heaven for the saving of Souls, it made me tremble to see the Sight . . .

Nathan Cole's description of George Whitefield's appearance before four thousand avid listeners in Middletown, Connecticut, in 1740 captures our attention at least partly because Cole's voice is one that is rare in early American literature.[1] The crude spelling and syntax signal a vernacular prose composed by an ordinary man, whose purpose is less to analyze the theological issues of the revival than to describe an exhilarating event. Lacking the literary refinements of a classical education, Cole portrayed his experience in the form of a "realistic narrative" framed against a concrete social background.[2] Although common in setting, the passage is hardly trivial, for it brings to life the impassioned world of the common people and conveys, in their own words, a sense of the irrepressible spontaneity that marked the revivals throughout the colonies. Thunderous noise, clouds of dust, horses in a lather, and unrecognizable shadowy figures dominate a vocabulary that manages to express, as no official account could possibly do, the powerful emotions evoked by the Great Awakening.

With Whitefield's celebrated speaking tours of the colonies there appeared an innovative style of communications that redefined the social context in which public address took place. The sheer size and heterogeneity of the audience exceeded anything in the annals of colonial popular assembly. To organize the mass meetings, both speaker and audience altered the roles and language they customarily adopted in public worship. In the process, a new model of social organization and public address developed—a model which could be applied to a broad range of social, political, and religious contexts.

Contemporary and historical accounts agree that the Awakening was the most momentous intercolonial popular movement before the Revolution. Indeed, the parallel between the popular engagement and "enthusiasm" evidenced alike

Reprinted from the *William and Mary Quarterly* 34 (1977), 519–41; copyright © Institute of Early American History and Culture.

in the revivals and the rebellion merits close attention. Unfortunately, however, attempts to explain the meaning those two movements had for their participants must confront the fact that the documentary evidence originates overwhelmingly from an elitist "rhetorical world" that excluded the common people from the presumed audience.[3] Although the informed writings of the Founding Fathers provide the official revolutionary vocabulary, they do not render in a realistic narrative form the ideological arousal of the common people, who, by the very rhetoric of those documents, were excluded from the message. How were revolutionary sentiments communicated with ideological force to an audience unversed in the rhetorical forms of the literature? And, conversely, how did the active popular self-consciousness manifested in the popular movements energize a republican vocabulary and push it in egalitarian directions the leaders had never intended? The documents are of little help here. More to the point, they actually create the problem of interpretation.

Cole's description of the popular enthusiasm of the revival suggests a different approach to the problem of popular culture and republican ideology. If *what* was communicated is qualified by the restrictive rhetoric through which the ideas were intended to be transmitted, it may help to ask instead *how* communications were conducted and how they changed during the second half of the eighteenth century? There could be no egalitarian culture as we know it today without an ideological predisposition toward the idea that the vulgar masses ought to be reached directly. By examining the changing style of communications in the revivals it is possible to gain insights into the nature of an egalitarian rhetoric through which, and only through which, republican ideas could be conveyed to an unlettered audience.

David Ramsay, a noted participant in and historian of the Revolution, recognized that, to understand the meaning of the Revolution, "forms and habits" must be regarded.[4] Before a republican vocabulary could communicate radical social meanings, a new rhetoric had to appear in which familiar terms were used to express unfamiliar thoughts. And this, it is argued here, is precisely what happened in the mass assemblies inaugurated by preachers like Whitefield. Despite the differences in intellectual substance between the revivals and the rebellion, those movements exhibited a close rhetorical affinity that infused religious and political ideas with powerful social significance and ideological urgency.

The point of departure for this article is Alan Heimert's study of *Religion and the American Mind*.[5] Published in 1966, the book had a generally cool reception. Critical essays by Edmund S. Morgan and Sidney E. Mead pointed out conceptual shortcomings in the work but failed to recognize its value in suggesting a method of historical analysis that focuses on the context of communications.[6] This failure had the unfortunate effect of foreclosing a line of inquiry into the subject of religion and the ideological origins of the Revolution.

Heimert's forward states his central thesis: religious "Liberalism was profoundly conservative, politically as well as socially, and . . . its leaders, insofar as they did in fact embrace the Revolution, were the most reluctant of rebels. Conversely, 'evangelical' religion, which had as its most notable formal expression the

'Calvinism' of Jonathan Edwards, was not the retrograde philosophy that many historians rejoice to see confounded in America's Age of Reason. Rather Calvinism, and Edwards, provided pre-Revolutionary America with a radical, even democratic, social and political ideology, and evangelical religion embodied, and inspired, a thrust toward American nationalism."[7] This assertion diverged dramatically from the conventional wisdom regarding the relations of religion and the Revolution. In demonstrating his thesis Heimert contended, in now notorious words, that it was necessary to read the sources "not between the lines, but, as it were, through and beyond them."[8] Only by doing this would it be possible to cut through the immediate idiom of political discourse that dominated the official Revolutionary debates and discover the underlying "relationship of ideology and political commitment to modes of persuasion."[9] In Heimert's view, these "modes of persuasion" were derived from the Evangelical rather than the Liberal tradition.

Against this thesis, and the method upon which it rests, Morgan and Mead launched an impressive assault. The conceptual framework they imposed on early America, and their way of reading historical documents, were molded largely by Perry Miller, and it was as an extension of Miller's work that they interpreted Heimert.[10] To them, Heimert's tactic of reading "beyond" the content of the documents to the styles they expressed smacked, in Morgan's word, of "fantasy."[11] They contended that the method not only detached the historian from the security of objective reference (that is, the content of the documents) but also ignored social and intellectual connections between revivalism and republicanism that were neither as sharp nor as consistent as Heimert supposed.

Influential as these criticisms have been in stifling consideration of *Religion and the American Mind*, we must ask whether in fact Heimert wrote the book the critics reviewed. If Heimert's study is simply an extension of Miller, then the problems with the book become insurmountable because, as the critics demonstrate, there is no clear and consistent link between revivalism and republicanism at the level of ideas. But if the book is viewed in a different context altogether—if Heimert was not seeking to establish direct intellectual links between religious thought and political rebellion—then the entire effort needs to be revaluated.

Perry Miller's fullest statement on religion and the ideological origins of the Revolution appeared in his essay "From the Covenant to the Revival," published in 1961.[12] Addressing the role of "Calvinistic" Protestantism (a term he applied indiscriminately to Liberals and Evangelicals) in the Revolution, Miller insisted that, with the exception of a few hopelessly optimistic Anglicans, the American people shared a religious tradition articulated in the Reformed vocabulary of "federal" theology.[13] Under the influence of this austere covenantal tradition the colonists could never be moved by self-congratulatory appeals to natural rights and enlightened self-interest. Rather, the dynamic for revolution issued from a deep sense of moral corruption and degradation that found a target in English oppression but, more important, spoke to the sins of colonial society itself. For generations of colonists schooled in the language of covenant, judgment, and collective accountability, the jeremiad functioned as the "form of discourse" capable of driving them to a moral revolution. Considered as an intellectual movement, the

Revolution represented a spiritual purge administered to a corrupt established order in the interest of restoring a pure order that would both free the colonists from a decadent oppressor and cleanse their own society. The Revolution was inspired by this highly unstable compound of pious contrition and political rebellion, moral reformation and patriotic resistance.

Miller's essay came to exert an enormous influence on assessments of the role of religion in the Revolution.[14] Yet nowhere did it reflect a recognition of the social dislocations and divisions which we now know proliferated in eighteenth-century America.[15] Miller's framework fails to show how Americans sharing the "Puritan Ethic" could have been so sharply divided over the issue of independence or why, among the patriots, such confusion and contradiction raged over the question of what the Revolution was all about.[16] Finally, it is impossible in Miller's terms to account for receptivity to rebellion on the part of a populace of limited literacy.[17] To focus solely on the ideas set forth in surviving documents as the source of ideological change is to confuse a deep cultural transformation with its subsequent manifestation in a self-conscious, theoretical vocabulary.

In opposition to Miller, Heimert describes two clearly separate and distinctive revolutionary styles in eighteenth-century America, each originating in opposing "rhetorical strategies" that crystallized after the mass revivals.[18] On the one hand, there was the rebellion itself—the movement for independence from England, which Heimert concedes may well have proceeded from Liberal assumptions. On the other hand, there emerged with the rebellion an egalitarian impulse that pointed toward the creation of a society fundamentally incompatible with traditional conceptions of order, hierarchy, and deference.[19]

Approaching the problem of popular receptivity and concentrating on the verbal forms through which ideas were presented, Heimert locates the sources of this animating egalitarianism in the Great Awakening but concludes that it can be understood only by reading beyond the religious content of evangelical ideas to the new forms of public address established in the revivals. At some point prior to the popular reception of a revolutionary vocabulary, a new rhetoric must appear in which familiar terms can be used to mean something different—and this change in the *form*, as distinguished from the *content*, of communications marks the moment of a fundamental transformation of popular consciousness. Any revolution in world-view requires a new rhetoric. The most conspicuous and revolutionary product of the revivals was not to be found in doctrine, in the creation of new ecclesiastical or academic institutions, or even in resistance to the tyranny of established religion or monarchy. Evangelicalism's enduring legacy was a new rhetoric, a new mode of persuasion that would redefine the norms of social order. In Heimert's words, "quite apart from the question of Revolution, the contrasts between Liberal and Calvinist social thought were possibly of less ultimate significance than the remarkable differences between their oratorical strategies and rhetorical practices."[20]

Heimert's recognition of the revolutionary potentialities of the revivals suggests a closer look at evangelical oratory, particularly in relation to the forms of public worship that prevailed before the revivals. Despite differences in style and substance between Puritanism and southern Anglicanism, all churchmen believed traditionally with Samuel Willard that God did "Ordain Orders of Superiority and Inferiority among men."[21] This hierarchical world-view presupposed a society of face-to-face personal relationships in which people identified themselves with reference to those around them and acted according to their rank in the community. Forms of attire, the "seating" of public meetings, and patterns of speech were among the more conspicuous indications of a pervasive social stratification that separated the leaders from the rank and file. As Stephen Foster observes, "mutuality, subordination, and public service constituted a kind of sacred trinity of all respectable societies, Puritan or otherwise."[22]

The social institutions of colonial America were designed to sustain this prevailing perception of proper social organization. In this traditional social ethic, itinerancy was inconceivable because, in Increase Mather's words, "to say that a Wandering Levite who has no flock is a Pastor, is as good sense as to say, that he that has no children is a Father."[23] What made a pastor was not simply the preaching of the word but also a direct, authoritarian identification with a specific flock. To ignore the personal and deferential relationship of a minister with his congregation would be to threaten the organic, hierarchical principles upon which both family and social order rested.

That ministers be "settled" was no idle proposition but rather an insistence carrying with it responsibility for the whole social order. An institution as critically important as the church could deny the forms of social hierarchy only at the peril of undermining the entire organization of social authority. In terms of communications this meant that speaker and audience were steadily reminded of their *personal* place in the community; in no context were they strangers to one another, for no public gatherings took place outside of traditional associations based upon personal acquaintance and social rank.[24]

Within this world of public address Liberals and Evangelicals alike realized that something dramatically different was appearing in the revivalists' preaching performances. The problem raised by the revivals was not their message of the new birth. Indeed, it was the familiar message of regeneration that lulled leaders into an early acceptance and even endorsement of the revivals. The problem, it soon became clear, was the revolutionary setting in which the good news was proclaimed. The secret of Whitefield's success and that of other evangelists (no less than of Patrick Henry in the 1770s) was not simply a booming voice or a charismatic presence. It was a new style: a rhetoric of persuasion that was strange to the American ear. The revivalists sought to transcend both the rational manner of polite Liberal preaching and the plain style of orthodox preaching in order to speak directly to the people-at-large.[25] Repudiating both the conventions of the jeremiad and the ecclesiastical formalities, they assaulted the old preaching style no less devastatingly than they attacked the doctrines of covenant theology. Their technique of mass address to a voluntary audience forced a dialogue between speaker and hearer that disregarded social position and local setting.

Immensely significant were the separation of the revivalists from local ministerial rule and their unfamiliarity with the audience. Until then, preachers, like political leaders, had to know whom they were addressing. Because the very act of public speaking signified social authority, they were expected to communicate through the existing institutional forms. When public speakers in positions of authority communicated outside of the customary forms, they set themselves, by that act itself, in opposition to the established social order. The eighteenth-century leaders' obsession with demagogy and "enthusiasm" can only be understood in the context of a deferential world-view in which public speakers who were not attached to the local hierarchy created alternative settings that represented a threat to social stability. The frenzy raised by the itinerants was not born of madness but was derived from the self-initiated associations of the people meeting outside of regularly constituted religious or political meetings and, in so doing, creating new models of organization and authority. As the Harvard faculty clearly recognized in their censure of Whitefield, the "natural effect" of his preaching was that "the People have been thence ready to despise their own Ministers."[26]

In gathering their large and unfamiliar audiences the revivalists utilized the only form of address that could be sure to impress all hearers: the spoken word proclaimed extemporaneously in everyday language. As historians immersed in printed documents, we scarcely recognize the dominance of speech and oratory in aural cultures—an orality that, by definition, never survives in the written record. Alphabetic writing and print emerged, after all, as an *imitation* of spoken words, and so they have remained ever since. Recognition of the powerful social and psychological imperatives of direct oral address has led Walter Ong to observe that "writing commits the words to space. But to do so, it makes words less real, pretends they are something they are not: quiescent marks."[27] Print and typographic culture create highly visual, sequential, and analytic patterns of thought which aural cultures, attuned to easily remembered forms of speech, cannot readily comprehend.[28] Unlike print, which is essentially passive, reflective, and learned, sound is active, immediate, and spontaneously compelling in its demand for a response. Speech remains in the deepest sense an event or psychological encounter rather than an inert record—an event that is neither detached from personal presence nor analyzed, but is intrinsically engaged and calculated to persuade. Print cannot match the persuasive power of the spoken word whose potential audience includes everyone who can understand the language. It is no wonder that literate elites have feared persuasive orators, from Plato condemning the sophists to Charles Chauncy damning the demagogues of the revival. Once orators are allowed the opportunity to address the people, there is, in Chauncy's words, "no knowing how high it [their influence] may rise, nor what it may end in."[29]

To portray the word as event, as a vital indwelling principle, the revivalists employed what Miller termed a "rhetoric of sensation"[30]—a new rhetoric that, through its recognition of the singular power of the spoken word delivered to a mass audience, differed fundamentally from the Old Light or rational preaching which was written out like a lecture and was more concerned, in the revivalists' words, with "ornament" than with the "affections." The animadversions of Liberals against what they called the revivalists' "mighty noise," which not only stimulated enthusiasm but also challenged the social order, were certainly justified from their perspective.[31] Ong makes the important point that "script, and particularly the alphabet, provides a heightened experience of order. The world of thought is itself a beautifully intricate world, and the world of words is likewise impressively, if mysteriously, organized. . . . To attack the printed word would be to attack *the* symbol of order."[32]

Looking to the New Testament as their model, the revivalist rediscovered the effectiveness of extemporaneous address in their struggle against the Standing Order. Recent analyses of New Testament rhetoric demonstrate the prevailing orality of the gospel. Amos Wilder, for example, notes that "Jesus never wrote a word. . . . In secular terms we could say that Jesus spoke as the birds sing, oblivious of any concern for transcription. Less romantically we can say that Jesus' use of the spoken word alone has its own theological significance."[33] Throughout the gospels the Word is the oral word, and the Good News is uttered through ordinary speech. In his classic study of the Western Literary tradition Eric Auerbach pointed out that "in the last analysis the differences in style between the writers of antiquity and early Christianity are conditioned by the fact that they were composed from a different point of view and for different people."[34]

Returning not only to the social doctrine of the gospel but to its rhetoric as well, the evangelists excited the people to action by "calling them out" and ex-horting them to experimental Christianity. Radical attacks on an "unconverted ministry" that acted more like "Letter-learned . . . Pharisees" than preachers of the Word take on additional meaning in the social context of eighteenth-century established religion.[35] The danger that the Liberals sensed in the revivals was rhetorical as well as doctrinal. The Anglican commissary Alexander Garden cor-rectly, and sarcastically, identified this threat: *"What went you out, my Brethren, to see, or rather to hear? Any new Gospel, or message from Heaven? Why, no? but the old one explained and taught in a new and better Manner."*[36] Pointing to the spirit of this new manner, one opponent of the revivals observed that "it abhors Reason, and is always for putting out her Eyes; but loves to reign Tyrant over the Passions, which it manages by Sounds and Nonsense."[37] The identification of sight with rea-son, and of sound with the passions, is here obvious and comes very near to the center of the raging controversy surrounding the itinerants. At stake was nothing less than the rules and conventions governing public address and social authority.

The revivalists' repudiation of polite style and their preference for extempo-raneous mass address cut to the very core of colonial culture by attacking the habit of deference to the written word and to the gentlemen who mastered it. Evangelical rhetoric performed a dual function: it proclaimed the power of the spoken word directly to every individual who would hear, and it confirmed a shift in authority by organizing voluntary popular meetings and justifying them in the religious vocabulary of the day. Partly through doctrine, but even more through the rhetorical strategy necessitated by that doctrine, the popular style of the revivals challenged the assumption of hierarchy and pointed to a substitute basis for authority and order in an open, voluntary system.

The popular rhetoric of the evangelists contrasted sharply with the much more formal modes of address preferred by upholders of established authority. Nowhere were the social divisions of American society more clearly reflected than in the leaders' utilization of a printed form of discourse that separated the literati from the common people. Throughout the eighteenth century, public communications were not only increasingly printed but were tuned to a genteel European literary style governed by canons of correct usage. As George Philip Krapp observed in his seminal history of the English language, "pronunciation, grammar and spelling were not then tests of respectability [in the seventeenth century] . . . in the degree to which they have since become. What seems now like illiterate speech, the speech of persons who do not reflect how they speak, was then merely the normal speech of the community."[38] With no printed dictionaries to provide authority for correct spelling and usage, seventeenth-century vernacular literature exhibited a high degree of variability. As the spread of printing in the eighteenth century gave increased importance to writing, however, there emerged a concomitant movement toward standardization of spelling and usage. Following the appearance of Samuel Johnson's dictionary in 1755, language came to be thought of as written rather than spoken, and educated elites on both sides of the ocean adopted a written style intended to communicate with their literate peers.[39] Linguistic divisions between the well-bred and the vulgar became increasingly clear to both sectors of the colonial society. One revealing example of a distinctive lower-class style is a radical essay, *The Key of Libberty,* written (though never accepted for publication) in 1797 by James Manning, an untutored Massachusetts farmer who "neaver had the advantage of six months schooling in my life." In organization, spelling, and grammar the essay stands in stark contrast to the polished style of the whig patriots. It was, as Manning recognized, "not in the language and stile of the Larned for I am not able."[40]

Linguistic uniformity conspired with classical education to establish a learned discourse that effectively separated the literate elite from the common folk. Hugh Blair, whose handbook, *Lectures on Rhetoric and Belles Lettres,* came to epitomize the style for aspiring gentlemen, averred that the educated class "is now so much accustomed to a correct and ornamental style, that no writer can, with safety, neglect the study of it."[41] To encourage such a style Blair pointed to the patrician cultures of classical Greece and Rome, and urged his fellow literati "to render ourselves well acquainted with the style of the best authors. This is requisite, both in order to form a just taste in style, and to supply us with a full stock of words on every subject."[42] The classical heritage provided a vocabulary and mode of discourse which leaders had to learn if they were to communicate through the proper forms.[43]

Classical learning inculcated a set of social and cultural attitudes about the nature of speaker and audience that went far beyond the content of literature. A formal, analytical style conveyed social as well as literary prerogatives. For centuries, masters of print and the written word enjoyed social power and prestige partly because the people were awed by a sequential form of communications they could not understand. The eighteenth-century rise in learned treatises, tightly argued pamphlets, and belletristic writing reflected an effort, in Mather Byles's words, to "cultivate *polite* Writing, and form and embellish the Style of our ingenious Countrymen.—"[44] But Byles's "ingenious Countrymen" did not include the common folk.

The eighteenth-century shift in the direction of print and polite style was reflected in the growing appeal of rational religion among the educated elite. Cotton Mather typified this shift as early as 1726 in his *Manuductio ad Ministerium,* which, as Miller recognized, "in its catholicity of taste and urbanity suggests the spirit of current periodical essays rather than the utilitarian aim of a preaching manual."[45] Followers of deism, which carried the Liberal print-centered rationalism to an extreme, tended, in Ong's words, "to think of God himself as no longer a communicator, one who speaks to man, but as a Great Architect. . . . a manipulator of objects in visual-tactile space."[46] Treating communications as written rather than spoken, and locking words in printed space, rational Protestantism was incapable of penetrating the soul of an aural society; its ideas set forth in printed sermons and treatises could never inform a popular mentality attuned to the spoken word.

Attached to the elitist typographic culture were social imperatives. As long as social identities depended on a traditional social order for context and location within a finely graded hierarchy, communications had to be transacted through an elitist rhetoric. Power became so closely tied to print that advanced literacy and a classical education were virtually prerequisite to authority, and a college education guaranteed rapid advance in the social hierarchy.[47] By 1776 there were nearly three thousand college graduates in the colonies who, through the remarkable improvements in post and press, were able to communicate with one another on a scale and with a frequency unimaginable in the seventeenth century.[48] The cosmopolitan "better sort" formed a close-knit community that provided both authors and audience for the wave of printed literature that began to surge in the late eighteenth century. Pamphlets written by educated gentlemen, primarily lawyers, merchants, ministers, and planters, were addressed to their peers.[49] The common people were not included in the audience, but it was assumed that they would continue to defer to the leaders. There was no recognition that the pamphleteers' impassioned celebration of republicanism would require a new rhetoric of communications reflecting a profound shift in the nature of social authority—a rhetoric, in brief, that threatened to undermine the exclusive world in which the pamphlets were originally conceived.

With the coming of independence the American leadership could congratulate itself on the creation of a unique republican world-view through their publications. At the same time, however, these leaders could neither anticipate nor appreciate an egalitarian rhetoric that would soon compel them to relinquish their traditional claims to power and authority in the new republic. As a model of society, the neoclassical world of the colonial gentlemen was essentially stable; their exclusion of the common people meant that their writings could not reflect a changing self-consciousness initiated from below. The very outlook that created a learned and articulate "Republic of Letters" served, at the same time, to limit the writers' historical consciousness. Quite simply, the people were neither heard nor understood in their own terms.

The creation of an egalitarian rhetoric owed nothing to the classical heritage. If we are to understand the cultural significance of the Revolution, we must move beyond the rhetorical world of informed publications to the social world of popular assembly. We must *listen* as the "inarticulate" would have listened and determine to what extent religious and political meetings had a common rhetorical denominator that reached a revolutionary crescendo in the movement for independence.[50] For Philip Davidson, whose work continues to stand as the best general description of communications in the Revolutionary period, there was an unmistakably oral orientation to patriot "propaganda."[51] Throughout the colonies there existed a broad range of dramatic and oral communications in which, in William Eddis's words, "the busy voice of preparation echoes through every settlement."[52] The mobilization of the people was accomplished through extra-institutional mass meetings which, Merrill Jensen recognizes, were "of even greater long-range importance than mob action."[53]

The Founding Fathers were reluctant, for obvious reasons, to dwell on the oral dynamic unleashed in the course of rebellion; the same cannot be said of the loyalist opposition. Jonathan Sewall recognized both the evangelical and oral connections with republicanism: "there is an Enthusiasm in politics, like that which religious notions inspire, that drives Men on with an unusual Impetuosity, that baffles and confounds all Calculation grounded upon rational principles. Liberty, among Englishmen, is a Word, whose very Sound carries a fascinating charm."[54] Loyalist literature is replete with complaints that American towns were increasingly "filled with mock orations and songs, which for composition and sentiment would disgrace the most stupid and abandoned. . . ."[55]

Whigs and loyalists used against one another the same arguments from constitution, law, and natural rights, but the charge of demogogic orality was a one-way criticism. The loyalist opposition never mustered a counterattack until after 1773; and when it finally appeared, it was almost exclusively printed. Like earlier Liberal rhetoric, that of the loyalists disdained the "wild uproars" of the whigs which culminated in nothing less than a "Yell of Rebellion," and concentrated instead on pen and press.[56] In Davidson's words, "the Tory appeal was a written appeal; the dearth of oral, dramatic, and pictorial suggestions is striking."[57]

Insofar as the whig gentlemen favored traditional modes of public address, they failed to plumb the depths of a popular revolutionary spirit that was oral and egalitarian rather than printed and elitist. Bernard Bailyn, who has examined the ideological origins of the Revolution more deeply than any other scholar, relies almost exclusively on printed sources as a sufficient explanation for the development of a Revolutionary mentality. It was "the opposition press, as much as any single influence," Bailyn argues, "that shaped the political awareness of eighteenth-century Americans."[58] Although this is true for the informed populace, the link between print culture and the people, between pamphlets and popular ideology, is assumed, not demonstrated. Despite the rhetorical incompatibility of a popular culture and tightly reasoned pamphlets, the existence of a distinctive popular ideology is denied.[59] But as Patrick Henry pointed out, "the middle and lower ranks of people have not those illumined ideas which the well-born are so happily possessed of—they cannot so readily perceive latent objects."[60] Henry's refusal to enter into "the labyrinths of syllogistic [Latin] argumentative deductions" in his public address may well account for the power of his oratory, which more than one commentator has likened to that of the revivalists in style and impact.[61]

The problem with Bailyn's analysis is not that it is wrong in the way it portrays ideology; indeed, it represents a brilliant plea for the late eighteenth century as an "age of ideology." The problem is pamphlets: although central to the rebellion and to the articulation of classical republican theory in the colonies, they are not sufficient to explain the process of an egalitarian cultural transformation. Bailyn concentrates on the pamphlets and the "real whig" country ideology as the formative sources of the rebellion. Having set the ideological background for rebellion, he describes some of the manifestations of the "transforming radicalism" unleashed by the Revolution.[62] But the instances of transforming radicalism which Bailyn isolates are described far more effectively than they are explained in terms of their cultural sources. Pamphlets could never represent the primary source of radical republicanism, any more than the revivals could have issued from printed sermons or the loyalist critique of the rebellion organize itself through oral popular appeals.

Recognizing the failure of pamphlets to capture the growing revolutionary sentiment in America, a writer for the *Pennsylvania Packet* argued in 1776 that "our cause will never appear to advantage in a pamphlet. . . . When you write a pamphlet you are expected to say the best, if not all that can be said on the subject, and if it contains [only] a few weighty arguments the author is despised and the subject suffers."[63] The writer was referring, of course, to pamphlets generally. Not every pamphlet was limited by the rhetorical constraints of a classical style. What made Thomas Paine's *Common Sense* so unlike the prevailing pamphlet literature of the day was its scorn for the best literary canons and its repudiation of the language and forms of classical discourse. Coming from a lower-class Quaker background, Paine lacked the formal Latin education common to other pamphleteers; in its place he managed to establish a new style that anticipated the wave of nineteenth-century literature intended for the people generally.[64]

Another major atypical pamphlet to appear in the colonies before independence was *An Oration on the Beauties of Liberty,* published in 1773 by the Baptist minister and linen-draper John Allen. Like Paine, Allen was a recent arrival from England at the time *An Oration* was printed, and, like *Common Sense,* the tract enjoyed immense popularity in the colonies.[65] In style it bears repeated resemblances to the "enraged" language which scholars have found throughout *Common Sense.*[66] Also, as in *Common Sense,* the references and quotations are not drawn, as in the other pamphlets, from classical republicanism or British constitutional theory, but rather from the Bible. There is not one page of *An Oration* that does not supply biblical precedent or injunction for the assault on privilege and tyranny. Ahab, the golden calf, Zedekiah, Cain, Abel, and Rehoboam constituted a familiar vocabulary that was "opened up" and explained repeatedly in colonial sermons. To liken a ruler to Ahab or a social order to Babylon was to call for a revolution.

Perhaps the most important aspect of *An Oration* is that it was obviously meant to be heard as well as read.[67] Its full impact can be felt only when one *listens* to the rhetoric. Addressing the common people, Allen repeatedly relied on a coarse prose, rather than on logical syllogisms or authorities from a printed past. Reminding the people that rulers and ministers were "servants" who must "hear" a free and "affectionate" people, Allen demanded, "Has not the voice of your father's blood cry'd yet loud enough in your ears, in your hearts? . . . Have you not heard the voice of blood in your own streets . . . ?"[68] In striking contrast to virtually all the other pamphleteers, but like Paine later, Allen aimed his rhetoric beyond the literate elite to the rank and file.

If action proceeds from a cultural perception of public events in terms of symbolic forms, then analyses of the mobilization of ideas into ideology and action must recognize, at least in part, the cultural preconditions for receptivity, particularly on the popular level. A discontinuous ("revolutionary") cultural change could, by definition, never emerge from a continuing intellectual tradition; there must be a break somewhere. Where are the sources of such a radical ideology to be discovered?

Without denying the influence of typographic culture on the leaders of the rebellion and in the formation of the new governments, it might be helpful to think of republicanism in a pluralistic context as absorbing both traditional and egalitarian perceptions of social order. The theoretical work of J. G. A. Pocock builds upon an understanding of the unavoidable "multivalency" of language that derives from the different experiences of speakers and hearers.[69] Recognizing the truism that words do not necessarily mean what either the speaker or the historian believe they mean, Pocock does not examine language and ideas as fixed entities, but rather insists that language and communications not be separated from the circumstances and comprehension of their individual users. When "conceptual and social worlds" are placed in conjunction, no singular "constellation of ideas" or "climate of opinion" appears to have embodied an identical meaning for all social ranks.[70] To get at the popular meaning of republican ideology requires moving beyond the verbal content of the documents themselves to the social world in which they were transmitted.

Pocock's insights, placed in the context of the American Revolution, reveal that not one but two ideological explosions propelled the colonies into a new nation. Both leaders and followers were possessed of an extraordinarily powerful ideology that at points converged on common antagonists and a common vocabulary, and at other points diverged dramatically. No ideology that is pieced together solely from the literate world of print can fully comprehend the radical dynamic of the Revolution. It is incapable of accounting for the enormously creative power of *vox populi* to organize a social order bound together in voluntary associations based on discussion and public address. Resisting John Adams and others who located the Revolution's *raison d'être* among the classical world-view of the elite, Benjamin Rush issued the following advice to historians: "I hope with the history of this folly, some historian will convey to future generations, that many of the most active and useful characters in accomplishing this revolution, were strangers to the formalities of a Latin and Greek education."[71]

The social conditions that allowed for the popular upsurge in the revivals and rebellion did not permit unstructured public address to degenerate into "anarchy" and mass rebellion, as the Standing Order had always feared. Perhaps the enduring legacy of the Revolution lay in its demonstration that distinctive ideologies *could* work in concert. The typographic ideology of the real whig tradition was, as Bailyn and others demonstrate, an "inner accelerator" of a transforming radicalism, but only in the sense that the aroused elite were compelled by the logic of their argument for rebellion to create, in law and politics, an egalitarian vocabulary, and, in communications, the secular equivalents of the revival in voluntary political parties and free presses.[72] Beneath that impulse, however, we must also recognize typographic ideology and the rebellion as accelerating a movement *already in progress*, a movement that originated among the lower rather than the upper strata of colonial society, and that, combined with profound social strains which increased throughout the eighteenth century, opened the way for the "enchanting sound" of mass public address.[73]

While the whig justification of the rebellion pointed to an "invisible government" of ministers, cliques, and venal officials, another conspiracy, recognized as early as 1773 by the loyalist Boucher, was equally "invisible" and far more powerful. Attacking the foundations of traditional social order, this conspiracy derived its "invisibility" from its essentially extemporaneous nature. In Boucher's words: "As though there were some irrefutable charm in all extemporaneous speaking, however rude, the orators of our committees and sub-committees, like those in higher spheres, *prevail with their tongues*. To public speakers alone is the government of our country now completely committed. . . . An empire is thus completely established within an empire; and a new system of government of great power erected, even before the old one is formally abolished."[74] An empire premised on talk, wholly lacking in the formal coercive structure that kings, churches, aristocracies, standing armies, and mercantile controls provided, did indeed represent a revolutionary departure in the principles of government and social order. Voluntaryism, the very linchpin of social, religious, and political organization in the new republic, was perhaps the clearest manifestation of this revolutionary system of authority.[75] Of course, public address did not replace print, nor was the populace hostile to print and literacy *per se*, but only to a print culture that was elitist and hierarchical. Still, it is no accident that early republicanism represented the "Golden Age of Oratory," because mass address was, for a time, the most effective means of reaching the new audience and utilizing the egalitarian style seized upon by republican orators and revivalists as the creative force within the popular ideology.[76]

The rhetorical transformation in the revivals signified an emerging popular culture asserting itself against a paternalistic social ethic. In the course of the Revolution, the social order prefigured in evangelical assemblies was suffused with secular and political meanings articulated in the world-view of republicanism. This new order, in Michael Kammen's description, was not so much a "seamless web" as an "unstable pluralism" defying reduction to any one ideology or social system.[77] The rhetorical division resulting from the revivals played a major role in generating subsequent tensions and conflicts in American society. These tensions, moreover, reflected not so much opposing ideas with conflicting literary traditions as entirely different social outlooks and attitudes toward social authority, all deriving legitimacy from the individualism implicit in a mass democratic society. Evangelical attacks on a settled and educated ministry may have expressed a pristine "anti-intellectualism" in the colonies,[78] but it was an anti-intellectualism that was positive and creative—indeed, revolutionary. Without it there would have been no creation of an egalitarian American republic.

The oral explosion and egalitarian style evidenced in the revivals were not limited to religion, nor was the articulation of a radical ideology the conscious objective of itinerant evangelists. The primary concern of the revivals was the saving of souls, and the rhetorical innovations that lent force to the movement were not fully perceived or verbalized for what they could come to represent: a revolutionary shift in world-view. As a movement initiated from below, the social experience of the revivals existed in fact before the emergence of a literate rationale. This does not mean that the experience proceeded from irrational impulses but, rather, that the terms necessary for rational comprehension and formal legitimation had to be invented. What opponents of the revivals termed a "spirit of superstition" was, for Jonathan Edwards, a new "sense" that could not easily be rendered into the existing forms of speech: "Some Things that they are sensible of are altogether new to them, their Ideas and inward Sensations are new, and what they therefore knew not how to accommodate Language to, or to find Words to express."[79] Edwards's concern was to fit the new social experience of the revivals to its proper spiritual vocabulary, while acknowledging that no language could fully express the essence of religious faith.

What Edwards and other churchmen failed to recognize was that the "spirit of liberty" manifest in the revivals would not be contained in religious categories. In the movement for independence both leaders and followers adopted a political vocabulary that expressed the egalitarian impulse in the secular language of republicanism. This vocabulary was largely provided, as Bailyn and Caroline Robbins demonstrate, through the Commonwealth tradition. But the ethos and ideological fervor of republicanism did not derive so much from the injection of Commonwealth vocabulary into colonial pamphlets as from the translation of the evangelical experience into a secular theoretical vocabulary that more adequately embodied, for some, the revolutionary thrust first widely experienced in the revivals. Words that were abstracted from their restrictive, deferential context came to mean something else. In Tocqueville's observation, Americans had a penchant for abstract words because only by using a vocabulary lacking specificity could they communicate radical ideas that destroyed a conventional style. "An abstract word," Tocqueville noted, "is like a box with a false bottom; you may put in it what ideas you please and take them out again unobserved."[80] The "country" publicists did not provide the textbook of revolution, so much as a lexicon of revolution, the meaning of which could be grasped only within a persuasion that celebrated the sovereignty of the new political audience.

NOTES

1. Michael J. Crawford, ed., "The Spiritual Travels of Nathan Cole," *William and Mary Quarterly*, 3d Ser., XXXIII (1976), 93. The crowd estimate at Middletown is taken from *George Whitefield's Journals* (Philadelphia, 1960), 479.

2. Hans W. Frei distinguishes a "realistic narrative" in the following terms: "Realistic narrative is that kind in which subject and social setting belong together, and characters and external circumstances fitly render each other. . . . [R]ealistic narrative, if it is really seriously undertaken and not merely a pleasurable or hortatory exercise, is a sort in which in style as well as content in the setting forth of didactic material, and in the depiction of characters and action, the sublime or at least serious effect mingles inextricably with the quality of what is casual, random, ordinary, and everyday" (*The Eclipse of Biblical Narrative: A Study in Eighteenth and Nineteenth Century Hermeneutics* [New Haven, Conn., 1974], 13–14).

3. The term "rhetorical world" is taken from Gordon S. Wood, "The Democratization of Mind in the American Revolution," in *Leadership in the American Revolution*, Library of Congress Symposia (Washington, D.C., 1974), 72.

4. David Ramsay, *The History of the American Revolution* (1789), in Edmund S. Morgan, ed., *The American Revolution: Two Centuries of Interpretation* (Englewood Cliffs, N.J., 1965), 8.

5. Alan Heimert, *Religion and the American Mind: From the Great Awakening to the Revolution* (Cambridge, Mass., 1966).

6. Edmund S. Morgan's review in *WMQ*, 3d Ser., XXIV (1967), 454–459, and Sidney E. Mead, "Through and beyond the Lines," *Journal of Religion*, XLVIII (1968), 274–288. The prominent exception to the negativity of the reviews is William G. McLoughlin's "The American Revolution as a Religious Revival: 'The Millennium in One Country,'" *New England Quarterly*, XL (1967), 99–110.

7. Heimert, *Religion and the American Mind*, viii.

8. *Ibid.*, 11. Heimert's terminology is not meant to imply that one reads beyond the documents by ignoring documentation (as nearly 2,000 footnotes fully attest). Rather, it is the recognition, recently articulated by Gene Wise, that to get at the meaning of verbal statements "one would have to go beyond the documents to the original experience they came out of" (*American Historical Explanations: A Strategy for Grounded Inquiry* [Homewood, Ill., 1973], 73).

9. Heimert, *Religion and the American Mind*, vii.

10. Mead is most explicit here in the opening comments of his review: "Essentially Mr. Heimert's work seems to me to be a 639-page expansion, with massive footnoting of some suggestions imaginatively adumbrated in 1961 by Perry Miller. . . . The voice seems to be that of Jacob, but the hand that tapped the typewriter was that of Esau" ("Through and beyond the Lines," *Jour. of Religion*, XLVIII [1968], 274).

11. Morgan states in his review: "The world he offers us has been constructed by reading beyond the lines of what men said; and what he finds beyond the lines is so far beyond, so wrenched from the context, and so at odds, with empirical evidence, that his world, to this reviewer at least, partakes more of fantasy than of history" (*WMQ*, 3d Ser., XXIV [1967], 459).

12. In James Ward Smith and A. Leland Jamison, eds., *The Shaping of American Religion* (Princeton, N.J., 1961), 322–368.

13. *Ibid.*, 325.

14. See, in particular, Edmund S. Morgan, "The Puritan Ethic and the American Revolution," *WMQ*, 3d Ser., XXIV (1967), 3–43, and Bernard Bailyn, *The Ideological Origins of the American Revolution* (Cambridge, Mass., 1967), 7, 32, 140, 193, 250. It is instructive to note exactly where Miller's "From the Covenant to the Revival" fits in Heimert's work. In *Religion and the American Mind* the essay is cited only three times, and never expanded on. Even more revealing, in his introductory essay to the volume of Great Awakening documents jointly edited with Miller (*The Great Awakening: Documents Illustrating the Crisis and Its Consequences* [Indianapolis, 1967]), Heimert includes Miller in every historiographical citation, but not one of those citations is to "From the Covenant to the Revival."

15. See Kenneth A. Lockridge, "Social Change and the Meaning of the American Revolu-

tion," *Journal of Social History*, VI (1973), 403–439, and Jack P. Greene, "The Social Origins of the American Revolution: An Evaluation and Interpretation," *Political Science Quarterly*, LXXXVIII (1973), 1–22.

16. See John R. Howe, Jr., "Republican Thought and the Political Violence of the 1790s," *American Quarterly*, XIX (1967), 147–165.

17. Drawing upon a sampling of colonial will signatures, Kenneth A. Lockridge concludes that "the literacy of that American generation which took the colonies into the Revolution was less than perfect. It seems probable that one-quarter of the generation born around 1730 . . . was totally illiterate. Including New England in the total would not much alter the level of enduring illiteracy since two-thirds of the population lived outside of New England" (*Literacy in Colonial New England: An Enquiry into the Social Context of Literacy in the Early Modern West* [New York, 1974], 87).

18. I use the term "mass revival" here intentionally to distinguish multi-community meetings addressed by itinerating preachers, who were often uneducated and of low social origins, from local revivals conducted by a settled pastor. Heimert's concentration on Jonathan Edwards and the established New England ministry tends, I believe, to work at cross-interests to his point concerning the stylistic innovation of the revivals. Historians would do better to concentrate on Whitefield and the awakening he inspired through his public addresses to unprecedented thousands of auditors. The fundamental problem raised by the revivals was not Edwards's treatises but the itinerants' practices.

19. Heimert, *Religion and the American Mind*, 14, 532. To avoid terminological confusion I will use the term "rebellion" to refer to independence from England and "revolution" to describe the radical internal impulse to reorder American society in an egalitarian direction. Similarly, the classical (deferential) theory of republicanism richly described in Gordon S. Wood, *The Creation of the American Republic, 1776–1787* (Chapel Hill, N.C., 1969), 3–124, and J. G. A. Pocock, "The Classical Theory of Deference," *American Historical Review*, LXXXI (1976), 516–523, must be distinguished from the more radical egalitarian "republicanism" that ultimately came to mean, in Wood's terms, "nothing less than a reordering of eighteenth-century society and politics as they had known and despised them . . ." (*Creation of the American Republic*, 48).

20. Heimert, *Religion and the American Mind*, 18.

21. Perry Miller and Thomas H. Johnson, eds., *The Puritans* (New York, 1938), 251. For a discussion of the inherited social ethic which the revivals challenged see especially William G. McLoughlin, *Isaac Backus and the American Pietistic Tradition* (Boston, 1967), 1–22; Rhys Isaac, "Religion and Authority: Problems of the Anglican Establishment in Virginia in the Era of the Great Awakening and the Parsons' Cause," *WMQ*, 3d Ser., XXX (1973), 3–36; and Isaac, "Evangelical Revolt: The Nature of the Baptists' Challenge to the Traditional Order in Virginia, 1765 to 1775," *ibid.*, XXXI (1974), 345–368.

22. Stephen Foster, *Their Solitary Way: The Puritan Social Ethic in the First Century of Settlement in New England* (New Haven, Conn., 1971), 18.

23. Quoted in Cedric B. Cowing, *The Great Awakening and the American Revolution: Colonial Thought in the Eighteenth Century* (Chicago, 1971), 23.

24. On the cultural implications of a face-to-face traditional society see Rhys Isaac, "Dramatizing the Ideology of Revolution: Popular Mobilization in Virginia, 1774 to 1776," *WMQ*, 3d Ser., XXXIII (1976), 364–367. I am indebted to Professor Isaac for sharing his article with me prior to its publication and for clarifying many of the points raised in this essay.

25. Although Puritan rhetoric rejected the ornamental tropes and "witty" figures common to classical (Ciceronian) rhetoric, the New England plain style remained a literate rhetoric born in the schools and designed to instruct a reading public. The plain style was not intended to persuade essentially illiterate audiences unused to the logic of rational discourse. See Walter J. Ong, *Ramus: Method and the Decay of Dialogue* (Cambridge, Mass., 1958), 212–213.

26. Heimert and Miller, eds., *Great Awakening*, 352.

27. Walter J. Ong, *Why Talk? A Conversation about Language* (San Francisco, 1973), 17.

28. On the relationship of literacy and analytical thought see Jack Goody and Ian Watt, "The Consequences of Literacy," *Comparative Studies in Society and History*, V (1963), 304–345, and Jack Goody, "Evolution and communication: the domestication of the savage mind," *British Journal of Sociology*, XXIV (1973), 1–12.

29. Heimert and Miller, eds., *Great Awakening*, 256.

30. Perry Miller, *Errand into the Wilderness* (Cambridge, Mass., 1956), 167–183. Heimert brilliantly develops this theme in his chapter on "The Danger of an Unconverted Ministry," which he singles out as the "principal hinge" of his study (*Religion and the American Mind*, 159–236).

31. John Caldwell, *The Nature, Folly, and Evil of rash and uncharitable Judging. A Sermon Preached at the French Meeting-House in Boston . . .* (1742), in Richard L. Bushman, ed., *The Great Awakening: Documents on the Revival of Religion, 1740–1745* (New York, 1969), 159.

32. Walter J. Ong, *The Presence of the Word: Some Prolegomena for Cultural and Religious History* (New Haven, Conn., 1967), 136.

33. Amos N. Wilder, *Early Christian Rhetoric: The Language of the Gospel* (Cambridge, Mass., 1971), 13.

34. Eric Auerbach, *Mimesis: The Representation of Reality in Western Literature*, trans. Willard R. Trask (Princeton, N.J., 1953), 46.

35. Gilbert Tennent, *The Danger of an Unconverted Ministry, Considered in a Sermon on Mark VI. 34* (1741), in Heimert and Miller, eds., *Great Awakening*, 73.

36. Alexander Garden, *Regeneration, and the Testimony of the Spirit. Being the Substance of Two Sermons . . .* (1740), *ibid.*, 58.

37. *A true and genuine Account of a WANDERING SPIRIT, raised of late . . . , ibid.*, 149.

38. George Philip Krapp, *The English Language in America*, I (New York, 1925), ix.

39. See, for example, H. L. Mencken, *The American Language: An Inquiry into the Development of English in the United States*, 4th ed. (New York, 1936), 380, and James Root Hulbert, *Dictionaries: British and American*, rev. ed. (London, 1968), 10.

40. Samuel Eliot Morison, ed., "William Manning's *The Key of Libberty*," *WMQ*, 3d Ser., XIII (1956), 202–254.

41. Hugh Blair, *Lectures on Rhetoric and Belles Lettres*, I (Philadelphia, 1862), 215. Blair's lectures and essays were gathered together for publication in 1783.

42. *Ibid.*, 214.

43. Walter Ong observes in "Latin and the Social Fabric," that "using Latin was like playing a game whose rules could never be changed. . . . Latin was not merely one subject among many or even among several . . . Latin effected the transit from ignorance to tribal or communal wisdom. . . . Youngsters were given to understand that the treasures of all understanding were stored in the ancient tongues" (*The Barbarian Within* [New York, 1962], 206, 215). For descriptions of the classical grounding of colonial thought and education see Richard M. Gummere, *The American Colonial Mind and the Classical Tradition* (Cambridge, Mass., 1963); Robert Middlekauff, "A Persistent Tradition: The Classical Curriculum in Eighteenth-Century New England," *WMQ*, 3d Ser., XVIII (1961), 54–67; Meyer Reinhold, ed., *The Classick Pages: Classical Reading of Eighteenth-Century Americans* (University Park, Pa., 1975); and Wood, *Creation of the American Republic*, 48–53.

44. Miller and Johnson, eds., *The Puritans*, 689. For a description of the increasingly high incidence of colonial borrowing from polite British culture see T. H. Breen, *The Character of the Good Ruler: A Study of Puritan Political Ideas in New England, 1630–1730* (New Haven, Conn., 1970), 203–239, and Jack P. Greene, "Search for Identity: An Interpretation of the

Meaning of Selected Patterns of Social Response in Eighteenth-Century America," *Jour. Soc. Hist.,* III (1970), 189–200.

45. Miller and Johnson, eds., *The Puritans,* 669. See also Johnson's discussion of Puritan rhetoric, *ibid.,* 64–79.

46. Ong, *Presence of the Word,* 73. The same print-centered ("visual") mode of perception is apparent in the Lockean epistemology that underlay Liberal assumptions in both religious and political contexts. See Ernest Tuveson, "Locke and the 'Dissolution of the Ego,'" *Modern Philology,* LII (1955), 164–165.

47. On the social meaning and political significance of a classical education in the colonies see James Axtell, *The School upon a Hill: Education and Society in Colonial New England* (New Haven, Conn., 1974), 201–244; James J. Walsh, *Education of the Founding Fathers of the Republic: Scholasticism in the Colonial Colleges . . .* (New York, 1935); and Robert M. Zemsky, "Power, Influence, and Status: Leadership Patterns in the Massachusetts Assembly, 1740–1755," WMQ, 3d Ser., XXVI (1969), 511–512.

48. Axtell, *School upon a Hill,* 213. For classic descriptions of the expanding networks of communications in 18th-century America see Frank Luther Mott, *American Journalism: A History of Newspapers in the United States Through 250 Years, 1690–1940* (New York, 1941), 3–110, and Wesley Everett Rich, *The History of the United States Post Office to the Year 1829* (Cambridge, Mass., 1924), 3–67.

49. Gordon S. Wood observes that "even more indicative of the limited elitist conception of the audience was the extraordinary reliance on personal correspondence for the circulation of ideas. It is often difficult to distinguish between the private correspondence and the public writings of the Revolutionaries, so much alike are they" ("Democratization of Mind," *Leadership in the American Revolution,* 67–72).

50. That the revivals did, in fact, continue to grow is most clearly reflected in the rapid growth of the dissenter movements in the colonies. Thomas Jefferson, for example, observed that by the time of the Revolution "two-thirds of the people [of Virginia] had become dissenters" (*Notes on the State of Virginia,* ed. William Peden [Chapel Hill, N.C., 1955], 158). More generally, Isaac Backus noted that, by 1795, the number of Separate Baptist preachers had grown to 1,125 (*A History of New England with Particular Reference to the Baptists,* ed. David Weston, 2d ed. [Newton, Mass., 1871], 401).

51. Philip Davidson, *Propaganda and the American Revolution, 1763–1783* (Chapel Hill, N.C., 1941). Despite his penetrating description of Revolutionary communications, Davidson failed to recognize that the sort of mass society in which a manipulative propaganda could flourish did not exist in pre-Revolutionary America. What made the pamphlets significant was not the writers' intent to hoodwink the people but rather their exclusion of the people from the presumed audience. Both the term and the practice of mass propaganda originated after the Revolution. See David Hackett Fischer, *The Revolution of American Conservatism: The Federalist Party in the Era of Jeffersonian Democracy* (New York, 1963), 144–149.

52. William Eddis, *Letters from America,* ed. Aubrey C. Land (Cambridge, Mass., 1969), 100.

53. Merrill Jensen, "The American People and the American Revolution," *Journal of American History,* LVII (1970), 15. For suggestive descriptions of how these "mass meetings" aroused "popular enthusiasm" for independence see Davidson, *Propaganda and the American Revolution,* 173–208; Isaac, "Dramatizing the Ideology of Revolution," *WMQ,* 3d Ser., XXXIII (1976), 357–385; and Robert Middlekauff, "The Ritualization of the American Revolution," in Stanley Coben and Lorman Ratner, eds., *The Development of an American Culture* (Englewood Cliffs, N.J., 1970), 31–43.

54. "A Letter from Jonathan Sewall to General Frederick Haldimand," May 30, 1775, in Jack P. Greene, ed., *Colonies to Nation, 1763–1789: A Documentary History of the American Revolution* (New York, 1975), 267.

55. Margaret Wheeler Willard, ed., *Letters on the American Revolution* (New York, 1925), 81. See also Ramsay, *History of the American Revolution,* 16–17.

56. Daniel Leonard, "To the Inhabitants of the Province of the Massachusetts-Bay," (1775), in Leslie F. S. Upton, ed., *Revolutionary Versus Loyalist: The First American Civil War, 1774–1784* (Waltham, Mass., 1968), 39.

57. Davidson, *Propaganda and the American Revolution*, 298, 301.

58. Bernard Bailyn, *The Origins of American Politics* (New York, 1967), 38–39. Bailyn attributes many of the ideas presented in the "opposition press" to the English "real whig" tradition. This is of some importance because, like the American whigs, the English libertarian persuasion was almost exclusively print-centered. As Caroline Robbins observes, "the Real whigs, the liberals, seem to have been associated in certain areas and institutions around a few persuasive men. They were related by a bewildering series of marriages. . . . They relied on conversation, on letters among themselves or occasionally in the public press, on the dissemination of the printed word. . . . [T]hey followed a hit-and-miss method, consistent only in their determined faith in the printed tracts and treatises continually produced by them" (*The Eighteenth-Century Commonwealthman: Studies in the Transmission, Development and Circumstance of English Liberal Thought from the Restoration of Charles II until the War with the Thirteen Colonies* [Cambridge, Mass., 1959], 381, 382, 383).

59. Bernard Bailyn argues that "the outbreak of the Revolution was not the result of social discontent. . . . Nor was there a transformation of mob behavior or of the lives of the 'inarticulate' in the pre-Revolutionary years that accounts for the disruption of Anglo-American politics" ("The Central Themes of the American Revolution: an Interpretation," in Stephen G. Kurtz and James H. Hutson, eds., *Essays on the American Revolution* [Chapel Hill, N.C., 1973], 12).

60. William Wirt Henry, ed., *Patrick Henry: Life, Correspondence and Speeches*, III (New York, 1891), 462.

61. Heimert, *Religion and the American Mind*, 232, 233; Rhys Isaac, "Preachers and Patriots: Popular Culture and the Revolution in Virginia," in Alfred F. Young, ed., *The American Revolution: Explorations in the History of American Radicalism* (DeKalb, Ill., 1976), 152–154.

62. Bailyn states that "the radicalism the Americans conveyed to the world in 1776 was a transformed as well as a transforming force. . . . Institutions were brought into question and condemned that appeared to have little if any direct bearing on the immediate issues of the Anglo-American struggle" (*Ideological Origins of the American Revolution*, 161, 232).

63. Quoted in Thomas R. Adams, *American Independence, the Growth of an Idea: A Bibliographic Study of the American Political Pamphlets Printed Between 1764 and 1776 . . .* (Providence, R.I., 1965), xiv–xv.

64. This point is effectively developed in Eric Foner, *Tom Paine and Revolutionary America* (New York, 1976), xv–xvi, 80–87.

65. *An Oration Upon the Beauties of Union* (Boston, 1773) was exceeded in separate editions by only two pamphlets including the "runaway best seller" *Common Sense*. For tabulations see Adams, *Amercian Independence*, xi–xii.

66. See, for example, Bernard Bailyn, "Common Sense," in *Fundamental Testaments of the American Revolution*, Library of Congress Symposia (Washington, D.C., 1973), 7–22.

67. John M. Bumsted and Charles E. Clark, "New England's Tom Paine: John Allen and the Spirit of Liberty," *WMQ*, 3d Ser., XXI (1964), 570.

68. Allen, *An Oration on the Beauties of Liberty*, 19, 27.

69. See, especially, J. G. A. Pocock, *Politics, Language and Time: Essays on Political Thought and History* (New York, 1971), 3–41.

70. *Ibid.*, 15.

71. Quoted in Meyer Reinhold, "Opponents of Classical Learning in America during the Revolutionary Period," American Philosophical Society, *Proceedings*, CXII (1968), 230.

72. Bailyn, *Ideological Origins of the American Revolution*, 95.

73. Garden, *Regeneration, and the Testimony of the Spirit,* in Heimert and Miller, eds., *Great Awakening,* 47.

74. Jonathan Boucher, *A View of the Causes and Consequences of the American Revolution in Thirteen Discourses* . . . (New York, 1967 [orig. publ. London, 1797]), 320, 321. See David Ammerman's discussion of "government by committee," in *In the Common Cause: American Response to the Coercive Acts of 1774* (Charlottesville, Va., 1974), 103–124, and Wood, *Creation of the American Republic,* 319–328.

75. On the frontier the essentially oral, voluntary association was most clearly manifested in the revivals which, as Donald G. Matthews suggests, represented a critical "organizing process" in the new nation. See Matthews, "The Second Great Awakening as an Organizing Process, 1780–1830," *Am. Qtly.,* XI (1969), 23–43. Similarly, Leonard L. Richards points out how, in the voluntary reform efforts of the "evangelical crusade," evangelical abolitionists effectively utilized the "revolution in communications and the creation of mass media" to bypass traditional social channels and organize voluntary associations within "impersonal, large-scale organizations" (*"Gentlemen of Property and Standing": Anti-Abolition Mobs in Jacksonian America* [New York, 1970], 167).

76. Wood points this out in *Creation of the American Republic,* 621–622, and "Democratization of Mind," in *Leadership in the American Revolution,* 78–82. Perhaps not sufficiently emphasized in studies of early American literature is the abrupt decline in public significance of pamphlets, letters, treatises, and printed sermons after the Revolution.

77. Michael Kammen, *People of Paradox: An Inquiry Concerning the Origins of American Civilization* (New York, 1972), 89–96. The social ramifications of this cultural pluralism are treated in Robert H. Wiebe, *The Segmented Society: An Introduction to the Meaning of America* (New York, 1975).

78. Richard Hofstadter, *Anti-Intellectualism in American Life* (New York, 1962), 55–141.

79. Jonathan Edwards, *The Distinguishing Marks of a Work of the Spirit of God* . . . (1741), in Bushman, ed., *Great Awakening,* 123. On Edwards's use of language see Harold P. Simonson, *Jonathan Edwards: Theologian of the Heart* (Grand Rapids, Mich., 1974), 91–118.

80. Alexis de Tocqueville, *Democracy in America,* eds. J. P. Mayer and Max Lerner (New York, 1966), 482. See also Robert E. Shalhope, "Toward a Republican Synthesis: The Emergence of an Understanding of Republicanism in American Historiography," *WMQ,* XXIX (1972), 72–73.

Jon Butler

Enthusiasm Described and Decried: The Great Awakening as Interpretative Fiction

In the last half century, the Great Awakening has assumed a major role in explaining the political and social evolution of prerevolutionary American society. Historians have argued, variously, that the Awakening severed intellectual and philosophical connections between America and Europe (Perry Miller), that it was a major vehicle of early lower-class protest (John C. Miller, Rhys Isaac, and Gary

Reprinted from Butler, Jon, "Enthusiasm Described and Decried: The Great Awaking as Interpretative Fiction," *Journal of American History* 69(2) (Sept. 1982), 305–325.

B. Nash), that it was a means by which New England Puritans became Yankees (Richard L. Bushman), that it was the first "intercolonial movement" to stir "the people of several colonies on a matter of common emotional concern" (Richard Hofstadter following William Warren Sweet), or that it involved "a rebirth of the localistic impulse" (Kenneth Lockridge).[1]

American historians also have increasingly linked the Awakening directly to the Revolution. Alan Heimert has tagged it as the source of a Calvinist political ideology that irretrievably shaped eighteenth-century American society and the Revolution it produced. Harry S. Stout has argued that the Awakening stimulated a new system of mass communications that increased the colonists' political awareness and reduced their deference to elite groups prior to the Revolution. Isaac and Nash have described the Awakening as the source of a simpler, non-Calvinist protest rhetoric that reinforced revolutionary ideology in disparate places, among them Virginia and the northern port cities. William G. McLoughlin has even claimed that the Great Awakening was nothing less than "the Key to the American Revolution."[2]

These claims for the significance of the Great Awakening come from more than specialists in the colonial period. They are a ubiquitous feature of American history survey texts, where the increased emphasis on social history has made these claims especially useful in interpreting early American society to twentieth-century students. Virtually all texts treat the Great Awakening as a major water-shed in the maturation of prerevolutionary American society. *The Great Republic* terms the Awakening "the greatest event in the history of religion in eighteenth-century America." *The National Experience* argues that the Awakening brought "re-ligious experiences to thousands of people in every rank of society" and in every region. *The essentials of American History* stresses how the Awakening "aroused a spirit of humanitarianism," "encouraged the notion of equal rights," and "stimu-lated feelings of democracy" even if its gains in church membership proved episodic. These texts and others describe the weakened position of the clergy pro-duced by the Awakening as symptomatic of growing disrespect for all forms of authority in the colonies and as an important catalyst, even cause, of the Ameri-can Revolution. The effect of these claims is astonishing. Buttressed by the stan-dard lecture on the Awakening tucked into most survey courses, American under-graduates have been well trained to remember the Great Awakening because their instructors and texts have invested it with such significance.[3]

Does the Great Awakening warrant such enthusiasm? Its puzzling historiog-raphy suggests one caution. The Awakening has received surprisingly little sys-tematic study and lacks even one comprehensive general history. The two studies, by Heimert and Cedric B. Cowing, that might qualify as general histories actually are deeply centered in New England. They venture into the middle and southern colonies only occasionally and concentrate on intellectual themes to the exclusion of social history. The remaining studies are thoroughly regional, as in the case of books by Bushman, Edwin Scott Gaustad, Charles Hartshorn Maxson, Dietmar Rothermund, and Wesley M. Gewehr, or are local, as with the spate of articles on New England towns and Jonathan Edwards or Isaac's articles and book on Vir-ginia.[4] The result is that the general character of the Great Awakening lacks sustained, comprehensive study even while it benefits from thorough local examinations. The relationship between the Revolution and the Awakening is described in an equally peculiar manner. Heimert's seminal 1966 study, despite fair and unfair criticism, has become that kind of influential work whose awesome reputation apparently discourages further pursuit of its subject. Instead, historians frequently allude to the positive relationship between the Awakening and the Revolution without probing the matter in a fresh, systematic way.[5]

The gap between the enthusiasm of historians for the social and political significance of the Great Awakening and its slim, peculiar historiography raises two important issues. First, contemporaries never homogenized the eighteenth-century colonial religious revivals by labeling them "the Great Awakening." Although such words appear in Edwards's *Faithful Narrative of the Surprising Work of God*, Edwards used them alternately with other phrases, such as "general awakening," "great alteration," and "flourishing of religion," only to describe the Northampton revivals of 1734–1735. He never capitalized them or gave them other special emphasis and never used the phrase "the Great Awakening" to evaluate all the prerevolutionary revivals. Rather, the first person to do so was the nineteenth-century historian and antiquarian Joseph Tracy, who used Edwards's otherwise unexceptional words as the title of his famous 1842 book, *The Great Awakening*. Tellingly, however, Tracy's creation did not find immediate favor among American historians. Charles Hodge discussed the Presbyterian revivals in his *Constitutional History of the Presbyterian Church* without describing them as part of a "Great Awakening," while the influential Robert Baird refused even to treat the eighteenth-century revivals as discrete and important events, much less label them "the Great Awakening." Baird all but ignored these revivals in the chronological segments of his *Religion in America* and mentioned them elsewhere only by way of explaining the intellectual origins of the Unitarian movement, whose early leaders opposed revivals. Thus, not until the last half of the nineteenth century did "the Great Awakening" become a familiar feature of the American historical landscape.[6]

Second, this particular label ought to be viewed with suspicion, not because a historian created it—historians legitimately make sense of the minutiae of the past by utilizing such devices—but because the label itself does serious injustice to the minutiae it orders. The label "the Great Awakening" distorts the extent, nature, and cohesion of the revivals that did exist in the eighteenth-century colonies, encourages unwarranted claims for their effects on colonial society, and exaggerates their influence on the coming and character of the American Revolution. If "the Great Awakening" is not quite an American Donation of Constantine, its appeal to historians seeking to explain the shaping and character of prerevolutionary American society gives it a political and intellectual power whose very subtlety requires a close inspection of its claims to truth.

How do historians describe "the Great Awakening"? Three points seem especially common. First, all but a few describe it as a Calvinist religious revival in which converts acknowledged their sinfulness without expecting salvation. These colonial converts thereby distinguished themselves from Englishmen caught up in contemporary Methodist revivals and from Americans involved in the so-called Second Great Awakening of the early national period, both of which imbibed Arminian principles that allowed humans to believe they might effect their own salvation in ways that John Calvin discounted.[7] Second, historians emphasize the breadth and suddenness of the Awakening and frequently employ hurricane metaphors to reinforce the point. Thus, many of them describe how in the 1740s the Awakening "swept" across the mainland colonies, leaving only England's Caribbean colonies untouched.[8] Third, most historians argue that this spiritual hurricane affected all facets of prerevolutionary society. Here they adopt Edwards's description of the 1736 Northampton revival as one that touched "all sorts, sober and vicious, high and low, rich and poor, wise and unwise," but apply it to all the colonies. Indeed, some historians go farther and view the Great Awakening as a veritable social and political revolution itself. Writing in the late 1960s, Bushman could only wonder at its power: "We inevitably will underestimate the effect of the Awakening on eighteenth-century society if we compare it to revivals today. The Awakening was more like the civil rights demonstrations, the campus disturbances, and the urban riots of the 1960s combined. All together these may approach, though certainly not surpass, the Awakening in their impact on national life."[9]

No one would seriously question the existence of "the Great Awakening" if historians only described it as a short-lived Calvinist revival in New England during the early 1740s. Whether stimulated by Edwards, James Davenport, or the British itinerant George Whitefield, the New England revivals between 1740 and 1745 obviously were Calvinist ones. Their sponsors vigorously criticized the softcore Arminianism that had reputedly overtaken New England Congregationalism, and they stimulated the ritual renewal of a century-old society by reintroducing colonists to the theology of distinguished seventeenth-century Puritan clergymen, especially Thomas Shepard and Solomon Stoddard.[10]

Yet, Calvinism never dominated the eighteenth-century religious revivals homogenized under the label "the Great Awakening." The revivals in the middle colonies flowed from especially disparate and international sources. John B. Frantz's recent traversal of the German revivals there demonstrates that they took root in Lutheranism, German Reformed Calvinism (different from the New England variety), and Pietism (however one wants to define it). Maxson stressed the mysticism, Pietism, Rosicrucianism, and Freemasonry rampant in these colonies among both German and English settlers. In an often overlooked observation, Maxson noted that the Tennents' backing for revivals was deeply linked to a mystical experience surrounding the near death of John Tennent and that both John Tennent and William Tennent, Jr., were mystics as well as Calvinists. The revivals among English colonists in Virginia also reveal eclectic roots. Presbyterians brought Calvinism into the colony for the first time since the 1650s, but Arminianism underwrote the powerful Methodist awakening in the colony and soon crept into the ranks of the colony's Baptists as well.[11]

"The Great Awakening" also is difficult to date. Seldom has an "event" of such magnitude had such amorphous beginnings and endings. In New England, historians agree, the revivals flourished principally between 1740 and 1743 and had largely ended by 1745, although a few scattered outbreaks of revivalism occurred there in the next decades. Establishing the beginning of the revivals has proved more difficult, however. Most historians settle for the year 1740 because it marks Whitefield's first appearance in New England. But everyone acknowledges that earlier revivals underwrote Whitefield's enthusiastic reception there and involved remarkable numbers of colonists. Edwards counted thirty-two towns caught up in revivals in 1734–1735 and noted that his own grandfather, Stoddard, had conducted no less than five "harvests" in Northampton before that, the earliest in the 1690s. Yet revivals in Virginia, the site of the most sustained such events in the sourthern colonies, did not emerge in significant numbers until the 1750s and did not peak until the 1760s. At the same time, they also continued into the revolutionary and early national periods in ways that make them difficult to separate from their predecessors.[12]

Yet even if one were to argue that "the Great Awakening" persisted through most of the eighteenth century, it is obvious that revivals "swept" only some of the mainland colonies. They occurred in Massachusetts, Connecticut, Rhode Island, Pennsylvania, New Jersey, and Virginia with some frequency at least at some points between 1740 and 1770. But New Hampshire, Maryland, and Georgia witnessed few revivals in the same years, and revivals were only occasionally important in New York, Delaware, North Carolina, and South Carolina. The revivals also touched only certain segments of the population in the colonies where they occurred. The best example of the phenomenon is Pennsylvania. The revivals there had a sustained effect among English settlers only in Presbyterian churches where many of the laity and clergy also opposed them. The Baptists, who were so important to the New England revivals, paid little attention to them until the 1760s, and the colony's taciturn Quakers watched them in perplexed silence. Not even Germans imbibed them universally. At the same time that Benjamin Franklin was emptying his pockets in response to the preaching of Whitefield in Philadelphia—or at least claiming to do so—the residents of Germantown were steadily leaving their churches, and Stephanie Grauman Wolf reports that they remained steadfast in their indifference to Christianity at least until the 1780s.[13]

Whitefield's revivals also exchanged notoriety for substance. Colonists responded to him as a charismatic performer, and he actually fell victim to the Billy Graham syndrome of modern times: his visits, however exciting, produced few permanent changes in local religious patterns. For example, his appearances in Charleston led to his well-known confrontation with Anglican Commissary Alexander Garden and to the suicide two years later of a distraught follower named Anne LeBrasseur. Yet they produced no new congregations in Charleston and had no documented effect on the general patterns of religious adherence elsewhere in the colony. The same was true in Philadelphia and New York City despite the fact that Whitefield preached to enormous crowds in both places. Only Bostonians responded differently. Supporters organized in the late 1740s a new "awakened" congregation that reputedly met with considerable initial success, and opponents adopted a defensive posture exemplified in the writings of Charles Chauncy that profoundly affected New England intellectual life for two decades.[14]

Historians also exaggerate the cohesion of leadership in the revivals. They have accomplished this, in part, by overstressing the importance of Whitefield and Edwards. Whitefield's early charismatic influence later faded so that his appearances in the 1750s and 1760s had less impact even among evangelicals than they had in the 1740s. In addition, Whitefield's "leadership" was ethereal, at best, even before 1750. His principal early importance was to serve as a personal model of evangelical enterprise for ministers wishing to promote their own revivals of religion. Because he did little to organize and coordinate integrated colonial revivals, he also failed to exercise significant authority over the ministers he inspired.[15]

The case against Edwards's leadership of the revivals is even clearer. Edwards defended the New England revivals from attack. But, like Whitefield, he never organized and coordinated revivals throughout the colonies or even throughout New England. Since most of his major works were not printed in his lifetime, even his intellectual leadership in American theology occurred in the century after his death. Whitefield's lack of knowledge about Edwards on his first tour of America in 1739–1740 is especially telling on this point. Edwards's name does not appear in Whitefield's journal prior to the latter's visit to Northampton in 1740, and Whitefield did not make the visit until Edwards had invited him to do so. Whitefield certainly knew of Edwards and the 1734–1735 Northampton revival but associated the town mainly with the pastorate of Edwards's grandfather Stoddard. As Whitefield described the visit in his journal: "After a little refreshment, we crossed the ferry to Northampton, where no less than three hundred souls were saved about five years ago. Their pastor's name is Edwards, successor and grandson to the great Stoddard, whose memory will be always precious to my soul, and whose books entitled 'A Guide to Christ,' and 'Safety of Appearing in Christ's Righteousness,' I would recommend to all."[16]

What were the effects of the prerevolutionary revivals of religion? The claims for their religious and secular impact need pruning too. One area of concern involves the relationship between the revivals and the rise of the Dissenting denominations in the colonies. Denomination building was intimately linked to the revivals in New England. There, as C. C. Goen has demonstrated, the revivals of the 1740s stimulated formation of over two hundred new congregations and several new denominations. This was accomplished mainly through a negative process called "Separatism," which split existing Congregationalist and Baptist churches along prorevival and antirevival lines. But Separatism was of no special consequence in increasing the number of dissenters farther south. Presbyterians, Baptists, and, later, Methodists gained strength from former Anglicans who left their state-supported churches, but they won far more recruits among colonists who claimed no previous congregational membership.[17]

Still, two points are important in assessing the importance of revivals to the expansion of the Dissenting denominations in the colonies. First, revivalism never was the key to the expansion of the colonial churches. Presbyterianism expanded as rapidly in the middle colonies between 1710 and 1740 as between 1740 and 1770. Revivalism scarcely produced the remarkable growth that the Church of England experienced in the eighteenth century unless, of course, it won the favor of colonists who opposed revivals as fiercely as did its leaders. Gaustad estimates that between 1700 and 1780 Anglican congregations expanded from about one hundred to four hundred, and Bruce E. Steiner has outlined extraordinary Anglican growth in the Dissenting colony of Connecticut although most historians describe the colony as being thoroughly absorbed by the revivals and "Separatism."[18]

Second, the expansion of the leading evangelical denominations, Presbyterians and Baptists, can be traced to many causes, not just revivalism or "the Great Awakening." The growth of the colonial population from fewer than three hundred thousand in 1700 to over two million in 1770 made the expansion of even the most modestly active denominations highly likely. This was especially true because so many new colonists did not settle in established communities but in new communities that lacked religious institutions. As Timothy L. Smith has written of seventeenth-century settlements, the new eighteenth-century settlements welcomed congregations as much for the social functions they performed as for their religious functions. Some of the denominations reaped the legacy of Old World religious ties among new colonists, and others benefited from local anti-Anglican sentiment, especially in the Virginia and Carolina backcountry. As a result, evangelical organizers formed many congregations in the middle and southern colonies without resorting to revivals at all. The first Presbyterian congregation in Hanover County, Virginia, organized by Samuel Blair and William Tennent, Jr., in 1746, rested on an indigenous lay critique of Anglican theology that had turned residents to the works of Martin Luther, and after the campaign by Blair and Tennent, the congregation allied itself with the Presbyterian denomination rather than with simple revivalism.[19]

The revivals democratized relations between ministers and the laity only in minimal ways. A significant number of New England ministers changed their preaching styles as a result of the 1740 revivals. Heimert quotes Isaac Backus on the willingness of evangelicals to use sermons to "'insinuate themselves into the affections' of the people" and notes how opponents of the revivals like Chauncy nonetheless struggled to incorporate emotion and "sentiment" into their sermons after 1740. Yet revivalists and evangelicals continued to draw sharp distinctions between the rights of ministers and the duties of the laity. Edwards did so in a careful, sophisticated way in *Some Thoughts concerning the Present Revival of Religion in New England*. Although he noted that "disputing, jangling, and contention" surrounded "lay exhorting," he agreed that "some exhorting is a Christian duty." But he quickly moved to a strong defense of ministerial prerogatives, which he introduced with the proposition that "the Common people in exhorting one another ought not to clothe themselves with the like authority, with that which is proper for ministers." Gilbert Tennent was less cautious. In his 1740 sermon *The Danger of an Unconverted Ministry*, he bitterly attacked "Pharisee-shepherds" and "Pharisee-teachers" whose preaching was frequently as "unedifying" as their personal lives. But Gilbert Tennent never attacked the ministry itself. Rather, he argued for the necessity of a *converted* ministry precisely because he believed that only preaching brought men and women to Christ and that only ordained ministers could preach. Thus, in both 1742 and 1757, he thundered against lay preachers. They were "of dreadful consequence to the Church's peace and soundness in principle. . . . [F]or Ignorant Young Converts to take upon them authoritatively to Instruct and Exhort publickly tends to introduce the greatest Errors and the greatest anarchy and confusion."[20]

The 1740 revival among Presbyterians in New Londonderry, Pennsylvania, demonstrates well how ministers shepherded the laity into a revival and how the laity followed rather than led. It was Blair, the congregation's minister, who first criticized "dead Formality in Religion" and brought the congregation's members under "deep convictions" of their "natural unregenerate state." Blair stimulated "soul exercises" in the laity that included crying and shaking, but he also set limits for these exercises. He exhorted them to "moderate and bound their passions" so that the revival would not be destroyed by its own methods. Above this din, Blair remained a commanding, judgmental figure who stimulated the laity's hopes for salvation but remained "very cautious of expressing to People my Judgment of the Goodness of their States, excepting where I had pretty clear Evidences from them, of their being savingly changed."[21]

Did itinerants challenge this ministerial hegemony? McLoughlin has framed such an argument in exceptionally strong terms. He has argued that the itinerant significantly changed the early American social and religious landscape because he usually lacked formal education, "spoke to other men as equals" in a traditionally deferential society, "eschew[ed] the parish church," refused to "order or command his hearers to conform," and was "clothed only with spiritual authority [so that] his power was based solely on his ability to persuade the individual listener to act upon his own free will."[22]

Actually, itinerancy produced few changes in colonial American society and religion and is frequently misunderstood. Although some itinerants lacked institutionally based formal educations, none are known to have been illiterate. The most famous itinerant of the century, Whitefield, took an Oxford degree in 1736, and the most infamous, Davenport, stood at the top of his class at Yale in 1732. Itinerants usually bypassed the local church only when its minister opposed them; when the minister was hospitable the itinerants preached in the church building. One reason itinerants eschewed the coercive instruments of the state was that they never possessed them before the Revolution. But after the Revolution the denominations they represented sought and received special favors from the new state governments, especially concerning incorporation, and won the passage of coercive legislation regarding morality and outlawing blasphemy. Finally, itinerants seldom ventured into the colonial countryside "clothed only with spiritual authority." Instead, itinerants acknowledged the continuing importance of deference and hierarchy in colonial society by stressing denominational approbation for their work. Virtually all of them wore the protective shield of ordination—the major exceptions are a few laymen who itinerated in New England in the early 1740s and about whom virtually nothing is known—and nearly all of them could point to denominational sponsorship. Even Virginia's aggressive Samuel Davies defended himself to the Bishop of London, Gov. William Gooch, and the sometimes suspicious backcountry settlers to whom he preached by pointing to his ordination and sponsorship by the Presbytery of New Castle. Only Davenport ventured into the countryside with little more than the spirit (and his

Yale degree) to protect him. But only Davenport was judged by a court to have been mentally unstable.[23]

In this context, it is not surprising that the eighteenth-century revivals of religion failed to bring significant new power—democracy—to the laity in the congregations. Although Gilbert Tennent argued that the laity had an obligation to abandon unconverted, unedifying ministers in favor of converted ones, it is not possible to demonstrate that the revivals increased the traditional powers that laymen previously possessed or brought them new ones. Congregations throughout the colonies had long exercised considerable power over their ministers through their effective control of church spending and fund-raising as well as through the laity's ability simply to stop attending church services at all. As examples, witness alone the well-known seventeenth-century disputes between ministers and their listeners in Sudbury and Salem Village in Massachusetts and the complaints against ministers brought by the laity to the Presbytery of Philadelphia between 1706 and 1740. Yet, although the revivals should have increased this lay willingness to complain about ministerial failings, no historian ever has demonstrated systematically that this ever happened.[24]

Nor did the revivals change the structure of authority within the denominations. New England Congregationalists retained the right of individual congregations to fire ministers, as when Northampton dismissed Edwards in 1750. But in both the seventeenth and eighteenth centuries, these congregations seldom acted alone. Instead, they nearly always consulted extensively with committees of ordained ministers when firing as well as when hiring ministers. In the middle colonies, however, neither the prorevival Synod of New York nor the antirevival Synod of Philadelphia tolerated such independence in congregations whether in theory or in practice. In both synods, unhappy congregations had to convince special committees appointed by the synods and composed exclusively of ministers that the performance of a fellow cleric was sufficiently dismal to warrant his dismissal. Congregations that acted independently in such matters quickly found themselves censured, and they usually lost the aid of both synods in finding and installing new ministers.[25]

Did the revivals stir lower-class discontent, increase participation in politics, and promote democracy in society generally if not in the congregations? Even in New England the answer is, at best, equivocal. Historians have laid to rest John C. Miller's powerfully stated argument of the 1930s that the revivals were, in good part, lower-class protests against dominant town elites. The revivals indeed complicated local politics because they introduced new sources of potential and real conflict into the towns. New England towns accustomed to containing tensions inside a single congregation before 1730 sometimes had to deal with tensions within and between as many as three or four congregations after 1730. Of course, not all of these religious groups were produced by the revivals, and, as Michael Zuckerman has pointed out, some towns never tolerated the new dissidents and used the "warning out" system to eject them. Still, even where it existed, tumult should not be confused with democracy. Social class, education, and wealth remained as important after 1730 in choosing town and church officers as they had been before 1730, and Edward M. Cook, Jr., notes that after 1730 most new revival congregations blended into the old order: "dissenters [took] their place in town affairs once they stopped threatening the community and symbolically became loyal members of it."[26]

Recently, however, the specter of lower-class political agitation rampaging through other colonies disguised as revivals of religion has been raised in Nash's massive study of the northern colonial port cities and in Isaac's work on prerevolutionary Virginia. But in direct if quite different ways, both historians demonstrate the numerous difficulties of linking lower-class protest and political radicalism with "the Great Awakening." Nash notes that the link between lower-class political protest and revivalism was strongest in Boston. There, a popular party closely associated with the revivals attacked the city's propertied elite through the election process while the revivals prospered in the early 1740s. But the unfortunate lack of even a single tax list for the period and the lack of records from either the political dissidents or the revival congregations make it impossible to describe the social composition of either group with precision, much less establish firm patterns of interrelatedness. As a result, historians are forced to accept the nightmares of the antirevivalist Chauncy and the fulminations of the *Boston Evening Post* as accurate descriptions of all the agitators' religious and political principles.[27]

Yet Nash also carefully points out the minimal political impact of the revivals in New York City and Philadelphia even at the height of "the Great Awakening." The New York City revivals simply did not continue in a sustained fashion after the departure of Whitefield and Gilbert Tennent and, at best, were only loosely connected to the city's equally erratic popular political tumults of the 1740s. This link between revivals and popular political tumult is even weaker in Philadelphia where Nash argues pointedly that the revivals produced no popular political upheaval at all. Indeed, as Nash puts it, enthusiastic religion "remained a cohesive, socially stabilizing force" in the Quaker city. In fact, Nash's findings fit well with other recent studies debunking the extent and influence of the revivals in rural parts of the middle colonies. Herman Harmelink III has argued that Theodore Jacob Frelinghuysen's famed Raritan Valley "awakening" of the 1720s was no revival at all but a bitter personal quarrel that Frelinghuysen dressed in revival garb to justify his own petulant behavior. And as we have noted already, Wolf has cautioned against overenthusiastic evaluations of German involvement in Pennsylvania's prerevolutionary revivals. Unfortunately, the records of all the New Jersey and Pennsylvania Presbyterian congregations that underwent revivals before 1760 are only fragmentary and have so far prevented historians from pursuing the careful studies of communities in the middle colonies that are now so common for New England.[28]

Isaac's recent work on Virginia demonstrates that the Baptist revival movement there in the 1760s and 1770s shattered the old Anglican-aristocratic alliance so thoroughly that its political importance hardly can be questioned. But two points are especially significant in assessing the relationship of Isaac's work to the problem of "the Great Awakening." First, Isaac nowhere argues that the Virginia revivals demonstrate either the power or even the existence of a broadly based revival movement in the prerevolutionary colonies. Indeed, as he describes the process, Virginia's Baptists succeeded out of a nearly unique ability to confront a political and religious aristocracy that also was virtually unique in the colonies. Second, we do not yet know how democratic and egalitarian these Baptists were within their own ranks. For example, we do not know if poor, uneducated Baptists became elders and preachers as frequently as did richer, better-educated Baptists. Nor do we know how judiciously Baptists governed non-Baptists in the southside and backcountry counties where they were strong but where many settlers eschewed any denominational affiliation.[29]

Certainly Virginia Baptists flunked the slavery test. Slavery was the colony's most coercive insitution, and the Baptist fight against religious persecution there led some early revivalists like John Leland to attack slavery because it exemplified the evils of aristocratic coercion in that society. Thus, the Virginia Baptist General Committee, a denominational body of uncertain composition, condemned slavery as "contrary to the word of God" in 1785. But James David Essig notes that only a single Baptist congregation honored this condemnation and that the General Committee moved away from its own stand in 1793 by arguing that the slavery question should be answered by the legislature rather than by congregations. As a result, in 1796, the one Virginia Baptist association in which the slavery subject was raised refused to discuss it on the grounds that its "only business is to give advice to the Churches respecting religious matters."[30]

Nor did other revivalists improve this antislavery record. Whitefield complained bitterly that Americans badly mistreated slaves. He preached to blacks and at his death won Phyllis Wheatley's appreciation in a commemorative poem. But in the case of apparent radicals like Hugh Bryan and Jonathan Bryan of South Carolina, Whitefield seems largely to have reinforced existing urges to educate and free slaves; certainly he never risked his own charismatic appeal in a campaign to destroy the institution. Likewise, Davenport's radicalism did not prevent him from owning a newly imported slave girl named Flora in the 1740s. And if he became frustrated with her, his dissatisfaction did not rest on the knowledge that she symbolized the gap between the revivals and morality but stemmed from her inablity to "give but a broken account" of a religious experience she underwent after hearing a sermon by Eleazer Wheelock. She was "so new a negro" she could not describe it. In fact, it was Anglicans active in the Society for the Propagation of the Gospel in Foreign Parts and in the Bray associates, not colonial revivalists or even Quakers, who developed the first significant programs to ease the burden of slavery for captured Africans in America, although they too failed to understand that American slavery brooked no significant compromise with charity.[31]

What, then, of the relationship between the revivals and the American Revolution? Obviously, the revivals provided little focus for intercolonial unity in the way some historians have described. They appeared too erratically in too few colonies under too many different auspices to make such generalizations appropriate. The eighteenth-century colonial wars are more appropriate candidates for the honor. They raised significant legislature opposition to the crown in many colonies and cost many colonists their lives, especially in the last and most "successful" contest, the French and Indian War. Nor is it possible to demonstrate that specific congregations and denominations associated with the revivals originated anti-British protest that became uniquely important to the Revolution. Nathan O. Hatch has noted that Andrew Crosswell's revivalist congregation in Boston had all but collapsed by 1770, and no historian ever has demonstrated that similar congregations elsewhere served as isolated cells of anti-British protest. The connection is equally difficult to make with denominations. Connecticut New Lights and Pennsylvania Presbyterians played important roles in the colonial protests, but their activity does not, in itself, link revivals to the Revolution in any important way. First, the revivals in both places occurred a quarter of a century before the Revolution began. Second, neither group expanded in the 1740s or sustained its membership later exclusively because of the revivals. Third, the British probably angered laymen of both groups because the latter were important politicians rather than because they were New Lights and Presbyterians. Or, put another way, they were political leaders who happened to be New Lights and Presbyterians rather than Presbyterians and New Lights who happened to be politicians.[32]

This is not to say that colonial revivalism did not reinforce anti-British protest in some way. Heimert has argued that the Calvinism of the revivals "provided pre-Revolutionary America with a radical, even democratic, social and political ideology" and contained millennialist themes that bore equally dangerous implications for British rule. But the secret to the success of anti-British and revolutionary protests lay in the expanse of their ideological foundations. Millennialism was indeed important to the American revolutionaries because, as Hatch has argued, it crossed Old Light–New Light boundaries, while Bernard Bailyn has demonstrated in his capsule biographies of the New England clergymen Andrew Eliot, Jonathan Mayhew, and Stephen Johnson that both Calvinism and theological liberalism produced positive responses on questions of democracy and the Revolution. And, of course, some historians still argue for the importance of the secular Enlightenment in shaping revolutionary ideology, whether it be in the thought of John Locke, John Trenchard, and Thomas Gordon, or in newfound Scottish philosophers.[33]

Some historians have argued that the eighteenth-century revivals had a more subtle, yet still profound, effect on the colonies in fostering a new system of mass communications among settlers. Stout has written that itinerancy and extemporaneous preaching—but specifically not the intellectual content of the sermons preached—stimulated social and political egalitarianism in the colonies. They created a "spirit of liberty" that tore at traditional social and political deference and fitted Americans superbly for the contests of the 1760s and 1770s. Here again problems of timing and effect intrude. The political ramifications of extemporaneous sermons delivered by itinerant or resident preachers were unclear at best and were delayed for as long as twenty-five years. Moreover, the Revolution they presumably underwrote made only the most modest contributions to social egalitarianism and democracy, of which they probably were not the sole cause.[34]

Yet the real Achilles heel of Stout's interpretation may center on the extent of extemporaneous preaching itself. Stout—and McLoughlin, who has echoed him—did not study the frequency of extemporaneous preaching in the revivals. They built their argument on the assumption that it was the key to the revivals and the dominant mode of revival preaching, just as revival critics claimed. This may not be the case, however. As used in the eighteenth century, the term "extempore preaching" did not mean preaching without preparation. Rather, it meant preaching without a written text or notes in a way that, according to Stout, allowed the minister greater flexibility in shaping his subject and communicating with his audience. Although extemporaneous preaching was notorious at the height of the 1740 revivals, not all revival ministers engaged in the practice. Edwards probably never gave extemporaneous sermons despite the fact that he relaxed his sermon style after 1740. Gilbert Tennent, who appears to have preached extemporaneously through about 1743, apparently reduced this practice in the next decade. In 1762, Gilbert Tennent opposed the appointment of a man who preached extemporaneously as an assistant minister in Tennent's Philadelphia congregation, and he attacked extemporaneous preaching in an important but unpublished treatise he wrote in the same year. In the surviving draft of this document, Gilbert Tennent argued that ministers who favored extemporaneous preaching frequently overstressed emotion and that, ideally, ministers ought to mix their preaching styles by preaching with notes "in the morning to inform the mind" and by preaching extemporaneously "in the afternoon to affect the Heart." But in an observation obviously meant to deflate proponents of extemporaneous preaching, he also commented that in his own experience "the Difference between the two modes of preaching with or without notes is So Small, that if you Shutt your eyes or Sit where you don't See the Speaker, you will be often at a Loss to Distinguish which mode is used."[35]

The caution of Edwards and Gilbert Tennent in eschewing or abandoning extemporaneous preaching and the fact that nearly all reports about its frequency come from revival critics raise important questions about its real influence in the colonies. Did Whitefield, for example, memorize texts, speak from brief notes, or simply begin preaching without previously having given the sermon extended thought? Did other ministers speak extemporaneously on some occasions but revert, on others, to reading their sermons or delivering them from extensive notes? And between 1730 and 1770 did ministers adopt or abandon extemporaneous preaching in different denominations at different times? Since we do not yet have the answers to these questions, generalizations about the political implications of extemporaneous preaching in the revivals are premature.

What, then, ought we to say about the revivals of religion in prerevolutionary America? The most important suggestion is the most drastic. Historians should abandon the term "the Great Awakening" because it distorts the character of eighteenth-century American religious life and misinterprets its relationship to prerevolutionary American society and politics. In religion it is a deus ex machina that falsely homogenizes the heterogeneous; in politics it falsely unites the colonies in slick preparation for the Revolution. Instead, a four-part model of the eighteenth-century colonial revivals will highlight their common features, underscore important differences, and help us assess their real significance.

First, with one exception, the prerevolutionary revivals should be understood primarily as regional events that occurred in only half the colonies. Revivals occurred intermittently in New England between 1690 and 1745 but became especially common between 1735 and 1745. They were uniformly Calvinist and produced more significant local political ramifications—even if they did not democratize New England—than other colonial revivals except those in Virginia. Revivals in the middle colonies occurred primarily between 1740 and 1760. They had remarkably eclectic theological origins, bypassed large numbers of settlers, were especially weak in New York, and produced few demonstrable political and social changes. Revivals in the southern colonies did not occur in significant numbers until the 1750s, when they were limited largely to Virginia, missed Maryland almost entirely, and did not occur with any regularly in the Carolinas until well after 1760. Virginia's Baptist revivalists stimulated major political and social changes in the colony, but the secular importance of the other revivals has been exaggerated. A fourth set of revivals, and the exception to the regional pattern outlined here, accompanied the preaching tours of the Anglican itinerant Whitefield. These tours frequently intersected with the regional revivals in progress at different times in New England, the middle colonies, and some parts of the southern colonies, but even then the fit was imperfect. Whitefield's tours produced some changes in ministerial speaking styles but few permanent alterations in institutional patterns of religion, although his personal charisma supported no less than seven tours of the colonies between 1740 and his death in Newburyport, Massachusetts, in 1770.[36]

Second, the prerevolutionary revivals occurred in the colonial backwaters of Western society where they were part of a long-term pattern of erratic movements for spiritual renewal and revival that had long characterized Western Christianity and Protestantism since its birth two centuries earlier. Thus, their theological origins were international and diverse rather than narrowly Calvinist and uniquely American. Calvinism was important in some revivals, but Arminianism and Pietism supported others. This theological heterogeneity also makes it impossible to isolate a single overwhelmingly important cause of the revivals. Instead, they appear to have arisen when three circumstances were present—internal demands for renewal in different international Christian communities, charismatic preachers, and special, often unique, local circumstances that made communities receptive to elevated religious rhetoric.[37]

Third, the revivals had modest effects on colonial religion. This is not to say that they were "conservative," because they did not always uphold the traditional religious order. But they were never radical, whatever their critics claimed. For example, the revivals reinforced ministerial rather than lay authority even as they altered some clergymen's perceptions of their tasks and methods. They also stimulated the demand for organization, order, and authority in the evangelical denominations. Presbyterian "New Lights" repudiated the conservative Synod of Philadelphia because its discipline was too weak, not too strong, and demanded tougher standards for ordination and subsequent service. After 1760, when Presbyterians and Baptists utilized revivalism as part of their campaigns for denominational expansion, they only increased their stress on central denominational organization and authority.[38]

Indeed, the best test of the benign character of the revivals is to take up the challenge of contemporaries who linked them to outbreaks of "enthusiasm" in Europe. In making these charges, the two leading antirevivalists in the colonies, Garden of Charleston and Chauncy of Boston, specifically compared the colonial revivals with those of the infamous "French Prophets" of London, exiled Huguenots who were active in the city between 1706 and about 1730. The French Prophets predicted the downfall of English politicians, raised followers from the dead, and used women extensively as leaders to prophesy and preach. By comparison, the American revivalists were indeed "conservative." They prophesied only about the millennium, not about local politicans, and described only the necessity, not the certainty, of salvation. What is most important is that they eschewed radical change in the position of women in the churches. True, women experienced dramatic conversions, some of the earliest being described vividly by Edwards. But, they preached only irregularly, rarely prophesied, and certainly never led congregations, denominations, or sects in a way that could remotely approach their status among the French Prophets.[39]

Fourth, the link between the revivals and the American Revolution is virtually nonexistent. The relationship between prerevolutionary political change and the revivals is weak everywhere except in Virginia, where the Baptist revivals indeed shattered the exclusive, century-old Anglican hold on organized religious activity and politics in the colony. But, their importance to the Revolution is weakened by the fact that so many members of Virginia's Anglican aristocracy also led the Revolution. In other colonies the revivals furnished little revolutionary rhetoric, including even millennialist thought, that was not available from other sources and provided no unique organizational mechanisms for anti-British protest activity. They may have been of some importance in helping colonists make moral judgments about eighteenth-century English politics, though colonists unconnected to the revivals made these judgments as well.[40]

In the main, then, the revivals of religion in eighteenth-century America emerge as nearly perfect mirrors of a regionalized, provincial society. They arose erratically in different times and places across a century from the 1690s down to the time of the Revolution. Calvinism underlay some of them, Pietism and Arminianism others. Their leadership was local and, at best, regional, and they helped reinforce—but were not the key to—the proliferation and expansion of still-regional Protestant denominations in the colonies. As such, they created no intercolonial religious institutions and fostered no significant experiential unity in the colonies. Their social and political effects were minimal and usually local, although they could traumatize communities in which they upset, if only temporarily, familiar patterns of worship and social behavior. But the congregations they occasionally produced usually blended into the traditional social system, and the revivals abated without shattering its structure. Thus, the revivals of religion in prerevolutionary America seldom became proto-revolutionary, and they failed to change the timing, causes, or effects of the Revolution in any significant way.

Of course, it is awkward to write about the eighteenth-century revivals of religion in America as erratic, heterogeneous, and politically benign. All of us have walked too long in the company of Tracy's "Great Awakening" to make our journey into the colonial past without it anything but frightening. But as Chauncy wrote of the Whitefield revivals, perhaps now it is time for historians "to see that Things have been carried too far, and that the Hazard is great . . . lest we should be over-run with *Enthusiasm.*"[41]

NOTES

1. Perry Miller, *Errand into the Wilderness* (Cambridge, 1956), 153–66; Richard L. Bushman, *From Puritan to Yankee: Character and the Social Order in Connecticut, 1690–1765* (Cambridge, 1967), 183–232; John C. Miller, "Religion, Finance, and Democracy in Massachusetts," *New England Quarterly,* 6 (March 1933), 29–58; Rhys Isaac, "Evangelical Revolt: The Nature of the Baptists' Challenge to the Traditional Order in Virginia, 1765–1775," *William and Mary Quarterly,* 31 (July 1974), 345–68; Rhys Isaac, *The Transformation of Virginia, 1740–1790* (Chapel Hill, 1982), 161–80, 192–98, 243–69; Gary B. Nash, *The Urban Crucible: Social Change, Political Consciousness, and the Origins of the American Revolution* (Cambridge, 1979), 204–27; Richard Hofstadter, *America at 1750: A Social Portrait* (New York, 1973), 217; William Warren Sweet, *The Story of Religion in America* (New York, 1950), 138, 172; Kenneth A. Lockridge, *Settlement and Unsettlement in Early America: The Crisis of Political Legitimacy before the Revolution* (New York, 1981), 43–44.

2. Alan Heimert, *Religion and the American Mind from the Great Awakening to the Revolution* (Cambridge, 1966); Harry S. Stout, "Religion, Communications, and the Ideological Origins of the American Revolution," *William and Mary Quarterly,* 34 (Oct. 1977), 519–41; Rhys Isaac, "Dramatizing the Ideology of the Revolution; Popular Mobilization in Virginia, 1774 to 1776," *ibid.,* 33 (July 1976), 357–85; Rhys Isaac, "Preachers and Patriots: Popular Culture and the Revolution in Virginia," in *The American Revolution: Explorations in the History of American Radicalism,* ed. Alfred F. Young (DeKalb, Ill., 1976), 125–56; William G. McLoughlin, "'Enthusiasm for Liberty': The Great Awakening as the Key to the Revolution," in Jack P. Greene and William G. McLoughlin, *Preachers and Politicians: Two Essays on the Origins of the American Revolution* (Worcester, Mass., 1977), 47–73; Nash, *Urban Crucible,* 345, 350, 384.

3. Bernard Bailyn et al., *The Great Republic: A History of the American People* (2 vols., Lexington, Mass., 1981), I, 137–41; John M. Blum et al., *The National Experience: A History of the United States* (2 vols., New York, 1973), I, 63–65; Richard N. Current et al., *The Essentials of American History* (New York, 1980), 27–28. For examples from other textbooks, see Edwin C. Rozwenc and Thomas Bender, *The Making of American Society* (New York, 1978), 128–30; Mary Beth Norton et al., *A People and a Nation: A History of the United States* (Boston, 1982), 80–82; Henry F. Bedford and Trevor Colbourn, *The Americans: A Brief History to 1877* (New York, 1980), 36–37; Arthur S. Link et al., *The American People: A History* (2 vols., Arlington Heights, Ill., 1981), I, 134–35; Robert Kelley, *The Shaping of the American Past* (2 vols., Englewood Cliffs, N.J., 1982), I, 83–85; John A. Garraty, *The American Nation: a History of the United States to 1871* (New York, 1979), 46–47.

4. Heimert, *Religion and the American Mind;* Cedric B. Cowing, *The Great Awakening and the American Revolution: Colonial Thought in the Eighteenth Century* (Chicago, 1971); Bushman, *From Puritan to Yankee,* 183–220; Edwin Scott Gaustad, *The Great Awakening in New England* (New York, 1957); Charles Hartshorn Maxson, *The Great Awakening in the Middle Colonies* (Chicago, 1920); Dietmar Rothermund, *The Layman's Progress: Religious and Political Experience in Colonial Pennsylvania, 1740–1770* (Philadelphia, 1961); Wesley M. Gewehr, *The Great Awakening in Virginia, 1740–1790* (Durham, N.C., 1930); John W. Jeffries, "The Separation in the Canterbury Congregational Church: Religion, Family, and Politics in a Connecticut Town," *New England Quarterly,* 52 (Dec. 1979), 522–49; J. M. Bumsted, "Religion, Finance,

and Democracy in Massachusetts: The Town of Norton as a Case Study," *Journal of American History*, 57 (March 1971), 817–31; James Walsh, "The Great Awakening in the First Congregational Church of Woodbury, Connecticut," *William and Mary Quarterly*, 28 (Oct. 1971), 543–62; Gerald F. Moran, "Conditions of Religious Conversion in the First Society of Norwich, Connecticut, 1718–1744," *Journal of Social History*, 5 (Spring 1972), 331–43; Robert Sklar, "The Great Awakening and Colonial Politics: Connecticut's Revolution in the Minds of Men," *Connecticut Historical Society Bulletin*, 28 (July 1963), 81–95; Martin E. Lodge, "The Crisis of the Churches in the Middle Colonies, 1720–1750," *Pennsylvania Magazine of History and Biography*, 95 (April 1971), 195–220; Herman Harmelink III, "Another Look at Frelinghuysen and His 'Awakening,'" *Church History*, 37 (Dec. 1968), 423–38. For a superb guide to the vast bibliography of Jonathan Edwards studies, see Norman Fiering, *Jonathan Edwards's Moral Thought and Its British Context* (Chapel Hill, 1981), 371–79.

5. See, for example, Patricia Tracy, *Jonathan Edwards, Pastor: Religion and Society in Eighteenth-Century Northampton* (New York, 1979), 194. For exceptions to this pattern, see Heimert, *Religion and the American Mind*; Cowing, *Great Awakening*; McLoughlin, "'Enthusiasm for Liberty,'" 47–73.

6. Charles Hodge, *Constitutional History of the Presbyterian Church in the United States of America* (2 vols., Philadelphia, 1851), II, 2–122; Robert Baird, *Religion in America, or an Account of the Origins, Progress, Relation to the State, and Present Condition of the Evangelical Churches in the United States* (New York, 1844), 273–75. Edwards used numerous phrases and labels to describe the revivals in Northampton in *A Faithful Narrative of the Surprising Work of God*. Among them are "general awakening," "great awakenings," "very general awakening," "great alteration," "revival of religion," "flourishing of religion," "a very great awakening," "awakenings," "legal awakenings," "first awakenings," "awakenings and encouragements," and "God's works." Jonathan Edwards, *A Faithful Narrative of the Surprising Work of God*, in *The Great Awakening*, ed. C. C. Goen (New Haven, 1972), 145, 150, 153, 155, 156, 160, 162, 163, 164, 167, 168, 210. In none of these instances did Edwards use these phrases to describe religious revivals in all or most of the colonies. This is true as well of his writing in *Some Thoughts concerning the Present Revival of Religion in New England* (1743), in his preface to Joseph Bellamy's *True Religion Delineated* (1750), and in letters describing revivals written between 1741 and 1751. *Great Awakening*, ed. Goen, 289–530, 533–66, 569–72. Although Joseph Tracy entitled his book *The Great Awakening*, he seldom used the label in the text. Joseph Tracy, *The Great Awakening: A History of the Revival of Religion in the Time of Edwards and Whitefield* (Boston, 1842), 1, 35, 119, 223, 413, 431.

7. *The Great Awakening: Documents on the Revival of Religion, 1740–1745*, ed. Richard L. Bushman (New York, 1970), xii; Heimert, *Religion and the American Mind*, viii, 3–4. J. M. Bumsted dissents from this formulation by stressing the influence of Pietism in the Awakening, as does Charles Hartshorn Maxson. J. M. Bumsted, *The Great Awakening: The Beginnings of Evangelical Pietism in America* (Waltham, Mass., 1970), 1–3; Maxson, *Great Awakening in the Middle Colonies*, 1–10.

8. *Great Awakening*, ed. Bushman, xi; Darrett B. Rutman, *The Great Awakening: Event and Exegesis* (New York, 1970), 1–8; *The Great Awakening: Documents Illustrating the Crisis and Its Consequences*, ed. Alan Heimert and Perry Miller (Indianapolis, 1967), xiii–xvi; James A. Henretta, *The Evolution of American Society, 1700–1815* (Lexington, Mass., 1973), 131–38; David S. Lovejoy, *Religious Enthusiasm and the Great Awakening* (Englewood Cliffs, N.J., 1969), 3.

9. Edwards, *Faithful Narrative*, 157; *Great Awakening*, ed. Bushman, xi.

10. Gaustad, *Great Awakening in New England*, 7–9, 97, 107, 134–40; Heimert, *Religion and the American Mind*, 4, 38–58.

11. Gaustad, *Great Awakening in New England*, 111; Tracy, *Jonathan Edwards*, 184–88; John B. Frantz, "The Awakening of Religion among the German Settlers in the Middle Colonies," *William and Mary Quarterly*, 33 (April 1976), 266–88; Gewehr, *Great Awakening in Virginia*, 254; Maxson, *Great Awakening in the Middle Colonies*, 1–10, 28, 32. For an outstanding ac-

count of the complex causes that led some middle-colony Presbyterians to oppose revivals, see Elizabeth I. Nybakken, "New Light on the Old Side: Irish Influences in Colonial Presbyterianism," *Journal of American History*, 68 (March 1982), 813–32.

12. Paul R. Lucas, *Valley of Discord: Church and Society along the Connecticut River, 1636–1725* (Hanover, N.H., 1976), 199–202; Gaustad, *Great Awakening in New England*, 16–20; Sidney Ahlstrom, *A Religious History of the American People* (New Haven, 1972), 314–29; Timothy L. Smith, *Revivalism and Social Reform: American Protestantism on the Eve of the Civil War* (Baltimore, 1980), 254.

13. For brief treatments of the revivals in colonies where their impact was actually minimal, see William Howland Kenney III, "Alexander Garden and George Whitefield: The Significance of Revivalism in South Carolina, 1738–1741," *South Carolina Historical Magazine*, 71 (June 1970), 1–16; and David T. Morgan, Jr., "The Great Awakening in North Carolina, 1740–1775: The Baptist Phase," *North Carolina Historical Review*, 45 (July 1968), 264–83. Maxson has little to say about the revivals in New York. Maxson, *Great Awakening in the Middle Colonies*, 47–50, 59–60, 65–66, 82, 88–89, 114–15, 119–23. On George Whitefield's slim crowds in New York, see Martin E. Lodge, "The Great Awakening in the Middle Colonies" (Ph.D. diss., University of California, Berkeley, 1964), 185–86. For comments on the oddities of the revivals in Pennsylvania and Germantown, see Jon Butler, *Power, Authority, and the Origins of American Denominational Order: The English Churches in the Delaware Valley, 1680–1730* (Philadelphia, 1978), 52, 77; and Stephanie Grauman Wolf, *Urban Village: Population, Community, and Family Structure in Germantown, Pennsylvania, 1683–1800* (Princeton, 1976), 228–42.

14. Heimert, *Religion and the American Mind*, 51, 119, 160; Kenney, "Alexander Garden and George Whitefield," 1–16.

15. Gaustad, *Great Awakening in New England*, 25–28; Maxson, *Great Awakening in the Middle Colonies*, 40–53, 104–11; Gewehr, *Great Awakening in Virginia*, 7–8, 16; *Great Awakening*, ed. Bushman, 19–38; Nash, *Urban Crucible*, 204–20. Alan Heimert, however, notes that Whitefield's role "was very much a symbolic one." Heimert, *Religion and the American Mind*, 36.

16. *George Whitefield's Journals* (London, 1960), 476. Edwards's invitation to Whitefield is described in *Great Awakening*, ed. Goen, 48. For discussions of Edwards's influence see Charles Anghoff, ed., *Jonathan Edwards: His Life and Influence* (Rutherford, N.J., 1975); and Joseph A. Conforti, "Samuel Hopkins and the New Divinity: Theology, Ethics, and Social Reform in Eighteenth-Century New England," *William and Mary Quarterly*, 34 (Oct. 1977), 572–89.

17. This is the thesis of C. C. Goen, *Revivalism and Separatism in New England, 1740–1800: Strict Congregationalists and Separate Baptists in the Great Awakening* (New Haven, 1962). A "separation" did occur among Presbyterians in Philadelphia. See Maxson, *Great Awakening in the Middle Colonies*, 77.

18. On Presbyterian expansion before 1740, see Leonard J. Trinterud, *The Forming of an American Tradition: A Re-examination of Colonial Presbyterianism* (Philadelphia, 1949) 15–52; and Butler, *Power, Authority, and the Origins of American Denominational Order*, 43–52. On Anglican growth, see Edwin Scott Gaustad, *Historical Atlas of Religion in America* (New York, 1976), 3–4; Bruce E. Steiner, "New England Anglicanism: A Genteel Faith?" *William and Mary Quarterly*, 27 (Jan. 1970), 122–35; and Bruce E. Steiner, "Anglican Officeholding in Pre-Revolutionary Connecticut: The Parameters of New England Community," *ibid.*, 31 (July 1974), 369–406.

19. Timothy L. Smith, "Congregation, State, and Denomination: The Forming of the American Religious Structure," *William and Mary Quarterly*, 25 (April 1968), 155–76. Although many American historians infer that denominational growth stemmed from revivalism and a commitment to evangelicalism, the evidence does not allow them to say that the organization of each new congregation stemmed from a local revival. For example, the controversies in Hanover County, Virginia, clearly centered on doctrinal issues rather than revivalism. Gewehr, *Great Awakening in Virginia*, 3–39.

20. Heimert, *Religion and the American Mind*, 206. See also *Ibid.*, 206–17; Jonathan Edwards, *Some Thoughts concerning the Present Revival of Religion in New England*, in *Great Awakening*, ed. Goen, 279–383, 401–05, 483–89; Gilbert Tennent, *The Danger of an Unconverted Ministry*, in *Great Awakening*, ed. Heimert and Miller, 90, 97; Rothermund, *Layman's Progress*, 160; Maxson, *Great Awakening in the Middle Colonies*, 146. Harry S. Stout drew my attention to the impact of the revivals on sermon styles.

21. Samuel Blair, *A Short and Faithful Narrative of the Late Remarkable Revival of Religion in the Congregation of New-Londonderry*, in *Great Awakening*, ed. Bushman, 71–77.

22. McLoughlin, "'Enthusiasm for Liberty,'" 69.

23. *Ibid.* Two historians have taken James Davenport seriously, although both point out that he lacks a full study. See Goen, *Revivalism and Separatism in New England*, 19–27; Nash, *Urban Crucible*, 208–20. Whitefield preached in established, tax-supported churches when he got the chance, as happened at Northampton during his visit to Edwards in 1740. See *Great Awakening*, ed. Goen, 48–49. On itinerant preachers and their use of existing pulpits in Virginia, see Gewehr, *Great Awakening in Virginia*, 69–72. The evangelical demand for coercive legislation from the individual states on matters of morality and blasphemy after 1783 is described in William G. McLoughlin, "The Role of Religion in the Revolution: Liberty of Conscience and Cultural Cohesion in the New Nation," in *Essays on the American Revolution*, ed. Stephen G. Kurtz and James H. Hutson (Chapel Hill, 1973), 197–255.

24. Sumner Chilton Powell, *Puritan Village: The Formation of a New England Town* (Middletown, Conn., 1963), 116–32; Paul Boyer and Stephen Nissenbaum, *Salem Possessed: The Social Origins of Witchcraft* (Cambridge, 1974), 60–79.

25. J. William T. Youngs, *God's Messengers: Religious Leadership in Colonial New England, 1700–1750* (Baltimore, 1976), 53–55, 74; Butler, *Power, Authority, and the Origins of American Denominational Order*, 57–58.

26. Bushman, *From Puritan to Yankee*, 196–232; Michael Zuckerman, *Peaceable Kingdoms: New England Towns in the Eighteenth Century* (New York, 1970), 140, 224; Edward M. Cook, Jr., *The Fathers of the Towns: Leadership and Community Structure in Eighteenth-Century New England* (Baltimore, 1976), 140–41; Miller, "Religion, Finance, and Democracy," 29–58.

27. Nash, *Urban Crucible*, 204–19; Gaustad, *Great Awakening in New England*, 80–101; Isaac, *Transformation of Virginia*.

28. Nash, *Urban Crucible*, 219–21; Harmelink, "Another Look at Frelinghuysen and his 'Awakening,'" 423–38. In contrast to the case in New England, in New Jersey and Pennsylvania not a single Presbyterian congregation possesses a full set of church records for the years 1720–1760, and the fragmentary records that have survived seldom have been published, although most of the latter are available in their original form or in copies at the Presbyterian Historical Society, Philadelphia.

29. Isaac, *Transformation of Virginia*, 181–269.

30. James David Essig, "A Very Wintry Season: Virginia Baptists and Slavery, 1785–1797," *Virginia Magazine of History and Biography*, 88 (April 1980), 170–85.

31. Arnold A. Dallimore, *George Whitefield: The Life and Times of the Great Evangelist of the Eighteenth-Century Revival* (London, 1970), 495–509; Frank J. Klingberg, *An Appraisal of the Negro in Colonial South Carolina: A Study in Americanization* (Washington, 1941), 27–54, 101–22; John C. Van Horn, "'Pious Designs': The American Correspondence of the Associates of Dr. Bray, 1731–1775" (Ph.D. diss., University of Virginia, 1979), 56–100, 197; James Davenport to Eleazer Wheelock, July 9, 1740, American Colonial Clergy section, Gratz Collection (Historical Society of Pennsylvania, Philadelphia). The erratic Quaker path to humanitarian relief for slaves is traced in Sydney V. James, *A People among Peoples: Quaker Benevolence in Eighteenth-Century America* (Cambridge, 1963), 103–40. Various aspects of Anglican relief are described in Frank J. Klingberg, *Anglican Humanitarianism in Colonial New York* (Philadelphia, 1940), 130–40; Klingberg, *Appraisal of the Negro*, 1–54; and Sheldon S. Cohen, "Elias Neau, Instructor to New York's Slaves," *New-York Historical Society Quar-*

terly, 55 (Jan. 1971), 7–27. Paradoxically, Elie Neau was a French Protestant whose work with slaves stemmed from new forms of piety and religious enthusiasm created by the expulsion of Protestants from France in 1685. See Emile G. Leonard, "La piété de l'église des galleres' sous Louis XIV," in *Melanges offerts à M. Paul-E. Martin* (Geneva, Switzerland, 1961), 97–111; and Jon Butler, ed., "Les 'Hymnes ou cantiques sacrez' d'Elie Neau: Un nouveau manuscrit du 'grand mystique des galères,'" *Bulletin de la Société de l'Histoire du Protestantisme Français,* 124 (July–Sept. 1978), 416–23.

32. Nathan O. Hatch, "New Lights and the Revolution in Rural New England," *Reviews in American History,* 8 (Sept. 1980), 323; Heimert, *Religion and the American Mind,* 346–47; James H. Hutson, *Pennsylvania Politics, 1746–1770: The Movement for Royal Government and Its Consequences* (Princeton, 1972), 100–02, 211–13, 240–43.

33. Heimert, *Religion and the American Mind,* viii; Nathan O. Hatch, *The Sacred Cause of Liberty: Republican Thought and the Millennium in Revolutionary New England* (New Haven, 1977); Carl L. Becker, *The Declaration of Independence: A Study in the History of Political Ideas* (New York, 1922); Garry Wills, *Inventing America: Jefferson's Declaration of Independence* (Garden City, N.Y., 1978); Bernard Bailyn, *The Ideological Origins of the American Revolution* (Cambridge, 1967), 55–93; Bernard Bailyn, "Religion and Revolution: Three Biographical Studies," *Perspectives in American History,* 4 (1970), 83–169.

34. Stout, "Religion, Communications, and the Ideological Origins of the American Revolution," 519–41.

35. *Ibid.;* McLoughlin, "'Enthusiasm for Liberty,'" 47–73; Gilbert Tennent, "Thoughts on Extempore Preaching," 1762 (Presbyterian Historical Society, Philadelphia); Tracy, *Jonathan Edwards,* 82–88; Maxson, *Great Awakening in the Middle Colonies,* 86. Maxson is the only historian who appears to have noticed Gilbert Tennent's manuscript and its significance. The manuscript itself actually contains drafts of two different statements. One is an attack on extemporaneous preaching, which was written in response to Roderick Mackenzie, *Reading No Preaching* (Philadelphia, 1761). The other is Tennent's defense of his refusal to accept George Duffield as his assistant in Philadelphia in 1762. For the latter, see Trinterud, *Forming of an American Tradition,* 160–61.

36. Heimert is sensitive both to the slippages in Whitefield's popularity and to his continuing symbolic importance in at least some quarters. Thus, he reports the bizarre occasion in 1775 during which military officers preparing to attack Canada accompanied the minister Samuel Spring into Whitefield's tomb at Newburyport, Massachusetts, "took the lid from Whitefield's coffin, removed Whitefield's collar and wrist bands, cut them in small pieces, and divided them among the officers." Heimert, *Religion and the American Mind,* 483.

37. The best discussion of revivalism and enthusiasm in Western religion is Ronald Knox, *Enthusiasm: A Chapter in the History of Religion* (New York, 1961). The eighteenth-century revivals in Europe and America lack a modern general history. Maxson attempted to place the Pennsylvania revivals in an international perspective but was handicapped by the lack of parallel scholarly studies. Maxson, *Great Awakening in the Middle Colonies,* 1–10, 80–83, 112–31.

38. Trinterud, *Forming of an American Tradition,* 122–34; Sandra Rennie, "The Role of the Preacher: Index to the Consolidation of the Baptist Movement in Virginia from 1760 to 1790," *Virginia Magazine of History and Biography,* 88 (Oct. 1980), 430–41. See also Nybakken, "New Light on the Old Side," 813–32.

39. The best-known pieces linking the French Prophets with the colonial revivalists are Alexander Garden, *Take Heed How Ye Hear* (Charleston, S. C., 1741); and *The Wonderful Narrative; Or, a Faithful Account of the French Prophets, Their Agitations, Extasies, and Inspirations* (Boston, 1742). Charles Chauncy has long been considered the author of the latter. Like other revivalists, Edwards was sometimes forced to acknowledge the accusations, although he never dealt with them forcefully. See Edwards, *Some Thoughts concerning the Present Revival,* 313, 330, 341. The most authoritative modern treatment of the Prophets is Hillel Schwartz, *The French Prophets: The History of a Millenarian Group in Eighteenth-Century*

England (Berkeley, 1980). Women's participation in the eighteenth-century revivals, as well as in organized religion in the colonies, should be distinguished from their leadership. The religious group in which women exercised some leadership roles most consistently was uninvolved in the revivals—the Quakers. See Mary Maples Dunn, "Saints and Sisters: Congregational and Quaker Women in the Early Colonial Period," *American Quarterly*, 30 (Winter 1978), 582–601; Mary Beth Norton, *Liberty's Daughters: The Revolutionary Experience of American Women, 1750–1800* (Boston, 1980), 97, 129–33, 140–41; Barbara L. Epstein, *The Politics of Domesticity: Women, Evangelism, and Temperance in Nineteenth-Century America* (Middletown, Conn., 1981), 11–44.

40. Bernard Bailyn has demonstrated how thoroughly the issue of morality in British politics transcended organized religion and revivalism. Bailyn, *Ideological Origins of the American Revolution*, 55–93.

41. Charles Chauncy, *A Letter from a Gentleman in Boston, to Mr. George Wishart*, in *Great Awakening*, ed. Bushman, 121.

CHAPTER
6

The Challenge of a Woman's Religion

Charles E. Hambrick-Stowe's essay describes one of the most powerfully gifted female preachers in colonial American history. Women occupied a difficult place in colonial American religious institutions. Often, women dominated congregations numerically, yet, except among Quakers, women lacked a substantial formal role in church government, preaching, and other ritual activities, almost all of which were limited to men exclusively. Does Osborn's career tell us how other women might have handled their situation? What was the central argument in her defense of female preaching? Was her message different from the salvation preaching of "Puritan" clergymen? Why were figures like Osborn neglected for so long?

Additional Reading: Laurel Thatcher Ulrich, *Good Wives: Image and Reality in the Lives of Women in Northern New England 1650–1750* (New York, 1982) describes women's lives, including their religious roles, in New England, while Susan Juster, *Disorderly Women: Sexual Politics and Evangelicalism in Revolutionary New England* (Ithaca, 1994) describes the rise and fall of women's religious authority among eighteenth-century New England Baptists. Jean R. Soderlund, "Women's Authority in Pennsylvania and New Jersey Quaker Meetings 1680–1760," *William and Mary Quarterly,* 44 (1987): 722–749, explains the extent and limitations of women's authority in the one denomination where women exercised substantial power. Joan R. Gunderson, "The Non-Institutional Church: The Religious Role of Women in Eighteenth-Century Virginia," *Historical Magazine of the Protestant Episcopal Church,* 51 (1982): 347–357, describes the role of women in eighteenth-century Virginian Anglicanism.

Charles E. Hambrick-Stowe # The Spiritual Pilgrimage of Sarah Osborn (1714–1796)

Sarah Osborn does not appear in the definitive biographical dictionary, *Notable American Women.* She is not in the pages of Sydney Ahlstrom's *A Religious History of the American People,* nor of any more recent standard American religious history text. She failed to catch the attention of the editors and authors of the recent *Encyclopedia of the American Religious Experience* or *Dictionary of Christianity in America.* The great New Divinity pastor-theologian Samuel Hopkins in some measure owed his career to Sarah Osborn, but studies of him mention her only in passing or not at all. Scholars have learned of her through the work of Mary Beth Norton and in the documentary history, *Women and Religion in America,* but the Sarah Osborn most often mentioned in connection with early New England is the one accused as a witch at Salem who died in Boston prison 10 May 1692.[1]

The Sarah Osborn who deserves more of our attention, however, is one of the significant women in early American religious history. Her experience was rooted in the older Puritanism of the seventeenth century, came to epitomize the spirit of the Great Awakening and of New England piety in the Revolutionary era, and anticipated certain themes of the Second Great Awakening which was beginning to ignite as her life drew to a close. Before discussing the spiritual pilgrimage of Sarah Osborn in this broad threefold context, it will be helpful to introduce her briefly.

1.

Born in London, 22 February 1714, to Benjamin and Susanna (Guyse) Haggar, eight-year-old Sarah immigrated in 1722 with her mother, joining her father who had come a bit earlier to Boston. After a sojourn in the vicinity of Taunton, the family moved permanently to Rhode Island, with Sarah now in her early teens. Her mother, whose brother was a minister in London, was drawn to Newport by the ministry of Nathaniel Clap, who in those very years was mired in the controversy that issued in the separation of a substantial part of his membership to form the Second Church. As dour and rigid as the venerable Calvinist may have appeared to some, Sarah was instantly devoted to him. She recalled how on a visit prior to the move he had given her mother "a little book of spiritual songs for me" inscribed from "one who was a hearty well wisher to my soul." Young Sarah's response was typical of the Puritan piety that infused her soul: "These words immediately seized me, and filled me with shame to think that one whom I never knew should take such care of my precious soul, while I was so careless myself." After Second Church was officially gathered with its own pastor in 1728, its leaders succeeded in ousting Clap and his small band of more conservative followers and possessed the meeting house for themselves. Sarah's parents continued to wor-

Reprinted with permission from *Church History* 61 (December 1992), 408–21.

ship in the old building with the new church. They disapproved of Sarah's loyalty to Clap, but the teenager would occasionally sneak out "to hear Mr. Clap preach at his own house, where I inclined to go constantly." At eighteen, also against the wishes of her parents, Sarah married Samuel Wheaton, who promptly died at sea shortly after the birth of their child. In her twenties "the widow's God remarkably provided for me" from 1733 until 1742 when she married a widower with two children, Henry Osborn. Unfortunately, her new husband proved to be a continual failure in business and poverty dogged Sarah all her life.[2]

Sarah Osborn kept school to make ends meet in the bustling commerce-oriented town of Newport and thanked God for "the veins of mercy, which I could see running through all my afflictions." Along with physical ailments, personal loss, and financial insecurity, she struggled more deeply with spiritual yearnings, doubts, awakenings, and lapses. After a decisive experience of repentance in which she was "filled with terrors" and "saw [her]self utterly lost without a Christ," she was by grace enabled to "accept him upon his own terms." She consulted with her mentor Nathaniel Clap and was admitted to membership in First Church in 1737. Sarah Osborn was thus already converted when the primary wave of the Great Awakening hit Newport in 1740. But, as was so indicative of the cyclical pattern of Puritan piety, by then she found herself "sunk by degrees lower and lower, till I had at last almost lost all sense of my former experiences." At times they "seemed like dreams or delusions," while "at others again, I had some revivals." For Sarah Osborn the Awakening was her re-awakening. She attended the evangelistic preaching of God's "dear servant [George] Whitefield . . . which in some measure stirred me up" and of Presbyterian New Light itinerant Gilbert Tennent which "it pleased God to bless . . . so to me, that it roused me."[3] Thus soundly converted she never looked back, working tirelessly to keep the Great Awakening alive, to stir the embers of New England piety into flame in the "Babylon" of "poor Rhode-Island."[4]

Osborn organized a "Religious Female Society" which became the backbone of Newport's First Church during the Awakening decade of the 1740s. This group of zealous women sustained the church during the lackluster ministry of Clap's successor and was then at the center of a fresh outbreak of revival in 1766 and 1767. Sarah Osborn and her friends engineered the calling of Jonathan Edwards's New Light protégé Samuel Hopkins as pastor in 1769. And it was they who kept the struggling church alive as many ardent patriots (including Hopkins himself) fled during the British occupation of the city. While prestigious and theologically moderate Second Congregation Church, from 1755 until the 1776 evacuation under the general pastorate of future Yale president Ezra Stiles, boasted almost seven hundred full members and many hundreds more adherents, First Church had fewer than two hundred worshippers. Only seventy of these were members, fifty of whom were women who looked to Osborn as their leader.[5] She welcomed prayer groups of all kinds to meet in her home, ranging from young men and women to free blacks and slaves; even Baptists were welcome. At the high-water mark of the 1766–1767 revival people gathered in such numbers, every night but Saturday, that "the House will not contain them"—as many as 525 per week, probably a larger crowd than her pastor had ever addressed.[6]

Sarah Osborn was also an astonishingly prodigious author, writing, for example, book-length devotional commentaries on Genesis and each of the synoptic gospels in addition to her journals and spiritual autobiography. In all, Samuel Hopkins, who edited some of her work for publication, recorded that she wrote "more than fifty volumes, the least containing near 100 pages, the bigger part above 200, and a number 300, and more, besides letters to her friends, and other occasional writings," such as her poem, "The Employment and Society of Heaven." One piece, a letter of spiritual advice to a friend, was published during her lifetime as a little fifteen-page book, *Nature, Certainty, and Evidence of true Christianity.*[7] Hopkins published her autobiography, written as a spiritual exercise when she turned thirty ("Life of Mrs. Sarah Osborn"), along with "Extracts from her Diary" and other biographical material as her *Memoirs* soon after her death. A few years later a collection of *Familiar Letters* of Osborn and her close friend, Susanna Anthony, was published in Newport. Finally, Osborn's 1767 letter to her ministerial advisor Joseph Fish of Stonington, Connecticut, defending her public leadership of prayer and study groups was edited by Mary Beth Norton and published in a scholarly journal in 1976. This was one of many letters exchanged between Osborn and Fish during the 1760s preserved at the American Antiquarian Society.[8] Even in old age, after the Revolution, when because of infirmity she could no longer attend worship or lead her devotional groups, groups and individuals continued to gather at Sarah Osborn's home in order to be near her.

2.

Sarah Osborn was an eighteenth-century woman, and her family had no roots in the New England of the Mathers. Even as a young girl, however, she was drawn to the piety of seventeenth-century Puritanism. Her love for old Nathaniel Clap, a third generation New Englander born in 1668, her loyalty to him in conflict, and the fact that she looked to him as her spiritual father until his death in 1745 suggests this religious orientation. George Whitefield said of Clap, who was 72 in 1740, "He looked like a good old Puritan, and gave me an idea of what stamp those men were, who first settled New England."[9]

Clap's sermons which affected Sarah Osborn so deeply essentially represented the "plain style" of the preachers who were old men when Clap was a youth—this, despite the fact that he was a 1690 graduate of Harvard College. She recalled that when in the throes of conversion, during worship it seemed as if "Mr. Clap . . . told me the very secrets of my heart in his sermon, as plain as I could have told them to him, and indeed more so. His sermon was very terrible to me. My sins, from my cradle, were ranked in order before my eyes, and they appeared dreadful. I saw the depravity of my nature; and how I was exposed to the infinite justice of an angry God." As humbling as was the Puritan homiletic "use of terror," salvation was experienced as intense joy. Sarah Osborn went to her pastor for what Puritans referred to as "private conference" when grace was beginning to shine upon her. As he "lifted up his hands, giving me his blessing," his prayer "filled me with joy unspeakable." Back home in "closet prayer," Osborn experienced the kind of "ecstacies of joy" associated with Edward Taylor in his meditative poetry. "But O, what a rapture I was in, when I renewed my solemn engagements to be the Lord's! . . . O, how was I ravished with his love! . . . O, why me, Lord! Why am I not in hell! Why among the living to praise the Lord! . . . O, amazing grace! Hast thou snatched me as a brand out of the burning!"[10] This biblically-rooted cycle of being emptied and filled, of feeling humbled and exalted, of God's judgment and grace, of divine wrath and love typified Puritan Calvinism as it was inherited from the seventeenth century.

Osborn adopted the well-established devotional disciplines of journal-keeping and spiritual autobiography. Seventeenth-century Puritans used the New Year or significant birthdays as occasions for meditative self-examination, and it was for her thirtieth birthday that Sarah Osborn wrote her life story. Her aims were twofold: "to stir up gratitude in the most ungrateful of all hearts, even mine, to a glorious and compassionate Savior, for all his benefits towards so vile a monster in sin as I am: And for the encouragement of any who may providentially light on these lines after my decease." On another occasion, in 1753, in her letter counseling a friend who was vexed in her quest for assurance of grace, Osborn again set down some of the high points of her spiritual pilgrimage. This time her aim was to provide touchstones by which the woman could find her way and perhaps conclude, "surely God has done thus and thus for me also." The narratives describe the sort of remarkable providences, near-death experiences, lapses into sin and fresh infusions of grace that typified this traditional genre. Her memoirs are comparable in this regard to those of her more famous contemporary, the *Life of David Brainerd,* edited and published by Jonathan Edwards as a model of piety. Brainerd, who died in his thirtieth year, consciously sought to replicate the traditional patterns. For example, he wrote a preface and helped Thomas Prince edit "old Mr. Shepard's" diary, published in 1747 as *Meditations and Spiritual Experiences of Mr. Thomas Shepard.* It is probable that Sarah Osborn was likewise familiar with some of the personal writings of the Puritans, such as those preserved in Cotton Mather's *Magnalia Christi Americana* (1702).[11]

Osborn's diaries are filled with the language and spiritual-psychological patterns of Puritan piety. She used Saturday night and the early morning of the Sabbath for "the work of self examination, to see how the case stood between God and my soul." On Monday she meditated on the text and message of the sermon she had heard. One week, for example, after a sermon on "the look he gave . . . Peter" (Luke 22:61), Osborn prayed: "O dear Jesus! Still look me into deeper repentance. Look me into faith. Look me into flaming love and zeal. Look me into constant and universal obedience. . . . Do but look, dear Lord." On New Year's eve and birthdays she confessed her sins, thanked God for abundant mercies, contemplated her mortality—"O let me be in an actual preparation for death, which may come long before the return of another year"—and renewed her covenant. In her Female Society and in other settings private and public, she participated regularly in days of fasting and thanksgiving. Her prayers reflect the Puritans' providential view of human and natural events, as when during an earthquake "my soul darted up to God, in ejaculation, that he would sanctify this shock, for the awakening of his people." And her faith was solidly grounded in what the Puritans called the "means of grace"—Scripture, worship, reading, meditation, prayer, sacraments, church membership. "It is the God of ordinances I want to find . . . by the influences of thy blessed Spirit of grace." She wrote often of the powerful effect witnessing a baptismal service had on her; and before joining the church she "longed for the ordinance of the Lord's supper." In Communion she "saw a crucified Saviour pouring out his precious blood to redeem his people from their sins. And . . . O, how did my heart melt, and my eyes flow with tears." With the Puritans, Osborn believed in Christ's real spiritual presence in the Supper. "When feeding upon his broken body, I was filled with astonishment. . . . His blood was sweet to me, as it was shed for the remission of sins."[12]

Sarah Osborn found comfort and strength in the writings of the old Puritans. When her eleven-year-old son, serving an apprenticeship some twenty miles away from home, lay sick and dying in 1744, she hurried to him with a Bible and her copy of Joseph Alleine's *Heaven's Alarm to Unconverted Sinners.* Her family may have brought this religious best-seller (first published in London, 1673) with them from England, or she could have bought one of the recent Boston editions (1727, 1739, 1743; or Philadelphia, 1741). Her use of the book reflects Puritanism's print-oriented piety and the persistence of these traditions in the age of the Great Awakening. Alleine's devotional manual guided her prayers for physical recovery, but even more "for that precious jewel, his immortal soul." She wrote that "in his dying moments I had an awful sense of his deplorable condition, if his naked soul should launch into a boundless eternity, without a God to go to." In prayer, however, she found assurance "of the fulness and sufficiency of Christ to make satisfaction" and welcome his soul to heaven. "While friends were putting on his grave clothes, I went into the field and walked, where, with more secrecy and freedom, I could breathe out my soul to God. And the sweetness of that season I cannot express. God discovered himself to be my God, my covenant God, my Father, my Friend."[13]

Alleine's *Alarm to Unconverted Sinners* was one of scores of classic devotional manuals from both sides of the Atlantic that continued to circulate in old and new editions in the 1730s and 1740s. Having gone through dozens of editions before 1710, with hundreds of thousands of copies in print, these "steady sellers," as David Hall has called them, exhibited great staying power in the New England book market. America's first religious periodical, Thomas Prince's *The Christian History,* published weekly in 1743 and 1744, made available such old material that was out of print. The journal was an unwieldy collection of (a) extracts from the devotional-theological writings of "the most famous Old Writers" of Puritan England, Scotland, and "the first Settlers of new-England and their children"; (b) "Manuscript original Letters now in the Hands of the Rev. Mr. Prince" written by ministers and other observers of mini-revivals "in almost all Parts of the Land" between 1660 and 1720; and (c) reports from Scotland and the British North American colonies concerning the Great Awakening of the 1730s and 1740s. By printing these types of materials, Prince sought to illustrate the traditionalism of the Awakening. Specifically, he wished to demonstrate that "the pious Principles and Spirit" of the "Old Writers" were "at this Day revived," and "also [to] guard against all extreams."[14]

The fact is, the Great Awakening was not simply the revolutionary, future-oriented phenomenon most historians have interpreted it as being. Richard Brown, in his recent study of how information was diffused within American society from the colonial to the early national period, affirms on the one hand that the revival advanced American individualism, and thus was a change-agent. On the other hand, he expresses doubt that "a single movement, even one so profound and so extensive as the Great Awakening, could shatter the common culture and information system that sustained it." Indeed, scholars are beginning to describe the Awakening as a "renaissance" of older traditions; some, for example, have discovered the seventeenth-century Scottish roots of that "uniquely American" revivalist phenomenon, the camp meeting. David Hall argues that during the period of the Awakening, the old "mentality of wonders, the story line of deliverance and confession, and the moral allegory of a land swept clean of sin . . . flourished once more among ordinary people." For these traditional believers, he states, "printers continued to publish . . . books like Alleine's *Alarm to Unconverted Sinners.*" Sarah Osborn fits this new interpretation of the Great Awakening's traditionalism.[15]

3.

Sarah Osborn participated in the Great Awakening of 1740, as already noted, by attending the revival services of George Whitefield and Gilbert Tennent. Her correspondence with Tennent contributed even more to her assurance of salvation. She read Jonathan Edwards's *Treatise Concerning Religious Affections* (1746), found it "a lovely piece" and quoted from it in her diary. Osborn spoke the language of the movement, which became the perennial language of evangelicalism. For example, in 1743, remembering how she had experienced God's "amazing grace" as a teenager, and 36 years before John Newton wrote his classic hymn, Osborn wrote: "O, amazing grace, that God should spare such a wretch as me!" At the same time, the exuberant freedom of the Awakening enabled her occasionally to think of God in ways more deeply personal and feminine than her tradition would suggest, as when she referred to "the womb of divine Providence" and "the bosom of God."[16]

Osborn shared the central concern of the Great Awakening, specifically, the need of every soul for spiritual rebirth, for a personal experience of salvation by faith alone. Her aged pastor had imparted to her the sense of spiritual immediacy which characterized the revivals, having once urged her to "give myself up to [God] *then.*" The Awakening, to a greater degree than the Puritanism of the late seventeenth century with its Halfway Covenant, brought a sense of the separation of the saved from the generality of people in the world. Ecclesiastically, this fostered the division of New England Congregationalism into New Light and Old Light camps and the splintering of some congregations. The "come-outer" spirit was evident in Osborn's criticism of the "Arminian" theology which appealed to the merchant class of cities like Newport, Boston, and Salem. After hearing an urbane liberal clergyman preach she once complained to her friend Susanna Anthony, "I cannot thank the minister, nor the sermon, for any good obtained thereby." Protesting the sermon's theme, "Do, and live," she pointed to the evangelical truth that "if salvation came by the law, then Christ is dead in vain." Osborn stood for "salvation, only through faith in Christ Jesus." With other New Lights, she did not stop there, for this faith "purifies the heart, works by love, and influenceth the whole man, to a life of universal obedience." But the Enlightenment elevation of the inherent goodness of humanity she saw as "hurtful to man, as it tends to draw him from Christ, the only hope of sinners." It was the evangelical theology of rebirth—not the optimistic theology of human goodness—that empowered Sarah Osborn as a woman. In Sarah Osborn the Great Awakening's theology of personal salvation also gave birth to joy and solidarity with others of the elect, most intimately those in her Female Society. "Never was adorable, sovereign mercy, more richly displayed, than in choosing rebel me, to be one of the happy few!" She insisted, further, that the "Gatherings at our House . . . in no way tend to separations, rents, or diversions, but rather are a Sweet sementing bond of union."[17]

Sarah Osborn's contribution to the Great Awakening in Rhode Island was her effort to sustain the revivals over the decades of the 1750s and 1760s. She did this through her work with groups of seekers and Christians and by bringing New Light and New Divinity preachers to Newport. She labored under the handicap of having as pastor of First Church for twenty years one William Vinal, of whom she makes no mention in her writings. Vinal's ineffective and increasingly alcoholic ministry culminated in his resignation under pressure in 1768. At the heart of Osborn's efforts was her Religious Female Society, which she founded "after I was revived" and found herself "longing to be made useful in the world." She was approached by "a number of young women, who were awakened to a concern for their souls" who "proposed to join in a society, provided I would take care of them." Such devotional fellowship groups were common in seventeenth-century New England, but they took on even greater importance in the mid-eighteenth century, as the effectiveness of the Methodist class meetings also attests. Osborn traveled periodically through southern New England to join similar "private religious meeting[s]" in fasting and prayer for "the outpouring of the Spirit of God on that place." She also looked upon her pupils at school as subjects for evangelism, determining to "pray with them, as well as for them," and she catechized children in her home several afternoons a week. In 1766 and 1767, ironically at the end of Vinal's tenure, the efforts of Sarah Osborn and her friends bore fruit as a fresh revival swept Newport. Hopkins wrote that hundreds of women—and now men—"repaired to her as a known, pious, benevolent Christian, to whom they could have easy access" for "counsel and prayers." She scheduled these groups carefully, in order to avoid scandal. The Sabbath evening "a number of young men" met at her house; Monday evening was for teenage girls; Tuesday "a large number of boys" came; Wednesday was her regular Female Society meeting; Thursday and Saturday afternoon she catechized children; and Friday evening "a number of heads of families" gathered "for prayer and religious conversation." She reserved Saturday mornings for her friend, Susanna Anthony. When "poor Blacks" sought a time with her for biblical instruction and prayer, she found room for slaves on the Sabbath evening in another room from the young white men, and welcomed an "Ethiopian Society" of free blacks to her kitchen on Tuesday evenings. Mary Beth Norton argues that the 1766 revival actually began the previous spring in the Sabbath evening black fellowship, for Osborn suggests in an April 1765 letter to Joseph Fish that the spiritual excitement of the slaves drew "white lads and neighbors daughters also [to] press in."[18]

A woman who gained such influence inevitably worried those for whom order was the highest priority, especially when her ministry extended beyond women and children to heads of households, young men, and blacks. In 1767 Osborn felt constrained to defend her practices in a letter to her supportive but cautious ministerial advisor, Joseph Fish. She explained that in order to avoid "moving beyond my line," when meeting with men and older teenaged boys "I by no means Set up for their instructor." She assured Fish that blacks were never "lifted up with pride," that she stressed obedience with them, and that several had been converted. Brushing off rude remarks from Newport's aristocracy about "keeping a Negro House," she expressed pleasure at being able to share the gospel with the poorest of people. As for the view that women should not undertake such work, Sarah Osborn continually offered to relinquish any of her groups for a minister to take over, but none ever came forward. Finally, she insisted that her schedule was not physically too hard, for these "sweet refreshing evenings" were "my resting reaping times." In the light of all this, she asked, "who would advise me to shut up my Mouth and doors and creep into obscurity?"[19]

Sarah Osborn and the Female Society were responsible for their church's invitation to Samuel Hopkins to preach as a probationary candidate for First Church's pulpit after his embarrassing dismissal from Great Barrington. Osborn had for years been "reading and thinking on" authors like Joseph Bellamy, the New Divinity theologian who sought to advance the pro-revival theology of Jonathan Edwards. Osborn was already using Hopkinsian-Calvinist-New Divinity theological language in her writings, referring often to Christ as "the glorious God-man Mediator" and to the Christian life as one of "disinterested benevolence." The church was a troubled and dwindling fellowship, however, in the wake of William Vinal's resignation. Hopkins's trial period turned into a nightmare, with a large faction of men of a more moderately Calvinist stamp opposing a permanent call. Osborn prayed and lobbied steadfastly that "it may yet be [God's] will, to give me Mr. H. for my minister!" She counseled Hopkins to "wait, dear Sir, awhile longer," for "I scarce ever received any signal mercy, but which was sweetened, by the trials that went before it," and she resolved "we will pray more frequently, more earnestly." In the end, after a negative vote, it was Hopkins's farewell sermon that won over enough men to change their votes and call him as pastor. The victory of Osborn and Hopkins was significant, for it positioned the learned New Divinity pastor for a productive publishing and teaching career as the most influential Congregational systematic theologian of the Revolutionary period. By persevering in the ordeal of securing Hopkins as pastor, Osborn encouraged the extension of Great Awakening-rooted theology, and the hope of more 1740 and 1766 style revivals.[20]

4.

The Great Awakening can no longer be understood as a single event or even a decade of revivals from the 1730s to the 1740s. As Jon Butler points out, "revivals linked to it started in New England long before 1730 and yet did not appear with force in Virginia until the 1760s." In the 1760s and 1770s, indeed, Sarah Osborn was still dedicated to their perpetuation in Newport. This is to deny neither the significance of 1740, nor the real theological developments and sociopolitical and economic change in New England society over the course of the eighteenth century. Still, Osborn rejoiced that Hopkins returned to Newport after the British occupation "with a tenfold lustre in his ministrations" and "zeal for God." Newport's destruction by the British—Hopkins's meeting house and parsonage were among the heavily damaged buildings—was indicative of a world that needed rebuilding. The Hopkinsian doctrine of "disinterested benevolence" would play a special role in the creation of the new republic through the movements of the late 1790s and early 1800s commonly referred to as the Second Great Awakening. In all this, the evangelical spirit which took root in Puritan piety and flourished in the pre-Revolutionary decades of the Great Awakening again flowered in recognizable forms. The spiritual pilgrimage of Sarah Osborn, which substantiates the notion of an extended Awakening period, continued after her death, as more of her writings were published in 1799 and 1807.[21]

Contrary to—or at least supplemental to—the conventional thesis that the Great Awakening spawned American individualism, New Divinity revivalism argued for communalism, social responsibility, and moral reform. Sarah Osborn opposed "the hateful principle of self-love," the very force that was beginning to drive the American economy.[22] While Adam Smith's nascent capitalism and the democracy of the new United States Constitution were based on the idea of competing self-interested individuals and groups, post-Revolutionary promoters of a new Awakening struggled to redefine and refashion the old Calvinist, Puritan, and Edwardsian idea of the covenanted community under the sovereignty of God. Hopkins and other evangelical Congregationalists poured their energy into this task by organizing countless societies for mission, evangelism, education, and social and moral reform which would compete for influence in the public realm.

Hopkins used the example of Sarah Osborn to fight against the socioeconomic transformation of the young republic which Charles Sellers has recently described in *The Market Revolution*. As Sellers observes, "the New-Light women's prophetic leader Sarah Osborn knew market vicissitude firsthand," through the death of her first husband, the business incompetency of her second, and her struggle to support her family by teaching. By publishing her writings Hopkins elevated Osborn as a person of piety and true virtue, one who lived not for self but others. While Newport gloried in the quest for luxury, Osborn glorified God for the lessons of poverty. Again and again in her diaries she records God's providence, when "business is now failing every day," in suddenly saving her family from bankruptcy. "I have often thought God has so ordered it throughout my days . . . that I should be in an afflicted, low condition, as to worldly circumstances . . . on purpose to suppress that pride of my nature, which doubtless would have been acted out greatly to his dishonor, had I enjoyed health, and had prosperity." While Newport strove for prosperity, Osborn prayed she might "be made useful in the world" by organizing societies. While Newport got rich "by the blood of the poor Africans" through the slave trade, Osborn taught blacks how to read and pray. While capitalism promoted efficiency, Osborn advanced the work of the Spirit which later came to epitomize the Second Great Awakening in its Methodist and Finneyite manifestations: sanctification and "perfection of holiness." "Lord, I am not sueing for riches," she prayed, "but for sanctifying grace." "And who can tell but he may have yet far greater degrees of grace to bestow on thee? . . . for he is thy sanctification as well as redemption."[23] Her life and ministry are thus illustrative of broad developments and continuities from colonial days to nineteenth-century America.

Sarah Osborn used her freedom as a born-again eighteenth-century woman to reestablish an apparently outdated communal and spiritual ideal. Charles Sellers states: "Against the male egotism of market relations, she and her Newport sisters were defending the altruism that validated their nurturant role in the traditional family and community."[24] This ideal itself was reborn in the Second Great Awakening. Abolition (of which Hopkins was an early advocate), temperance, women's rights, prison reform, and world mission required individuals willing to give themselves in community effort. Within the tumultuous antebellum world of slavery and the Industrial Revolution many believers organized into societies, as Sarah Osborn had done, in order to do the work of the Lord.

Samuel Hopkins published the writings of Sarah Osborn in 1799, and there was still a market for an edition of her letters in 1807, for the same reason Thomas Prince and other leaders of the Great Awakening republished many of the Puritan classics in the 1730s and 1740s. It was not so much nostalgia, a clinging to "old time religion," but rather the enduring power, amidst social change, of the evangelical ideals of the new birth and life for others under the sovereignty of God. Promoters of the Second Great Awakening felt her life had something to say to their new century. Sarah Osborn herself would have been humbled, yet pleased. As she prayed at the end of her spiritual autobiography, "If a word in these lines ever prove useful to one soul, after my decease, it will be ten thousand times more than I deserve from the hands of a bountiful God: To him alone be all the glory."[25]

NOTES

1. See Edward T. James, ed., *Notable American Women: A Biographical Dictionary*, 3 vols. (Cambridge, Mass., 1971); Sydney Ahlstrom, *A Religious History of the American People* (New Haven, 1972); Charles H. Lippy and Peter W. Williams, eds., *Encyclopedia of the American Religious Experience*, 3 vols. (New York, 1988); Daniel G. Reid, et al., eds., *Dictionary of Christianity in America* (Downers Grove, Ill., 1990); Mary Beth Norton, ed., "'My Resting Reaping Times': Sarah Osborn's Defense of Her 'Unfeminine' Activities, 1767," *Signs: Journal of Women in Culture and Society* 2 (1976): 515–529; Mary Beth Norton, *Liberty's Daughters: The Revolutionary Experience of American Women, 1750–1800* (Boston, 1980), pp. 129–133,

140–141; Rosemary Radford Ruether and Rosemary Skinner Keller, eds., *Women and Religion in America*, 3 vols. (San Francisco, 1983) 2:316, 320, 321, 326, 348–351. On Hopkins, see Joseph A. Conforti, *Samuel Hopkins and the New Divinity Movement* (Grand Rapids, Mich., 1981), p. 103; Allen C. Guelzo, *Edwards on the Will: A Century of American Theological Debate* (Middletown, Conn., 1989). On the other Sarah Osborne, see Paul Boyer and Stephen Nissenbaum, *Salem Possessed: The Social Origins of Witchcraft* (Cambridge, Mass., 1974), pp. 193–194.

2. Sarah Osborn, *Memoirs of the Life of Mrs. Sarah Osborn*, Samuel Hopkins, ed. (Worcester, Mass., 1799), pp. 5–9, 14–20, 50.

3. Ibid., pp. 19, 24–26, 30, 35, 43.

4. Sarah Osborn and Susanna Anthony, *Familiar Letters, Written by Mrs. Sarah Osborn, and Miss Susanna Anthony, Late of Newport, Rhode-Island* (Newport, R.I., 1807), p. 70. Conforti, *Hopkins and the New Divinity Movement*, p. 95.

5. Conforti, *Hopkins and the New Divinity Movement*, pp. 93–103. Charles Sellers, *The Market Revolution: Jacksonian America, 1815–1846* (New York, 1991), p. 205.

6. Norton, ed., "'My Resting Reaping Times,'" pp. 519–520. Osborn, *Memoirs*, pp. 76–83.

7. Sarah Osborn, *Nature, Certainty, and Evidence of true Christianity* (Boston, 1755).

8. An extract from Norton, ed., "'My Resting Reaping Times'" also appears in Ruether and Keller, eds., *Women and Religion in America*, 2:348–351. See also Norton, *Liberty's Daughters*, pp. 129–133, for several quotations from the Osborn-Fish correspondence.

9. Quoted in William B. Sprague, ed., *Annals of the American Pulpit* (New York, 1859), 1:350.

10. Osborn, *Memoirs*, pp. 21, 31–33. For Taylor's poetry, see Charles E. Hambrick-Stowe, *Early New England Meditative Poetry: Anne Bradstreet and Edward Taylor* (New York, 1988). On Puritan devotional exercises generally, see Charles E. Hambrick-Stowe, *The Practice of Piety: Puritan Devotional Disciplines in Seventeenth-Century New England* (Chapel Hill, N.C., 1982) and Charles Lloyd Cohen, *God's Caress: The Psychology of Puritan Religious Experience* (New York, 1986). Kenneth Silverman's biography, *The Life and Times of Cotton Mather* (New York, 1984), offers a sensitive interpretation of this spirituality in the life of the most prominent third generation New Englander.

11. Osborn, *Memoirs*, p. 6. Osborn, *Nature, Certainty, and Evidence of True Christianity*, p. 14. Jonathan Edwards, *Life of David Brainerd*, Norman Pettit, ed. (New Haven, 1985), pp. 451, 460, 513. See also Michael J. Crawford, ed., "The Spiritual Travels of Nathan Cole," *The William and Mary Quarterly*, 3rd ser., 33 (1976): 89–126.

12. Osborn, *Memoirs*, pp. 84, 87–88, 112, 177–178, 120, 14, 16, 28, 35–36. Osborn and Anthony, *Familiar Letters*, p. 12.

13. Osborn, *Memoirs*, pp. 65–67. David D. Hall, *Worlds of Wonder, Days of Judgment: Popular Religious Belief in Early New England* (New York, 1989), p. 49. Examples of other seventeenth-century bestsellers that were republished in Boston during the Great Awakening are: William Dyer, *Christ's Famous Titles, and A Believer's Golden Chain* (1731); Andrew Jones, *The Black Book of Conscience* (1732); [Joshua Scottow], *Old Men's Tears* (1733); John Corbet, *Enquiry into the State of his Own Soul* (1743); [Thomas Wilcox], *A Choice Drop of Honey, From the Rock Christ* (1734, 1741); Jeremiah Burroughs, *The Rare Jewel of Christian Contentment* (1731); Thomas Gouge, *The Young Man's Guide* (1743); John Owen, *Eshcol: A Cluster of the Fruit of Canaan* (1744); Daniel Burgess, *Rules for Hearing the Word of God* (1742); James Janeway, *Heaven Upon Earth* (1730); Richard Baxter, *A Call to the Unconverted to Turn and Live* (1731); Thomas Prince, ed., *The Memoirs of Capt. Roger Clap* (1731); and several works of Thomas Shepard, *The Sound Beleever* (1736, 1742), *The Sincere Convert* (1735, 1742, 1743), *The Saints' Jewel* (1743), and *Three Valuable Pieces* (1747).

14. Thomas Prince, *The Christian History* (Boston, 1744), pp. 1–2, 113, 155, 162, 185.

15. Richard D. Brown, *Knowledge is Power: The Diffusion of Information in Early America, 1700–1865* (New York, 1989), pp. 272–273. Jon Butler, *Awash in a Sea of Faith: Christianizing*

the American People (Cambridge, Mass., 1990), pp. 164–193. Marilyn J. Westerkamp, *Triumph of the Laity: Scots-Irish Piety and the Great Awakening, 1625–1760* (New York, 1988). Leigh Eric Schmidt, *Holy Fairs: Scottish Communions and American Revivals in the Early Modern Period* (Princeton, 1989). Michael J. Crawford, *Seasons of Grace: Colonial New England's Revival Tradition in Its British Context* (New York, 1991). Hall, *Worlds of Wonder*, p. 244. For the conventional presentation of the Great Awakening as a modernizing phenomenon, a decisive break in time, see Richard L. Bushman, *From Puritan to Yankee* (Cambridge, Mass., 1967), p. 207; Perry Miller, "Jonathan Edwards and the Great Awakening," *Errand into the Wilderness* (Cambridge, Mass., 1956), pp. 153–166; Edwin Scott Gaustad, *The Great Awakening in New England* (New York, 1957), pp. 1–15, 102–140; Alan Heimert, *Religion and the American Mind* (Cambridge, Mass., 1966), pp. 27–94; Wesley M. Gewehr, *The Great Awakening in Virginia, 1740–1790* (Gloucester, Mass., 1965; orig. 1930), pp. 3–18; David S. Lovejoy, *Religious Enthusiasm in the New World* (Cambridge, Mass., 1985), pp. 178–214; William G. McLoughlin, "'Enthusiasm for Liberty': The Great Awakening as the Key to the Revolution," *Preachers and Politicians* (Worcester, Mass., 1977), pp. 47–73; Harry S. Stout, *The New England Soul: Preaching and Religious Culture in Colonial New England* (New York, 1986), pp. 185–211; Martin E. Marty, *Religion, Awakening, and Revolution* (n.p., 1977), pp. 79–80, 93.

16. Osborn, *Memoirs*, pp. 325, 10, 39. Osborn and Anthony, *Familiar Letters*, p. 96. Similarly, eleven years before Toplady wrote "Rock of Ages" Osborn used the biblically rooted phrase in *Nature, Certainty, and Evidence of true Christianity*, p. 6: "Now the Foundation of my Hopes are laid upon the Rock of Ages."

17. Osborn, *Memoirs*, p. 44. Osborn and Anthony, *Familiar Letters*, pp. 36, 86–87. Norton, ed., "'My Resting Reaping Times,'" p. 525.

18. Osborn, *Memoirs*, pp. 49, 62, 50, 76, 81–82. Norton, ed. "'My Resting Reaping Times,'" p. 519. Conforti, *Hopkins and the New Divinity Movement*, p. 100. Norton, *Liberty's Daughters*, p. 130.

19. Norton, ed., "'My Resting Reaping Times,'" pp. 518–521, 522, 524–526.

20. Osborn, *Memoirs*, p. 295. Osborn and Anthony, *Familiar Letters*, pp. 75, 96–97. Conforti, *Hopkins and the New Divinity Movement*, pp. 95–106.

21. Butler, *Awash in a Sea of Faith*, pp. 164–166, 179–181. Osborn and Anthony, *Familiar Letters*, pp. 110–111. Conforti, *Hopkins and the New Divinity Movement*, pp. 131–132.

22. Osborn and Anthony, *Familiar Letters*, p. 31.

23. Osborn, *Memoirs*, pp. 78, 252, 55, 49, 178, 270, 134. Sellers, *Market Revolution*, p. 206. Osborn, *Memoirs*, p. 130.

24. Sellers, *Market Revolution*, pp. 204–208.

25. Osborn, *Memoirs*, p. 56.

P A R T   I I

THE NINETEENTH CENTURY

The nineteenth century witnessed an astonishing explosion of religious expansion and creativity in the United States. Contrary to many myths about religious "decline" after the colonial period, the number of Americans who belonged to religious groups expanded dramatically. Only about 15 percent of American adults belonged to any religious group at the time of the American Revolution in the 1770s and 1780s, but this figure rose to about 45 percent by the 1890s. This dramatic expansion in religious belonging substantially outstripped America's remarkable population growth as well as its geographical expansion (this growth was not even, however, and the West remained the least involved with organized religion well into the twentieth century).

The religious expansion also brought far more religious groups to an already religiously pluralistic society. Some of the new groups arrived through immigration. Catholics and Jews greatly expanded their presence in American society; indeed, by the end of the nineteenth century, it was not sufficient to ask whether one was a Jew or Catholic, but whether one might be a Russian rather than a German Jew, or a Polish rather than an Italian or German Catholic.

Other new groups emerged because America proved so spiritually creative. If the Shakers, who first arrived in the 1780s, were a British import that prospered in America, the Mormons, who quickly expanded after Joseph Smith published the *Book of Mormon* in 1830, were entirely native born. Spiritualists (also originally British), Adventists (who believed the world would end in 1843 and whose disappointed followers later formed the Seventh Day Adventists), Christian Scientists (who emerged out of the "New Thought" movement under the leadership of Mary Baker Eddy), "fundamentalists" (conservative evangelical Protestants whose theology also bore British origins), and the African-American denominations that expanded so powerfully throughout the South after slavery's collapse in 1865—the African Methodist Episcopal Church, the African Methodist Episcopal Church Zion, the National Baptist Convention—all had utterly transformed the American spiritual landscape by 1900. They did far more than add important numbers to religious groups in nineteenth-century America: They added extraordinary richness to America's religious expression.

CHAPTER
7

Immigrants and Religion in America

At the time of the founding of the American Republic, the vast majority of citizens (and their slaves) were nominally Protestant. But all of this would change amidst a sea of "New," predominantly Catholic, immigrants in the nineteenth century. Already by 1850, the Roman Catholics were the largest single American denomination, and they would continue to expand exponentially throughout the century. Inevitably this Catholic influx would both enrich and complicate American life in ways that the Founders could not have foreseen. The Catholic immigrant experience proved to be conflicted on many fronts. Internally, Catholic priests and laity often found themselves divided over the question of "Americanism" and the extent to which Catholic congregations would be governed by a hierarchy that was disproportionately Irish and closely allied with the papacy in Rome. Externally, Catholics battled a quasi-official "Protestant Establishment" that sought to "melt" Catholic identity into a Protestant-based "American Way of Life" on every front from government and health care to public education. In the end, the Catholic immigrants would survive, faith intact, to become the wealthiest, most politically powerful Christian denomination in the nation.

In his presidential address to the American Society of Church History, Jay P. Dolan traces the close relationship between ethnicity and religion among immigrant groups. How closely attached were the immigrants to their gods? Is it possible that "religion" and "ethnicity" were one and the same thing for many new immigrant groups? What does Professor Dolan rely upon for evidence?

Additional Reading: Jon Butler, *The Huguenots in America: A Refugee People in New World Society* (Cambridge, Mass., 1983) describes the failure of French Protestants to prosper as a separate religious or ethnic group in the American colonies. Jay P. Dolan, *The Immigrant Church: New York's Irish and German Catholics, 1815–1865* (Baltimore, 1975) and Robert A. Orsi, *The Madonna of 115th Street: Faith and Community in Italian Harlem, 1880–1950* (New Haven, 1985) describe the rich and varied experience of Catholics in New York City, while Timothy L. Smith, "Religion and Ethnicity in America," *American Historical Review,* 83 (1978): 1155–1185, describes religion's frequent benefit from immigration to America. The best study of general prejudice against immigrants, much of it religiously based, remains John Higham, *Strangers in the Land: Patterns of American Navitism, 1860–1925* (New Brunswick, 1955).

Jay P. Dolan

The Immigrants and Their Gods: A New Perspective in American Religious History

Twenty years ago Jerald Brauer wrote an essay on the writing of American church history entitled, "Changing Perspectives on Religion in America." In this essay he noted that "change in perspective marks the writing of the history of religion in America." After discussing the work of Robert Baird and William Warren Sweet, the two historians whose perspectives most influenced the writing of American church history in the nineteenth and twentieth centuries respectively, Brauer then directed his attention to a third and new perspective. This new perspective had developed in the post-World War II era and was the result of the work of Sidney E. Mead, Sydney E. Ahlstrom, Winthrop S. Hudson, and others. Brauer described the new perspective by pointing out how it differed from the work of Sweet. It was clear to Brauer, however, that no one historian or school of historians had yet emerged whose perspective was able to dominate the landscape in the manner that Baird and Sweet had. There really was no new single perspective, but a variety of approaches and interpretations. In other words, in the late 1960s the discipline of American church history was in a state of flux, and "a number of young historians" were, in Brauer's words, "anxious to develop a new perspective through which to view the development and nature of Christianity in America."[1] Twenty years have passed since Brauer wrote those words, and since then a great amount of work has been done in American religious history and a new generation of historians has emerged. Nonetheless, the discipline is still in a state of flux and no one has been able to present a perspective or interpretation that commands the landscape.

I do not pretend to claim that I have found the magical interpretative key of church history past. In fact, no single interpretation or theory can explain adequately the more than three hundred years of American religious history. Nonetheless, I want to suggest a new perspective through which historians can view the historical development of religion in the United States. In order to appre-

Reprinted with permission from *Church History* 57 (March 1988), 61–72.

ciate the usefulness of this perspective some general remarks about the present state of American religious history are in order.

In the past twenty years an explosion of historical information has taken place. So many articles and books have been published that it has become virtually impossible for any one person to keep up with this information explosion. The positive side of this development is that we know a great deal more about the history of religion in the United States than we did twenty years ago. Moreover, historians have developed new approaches to the study of religious history which have challenged our assumptions and provided new models for doing history. New questions are being asked about the past and new trends in the study of religious history are evident.[2] This situation is as true of the historical study of religion in Europe as it is of American religious history, perhaps even more so. But there is also a dark side to this explosion of historical information. Because of this explosion any hope for synthesis or coherence has vanished. Thus, a central problem for historians is now to organize and integrate all this new information with the canon of American religious history.

This problem of the whole and its parts, or the one and the many, is common to all areas of history and has been discussed by many historians. Bernard Bailyn summed up one aspect of the problem in the following manner. "Modern historiography in general," he wrote, "seems to be in a stage of enormous elaboration. Historical inquiries are ramifying in a hundred directions at once, and there is no coordination among them. Even if one reduces the mass of new writings in the early modern period to the American field, and still further to the publications of card-carrying historians, the sheer amount of the writing now available is overwhelming." He then went on to note that "the one thing above all else that this outpouring of historical writings lacks is coherence."[3] For Bailyn and numerous others, defining the relationship between the whole and its parts is a major issue for historians. How then can we achieve coherence in the writing of history?

One way that historians of American religion can move toward a more coherent synthesis is to avoid a narrow, parochial approach to history. This faulty approach is found in all areas of history when such issues as nationalism and religious sectarianism motivate historians. The myopic vision of sectarian church history was commonplace not too long ago. It was divisive, narrow, and unappealing except to the zealot. Though it has not disappeared entirely, such an understanding of history is much less common today.

Denominational history is still very much in vogue and will remain so as long as the need exists for a more complete understanding of a specific religious tradition. Such histories are the building blocks from which any future synthesis will be constructed. But denominational history does not have to be parochial, and above all it should not be sectarian and apologetical. One way to avoid the intrinsically narrow nature of denominational history is to integrate such studies into the larger framework of American history in such a manner that they become central to the American experience.

To move toward more coherence in the writing of American religious history requires more than just avoiding narrow denominational history and sectarian myopia. It requires the grand vision. Historians must use a wide-angle lens when they look back at the past and seek to discover the dominant themes that shaped historical development. Such grand themes by their very nature clear away the debris of history and bring clarity and coherence to the past. They also transcend denominational boundaries and for this reason become more central to the American experience and thus more important to historians in search of a usable past.

Puritanism has become one of the grand themes of American colonial history. This theme served to organize that period of history, and the more Puritan studies progressed, the more understandable the past became. In fact, the theme of Puritanism unified colonial historiography to such an extent that it eventually dominated the field. At about the same time, however, historians began to look beyond Puritanism and the region of New England in order to understand colonial history more fully. Nonetheless, the study of Puritanism continues to have a unifying effect on the writing of colonial religious history.

More recently, the theme of evangelicalism has emerged as a grand theme in the study of nineteenth-century America. Books and articles on American evangelicalism continue to drop off the press in heaps. Like the grand theme of Puritanism, evangelicalism cuts across denominational boundaries and tends to unify the mass of historical information pertaining to the nineteenth century.[4] The study of evangelicalism, like the study of Puritanism, concentrates on the Protestant expression of this religious tradition. But this exclusive focus on Protestantism does not have to be. The evangelical tradition also found a home among Roman Catholics, and Puritanism was rooted in Augustine as well as Calvin.

Fundamentalism is another case in point. The study of religious fundamentalism necessarily must move beyond the trials and debates of the 1920s in the Protestant community and include manifestations of fundamentalism in other religious traditions. Fundamentalism, like Puritanism and evangelicalism, is not just a Protestant phenomenon. Jews, Muslims, and Catholics also possess fundamentalist inclinations. Historians of American religion, the majority of whom are Protestant, must move beyond the boundaries of the Protestant tradition and begin to write history that is reflective of the ecumenical climate of the late twentieth century. The same can be said for historians of American Catholicism and American Judaism. Denominational history is needed, but if we ever are going to achieve some measure of coherence in American religious historiography, we will need histories that are conceptually more inclusive, more ecumenical.[5]

The popularity of Puritan studies and evangelical studies reflects the dominance of intellectual history among historians of American religion. One reason for this is the long-standing bond between church history and theology; in fact, in some institutions church history really translates into the history of theology. Another reason is the intrinsic appeal of intellectual history and the ability it affords scholars to limit their focus to the thought of prominent clergy or laypersons. Such a focus, however, necessarily restricts the value of these studies since it excludes the vast numbers of laypeople who make up the religious population of the United States. In recent years scholars have sought to move beyond the pulpit to the pew in order to probe more thoroughly the rich complexities of American religious history. The major reason for this trend has been the emergence of social history.

In the past quarter century, social history has bulled its way in the market-place and now occupies a very prominent position in the historical academy. This statement is as true for the study of European history as it is for American history. The impact of social history on European history has been significant. An explosion of historical information has occurred, but along with this explosion has come the grand synthesis, the major interpretive work. One stunning example is John Bossy's book, *The English Catholic Community 1570–1870*. Not only is this book a fine example of the social history of religion, but it also has offered an entirely new interpretation of English Catholicism in the post-Reformation period. The French historian Jean Delumeau has achieved something similar in his work, *Catholicism Between Luther and Voltaire*. A leading member of the *Annales* school of historical studies, Delumeau has combined the long view of history with the thematic approach and has written a book that offers a major reinterpretation of the Counter-Reformation period. As the work of Bossy and Delumeau suggests, the social history of religion, with its focus on the religious life of the laity, brings coherence and synthesis to historical studies.[6]

The influence of social history on American religious history has not been as significant as in European studies. Nonetheless, the impact is noticeable. Its influence is seen especially in colonial history, where community studies and other types of social histories of colonial religion have enhanced our understanding of the role of religion in American life. Social history also has made its mark in nineteenth-century historiography in such areas as the study of revivalism. The new history of American Catholicism also mirrors the influence of social history.[7] Another major development in recent years has been the emergence of women's studies. Though significant cultural changes help to account for this development, the inclusive nature of social history has encouraged historians to examine the place of women and the role of gender in American society. Historians of American religion have not been as quick to follow this development, but every indication is that the issue of women and religion is moving from the periphery to the center in American religious historiography.[8]

Another area that has benefitted from the renaissance in social history is immigration history. In the past quarter century immigration history has come into its own, and in the United States it now has its own journal and professional organization, as well as several research centers that concentrate on immigration studies. The number of published works in this area is most impressive, and the implications of these studies for American religious history cannot be overlooked.[9]

Immigration has never attracted very much attention from American religious historians. In fact, until recently the historical study of immigration attracted the attention of only a handful of scholars. This lack of attention is illustrated very dramatically in the following statistic: of all the dissertations written on immigration between 1899 and 1972, 50 percent were done in one decade, 1962–1972.[10] Thus the increased interest in immigration history clearly is linked to the recent renaissance in social history as well as to other social developments. Even with this renewed interest in the study of the immigrants, historians of American religion have remained reluctant to turn their attention in this direction. A search of books reviewed in the four major historical journals between 1965 and

1985 revealed a total of fifty-eight books that treated both immigration and religion or immigration and the church. That is a meager number indeed. The bulk of those books that treated both immigration and religion were published in the 1965–1975 period, and since then a noticeable decrease has occurred. Another statistic further illustrates the meager attention given to the study of religion and immigration: of the 3,534 dissertations written in immigration history between 1885 and 1983, only 128, or 3.6 percent, treated the theme of religion.[11] Such neglect is understandable given the past history of American religious historiography. But to continue such neglect is inexcusable.[12] It would mean that historians would be overlooking not only a very valuable area of study, but one that brings greater coherence and understanding to the field of American religious history.

Even though immigration was an important aspect of colonial history and remains very much a part of contemporary American life, I want to focus on the nineteenth century, pointing out how the study of the immigrant experience not only will enrich our understanding of that era of American religious history, but also will bring greater coherence to the study of religion in the nineteenth century. Puritanism, evangelicalism, and fundamentalism are intellectual or theological principles, systems of belief, and for this reason they are able to provide coherence or synthesis for a particular period of study. As a theme or organizing principle of study, immigration can function in a similar manner and provide historians with a perspective through which they can view the development of American religion.

First, immigration was a phenomenon that cut across denominational boundaries. It was not limited to Italian Catholics, Russian Jews, or Norwegian Lutherans. It was a typically American experience. The 1916 census of religious bodies points this out very clearly. Of the 200 denominations studied, 132 reported a part or all of their congregations using a foreign language—a remarkably high percentage. Equally striking is the revelation that forty-two languages were in use in these churches. Among Roman Catholics, twenty-eight foreign languages were spoken; the Methodists reported twenty-two different languages in use. Clearly, immigration affected all religious traditions in nineteenth-century America.[13] Because it transcends denominational boundaries, the theme of immigration provides historians with a perspective that enables them to examine issues that are common to many religious traditions. For this reason it brings greater coherence and synthesis to the historical study of American religion.[14]

Second, studying the immigrant experience in the United States will force historians to acquire a comparative perspective. Religion is such a distinguishing feature of American life, and yet rarely is it studied comparatively. Immigration can provide that comparative perspective for the nineteenth century and force historians to look beyond the American scene and ask if what happened in America may have differed from what went on in the Old World. Did the establishment of the Dutch Reformed tradition in the United States differ significantly from developments in the Netherlands, and if so, why? Did the American environment alter the folk religion of Italian Catholics, and if so, how? Questions like these and countless others will enlarge our vision and force us, as Carl Degler noted, to "emphasize aspects of our past that may have gone unnoticed," and "call for explanations where none was thought necessary before."[15] Only through such a comparative perspective will we find out how distinctive the American religious experience was. And in discovering this distinctiveness, historians will better understand the development of religion in the United States.

By studying the immigrant experience American religious historians also will be able to draw on the vast amount of published material produced by immigration historians in the past twenty years. Not only will this lead church historians beyond the confines of their own field, but it also will provide them with a rich source of historical information pertinent to the study of religion in American life. Historians of immigration have examined the old-world background of the newcomers, their patterns of settlement in the United States, and their efforts to adjust to American society and the stresses and strains this adjustment caused. The issues of language and Americanization also have attracted the attention of immigration historians.

All of these issues have relevance for religious history. Realizing this, many historians of immigration have incorporated the theme of religion into their work. Some historians have focused on the issue of conflict in the immigrant community. Not surprisingly, a good deal of attention in such studies centers on religious conflict. In recent years historians have begun to examine the persistence of old-world cultures in the New World. One of the major keepers of culture was the church; this role was manifested in architecture, theology, and devotional practices. The relationship between religion and politics in the immigrant community also has attracted the attention of scholars, and their work has demonstrated how influential religion was in shaping politics in the immigrant community. These are just some of the issues pertinent to American religious history which historians of immigration have studied. A survey of these studies clearly reveals that religion was central to the immigrant experience. It was especially important in rural areas where community was essential to the survival of immigrant culture. If there was no church, there was no colony; and without a colony, the culture of the immigrants would have disappeared.[16]

Because the issues immigration historians study transcend denominational boundaries, they have a unifying influence on religious history. The persistence of religion in the New World is not something unique to Polish or Italian Catholics. Norwegian Lutherans and English Methodists experienced it as well. By examining this issue within various denominations, historians will be able to study an experience common to all immigrant communities. In this manner historians can bring more unity to a field that of its nature tends to be very splintered. This is what I have tried to do in my own work in American Catholic history. Not only have I relied on the writings of historians of immigration, but I have used immigration as an organizing theme in my work. This method has enabled me to bring a greater measure of synthesis and coherence to the history of nineteenth-century American Catholicism.[17] I believe that if a similar approach is used in the study of nineteenth-century American religious history, scholars will gain a richer understanding of the field and religion will become more central to the study of American history.

Convinced of the need for more coherence in American religious historiography and the value of immigration as an organizing principle, I have begun a long-range project which will study the immigrants and their gods. This project will focus on Catholics, Protestants, and Jews and will seek to understand the role and meaning of religion in the lives of the immigrants. The expanding body of literature in immigration history will help to make such a study feasible. Much of this literature, however, is limited to the social history of the institutional church. Equally important is the religious behavior of the people, a topic of special interest for me. I am eager to discover the religious world of the people, not just the institutional nature of the church. In other words, I am in search of the religious mentality of nineteenth-century immigrants.

In order to understand the religion of the people, historians have examined prayer books, sermons, rituals, hymns, diaries, and an array of other sources. For historians of nineteenth-century immigration, another resource exists which can be most helpful in opening up the religious world of the people: the letters that the immigrants wrote to their family and friends in the old country.

For the past two years I have been reading immigrant letters, both published and unpublished, in an effort to understand the religious world of the immigrants. Though I am still in the midst of this research, I have read enough letters from a variety of people that I can make some observations about the immigrants and their gods.

God-talk was an integral part of the immigrant letter. The God of the immigrants was always present, watching over the people, and many letters refer to God in this manner. Some groups were more inclined to God-talk than others. Irish Catholics and Jews were reticent when it came to God-talk. Norwegian Lutherans, Dutch Reformed, and English Methodists liked to talk about God in their letters. Among the Irish, God-talk was more a decorative feature of their letters, with "thanks be to God" often being about as effusive as they could get. Among Norwegian Lutherans, however, it was common for a letter writer to speak about God in a lengthy sentence or two. Only rarely does a letter writer discourse at length about God or religion; those so inclined tended to be individuals of an evangelical persuasion who often would write at length about a conversion experience.

The God of the immigrants was very busy. The divinity watched over the people at all times, protecting them from all types of adversity. A Dutch Reformed traveller recounted his experience on board a sailing vessel and the fear that gripped him and his wife as the ship began to roll on its side during a storm. Then, he wrote, "most likely, in answer to the prayer of one or other pious passenger, the Lord God spared us and caused the storm to abate." For a Norwegian Lutheran in Texas, God was always arranging "everything so well."[18] In a letter to his family in Ireland a young Irish immigrant, Denis Hurley, noted the historic importance of the new year of 1876 and then wrote the following prayerful remark: "May Almighty God be equally propitious to us with his favors in the New as He has been in the old. May he preserve us from family broils, bitterness and contention, and enable us to live in unity, peace and harmony to the end of our lives."[19] At first glance Hurley's remarks appear innocuous, the pious thoughts of a lonely young man. Nonetheless, they paint a portrait of the divinity that was common among all the people whose letters I have read. The God of nineteenth-century immigrants was a personal God who was in close touch with the people. The divinity was not remote, but was a constant companion, guide, and savior in whom the immigrants learned to trust "for everything." The God of the immigrants was not a stern Calvinist who stirred up fear in the people, nor did the divinity resemble the Roman Catholic God of judgment who was ready to pounce on people because of their sins.

The immigrants were not immune to suffering and hardship. Disillusionment with the New World, loss of the harvest, sickness, and death itself were frequent themes in their letters. Despite the harshness of these experiences, the immigrants put such suffering in a religious context. A Dutch Catholic writing from Wisconsin to his mother, brothers, and sisters talked about the misfortunes that had struck his family. "Of the four children which we brought from Holland," he wrote, "Johanna is the only one left." He continued, "misfortunes in our family have been too many and too severe. But it is God's will, and we must carry our Cross no matter how heavy it is." A Norwegian woman spoke of the suffering she had to endure and then stated that "God often sends us sufferings and tribulations to test our faith if we have patience both in good fortune and adversity."[20] The immigrants shared a common understanding of suffering and it was obvious that they had learned this teaching very well. In the good times they thanked God for many blessings; in the bad times they also saw the hand of God at work.

Another common concern reflected in these letters is the immigrants' belief in the afterlife. Moreover, they had a distinctive understanding of what life would be like beyond the grave; the most frequent comparison was to a place of reunion. An Irish letter writer who held a strong belief in the afterlife as well as in God's providence assured his mother that they would meet again in heaven. A Norwegian immigrant ended his letter with greetings to his mother, daughter, and "all my relatives, acquaintances, and friends." He then prayed that "we sometime with gladness may assemble with God in the eternal mansions where there will be no more partings, sorrows, no more trials, but everlasting joy and gladness."[21] This understanding of the afterlife as a place of reunion mirrored the social experience of the immigrants and the sense of separation inherent in the immigrant experience.

One of the most striking features in these letters is the absence of Jesus. For the vast majority of letter writers he seemed not to exist and thus he was rarely mentioned. The letter writers did not talk about sin either. Another striking omission is the absence among Catholic writers of any reference to Mary or individual saints or any devotions thought to be so central to Catholic belief. In fact, in many instances it would be difficult to determine the religious affiliation of the letter writers based on their references to religion. Denominational distinctiveness seldom appears, and because of this absence the belief systems of these people appear to be remarkably similar. They are spartan in their simplicity, with God, suffering, and the afterlife forming the major religious themes. The immigrants manifested a strong belief in a personal God who was very involved in their lives.

The one noticeable denominational difference that does appear in the letters that I read was the preoccupation of some writers from the more hierarchically structured churches (the Episcopal and Roman Catholic in particular) with clergy, ritual, and church. Irish Catholics frequently talked about the clergy, and in very positive terms. On occasion they also mentioned some Catholic rituals, mostly the mass and the parish mission. Both Episcopalians and Roman Catholics talked about the absence of church and clergy. When they did so, however, it was not in a religious or spiritual manner. It was more a statement of fact than an expression of belief. Methodists seldom commented on church and clergy. Good evangelicals that they were, Methodist letter writers were more inclined to talk about revivals and conversion. They met God at revivals and in a conversion experience, whereas Roman Catholics and Lutherans met God when they encountered suffering and the providential hand of the divinity.[22]

One striking observation that emerges from this study is the difference between the religion of Roman Catholic immigrants articulated in prayer books and rituals, and that found in their letters. The letters reveal a very plain religion centered around a God who cares about people. The prayer books and rituals reveal what I have called the Catholic ethos—a belief system grounded in sin, authority, ritual, and the miraculous.[23] These four marks of the Catholic ethos are found in prayer books and rituals developed by the clergy, whereas the letters of the people articulated a more plain religion or ethos. In the people's writings the emphasis was on simplicity, and especially on the miraculous or transcendent aspect of religion. They were not preoccupied with sin in their letters, whereas the clergy emphasized conversion from sin. This striking difference leads to at least two conclusions: as valuable as they are, immigrant letters cannot be the only resource used in searching for the religious world of people; and, as revealing as it might be, the behavior of people at church-sponsored rituals does not completely express the religion of the people. They practiced their religion in other settings, and oftentimes the beliefs professed on these occasions—in this case in the course of reflection and writing—were more plain and uncomplicated. The churches and their clergy emphasized certain aspects of religion, whereas the people emphasized other features of their belief. But these different expressions of religion did not contradict one another; rather, one complemented the other.

For too long, historians of American religion have neglected the study of the immigrant experience. There is no reason to continue this neglect. Now is the time for the recovery of immigration as a theme and organizing principle in the writing of American religious history. Social historians of immigration have provided us with a substantial amount of historical information pertinent to the study of American religious history, and we cannot afford to overlook this work. Moreover, historians of American religion are desirous of writing a more representative history, one that incorporates the laity as well as the clergy. The study of immigration encourages this development by focusing the attention of historians on the religious world of the people. Its helpfulness is especially clear when the focus is on immigrant letters, but is also true when the historian studies the social history of the immigrant community and church. The study of immigration also provides historians with a grand view of history, for it enables them to study themes that transcend denominational boundaries and can readily be extended over long periods of time. In addition, the study of immigration provides scholars with a comparative perspective, not only between the Old World and the New, but between various immigrant groups and religious traditions as well. Such a perspective will enable scholars to understand more completely the uniqueness and complexity of religion in American life. Finally, the use of immigration as an organizing theme of study can bring greater coherence to a field which, because of its denominational traditions, is inclined to splinter into disconnected phenomena.

NOTES

1. Jerald C. Brauer, "Changing Perspectives on Religion in America," in *Reinterpretation in American Church History,* ed. Jerald C. Brauer (Chicago, 1968), p. 19.

2. See Jay P. Dolan, "The New Religious History," *Reviews in American History* 15 (1987): 449–454; and Jon Butler, "The Future of American Religious History: Prospectus, Agenda, Transatlantic *Problematique,*" *William and Mary Quarterly,* 3d ser., 42 (1985): 167–183.

3. Bernard Bailyn, "The Challenge of Modern Historiography," *American Historical Review* 87 (1982): 2–3; see also the essay by Carl N. Degler, "In Pursuit of an American History," *American Historical Review* 92 (1987): 1–12.

4. See the bibliographic essay by Leonard I. Sweet, "The Evangelical Tradition in America," in *The Evangelical Tradition in America,* ed. Leonard I. Sweet (Macon, Ga., 1984), pp. 1–84, where he discusses this abundant literature.

5. See Jay P. Dolan, *Catholic Revivalism: The American Experience 1830–1900* (Notre Dame, Ind., 1978), for the Catholic side of evangelicalism in the nineteenth century; and Charles Hambrick-Stowe, *The Practice of Piety: Puritan Devotional Disciplines in Seventeenth Century New England* (Chapel Hill, N.C., 1982), for a broader understanding of Puritanism.

6. John Bossy, *The English Catholic Community 1570–1870* (New York, 1976); and Jean Delumeau, *Catholicism Between Luther and Voltaire: A New View of the Counter-Reformation,* trans. Jeremy Moiser (Philadelphia, 1977).

7. See Butler, "Future of American Religious History," for a discussion of some of these studies.

8. A major reason for this movement is the three-volume work, Rosemary Radford Ruether and Rosemary Skinner Keller, eds., *Women and Religion in America* (San Francisco, 1982–1986), which includes essays and primary documents related to American religious history from colonial times to the mid-twentieth century.

9. See Rudolph J. Vecoli, "The Resurgence of American Immigration History," *American Studies International* 17 (1979): 49–66; and Thomas J. Archdeacon, "Problems and Possibilities in the Study of American Immigrations and Ethnic History," *International Migration Review* 19 (1985): 112–134.

10. Edward Kasinec, "Resources in Research Centers," in *Harvard Encyclopedia of American Ethnic Groups,* ed. Stephan Thernstrom (Cambridge, Mass., 1980), p. 876.

11. My thanks to Susan White for searching the following journals: *American Historical Review, Journal of American History, Church History,* and *Catholic Historical Review;* A. William Hoglund, *Immigrants and Their Children in the United States: A Bibliography of Doctoral Dissertations, 1885–1982* (New York, 1986), p. viii.

12. See Jay P. Dolan, "Immigration and American Christianity: A History of Their Histories," in *A Century of Church History: The Legacy of Philip Schaff,* ed. Henry Warner Bowden (Carbondale, Ill., 1988), for an examination of the treatment of immigration in American church history during the past century.

13. *Religious Bodies 1916* (Washington, D.C., 1919), pt. 1, pp. 76, 85, and pt. 2, p. 457.

14. Timothy L. Smith demonstrated this in his essay "Religion and Ethnicity in America," *American Historical Review* 83 (1978): 1155–85.

15. Degler, "In Pursuit of an American History," p. 7.

16. The *Journal of American Ethnic History* and the *Immigration History Newsletter* are publications of the Immigration History Society and provide information on recent publications in this field of study.

17. Jay P. Dolan, *The American Catholic Experience: A History From Colonial Times to the Present* (New York, 1985).

18. Henry S. Lucas, ed., *Dutch Immigrant Memoirs and Related Writings*, 2 vols. (Seattle, 1955), 2:89; Theodore C. Blegen, ed., *Land of Their Choice: The Immigrants Write Home* (St. Paul, Minn., 1955), p. 348. My thanks to Michael Hamilton, who greatly assisted me in the study of published collections of immigrant letters.

19. Correspondence of Denis and Michael Hurley, Carson, Nevada, to parents in Clonakilty, Ireland, 6 January 1876, Archives of City of Cork, Ireland.

20. Lucas, *Dutch Immigrant Memoirs*, 2:168; Blegen, *Land of Their Choice*, p. 187.

21. Unidentified letter, 7 March 1876, Schrier Collection, Ms. 8347, National Library, Dublin, Ireland; Blegen, *Land of Their Choice*, p. 430.

22. See Charlotte Erickson, *Invisible Immigrants: The Adaptation of English and Scottish Immigrants in Nineteenth-Century America* (Coral Gables, Fla., 1972), pp. 87–92, 127–128.

23. Dolan, *American Catholic Experience*, pp. 221–240.

CHAPTER
8

Female Language in the American Religious Experience

Women's rising importance in nineteenth-century American religion could be seen in a variety of settings. Women who continued to be denied positions in church government and worship formed an array of voluntary societies that concentrated on reform issues ranging from education and temperance to Sunday schools and women's rights. They usually comprised most of the members of these societies, and in many they also comprised the principal leadership of the societies.

This essay by Barbara Welter describes how female language overtook American Christianity in the nineteenth century, sometimes with peculiar effects. Welter calls this the "feminization of American religion." How does Welter define "feminization?" How does she measure its extent? May we be sure that other sorts of evidence, such as literary sources, quantitative data, and material culture, would support Welter's thesis?

Additional Reading: Mary Ryan, *Cradle of the Middle Class: The Family in Oneida County, New York, 1790–1865* (New York, 1981) and Teresa Anne Murphy, *Ten Hours Labor: Religion, Reform, and Gender in Early New England* (Ithaca, 1992) describe women's religious experience in the old Northeast. Two books offer superb examinations of women's roles in southern religious communities: Evelyn Brooks Higginbotham, *Righteous Discontent: The Women's Movement in the Black Baptist Church, 1880–1920* (Cambridge, Mass., 1993) and Stephanie McCurry, *Masters of Small Worlds: Yeoman Households, Gender Relations, and the Political Culture of the Antebellum South Carolina Low Country* (New York, 1995). Colleen McDannell, *The Christian Home in Victorian America, 1840–1900* (Bloomington, 1986) compares the Protestant and Catholic home and women's crucial roles in creating them. Stephen J. Stein, *The Shaker Experience in America: A History of the United Society of Believers* (New Haven, 1992), Ronald L. Numbers, *Prophetess of Health: Ellen G. White and the Origins of Seventh-Day Adventist Health Reform,* revised ed. (Knoxville, 1992), and Stephen Gottschalk, *The Emergence of Christian Sci-*

ence in American Religious Life (Berkeley, 1973) describe the powerful roles played by Anne Lee, Ellen White, and Mary Baker Eddy in founding three of America's most distinctive religious groups—the Shakers, the Seventh-Day Adventists, and the Christian Scientists.

Barbara Welter
The Feminization of American Religion: 1800–1860

The relationships among nineteenth-century reform movements in the United States, their overlapping of personnel, and their disparity and similarity in motivations and results are popular themes in social history.[1] In the women's movement, which concentrated on obtaining suffrage but had more specific and more diffuse goals as well, almost all of the leaders and most of the followers were active in other reforms. Indeed, the abolitionist, temperance, and peace societies depended on their women members to lick envelopes, raise money through fairs, and influence their husbands and fathers to join in the good work. Although sometimes frustrated and even betrayed by these other reform movements, the woman's movement on the whole benefitted from the organizational experience, political knowledge, and momentum generated by other reforms. At the same time American religion, particularly American Protestantism, was changing rapidly and fundamentally. Although not overtly tied to the woman's movement, these religious changes may have had more effect on the basic problems posed by women than anything which happened within the women's organizations or in related reform groups. Because of the nature of the changes and the importance of their results to women's role, American religion might be said to have been "feminized." The term is used here, like the term "radicalization," to connote a series of consciousness-raising and existential, as well as experiential, factors which resulted in a new awareness of changed conditions and new roles to fit these new conditions.

For the historian to attempt an analysis of the relationships between institutions and movements at a given point in time is a fascinating exercise in social history. It may well be an exercise in futility, however, because he lacks sufficient knowledge of the society he studies, or because the theories of change and social dynamics are applicable only to the present, or at least not to the particular segment of the past which he explores. The hazards of the sociological vocabulary, the limited number of sources (or the overwhelming magnitude of sources in some areas), and the difference between sociological and historical logistics and time are significant barriers.[2] Within these limitations this article proposes to discuss the process of "feminization," to apply this definition to religion in America in the first half of the nineteenth century, and to explore the results of a "feminized" religion.

From Barbara Welter, "The Feminization of American Religion" in Mary Hartman and Lois Banner (eds.), *Clio's Consciousness Raised* (New York, 1973); reprinted by permission of the author.

In some ways the allocation of institutions or activities to one sex or another is a continuation of the division of labor by sex which has gone on since the cave dwellers. At certain times survival required that the strongest members of society specialize in a given activity. Once the basic needs of survival were met, other activities, not of current critical importance, could be engaged in. These more expendable institutions became the property of the weaker members of society which, in western civilization, generally meant women.[3] In the period following the American Revolution, political and economic activities were critically important and therefore more "masculine," that is, more competitive, more aggressive, more responsive to shows of force and strength. Religion, along with the family and popular taste, was not very important, and so became the property of the ladies. Thus it entered a process of change whereby it became more domesticated, more emotional, more soft and accommodating—in a word, more "feminine."

In this way the traditional religious values could be maintained in a society whose primary concerns made humility, submission, and meekness incompatible with success because they were identified with weakness. At the same time American Protestantism changed in ways which made it more useful to American society, particularly to the women who increasingly made up the congregations of American churches. Feminization, then, can be defined and studied through its results—a more genteel, less rigid institution—and through its members—the increased prominence of women in religious organizations and the way in which new or revised religions catered to this membership.

American churches had regarded it as their solemn duty to lead in building a godly culture, and the "city on the hill" which symbolized American aspirations had clusters of church steeples as its tallest structures.[4] In the nineteenth century the skyscraper would replace the steeple as a symbol of the American dream, and the ministers of God fought against this displacement. Politics captured the zeal and the time once reserved to religion, and the pulpits thundered against those men who mistakenly served power itself and not the Source of Power. The women's magazines and books of advice also warned against politics as a destroyer of the home. Cautionary tales equated the man who squandered his energy in political arguments with the man who drank or gambled; both were done at the expense of the home and religion.[5] Women and ministers were allies against this usurper, from which they were both excluded. Women were forbidden to go into politics because it would sully them; the church was excluded for similar reasons. Increasingly, in a political world, women and the church stood out as anti-political forces, as they did in an increasingly materialistic society, dominated by a new species, Economic Man. For women and the church were excluded from the pursuit of wealth just as much as they were kept out of the statehouse, and for the same rhetorical reasons. Both women and the church were to be above the counting house, she on her pedestal, the church in its sanctuary. Wealth was to be given them as consumers and as reflections of its makers.[6]

Democracy, the novel by Henry Adams, gives a fascinating insight into what happens when a woman ventures near the source of power, politics, and Washington. In venturing so near the sun she burns her wings and, limping badly, heads for home.[7] Human nature as defined by the church and human nature as defined by the state seemed totally different in the eighteenth century when the idea of original sin conflicted with the Jeffersonian hopes for perfectability through democracy. During the nineteenth century the churches moved toward the eighteenth-century premise of progress and salvation. Democracy, on the other hand, seems to have reverted to a more cynical or perhaps realistic view of human nature, closer to the Calvinist tradition. Women, however, precisely because they were above and beyond politics and even beyond producing wealth, much less pursuing it, could maintain the values of an earlier age. If women had not existed, the age would have had to invent them, in order to maintain the rhetoric of eighteenth-century democracy. As the religious view of man became less harsh, it meshed nicely with the hopes of Jefferson and Jackson.

The hierarchy, ministers, and theologians of most religions remained male. There were almost no ordained female ministers—Antoinette Brown Blackwell was an exception and not too happy a one—and few evangelical or volunteer female ministers.[8] When Orestes Brownson growled about a "female religion" he was referring largely to the prominent role which women played in congregations and revivals. However, he was also sniping at the tame minister, whom he caricatured with such scorn as a domesticated pet of spinsters and widows, fit only to balance teacups and mouth platitudes. Brownson's solution, to join the Church of Rome, undoubtedly was motivated by a number of personal and ideological reasons. Not the least of these, however, in the light of his contempt for feminine and weak Protestantism, was the patriarchal structure of the Catholic Church.[9]

Besides their prominence during services, women increasingly handled the voluntary societies which carried out the social office of the churches, by teaching Sunday school, distributing tracts, and working for missions. This was only the external sign of the internal change by which the church grew softer and the religious life less rigorous. Children could be baptized much earlier. The idea of infant damnation, which Theodore Parker rightly said would never have been accepted had women been in charge of theology, quietly died around the middle of the century.[10] These changes were of great benefit to women's peace of mind. Now, if a diary recorded the loss of a child, at least the loss was only a temporary one. Women had found the prospect of parting forever from a beloved child, because there had been no baptism or sign of salvation, almost unbearable. The guilt with which these women so often reproached themselves at least need not concern eternal suffering, and the difference mattered to a believer.

The increasing softness and flexibility in the American churches were reflected in their role in social stratification as well as in their theology. The highly touted classless society of the Revolution was becoming increasingly stratified and self-conscious. The churches represented all different stages in the transition from wilderness to social nicety. The revivals had to fight not only hardness of heart but the lack of social prestige they entailed. Anglo-Catholicism had stood for a softer life both materially and spiritually since at least the time of the Glorious Revolution. it was also to a degree partially identified with higher social and economic status. The Episcopal Church and the Presbyterian Church were increasingly the churches of the well-to-do, and they offered their members a higher social status to correspond with their wealth. Women used their membership in a more prominent church as an important means of establishing a pecking order within the community.[11]

The male principle was rarely challenged by Trinitarians or Unitarians—whether three or one, God was male (and probably white). However, during the first half of the nineteenth century two ideas gained popularity which showed an appreciation for the values of femaleness—the first was the idea of the Father-Mother God and the second was the concept of the female Saviour. The assignation to God of typically female virtues was nothing new. Presumably a God who was defined as perfect would have all known virtues, whether or not he had a beard. The Shakers went farther, however, and insisted that God had a dual nature, part male and part female.[12] Theodore Parker used the same theme, in pointing out the need for female virtues, particularly the lack of materialism, and finding these virtues in a Godhead which embodied all the symbols of mother's mercy along with father's justice.[13] Joseph Smith consoled his daughter with the thought that in heaven she would meet not only her own mother, who had just died, but she would also "become acquainted with your eternal Mother, the wife of your Father in Heaven." Mormon teaching posited a dual Parenthood within the Godhead, a Father and a Mother, equally divine.[14]

This duality of God the Father with a Mother God almost necessitated the idea of a female counterpart of Christ. Hawthorne in *The Scarlet Letter* has Hester muse on the coming of a female saviour. She reflects that because of her sin she is no longer worthy to be chosen.[15] The female saviour is an interesting amalgam of nineteenth-century adventism, the need for a Protestant counterpart to the cult of the Virgin, and the elevation of pure womanhood to an almost supernatural level. If the world had failed its first test and was plunging into an era of godlessness and vice, as many were convinced, then a second coming seemed necessary. Since the failure of the world also represented a failure of male laws and male values, a second chance, in order to effect change, should produce a different and higher set of laws and values.[16] The role was typecast for the True Woman, as the Shakers and the Mystical Feminists (and later the Christian Scientists) were quick to point out.

The changes in interpretation of Christ which made him the greatest of humans and stressed his divinity in the sense that all men are divine were also interpreted as feminine. The new Christ was the exemplar of meekness and humility, the sacrificial victim.[17] Woman too was the archetypal victim, in literary and religious symbolism. If Christ was interpreted as a human dominated by love, sacrificing himself for others, asking nothing but giving everything and forgiving his enemies in the bargain, he was playing the same role as the true woman in a number of typical nineteenth-century melodramatic scenarios. As every reader of popular fiction knew in the early nineteenth century, woman was never more truly feminine than when, on her deathbed, the innocent victim of male lust or greed, she forgave her cruel father, profligate husband, or avaricious landlord. A special identification with suffering and innocence was shared by both women and the crucified Christ. "She was a great sufferer," intoned one minister at a lady's funeral, "and she loved her crosses."[18]

The minister who interpreted this feminized Christ to his congregation spoke in language which they understood. By 1820 sermons were being preached on the "godless society" which spent its time and money on politics and the pursuit of wealth, and appeared in church "only at weddings and funerals."[19] Observers of the American scene noted frequently that American congregations were composed primarily of women and that ministers spoke to their special needs. Mrs. Trollope cast her cold eye over the flounce-filled pews and remarked that "it is only from the clergy that the women of America receive that sort of attention which is so dearly valued by every female heart throughout the world. . . . I never saw, or read, of any country where religion had so strong a hold upon the women, or a slighter hold upon the men."[20] One reason for this prominence was, she felt, that only the clergy listened to women, all other ranks of man's society and interests were closed to them.

The hymns of this period also reflect the increasing stress on Christ's love and God's mercy. The singer is called upon to consider Christ his friend and helper. (To some degree, if the period before the Civil War is seen as one of feminization for Protestantism, the period following it might be termed a period of juvenilization, for increasingly the child as the hope and redeemer of his parents and society is stressed.) Woman's active role in the writing of hymns used in the Methodist, Presbyterian, Episcopal and Congregational hymnals at this time is very small. They contributed almost no music but did quite a few translations, particularly from the German. They were represented best in the lyrics to children's hymns.[21] It is perhaps significant that a hymn which became extremely popular at weddings had words written by a woman. "O Perfect Love" exhorts the young couple to emulate the perfect love of Christ in their own marriage:

> O perfect life, be thou their full assurance
> Of tender charity and steadfast faith,
> Of patient hope, and quiet, brave endurance,
> With childlike trust that fears nor pain nor death.

This was a pattern for domestic bliss much favored by women and the church, since it required the practice of those virtues they both cherished so highly—and which were found increasingly in only one partner of marriage. The implication is one which was made more explicit in the women's magazines: the burden of a marriage falls on the wife; no matter how hard her bed, it is her duty to lie on it. Marriage, and life itself, were at best endurance contests and should be entered in a spirit of passive acceptance and trust.

Another great favorite, "Nearer My God, to Thee," written by Sarah Adams in 1841, carried the same message: "E'en though it be a cross, that raiseth me; Still all my song would be, Nearer, My God, to thee, nearer to thee."[22] The hymns of the Cary sisters, Phoebe and Alice, repeated this theme with variations: "No Trouble Too Great But I Bring It to Jesus," and "To Suffer for Jesus Is My Greatest Joy," for example.[23] Another favorite stressed the total dependence of the singer on Jesus: "I Need Thee Every Hour."[24] The lyrics to this lend themselves all too well to the *double entendre* as those of us forced to sing it in Sunday Schools remember to our shame, but in fairness to our interpretations it is true that the imagery in many of these hymns seems very physical. In the desire to stress the warmth and humanity of Christ, he becomes a very cozy person; the singer is urged to press against him, to nestle into him, to hold his hand, and so forth. A love letter to Christ was the only kind of love letter a nice woman was allowed to publish, and sublimation was as yet an unused word. If Julia Ward Howe had called her book of love lyrics a book of hymns even Hawthorne (who thought her husband should have whipped her for the book) would have approved.

The ultimate in such expressions of total absorption in Christ and a yielding up of an unworthy body and soul to his embrace is the widely-sung "Just As I Am, Without One Plea."

> Just as I am, without one plea,
> But that thy blood was shed for me,
> And that thou bidd'st me come to thee,
> O Lamb of God, I come, I come.
>
> Just as I am, though tossed about
> With many a conflict, many a doubt;
> Fightings and fears within, without,
> O Lamb of God, I come, I come.
>
> Just as I am, poor, wretched, blind;
> Sight, riches, healing of the mind,
> Yea, all I need, in thee to find,
> O Lamb of God, I come, I come . . .
>
> Just as I am: thy love unknown
> Has broken every barrier down;
> Now to be thine, yea, thine alone.
> O Lamb of God, I come, I come.[25]

Since so many of women's problems were presumably physical and thus, like the weather, beyond help, it behooved them to endure what they could not cure. The "natural" disasters of childbirth, illness, death, loss of security through recurrent financial crises—all made "thy will be done" the very special female prayer, especially since submission was considered the highest of female virtues. In their hymns women expressed this theme of their lives, as a kind of reinforcement through repetition. However the woman who wanted a more active role in religion than enduring, or even than teaching Sunday school, had several possibilities open to her at this time. She could become a missionary, she could practice an old religion in a new setting, or she could join a new religion which gave women a more active role.

The Christianizing of the West, indeed the domesticating of the West, was probably the most important religious, cultural, and political event of the first half of the nineteenth century.[26] So long as the West was unhampered by the appurtenances of civilization, including women with their need for lace curtains, for coffee cups and Bibles and neighbors within chatting distance—it was an unknown and possibly dangerous phenomenon. All the Protestant religions and Catholicism as well considered it their special duty to bring God and women westward as soon as possible. Law, order, and consumers were enhanced by the presence of churches and women. Missionary work appealed to women as a way to have an adventure in a good cause, although the Mission Boards which passed on applications were firm in ruling out "adventure" as a satisfactory motive. Missions to far off China or Burma were usually denied to the single woman, but the determined girl could quickly find a husband in other zealous souls determined on the same career. The majority of American missionaries in the period before the Civil War stayed within the continent, taking the Christianizing of the Indians as their special challenge and duty.[27]

Mary Augusta Gray reflected on the interior dialogue with which she came to her missionary vocation:

> Ever since the day when I gave myself up to Jesus, it had been my daily prayer, "Lord, what wilt thou have me do?" and when the question, "Will you go to Oregon as one of a little band of self-denying missionaries and teach these poor Indians of their Saviour?" was suddenly proposed to me, I felt that it was the call of the Lord and I could not do otherwise.[28]

The missionaries to China usually went with a sense of doom and impending martyrdom, and the heroic exploits of such women as Ann Hasseltine Judson were fodder for this belief. Mrs. Judson had died, as she knew she would, far from home but near to Jesus, and thus her story became one much favored in children's biographical literature.[29] However even the home missions carried the same possibility for martyrdom, as the fate of Narcissa and Marcus Whitman proved.[30] There is no question but that the aspiring missionary was aware of this possibility and that he welcomed it. Part of the reason for this is perhaps the theology of the period which taught that the death of a martyr assured heaven. The desire for death in the service of the Lord seems in the cases of some missionary women to be their strongest motive.

Eliza Spaulding, a Connecticut girl who had been converted at an early age, found that distributing tracts and doing visiting among the poor was not enough for her. She asked divine guidance about her future and received the impulse to go to Oregon. When her husband tried to dissuade her she replied: "I like the command just as it stands, 'Go ye into all the world,' with no exception for poor health. The dangers in the way and the weakness of my body are his; duty is mine." Mrs. Spaulding survived the trip, leaving the following diary entry:

> Oh, that I had a crust of bread from my mother's swill pail. I cannot sit on that horse in the burning sun any longer. I cannot live much longer. Go on, and save yourself and carry the Book to the Indians. I shall never see them. My work is done. But bless God that He has brought me thus far. Tell my mother that I am not sorry I came.

Her husband wrote to the Mission Board: "Never send another white woman over these mountains, if you have any regard for human life," but of course they did, for the women clamored to come to the Indians and to death, if need be.[31]

Although the West has been seen as a fertile ground for democratic innovations, this was not necessarily true for women's role. Simply because of the lack of numbers, most western churches gave women the freedom to participate in church services, and the West was the natural breeding place for such women evangelists as Carry A. Nation and Aimee Semple MacPherson. However there was still pressure to conform to the traditional female role within religion, as Narcissa Whitman wrote shortly before her death:

> In all the prayer meetings of this mission the brethren only pray. I believe all the sisters would be willing to pray if their husbands would let them. We are so few in number, it seems as if they would wish it, but many prefer the more dignified way. My husband has no objection to my praying, but if my sisters do not, he thinks it quite as well for me not to.[32]

In the West, but especially in the East, the spirit of revival was strong during this period. The language, like that of the hymns, was sexual in its imagery and urged the penitent to "stop struggling and allow yourself to be swept up in His love." Obviously this kind of imagery had a familiar ring to women, for it was in similar language that they were encouraged to submit to their husbands. Whether in the divine or human order, woman was constantly urged to be swept away by a torrent of energy, not to rely on her own strength which was useless, to sink into the arms of Jesus, to become absorbed and assimilated by the Divine Will—in other words, to relax and enjoy it. The fantasies of rape were nourished by this language and by the kind of physical sensations which a woman expected to receive and did receive in the course of conversion. "A trembling of the limbs," "a thrill from my toes to my head," "wave after wave of feeling," are examples of female reaction to the experience of "divine penetration."[33]

Mrs. Maggie N. Van Cott, who called herself the first lady licensed to preach in the Methodist Episcopal Church in the United States, told in her autobiography of receiving the "great blessing of fullness" as a result of which she was "perfectly emptied of self and filled with the Spirit of God." In showing her the way, God had announced "I am a jealous God; thou shalt have no other Gods before me," which she interpreted to mean that her Master wanted her complete devotion.[34]

Ellen G. White had a similar vision in which she was shown a steep frail staircase, at the top of which was Jesus. As she fell prostrate, her guide gave her a green cord "coiled up closely," which she could uncoil to reach Him. From that time "my entire being was offered to the service of my Master."[35]

Particularly interesting are those first-person accounts which discuss these experiences and then go on to say how little her husband understands her and how he tries to interfere with this wholehearted commitment to Christ. "Oh, the bliss of that moment, when my soul was enabled to cast all her care upon Jesus and feel that *her* will was lost in the will of God," rhapsodized Myra Smith at 4:14 a.m. one Sunday. Soon after she wrote: ". . . I find sweet comfort in doing the will of God instead of my own. . . . I feel that God calls me to labor in a more special manner than he usually does females. . . . I am not understood by my husband and children but I don't murmur, or blame them for it. I know they can't tell why

I seem at times lost to everything around me."[36] Richard Hofstadter points out that revivalism was one of the manifestations of a pervasive anti-intellectualism in mid-nineteenth-century America.[37] However it can be further annotated by means of the popular custom of dividing qualities into male and female categories. By this nomenclature all the intuitive and emotional qualities are most natural to women, all the cerebral and intellectual policies of linear thought the prerogative of men. When in terms of religion a more intuitive, heartfelt approach was urged it was tantamount to asking for a more feminine religious style.[38]

Although at the intellectual and, therefore, presumably "masculine" end of the scale, Transcendentalism might also be considered representative of certain feminine standards. One hanger-on to Transcendental circles and ardent feminist, Caroline Dall, saw Anne Hutchinson as the first Transcendentalist and, by extension, the first feminist in the American colonies.[39] Her argument was that antinomianism was an open door to the exercise of individual rights, by either sex or by any group. If God, not the ordained clergy, picks His spokesmen, then women are as likely as any to be among the chosen, for as any popular novel or sermon would have it, women are more religious, more noble, more spiritual than men— so all the more likely to be a vehicle for God's message. Besides, if one adheres to the principle of autonomous conversion, then there is no way to second-guess the Almighty; any soul may receive Him, no sex barred. In the Quaker religion the Inner Light was expected to be equally indiscriminate in the choice of vessels to illuminate, and the Society of Friends practiced theoretical religious equality from its beginnings.

The Transcendentalists accepted a similar definition of equality before God. All souls were equally divine, without regard to sex or race. As Nathaniel Frothingham points out, Transcendentalism was a part of the Woman's Rights Movement in the most profound sense in that it posited her as an innate equal, whose potential had been hampered by society. Ralph Waldo Emerson went through a number of phrases in the formulation of his own position on women. His theoretical approach, contained in a number of essays, was sometimes at variance with the way in which he actually coped with his Aunt Mary, his two wives, and the irritatingly untheoretical presence of Margaret Fuller. In an essay, "Woman," Emerson tried to analyze the religious style of females. He concluded that ". . . the omnipotence of Eve is in humility." This, he continued, was the direct opposite of male style, which was to stress the necessity and potency of the male to the object loved. Religion perforce requires humility, since God does not depend on human strength. Women also, according to Emerson, possess to a high degree that "power of divination" or sympathy which the German Romantics prized so highly. They have "a religious height which men do not attain" because of their "sequestration from affairs and from the injury to the moral sense which affairs often inflict. . . ." It was therefore not surprising that "in every remarkable religious development in the world, women have taken a leading part."[40]

The idea of a regenerated reconstituted society was important to most members of the Hedge Club, and they looked optimistically towards an America in which man would leave behind his chains and emerge closer to nature and nature's God. The concept of ideal manhood and of ideal womanhood was often discussed at these meetings, and, of course, in Margaret Fuller's Conversations.[41] Womanhood was believed to be, in principle, a higher, nobler state than manhood, since it was less directly related to the body and was more involved with the spirit; women had less to transcend in their progress. "I trust more and more every opportunity will be offered to women to train and use their gifts, until the world finds out what womanhood is," wrote William Henry Channing. "My hope for society turns upon this; the regeneration of the future will come from the exalting influence of woman."[42] Most of these Transcendentalists were unconvinced about woman's role in politics, but they were totally convinced that she represented the highest and best parts of man.

Margaret Fuller contributed another important idea to the feminization of religion in her stress on the importance of the will. As historians such as John William Ward have pointed out, this belief in the power of the American will was typical of Jacksonian America. Like other aspects of the so-called American character, however, it did not necessarily hold true for all groups within the society. (David Riesman, for example, has reconsidered some of his statements about American character because of the remoteness of the female half of the population from his producer economy.)[43] For Margaret Fuller the will was the instrument to power for women even more than for men, and she set out to convince her world of this fact. Woman traditionally was urged to negate her will, or at least to yield it up to her father, her husband, and her God. Margaret Fuller told her to actively pursue her goals, to "elect" her destiny. Miss Fuller possessed Emerson's "spark of divinity" by which she was able to convince the young girls and wives who flocked to her that they too were divine and could go out and accomplish great (but unnamed) things. This preaching to women of their worth before God and man was sound Transcendental doctrine, but the stress on female worth, on transcendent womanhood, was a personal interpretation of Margaret Fuller. She gloried in her role of Sibyl and relished all references to her as Delphic and/or Oracular.[44] The cult of the will, as Donald Myers writes, found its triumph in Christian Science, also the religion of a woman, in which even death bows to positive thought.[45] Margaret Fuller's intent and fervid preoccupation with the making-over of the self presented a considerable threat to the men in her circle. For if sex itself, as well as health, family, education, income, all counted for nothing—what standards remained? It was perhaps the vicious circle of antinomianism after all; a religion open to the vagaries of God's choice or the boundaries of the human will is a religion without class lines and certainly without sex discrimination.

The Transcendentalists sought concrete expression of their philosophy in the community of Brook Farm, and the setting up of ideal communal societies was one way in which nineteenth-century religion expressed its dissatisfaction with past religious styles and its hope for the future. The equal rights of Transcendentalism were much in evidence at Brook Farm. One participant in that noble experiment recalled hearing a lecture on women's rights during his time in residence. The young lady speaker:

> . . . was much put out, after orating awhile, to note that her glowing periods were falling on dull ears. Our womenfolk had all the rights of our men-folk.

They had an equal voice in our public affairs, voted for our offices, filled responsible positions, and stood in exactly the same footing as their brethren. If
women were not so well off in the outer world, they had only to join our community or to form others like it.[46]

In the constitution of Brook Farm, as in many other communal societies, there
are promises to the women members that they would be liberated from the
tyranny of men and of the stove, and given greater freedom to develop their own
identities. Charles Nordhoff, writing on the influence of women in utopian communities in 1875, found that women's participation in discussion gave them "contentment of mind, as well as enlarged views and pleasure in self-denial." Women
in communal life found stability, which they needed and wanted, and many small
comforts provided by the men for which "the migrating farmer's wife sighs in
vain." The simplicity of dress typical of many groups was "a saving of time and
trouble and vexation of spirit." Their greatest contribution to communal society
was their "conservative spirit," which operated in the aggregate as it had in
family life. Nordhoff concluded that women expressed the basic excuse for being
of the communist society, for her "influence is always toward a higher life."[47]

When the commune moved from the planning stages to the land itself, somehow or other, women ended up in the kitchen or the laundry. Men might serve on
these committees, but the overriding principle of the division of labor mandated
their presence outdoors. In the communal societies whose records I studied, there
is no record of any complaint on the part of the women, nor was there any
recorded instance of women challenging their husbands on a given vote. There
seems also to be no pattern of a woman's bloc.[48] But the actual role of women is
less important than the way in which the changed pattern of social life was supposed to bring true equality to both sexes and liberate man from his own tyranny
at the same time woman was freed from the conventional bonds of family life.

The Fourierist philosophy, which, so far as recorded sources tell, was never
completely followed in the United States, provided for a good deal of sexual freedom within a definition of human nature which relied on "natural affinities."
Parts of the human race were exempted from monogamy because they had "natural affinities" towards several members of the opposite sex. The fact that women,
as well as men, might be expected to have these preferences was regarded as "peculiarly French," and not relevant to the American Phalanx.[49]

Within the Americanized version of Fourierism there was much "wholesome
intercourse" between the sexes. The opportunity to work and study and talk together was rare enough for middle-class American youth, and the Phalanxes gave
them much more freedom than most families allowed. The great charm of the
communal life, one remembered fondly long after the community itself was a
thing of the past, "was in the free and natural intercourse for which it gave opportunity, and in the working of the elective affinities."[50] The young women who participated in these experiments were emboldened to pursue lives as teachers or reformers after they left the Phalanx. The Transcendental idea of the infinite worth
of the individual and his ability to work out his destiny was greatly appealing to
these young women. Even if women continued to do woman's work and find

their greatest individual destiny in monogamous marriage, there was a statement of equality and of alternatives on the record.

The experiment at Oneida, conducted by John Humphrey Noyes as an example of his Perfectionist religion, was a particularly interesting application of new religion to women. One of the avowed purposes of the Oneida Community was to give women "extended rights" within "an extended family." The way in which Noyes defined these rights was sharply criticized by his contemporaries and has not received very sympathetic treatment from historians. In many ways he really was, as he claimed to be, "Woman's best friend." Noyes believed that the search for complete perfection began with control over one's own body. For women this was a complicated phenomenon, involving not only the marital rights but the right to choose whether she wished to have children. Noyes spoke very cogently about the trauma of the nineteenth-century woman, who bore her children with such pain and hope, and saw them die as infants.[51] In a society which defined woman as valuable largely in relation to her ability to bear children, it was logical that women thought of their own worth in those terms. When a child died it was an affirmation of personal guilt and possibly sin. What have I done, the bereaved mother asked her God, that I should be punished? Pages of women's diaries are filled with personal recriminations. For months she flagellated herself with the remedies she might have used, the errors of judgment she could have avoided, the ways in which she might have offended a jealous God. Noyes proposed to define her worth in different terms: she was a loving companion and "yoke-fellow" on the road to perfection. Childbearing was only part of her duty, to be engaged in sparingly and under controlled conditions, and to be separated from sex.[52] In terms of woman's self-image this proposal was one of the most radical of the century.

The form of birth control used by Noyes, which he called "male continence," consisted in "self-control" which prolonged intercourse but stopped the act short of ejaculation. Interestingly enough, this insistence on control was only for the man; there was no limit to the amount of pleasure a woman was allowed to get from the act. Moreover, sexual intercourse was accepted as a good in itself, completely outside the propagation of the species, and as an important means of self-expression for both sexes. Noyes went so far in identifying the sex act with perfectionism as to assert that sexual intercourse was practiced in heaven. This insistence on the joys of sex was rare enough, but, couched in terms of a conjugal relation which promised equal rights of choice and no penalty of childbearing on the woman, it was extraordinary. Perfectionism stressed the "giving, not the claiming," the act of loving, rather than the social and economic benefits of marriage.[53] In these ways, it acceded to the feminine spirit and role. The nineteenth-century belief that "love is a game, nothing more to a man / But love to a woman is life or death," that "love is woman's whole existence," was applied by Noyes to both sexes. "We should pray, give us this day our daily love, for what is love but the bread of the heart. We need love as much as we need food and clothing, and God knows it. . . ."[54] In the popular jargon of phrenology, Noyes separated "amativeness" from both "union for life" and "procreativeness." In the phrenological manuals, amativeness was considered to be particularly well developed in men;

the other two qualities, along with "philoprogenitiveness" to be peculiarly suited to female skulls.[55] Noyes stressed love for both sexes and freedom of choice for both, which gave to women the continuation of her preoccupation with love plus the right to a repetitive use of her loving. Marriage at Oneida was a working out of the feminine rhetoric of love on a sequential basis.

Although Mormonism was treated as a great foe of women's rights, and even its female proponents agreed that it placed the male in a dominant role, it had certain components which made it part of the overall movement towards "feminization." Like Perfectionism it claimed to be acting in the name of a better life for women. "No prophet or reformer of ancient or modern times has surpassed, nay, has equalled, the Prophet Joseph Smith in the breadth and scope of the opportunities which he accorded womanhood," wrote a dutiful and satisfied daughter of both the Prophet and Zion.[56] Mormonism required its followers to accept the words of their spiritual Father without murmur, and to obey the precepts of authority. The important concept of the Mormon priesthood is one which excludes women (as well as blacks by some interpretations). However, Joseph Smith, when the women of his group asked him for a written constitution for their Relief Society, told them he would give them "something better for them than a written constitution. . . . I will organize the sisters under the priesthood after a pattern of the priesthood. . . . The Church was never perfectly organized until the women were thus organized."[57]

Thus the woman of the Church of Jesus Christ of the Latter Day Saints claimed that they were admitted as "co-workers and partners" in the important work of attaining salvation. They were in the priesthood only when taken by their husbands and only with their husband could they enter into a special heaven. Their consent was required for plural marriage, which became their passport— again, only with their husbands—to the highest stages of celestial bliss. And yet, patriarchal as it was, women were not ignored by this new religion. Indeed, they were given explicit and critical directions for salvation. No man could get to heaven alone, by any combination of faith or good works; he had to come bringing his family with him. Women could legitimately claim that Mormonism recognized their importance more than any other religion because it tied them to their husbands for all time and eternity. Motherhood was stressed in Utah even more than in the rest of American society, but it was the importance of producing souls not bodies that counted. Since every woman, in theory, could be united to the man of her choice, she could go to heaven with her love, not her forced compromise. Recognizing the fact that society gave women status only as a married woman and as a mother, the Mormons gave each woman the opportunity to have that coveted status in this life and in the next. What is surprising is not the formulation of Celestial Marriage, but the fervor with which Mormon women defended it as important to their ideas of themselves as valuable and valid persons.[58]

Like the Church of the Latter Day Saints, Roman Catholicism during this pre-Civil War period had both masculine and feminine manifestations. The patriarchal system of authority, which so pleased Orestes Brownson, has already been mentioned. The diatribes against Rome which were prevalent in the 1830s and 1840s stressed this authoritarian and anti-democratic aspect of the Church. In other words, Catholics were not allowed to exercise their masculine prerogatives of intellectual autonomy and independent judgment. When a modest number of conversions to Roman Catholicism occurred during the last days of Brook Farm, some observers found the cause to be the discouragement and disappointment which the failure of that experiment created in its members. Most of the converts were female, and disparaging statements were made about the need to abandon the heritage of the New England Protestant (masculine) Church to find solace in a more soothing, structured (feminine) religion.[59]

The letters of the converted Fourierists do nothing to deny that they found the Church of Rome more suitable to their needs, but their emphasis is not on feminine dependence but on womanly warmth. Sophia Ripley wrote to a sympathetic friend that she found "the coldness of heart in Protestantism and my own coldness of heart in particular" to be repugnant. After her conversion she saw herself clearly for the first time: "I saw that all through life my ties with others were those of the intellect and imagination, and not human heart ties; that I do not love anyone. I never did, with the heart, and of course never could have been worthy in any relation." Catholicism united her for the first time with humanity, and that chill intellectual pride which New Englanders wore like Lady Eleanor's mantle at last melted away. "I saw above all that my faith in the Church was only a reunion of my intellect with God," and not a union of hearts. To her mentor Bishop Hughes she poured out her fears that "this terrible deathlike coldness" had produced a "heart of stone" which even the love of Christ could not melt. He reassured her that if she had been born in the Church perhaps her nature would have been softened, but she must offer to God not the heart she coveted but the heart she had: "Oh God, take this poor cold heart of mine, and make of it what thou wilt. . . . This heart of yours is a cross which you must bear to the end if needs be."[60] Catholicism, then, at least to some of its members, incorporated the love and warmth so characteristic of women and so necessary to them.

Like Mormonism, Roman Catholicism was also regarded as a religion for the many, not the few. This sense of religion as a means of keeping down intellectual arrogance and spiritual pride is one which accords with a subtle but important aspect of female definition during this period. In Hawthorne's stories and novels the woman is the symbol of the earth, the tie with domestic detail and bodily warmth which prevents man from soaring too high or sinking too low.[61] Louis Auchincloss has called women "guardians and caretakers" because of their role in preserving literary and cultural traditions.[62] Inasmuch as religion is concerned they might as well be termed "Translators and Vulgarizers." In the Transcendental novel, *Margaret*, Sylvester Judd says of woman: "She translates nature to man and man to himself."[63] Women, in religion, as in popular taste, take the bold and bitter and make it bland. One critic of American conformity blames the low standards of American culture on the fact that women are the audience and arbiters. "Averse to facing the darker brutal sides of existence, its uncertainty and irrationality, they prefer the comforting assurance that life is just bitter enough to bring out the flavor of its sugared harmonies."[64] Women in the first half of the nineteenth century took Christianity and molded it to their image and likeness.

"The curse of our age is its femininity," complained Orestes Brownson. "Its lack, not of barbarism, but of virility."[65] These changes, which annoyed Brownson as much in literature as in religion, made women as well as men conscious of their virtues. Womanhood and virtue became almost synonymous. Although the values of the nineteenth century have predominated during the twentieth century, it becomes increasingly more clear that they are not the only values and that the so-called feminine virtues may assume more than rhetorical significance. The giving over of religion to women, in its content and in its membership, provided a repository for these female values during the period when the business of building a nation did not immediately require them. In order to do this, it was necessary first to assign certain virtues to women and, then, to institutionalize these virtues. The family, popular culture, and religion were the vehicles by which feminine virtues were translated into values.

Religion carried with it the need for self-awareness, if only for the examination of conscience. Organizational experience could be obtained in many reform groups, but only religion brought with it the heightened sense of who you were and where you were going. Women in religion were encouraged to be introspective. What they found out would be useful in their drive towards independence. The constant identification of woman with virtue and with religion reenforced her own belief in her power to overcome obstacles, since she had her own superior nature and God's own Church, whichever it might be, behind her. Religion in its emphasis on the brotherhood of man developed in women a conscious sense of sisterhood, a quality absolutely essential for any kind of meaningful woman's movement. The equality of man before God expressed so effectively in the Declaration of Independence had little impact on women's lives. However the equality of religious experience was something they could personally experience, and no man could deny it to them.

NOTES

1. Martin Duberman has done this very effectively in his introduction to *The Anti-Slavery Vanguard: New Essays on the Abolitionists* (Princeton, 1965) and his biography of James Russell Lowell (Boston, 1966). Alice Felt Tyler, *Freedom's Ferment: Phases of American Social History to 1860* (Minneapolis, 1944) and Arthur M. Schlesinger, Sr., *The American as Reformer* (Cambridge, 1951) attempt a synthesis of the reform movements of the nineteenth century. A contemporary account of the nature of the reformer by Ralph Waldo Emerson, "Man the Reformer," in Ralph Waldo Emerson, *Nature, Addresses, and Lectures,* ed. Edward Waldo Emerson (Boston, 1903) is the first and perhaps the best attempt at this kind of social history.

2. For example, Max Weber, *The Theory of Social and Economic Organization,* translated by A.M. Henderson (Glencoe, Ill., 1957); Robert Merton, *Social Theory and Social Structure,* Rev. Ed. (Glencoe, Ill., 1960); Talcott Parsons, *Structure and Process in Modern Society* (Glencoe, Illinois, 1960); Richard H. Tawney, *Religion and the Rise of Capitalism* (New York, 1922); W. Seward Salisbury, *Religion in American Culture* (Homewood, Ill., 1964); Hadley Cantril, *The Psychology of Social Movements* (New York, 1941); Cyclone Covey, *The American Pilgrimage* (Stillwater, Oklahoma, 1960); and David O. Moberg, *The Church as a Social Institution: The Sociology of American Religion* (Englewood Cliffs, N.J., 1962).

3. See especially Robert Briffault, *The Mothers: The Matriarchal Theory of Social Origins* (New York, 1931) and Johann Jakob Bachsfen, *Myth, Religion and Mother Right,* translated by Ralph Manheim (Princeton, New Jersey, 1967).

4. For basic histories of American religion see Winthrop Hudson, *American Protestantism* (Chicago, 1961); W. W. Sweet, *The Story of Religions in America* (New York, 1930); W. L. Sperry, *Religion in America* (New York, 1946); T. C. Hall, *The Religious Background of American Culture* (Boston, 1930); J. W. Smith and A. L. Jamison, eds., *Religion in American Life* (Princeton, 1961); and E. S. Bates, *American Faith: Political and Economic Foundations* (New York, 1940).

5. For example, Eliza W. Farnham, *Woman and Her Era*, 2 vols. (New York, 1964), and Charlotte Perkins Stetson Gilman, *His Religion and Hers: A Study of the Faith of Our Fathers and the Work of Our Mothers* (New York and London, 1923).

6. A classic account is in Thorstein Veblen, *The Theory of the Leisure Class* (New York, 1919). In nineteenth-century tariff policy, women are urged to consume only goods manufactured at home. In his report on manufactures in 1790, Alexander Hamilton urged the adoption of manufacturing as a means of providing employment for women, an argument approved of by the nineteenth-century economist Matthew Carey. However, the use of women as cheap labor paid scarcely any lip service to these rhetorical rationalizations, and Veblen's theory of women as consumers and symbols of prosperity increasingly applied only to the middle classes.

7. Henry Adams, *Democracy: An American Novel* (New York, 1882).

8. The best brief sketch of Antoinette Brown Blackwell is by Barbara M. Solomon in *Notable American Women: 1607–1950*, 3 vols., Vol. I (Cambridge, Mass., 1970), 158–60, hereafter referred to as NAW. Other biographies are Laura Kett, *Lady in the Pulpit* (New York, 1951), and Elinor Rice Hays, *Those Extraordinary Blackwells* (New York, 1967). Mrs. Blackwell became increasingly dissatisfied with pastoral work and the Congregational Church and by 1854, after one year's service, resigned her pulpit to do volunteer work among the poor and mentally disturbed. In later life, after her family was raised, she returned to the ministry, where she campaigned for woman suffrage. Mrs. Blackwell was a philosopher rather than a theologian and, like her sister-in-law Elizabeth, was more concerned with the application of her profession to women's life than in achieving distinction in her own field.

9. *The Works of Orestes A. Brownson, Collected and Arranged by Henry F. Brownson*, 20 vols. (New York, 1966) give a complete picture of Brownson's views on women. Briefly, he was opposed to the "woman worship" of his age, and horrified at the woman's movement because it preached interference with marriage and procreation. "Of course we hold that the woman was made for the man, not the man for the woman, and that the husband is the head of the wife, even as Christ is the head of the Church. . . ." (Vol. XVIII, p. 386) He saw the weakening of American family life as the greatest crisis of the age, and the women's movement, in its stress on individual rights, hastened the dissolution of the family as a social unit and contributed to the disastrous trend of isolation. (Vol. XVIII, 388.) Moreover, the woman's movement was yet another indication of the increasing "spirit of insubordination" in society and like other such movements required "no self-sacrifice or submission of one's will." (Vol. XVIII, 416.) He was convinced that its leaders were not only opposed to the Christian family, "but to Christianity itself." (Vol. XVIII, 414.)

10. Quoted in Henry Steele Commager, *Theodore Parker* (Boston, 1936), 150 and in Theodore Parker, *A Discourse of Matters Pertaining to Religion* (Boston, 1842), 201. The issue of infant damnation led several Congregational ministers into the more permissive theology of Unitarianism, including Sheba Smith and Antoinette Brown Blackwell. Barbara M. Cross, *Horace Bushnell: Minister to a Changing America* (Chicago, 1958) deals with one minister's solution to the tensions of change. Unitarian theology is covered fully in E. M. Wilbur, *History of Unitarianism*, 2 vols. (Cambridge, Mass., 1945–1952).

11. E. Digby Baltzell, *The Protestant Establishment: Aristocracy and Caste in America* (New York, 1964); Henry F. May, *Protestant Churches and Industrial America* (New York, 1949); Louis Wright, *Culture on the Moving Frontier* (Bloomington, Indiana, 1955), and David O. Moberg, *Church As a Social Institution* (Englewood Cliffs, N.J., 1962).

12. *Testimony of the Life, Character, Revelations and Doctrines of Our Ever Blessed Mother, Ann Lee and the Elders With Her; Through whom the word of eternal life was opened on this day of*

Christ's Second Appearing; Collected from living witnesses, by order of the ministry, in union with the Church (Hancock, Massachusetts, 1816). A basic history of the Shakers is Marguerite Melcher, *The Shaker Adventure* (Princeton, 1941).

13. Theodore Parker, "A Sermon of the Public Function of Woman," Preached at the Music Hall, March 27, 1953 (Boston, 1853) and in many other sermons.

14. Susa Young Gates, *History of the Young Ladies' Mutual Improvement Association of the Church of Jesus Christ of Latter Day Saints* (Salt Lake City, 1911), 16ff. Eliza R. Snow Smith, wife of both Joseph Smith and Brigham Young, wrote a hymn on this theme, "O My Father," in *Poems, Religious, Historical and Political* (Salt Lake City, 1877), 173.

15. Nathaniel Hawthorne, *The Scarlet Letter* (Boston, 1850), "Earlier in life, Hester had vainly imagined that she herself might be the destined prophetess, but had long since recognized the impossibility that any mission of divine and mysterious truth should be confided to a woman stained with sin, bowed down with shame, or even burdened with a life-long sorrow. The angel and apostle of the coming revelation must be a woman indeed, but lofty, pure, and beautiful, and wise, moreover, not through dusky grief, but the ethereal medium of joy; and showing how sacred love should make us happy, by the truest test of a life successful to such an end." (240) This new saviour will reveal "a new Truth" to re-order the relations between men and women.

16. This idea is set out most clearly in Eliza W. Farnham, *Woman and Her Era*, 2 vols. (New York, 1964).

17. A history of the major theological and social changes in Christianity could be written in which the primary sources were biographies of Christ. A perceptive treatment of this subject is Edith Hamilton, *Witness to the Truth: Christ and His Interpreters* (New York, 1948). Another sort of survey is *Christ In Poetry*, an anthology compiled and edited by Thomas Curtis Clark and Hazel Davis Clark (New York, 1952). Two popular nineteenth-century biographies were Lyman Abbott, *Jesus of Nazareth: His Life and Teachings* (New York, 1869) and Frederic William Farrar, *The Life of Christ* (New York, 1874). A sample of the "Sunday School" biography is Caroline Wells Dall, *Nazareth* (Washington, D.C., 1903). Mrs. Dall saw the mission of the Saviour as the revelation of "the universal Fatherhood of God, the common brotherhood of man" and the repudiation of the "old dogma of a corrupt nature by showing how Godlike a human life could be," 24.

18. C. A. Bartol, "The Image Passing Before Us: A Sermon After the Decease of Elizabeth Howard Bartol" (Boston, 1883).

19. Theodore Parker had several sermons on this subject, including "A Sermon of Merchants" (November 22, 1846); "A Sermon on the Moral Condition of Boston" (February 11, 1849); "A Sermon on the Spiritual Condition of Boston" (February 18, 1849); and "A Sermon of the Moral Dangers Incident to Prosperity" (November 5, 1854).

20. Frances Trollope, *Domestic Manners of the Americans* (New York, 1949; original edition 1832), 75. This American phenomenon (which has parallels in most Western countries) of women forming the majorities of church congregations, has been explained in various ways. The way most favored by the nineteenth century involved the natural predeliction of women for good and therefore for religion. One twentieth-century writer believes that church-going is accounted for largely by a "psychology of Bereavement." The Puritans were bereft of England, the nineteenth-century woman was bereft of her children (or her personhood), and so forth. Therefore insofar as the individual American was pleased with himself, self-confident, and victorious over nature or property he had, presumably, increasingly less need for church—Cyclone Covey, *The American Pilgrimage*, 44–69. Another sociological explanation believes that women are "conditioned to react in terms of altruism and cooperation rather than of egocentrism and competition," and therefore are prime candidates for submission to external authority in both worlds—W. Seward Salisbury, *Religion in American Culture*, 88. Other explanations stress the supposed attraction of children to authority figures of the opposite sex. God is the father, ergo Oedipus aeternus. Woman's supposed innate masochism might, it could be argued, produce more guilt feelings than are

produced in males, and religion is supposed to remove feelings of guilt. In any case, whether psychological or cultural, the historic fact of female-dominated churches and male-dominated clergy remains.

21. Hymn books consulted were: Baron Stow and S. F. Smith, *The Psalmist: a new collection of hymns for the use of the Baptist Church* (Boston, 1843); *Psalms and Hymns Adapted to Social, Private and Public Worship in the Presbyterian Church in the United States of America: Approved and authorized by the General Assembly* (Philadelphia, 1843); *Hymns of the Protestant Episcopal Church in the United States of America: Set Forth in the General Convention of Said Church in the Year of Our Lord, 1789, 1808, 1826* (Philadelphia, 1827); *Collection of Hymns for Public and Private Worship: Approved by the General Synod of the Evangelical Lutheran Church* (Columbus, Ohio, second edition, 1855); Abiel A. Livermore, ed., *Christian Hymns for Public and Private Worship* (Boston, 1846); Samuel Longfellow and Samuel Johnson, *A Book of Hymns for Public and Private Devotion* (Cambridge, 1846) (Unitarian); *Plymouth Collection of Hymns and Tunes; for the use of Christian Congregations* (New York, 1855); *Hymnal of the Presbyterian Church: Ordered by the General Assembly* (Philadelphia, 1866); *The Hymnal: Published by the Authority of the General Assembly of the Presbyterian Church in the United States of America* (Philadelphia, 1895); *Hymns of the Faith with Psalms* (Boston, 1887) (Congregational); *The Baptist Hymn and Tune Book* (Philadelphia, 1871); *Hymns: Approved by the General Synod of the Lutheran Church in the United States* (Philadelphia, 1871, revised from the edition of 1852); *Hymns for Church and Home* (New York, 1860) (Episcopal); and *Hymnal: According to the Use of the Protestant Episcopal Church in the United States of America printed under the authority of the General Convention* (Oxford, 1892; original edition 1872).

22. "O Perfect Love" was written by Charlotte Elliott, a pious English invalid, who also wrote the popular revival hymn "Just As I Am"—Harvey B. Marks, *The Rise and Growth of English Hymnody* (New York, London and Edinburgh, 1937), 127. Sarah Adams, perhaps the most famous of the nineteenth-century hymn writers, had the dubious distinction of seeing her most popular hymn, "Nearer, My God to Thee," identified with imperialism and patriotism. It was reputedly quoted by McKinley on his deathbed, was Theodore Roosevelt's favorite hymn, and was sung by the gallant men on the sinking *Titanic*—Louis F. Benson, *The English Hymn: Its Development and Use in Worship* (Richmond, Virginia, 1962; original edition, 1915), 272.

23. Mary Clemmer, ed. *The Poetical Works of Alice and Phoebe Cary: With a Memorial of Their Lives* (New York, 1876), 172; Alice Cary, *Ballads, Lyrics and Poems* (New York, 1866), 276.

24. "I Need Thee Every Hour" was written by Mrs. Annie S. Hawks, and was considered a particularly appropriate hymn for Women's Circles and Mothers' Meetings—Edward S. Ninde, *The Story of the American Hymn* (New York, 1921), 150.

25. Charlotte Elliott in Marks, *Rise and Growth of English Hymnody,* 128.

26. The Christianizing of the West is seen as a central theme in virtually all standard accounts of the American religious experience. T. Scott Miyakawa, *Protestants and Pioneers: Individualism and Conformity on the American Frontier* (Chicago and London, 1944) applies Frederick Jackson Turner's frontier thesis to the religious life of the West, and agrees with Turner that in this, as in other areas, the frontier "either drastically altered or rejected the older cultural traditions," 226. Nineteenth-century witnesses to the propagation of the faith included the travel accounts of Robert Baird, *Religion in America: or, an Account of the Origins, Progress, Relation to the State and Present Condition of the Evangelical Churches in the United States* (New York, 1844); Caroline Kirkland, *The Evening Book: Or, Fireside Talk on Morals and Manners, with Sketches of Western Life* (New York, 1852); Harriet Martineau, *Retrospect of Western Travel,* 3 volumes (London, 1838); and *Society in America,* 3 volumes (London, 1837), as well as the critical Mrs. Trollope.

27. Robert F. Berkhofer, Jr., *Salvation and the Savage: An Analysis of Protestant Missions and American Indian Response, 1787–1862* (Lexington, Kentucky, 1965) and R. Pierce Beaver, *Church, State, and the American Indians: Two and a Half Centuries of Partnership in Missions Between Protestant Churches and Government* (St. Louis, 1966).

28. Mrs. Owens, ed., "Diaries of Pioneer Women of Clatsop County," *Oregon Pioneers Association*, Vol. XXIV (1896), 89–94.

29. Adoniram Judson, a baptist missionary, brought three wives to join him in his labors in Burma: Ann Hasseltine (1789–1826), followed by Sarah Hall Boardman (1803–1845) and Emily Chubbuck (1817–1854) who returned to the United States after her husband's death in 1850. The combined trials of these three women culminating in their early deaths were considered excellent propaganda for the Mission Boards—James D. Knowles, *Memoir of Mrs. Ann H. Judson, Late Missionary to Burma* (New York, 1829); Arabella W. Stuart, *The Lives of Mrs. Ann H. Judson and Mrs. Sarah B. Judson, with a Biographical Sketch of Mrs. Emily C. Judson* (New York, 1851); Gordon L. Hall, *Golden Boats from Burma* (New York, 1961); Emily Forester [Judson], *Memoir of Sarah B. Judson* (New York, 1848); Walter N. Wyeth, *Sarah B. Judson* (Boston, 1889); Asahel Clark Kendrick, *The Life and Letters of Mrs. Emily C. Judson* (New York, 1860). Another popular missionary heroine was Harriet Atwood Newell (1793–1812), who was the first American to die on a foreign mission—NAW, Vol. II, Mary Summer Benson, "Harriet Atwood Newell," 619–620; Harriet Newell, *The Life and Writings of Mrs. Harriet Newell* (Boston, 1831).

30. The Whitmans were married in 1836 and almost immediately embarked for Oregon. Narcissa survived the hazards of frontier life, the loss of her daughter by drowning, increasing blindness and constant harassment by Indians and rival religious groups only to die with her husband in a massacre at Waiilatpu in 1847—Clifford M. Drury, *First White Women over the Rockies*, 3 volumes (New York, 1963–66); Jeanette Eaton, *Narcissa Whitman* (New York, 1941); Opal Sweazea Allen, *Narcissa Whitman* (New York, 1959); and the *Proceedings* of the Oregon Pioneers Association, *passim*.

31. Eliza Spalding, whose health continued to decline with each year in the West, died of tuberculosis in 1851 at the age of forth-three—Clifford M. Drury, *The First White Women over the Rockies* I, 173–233; "Diary of Mrs. E. H. Spalding," Oregon Pioneers Association, Vol. XXIV (1896), 106–110.

32. T. E. Elliott, ed., Narcissa Prentiss Whitman, "The Coming of the White Woman, 1836," as told in the *Letters and Journal of Narcissa Prentiss Whitman* (Portland, 1937), 108.

33. Histories of revivalism in the United States are numerous. One of the best is Timothy L. Smith, *Revivalism and Social Reform in Mid-Nineteenth Century America* (New York and Nashville, 1957). An interesting psychological study is Sidney George Dimond, *The Psychology of the Methodist Revival: An Empirical and Descriptive Study* (London, 1926). Other sources are Paulus Scharpff, *History of Evangelism: Three Hundred Years of Evangelism in Germany, Great Britain, and the United States of America*, translated by Helga Bender Henry (Grand Rapids, Michigan, 1966); F. G. Beardsley, *A History of American Revivals* (The Tract Society, n.p., 1912); Bernard A. Weisberger, *They Gathered At the River: The Story of the Great Revivals and Their Impact Upon Religion in America* (Boston and Toronto, 1958): C. A. Johnson, *The Frontier Camp Meeting* (Dallas, Texas, 1955); and Whitney R. Cross, *The Burned-over District: The Social and Intellectual History of Enthusiastic Religion in Western New York, 1800–1850* (Ithaca, New York, 1950). The most famous nineteenth-century account of revivals was by the man who made them, Charles G. Finney, *Lecturers on Revival* (Boston, 1836).

34. Mrs. Maggie N. Van Cott, *The Harvest and the Reaper: Reminiscences of Revival Work* (New York, c.1883), 49, 67–9.

35. Ellen G. White, *Life Sketches* (Mountain View, California, 1915; first edition, 1860), 32–34.

36. MS Diary of Myra S. Smith, June 19, 1859, Elizabeth and Arthur Schlesinger Library, Radcliffe College, Cambridge, Massachusetts.

37. Richard Hofstadter, *Anti-Intellectualism in America* (New York, 1963).

38. Barbara Welter, "Anti-Intellectualism and the American Woman: 1800–1860," *Mid-America*, Vol. 48 (October, 1966), 258–70.

39. Caroline Dall, "Transcendentalism in New England: A Lecture Given before the Society for Philosophical Enquiry, Washington, D.C., May 7, 1895," in *The Journal of Speculative Philosophy*, Vol. XXIII, No. 1 (1897), 1–38. C. Gregg Singer, *A Theological Interpretation of American History* (Nutley, New Jersey, 1964) saw Transcendentalism as a direct repudiation of Puritanism, because it glorified man instead of God.

40. Octavius Brooks Frothingham, *Recollections and Impressions, 1822–1890* (New York and London, 1891), 136. Ralph Waldo Emerson, *The Complete Writings of Ralph Waldo Emerson* (New York, 1929, 1st edition 1875), "Woman," 1178–84.

41. Caroline Dall, in her voluminous diaries and notes, recorded many impressions of these conversations besides the ones she published—Caroline Healy Dall MSS, Massachusetts Historical Society and Radcliffe Women's Archives.

42. Octavius Brooks Frothingham, *Memoir of William Henry Channing* (Boston and New York, 1886), 296.

43. David Riesman, Introduction to Jessie Bernard, *Academic Women* (New York 1966). The late David Potter also reconsidered his assessment of the American character in his essay, "American Women and the American Character" in John A. Hague, ed., *American Character and Culture* (De Land, Florida, 1964), 65–84.

44. See in particular Margaret Fuller (Ossoli), *Woman in the Nineteenth Century* (New York, 1845), *Life Without and Life Within*, edited by A. B. Fuller (Boston, 1859) and Caroline W. Healey (Dall), *Margaret and Her Friends: Or, the Conversations with Margaret Fuller Upon the Mythology of the Greeks and Its Expression in Art* (Boston, 1896).

45. Donald Meyer, *The Positive Thinkers* (Garden City, New York, 1965).

46. John Van Der Zee Sears, *My Friend at Brook Farm* (New York, 1918), 89.

47. Charles Nordhoff, *The Communist Societies of the United States* (New York, 1912; original edition 1875), 412.

48. New Harmony (Indiana), Yellow Springs Community (Ohio), Brook Farm (Massachusetts), North American Phalanx (New Jersey), Ceresco (Wisconsin), Northampton Association (Massachusetts), Fruitlands (Massachusetts), Oneida (New York) and Modern Times (New York).

49. John Thomas Codman, *Brook Farm: Historic and Personal Memoirs* (Boston, 1894), 111, and articles in *The Dial* and *The Harbinger*, throughout their publication, translating and commenting on Fourier. Fourier's ideas on the role of women in the new society can be found in Francois Marie Charles Fourier, *Theory of Social Organization* (New York, 1876).

50. Amelia Russell, "Home Life of the Brook Farm Association," *The Atlantic Monthly*, Vol. 42 (October, 1878, pp. 457–66) and (November, 1878, pp. 556–63), 561.

51. Robert Allerton Parker, *A Yankee Saint: John Humphrey Noyes and the Oneida Community* (New York, 1935), is an excellent biography with many quotations from Noyes' writings.

52. *Ibid.*, 67.

53. *Ibid.*, 182–3.

54. *Ibid.*, 183.

55. Phrenology was a nineteenth-century mixture of science, religion, and cultural reinforcement; both conservatives and liberals used its terminology, sometimes seriously, sometimes with tongue in cheek. Among the most popular phrenological manuals were Jessie A. Fowler, *A Manual of Mental Science* (London and New York, 1897); G. Spurzheim, *Outlines of Phrenology* (Boston, 1832); and Lorenzo N. Fowler, *Marriage* (New York, 1847).

56. Susa Young Gates, *History of the Young Ladies' Mutual Improvement Association*, 2.

57. *History of the Relief Society of the Church of Jesus Christ of Latter Day Saints* (Salt Lake City, 1966), 18.

58. For example, see the testimony of Joseph Smith's wives in Don Cecil Corbett, *Mary*

Fielding Smith: Daughter of Britain; Portrait of Courage (Salt Lake City, 1966), and the women in Edward W. Tullidge, *The Women of Mormonism* (New York, 1877). Tullidge quotes Eliza Snow Smith as saying that the Mormon Church "is the oracle of the grandest emancipation of womanhood and motherhood," 194. Mrs. Hannah T. King, in 1870, proposed a resolution opposing the federal bill outlawing polygamy which ended with an acknowledgment of the Church of the Latter Day Saints "as the only reliable safeguard of female virtue and innocence; and the only sure protection against the fearful sin of prostitution . . .", 385. There is also a considerable literature of anti-Mormonism, in which the Mormons are portrayed as despoilers of female virtue and degenerates of the worst sort, very much in the Maria Monk tradition.

59. Octavius Brooks Frothingham, *George Ripley* (Boston, 1882), 236–7.

60. MSS Letters of Sophia Dana Ripley and Charlotta Dana, Dana Papers, Massachusetts Historical Society, Boston, Massachusetts; March, 1848.

61. For example, Ellen in *Fanshawe,* Phoebe in *The House of the Seven Gables,* and Annie in "The Artist of the Beautiful" all represent the principle of the common humanity of the ordinary man rather than the singular arrogance of the individual.

62. Louis Auchincloss, *Pioneers and Caretakers: A Study of Nine American Women Novelists* (Minneapolis, 1965).

63. Sylvester Judd, *Margaret: A Tale of the Real and Ideal* (Boston, 1882; first edition, 1851), 378–9.

64. Morris Raphael Cohen, *American Thought: A Critical Sketch* (New York, 1962; original edition, 1954), 41.

65. Orestes Brownson, *Works*, "Literature, Love and Marriage," Vol. XIV, 421.

CHAPTER
9

The Rise of an American Original: Mormonism

Of the many "Made in America" religions, the most enduring and influential has been the Church of Jesus Christ of Latter-Day Saints (the Mormons). From "cultic" origins in the "burned over district" of western New York (so named for its nonstop revival activity), the movement grew rapidly under its charismatic founder, Joseph Smith. A series of visions led Smith to translate golden tablets received from the angel, Moroni, into *The Book of Mormon* (1830), a new revelation that would stand alongside the Christian scriptures as the central text of Smith's new movement. Following Smith's assassination in 1844, Brigham Young (1801–1877) took over leadership of the fledgling movement and led them on a great migration from Nauvoo, Illinois, to the western territory of Utah. There the church would grow at a fantastic rate, placing the Mormons' stamp on the region just as surely as the Puritans dominated New England a century earlier.

From their inception, the Mormons proved to be controversial under the larger Christian umbrella. In the essay below, Gordon S. Wood, author of the classic *The Creation of the American Republic,* examines the birth of Mormonism in the context of the creative fervor unleashed by the Revolution. What did Mormonism share in common with evangelicalism? What is it that made Mormonism unique? Is it possible that Wood has overstated the parallels between Mormonism and evangelicalism? What is important about their possible links? Did Mormonism prosper because of them?

Additional Reading: Books published in the past fifteen years have transformed our understanding of Mormonism's origins and early history. Leonard J. Arrington and Davis Bitton, *The Mormon Experience: A History of the Latter-Day Saints* (New York, 1979) offers an excellent general history. Richard L. Bushman, *Joseph Smith and the Beginnings of Mormonism* (Urbana, 1984) unravels Joseph Smith's early career, and Jan Shipps, *Mormonism: The Story of a New Religious Tradition* (Urbana, 1985) describes how the Mormons transformed themselves from an upstart "cult" to a "tradition." D. Michael Quinn, *Early Mormonism and the Magic World View* (Salt Lake City, 1987) and John L. Brooke, *The Refiner's Fire: The Making of Mormon Cosmology, 1644–1844* (New York, 1994) illustrate the links between Mormonism and various occult traditions, many of which evaporated as the movement evolved.

Gordon S. Wood # Evangelical America and Early Mormonism

It is one of the striking facts of American history that the American Revolution was led by men who were not very religious. At best the Founding Fathers only passively believed in organized Christianity and at worst they scorned and ridiculed it. Although few were outright deists, most, like David Ramsay, described the Christian church as "the best temple of reason." Washington was a frequent churchgoer, but he scarcely referred to God as anything but "the Great Disposer of events." Like the principal sources of their Whig liberalism—whether John Locke or the Commonwealth publicist "Cato"—they viewed religious enthusiasms as a kind of madness, the conceit "of a warmed or overweening brain." Jefferson's hatred of the clergy knew no bounds and he repeatedly denounced the "priestcraft" for converting Christianity into "an engine for enslaving mankind, . . . into a more contrivance to filch wealth and power to themselves."[1] For Jefferson and his liberal colleagues sectarian Christianity was the enemy of most of what they valued—the free and dispassionate inquiry of reason into the workings of nature. As enlightened men they abhorred "that gloomy superstition disseminated by ignorant illiberal preachers" and looked forward to the day when "the phantom of darkness will be dispelled by the rays of science, and the bright charms of rising civilization." When Hamilton was asked why the members of the Philadelphia Convention had not mentioned God in the Constitution, he allegedly replied, speaking for many of this remarkable generation of American leaders, "we forgot."[2]

By 1830, less than a half century later, it was no longer so easy to forget God. The Americans' world had been radically transformed. The Enlightenment seemed to be over, and evangelical Protestantism had seized control of much of the culture. The United States, said Tocqueville, had become the most thoroughly Christian nation in the world.[3]

That year, 1830, was in fact a particularly notable one in the history of American religion. In that year the great preacher Charles G. Finney came to Rochester, New York, the fastest growing community in the United States, and launched a revival that eventually shook the nation. In that same year the Shakers had more members than at any other time of their history. In 1830 the religious fanatic Robert Matthews experienced the revelation that turned him into a wandering Jewish prophet predicting the imminent end of the world. At the same time,

From Gordon S. Wood, "Evangelical America and Early Mormonism," *New York History* 61 (1980), 359–86; reprinted Courtesy of the New York State Historical Association, Cooperstown, New York.

Alexander Campbell broke from the Baptists and began publication of the *Millennial Harbinger* in preparation for his momentous alliance with Barton Stone and the creation of the Disciples of Christ. And in that same crucial year, 1830, Joseph Smith published the *Book of Mormon*.[4]

These remarkable religious events of 1830 were only some of the most obvious manifestations of a firestorm of evangelical enthusiasm that had been sweeping through American society for at least a generation. This movement—generally called the Second Great Awakening—was itself the expression of something bigger and more powerful than even religion. Evangelical revivalism, utopian communitarianism, millennial thinking, multitudes of dreams and visions by seekers, and the birth of new religions were in fact all responses to the great democratic changes taking place in America between the Revolution and the Age of Jackson. The remains of older eighteenth-century hierarchies fell away, and hundreds of thousands of common people were cut loose from all sorts of traditional bonds and found themselves freer, more independent, more unconstrained than ever before in their history.

It is not surprising that 1830—the same year in which so many spectacular religious events occurred—was also the year in which the Americans' drinking of alcoholic spirits reached its peak: In 1830 Americans consumed nearly four gallons of alcohol per person, the highest rate of consumption in any year in all of American history.[5] The drinking of spirits and the search for spiritualism were but different reactions to a common democratic revolution and the chaos it had created. By 1830 Americans had experienced a social and cultural upheaval scarcely matched in their history.

The national outpouring of religious feeling during the early decades of the nineteenth century was very much a part of this upheaval. This Second Great Awakening brought religion to the remotest areas of America, popularized religion as never before, and created a religious world unlike anything in Christendom. It was not just a continuation of the first Awakening of the mid-eighteenth century. It was more popular, more evangelical, more ecstatic, more personal, more secular, and more optimistic. It combined the past and present, communalism and individualism, folkways and enlightenment in odd and confusing ways. The sovereignty of Christ was reaffirmed, but people were given personal responsibility for their salvation as never before. Nearly everyone yearned for Christian unity, but never before or since was American Christendom so divided. For many the world was coming to an end, but at the same time everything in the here and now seemed possible. It was the time of greatest religious chaos and originality in American history. During this unique moment in annals of American religion, Mormonism was born.

At the time of the Revolution no one foresaw what would happen to American religion. Many of America's religious leaders, including the Calvinist clergy, endorsed the Revolution and its enlightened liberal impulses wholeheartedly. For most Protestant groups the great threat to religion came from the Church of England, and enlightened rationalists like Jefferson and Madison had little trouble in mobilizing Protestant dissenters against the established Anglican church. The

Enlightenment's faith in liberty of conscience that justified this disestablishment of the Anglican church scarcely seemed dangerous to American religion. Even in Connecticut and Massachusetts, where religious establishments existed but were Puritan, not Anglican, Presbyterian and Congregational clergy invoked enlightened religious liberty against the dark twin forces of British civic and ecclesiastical tyranny without fear of subverting their own peculiar alliances between church and state. The Revolution and enlightened republicanism blended with evangelical Protestantism to promise all Americans, secular- and religious-minded alike, the moral regeneration the country needed.

Yet the Revolution was scarcely over before many clergymen began having second thoughts about what separation of church and state and religious freedom really meant. Few could share Jefferson's enlightened belief, expressed in his 1786 Virginia Act for Establishing Religious Freedom, that religion was only a matter of opinion having no more relation to government than "our opinions in physics or geometry." Since religion was the principal promoter of morality and virtue, without which no republic could long exist, it now seemed increasingly dangerous "to carry the idea of religious liberty so far, as . . . to rob civil government of one of its main supports."[6] The enlightened liberalism of the Revolutionary leaders appeared to be having more devastating effects on religion than many clergy had expected.

By the 1790s organized religion was in disarray. The Revolution had destroyed churches, interrupted ministerial training, and politicized people's thinking. The older established churches, now either dismantled or under attack, were unequipped to handle a rapidly growing and moving population. The proportion of college graduates entering the ministry fell off, and the number of church members declined drastically, with, it is estimated, scarcely one in twenty Americans being members of a church.[7] At the same time the influence of enlightened liberalism was growing. It underlay the First Amendment and infected the thinking of gentlemen everywhere. It ate away the premises of Calvinism, indeed, of all orthodox Christian beliefs. It told people they were not sinful but naturally good, possessed of a moral sense or instinct, and that evil lay in the corrupt institutions of both church and state. For some enlightened gentlemen Christianity became simply the butt of dinner party jokes. Everywhere orthodox clergymen tried to reconcile their traditional beliefs with liberal rationalism and to make sense of what Jefferson called "the incomprehensible jargon of the Trinitarian arithmetic, that three are one, and one is three."[8] This rational deism could not be confined to the drawing rooms of the gentry but even spilled into the streets. The anti-religious writings of Ethan Allen, Thomas Paine, Comte de Volney, and Elihu Palmer, reached out to new popular audiences and gave many ordinary people the sense that reason and nature were as important (and mysterious) as revelation and the supernatural. By the early nineteenth century, enlightened leaders like Jefferson and young John C. Calhoun were enthusiastically predicting that the whole country was rapidly on its way to becoming Unitarian.[9]

All this accumulated evidence of religious apathy and growing rationalism has convinced many historians that the decade and a half following the Revolution were "the most irreligious period in American history," "the period of the lowest ebb-tide of vitality in the history of American Christianity." The early Republic has even been called "a heathen nation—one of the most needy mission fields in the world."[10]

We are now only beginning to realize how misleading these common historical interpretations of popular infidelity and religious indifference in post-Revolutionary America are.[11] The mass of American people had not lost their religiosity during the Enlightenment. Certainly the low proportion of church membership is no indication of popular religious apathy, not in America where church membership had long been a matter of an individual's conversion experience and not, as in the Old World, a matter of birth. To be sure, there were fierce expressions of popular hostility to the genteel clergy with their D.D.'s and other aristocratic pretensions. It was this egalitarian anti-clericalism rather than any widespread rejection of Christianity that lay behind the popular deism of these years. For most common people, Christianity remained the dominant means for explaining the world; all they wanted was for it to be adapted to their newly aroused and newly legitimated needs.

During the last quarter of the eighteenth century, powerful currents of popular evangelical feeling flowed beneath the refined and aristocratic surface of public life, awaiting only the developing democratic revolution to break through the rationalistic crust of the Enlightenment and to sweep over and transform the landscape of the country. Once ordinary people found that they could change traditional religion as completely as they were changing traditional politics, they had no need for deism or infidelity. By 1800 there was as little chance of all Americans becoming rational Unitarians as there was of their all becoming high-toned Federalists. Evangelical Christianity and the democracy of these years, the very democracy with which Jefferson rode to power and destroyed Federalism, emerged together and were interrelated.

This democracy and the popular evangelicism of the early nineteenth century were both products of a social disintegration unequalled in American history. All the old eighteenth-century aristocratic hierarchies, enfeebled and brittle to begin with, now collapsed under the impact of long developing demographic and economic forces. The population grew at phenomenal rates and spread itself over half a continent at speeds that astonished everyone. Between 1790 and 1820 New York's population quadrupled, and Kentucky's multiplied nearly eight times. People were on the move as never before, individuals sometimes uprooting themselves four or five or more times in a lifetime. Joseph Smith's father moved his family seven times in fourteen years.[12] Ohio in a single decade grew from a virtual wilderness to become larger than most of the colonies had been at the time of the Revolution. This growth and movement of people combined with the spread of market economies to shatter all sorts of paternalistic social relationships and to excite the acquisitive impulses of countless individuals. Young people left their parents, women found new roles for themselves, servants stopped living in households, apprentices and journeymen grew apart from their masters and became employees, and numerous patrons and clients switched roles. In thousands of different ways connections that had held people together for centuries were strained and severed, and people were set loose in unprecedented numbers.

The effects and symptoms of this social disintegration appeared everywhere in the early Republic. Urban rioting became more prevalent, more destructive, and more class-conscious. Major strikes of employees against employers occurred for the first time in American history. Poverty in both the countryside and the cities increased dramatically. Everything seemed to be coming apart, and murder, suicide, theft, and the phenomenal drinking of Americans became increasingly common responses to the burdens that the new individualism and the expectation of gain were placing on people.

The ideology of the Revolution aggravated this social disintegration but at the same time helped make it meaningful. The egalitarianism of the Revolution explained and justified for common people their new independence and distance from one another. The change and disruptions were offset by the Revolutionary promises for the future of the country. Improvement became an everyday fact of life for unprecedented numbers of people. Traditional structures of authority crumbled under the momentum of the Revolution, and common people increasingly discovered that they no longer had to accept the old distinctions that had separated them from the upper ranks of the gentry. Ordinary farmers, tradesmen, and artisans began to think they were as good as any gentleman and that they actually counted for something in the movement of events. Were not the people being equated with God with every last humble one of them being celebrated for possessing a spark of divinity? Were not half-literate ploughmen being told they had as much moral sense and insight into God as professors and doctors of divinity?[13]

As the traditional connections of people fell away, many Americans found themselves in a marginal or what anthropologists call a liminal state of transition and were driven to find or fabricate new ways of relating to one another. Fraternity became as important to Revolutionary Americans as liberty and equality. Never in Western history did so much intellectual effort go into exploring the bonds that tie individuals together. From Lord Shaftesbury to Francis Hutcheson to Adam Smith eighteenth-century philosophers were drawn upon to explain and reinforce what seemed to be the natural affections and moral sympathy that even unrelated individuals had for each other. People were urged to transcend their parochial folk and kin loyalties and to reach out to embrace even distant strangers. The Enlightenment's stress on modern civility came together with the traditional message of Christian charity to make the entire period from the Revolution to the Age of Jackson a great era of benevolence and communitarianism. Figures as diverse as Jefferson, Samuel Hopkins, and Thomas Campbell told people that all they had to do in the world was to believe in one God and to love other people as themselves.[14]

By the early nineteenth century a radical and momentous transformation had taken place. Countless numbers of people involved in a simultaneous search for individual autonomy and for new forms of community experienced immense psychological shifts. While educated gentry formed new cosmopolitan connections, increasing numbers of common people found solace in the creation of new egalitarian and affective communities. From the Revolution on, all sorts of associations—from mutual aid societies to Freemasonry—arose to meet the needs of newly detached individuals; but most important for ordinary folk was the creation of unprecedented numbers of religious communities. The disintegration of older structures of authority released torrents of popular religiosity into public life. Visions, dreams, prophesyings, and new emotion-soaked religious seekings acquired a validity they had not earlier possessed. The evangelical pietism of ordinary people, sanctioned by the democratic revolution of these years, had come to affect the character of American culture in ways it had not at the time of the Revolution. It now became increasingly difficult for enlightened gentlemen to publicly dismiss religious enthusiasm as simply the superstitious fanaticism of the illiterate and lowborn.

Yet this transformation was not simple and stark. The world did not simply turn upside down and replace the skeptical Founding Fathers with new evangelical-minded popular leaders. The reason of the Enlightenment was not suddenly supplanted by the revelations of Protestant Christianity. To be sure, some of the leading Revolutionary figures, including John Jay, Benjamin Rush, and Noah Webster, did experience a religious rebirth in the early nineteenth century and abandon enlightened rationalism in favor of traditional Christianity.[15] But more than such dramatic changes of mind were involved. What came after contained much of what had existed before.

The Enlightenment was not repudiated but popularized. The great democratic revolution of the period forged a new popular amalgam out of traditional folk beliefs and the literary culture of the gentry. Through newspapers, almanacs, chapbooks, lectures and other media, ordinary people increasingly acquired smatterings of knowledge about things that hitherto had been the preserve of educated elites. And at the same time they were told that their newly-acquired knowledge was just as good as that possessed by those with college degrees. "Hitherto," said Dr. Daniel Drake in 1821 to a group of Ohio medical students, "the philosophers have formed a distinct *caste* from the people; and like kinds have been supposed to possess a divine right of superiority. But this delusion should be dispelled, is indeed fast disappearing, and the distinction between scientific and the unscientific dissolved. . . . All men to a certain extent may become philosophers."[16] Under such egalitarian circumstances, truth itself became democratized, and the borders the eighteenth century had painstakingly worked out between science and superstition, naturalism and supernaturalism, were now blurred. Animal magnetism seemed as legitimate as gravity. Dowsing for hidden metals appeared as rational as the workings of electricity. Scholarly studies of the origins of the Indians and the mounds of the northwest seemed no more plausible than popular speculations about the lost tribes of Israel. And crude folk remedies were even thought to be as scientific as the bleeding cures of enlightened medicine.[17]

The result was an odd mixture of credulity and skepticism among people. Where everything was believable, everything could be doubted. All claims to expert knowledge were suspect, and people tended to mistrust, as George Tucker complained in 1827, anything outside of "the narrow limits of their own observation." Yet because people prided themselves on their shrewdness and believed they now understood so much, they could be easily impressed by what they did not understand. A few strange words like hieroglyphics spoken by a preacher or a documentary patent displayed by a medicine seller could carry great credibility. In such an atmosphere, hoaxes of various kinds of quackery in all fields flourished.[18]

Like the culture as a whole, religion was powerfully affected by these popularizing developments. Subterranean folk beliefs and fetishes emerged into the open and blended with traditional Christian practices to create a wildly spreading evangelical enthusiasm. Ordinary people cut off from traditional social relationships were freer than ever before to express publicly hitherto repressed or vulgar emotions. Thousands upon thousands became seekers looking for signs and prophets and for new explanations for the bewildering experiences of their lives. These marginal people came together without gentry leadership anywhere they could—in fields, barns, or homes—to lay hands on one another, to offer each other kisses of charity, to form new bonds of fellowship, to set loose their feelings both physically and vocally, and to Christianize a variety of folk rites. From the "love feasts" of the Methodists to the dancing ceremonies of the Shakers, isolated individuals found in the variety of evangelical "bodily exercises" ungenteel and sometimes bizarre but emotionally satisfying ways of relating to God and to each other. When there were no trained clergy to minister to the yearnings of these lost men and women, they recruited leaders from among themselves. New half-educated enterprising preachers emerged to mingle exhibitions of book-learning with plain talk and appeals to every kind of emotionalism. They developed and expanded revivalistic techniques because such dynamic folk-like processes were better able to meet the needs of rootless egalitarian-minded men and women than were the static churchly institutions based on eighteenth-century standards of deference and elite monopolies of orthodoxy.[19] These common people wanted a religion they could personally and bodily feel. They wanted sermons free from "literary quibbles and philosophical speculations." Each person wanted, as one spiritual song put it, to literally and physically "see bright angels stand/and waiting to receive me."[20]

We are now only beginning to appreciate the power and immensity of this Second Great Awakening. There was nothing like it on this popular scale since the religious turbulence of seventeenth-century England or perhaps the Reformation. It was very much a movement from below, fed by the passions of very ordinary people. To describe it therefore, as some historians have done, as a conservative anti-democratic movement is to miss its popular force and significance.[21] To be sure, some Congregational clergy in New England saw in evangelical Christianity a means by which Federalists might better control the social disorder resulting from the Revolution. But these Federalist clergy like Timothy Dwight scarcely comprehended, let alone were able to manage, this popular religious upheaval.[22] In New England, the clergy scrambled to keep up with the surging emotional needs of people—by creating new colleges and academies to train ministers, by restructuring the churches, and by founding missionary societies; but elsewhere, especially in the fluid western areas, the religious yearnings of people simply overwhelmed the traditional religious institutions.[23] Between 1803 and 1809, for example, more than half the Presbyterian clergy and church membership of Kentucky were swept away by the torrents of revivalism.[24]

This genuine folk movement spawned hundreds and thousands of camp meetings and religious communities throughout the early Republic. By focusing on the most bizarre behavior of the revivals, like the "jerks" and "laughing jags," or on the most exotic expressions of the communalism, like the Shakers, we have sometimes missed its popular strength and scope. It is obvious that this religious enthusiasm tapped long existing veins of folk culture, and many evangelical leaders had to struggle to keep the suddenly released popular passions under control. Some enthusiasts drew on folk yearnings that went back centuries and in the new free atmosphere of republican America saw the opportunity to establish long-desired utopian worlds in which all social distinctions were abolished, diet was restricted, and women and goods were shared.[25] But for every such ascetic or licentious utopian community there were hundreds of other evangelical communities that clung, however tenuously, to one or another of the Old World religions. Presbyterian, Methodist, and Baptist evangelicals all participated in the Awakening and constituted its main force. Yet in the end, perhaps, our fascination with the unusual sects and prophets is not mistaken, for the radical enthusiasts and visionaries represented the advanced guard of this popular evangelical movement, with which they shared a common hostility to orthodox authority.

All of the evangelicals—from the Shakers to the Baptists—rejected in one degree or another the ways in which traditional society organized itself and assigned prestige. Thousands of ordinary people—farmers, bricklayers, millers, carpenters, petty businessmen of every sort, and their mothers, wives, and sisters—found in evangelicalism a counter-culture that condemned the conventional society and offered them alternative measures of social esteem.[26] Being called by polite society "the scum of the earth, the filth of creation," these evangelicals made their fellowship, their conversion, experiences, and their peculiar folk rites their badges of respectability.[27] They denounced the dissolute behavior they saw about them—the profanity, drinking, gambling, dancing, horseracing and other amusements shared by both the luxurious aristocracy at the top of the society and the unproductive rabble at the bottom. By condemning the vices of those above and below them, evangelicals struck out in both social directions at once and thereby began to acquire a nineteenth-century "middle-class" distinctiveness.

The American Revolution itself was invoked by this evangelical challenge to existing authority, and Christianity for some radicals became republicanized. As in government so in religion: The people were their own theologians and could no longer rely on others to tell them what to believe. We must, declared the renegade Baptist Elias Smith in 1809, be "wholly free to examine for ourselves, what is truth, without being bound to a catechism, creed, confession of faith, discipline or any rule excepting the scriptures.[28] From northern New England to southern Kentucky Christian fundamentalists called for an end to priests, presbyters, associations, doctrines, confessions—anything and everything that stood between the people and Christ. The people were told they were quite capable of running their own churches; and even clerical leaders of the conservative denominations like Presbyterian Samuel Miller were forced to concede greater and greater lay control.[29] Those who tried to resist this democratic religious thrust had to contend with the Enlightenment itself; for there was little essential difference between Jefferson's desire to knock down "the artificial scaffolding reared to mask from the view the simple structure of Jesus" and the primitive restorationist message preached by the most radical evangelicists.[30]

Everywhere the people were "awakened from the sleep of ages" and saw "for the first time that they were responsible beings," who might even be capable of their own salvation.[31] Although Calvinists and others still stressed the grace and sovereignty of God, conversion more and more seemed to be within the grasp of all who desired it. The new groups of Universalists who promised salvation for everyone were widely condemned, but they were only starkly drawing out the logic implied by others. Sin was no longer conceived as something inherent in the depravity of man but as a kind of failure of man's will and thus fully capable of being eliminated by individual exertion. Thus the immediate and personal awareness of God bred by revivalism led not to a quiet and introverted mysticism but to stirring and engaging activism.

Because the criteria of religious affiliation were now so personal, so emotional, so subjective, individuals moved easily from one religious group to another in a continual search for signs, prophets, or millennial promises that would make sense of their disrupted lives. With no group sure of holding its communicants, competition among the sects was fierce. Each claimed to be right, called each other names, argued endlessly over points of doctrine, mobbed and stoned each other, and destroyed each other's meeting houses.[32] Nowhere else in Christendom was religion so broken apart. Not only were the traditional Old World churches fragmented, but the new fragments themselves shattered in what seemed at times to be an endless process of fission. There were not just Presbyterians, but Old and New School Presbyterians, Cumberland Presbyterians, Springfield Presbyterians, Reformed Presbyterians, and Associated Presbyterians; not just Baptists, but General Baptists, Regular Baptists, Free Will Baptists, Separate Baptists, Dutch River Baptists, Permanent Baptists, and even Two-Seed-in-the-Spirit Baptists. Some groups cut their ties completely with the Old World churches and gathered themselves around a dynamic leader like Barton Stone or Thomas Campbell. Other seekers formed only single congregations, and isolated clergymen—free-lance revivalists with folk names such as "Crazy Dow" or "Father Havens"—roamed the countryside in search of lost souls.[33]

In some areas, churches as such scarcely seemed to exist, and the traditional identification between religion and society, never very strong in America to begin with, now finally dissolved. The church became for many little more than the building in which religious services were conducted. Religion that made each person alone responsible for his theology and salvation, as Lyman Beecher and other evangelicals acutely came to see, left nothing holding "society against depravity within and temptation without" except the force of God's law "written upon the heart" of each individual. Only the self-restraint of individuals—their "character"—now remained to keep this new society together.[34] By concentrating on the saving of individual souls, the contending denominations abandoned their traditional institutional and churchly responsibilities for organizing the world along godly lines.

From the disruptions and bewilderments of their lives many people could readily conclude that the world was on the verge of some great transformation—nothing less than the Second Coming of Christ and the Day of Judgment predicted in the Bible. Millennialism of various kinds, both scholarly and popular, flourished in the turbulent decades following the Revolution and became the means by which many explained and justified the great social changes of the period. Although old and new millennial ideas mingled confusedly, some of the adventist beliefs in the early nineteenth century now assumed a character appropriate to the realities of a new improving American society. Older popular Christian beliefs in the millennium had usually assumed that Christ's coming would precede the establishment of a new kingdom of God. Christ's advent would be forewarned by signs and troubles, culminating in a horrible conflagration in which everything would be destroyed. Christ would then rule over the faithful in a New Jerusalem for a thousand years until the final Day of Judgment. Those who held such millennial beliefs generally saw the world as so corrupt and evil that only the sudden and catastrophic intervention of Christ could create the new world. But in the America of the early nineteenth century, such older cataclysmic interpretations of the millennium began to be replaced by newer ideas which pictured the Second Coming of Christ following, rather than preceding, the thousand years of glory and bliss. And such an approaching age of perfection seemed to be beginning in American itself.[35]

This new millennialism of many post-Revolutionary Americans represented both a rationalizing of revelation and a Christianizing of the Enlightenment belief in secular progress. It was optimistic and even worldly; it promised not the sudden divine destruction of a corrupt world but a step-by-step, man-dominated progression toward perfection in this world. Since the United States was itself leading mankind toward the earth's final thousand years of bliss, millennial hopes came to focus on contemporary events occurring in America as signs of the approaching age of perfection—a perfection that would be brought about, some said, "not by miracles but by means," indeed, "BY HUMAN EXERTIONS."[36] Every advance in America's material progress—even new inventions and canal-building—was now interpreted in millennial terms. Such millennial beliefs identified the history of redemption with the history of the new Republic. They reconciled Christianity with American democracy, and they explained and justified the troubled lives and the awakened aspirations of countless numbers of ordinary Americans for whom the world had hitherto never offered any promise of improvement. Such popular millennial thinking not only reinforced nineteenth-century Americans' sense of their peculiar mission in history but kept alive an older folk world in which prophets and prophesying were still conceivable and important.

"In the midst of this war of words and tumult of opinions"—rivalling the early days of the Reformation—it is no wonder that troubled seekers like young Joseph Smith were asking "What is to be done? Who of all these parties are right; or, are they all wrong together? If any one of them be right, which is it, and how shall I know it?"[37]

The inevitable reactions to this extreme sectarianism and religious individualism were diverse, and they came from both the left and the right. Some radical evangelicals thought they could end the religious chaos by appealing to the Bible as the lowest common denominator of Christian belief. The Scriptures were to be to democratic religion what the Constitution was to democratic politics—the fundamental document that would bind all American Christians together in one national community. The biblical literalism of these years became, in fact, popular religion's ultimate concession to the Enlightenment—the recognition that religious truth now needed documentary "proof." In that democratic age where all traditional authority was suspect, some concluded that individuals possessed only their own reason and the scriptures—the "two witnesses," said Joseph Smith's grandfather, "that stand by the God of the whole earth." The only difficulty, of course, as Joseph Smith himself came to perceive, was that "the different sects understood the same passages of scripture so differently as to destroy all confidence in settling the question by an appeal to the Bible."[38] Only some final interpreter, some supreme court of Christianity, could end the confusion. But, as radical evangelicals like the maverick Methodist James O'Kelley realized, if such an ultimate authoritative interpreter existed here on earth, "he must be a Prophet or Apostle." Although young Smith was told "that there were no such things as visions or revelations in these days," the time was obviously ripe for the emergence of the greatest of America's prophets.[39]

The reaction from the right to the excesses of revivalism was also concerned with reestablishing religious authority. It began during the second decade of the nineteenth century among conservative churches, particularly High Church Episcopalians and Old School Presbyterians, but did not become important until the second quarter of the century. These conservative groups wanted to offset the personal and emotional character of revivalism by restoring the corporate rituals and doctrines of the historic churches. They reemphasized the sacerdotal authority of the clergy and called for a strengthening of bishops, presbyters, and general ecclesiastical leadership and organization. They reaffirmed the organic nature of church society and traced the historic roots of their churches as far back as they could, even to apostolic times. And, as much as the Christian fundamentalists, they rejected the sectarianism of the day. They thought that American "denominationalism"—the division of the visible church into different contending denominations—violated the traditional ideal of a single, catholic, and apostolic church.[40] Although these High Church Episcopalians and Old School Presbyterians had little in common, either socially or intellectually, with the primitive "Christians" that eventually made up the Disciples of Christ, they were alike in their desire to recreate a single, visible church that would encompass all Christians. While conservative churchmen sought to realize this goal by strengthening the institutions and creeds of the churches, the Disciples thought that only the tearing away of the various trappings of the different churches could expose the scriptural foundations common to all Christians. It would be the Mormons' peculiar contribution to this aim of regaining the one apostolic Christian church to do both—to combine the radical and conservative efforts to end sectarianism.

This, then, was the evangelical world out of which Mormonism arose. The Church of Jesus Christ of Latter-day Saints, for all its uniqueness, was very much a product of its time, but not in any simple or obvious way. Mormonism was undeniably the most original and persecuted religion of this period or of any period of American history. It defied as no other religion did both the orthodox culture and evangelical counter-culture. Yet at the same time it drew heavily on both these cultures. It combined within itself different tendencies of thought. From the outset it was a religion in tension, poised like a steel spring by the contradictory forces pulling within it.

Mormonism was both mystical and secular; restorationist and progressive; communitarian and individualistic; hierarchical and congregational; authoritarian and democratic; antinomian and arminian; anti-clerical and priestly; revelatory and empirical; utopian and practical; ecumenical and nationalist. Alexander Campbell was not exaggerating by much when he charged in 1831 that "this prophet Smith" had brought together in the Book of Mormon "every error and almost every truth discussed in New York for the last ten years." Mormonism set out to meet a wide variety of popular needs. It spoke, said John Greenleaf Whittier, "a language of hope and promise to weak, weary hearts, tossed and troubled, who have wandered from sect to sect, seeking in vain for the primal manifestations of the divine power."[41]

Mormonism was a new religion, but it was not to be simply another denomination among the many others of America. The Church did not see itself as just another stage in the ongoing Protestant Reformation. It marked a new beginning in the Christian faith. Like the Disciples of Christ, with which it had much in common, Mormonism was to be "the only true and living church upon the face of the whole earth."[42] But unlike the primitive gospelers, Mormonism did not seek to strip Christianity of its complexities and to ground itself in the literalism of the Bible in order to have the broadest common basis of appeal. Instead, it added new complexities and institutions to Christianity, new rituals and beliefs, and new revelations and miracles. Most important, it added an extraordinary complement to the Scriptures. The Book of Mormon published in 1830 was undoubtedly the most distinctive and important force in establishing the new faith.

The Book of Mormon together with Joseph Smith's revelations gave to Mormonism a popular authoritative appeal that none of the other religions could match. Even the primitive gospelers' return to the simplicity of the New Testament had not ended their quarreling over interpreting the Scriptures. The Book of Mormon cut through these controversies and brought the Bible up-to-date. It was written in plain biblical style for plain people. It answered perplexing questions of theology, clarified obscure passages of the Bible, and carried its story into the New World. And it did all this with the assurance of divine authority. The Book of Mormon brought to the surface underlying currents of American folk thought that cannot be found in the learned pamphlets or public orations of the day. It reveals in fact just how limited and elitist our understanding of early nineteenth-century popular culture really is.[43] The Book of Mormon is an extraordinary work of popular imagination and one of the greatest documents in American cultural history.

Its timing in 1830 was providential. It appeared at precisely the right moment in American history; much earlier or later and the Church might not have taken hold. The Book of Mormon would probably not have been published in the eighteenth century, in that still largely oral world of folk beliefs prior to the great democratic revolution that underlay the religious tumult of the early Republic. In the eighteenth century, Mormonism might have been too easily stifled and dismissed by the dominant enlightened gentry culture as just another enthusiastic folk superstition. Yet if Mormonism had emerged later, after the consolidation of authority and the spread of science in the middle decades of the nineteenth century, it might have had problems of verifying its texts and revelations. But during the early decades of the nineteenth century the time was ideally suited for the establishment of the new faith. The democratic revolution was at its height, all traditional authorities were in disarray, and visions and prophesying still had a powerful appeal for large numbers of people. A generation or so later it might have been necessary for Smith and his followers to get some university professors to authenticate the characters on the golden plates. But Martin Harris's failure to get such "professional" and "scientific" verification in the 1820s did not matter. After all, ordinary ploughmen had as much insight into such things as did college professors.[44]

Yet the American ploughmen of the 1820s were no longer the simple folk of the eighteenth century. They had been touched by the literary culture and rationality of the Enlightenment, and despite their lingering superstitions they had their own small shrewdness and their own literal-minded standards of proof. The odd tales of "Joe Smith," this "ignorant plough-boy of our land" who had a local reputation as a "fortune teller," staggered the wits of many in that credulous but skeptical age.[45] To think that "angels appear to men in this enlightened age! Damn him," critics said; "he ought to be tarred and feathered for telling such a damned lie!" In that enlightened age even ordinary farmers no longer dared to invoke "apparitions, or ghosts" in religion, wrote Emily Austin, an early but temporary convert to Mormonism; "for the very reason that we see no just grounds on which to build our faith." For many the Book of Mormon provided those "just grounds" of faith, though not in the end for Emily Austin; for when she eventually concluded that the Book of Mormom lacked "the spirit of conviction," her faith fell away. But for hundreds and thousands of other seekers "Joe's Gold Bible" offered what one of Smith's early revelations called "the surety that these things are true" for "this unbelieving and stiffnecked generation." One Methodist preacher who converted to Mormonism reputedly even reasoned that "the New Bible" was four times better substantiated than the New Testament because "the disciples of Joseph Smith had four living witnesses to sustain the Book of Mormon."[46]

It is not surprising that opponents of the new faith spent so much energy trying to discredit the origins of the new scripture, for it was precisely this kind of "surety," this concrete material evidence, that gave Joseph Smith's prophesying a legitimacy that the visions and predictions of the many other prophets of the day could not equal. The Book of Mormon nicely answered the warnings of the rational genteel world against "running into extremes, and making ourselves wise above what is written."[47] It had a particular appeal for people emerging from a twilight folk world of dreams and superstitions and anxious to demonstrate their literacy and their enlightenment. Such a tangible document fit the popular belief that what was written was somehow truer and more authentic than what was spoken.

In other ways, too, Mormonism brought the folk past and enlightened modernity together. It sought to reconcile the ecstatic antinomian visions of people with the discipline of a hierarchical church. It drew upon the subjective emotionalism and individualism of revivalism and institutionalized them. Mormonism, in fact, can be understood as a popular version of the elitist churchly reaction to revivalism that began in the second and third decades of the nineteenth century. Just as High Church Episcopalians were looking back to the earliest days of their church for new apostolic authority, so too did Mormons appeal to ancient, pre-Reformation history as set forth in the Book of Mormon. Mormonism offered people the best of both the popular world of millenarian evangelicism and the respectable world of priestly churches. Almost overnight, Mormonism created an elaborate hierarchy, mysterious rituals, and a rich churchly tradition that reached back to apostolic times.[48]

In dozens of different ways Mormonism blended the folk inclinations and religiosity of common people with the hardened churchly traditions and enlightened gentility of modern times. Like many other religious groups, the Mormons built a separate community of gathered saints, but at the same time they rejected the idea that they were just another sect representing a particular social fragment. They reversed America's separation of church and state and tried to reestablish the kind of well-knit commonwealth that John Winthrop had envisioned two hundred years earlier. Mormonism readily responded to the ancient popular yearnings for ascetic communal living and sharing, but at the same time, unlike Shakerism, it recognized the modern Americans' individualistic desires for property-owning. Since in the eyes of the gentry the Mormons were "the miserable Mormons," drawn from "the lowest and most ignorant walks of life," they, like other evangelicals, sought to establish among themselves new standards of respectability and prided themselves on what would become "middle-class" decorum and moral behavior.[49] Mormonism answered the powerful anti-clerical, egalitarian feelings of people by erecting a church without a professional clergy and by making every man a priest.

Its theology, too, mingled supernatural folk wisdom with modern rationalism. It allied the deep lying popular emotionalism of the period with the Enlightenment's faith in useful knowledge and education. By drawing on the folk habit of identifying the physical and spiritual worlds, Mormonism gave God a more corporeal human character and at the same time made man more divine. Its beliefs fit the needs of lost, lonely people unsure of who they were and where they were going. It sought to counter the disruptive mobility of the times by strengthening the extended family. The baptism of the dead even reached across generations and recaptured for people the sense of ancestral continuity that modern rootlessness had destroyed. This practice, in fact, did for ordinary people what the formation of genealogical societies in the 1840s did for anxious elites. Mormonism recognized the uneasiness, the guilt, and the sinful feelings of people created by their social and geographical displacements, but at the same time it promised these people redemption through their own efforts. However much Mormonism harked back to ancient folkways, it was a religion designed for the future.

Like many other popular faiths of the period on both sides of the Atlantic,

Mormonism was thoroughly millennialist. "We believe," wrote Smith, "in the literal gathering of Israel and in the restoration of the Ten Tribes. That Zion will be built upon this continent. That Christ will reign personally upon the earth, and that the earth will be renewed and receive its paradisiac glory."[50] Again in its millennial ideas, as in so many other ways, early Mormonism combined disparate traditions. As scholars have noted, its belief in the Second Coming cannot be easily fitted into any single pattern of millennialism.[51] Early Mormons followed the traditional belief in the corruption of the world and the imminence of Christ's arrival, and they searched the times for signs and omens of the cataclysmic event. At the same time, however, they shared in the more modern millennialist idea that the kingdom of God could be built in this world and that the everyday material benefits of progress were but the working out of God's purpose. Although other millenarians on both sides of the Atlantic emphasized the special role of their respective nations in the coming age of perfection, no American believers in Christ's Second Coming ever identified the New Jerusalem so particularly and so concretely with America as did the Mormons. Zion was literally to arise within the borders of the United States.[52]

The identification between Mormonism and America was there at the beginning. No doubt it was and is a unique faith, but it is also uniquely American. It was born at a peculiar moment in the history of the United States, and it bears the marks of that birth. Only the culture of early nineteenth-century evangelical America could have produced it. And through it we can begin to understand the complicated nature of that culture.

NOTES

1. Henry May, *The Enlightenment in America* (New York, 1976), p. 73; [John Trenchard and Thomas Gordon], *Cato's Letters . . .* (London, 1748), IV, No. 123; John Locke, *An Essay Concerning Human Understanding* (London, 1695), bk IV, ch. 19.

2. George H. Knoles, "The Religious Ideas of Thomas Jefferson," *The Mississippi Valley Historical Review* 30 (1943–44), 194; Nicholas Collins, "An Essay on those inquiries in Natural Philosophy which at present are most beneficial to the United States of North America," American Philosophical Society, *Trans.* 2 (1793), vii; Douglass Adair, *Fame and the Founding Fathers* (New York, 1974), p. 147n.

3. Alexis de Tocqueville, *Democracy in America*, ed. Phillips Bradley (New York, 1956), I, 303.

4. Paul E. Johnson, *A Shopkeeper's Millennium: Society and Revivals in Rochester New York, 1815–1837* (New York, 1978); Henri Desroche, *The American Shakers* (Amherst, Mass., 1971), p. 132; William L. Stone, *Matthias and His Impostures . . .* (New York, 1835); Winfred Ernest Garrison and Alfred T. DeBroot, *The Disciples of Christ: a History* (St. Louis, Mo., 1958), pp. 180–230.

5. W. J. Rorabaugh, *The Alcoholic Republic: An American Tradition* (New York, 1979), p. 10.

6. Gordon S. Wood, *The Creation of the American Republic, 1776–1787* (Chapel Hill, 1969), p. 427; Henry Cumings, *A Sermon Preached . . . May 28, 1783* (Boston, 1783), p. 47.

7. Russel B. Nye, *The Cultural Life of the New Nation, 1776–1830* (New York, 1960), p. 230; Franklin Hamlin Littell, *From State Church to Pluralism: A Protestant Interpretation of Religion in American History* (New York, 1962), p. 32.

8. G. Adolph Koch, *Religion of the American Enlightenment* (New York, 1968), p. 83; Jefferson to Timothy Pickering, 27 Feb. 1821, in A. A. Lipscomb and A. E. Bergh, eds., *The Writings of Thomas Jefferson* (Washington, D.C., 1903–04), XV, 323.

9. Jefferson to Benjamin Waterhouse, 26 June 1822, *ibid.*, p. 385; Clarence Gohdes, "Some Notes on the Unitarian Church in the Ante-Bellum South," in David Kelly Jackson, eds., *American Studies in Honor of William Kenneth Boyd* (Durham, N.C., 1940), p. 327.

10. John W. Chandler, "The Communitarian Quest for Perfection," in Stuart C. Henry, ed., *A Miscellany of American Christianity* (Durham, N.C., 1963), p. 58; William Warren Sweet, *The Story of Religions in America* (New York, 1930), p. 322; Littell, *From State Church*, p. 29.

11. Douglas H. Sweet, "Church Vitality and the American Revolution: Historiographic Consensus and Thoughts Towards a New Perspective," *Church History* 45 (1976), 343–57.

12. I owe this fact to Richard L. Bushman who is preparing a book on "The Beginnings of Mormonism."

13. Koch. *Religion of the American Enlightenment*, p. 181; Jefferson to Peter Carr, 10 Aug. 1787, Lipscomb and Bergh, eds., *Writings of Jefferson*, VI, 257–58.

14. Conrad E. Wright, "Christian Compassion and Corporate Beneficence: The Institutionalization of Charity in New England, 1770–1810" (unpublished diss., Brown University, 1980). On the similarity of the messages of Jefferson, Hopkins, and Campbell see H. Shelton Smith, Robert T. Handy, and Lefferts A. Loetscher, *American Christianity: An Historical Interpretation with Representative Documents* (New York, 1960), I, 516, 543–44, 579–86. For a recent interpretation stressing the communitarian aspects of Jefferson's thought see Garry Wills, *Inventing America: Jefferson's Declaration of Independence* (New York, 1978). The anthropologist most responsible for the concept of "liminality" is Victor Turner. See his *The Ritual Process: Structure and Anti-Structure* (Chicago, 1969).

15. Frank Monaghan, *John Jay* (New York, 1935), pp. 427–36; Benjamin Rush to Granville Sharp, 8 Oct. 1801, in John A. Woods, ed., "The Correspondence of Benjamin Rush and Granville Sharp 1773–1809," *Journal of American Studies* I (1967), 35–36; Richard M. Rollins, *The Long Journey of Noah Webster* (Phila., 1980).

16. Daniel Drake, "Introductory Lecture for the Second Session of the Medical College of Ohio" (1821), in Henry D. Shapiro and Zane L. Miller, eds., *Physician to the West: Selected Writings of Daniel Drake . . .* (Lexington, Ky., 1970), p. 171.

17. Stone, *Matthias*, p. 298; Herbert Leventhal, *In the Shadow of the Enlightenment: Occultism and Renaissance Science in Eighteenth-Century America* (New York, 1976), pp. 114–15; Robert Silverberg, *Mound Builders of Ancient America* (Greenwich, Conn., 1968); Curtis Dahl, "Mound Builders, Mormons, and William Cullen Bryant," *New England Quarterly* 34 (1961), 178–90; Marion Barber Stowell, *Early American Almanacs: The Colonial Weekday Bible* (New York, 1977), pp. 183–89.

18. Joseph Atterley [George Tucker], *A Voyage to the Moon* (New York, 1827; reprinted, Boston, 1975), p. 11; Charles C. Sellers, *Lorenzo Dow: The Bearer of the Word* (New York, 1928), p. 245; Daniel Drake, *The People's Doctors . . .* (Cincinnati, 1830), in Shapiro and Miller, eds., *Physician to the West*, pp. 197–99; Neil Harris, *Humbug: The Art of P. T. Barnum* (Boston, 1973), pp. 67–89.

19. See especially Rhys Isaac, "Evangelical Revolt: The Nature of the Baptists' Challenge to the Traditional order in Virginia, 1765 to 1775," *William and Mary Quarterly*, 3d Ser., 31 (1974), 345–68; Donald G. Matthews, *Religion in the Old South* (Chicago, 1977). On the folk aspects of Methodist preachers, see Donald E. Byrne, Jr., *No Foot of Land: Folklore of American Methodist Itinerants* (Metuchen, N.J., 1975).

20. Gordon E. Finnie, "Some Aspects of Religion on the American Frontier," in Henry, ed., *Miscellany*, p. 92n; Ralph H. Gabriel, "Evangelical Religion and Popular Romanticism in Early Nineteenth-Century America," *Church History* 19 (1950), 39. On the literal personifi-

cation of God and saints in folk sermons see Bruce Rosenberg, *The Art of the American Folk Preacher* (New York, 1970), p. 17.

21. Dixon Ryan Fox, "The Protestant Counter-Reformation in America," *New York History* XVI (1935), 19–35; Clifford S. Griffin, "Religious Benevolence as Social Control, 1815–1860," *Mississippi Valley Historical Review* XLIV (1957), 423–44; Charles I. Foster, *An Errand of Mercy: The Evangelical United Front, 1790–1837* (Chapel Hill, N.C., 1960).

22. For a recent book on this theme see Stephen E. Berk, *Calvinism versus Democracy: Timothy Dwight and the Origins of American Evangelical Orthodoxy* (Hamden, Conn., 1974).

23. Donald M. Scott, *From Office to Profession: The New England Ministry, 1750–1820* (Phila., 1978), p. 52.

24. Ralph E. Morrow, "The Great Revival, the West, and the Crisis of the Church," in John Francis McDermott, ed., *The Frontier Re-Examined* (Urbana, Ill., 1967), p. 78.

25. For a remarkable revelation of some of these deep-rooted folk yearnings in a sixteenth-century Italian village, see Carlo Ginzburg, "Cheese and Worms: The Cosmos of a Sixteenth-Century Miller," in James Obelkevich, ed., *Religion and the People, 800–1700* (Chapel Hill, 1979), pp. 87–167.

26. Mathews, *Religion in the Old South*, pp. 34–38.

27. William Gribbin, *The Churches Militant: The War of 1812 and American Religion* (New Haven, 1973), p. 102.

28. Elias Smith, *The Loving Kindness of God Displayed in the Triumph of Republicanism in America* . . . (n.p., 1809), p. 27. On republican radicalism among evangelicals see the insightful study by Nathan O. Hatch, "The Christian Movement and the Demand for a Theology of the People," *Journal of American History*, forthcoming.

29. Belden C. Lane, "Presbyterian Republicanism: Miller and the Eldership as an Answer to Lay-Clerical Tensions," *Journal of Presbyterian History* 56 (1978), 311–14.

30. Jefferson to Pickering, 27 Feb. 1821, in Libscomb and Bergh, eds., *Writings of Jefferson*, XV, 323.

31. John Rogers, *The Biography of Elder Barton Warren Stone* . . . (Cincinnati, 1847), p. 45.

32. For examples of religious conflict see Beverley W. Bond, Jr., *The Civilization of the Old Northwest* (New York, 1934), p. 486; Finnie, "Religion on the American Frontier," in Henry, ed., *Miscellany*, pp. 90–91.

33. Sellers, *Dow*, p. 23. On these religious developments see in general Whitney R. Cross, *The Burned-Over District: The Social and Intellectual History of Enthusiastic Religion in Western New York, 1800–1850* (New York, 1965); T. Scott Miyakawa, *Protestants and Pioneers: Individualism and Conformity on the American Frontier* (Chicago, 1964); John B. Boles, *The Great Revival, 1787–1805* . . . (Lexington, Ky., 1972); Richard Carwardine, *Trans-Atlantic Revivalism: Popular Evangelicalism in Britain and America 1790–1865* (Westport, Conn., 1978).

34. [Lyman Beecher] "The Necessity of Revivals of Religion to the Perpetuity of Our Civil and Religious Institutions," *Spirit of the Pilgrims* 4 (1831), 471.

35. On millennialism see J. F. Maclear, "The Republic and the Millennium," in Elwyn A. Smith, ed., *The Religion of the Republic* (Phila., 1971), pp. 183–216; David E. Smith, "Millenarian Scholarship in America," *American Quarterly* 17 (1965), 535–49; Ernest Lee Tuveson, *Redeemer Nation: The Idea of America's Millennial Role* (Chicago, 1968); James West Davidson, *The Logic of Millennial Thought: Eighteenth-Century New England* (New Haven, 1977); J. F. C. Harrison, *The Second Coming: Popular Millenarianism, 1780–1850* (New Brunswick, N.J., 1979); Sacvan Bercovitch, *The American Jeremiad* (Madison, Wisc., 1978).

36. Timothy Dwight (1813) and Elephalet Nott (1806) cited in Davidson, *Millennial Thought*, pp. 275, 276.

37. Joseph Smith, *The Pearl of Great Price* (Salt Lake City, 1974), p. 47.

38. Asael Smith (1799), in William Mulder and A. Russell Mortensen, eds., *Among the Mor-*

mons: *Historic Accounts by Contemporary Observers* (New York, 1958), p. 24; Smith, *Pearl of Great Price*, p. 47.

39. James O'Kelley, *A Vindication of the Author's Apology* . . . (Raleigh, N.C., 1801), p. 49; Smith, *Pearl of Great Price*, p. 49.

40. H. Shelton Smith, Robert T. Handy, and Lefferts A. Loetscher, *American Christianity* . . . (New York, 1963), II, 66–74.

41. Harrison, *Second Coming*, pp. 184, 191. The best single-volume history of Mormonism is Leonard J. Arrington and Davis Bitton, *The Mormon Experience: A History of the Latter-day Saints* (New York, 1979).

42. *The Doctrine and Covenants of the Church of Jesus Christ of Latter-Day Saints, Containing Revelations Given to Joseph Smith, the Prophet* (Salt Lake City, 1974), Section 1:30.

43. Richard L. Bushman, "The Book of Mormon and the American Revolution," *Brigham Young University Studies* 17 (1976), 3–20, shows how little the Book of Mormon reflected the elitist public literature of the day.

44. Donna Hill, *Joseph Smith, The First Mormon* (New York, 1977), pp. 75–78. For Smith, Columbia Professor Charles Anthon's inability to read the language on the plates only fulfilled the prophecy of Isaiah 29:11 that the book was "sealed . . . to one that is learned."

45. Emily Austin, *Mormonism; or Life Among the Mormons* (Madison, Wisc., 1882), pp. 31–32; Nancy Towle, *Vicissitudes Illustrated* (Portsmouth, N.H., 1833), in Mulder and Mortensen, eds., *Among the Mormons*, p. 61.

46. Martin Harris, in Mulder and Mortensen, eds., *Among the Mormons*, p. 30; Austin, *Mormonism*, pp. 53, 62; *Doctrine and Covenants*, Section 5:12, 8; Robert Frederick West, *Alexander Campbell and Natural Religion* (New Haven, 1948), pp. 183–84.

47. Stone, *Matthias*, p. 313.

48. Parley Parker Pratt in the late 1820s heard the restorationist message of the Christian Campbellites and was amazed. "But still one great link was wanting to complete the chain of the ancient order of things; and that was, the *authority* to minister in holy things–the apostleship, the power which should accompany the form." Mormonism gave him that link. Parley Parker Pratt, *Autobiography* (New York, 1874), pp. 32, 39, 43.

49. Stone, *Matthias*, p. 39. For a non-Mormon's sympathetic interpretation of Mormon culture see Thomas F. O'Dea, *The Mormons* (Chicago, 1957).

50. Joseph Smith, "The Wentworth Letter," in Mulder and Mortensen, eds., *Among the Mormons*, pp. 16–17.

51. Tuveson, *Redeemer Nation*, p. 175; Klaus J. Hansen, *Quest for Empire: The Political Kingdom of God and the Council of Fifty in Mormon History* (Lincoln, Neb., 1974), pp. 13–14; Harrison, *Second Coming*, p. 181.

52. Robert Flanders, "To Transform History: Early Mormon Culture and the Concept of Time and Space," *Church History* 40 (1971), 108–17.

CHAPTER
10

What Religious Pluralism Meant

Mormonism, though the most numerous new religious tradition, was not the only religious experiment to thrive in the republican air of the United States. In fact, "outsiders" of all sorts became insiders under the new rules of separation of church and state. Some of these, like the "Millerites," were "Adventist" and apocalyptic, believing that Christ's return was imminent. Others, like the "Shakers" or the Oneida Community of John Humphrey Noyes were communitarian and turned their backs on the capitalism that so enthralled the majority of American citizens. Some were celibate, others practiced "free love." In all cases, the new movements stood outside of the Euro-American Christian mainstream and sought alternative ways of living and worshipping.

In the essay by Professor R. Laurence Moore, we see how the very act of defining oneself as an "outsider" gave credence and legitimacy to a religious movement. How does Professor Moore define "insiders" and "outsiders"? Is he suggesting, then, that the Revolution made "outsiders" of all Americans? Is it possible to make generalizations about a national religious situation when only a few denominations are emphasized?

Additional Reading: The literature on "Outsiders" is large and growing rapidly. Among the more important recent studies are: R. Laurence Moore, *In Search of White Crows: Spiritualism, Parapsychology, and American Culture* (New York, 1977); Anne Braude, *Radical Spirits: Spiritualism and Women's Rights in Nineteenth-Century America* (Boston, 1989); Stephen J. Stein, *The Shaker Experience in America* (New Haven, 1992); Spencer Klaw, *Without Sin: The Life and Death of the Oneida Community* (New York, 1993); and Paul Boyer, *When Time Shall Be No More: Prophecy Belief in Modern American Culture* (Cambridge, Mass., 1992).

R. Laurence Moore

Insiders and Outsiders in American Historical Narrative and American History

This essay had its origin in a slightly frivolous but nagging question that a previous research project had left unanswered. In a monograph about American spiritualism, I had made the assumption often associated with scholars who pursue American Studies that no historical belief or activity can be wholly deviant with respect to the age in which it appeared. Everything, after all, is a product of its cultural milieu and, therefore, has some more or less normal meaning within the culture. That assumption, among other things, steered me away from the tendency evident in some earlier historical accounts to interpret nineteenth-century spiritualists as either "kooks" or charlatans. Spiritualists, it clearly appeared, had given expression to many central intellectual currents of their time. For that reason, millions of Americans in all social classes had taken a strong and sympathetic interest in their claims. Arguing that American spiritualist leaders were close to the center of the American belief structure (they were "insiders"), the book insisted, I suppose, on interpreting American psychics as part of the mainstream.[1]

Despite the book's demonstration of the importance and prevalence of spiritualist belief in nineteenth-century America, however, considerable evidence remained to suggest that the argument that rendered spiritualist perspectives "normal" or "typical" was downright perverse. Anyone who has read the writings of the leading proponents of spiritualist belief—or, for that matter, of the abolitionists and feminists with whom they frequently allied—is aware of their heavy reliance on what can appropriately be called a rhetoric of deviance.[2] In their public and private statements, they constantly claimed that they were outcasts (or "outsiders"). Since they had good and tangible reasons to talk about themselves as the victims of verbal and physical abuse, I had to ask myself whether efforts by the historian "to mainstream" spiritualist belief distorted the way in which historical actors perceived themselves or sought to resolve in too simple a way ambiguities inherent in their self-perceptions. A reading of the "objective facts" about the popularity of spiritualist activities seemed to bear an antagonistic, certainly confusing, relationship to any number of realities vigorously asserted by all of the parties in the controversy. Were spiritualists inside the nineteenth-century mainstream (because they created a broad popular movement) or outside it (because they constantly emphasized the powerful opposition they aroused)?

This nagging question would remain frivolous if the only thing at stake were the proper interpretation of American spiritualism. More general problems, however, are involved in the questions we pose about insiders and outsiders in America's past and present. American historical narrative has depended, perhaps

From R. Laurence Moore, "Insiders and Outsiders in American Historical Narrative and American History," *American Historical Review* 87 (1982), 390–423; reprinted by permission of the American Historical Association.

to an unusual degree, on tales about people identified by one of these two labels or their equivalents. Given the "Balkanization" of the American past evident in our recent narratives, that dependence may even be increasing. In a period when the ideas of national character, an integrated society, and a shared national culture have come "under withering attack," narrative all the more seems to need a center,[3] and reference to a mainstream, our currently popular metaphor that automatically divides the world into insiders and outsiders, provides one. The boundaries of a particular mainstream may be broad and fluid, but the metaphor nonetheless leads historians to distinguish between the people in its central currents and those in side channels and backwaters.

When historians write about insiders and outsiders, about mainstreams and eddies, they are doing more than locating a center. Historical stories about insiders and outsiders are constructed from the implicit and explicit assumptions that historians make about how power and status have been distributed in American life, about how values have been created and disseminated in a plural society. Historians locate the mainstream according to how they conceptualize majority and minority groups and according to how they analyze such sociological categories as marginal and elite groups and sub- and dominant cultures. Their division of historical landscapes into insiders and outsiders, ingroups and outgroups, conceals a multitude of judgments about American socioeconomic structure.

Historians are, of course, supposed to disagree about these matters, and the point of the ensuing discussion does not mean to suggest how we might attain a steady definition in our narratives for terms like "typical" or "dominant." Quite the contrary. Its point is to clarify some of the reasons why our disagreements about these matters have no ultimate resolution. It is also to suggest some ways in which we can make better sense of the historical contests between insiders and outsiders and to clarify the meaning of those contests within the context of American pluralism. To do these things, I will pay attention not only to the ways in which historians have used insider and outsider labels but also to the ways in which historical actors have used them. For both historians and historical actors often tend to conceal or neglect ambiguities that are essential to the meaning and importance of those and closely related forms of identification.

The organization of this essay is perhaps sufficiently eccentric to warrant a few initial sentences about the direction and aim of the argument. First, I will try to clarify the ideological perspectives that often lurk behind historians' use of insider and outsider labeling and to show in what ways the most familiar patterns of American historical narrative stereotype the role of outsiders. In the next section, I will examine some examples of insider and outsider rhetoric used by historical figures and suggest that historians' stereotypes, though all derivable from the rhetoric, often neglect important counterimages, which are frequently suppressed in the rhetoric but are nevertheless essential to its meaning. The following, and longest, section discusses some common consequences of the neglect of ambiguities in outsider identity. What mistakes of historical judgment can result when counterimages are not given due weight? In what ways can the historian's estimate of the political (or social or economic or intellectual) significance (or insignificance) of various outsider groups encourage a misreading of the meaning of outsider rhetoric? What can be misleading about the outsider's estimate of his own deviance? That section, though restricted to illustrations drawn from my current research in American religious history, suggests the need to redress a general interpretive neglect of the strategical uses of insider and outsider rhetoric. The final section of the essay draws out the reasons why contests between insiders and outsiders have an importance in America's pluralist past that cannot be analyzed solely in terms of objective conditions that determine America's socioeconomic structure. In that concluding part, I shall have something to say about what is wrong with the way we often try to understand typical or dominant culture in America.

The nagging question I asked earlier about nineteenth-century American spiritualists is, in fact, badly posed because attempts to answer it cannot at the same time address what we must often distinguish as levels of perceived reality and levels of factual reality. The latter relates to conditions that do not change as a result of what people, past or present, say about them. What follows is an attempt to ask better questions.

What common roles have insiders and outsiders generally played in twentieth-century historical narrative? The Progressive historians are the appropriate starting point for discussion. Strongly influenced by Marxist dialectical ideas, they were perhaps the first American historians to make outsider groups important to an interpretation of American life. Certainly they were the first to take much explicit interest in the sociostructural determinants of group conflict. In the histories of Charles A. Beard and Vernon Louis Parrington, the dominant, though not necessarily typical, culture in America was economically determined, reflecting the value system of the largest property holders. Since financiers and industrialists commanded vast reserves of economic and political power, the conservative norms imbedded in the dominant culture determined much of what happened in American life. But, thanks to the struggles of the economic underdogs, they did not determine everything. Inspired in different eras by such people as Thomas Paine, Andrew Jackson, William Jennings Bryan, and Eugene Debs, outsiders—the humble folk who individually had no economic power—arose periodically to challenge the overlordship of the propertied comfortable classes.

Progressive patterns of narrative often present historical outsiders as both victims and heroes. Outsiders suffered from injustices imposed upon them by the insiders who controlled the mainstream institutions of economic and social power. Because of the circumstances of their lives—their low wages, the declining importance of their skills, their recent entry into Anglo-American culture—they could not take their "power, status, or sense of reality for granted." They were not, however, defeated or unimportant. Despite their victimization, they bore a counterimage of the American mainstream, one ironically derived from a close reading of the egalitarian principles of the Declaration of Independence. "Outgroups," to quote Robert Kelley, whose recent noneconomic structuring of American conflict nonetheless fits a Progressive pattern, were "the ones among whom the basic ideals of the democratic order have been most energetically agitated."[4] Underdogs never successfully overturned the economic base of class dominance, but they did manage to organize effectively, especially in the Democratic party. Their struggle to shift the mainstream from what it was at any time in the past closer to what they thought it was and is supposed to be has never ended.

A markedly different configuration of insiders and outsiders is apparent in the narratives of Consensus-minded American historians. In the fashions of Consensus history, economically privileged groups have not foisted the dominant American culture upon powerless outsiders. Rather, the dominant culture in America has always been the result of a widely shared liberal viewpoint that grew naturally from the historical circumstances that gave birth to the American republic. Louis Hartz, whose classic book turned Alexis de Tocqueville's tyranny of the majority into Lockean unanimity, argued this point of view most persuasively.[5] But the general tendency of all Consensus narrative is to turn the mainstream into a broad and almost irresistible current. No longer conceptualized as the private swimming hole of economic elites, the center becomes a public bath to which almost all people, regardless of ties to minority or special interest groups, gain entry. In historical narrative, these assumptions work in a decisive way to undercut the role of outsiders as heroes and alter as well the meaning and significance of their victimization.

Consensus narrative turns most Americans into insiders who experienced outsiderhood, if at all, as a temporary form of identification. Focusing on the ever-widening mainstream, it argues that Americans were essentially alike even when they talked as if they were unlike. True outsiders—that is, alienated malcontents and socially marginal people—were not harbingers of progressive change. They were threats. They were the ones who might suddenly rally around the political banner of a Senator Joseph McCarthy. The narrative use that Richard Hofstadter made of the anti-intellectual and paranoid behavior of outgroups very much shaped the Consensus interpretation of "real" outsiderhood as a kind of social disease. Insofar as that form of identity gathered strength in any particular period, it disrupted the comity necessary to the stability of American pluralism. In Consensus narrative, the victimization of true outsiders turns them not into heroes but into villains of varying degrees of malevolence.[6]

Many American historians who began to write in the 1960s noted what they believed was a fundamental dilemma in Consensus narrative. On the one hand, with the significant exception of Daniel Boorstin's books, most Consensus history written in the 1950s had intended to make criticisms of the American liberal imagination.[7] The existence of malcontented outsiders, whose status anxieties led them to support extremist politics, suggested the need to transcend the social attitudes accepted by the average insider American citizen. Unfortunately, and this is the other hand, Consensus narratives never specified how that might be done. The logic of the narratives seemed to legitimize the politics of compromisers and technicians who had neither personal reasons for challenging nor the necessary ideological perspectives to challenge the status quo. If the Consensus interpretation is right, American insiders had succeeded in making too many people share their hostility to ideological divisiveness. Neither the majority who shared their views nor the dissolute and sometimes disruptive remainder appeared likely to become the agents of truly progressive change.

Having made that observation, many young Radical historians began to take steps that restored heroic stature to historical outsiders. The task was not always easy, for the Radicals' perspective on the past was not nearly so sanguine as the one of the more Whiggish Progressives. Although "New Left" historians agreed with the Progressives that economic and social power, rather than a majoritarian viewpoint, had determined what was dominant culture in America's past, they emphasized more strongly the strength of that power. In fact, in one way that emphasis represented less a return to Progressive narrative than a reinforcement of the Consensus interpretation. Much like Hartz, Gabriel Kolko and Howard Zinn plotted narratives that showed liberal belief strangling the American political imagination.[8] In their view, a numerically tiny governing class created the mainstream. Power elites exercised hegemony at any point in our past because they owned a disproportionate amount of the country's wealth, received a disproportionate share of the country's yearly income, and contributed a disproportionate number of members to the country's controlling institutions. Most other people in any historical era were simply "co-opted" into the mainstream and fell into a state of false consciousness. The mainstream side won by taming or splintering dissenting viewpoints in ways that nullified any real threat to the status quo.

Although citations to the work of C. Wright Mills and Antonio Gramsci certainly encouraged a reading of the past that diminished the political achievements that Progressive historians wanted to credit to historical outsiders, transforming what were once considered great victories into empty reforms that actually strengthened the economic position of power elites, recent Radical histories have focused more attention on outsiders than the narratives of any other school of American historiography have. Indeed, politically conscious outsiders—the ones whose struggles resulted in something that historians might regard as "a politically significant cultural achievement."[9]—became *the* subject of American history in the 1960s and 1970s, as scholars paid attention to many outgroups that the Progressive historians had barely noticed—feminists, blacks, native Americans, and immigrants with preindustrial values. The narrative assertion that some of these outgroups had maintained a value system at odds with the dominant culture underlines what is, after all, a crucial distinction between Consensus and Radical narratives. According to the New Left historians, America's hegemonic bourgeois culture did not arise naturally out of shared historical experiences. It was the fabrication of specific class interests. The efforts of outgroups to gain a critical awareness of their true interests were therefore terribly important. Those struggles gave the past whatever meaning it has for the present.[10] When Radical historians structure narrative around a politics of struggle generated by opposed people outside the mainstream, they are paying homage to the most durable legacy of Progressive historiography. The Radical historian's outsiders are almost always defeated heroes or victims. All the same, just as in Progressive history, they invariably carry the true version of the American dream in their heads.

Heroes, villains, victims—these roles, shaped in one way or another by historians' perspectives, are the common ones that outsiders play in twentieth-century historical narratives. Those narratives are not, of course, quite so formulaic as my discussion here might suggest. But it should at least clarify what kinds of underlying issues historians argue when they divide the historical landscape between insiders and outsiders. How do social values and norms get created? How and why do the values of one group get imposed on another group? Who benefits from what gets called "mainstream" values and who gets oppressed? Who in the society can effectively contest the "mainstream" norms? The ways in which historians use insiders and outsiders in their narratives invariably indicate their answers to these questions. That is to say, whether historians make the outsider John Brown a noble hero or a misguided victim or a disruptive villain depends in large part on their views about the working, or nonworking, of American society.

The last of the usual roles that outsiders play in narrative is, in fact, a nonrole. Obviously, Consensus-minded historians, because of the inclusive nature of their mainstream, often simply omit some outgroups from any serious consideration. Unless an outsider group threatened to become disruptive, it can have no particular importance in historical narrative. True outsiderhood in the Consensus view often become synonymous with historical significance. For somewhat less obvious reasons, Progressive and Radical historians can be almost equally dismissive of some types of outgroups. Although their mainstream is less inclusive, or is not given the same "legitimate" status that Consensus narratives accord to it, they focus their attention on outsiders whose politics supported what the historian judges to be a "progressive" trend. Other outgroups they ignore or treat with harsh condescension.[11] In addition, then, to the presentist assumptions implicit in the act of typecasting outsiders as heroes, villains, or victims, historians of all persuasions sometimes simply push, for various reasons, many outsiders to the fringes and margins of narrative. If they cannot serve a political or ideological point in narrative, outsiders are in danger of disappearing altogether from historical sight.

Historians defend their narrative treatments of outsiders by insisting that a particular treatment is faithful to the facts. In other words, some outsiders really are heroes (Emma Goldman), some really are paranoid (Whittaker Chambers), and some really are best left to sociologists and psychologists of deviance (the people who died with Jim Jones in Guyana). In defense of these claims, historians can get a lot of help from the historical actors in question. After all, historical outsiders usually saw themselves as fitting stereotypical roles of heroes or victims, though not, perhaps, of villains. And many defined themselves as social radicals, or as persecuted martyrs, or as alienated underdogs. But the trouble is that outsiders quite commonly assumed all of the identities at once. Historians have no trouble quoting John Brown in ways that show the famous abolitionist analyzing himself as a victim, a hero, or a crazed fool. Before quoting words that emphasize one identity at the expense of another, however, they have good reason to think about why outsider rhetoric—or, alternatively, insider rhetoric—allows such a variety of interpretations. The rhetoric is not simple, and seldom does it in any easy way provide confirmation of or negate the points that historians often want to make in their narratives.

A few examples of "typical" insider and outsider rhetoric suffice to make clear the nature of the interpretive problem. The first one, drawn from an essay by the Reverend S. M. Campbell written in 1867, is on one level the declaration of someone who perceived his own values to be the ones that dominated American society and culture. "This is a Christian Republic, our Christianity being of the Protestant type," he wrote. "People who are not Christians, and people called Christians, but who are not Protestants, dwell among us; but they did not build this house. We have never shut our doors against them but if they come, they must take up with such accommodations as we have."[12] Campbell's statement is obvious grist for any historical mill seeking to make Protestantism the dominant American culture of the mid-nineteenth century. Campbell's words imply that he, as a member of that dominant culture, took his status and identity in America for granted.

The second example, this time of outsider rhetoric, comes from the memoirs of John Humphrey Noyes. Noyes was descended from respectable New Englanders; by virtue of his breeding and education, he knew a good bit about the traditions to which Campbell referred. Still, the antinomian implications in Noyes's teachings about Christian perfectionism had led to the severance of his ties to the church to which he was first called. In remembering, long after the fact, the moment when he had lost his license to preach, he wrote, "I had now lost my free standing in the Free Church, in the ministry, and in the College [Yale]. My good name in the great world was gone. My friends were fast falling away. I was beginning to be indeed an outcast. Yet I rejoiced and leaped for joy. Sincerely I declared that I was glad when I got rid of my reputation."[13] Noyes called himself an outcast, and, by his other remarks, he invited historians to start plugging him into a narrative role either as victim, as disrupter, or as heroic protester. But his statement, if pressed too quickly into the service of any one of these narrative lines, can be misleading. Both Noyes's declaration of his outsiderhood and the opposite sort of declaration made by Campbell raise rather than settle a problem about locating American mainstreams.

As soon as we start to think about the occasion for each of these statements, the underlying reasons for such assertions, we begin to recognize almost mirror images of the explicit identifications. Campbell wrote what he did because he had grown unsure of his majority. He knew that significant groups were making claims that undercut his own claims to elite status. The self-proclaimed insider in this case defined a "mainstream" at the moment when the objective reality of that mainstream had in his own mind become problematic. A full interpretation of his statement requires our awareness of *his* awareness of cultural fragmentation. In 1867 substantial doubts existed as to whether a homogeneous Protestant mentality enjoyed much dominance, however that dominance is defined, in a country where most people did not belong to or attend a Protestant Church and where the largest and fastest-growing denomination was Roman Catholic. Campbell's statement grew from rejection as much as from self-confidence. He harbored fears about the diminished influence of men like himself.

In contrast, Noyes's explicit statement of rejection exuded self-confidence rather than fear, a sense of growing influence rather than a feeling of social isolation. Clearly, when Noyes emphasized the hostility directed at him, his alienation from his neighbors and their values, he was not proclaiming his insignificance or irrelevance. His words, contained in a journal written for future generations, were rather chosen for the effect they had in stressing his importance. His enthusiastic admission that he was an outcast proceeded from a deeply held belief that he had achieved, whatever the paradox, a status and respectability that both God and his enemies took seriously. He tied his rhetoric into the ancient tradition of religious sacrifice that a long line of Christian saints and martyrs had made sacred. He could be certain that his American readers would not miss the point.

Spotting these counterimages does not require any between-the-lines reading. Indeed, they are explicitly stated in other passages drawn from Campbell's and Noyes's works. Persecuted individuals like Noyes, who in more recent times have typically wrapped themselves in the flag, have frequently dropped the rhetoric of deviance to emphasize their embodiment of the "true" American spirit. Reverend Campbell, along with virtually all other Protestant ministers in the nineteenth century, could scarcely utter a paragraph proclaiming the dominance of Protestantism in America without adding another bewailing its decline. From early in the century, they regularly trotted out the Jeremiad sermon to attack "secular" editors and politicians who gave them no help in their efforts to curb the Catholic menace, combat infidelity, or enforce Christian moral standards. H. A. Boardman, the pastor of the Walnut Street Presbyterian Church in Philadelphia, stated flatly in 1840 that the "secular press" was "decidedly un-protestant, if not anti-protestant," and that "public sympathy" was with Catholics. "It is a remarkable fact," he said, that, if any one of the Protestant sects "rises up to withstand the bold and threatening aggressions of Romanism, it is sure to draw down upon itself the imputation of a self-aggrandizing and persecuting spirit."[14] The complaint had many echoes. People who saw themselves in one mood as guardians of dominant American values seized regularly on the language of the martyr. Insider and outsider identities are rarely unmixed. In fact, when the identifications are of most interest to historians, they are interlocked. The assertion that one is an outsider often implies the opposite, and vice versa.

This point can easily be pushed too far. Obviously, the rhetoric of self-proclaimed insiders and self-proclaimed outsiders tells us a great deal about the social and economic realities that prevailed in a given period of time. Whatever Campbell did or did not say, America was in some important factual respects a Protestant nation in the mid-nineteenth century. Protestants, even if that term only signified any non-Catholic who adhered to a vague sort of Christianity, could rely on the support of many institutions (the public schools, for example). Compared to Irish-Catholic immigrants, native-born Anglo-Americans had unproblematic identities, and they held the vast majority of key economic and political positions. And, whatever Noyes did or did not say, he confronted throughout his career customs and laws that were directly antagonistic to his goals. The burdens of outsiderhood, no matter what boost they give to a sense of self-importance, are quite real. The social costs that Noyes paid for his outsider identity were, relatively speaking, light, which no doubt explains the unusual cheerfulness in his remembrances of the circumstances that made him an outcast.

Although there most likely was some sort of connection between rhetoric and factual reality, there are particular reasons why these connections often became tenuous in conflicts between American insiders and American outsiders. The historian who quotes Campbell to prove that dominant American culture was purely and simply Protestant or who quotes Noyes to prove that "complex marriage" offended the moral standards of most Americans is asking for trouble. Mistakes start piling up once the historian forgets about the wide gap that is maintained in history between a factual reality, which keeps the same face, and a perceived reality, which does not. The assertions that historical actors made to identify insiders and outsiders have to be considered in part as metaphors and as strategic fictions. Such statements do not—cannot—tell us all there is to know about power and status in American life, for they were often the ways in which power and status were contested. A group that calls itself the moral majority or a political party that titles its journal *Mainstream* is trying to shape perception in a particular way.[15] The label does not necessarily describe the group's numerical strength. Indeed, such labels usually aim at trying to change the facts by taking what strategic advantage there is in being identified with the majority. The reasons behind this strategy may seem obvious—at least to anyone who has read Tocqueville on America. What American historians more often miss, however, in relating their stories about insiders and outsiders are the advantages that can be drawn from the identification as an outsider—advantages that significantly alter the roles, and nonroles, that historians have usually given outsiders in historical narrative.

Rhetoric from the past generally gives historians no choice but to treat some groups as insiders and others as outsiders. At the same time, historians cannot forget about the counterimages running through the rhetoric or about the impressive degree of popular and elite support that the values of outsiders often enjoyed. The question now becomes, What can happen if historians do?

In this section, I shall ignore differences between particular schools of historical narrative (but return to those in the conclusion) and concentrate on how stereotyped treatments of outsiders can cause blind spots in historical judgment. I know that common narrative stereotypes about outsiders capture some aspects of historical reality well enough. I am concerned with those instances in which the stereotypes mislead us about the meaning and uses of outsiderhood in American culture, for trying to characterize outsiderhood simply in terms of objectively measured distances from an objectively located, unshifting mainstream is impossible. No matter what rhetoric may seem to say, sometimes to be an outsider can really mean, both objectively and figuratively, to stand at the center of American experience.

The notion that historical outsiders stand at some measurable distance from the dominant (typical?) concerns of American life is perhaps most strongly reinforced in our conceptualization of the outsider as victim. We analyze victims as people who consciously or unconsciously violate social norms and are punished as a result. We can cite almost endlessly the words of historical outsiders who recall for us the ridicule of their friends and neighbors when they dared to be different. According to Joseph Smith, his relating the story of his controversial vision of 1820 "excited a great deal of prejudice against me . . . and was the cause of great persecution, which continued to increase."[16] The American historical record is filled with people who suffered savage discrimination because of clear differences between themselves and their surrounding culture. The sorriest tales relate to non-English-speaking immigrants, to native Americans, and to black slaves.

Clear and obvious differences do not, however, tell the whole story about many historical outsiders. The indisputable facts about the harassment and brutal murder of Joseph Smith make Smith an outsider in any historical narrative. Whether he remembered the stories about his early persecution with unfailing accuracy or not, his translation of the Book of Mormon and his founding of the Church of Jesus Christ of Latter-day Saints clearly caused him trouble in his upstate New York community. Those Americans who joined the Mormon Church crossed sharp boundaries drawn between themselves and surrounding "gentile" settlements and were eventually driven into exile. Yet historians know some equally important things about Joseph Smith and his followers. Those persecuted outsiders were clearly optimistic, pragmatic, and hardworking—a group of people whose religion "brought together various impulses and ideas of the emerging American *Weltanschauung.*"[17] If they were so like many other Americans, why did the practices of their religion, which did not for a long time include polygamy, cause such severe social consequences?

That question cannot be answered without taking into account the complexities of outsider identification and the ways in which Smith controlled his role as an outcast. That is to say, the deep divisions that sprang up between Mormons and many other Americans cannot be explained entirely by reference to differences between Smith's beliefs and those championed by powerful Protestant institutions. Labeling theories of deviance are surely useful for understanding the nineteenth-century Mormon controversy.[18] Outsiders (deviants) do get more or less arbitrarily stigmatized whenever the legally dominant part of the social order wants to draw boundaries. The theory explains why the persecuted outsiders in fact often share the basic value structure of the persecuting insiders. Groups whose objective deviance from existing norms is vast can safely be ignored by the dominant parts of society. What is not sufficiently emphasized in labeling theory, however, is the degree to which both parties to a controversy have active parts in drawing boundaries. Smith may innocently have crossed some lines that others suddenly made an important test of social conformity. But Smith did a great deal subsequently to keep those lines important. By the time he wrote "the Lord has constituted me so curiously that I glory in persecution," Smith had learned to exploit his identification as an outcast.[19] Like John Humphrey Noyes, he responded to persecution by letting his imagination elaborate and dwell upon what it meant to be a victim.

One of Mormonism's frustrated nineteenth-century critics complained that the "Mormons always have, and ever will thrive by persecution. They know well the effects it has upon them, and consequently crave to be persecuted."[20] We need not accept "crave" as the proper verb to recognize that Mormon history does seem to bear out the observation of Georg Simmel that "groups, and especially minorities, that exist in struggle and persecution, frequently rebuff approaches and tolerance from the other side, because otherwise the solidity of their opposition would disappear, and without this they could not further struggle."[21] More recently, Luther Gerlach and Virginia Hine have noted that "oppositional" movements often perceive more opposition to their cause than seems to exist objectively. That "unrealistic" notion of opposition results not from paranoia but from the functional benefits it can obtain for the movement's strength.[22] Persecution, real or imagined, can breed success.

Joseph Smith and other nineteenth-century Mormon leaders did not discover the principles of contemporary sociology and make them central to their plans; they did not in high and secret councils choose strategies that deliberately invited misunderstanding and persecution. They did, however, choose strategies that insisted on their distinctiveness. Knowing that they had considerable control over the way that other people perceived them, they reacted to the widely advertised belief that they were different by seeking to reinforce it. Their public speeches and writings made no attempt to reconcile the differences they had with the gentiles. They sought to maximize, rather than minimize, the importance of the innovative features of their church. Mormons, not gentiles, authored the notion of a separate Mormon culture. It was not distance from a mainstream that made that idea credible; it was, rather, the consequence of a conflict in which all parties found strategic reasons to stress not what Mormons had in common with other Americans, which was a great deal, but what they did not have in common. The mutual exaggeration of differences, which encouraged the idea that the differences could not be peacefully resolved, gives historians a considerable problem in trying to relate this controversy between insiders and outsiders to questions they have about dominant and subordinate value systems in American life.

A similar sort of problem is raised by the struggles of Roman Catholics, another important religious group that is usually given a victim's role in historical narratives about nineteenth-century America. These narratives, which strongly condemn nativist attacks upon Catholicism, end with the happy conclusion that the Church prospered in adversity. Indeed it did; but, as with the case of Mormonism, that result was not entirely fortuitous, nor did the persecution of the Church result solely from the affront it raised to Protestant "mainstream" norms.

Orestes Brownson, a native-born American who converted to Roman Catholicism, did not believe that opposition to the Church was inevitable. If Catholics would "quietly take their position as free and equal American citizens . . . , they will gain that weight and influence in the country to which their merit entitles them. All depends on ourselves."[23] Brownson was surely much too optimistic in this estimate, just as his famous antagonist, Bishop John Hughes of New York City, charged. But the Irish-born Hughes, whose influence on the course of American Catholicism was far greater than Brownson's, never gave Brownsons' advice much of a chance. Rather than urging Catholics to take a quiet place, Hughes learned early in his career that the tradition of outsiderhood had important uses. During the bitterly fought New York City school controversy of the mid-nineteenth century, Hughes played a central role in destroying the Public School Society and replacing it with a school administration less obviously hostile to Catholics. Although Hughes was as much a victor as anyone in the dispute, public statements stressed the opposition that his positions aroused rather than the support they received. Undeniably a powerful man, he rarely lost an opportunity to review the "vituperation, calumny, and slander" heaped on him.[24]

"Americanizers" in the Catholic Church were always critical of Hughes's militance and of what they regarded as his choice to separate Irish-born Catholic immigrants from the larger currents of American nationality. In 1967 Andrew Greeley wrote that Hughes "did not like American society. . . . He could see nothing but hostility and persecution." Another Catholic scholar, David O'Brien, has argued that Hughes encouraged a "ghetto mentality" among American Catholics, that he did little to assist "his immigrant followers to understand their surroundings and to live in peace with their neighbors."[25] Both judgments are in part correct, although they seriously underestimate the kinds of strength and influence Hughes managed to conceal under the label "victim." Hughes in fact liked America and often said so. Denying that America was de jure a Protestant country, he believed that the American Catholic Church had enjoyed great success. Nonetheless, he concentrated on the paradoxical strategy of pursuing the power of the "insider" by keeping the stigma of outsiderhood constantly attached to the people he tried to lead. Hughes and most other nineteenth-century American Catholic leaders developed a vested interest in supporting the claims of nativists that America was de facto overwhelmingly a Protestant country. By and large they left it to the outspoken "Americanizers" among them to dream idly of a Catholic America while they forged a more important myth that posited almost a natural connection between Catholic outsiderhood and Catholic power. They perpetuated vague notions about an American mainstream of Protestant values in order to make victimization a usable tradition.

Interpretive difficulties similar to those that are created in narrative versions of the outsider as victim appear in narratives that stereotype outsiders as agents of social change. The assumption that outsiders stand at a measurable distance from a set of dominant values encourages the conception of outsiderhood as something that inevitably promotes social change or disruption. Historical figures who did not share what are posited to be mainstream concerns must, it is argued, pose a threat to those concerns. Their discontent, whether it serves progressive or regressive ideologies, acts in narrative as a challenge to the status quo. The historian's own biases may make the pattern a useful form of narrative. But, as is true of our images of historical victims, those biases find much support in the statements of historical figures. Often the same historical statements that stress victimization tell of the holy causes for which victims struggled.

Perhaps we do not need reminding that the causes of historical outsiders were not always very holy. The persecutors (not merely the persecuted), the Know-Nothings (not merely the Catholics), the mobs that attacked the abolitionists (not merely the Garrisonians)—all at one time or another posed as beleaguered outgroups. But their posited victimization may suggest another oft-overlooked point: outsider rhetoric, regardless of the group or individual employing it, has some uses that are as likely to thwart change as to promote it. The quickest way to make this argument, although the main point has nothing to do with a particular political persuasion, is simply to note how often American conservatives of one kind or another have resorted to outsider rhetoric. The case of Henry Adams should remind us that people who possessed elite social status by any reasonable view of the facts did not necessarily perceive of themselves as part of the American "mainstream." If Adams seems to represent an extreme case, an eccentric attracted to a kind of conservatism that had never been comfortable with American institutions, then consider a recent representative of the more typical school of American free-enterprise conservatism. William Simon, a man of considerable wealth and a recent secretary of the treasury, suggested in memoirs published in 1978 that he was an outsider. "The United States," he wrote with a passion verging on bitterness, "is now ruled, almost exclusively, by a political-social-intellectual elite that is committed to the belief that the government can control our complex marketplace by fiat better than the people can by individual choice."[26]

It would be a mistake, I think, to write Simon's comment off as mere hypocrisy. In America's past, outsiders have taken their stand at the top and the bottom and the middle of the social scale. And, whatever our perception of the politics of any of them, they have all in some sense invented a mainstream against which to direct opposition. Obviously, some inventions are more "real" than others, and some oppositions more serious and less chosen than others. We should at least recognize, however, that a common strategy of exaggeration can be found in the writings of Eugene Debs as well as in those of Simon and that the exaggeration, rather than creating a verbal space for radicals to sustain their dreams, just as often created a verbal space for conservatives to vent their despair.

Every declaration of outsiderhood, even Simon's, is on one level made with the intention of changing something. But the rhetoric, whenever it expresses a well-developed form of self-identification, also means to conserve, in a nonpolitical sense. Victor Turner has shown in what ways a "liminal" or "underground" identity can act as a challenge to the existing social structure.[27] Yet, even the pose of the revolutionary can quickly become domesticated, not because the "system" somehow finds a way to crush revolutionary zeal but because the identity becomes important for itself. An outsider identification pursued by a group over time can provide the group with well-recognized social status within the structure of existing social arrangements. Mormon self-identity was initially shaped by the radical notion that those who followed Joseph Smith were preparing the way for the transformation of America into the Kingdom of God. But the longer Mormons waited for that kingdom, the more their outsider identification took on a life of its own. It concerned itself less with changing America than with preserving the social structures that made the identification significant. The Mormon sense of uniqueness was maintained by preserving—conserving—an oppositional relation to a perceived mainstream. At the same time, the effective desire to alter that mainstream lessened and to preserve—conserve—the status quo increased.

Andrew Hacker has noted that ethnicity, one form of American outsider identity, may be a form of consciousness that keeps people from making trouble for the system. The cultivation of ethnicity allows group members to make the best of their relatively low social standing by finding psychic satisfaction in their limited opportunities.[28] Much the same point could be made about the kind of consciousness sponsored by many nonfeminist women's groups in America's past and present. The conservative uses of outsiderhood must almost always qualify the use of the category in historical narrative to emphasize a potential force for change or disruption. An opposite potential also exists, even if it is rarely directly expressed in outsider rhetoric. Historical narrative may properly champion the cause of economic underdogs. But that commitment should not erase our awareness that outsiders often had a substantial investment in many of the same cultural and social values that maintained the status of insiders. The image of outsiders as agents of change, no more than the image of them as victims, does not capture their full importance for American historical narrative. Certainly, a priori judgments cannot tell us whether outsiders were more likely than insiders to promote the cause of social justice.

This point raises a third common problem in the narrative treatment of outsiders. Noticing outsiders only as agents of change often leads to almost total neglect of important outsider groups, a neglect that is yet another option that a great deal of historical rhetoric invites. Historical outsiders frequently used words to suggest what we now call marginal social status. The exaggeration of their differences from others cannot help but carry that implication. Whether historians decide to pick up the invitation should depend on what they conclude about the strategies involved in outsiders' declarations that "we are not like anyone else." The decision often depends, however, on other things, such as a historian's beliefs about progressive politics; and historians as a result fail to attend to values that, while not dominant among elites, were nonetheless quite typical in popular culture and enjoyed a degree of support among elites, regardless of the explicit statements in their public rhetoric. To illustrate what kinds of confusion strategical assertions about marginality may cause, not only to historians but even to the historical actors involved, there is no better case than the experiences of Christian Fundamentalists in the twentieth century. As before, the confusion occurs when counterimages contained in the rhetoric of deviance are ignored.

Christians who coupled insistence on a literal interpretation of Scripture with premillennialism began to find themselves written out of the Protestant mainstream in the late nineteenth century. In fact, ministers who favored a premillennial view of Christ's coming helped do the writing out, inasmuch as they had come to believe that they had scriptural reasons to accept the depiction of themselves as outsiders. The prophecies of the Book of Revelation suggested that the number of true Christians would dwindle to a small, suffering minority as the last days approached. The "small remnant" mentality grew stronger among premillennialists during the first part of the twentieth century.[29] National press reaction to the Scopes-Darwin trial in the 1920s was only one of the causes. By the end of the 1920s, leading Fundamentalist ministers were declaring that their efforts to prevent Christian Liberals from gaining a dominant position in the largest Protestant denominations had failed. This was by no means the case, but the perception was important in what happened next. With some considerable success in the 1930s and 1940s, the most uncompromising of the Fundamentalists tried to organize the faithful into separate churches and associations. Although they put a much different interpretation on their announced "failure" than Liberal Protestants did, they outdid everyone in attesting to the declining significance of Fundamentalism as a force in the "mainline" churches. That is to say, Fundamentalists joined with the Liberals, who by and large played the insiders in this particular struggle, in distorting the facts about the strength of Fundamentalist Christianity. Exaggeration, once again, was essential to outsider rhetoric.[30]

Many American historians in writing about the twentieth century have wanted to emphasize a theme of secularization. For that reason, in analyzing the consequences of the Scopes-Darwin trial in Dayton, Tennessee, they were more than happy to take the statements of Fundamentalists as evidence that their movement became something of a fringe cult after the 1920s, a refuge for the alienated and the dispossessed. The anti-Darwinism and the anti-intellectualism that historians correctly understood as basic to the Fundamentalist stand were not things they saw as helpful to a rational political order. Given all of the other troubles that stood in the way of the political enlightenment of Americans, historians wanted to write Americans beyond their religious backwardness as quickly as possible.

Unhappily for the proponents of secularization theory, various forms of conservative Christianity, which included Fundamentalists but also included groups more specifically labeled neo-evangelical and pentecostal, staged a dramatic comeback in the 1970s.[31] That, in any case, was what the media reported. The wealth of publicity that attended this "resurgence" put Fundamentalists and historians alike in something of a quandary. Fundamentalists faced an identity crisis. They had to settle what George Marsden has characterized as their "strikingly paradoxical tendency to identify sometimes with the 'establishment' and sometimes with the 'outsiders.'"[32] They had to worry about the cost of accepting an image—being tailored for them in the press—that settled the paradox by placing them firmly in the "mainstream" of Protestant Christianity. Recent issues of the glossy journals of conservative Christianity, themselves a sign of what can superficially be transformed as a result of media attention, have to an unusual degree been filled with hand-wringing discussions about the dangers of "respectability."[33] And with good reason. The outsider's stance, which in this case was frequently accompanied by a strident patriotism, had worked rather well for the Fundamentalists, keeping the faithful militant even in those churches where the movement had supposedly died. The wholesale switch to an insider's identity contained risks; among other things, it voided the assumption that until Christ's coming the hypocrites must control the churches. A peace treaty with Liberals clearly eliminates one primary reason why Fundamentalists had been influential. All of their previous rhetoric had implied that the acceptance of majority or mainstream status meant defeat.

The quandary of historians is of a different sort. Realizing that things rarely happen as suddenly as journalists like to think, historians must come to grips with the likelihood that the relative number of liberals and conservatives among Protestant believers has changed less dramatically over the last sixty years than historical narrative has suggested. Of course we have no reliable way to be absolutely sure. We can tally up leaders and militants in each camp, but those figures do not get us very far in estimating what sorts of belief attracted less active church members. Nonetheless, a decent regard for historical continuity suggests that, although recent media accounts have swayed the way liberals and conservatives have perceived their relative strength in the Protestant camp (not unimportant in itself), they have overstated the degree to which belief actually changed.[34] Therefore, judgments that have made Fundamentalism a movement of drastically dwindling significance in the twentieth century, although they have reflected fairly enough one image in the historical rhetoric, have ended by distorting historical reality in the worst possible way. Historians, by ignoring the contradictory elements in self-perception, the counterimages in Fundamentalist rhetoric, have caused a good chunk of the American population to disappear. Such benign neglect can serve admirable moral purposes in narrative. Yet it produces history that many Americans cannot recognize as their own.

The lines between historical insiders and outsiders may seem so hopelessly muddled in subjective perceptions that American historians ought simply to drop any suggestion of those categories in constructing narrative. We are stuck with some fundamental problems, and one of my purposes here has been to clarify the reasons why we can never definitely resolve such questions as when or even whether Roman Catholics entered *the* American mainstream. Even if we accept the common opinion that they did enter the mainstream sometime in the twentieth century, we cannot prove the case merely by referring to such undeniably important information as rising intermarriage among Catholic ethnic groups, the upward movement of average Catholic family income, or the election of John F. Kennedy as president. With respect to purported mainstream boundaries, these facts are important only to the degree that they prompted American Catholic and Protestant leaders to modify dramatically their nineteenth-century rhetorical patterns.[35] Making sense of those patterns is a more difficult chore than citing demographic information or election results. The same caveat applies to the study of other groups. The opinion of one historian that Utah's Senator Reed Smoot led a twentieth-century Mormon march into the American mainstream has to be viewed cautiously. Present-day Mormons, despite all of the chatter about their having become "super-Americans," still know how to keep their rhetorical distance from the mainstream when it suits their purposes.[36] And, to complicate the matter further, Mormons' use of a less strident language of differentiation does not in itself prove that the Mormon world view has undergone a transformation that in some easily defined, objective way has "normalized" their system of belief.

Given the almost endless variety of possible misinterpretation, the temptation to abandon the effort to make sense of the complex relationship among particular events, perception, and rhetoric is strong. But this relationship, with all of its inherent and attendant problems for historians, is the very thing that gives historical importance to questions about insiders and outsiders. We should not, therefore, reduce the narrative uses of insider and outsider categories but, instead, allow our narratives the chance to heighten rather than conceal the ambiguities. Perhaps the time has come for American historians to stop using the particular word "mainstream." It carries too many normative connotations about what values most Americans really did accept. Its casual and habitual use invariably deflects thought away from difficult problems about how to discuss typical or dominant values. An overused metaphor, it works to dismiss the fictional aspects of insider and outsider labeling and invites simplified conceptual versions of what is majority and minority culture in America.[37] Carried through, however, with a proper appreciation for the reasons why distortion and exaggeration are part of the meaning and why outsiders on one issue may be insiders on other issues, a narrative focus on contests between insiders and outsiders remains one of the best ways to analyze America's past. It works because the contests themselves were typically American, rather than necessarily the values that one side or the other proclaimed. Historical analysis of the contests is a means to open up, not settle prematurely, a multitude of questions about what were typical or dominant values in America's past. Such analysis must examine the social costs and benefits that attached to insider and outsider identifications on a case by case basis.

It is, of course, one thing to argue that the most common patterns of historical narrative do not fully reveal the complexity of these issues and quite another to posit an alternative. Any usable suggestions must derive from recognizing what is right and wrong in the typecasting of outsiders found in the major schools of American historiography. Actually, a good bit of what I have said here bears out some important themes of Consensus interpretation. This essay has, after all, pointed out that differences between ostensibly antagonistic groups have often been more apparent than real. It has, furthermore, supported the notion that centers of meaningful power really have been dispersed in American life. The rituals of outsiderhood, whatever they might seem to imply about alienation or victimization, have often been the means of finding or even maintaining a well-established, comfortable place in American life. The tradition of dissent, and the moral authority and respect dissent can command, have contributed to the relative stability of a plural system that even its architects had feared might quickly collapse.

I do think that many of the insights of Consensus historians are essentially correct. We know that at least some immigrant groups into this country, even in the late nineteenth century, shared more with the host country than was generally recognized.[38] We know, too, that many immigrant groups, having gone through a cultural assimilation, continued to resist what Milton Gordon called "structural assimilation."[39] We know that many "ethnics" stressed their differences from other groups in America, even when their sense of those groups remained vague, and cultivated in public rhetoric the feeling that "this country did not belong to them." This last sensibility continues to inform the strategies of the so-called new ethnicity. Michael Novak's *Rise of the Unmeltable Ethnics,* published a decade ago, fits into the well-established tradition of making outsiderhood count to one's advantage.[40] Novak's re-invention of the Protestant mainstream and his exaggeration of the differences between Catholics and Protestants were his ways of cutting WASP America down to size. People like Novak insisted, of course, that the American mainstream was shifting to include ethnic groups—that "America really was becoming America." But, if America ever did become America in Novak's sense, then our variegated national culture would be indistinguishable from a homogeneous one. Differences remain important only if someone asserts their existence and takes them seriously.

As it happens, a failure to appreciate this last point has seriously disabled Consensus interpretation. If Consensus historians have understood well enough that differences between groups have often been exaggerated, they have not been very sensitive to the reasons why many asserted, and even imagined, differences have so effectively divided people. A Consensus viewpoint might correctly spot "phony" aspects of Novak's ethnicity as judged by some objective standards, but it has trouble making sense of the ways in which "subjective" perception itself becomes "objective" historical information, to be analyzed and interpreted just like crime statistics or marriage patterns or election results. Suggesting that antagonism in American life was somehow always the result of misunderstanding, as Louis Hartz did, imposed severe handicaps on historical imagination. Consensus narrative tended to render cultural differences ("real" outsiderhood) either relatively rare—and, hence, historically unimportant—or rapidly disappearing—and, hence, of no great moment. Since Consensus interpretation could not adequately explain why Americans quarreled, it has encouraged us to think that they did not. The quarrels that did get noticed were deprived of substantive content. The argument that perception does not count dissolved differences. The possibility that competing groups turned similar values to very different uses was not explored.[41] These failures contributed to what was surely the biggest mistake in Consensus interpretation: the notion that the dispersal of power in America had led to a rough equality among groups. To say that self-proclaimed outsiders often gained an effective control over their lives and that self-proclaimed insiders were often insecure (as this essay has argued) is not to demonstrate that groups, of either the insider or the outsider variety, have had an equal say in American life.

Schools of historiography that have stressed conflict, therefore, began with a solid advantage over the Consensus school. Rather than making a disappearing line between insiders and outsiders the grand theme of American history, they have recognized that American experience is unintelligible without giving central importance to the lines insiders and outsiders drew, and consciously perpetuated. The aim of narrative should not be to drain those contests of meaning, because the participants had not realized their common commitment to Locke, but to explore the sorts of social meaning, real or imagined, they created. From the standpoint of this essay, what is weak in Progressive and Radical narrative is the tendency to turn all contests into sociopolitical struggles. Insiders were important only as the normal occupants of the most powerful positions in America and as the defenders of the status quo. Outsiders were important only as the economic underdogs who, because they had no social standing to protect, championed greater social justice. This sort of meaning is only one among many possibilities. As we have seen, outsiders may have had a significant social status and selfish interests to protect. They may have victimized as well as have been victims. And they may have had an importance to American culture even if they did not criticize things that some historians think they should have.

Undeniably, the number of American outsiders being recovered in historical narrative is growing at an impressive rate. That process has inevitably called attention to some of the complexities and ambiguities discussed in this essay. Radical historians especially have demonstrated that many groups and individuals, formerly thought to be without power or significant influence, had both. Thus, Herbert Gutman, in a postscript to a justly famous article, chided an earlier generation of labor historians for accepting the view that "the Gilded Age radical lives outside the mainstream of his times." In following the "route" of the Paterson, New Jersey, socialist leader Joseph McDonnell, Gutman found a way to "fit the Gilded Age labor radical into the mainstream of that era's history."[42]

For several reasons, however, I am not completely reassured by present trends. Outsiders are still taken up in narrative largely for the political significance they can be assigned. The full importance of outsiderhood in American historical experience will continue to go unrecognized until we are willing to see that not all, perhaps not most, outsiders have been "nice" or egalitarian-minded people. Once we finish studying the many historical groups whose protests remain politically important in our own time, we may find that we still have not got very close to writing a "people's history of the United States." Too much will remain buried, either with pity or contempt, under the label "fringe" or "marginal."

Second, to turn back to the question that began this essay, we do have to ask whether "mainstreaming" people who were once considered outsiders or passive victims is exactly the right narrative tactic. Constructing history so that Joseph McDonnell becomes one of the founders of the welfare state may only be Consensus history with a politically raised consciousness. It may reflect well enough some facts, yet still seriously distort the way people defined their own acts. The perceptions of historical actors, too, are facts. Inserting McDonnell narratively into an American mainstream can only undercut the oppositional strategy in his own self-identity.

Can historians ask questions about nineteenth-century spiritualists and Joseph McDonnells that can treat levels of factual and perceived reality together—questions that can assume the central cultural importance of contests between insiders and outsiders but that do not try to settle which side best reflected American norms? Clearly we can, but only if we stop assessing these contests solely for their impact on sociopolitical conflicts affecting American egalitarian principles. As a cultural process, contests between insiders and outsiders do not give the historian clear ways to divide the landscapes of the past into sub- and dominant cultures, but they do help us see that commonly held cultural values and norms did not always create common meanings or serve common purposes. To be sure, empirical research will reveal that many outsider groups had no influence, were truly deviant, and remained marginal to the major concerns of most American communities. Yet American historians cannot possibly discuss culture in America without recognizing the importance of the rhetoric and activities of opposition. (I do not therefore share the fashionable view that the study of outsiders, by showing us what America was not, can help us discern what America was.) By analyzing outsiders more carefully, we can more adequately address questions about the distribution of power and status in American life.

We cannot keep the historian's own perceptions out of the answers, and particular ideologies will no doubt continue to inform the shape of American historical narrative. Indeed, since I have argued that the perceptions of historical actors themselves not only fail as reliable guides to definitions of dominance or typicality but also confuse the interpretation of other empirical data, an ideological perspective may seem to be the only remaining way to begin a useful analysis of

American social structure. I am somewhat reluctantly drawn to that point of view. But particular ideologies will, I think, lead historians in more interesting directions, if they do not merely quote insider and outsider rhetoric to support or knock down Whiggish views of American history, if they actively pursue in their narratives the ambiguities that gave the rhetoric meaning in historical time. In so doing, they will preserve the best insights of the major schools of American historiography and find better reasons than narrative now provides to look closely at groups that have not yet commanded much historical attention. After all, outsiders were as American as cherry pie not because it makes sense to award the ones we admire posthumous admission into a mainstream but because their contests with insiders were the means by which many Americans invented themselves.

NOTES

1. Moore, *In Search of White Crows: Spiritualism, Parapsychology, and American Culture* (New York, 1977).

2. *Ibid.*, 90–101. For a discussion of the alliance of spiritualism and feminism, see William Leach, *True Love and Perfect Union: The Feminist Reform of Sex and Society* (New York, 1980), esp. 292–97.

3. John Higham and Paul Conkin, eds., *New Directions in American Intellectual History* (Baltimore, 1979), xii.

4. Kelley, *The Cultural Pattern in American Politics: The First Century* (New York, 1979), 27. For a preliminary statement of his argument, also see his "Ideology and Political Culture from Jefferson to Nixon," *AHR*, 82 (1977): 531–62; and see Geoffrey Blodgett, "Comment" on Kelley's essay, *ibid.*, 566–67.

5. Hartz, *The Liberal Tradition in America: An Interpretation of American Political Thought since the Revolution* (New York, 1955). For a general discussion of Consensus history, see Barnard Sternsher, *Consensus, Conflict, and American Historians* (Bloomington, Ind., 1975).

6. For examples of the kind of analysis I have in mind, see the essays in Daniel Bell, ed., *The Radical Right* (Garden City, N.Y., 1964); Richard Hofstadter, *Anti-Intellectualism in American Life* (New York, 1963), and *The Paranoid Style in American Politics and Other Essays* (New York, 1965); and Seymour Martin Lipset and Earl Raab, *The Politics of Unreason: Right-Wing Extremism in America, 1790–1970* (New York, 1970).

7. See David Potter, *People of Plenty: Economic Abundance and the American Character* (Chicago, 1954), 91–141; Richard Hofstadter, *The American Political Tradition and the Men who Made It* (New York, 1951), v–xi; and Hartz, *The Liberal Tradition in America*, 3–32.

8. Zinn wrote in his *Postwar America*, "All that I have said here supports the 'consensus' interpretation of American history which states, I believe, a profound truth about our society, that its progress and its political clashes have been kept within severe limits"; Zinn, *Postwar America, 1945–1971* (Indianapolis, 1973), xvi–xvii. Something of the same perspective informs Kolko's *The Triumph of Conservatism: A Reinterpretation of American History, 1900–1916* (New York, 1963) and James Weinstein's *The Corporate Ideal in the Liberal State, 1900–1918* (Boston, 1968).

9. I have taken this phrase from Eugene Genovese, Review of Leon Litwack, *Been in the Storm So Long: The Aftermath of Slavery* (New York, 1979), in the *New York Times Book Review*, June 10, 1979, p. 3.

10. See Herbert G. Reid, "Introduction," in Reid, ed., *Up the Mainstream: A Critique of Ideology in American Politics and Everyday Life* (New York, 1974), 2–9.

11. As a small example of this point, Christopher Lasch picked the word "grotesque" to describe nineteenth-century Mormon theology and the words "outlandish" and "trumped up" to characterize the "pseudo-historical myth" of Mormons as the chosen people. By using this sort of language, Lasch has reduced their significance to an illustration of ideological stupidity in American culture. See Lasch, "The Mormon Utopia," in his *The World Of Nations: Reflections on American History, Politics, and Culture* (New York, 1973), 60–61.

12. Campbell, "Christianity and Civil Liberty," *American and Presbyterian Theological Review*, 5 (1867): 390–91.

13. Noyes, "Confession of Religious Experience," as compiled in George Wallingford Noyes, ed., *Religious Experiences of John Humphrey Noyes, Founder of the Oneida Community* (New York, 1923), 125.

14. Boardman, "Is There Any Ground to Apprehend the Extensive and Dangerous Prevalence of Romanism in the United States?" in *Anti-Catholicism in America, 1841–1851: Three Sermons* (New York, 1977), 31, 33, 35.

15. One journal of American communism, published between 1956 and 1963, bore the title *Mainstream;* before 1956, the name of the journal was *Masses and Mainstream.*

16. Smith, *History of the Church of Jesus Christ of Latter-day Saints,* as quoted in Fawn M. Brodie, *No Man Knows My History: The Life of Joseph Smith, the Mormon Prophet* (2nd edn., New York, 1971), 23.

17. A. Leland Jamison, "Religions on the Christian Perimeter," in James Ward Smith and Jamison, eds., *The Shaping of American Religion,* 1 (Princeton, 1961): 214–15. Tolstoy, in an oft-quoted conversation with Andrew Dickson White, said that the Mormons taught *the* American religion.

18. See Kai Erikson, *Wayward Puritans: A Study in the Sociology of Deviance* (New York, 1966); Robert A. Dentler and Kai Erikson, "The Functions of Deviance in Groups," *Social Problems,* 7 (1959–60): 98–107; and Howard Becker, *Outsiders: Studies in the Sociology of Deviance* (New York, 1963).

19. Smith, "Address of May 26, 1844," in his *History of the Church of Jesus Christ of Latter-day Saints,* as quoted in Donna Hill, *Joseph Smith: The First Mormon* (Garden City, N.Y., 1977), 392.

20. Dr. Garland Hurt to George Manypenny, May 2, 1855, as quoted in Norman F. Furniss, *The Mormon Conflict, 1850–59* (New Haven, 1960), 51.

21. Simmel, "The Sociology of Conflict," *American Journal of Sociology,* 9 (1903–04): 680.

22. Gerlach and Hine, *People, Power, and Change: Movements of Social Transformation* (Indianapolis, 1970), chap. 11, esp. pp. 184–85. For the best discussion of the means used to build group commitment, see Rosabeth Kanter, *Commitment and Community: Communes and Utopias in Sociological Perspective* (Cambridge, Mass., 1972), esp. pt. 2.

23. Brownson, "Mission of America," *Brownson's Quarterly Review,* New York ser., 1 (1856): 414.

24. Hughes, Open Letter to Mayor James Harper of New York, May 17, 1844, in his *Complete Works of the Most Reverend John Hughes, D.D.,* 1 (New York, 1866): 454.

25. Greeley, *The Catholic Experience: An Interpretation of the History of American Catholicism* (Garden City, N.Y., 1967), 107, 117, 125; and O'Brien, "American Catholicism and the Diaspora," *Cross Currents,* 16 (1966): 310–15.

26. Simon, *A Time for Truth* (New York, 1978), 41.

27. Especially see the essays in his *Drama, Fields, and Metaphors: Symbolic Action in Human Society* (Ithaca, N.Y., 1974) and *The Ritual Process: Structure and Anti-Structure* (Chicago, 1969).

28. Hacker, Review of Stephan Thernstrom, ed., *Harvard Encyclopedia of American Ethnic*

Groups (Cambridge, Mass., 1980) in the *New York Times Book Review,* February 1, 1981, p. 29.

29. Pessimism was not the dominant tone in late-nineteenth-century premillennial journals and sermons. Dwight L. Moody, the best known of the premillennial ministers, was invariably upbeat. In contrast, James Brookes, in his journal *The Truth: or, Testimony for Christ,* stressed the decline of Protestant Christianity. He persisted in his work, he wrote, as "a help to the scattered witnesses for God's insulted truth, although it is certain that the protest will be unheeded, and that the voices of the witnesses, here and there, will be silenced amid the clamor of infidelity which will close the present age"; Brookes, Editorial, *The Truth,* 11 (1885): 530.

30. The separatist-minded Carl McIntire was the shrillest voice in asserting Fundamentalism's rout in the major Protestant denominations. The more moderate voice of William Bell Riley had, however, begun to stress the defeat of Fundamentalism by the end of the 1920s. Louis Gasper, in describing the mood of Fundamentalists in the 1930s, wrote, "For the most part they acted like martyrs and regarded themselves as the 'faithful remnant' of modern times suffering for Jesus Christ. This was a psychological stimulant, because they believed their faithfulness would be rewarded posthumously." Gasper, *The Fundamentalist Movement* (The Hague, 1963), 21.

31. For an influential book that guided much of what was subsequently said, see Dean M. Kelley, *Why Conservative Churches Are Growing* (New York, 1972). Also see Richard Quebedeaux, *The Young Evangelicals: Revolution in Orthodoxy* (New York, 1974), and *The New Charismatics: The Origins, Development, and Significance of Neo-Pentecostalism* (Garden City, N.Y., 1976).

32. Marsden, *Fundamentalism and American Culture: The Shaping of Twentieth-Century Evangelicalism, 1870–1925* (New York, 1980), 6.

33. See, for example, David F. Wells, "The Reformation: Will History Repeat Itself?" *Christianity Today,* October 25, 1974, p. 8. In the same journal, Timothy L. Smith remarked on the "fortress mentality," which he saw as still dominant among evangelicals; see "A Fortress Mentality: Shackling the Spirit's Power—An Interview with Timothy L. Smith," *ibid.,* November 19, 1976, pp. 23–24. Also suggestive are David Moberg, "Fundamentalists and Evangelicals in Society," in David F. Wells and John D. Woodbridge, eds., *The Evangelicals: What They Believe, Who They Are, Where They Are Changing* (Nashville, Tenn., 1975), 143–69; and Martin Marty, "Tensions within Contemporary Evangelicalism: A Critical Appraisal," *ibid.,* 170–88.

34. For an estimate of the continuity of Fundamentalists strength, see Joel A. Carpenter, "A Shelter in the Time of Storm: Fundamentalist Institutions and the Rise of Evangelical Protestantism, 1929–1942," *Church History,* 49 (1980): 62–75.

35. For a useful collection that offers varying perspectives on the Church's place in America, see Thomas T. McAvoy, ed., *Roman Catholicism and the American Way of Life* (Notre Dame, Ind., 1960).

36. For various issues relating to the "Americanness" of the Mormons, see Klaus Hansen, *Mormonism and the American Experience* (Chicago, 1981), esp. chaps. 2, 8; the essays in Marvin Hill and James Allen, eds., *Mormonism and American Culture* (New York, 1972); John Sorenson, "Mormon World View and American Culture," *Dialogue: A Journal of Modern Thought,* 8 (1973): 17–29; and Editorial Introduction: "In This [Fall] Issue," *Utah Historical Quarterly,* 45 (1977): 323. In a January 1979 syndicated column, the conservative columnist George F. Will wrote, "Mormons comprise the most singular great church to come into existence in the United States, and it is quintessentially American."

37. In addition to the national, sociopoliitcal mainstream, there is apparently a mainstream tendency in every subcategory of American life. Recent articles in the *New York Times* have announced that Hispanics are "beginning to have a broad impact on the economic, social, and cultural life of mainstream America," that "courses on ethics . . . have moved into the

mainstream of American universities and professional schools," that conservatism, once a "backwater of American intellectual and political life, has spilled into the mainstream," and the Village People "sociologically . . . attest to the continuing permeation of homosexual ideas into the mainstream." References pulled more or less randomly from scholarly works about America posit such things as "mainstream political discourse," "a Marxian mainstream," "mainstream feminism," and "mainstream Pentecostalism." With respect to normative overtones of the metaphor, remember that "mainstreaming," as an educational goal, is a "good thing"; it is the process by which the aspirations of "normal" men and women become realizable by everyone.

38. John W. Briggs, *An Italian Passage: Immigrants to Three American Cities, 1890–1930* (New Haven, 1978), 272–78.

39. Gordon, *Assimilation in American Life: The Role of Race, Religion, and National Origins* (New York, 1964), esp. chaps. 2, 3, 6.

40. Novak, *The Rise of the Unmeltable Ethnics* (New York, 1972), esp. 56, 62, 71, 291. During World War I, at the height of the frenzy to get the melting pot boiling, Arthur Preuss wrote, "The man or woman who would tamely submit to a large part of what goes under the name of Americanization is not fit to be in America"; Preuss, "Americanizing the Immigrant," *Fortnightly Review* [St. Louis], 25 (May 15, 1918), 156–59, as quoted in Richard M. Linkh, *American Catholicism and European Immigrants, 1900–1924* (New York, 1975), 22–23.

41. For one recent exploration of this possibility, see David Montgomery, *Workers' Control in America: Studies in the History of Work, Technology, and Labor Struggles* (New York, 1979), esp. Introduction, chap. 1.

42. Gutman, "A Brief Postscript: Class, Status, and the Gilded Age Radical—A Reconsideration," in his *Work, Culture, and Society in Industrializing America* (New York, 1976), 262, 290.

CHAPTER
11

Documents and Debate: On Whose Side?
God, Slavery, and the Civil War

Historians agree that the Civil War was the most convulsive—and defining—event in American history. Yet surprisingly, religion's role in this formative event has only recently begun to be explored. In this section we include two documents and two essays that describe religion's centrality to the contest over slavery and the Civil War. Frederick Douglass's powerful critique of slavery in the light of Christ's central teachings reveals both the profound ways in which African-American Christians developed their own reading of the Old and New Testaments and the astonishing and devastating influence of the slave-holding doctrines articulated by the Maryland Anglican Minister, Thomas Bacon, a century earlier—whose words Douglass quotes through the medium of Virginia's Episcopal Bishop, William Meade, who had reprinted Bacon's eighteenth-century tracts in Virginia in 1813 as a guide for Christian slaveholders.

The contrast with the essay by George Armstrong scarcely could be greater. Armstrong was a Presbyterian Minister in Norfolk, Virginia. His book, *The Christian Doctrine of Slavery in 1857*, from which we print the conclusion, "God's Work in God's Way," offered a typical Southern clergyman's defense of slavery on the eve of the Civil War. The essay opens with a brief but important racial epithet—Armstrong describes slaves as "deeply degraded"—then defends the view that the church had only one task with regard to the slave, to "make him a worthy worshipper among God's people on earth." Armstrong takes strong exception to the antislavery writings of Reverend Albert Barnes, a Northern antislavery leader who argued that slavery was unscriptural and should be abolished, and argues that a proper separation of church and state prevented the true Christian church from "intermeddling" in political questions, especially slavery. The essay concludes with ominous soundings about separation between North and South in America.

What are the central arguments about Christianity and slavery made by Douglass and Armstrong? How does each author employ scriptures to bolster his case? If you could have asked both men what they imagined an ideal Christian society to be, what do these essays suggest they might have said? What does each author see as religion's central purpose? How do their visions of religion and its obligations differ from that of Bacon, Meade, or Armstrong? How can we determine the representativeness of each of these essays in their own communities?

Additional Reading: There is a relatively large literature on religion and the slavery question. Several different aspects of religion's role in antislavery agitation are discussed in Daniel Walker Howe, *The Unitarian Conscience: Harvard Moral Philosophy, 1805–1861* (Cambridge, Mass., 1970) and David Blight, "Frederick Douglass and the American Apocalypse," *Civil War History,* 31 (1985), 309–328. Religious support for proslavery sentiment is outlined in Larry E. Tise, *Proslavery: A History of the Defense of Slavery in America, 1701–1840* (Athens, 1987) and in Eugene Genovese and Elizabeth Fox-Genovese, "The Divine Sanction of Social Order: Religious Foundations of the Southern Slaveholders' World View," *Journal of the American Academy of Religion,* 55 (1987), 211–233. James Henley Thornwell, *The rights and the duties of masters. A sermon preached at the dedication of a church erected in Charleston, S. C., for the benefit and instruction of the coloured population* (Charleston, 1850) offers an unusually sophisticated defense of slavery that has intrigued twentieth-century historians, though it is not as representative as Armstrong's more direct, petulant approach.

Frederick Douglass

Address on "Evangelical Flogging," Delivered at Market Hall, Syracuse, N.Y., September 24, 1847[1]

I like radical measures, whether adopted by Abolitionists or slaveholders. I do not know but I like them better when adopted by the latter. Hence I look with pleasure upon the movements of Mr. Calhoun and his party.[2] I rejoice at any movement in the slave States with reference to this system of Slavery. Any movement there will attract attention to the system—a system, as Junius once said to Lord Granby, "which can only pass without condemnation as it passes without observation." I am anxious to have it seen of all men: hence I am delighted to see any efforts to prop up the system on the part of the slaveholders. It serves to bring up the subject before the people and hasten the day of deliverance. It is meant otherwise. I am sorry that it is so. Yet the wrath of men may be made to praise God. He will confound the wisdom of the crafty, and bring to naught the counsels of the ungodly. The slaveholders are now marshaling their hosts for the propagation

Reprinted from Fredrick Douglass, "Address Delivered at Market Hall, Syracuse, New York, September 1847," *National Anti-Slavery Standard,* Oct. 28, 1847.

and extension of the institution—Abolitionists, on the other hand, are marshaling their forces not only against its propagation and extension, but against its very existence. Two large classes of the community hitherto unassociated with the Abolitionists, have come up so far towards the right as to become opposed to the farther extension of the crime. I am glad to hear it. I like to gaze upon these two contending armies, for I believe it will hasten the dissolution of the present unholy Union, which has been justly stigmatized as "a covenant with death, an agreement with hell." I welcome the bolt, either from the North or the South, which shall shatter this Union; for under this Union lie the prostrate forms of three millions with whom I am identified. In consideration of their wrongs, of their sufferings, of their groans, I welcome the bolt, either from the celestial or from the infernal regions, which shall sever this Union in twain. Slaveholders are promoting it—Abolitionists are doing so. Let it come, and when it does, our land will rise up from an incubus; her brightness shall reflect against the sky, and shall become the beacon light of liberty in the Western world. She shall then, indeed, become "the land of the free and the home of the brave."

For sixteen years, Wm. Lloyd Garrison and a noble army of the friends of emancipation have been labouring in season and out of season, amid smiles and frowns, sunshine and clouds, striving to establish the conviction through this land, that to hold and traffic in human flesh is a sin against God.[3] They have been somewhat successful; but they have been in no wise so successful as they might have been, had the men and women at the North rallied around them as they had a right to hope from their profession. They have had to contend not only with skillful politicians, with a deeply prejudiced and proslavery community, but with eminent Divines, Doctors of Divinity, and Bishops. Instead of encouraging them as friends, they have acted as enemies. For many days did Garrison go the rounds of the city of Boston to ask of the ministers the poor privilege of entering their chapels and lifting up his voice for the dumb. But their doors were bolted, their gates barred, and their pulpits [hermetically] sealed. It was not till an infidel hall was thrown open, that the voice of dumb millions could be heard in Boston.

I take it that all who have heard at all on this subject, are well convinced that the stronghold of Slavery is in the pulpit. Say what we may of the politicians and political parties, the power that holds the keys of the dungeon in which the bondmen is confined, is the pulpit. It is that power which is dropping, dropping, constantly dropping on the ear of this people, creating and molding the moral sentiment of the land. This they have sufficiently under their control that they can change it from the spirit of hatred to that of love to mankind. That they do it not, is evident from the results of their teaching. The men who wield the blood-clotted cow-skin come from our Sabbath schools in the Northern States. Who act as slave-drivers? The men who go forth from our own congregations here. Why, if the Gospel were truly preached among us, a man would as soon think of going into downright piracy as to offer himself as a slave-driver.

In Farmington, two sons of members of the Society of Friends are coolly proposing to go to the South and engage in the honourable office of slave-driving for a thousand dollars a year. People at the North talk coolly of uncles, cousins, and brothers, who are slaveholders, and of their coming to visit them. If the

Gospel were truly preached here, you would as soon talk of having an uncle or brother a brothel keeper as a slaveholder; for I hold that every slaveholder, no matter how pure he may be, is a keeper of a house of ill-fame. Every kitchen is a brothel, from that of Dr. Fuller's to that of James K. Polk's.[4] (Applause.) I presume I am addressing a virtuous audience—I presume I speak to virtuous females—and I ask you to consider this one feature of Slavery. Think of a million females absolutely delivered up into the hands of tyrants, to do what they will with them:—to dispose of their persons in any way they see fit. And so entirely are they at the disposal of their masters, that if they raise their hands against them, they may be put to death for daring to resist their infernal aggression.

We have been trying to make this thing appear sinful. We have not been able to do so yet. It is not admitted, and I hardly know how to argue against it. I confess that the time for argument seems almost gone by. What do the people want? Affirmation upon affirmation—denunciation upon denunciation,—rebuke upon rebuke?

We have men in this land now advocating evangelical flogging. I hold in my hand a sermon recently published by Rev. Bishop Meade, of Virginia.[5] Before I read that part in favour of evangelical flogging, let me read a few extracts from another part, relating to the duties of the slave. The sermon, by the way, was published with a view of its being read by Christian ministers to their slaves. White black birds! (Laughter.)

(Mr. Douglass here assumed a most grotesque look, and with a canting tone of voice, read as follows.)

"Having just shown you the chief duties you owe to your great Master in Heaven, I now come to lay before you the duties you owe to your masters and mistresses on earth. And for this you have one general rule that you ought always carry in your minds, and that is, to do all service for them, as if you did it for God himself. Poor creatures! you little consider when you are idle, and neglectful of your master's business; when you steal, waste, and hurt any of their substance; when you are saucy and impudent; when you are telling them lies and deceiving them; or when you prove stubborn and sullen, and will not do the work you are set about, without stripes and vexation; you do not consider, I say, that what faults you are guilty of towards your masters and mistresses, are faults done against God himself, who hath set your masters and mistresses over you in his own stead, and expects that you will do for them just as you would do for him. And pray, do not think that I want to deceive you, when I tell you that your masters and mistresses are God's overseers; and that if you are faulty towards them, God himself will punish you severely for it."[6]

This is some of the Southern religion. Do you not think you would "grow in grace and in the knowledge of truth."—(Applause.)

I come now to evangelical flogging. There is nothing said about flogging—that word is not used. It is called correction; and that word as it is understood at the North, is some sort of medicine.—(Laughter.) Slavery has always sought to hide itself under different names. The mass of the people call it "our peculiar institution." There is no harm in that. Others call it (they are the more pious sort,) "our Patriarchal institution." (Laughter.) Politicians have called it "our social system;" and people in social life have called it "our domestic institution." Abbott Lawrence has recently discovered a new name for it—he calls it "unenlightened labour."[7] (Laughter.) The Methodists in their last General Conference, have invented a new name—"the impediment."[8] (Laughter.) To give you some idea of evangelical flogging, under the name of correction, there are laws of this description,—"any white man killing a slave shall be punished as though he shall have killed a white person, unless such a slave die under moderate correction." It commences with a plain proposition.

"Now when correction is given you, you either deserve it, or you do not deserve it."—(Laughter.)

That is very plain, almost as safe as that of a certain orator:—"Ladies and Gentlemen, it is my opinion, my deliberate opinion, after a long consideration of the whole matter, that as a general thing, all other things being equal, there are fewer persons to be found in towns sparsely populated, than in larger towns more thickly settled." (Laughter.) The Bishop goes on to say—"Whether you really deserve it or not," (one would think that it would make some difference,) "it is your duty, and Almighty God requires that you bear it patiently. You may perhaps think that this is a hard doctrine," (and it admits of little doubt,) "but if you consider it right you must needs think otherwise of it." (It is clear as mud. I suppose he is now going to reason them into the propriety of being flogged evangelically.) "Suppose you deserve correction; you cannot but see it is just and right and you should meet with it. Suppose you do not, or at least so much or so severe; you perhaps have escaped a great many more, and are at least paid for all. Suppose you are quite innocent; is it not possible you may have done some other bad thing which was never discovered, and Almighty God would not let you escape without punishment one time or another? Ought you not in such cases to give glory to Him?"[9] (Glory!) (Much laughter.)

I am glad you have got to the point that you can laugh at the religion of such fellows as this Doctor. There is nothing that will facilitate our cause more than getting the people to laugh at that religion which brings its influence to support traffic in human flesh. It has deceived us so long that it has overawed us.

For a long time when I was a slave, I was led to think from hearing such passages as "servants obey, &c." that if I dared to escape, the wrath of God would follow me. All are willing to acknowledge my right to be free; but after this acknowledgment, the good man goes to the Bible and says "after all I see some difficulty about this thing. You know, after the deluge, there was Shem, Ham, and Japhet; and you know that Ham was black and had a curse put upon him; and I know not but it would be an attempt to thwart the purposes of Jehovah, if these men were set at liberty." It is this kind of religion I wish to have you laugh at—it breaks the charm there is about it. If I could have the men at this meeting who hold such sentiments and could hold up the mirror to let them see themselves as others see them, we should soon make head against this proslavery religion.

I dwell mostly upon the religious aspects, because I believe it is the religious people who are to be relied on in this Anti-Slavery movement. Do not misunderstand my railing—do not class me with those who despise religion—do not identify me with the infidel. I love the religion of Christianity—which cometh from above—which is pure, peaceable, gentle, easy to be entreated, full of good fruits, and without hypocrisy. I love that religion which sends its votaries to bind up the wounds of those who have fallen among thieves. By all the love I bear to such a Christianity as this, I hate that of the Priest and Levite, that with long-faced Phariseeism goes up to Jerusalem and worship, and leaves the bruised and wounded to die. I despise that religion that can carry Bibles to the heathen on the other side of the globe and withhold them from heathen on this side—which can talk about human rights yonder and traffic in human flesh here. I love that which makes it votaries do to others as they would that others should do to them. . . .[10]

There is another religion. It is that which takes off fetters instead of binding them on—that breaks every yoke—that lifts up the bowed down. The Anti-Slavery platform is based on this kind of religion. It spreads its table to the lame, the halt, and the blind. It goes down after a long neglected race. It passes, link by link till it finds the lowest link in humanity's chain—humanity's most degraded form in the most abject condition. It reaches down its arm and tells them to stand up. This is Anti-Slavery—this is Christianity. It is reviving gloriously among the various denominations. It is threatening to supersede those old forms of religion having all of the love of God and none of man in it. (Applause.)

I now leave this aspect of the subject and proceed to inquire into that which probably must be the inquiry of every honest mind present. I trust I do not misjudge the character of my audience when I say they are anxious to know in what way they are contributing to uphold Slavery.

The question may be answered in various ways. I leave the outworks of political parties and social arrangements, and come at once to the Constitution, to which I believe all present are devotedly attached—I will not say all, for I believe I know some who, however they may be disposed to admire some of the beautiful truths set forth in that instrument, recognize its proslavery features, and are ready to form a republic in which there shall be neither tyrant nor slave. The Constitution I hold to be radically and essentially slaveholding, in that it gives the physical and numerical power of the nation to keep the slave in his chains, by promising that power shall in any emergency be brought to bear upon the slave, to crush him in obedience to his master. The language of the Constitution is you shall be a slave or die. We know it is such and knowing it we are not disposed to have part nor lot with that Constitution. For my part I had rather that my right hand should wither by my side than cast a ballot under the Constitution of the United States.

Then, again, in the clause concerning fugitives—in this you are implicated. Your whole country is one vast hunting ground from Texas to Maine.

Ours is a glorious land; and from across the Atlantic we welcome those who are stricken by the storms of despotism. Yet the damning fact remains, there is not a rood of earth under the stars and the eagle on your flag, where a man of my complexion can stand free. There is no mountain so high, no plain so extensive, no spot so sacred, that it can secure to me the right of liberty. Wherever waves the star-spangled banner there the bondman may be arrested and hurried back to the jaws of Slavery. This is your "land of the free," your "home of the brave." From Lexington, from Ticonderoga, from Bunker Hill, where rises that grand shaft with its cap atone in the clouds, ask, in the name of the first blood that spurted in behalf of freedom, to protect the slave from the infernal clutches of his master. That petition would be denied, and he bid go back to the tyrant.

I never knew what freedom was till I got beyond the limits of the American eagle. When I first rested my head on a British Island, I felt that the eagle might scream, but from its talons and beak I was free, at least for a time. No slaveholder can clutch me on British soil. There I could gaze the tyrant in the face and with the [indignation] of a tyrant in my look, wither him before me. But republican, Christian America will aid the tyrant in catching his victim.

I know this kind of talk is not agreeable to what are called patriots. Indeed some have called me a traitor. That profanely religious Journal, "The Olive Branch," edited by the Rev. Mr. Norris, recommended that I be hung as a traitor.[11] Two things are necessary to make a traitor. One is, he shall have a country. (Laughter and applause.) I believe if I had a country, I should be a patriot. I think I have all the feelings necessary—all the moral material, to say nothing about the intellectual. I do not know that I ever felt the emotion, but sometimes thought I had a glimpse of it. When I have been delighted with the little brook that passes by the cottage in which I was born,—with the woods and the fertile fields, I felt a sort of glow which I suspect resembles a little, what they call patriotism. I can look with some admiration on your wide lakes, your fertile fields, your enterprise, your industry, your many lovely institutions. I can read with pleasure your Constitution to establish justice, and secure the blessings of liberty to posterity. Those are precious sayings to my mind. But when I remember that blood of four sisters and one brother, is making fat the soil of Maryland and Virginia,—when I remember that an aged grandmother who has reared twelve children for the Southern market, and these one after another as they arrived at the most interesting age, were torn from her bosom,—when I remember that when she became too much racked for toil, she was turned out by a professed Christian master to grope her way in the darkness of old age, literally to die with none to help her, and the institutions of this country sanctioning and sanctifying this crime, I have no words of eulogy, I have no patriotism. How can I love a country where the blood of my own blood, the flesh of my own flesh, is now toiling under the lash?— America's soil reddened by the stain from woman's shrinking flesh.

No, I make no pretension to patriotism. So long as my voice can be heard on this or the other side of the Atlantic, I will hold up America to the lightning scorn of moral indignation. In doing this, I shall feel myself discharging the duty of a true patriot; for he is a lover of his country who rebukes and does not excuse its sins. It is righteousness that exalteth a nation while sin is a reproach to any people.

But to the idea of what you at the North have to do with Slavery. You furnish the bulwark of protection, and promise to put the slaves in bondage. As the American Anti-Slavery Society says, "if you will go on branding, scourging, sundering family ties, trampling in the dust your down trodden victims, you must do it at your own peril." But if you say, "we of the North will render you no assistance: if you still continue to trample on the slave, you must take the consequences," I tell you the matter will soon be settled.

I have been taunted frequently with the want of valour: so has my race, because we have not risen upon our masters. It is adding insult to injury to say this.

You belong to 17,000,000, with arms, with means of locomotion, with telegraphs. We are kept in Ignorance[, our] three millions to [your] seventeen. You taunt us with not being able to rescue ourselves from your clutch. Shame on you! Stand aside—give us fair play—leave us with the tyrants, and then if we do not take care of ourselves, you may taunt us. I do not mean by this to advocate war and bloodshed. I am not a man of war. The time was when I was. I was then a slave: I had dreams, horrid dreams of freedom through a sea of blood. But when I heard of the Anti-Slavery movement, light broke in upon my dark mind. Bloody visions fled away, and I saw the star of liberty peering above the horizon. Hope then took the place of desperation, and I was led to repose in the arms of Slavery. I said, I would suffer rather than do any act of violence—rather than that the glorious day of liberty might be postponed.

Since the light of God's truth beamed upon my mind, I have become a friend of that religion which teaches us to pray for our enemies—which, instead of shooting balls into their hearts, loves them. I would not hurt a hair of a slave-holder's head. I will tell you what else I would not do. I would not stand around the slave with my bayonet pointed at his breast, in order to keep him in the power of the slaveholder.

I am aware that there are many who think the slaves are very well off, and that they are very well treated, as if it were possible that such a thing could be. A man happy in chains! Even the eagle loves liberty.

> Go, let a cage, with grates of gold,
> And pearly roof, the eagle hold;
> Let dainty viands be his fare,
> And give the captive tenderest care;
> But say, in luxury's limits pent,
> Find you the king of birds content?
> No, oft he'll sound the startling shriek,
> And dash the grates with angry beak.
> Precarious freedom's far more dear,
> Than all the prison's pamp'ring cheer!
> He longs to see his eyrie's seat,
>   Some cliff on ocean's lonely shore,
> Whose old bare top the tempests beat,
> And round whose base the billows roar,
> When tossed by gales, they yawn like graves,—
> He longs for joy to skim those waves;
> Or rise through tempest-shrouded air,
> All thick and dark, with wild winds swelling,
> To brave the lightning's lurid glare,
> And talk with thunders in their dwelling.[12]

As with the eagle, so with man. No amount of attention or finery, no dainty dishes can be a substitute for liberty. Slaveholders know this, and knowing it, they exclaim,—" The South are surrounded by a dangerous population, degraded, stupid savages, and if they could but entertain the idea that immediate, unconditional death would not be their portion, they would rise at once and enact the St.

Domingo tragedy.[13] But they are held in subordination by the consciousness that the whole nation would rise and crush them." Thus they live in constant dread from day to day.

Friends, Slavery must be abolished, and that can only be done by enforcing the great principles of justice. Vainly you talk about voting it down. When you have cast your millions of ballots, you have not reached the evil. It has fastened its root deep into the heart of the nation, and nothing but God's truth and love can cleanse the land. We must change the moral sentiment. Hence we ask you to support the Anti-Slavery Society. It is not an organization to build up political parties, or churches, nor to pull them down, but to stamp the image of Anti-Slavery truth upon the community. Here we may all do something.

> In the world's broad field of battle,
> In the bivouac of life,
> Be not like dumb driven cattle—
> Be a hero in the strive.[14]

NOTES

Several obvious typographical errors in the 1847 newspaper text have been corrected silently and the spelling has been modernized. Other corrections are enclosed in brackets. For another edition of the text, see *The Frederick Douglass Papers*, ed. John W. Blassingame (New Haven, 1979) 2: 93–105.

1. According to the *National Anti-Slavery Standard*, the text of this speech was based on a "Phonographic Report by Wm. H. Barr." Barr probably used one of the shorthand methods widely available in the nineteenth century to transcribe Douglass's address. Barr's transcription provides an interesting view of Douglass's speaking style.

2. During the debate over the Wilmot Proviso, which would have banned slavery in all territories acquired during the Mexican War of 1846, in 1847 John C. Calhoun had introduced Senate resolutions declaring that Congress lacked any constitutional right to legislate on slavery in the territories.

3. Together with Douglass, William Lloyd Garrison was one of the leading antebellum antislavery leaders.

4. Douglass probably was referring to Richard Fuller of Beaufort, South Carolina, who was one of the state's leading Baptist ministers and who was known in the north for his published slavery debate with Francis Wayland, *Domestic slavery considered as a Scriptural institution: in a correspondence between the Rev. Richard Fuller of Beaufort, S. C., and the Rev. Francis Wayland, of Providence, R. I.* (New York, 1845).

5. Douglass's reference to Meade's "recently published" sermon is confusing because Meade's edition of Thomas Bacon's sermons was printed in Winchester, Virginia, by John Heiskell in 1813 under the title *Sermons addressed to masters and servants: and published in the year 1743 [sic] / by Thomas Bacon; now republished with other tracts and dialogues on the same subject, and recommended to all masters and mistresses to be used in their families, by William Meade*. The editors of the *Frederick Douglass Papers* believe that Douglass was quoting from Meade's 1813 edition of Bacon's sermons and the passages do appear there, just as they do in Bacon's original publications.

However, it is more likely that Douglass was quoting Meade (actually, Bacon) from a copy of Samuel Brooke, *Slavery, and the Slaveholders' Religion; as opposed to Christianity* (Cincinnati, 1846). This pamphlet criticized the southern position on slavery and on pages

28–35 quoted extensively from Meade's 1813 edition of Bacon's sermons. But Brooke never mentioned Bacon and did not print the full title of Meade's work, which would have revealed Thomas Bacon's authorship of the text. As a result, Brooke's readers would have assumed that Meade was the author of the words Brooke quoted unless they had read the Meade book from which Brooke took his quotations.

Douglass quoted no material from Meade (or Bacon) that had not been quoted in Brooke's 1846 *Slavery, and the Slaveholders Religion,* and Douglass apparently had never referred to Meade until 1846, when he made a speech in Bristol, England, in September on "Slavery and the American Churches." It is most likely that Brooke alerted Douglass to Meade because Brooke's pamphlet was a compilation of southern laws, sermons, and agricultural advice that supported slavery, including Meade's 1813 publication. For other Douglass references to Meade, all of them made in 1846 and 1847, see *Frederick Douglass Papers,* 1: 396–397, 463, 472; 2: 132.

6. This material is quoted in Brooke, *Slavery and the Slaveholders Religion,* 30; Meade, *Sermons Addressed to Masters and Servants,* 104, and Thomas Bacon, *Two Sermons, Preached to a Congregation of Black Slaves, at the Parish Church of S[aint] P[eter's], in the Province of Maryland* (London, 1749), 30–31.

7. Abbot Lawrence was a Massachusetts Whig and onetime member of the American Colonization Society, which sought to return slaves to Africa.

8. The term "impediment" was used at the Methodist General Conference of 1844. See *Frederick Douglass Papers,* 2: 98.

9. This section on "correction" appeared in Brooke's *Slavery, and the Slaveholders Religion,* 34–35, in Meade's *Sermons Addressed to Masters and Servants,* 132–133, and in Bacon, *Two Sermons Preached to a Congregation of Black Slaves,* 71–72.

10. Several obscure references to nineteenth-century revivalism have been deleted here.

11. Rev. Thomas F. Norris of Boston edited the *Olive Branch* in the 1840s.

12. These verses may have been written by Douglass himself. See the *Frederick Douglass Papers,* 2: 104–105.

13. Douglass refers to the great—and greatly feared—slave revolts that erupted on the island of Santo Domingo in 1791.

14. The lines are from Henry Wadsworth Longfellow's poem, "A Psalm of Life," one of his most popular.

George D. Armstrong

The Christian Doctrine of Slavery: God's Work in God's Way

Where God has appointed a *work* for his Church, he has generally appointed the *way* also in which that work is to be done. And where this is the case, the Church is as much bound to respect the one appointment as the other. Both the *work* of the Church and the *way* are often more distinctly set forth in the life and ministry of

Reprinted from George D. Armstrong, *The Christian Doctrine of Slavery* (New York, 1857), 131–148.

Christ and his Apostles than in any positive precept. But in whatever manner the will of God is made known, that will is law to his Church.

In the case of a race of men in slavery, the *work* which God has appointed his Church—as we learn it, both from the example and the precepts of inspired men—is to labor to secure in them a Christian life on earth and meetness for his heavenly kingdom. The African slave, in our Southern States, may be deeply degraded; the debasing effects of generations of sin may, at first sight, seem to have almost obliterated his humanity, yet is he an immortal creature; one for whom God the Son died; one whom God the Spirit can re-fashion, so as to make him a worthy worshipper among God's people on earth, and a welcome worshipper among the ransomed in heaven; one whom God the Father waiteth to receive as a returning prodigal to his heart and to his home. And the commission of the Church, "go ye into *all the world* and preach the Gospel *to every creature,*" sends her a messenger of glad tidings to him as truly as to men for above him in the scale of civilization. On this point there can be no difference of opinion among God's people, North or South, who intelligently take the word of God as their "only rule of faith and obedience." This is *the work* of God, assigned by him to his Church, in so far as the slave race among us is concerned.

In what *way* is this work to be done? We answer, By preaching the same Gospel of God's grace alike to the master and the slave; and when there is credible evidence given that this Gospel has been received in faith, to admit them, master and slave, into the same Church—the Church of the Lord Jesus Christ, in which "there is neither bond nor free"—and to seat them at the same table of the Lord, that drinking of the same cup, and eating of the same loaf, they may witness to the world their communion in the body and blood of the same Saviour. And having received them into the same Church, to teach them the duties belonging to their several "callings" out of the same Bible, and subject them to the discipline prescribed by the same law, the law of Christ. And this, the teaching of the Church, is to be addressed not to her members only, but to the world at large; and her discipline of her members is to be exercised not in secret, but before the world, that the light which God has given her may appear unto all men. This is just *the way* in which Christ and his Apostles dealt with slavery. The instructions they have given us in their life and in their writings prohibit any other.

In this way must the Church labor to make "good masters and good slaves," just as she labors to make "good husbands, good wives, good parents, good children, good rulers, good subjects." With the ultimate effect of this upon the civil and political condition of the slave the Church has nothing directly to do. If the ultimate effect of it be the emancipation of the slave—we say—in God's name, "let it come." "If it be of God, we *cannot*"—and we *would not* if we could—"overthrow it, lest haply we be found even to fight against God." If the ultimate effect be the perpetuation of slavery divested of its incidental evils—a slavery in which the master shall be required, by the laws of man as well as that of God, "to give unto the slave that which is just and equal," and the slave to render to the master a cheerful obedience and hearty service—we say, let slavery continue. It may be, that such a slavery, regulating the relations of capital and labor, though implying some deprivation of personal liberty, will prove a better defense of the poor against the oppression of the rich, than the too great freedom in which capital is placed in many of the free States of Europe at the present day. Something of this kind is what the masses of free laborers in France are clamoring for under the name of "*the right to labor.*" Something of this kind would have protected the ejected tenantry of the Duke of Sutherland against the tyranny which drove them forth from the home of their childhood, and quenched the fire upon many a hearth-stone, and converted once cultivated fields into sheep-walks. It may be, that *Christian slavery* is God's solution of the problem about which the wisest statesmen of Europe confess themselves "at fault." "Bonds make free, be they but righteous bonds. Freedom enslaves, if it be an unrighteous freedom."[1]

To this way of dealing with slavery, thus clearly pointed out in God's words, does God in his providence "shut us up," for years to come. None but the sciolist in political philosophy can regard the problem of emancipation—even granting that this were the aim which the Christian citizen should have immediately in view—as a problem of easy solution. And thoughtful Christian men at the North, it has seemed to us, often lose sight of the greatest difficulties in the case. It is comparatively an easy matter to devise a scheme of emancipation in which all the just rights and the well-being of the master shall be provided for. But how shall we, as God-fearing men, provide for the just rights and well-being of the emancipated slave? To leave the partially civilized slave race, in a state of freedom, in contact with a much more highly civilized race, as all history testifies, is inevitable destruction to the former. Their writ of enfranchisement is their death-warrant. To remove one hundredth part of the annual increase of the slave race to Liberia, year by year, would soon quench for ever that light of Christian civilization which a wise philanthropy has kindled upon the dark coast of Africa. How shall we provide for the well-being of the enfranchised slave? Here is the real difficulty in the problem of emancipation.

We mean to express no opinion respecting the feasibility of the future emancipation of the slave race among us. As we stated in the outset, our purpose is to introduce no question on which the Bible does not give us specific instruction. And we have referred to the question of emancipation—a question which it belongs to the State, and not the Church, to settle—simply that the reader may see how completely God's word and God's providence are "at one," in so far as the present duty of the Church is concerned. Is slavery to continue? We want the best of Christian masters and the best of Christian slaves, that it may prove a blessing to both the one and the other. Is ultimate emancipation before us? We want the best of Christian masters to devise and carry out the scheme by which it shall be effected, and the best of Christian slaves, that their emancipation may be an enfranchisement indeed. And this is just what the Bible plan of dealing with slavery aims at. The *future* may be hidden from view in "the clouds and darkness" with which God oft veils his purposes; but there is light—heaven's light—upon the *present*. And it is with the *present alone* we have immediately to do.

This is *one way* of dealing with slavery, and so firmly convinced are we that it is *God's way* for his Church that we cannot abandon it.

Another way proposed is—confounding the distinction between slavery itself and the incidental evils which attach to it in our country, and at the present day, under the guise of dealing with "AMERICAN SLAVERY;" in *the teaching* of the Church to denounce slave-holding as a SIN, as "evil, always evil, and only evil," (*Barnes' Notes, 1 Cor. VII.* 21); and in *the discipline* of the Church to treat it as an *"offence,"* and "detach the Church from it, as it is detached from piracy, intemperance, theft, licentiousness, and duelling," (*Church and State*, p. 193), and so labor directly to put an end to slavery throughout the world.[2]

To all this we object—

FIRST.—There is a radical fallacy involved in the use which is made of the expression, "AMERICAN SLAVERY."

By American Slavery, Dr. Barnes means—and the same is true of all anti-slavery writers whose works we have seen—the aggregate of, 1. Slavery itself; and, 2. The incidental evils which attach to it in this country and at this day, considered as inseparable—an indivisible unit. This treatment of the subject is—

1. *Unphilosophical.* Nothing is more real than the distinction, as set forth in the writings of Paul. (See § 15.) The fact that Dr. B. can write about Jewish slavery, and Roman slavery, and American slavery, as different the one from the others, shows that there must be something common to them all, to which we give the common name, Slavery; and something peculiar to each, which we designate by the adjuncts Jewish, Roman, American. Dr. B. admits that Roman slavery, as encountered by the Apostles in their day, was far more cruel and oppressive than American slavery now is[3]—that is, that much of the incidental evil which once attached to slavery has disappeared. If much has already disappeared, why may not all that remains disappear in like manner? The change that has taken place, has been effected under the benign influence of Christianity. And just as certainly as we believe that Christianity is from God, and is destined to a final triumph in the world, just so certainly do we believe that slavery—if it is to continue to exist—must continue to be modified by it, until all its incidental evils disappear.

2. It is *unscriptural.* By this we mean, 1. It is an essentially different way of approaching the subject of slavery from that adopted by the Apostles. Paul never wrote a line respecting *Jewish* slavery—meaning thereby, slavery itself and the incidental evils which attached to it in his day and among the Jews—or *Roman* slavery; nor does he give the Churches any directions couched in any such language as this. He writes about *slavery,* which he treats as neither a sin nor an offence; and about *certain evils* attaching to slavery as he encountered it, which he treats as sinful, and requires the Church, in her own proper sphere, to labor to correct. 2. It ignores the very ground upon which the whole method of dealing with slavery prescribed in the Word of God, is predicted.

In his introduction to his "Scriptural Views of Slavery," Dr. Barnes justifies his dealing, as he does, with what he calls "American Slavery," upon the ground—

1. That slavery, as it exists in the United States, is slavery divested of all the incidental evils of which it is reasonable to suppose Christianity will ever divest it; and hence, that all which now belongs to it, ought to be considered as, for all practical purposes, essential to the system.[4]

This is certainly "American glorification"—"with a witness." For ourselves, we love our country; and we feel an honest, patriotic pride in her standing among the nations. But God forbid, that we should entertain the thought that her social institutions, either in law or in fact, shall never be brought more fully under the control of God's truth than they now are; that the wife shall never be better protected against the wrong often inflicted by the profligate husband; and the child against the cruelty of the drunken father; and all this, without destroying the essential character of the marital and parental relations as set forth in the Word of God; that our heart and our home relations shall never be more thoroughly Christian than they now are. And so, too, with respect to slavery. Had we heard such sentiments as those just quoted from Dr. B., as part of a Fourth-of-July oration of some beardless Sophomore, we would have comforted ourselves with the reflection—increasing years may give the young man wisdom. That we should read them from the pen of one who must have "gray hairs here and there upon him," we can account for only by calling to mind what Paul tells us of the effects of feeding on "unwholesome words."—1 *Tim. VI.* 3.

2. That what we have designated as God's way of dealing with slavery, is dealing with slavery *in the abstract,* and not as a *practical* matter.[5]

What Dr. B.'s idea of dealing with an institution *in the abstract* is, we know not. We have always supposed that such dealing implied the abstraction—i.e., the taking away or neglecting for the time being—something, either essential or incidental, belonging to such institution. But, surely, we are not dealing with American slavery—slavery as it exists among us, in the abstract—in any such sense as this.

We take slavery, and the whole of slavery, just as it exists among us, and, after Paul's example, we separate it into—1. That which is *essential,* i.e., that which must continue if slavery continues; and, 2. That which is *incidental,* i.e., that which may disappear and slavery yet remain. Having done this, we then, *in discussion, deal with both parts.* We prove from the Word of God, that the *first* is not in violation of his law; and show, just as clearly, that much of the *second* is in violation of that law. And *in our practical dealing with it, as a Church, we deal with both parts.* The *first* we treat as not sinful, and require both the parties to conform to its obligations; much of the *second*—and just so much of it as is in violation of God's law— we prohibit, with all the authority given by Christ to his Church over her members, and in every proper way, we seek to remove from the world at large. If this is not dealing with slavery in its entirety, we ask, What is? If this is dealing with slavery *in the abstract,* we ask, What have we abstracted?

We remarked that there was "a radical fallacy involved in the use which is made of the expression, *American slavery,*" as used by Dr. B. and other writers of the same school. The reader will now see just what was meant by that remark.

The only meaning which can properly attach to the expression *American slavery,* is that of slavery as it exists in these United States of America. In this sense of the expression, we are dealing with American slavery, just as truly, and just as fully, and with far more of *practical* wisdom, we think, than Dr. B. is. The real difference between us is, that we distinguish between that which is essential and that which is incidental, as Paul did, and we deal with each as it deserves, as Paul did. Whilst Dr. B., neglecting this distinction, and thus, practically, treating all as essential, deals with it as an indivisible unit; and he does this under the guise of dealing with "American slavery," foisting upon that phrase, in addition to its proper meaning, the idea of the indivisible unity of the mass. To take such a course as this, when the issues in question are such as they are, is nothing more nor less than "a begging of the question."

SECOND.—We object to the course proposed by Dr. B. and others, for dealing with slavery, because it requires the Church to obtrude herself into the province of the State, and this, in direct violation of the ordinance of God. A course which has never been taken in times past, without disastrous consequences to the Church which did the wrong, as well as to the State which permitted the wrong to be done. Many a thing which it is right and proper, and even the duty of the Christian citizen, in this our free country, to do, the Church, as such, has no right to intermeddle with. It is doubtless, the duty of the Christian citizen, for example, to use all proper means to inform himself respecting the qualifications of candidates for office, and having thus informed himself, to vote for the one whom he believes will best discharge the duties of the office. But will any Christian man, hence contend that it is right for the preacher, in the pulpit and on the Sabbath, to discuss the claims of rival candidates, and the Church, in her councils to direct her members how to vote? The Church and State has each its own appropriate sphere of operation assigned it of God, and neither can innocently intrude herself into the province of the other.

THIRD.—It leads to tampering with God's truth, and "wresting the Scripture," as Dr. B. has done in his Notes, by the application to them of principles and methods of interpretation, which destroy all certainty in human language. In order to make the Bible declare that slave-holding is a sin, when it plainly teaches just the contrary;[6] and to teach in the Church doctrines which we are forbidden to teach under the most solemn sanctions. (See § 12.) This course has led not a few, once fair and promising members of the Church, and even ministers, into open "blasphemy;" and Paul teaches us, that such is its natural tendency, (1 Tim. VI. 4.). We have no desire to walk in their way, or to meet their doom.

FOURTH.—It requires us to quit a method of dealing with slavery which has worked well in time past—all of real advantage to the slave that has ever been done by the Church has been done in this way—and to substitute for it a method which, to say the least of it, is a mere experiment, and an experiment which has wrought nothing but harm to the slave[7] thus far—and we say this, after watching its operation during a ministry of twenty years, all of it, in God's providence, spent in a slave-holding state.

For all these reasons, we can never adopt this second *way* proposed. GOD'S WORK IN GOD'S WAY, the Church at the South, in common with some portions of the Church of the North also,[8] have inscribed upon their banner; and under that banner do we mean to fight the "Lord's battles," grace assisting us, until he who bid us gird on our armor shall give us leave to put it off. Churches of God may cut us off from their communion. They cannot break our union with Christ, "the Head." Ministers of the Gospel, from whom we have a right to expect better things," may revile us—we "fear God rather than man." "A conscience void of offence before God," is above all price. With this whole subject of slavery, we mean to deal just as Christ and his Apostles dealt—to preach what they preached—to labor as they labored—to govern the Church of God as they governed it—in Christian fellowship and brotherhood with God's people at the North, and in other lands, *if we* MAY:— in faithfulness to Christ, though in opposition to all the world, *if we* MUST.

NOTES

The notes below are Armstrong's original notes, here converted from asterisks to numbers.

1. For an able examination of this point the reader is referred to *Slavery and the Remedy; or, Principles and Suggestions for a Remedial Code,* by Samuel Nott. Crocker and Brewster, publishers, Boston.

2. That the reader may see how far Dr. B. would go, we give his own words:—"A Church, located in the midst of slavery, though all its members may be wholly unconnected with slavery, yet owes an important duty to society and to God in reference to the system, and its mission will not be accomplished by securing merely *the sanctification of its members, or even by drawing within its fold multitudes of those who shall be saved. Its primary work as a Church* may have reference to an existing evil within its own geographical limits. The burden which is laid upon it may not be primarily *the conversion of the heathen,* or the diffusion of *Bibles* and *tracts* abroad. *The* work which God requires it to do, and for which *specifically* it has been planted there, may be to diffuse a definite moral influence in respect to an existing evil institution."—*Church and Slavery,* p. 21. To convert the Church of God into a kind of "omnibus," in which everything called a moral reform shall be free to ride on an equal footing with the Gospel, as Dr. B. does, (see *Church and Slavery,* pp. 159–164), is bad enough; but thus actually to turn the Gospel out upon the *pave,* until a certain moral reform has been carried home, is at once the folly of fanaticism and the fanaticism of folly.

3. "It is proper to concede that the state of things was such that they (the Apostles) must have encountered it (slavery), and that it then had all the features of cruelty, oppression, and wrong, which can ever exist to make it repellant to any of the feelings of humanity, or revolting to the principles of a Christian. It is fair that the advocates of the system should have all the advantage which can be derived from the fact that the Apostles found it in its most odious forms, and in such circumstances as to make it proper that they should regard and treat it as an evil, if Christianity regards it as such at all."—*Scriptural Views of Slavery,* pp. 250, 251. Compare this with a quotation given a little further on.

4. "If any system of slavery is sanctioned by the Bible, it may be presumed that that which exists in the United States is. This is a Christian land—a land, to a degree elsewhere unknown, under the influence of the Christian religion. It could hardly be hoped that a state of society could be found, in which slavery could be better developed, or where its developments would more accord with the principles of the Bible, than in our own land."—*Scriptural Views,* p. 14.

5. It is a subject of not infrequent complaint, that, in the examination of this subject (slavery), the adversaries of the system endeavor to show that slavery *as it exists* in our country, is contrary to the Bible, instead of confining themselves to the naked question, whether slavery *in the abstract* is right or wrong. The very question—the only one that is of any *practical* importance to us—is, whether slavery as it exists in the United States is, or is not, in accordance with the principles and the spirit of Christianity. As an *abstract* matter, there might indeed be some interest attached to the inquiry whether slavery, as it existed in the Roman empire in the time of the Apostles, or in Europe in the Middle Ages, was in accordance with the spirit of the Christian religion.—*Scriptural Views,* pp. 10, 12.

6. "As it appears to us too clear to admit of either denial or doubt, that the Scriptures do sanction slave-holding; that under the old dispensation it was expressly permitted by divine command, and under the New Testament is nowhere forbidden or denounced, but on the contrary, acknowledged to be consistent with the Christian character and profession,

(that is, consistent with justice, mercy, holiness, love to God, and love to man;) to declare it to be a heinous crime is a direct impeachment of the Word of God." "When Southern Christians are told that they are guilty of a heinous crime, worse than piracy, robbery, or murder, because they hold slaves, when they know that Christ and his Apostles never denounced slave-holding as a crime, never called upon men to renounce it as a condition of admission into the Church, they are shocked and offended without being convinced. They are sure that their accusers cannot be wiser or better than their Divine Master, and their consciences are untouched by denunciations which they know if well founded, must affect not them only, but the authors of the religion of the Bible."—*Hodge's Essays and Reviews*, pp. 503, 484.

7. In illustration of this remark, we quote from Fletcher—"Thirty years ago, we occasionally had schools for negro children; nor was it uncommon for masters to send their favorite young slaves to these schools; nor did such acts excite attention or alarm, and, at the same time, any missionary had free access to that class of our population. But when we found, with astonishment, that our country was flooded with abolition prints, deeply laden with the most abusive falsehoods, with the obvious design to excite rebellion among the slaves, and to spread assassination and bloodshed through the land; when we found these transient missionaries, mentally too insignificant to foresee the result of their conduct, or wholly careless of the consequences, preaching the same doctrines—these little schools, and the mouths of these missionaries, were closed. And great was the cry. Dr. Wayland knows whereabout lies the wickedness of these our acts! Let him and his coadjutors well understand that these results, whether for the benefit or injury of the slave, have been brought about by the work of their land."—*Studies on Slavery*, p. 41.

We could add much of similar character, from our own observation.

8. See the paper adopted by the General Assembly of the Presbyterian Church, O. S., in 1845. (*Assembly's Digest*, pp. 811–813.)

CHAPTER
12

The Occult in the American Religious Tradition

O ccultism is one of the oldest and most misunderstood traditions in American religion. The term "occult" has long had two general meanings: things that are secret or hidden from view, and things that have mysterious supernatural or religious significance. Within the history of both Christianity and Judaism, "occultism" has generally forwarded religious views and beliefs frowned upon by established authorities.

Occultism has existed in America since the seventeenth century. Among elites it took the form of alchemy, which attempted to transmute base metals (lead) into precious ones (gold) by unlocking hidden supernatural secrets through chemical experimentation (the son of the Puritan leader, John Winthrop, practiced it), or involvement in the Masonic movement, which followed so-called "Hermetic" principles descending from before the Middle Ages (Benjamin Franklin was a Mason). In the early nineteenth century, a far more popular form of occultism involved fortune-finding using "magical" sticks and formulas (the future Mormon prophet, Joseph Smith, apparently was convicted of this illegal activity in 1826).

Mary Farrell Bednarowski explains in this essay why a wide variety of occult beliefs—Spiritualism, Theosophy, and feminist witchcraft—has held such appeal for women across the nineteenth and twentieth centuries. Does Bednarowski consider women's religious experience to be fundamentally different from that of men? Did the theology of Spiritualism and Theosophy, if not feminist witchcraft, preclude men's involvement? What important historical differences separated these movements?

Additional Reading: Robert S. Ellwood, *Alternative Altars: Unconventional and Eastern Spirituality in America* (Chicago, 1979) offers a general history of "occult" religion in America, and Jon Butler, *Awash in a Sea of Faith: Christianizing the American People; Studies in Cultural History* (Cambridge, Mass., 1990) discusses "occultism" in the general context of American religious development. Catherine L. Albanese, *Nature Religion in America from the Algonkian Indians to the New Age* (Chicago, 1990) describes alternate religious traditions in both the nineteenth and twentieth centuries. Ann Braude, *Radical Spirits: Spiritualism and Women's Rights in Nineteenth-Century America* (Boston, 1989) is both the best general history of the Spiritualist movement and an extensive study of women's attraction to it. Two books that offer superb introductions to the fascinating world of early modern witchcraft trials are Paul Boyer and Stephen Nissenbaum, *Salem Possessed: The Social Origins of Witchcraft* (Cambridge, Mass., 1974), which studies the 1692 witch trials in Salem, Massachusetts, and Keith Thomas, *Religion and the Decline of Magic* (London, 1971), a book about sixteenth- and seventeenth-century England.

Mary Farrell Bednarowski   # Women in Occult America

Even a cursory survey of American religious history reveals that while women rarely had acknowledged authority in mainstream Judaism and Christianity, they have been prominent in a number of movements with occult characteristics, such as spiritualism, Theosophy, and feminist witchcraft. This chapter, a comparative study of these three movements—two with origins in the nineteenth century and one a product of the twentieth—has two purposes: first, to demonstrate the abiding concern for women's rights that has been part of a number of occult movements in America; and, second, to explicate the variety of forms of the occult in which this concern has been expressed, from the spirit messages of spiritualism to the Eastern esotericism of Theosophy, to the psychologically oriented occultism of feminist witchcraft.

A contemporary analysis provides some of the themes that become apparent in an investigation of occult movements which have taken up the causes of women. In the spring of 1975 *Quest: A Feminist Quarterly* published an edition on women and spirituality. One of the articles, "Spiritual Explorations Cross-Country," charted a summer tour by Susan Rennie and Kirsten Grimstad during which they found a "widespread and surging interest in . . . the spiritual aspects of life. . . . We found that wherever there are feminist communities, women are studying psychic and non-material phenomena. . . ." Grimstad and Rennie confessed an initial "indifference bordering on uneasiness and apprehension," later attributed to their culturally induced antagonism to anything that could not be validated "scientifically" and their "association of things spiritual with reactionary politics."[1] By the end of the tour they felt they had come to understand the feminist implications of this interest in an occult kind of spirituality:

> Women, feminists, are becoming sensitized and receptive to the psychic potential inherent in human nature—and they are realizing that women in particular

From Mary Farrell Bednarowski, "Women in Occult America," in Howard Kerr and Charles L. Crow (eds.), *The Occult in America: New Historical Perspectives* (Urbana, 1983), 177–196; copyright © 1983 by the Board of Trustees of the University of Illinois. Used with permission of the author and of the University of Illinois Press.

are the repository of powers and capabilities that have been suppressed, that have been casualties of western *man's* drive to technological control over nature. It is as if feminists have recognized an even deeper source of female alienation and fragmentation than the sex role polarization which has so effectively limited women's lives—the mind/body dualism progressively fostered by patriarchal culture. In acknowledging this side of our being, women are in effect striving for a total integration and wholeness. Accepting the wholeness that includes psychic awareness and exploration takes feminist consciousness into an entirely new dimension—it amounts to a new definition of reality.[2]

Although expressed in the language of contemporary feminism, this short article points to at least three prominent themes in all the movements under consideration, regardless of historical context and irrespective of different understandings of the meaning of "occult." These themes are seen in embryo form in spiritualism and are more fully articulated in Theosophy and feminist witchcraft. First, there is an indictment of male-dominated Western society as both "unnatural" and as antagonistic to woman's very nature. Second, there is an insistence on the need to heal the Cartesian split in the universe, to reintegrate spirit and matter, mind or soul and body, experience and reason. Third, there is an affirmation of woman's nature as defined by the particular movement as especially suited for the enterprise of restoring wholeness and balance to all the institutions of society. Interwoven with these themes is the implication that women must seek the development of their own spirituality outside the framework of institutionalized religion—that the mere reform of existing institutions is not enough. To repeat Grimstad and Rennie, they are talking about a "new definition of reality."

Before beginning an analysis of the distinct ways in which spiritualism, Theosophy, and feminist witchcraft have expressed concern for women through their particular understandings of the occult, it is useful both from a historical and a rhetorical point of view to note the strikingly similar assessments on the part of these movements as to how the male-centeredness of organized religion has produced a society which oppresses and denigrates women. W. J. Colville, a spiritualist, claimed that "people cannot entertain an exclusively masculine idea of Deity and at the same time believe that motherhood is as divine as fatherhood. The degradation of women is always supported most strongly where the belief is regnant that only males are fit to officiate at sacred altars."[3] A Theosophist, Helen Knothe, spoke of the need to "look for and find the divine aspect of woman," and "at the same time . . . prove the essential woman aspect of Divinity. . . . When women realize their own inherent Divinity, then shall they occupy the place which is rightfully theirs in the full light of Her love."[4] According to Z. Budapest, a feminist witch, "What people believe (faith—religions) is political because it influences their actions and because it is a vehicle by which a religion perpetuates a social system." Budapest interprets society as patriarchal in nature, stripped of woman's power, because "male energy pretends to power by disclaiming the female force."[5]

As for the particularities of these moments, there is no mistaking the vehemence of the feminism of nineteenth-century American spiritualism, although the movement never produced a very coherent theoretical basis for it, nor, as R. Laurence Moore points out, did the pro-feminist views of spiritualism have much influence outside the movement itself.[6] In fact, on the surface, it is difficult to ascertain exactly what accounts for the spiritualists' concern with women's rights. They had no interest in emphasizing the intuitive or mystical or emotional aspects of religion associated, rightly or wrongly, with feminine spirituality. Just the reverse, in fact: the spiritualists' intent was to demystify the universe and the supernatural in order to replace religious beliefs with scientific facts based on the physical manifestations of the spirits: "Religion indeed," said one spiritualist, "may quicken the aspirations of men after union with the Divine; but it is Science, earnest, deep-fathoming science, alone, that can determine the nature of that holy and wondrous Essence. . . ."[7] Spiritualism preached the kind of scientific evaluation of the spiritual with its emphasis on the sensory and the rational that twentieth-century feminists would come to see as particularly antagonistic to feminine spirituality. Further, the spiritualist pro-feminist stance did not emerge from an occult world view that sought to balance the cosmic principles of male and female, because the spiritualists did not consider themselves occultists—that label, they said, was imposed upon them from outside the movement. According to R. Laurence Moore, "People kept equating their interest in spirit voices with mysticism, or occultism or magic (or all three), whereas they insisted that it had nothing to do with any of these."[8]

From what bases, then, did the feminism of nineteenth-century American spiritualism arise? And how was it manifested within the movement? On the very simplest level, spiritualists saw themselves as champions not only of liberal religion but of liberal politics and social conventions as well. Henry James portrays graphically, if not sympathetically, the intertwining of both feminist and occult concerns in *The Bostonians*.[9] Robert Riegel cites the numerous feminists who were interested in both spiritualism and Theosophy, although he expresses puzzlement over the connection.[10] R. Laurence Moore mentions that when people's most important ideas have been rejected, as has certainly been the case with feminism and occultism most of the time in American society, "the temptation arose for them to make common cause with champions of other rejected ideas."[11] A short notice in the May 13, 1876, *Banner of Light*, a spiritualist weekly, underscores this thesis of the interconnectedness of liberal causes: the item publicized a "Mass Convention" of the spiritualists of Minnesota, promising a "feast of reason and a flow of soul," and inviting "all Spiritualists, together with Liberals of every name and kind. . . ."[12]

Spiritualists affirmed their pro-feminist bias with scatter-shot attacks aimed at a variety of institutions, the most frequent target being organized religion, which they believed had foundered because it had fallen into the hands of a powerful and degenerate elite—the ordained male clergy.[13] Male-dominated medicine also came in for accusations. During its more than fifty-year history the *Banner of Light* carried a substantial number of ads for alternate sources of medical aid, aimed against the "Medical Institution made up of a combination of speculating individuals, having no higher objective than money-making." One nontraditional clinic offered the services of "Mrs. R. E. Dillingham, Assistant, who will be present at all times, for the reception of ladies and will prescribe for them when more consistent and desirable."[14] There were also occasional ads for books on birth control techniques, whose chapter titles betray a pro-feminist bias. One such was Henry C. Wright's *The Unwelcome Child; or, The Crime of an Undesired Maternity.* One chapter, "A Protest of Humanity against Legalized Sensualism," was directed against the total sexual rights afforded husbands by the legal right of marriage.[15] That the spiritualists saw themselves pitted against the ministerial and medical professions is also evident from other sources. The biographer of Cora L. V. Scott, a healing and trance medium who began her career as a child in Wisconsin, mentions that she "aroused the antagonism of the regular physicians and clergymen in the neighborhood. The former was without patients and the latter lacked audiences."[16] The spiritualists were also concerned with politics and urged that women actively seek the vote to improve their lot. An article in the *Spiritualist,* a Wisconsin monthly of short duration, advised women, "Voting would make you more independent. Your feeling of dependence on men is proverbial. You are legally helpless, and men know it, and are apt to take advantage of it. Your relief is in the vote."[17]

Protests like those above give a good sense of the variety of areas in which spiritualist feminism expressed itself, but they fail to provide clues as to any underlying framework that would support a feminist stance other than general liberal, anti-institutional tendencies. Indeed, the movement never moved beyond the "attack" stage in its theory of feminism. That is not to say that spiritualism had only a superficial appeal for women—it provided them with access to mediumship, which was a legitimate form of spiritual leadership within the movement; it denied the truth of the doctrine of original sin and human depravity and woman as the "first transgressor" in Eden; and it expended a great deal of rhetoric on the need for equal rights for women in religion, politics, and marriage.[18]

Even if spiritualism did not provide a coherent underpinning for its feminism, it did make an attempt at pulling the universe together, at reintegrating spirit and matter in its search for "natural" laws that would prevail in both the material and the spiritual worlds. The spiritualists saw themselves as leaders in the search for such laws and proclaimed that "*the Spirit World* is after all, but a finer material world, as real, as substantial; and as directly within the province of universal law as that which we now inhabit."[19] The concern with universal laws had its significance for women in at least one area, that of marriage and the relationship between the sexes.

The spiritualists' preoccupation with the laws governing sexuality certainly stems in part from frequent accusations that they advocated free love and divorce. They denied these charges bitterly and attempted to make known what they considered their highly rational and moral views by an explanation of the "marriage law," which Lizzie Doten described as "a law of nature, which existed from the beginning. When God created the male and female, the very fact that he did create them male and female implanted the marriage law in their nature."[20] While this description does not in itself sound very revolutionary, the spiritualists believed that the marriage law operated on both the physical and the spiritual planes and that it drew together persons of like nature destined to be "spiritual affinities."

Unfortunately, the legal and social conditions of marriage in nineteenth-century America operated to prevent the union of spiritual affinities who discovered each other after an unhappy marriage. As a result, spiritualists expressed their antagonism to conventional morality, which prevented particularly the woman from seeking a divorce without irreparable harm to her reputation. The spiritualists insisted that the "marriage law" is "the divine law of reciprocal love" and "is above all legal or ecclesiastical statutes." To them it was inevitable that "the latter must in time pass away in order that the former may be left to free itself, before the highest ideal of the human species will appear on earth."[21] According to William H. Dixon, author of *Spiritual Wives*, "If a woman is free to make her own terms with God, why should she not be able to make her own terms with man?"[22]

Quite apart from any consideration of how much spiritualists put the rhetoric of free love into practice, it is interesting to see their attempt to get beyond what they considered the artificially imposed conventions of society and to seek out the "natural" and the cosmically rooted. That they sought to do so totally under the aegis of science is a measure of the intensity of appeal of the empirical method in mid-nineteenth-century America. Whether they realized it or not, the spiritualists were invoking the occult doctrine that like is attracted to like in their theory of spiritual affinities, and they made use of their understanding of universal law to try to free women from a double standard of morality.

The reality they posited other than the obviously physical was that of the spirits and the spheres they inhabited. Even though the women mediums in particular stressed that they had no control over the spirits, that they passively received and passed on the messages, the spiritualists nonetheless hoped to acquire the power that would proceed from a knowledge of the universal laws governing spirit and matter. Women had as much opportunity to seek this power as men, a power that would free them from the conventions of society and from helplessness in the face of the unfathomable.

No matter how unconventional their religious and social attitudes may have been in regard to women, the spiritualists never moved beyond the stereotype of nineteenth-century womanhood as more spiritual, sensitive, and passive than the male, and in need of protection. In fact, the typical female medium fits this description perfectly.[23] While they affirmed women's rights to religious, political, and social authority, there is almost no evidence that the spiritualists recognized that the very dependencies women were expected to cultivate as part of their nature prevented them from attaining the equality they sought. Lizzie Doten, for example, traveled all over America as a trance medium; she spoke in public on many controversial subjects including free love and the theology of Ralph Waldo Emerson, and she defended the lot of the working woman. But even as she defended the right of women—and men—to love freely (although not lustfully, as she pointed out), she still spoke of "the pure young girl," and the "yearning sympathy of her nature, pure as the water of a gushing rill," attracted to the "strong manly form . . . the arms stretched out with such tender and loving support."[24] Spiritualism questioned with great energy the fact that women were excluded from so many avenues to power, but never went so far as to question society's description of what a woman should be and what that description might have to do with her exclusion.

In contrast with spiritualism, Theosophy was from the beginning a movement admittedly and intentionally occult in nature. The doctrines of Theosophy proceeded from Helena Blavatsky's amalgam of Eastern religious doctrines and occult principles. Evident from the beginning and expressed in the first goal of the Theosophical Society—"to form a Universal Brotherhood of Humanity without distinction or race, colour, or creed"—the feminism of Theosophy had as its basis a belief in the need for the balance of the masculine and feminine principles in the cosmos and an adulation of the Mother Goddess. According to the Theosophists, in societies where women were deprived of their rights, the cosmic balance was upset and the disequilibrium brought with it all the ills that were so obvious in turn-of-the-century America—war, political corruption, economic inequity, and unhappiness between the sexes with its consequences in deteriorating family life. For the Theosophists who believed in spiritual evolution, the coming age must certainly bring with it an improvement in woman's lot in all aspects of society: "And now the Great Teachers will affirm the rights of woman. . . . Woman will have to be armed with courage, and, first of all, she will have to restrain her heart from unwise giving, for there must be the Golden Balance in everything."[25]

Theosophists' criticisms of society are often expressed in more abstract terms than those of spiritualism, reflecting their more cosmic concern with balance. In 1913 Charlotte Despard, a British Theosophist with an American audience, claimed that "the falsity of the present relations between man and woman lies at the base of many of the worst evils with which Humanity has had to struggle." Despard saw both the woman's movement as it existed just before World War I and the growth of Theosophy as evidence that society was in the grips of a spiritual awakening that would ensure the rights of women, and she outlined the essential changes that must occur before such developments could proceed: "(a) the recognition of a uniform moral standard, (b) not uniformity which is a foolish perversion of our demand, but unity, (c) that in the rebuilding of national and international life, women shall stand side by side with their brothers, and (d) that Public Opinion . . . be kept alive, instructed and active, until it takes place in the community of conscience in the individual."[26]

The same general tenor of the Theosophical argument for women's rights appears in a more contemporary source, the spring, 1976, issue of the *American Theosophist,* dedicated to a discussion of the "Feminine Principle." Editor William Quinn stresses, like Despard, that "co-equality of the feminine and the masculine principles is a fact—not a hypothesis. The fact is apparent not only in grandiose perceptions of the cosmos and in the interplay of the tremendous forces governing the universe, it is quite apparent at a more mundane level: that of the sexes."[27] Quinn attributes women's inequality to a predominance of the male principle over the female in American culture. The remedy is a reorientation toward wholeness and unity: "If the dual aspects are truly co-equal, then the idea of 'predominance of one' must be mutually exclusive of co-equality, for co-equality precludes imbalance."[28]

These rather abstractly phrased and sometimes implicit indictments of society that are typical of Theosophical feminism did not obviate the need for criticism directed at specific institutions, however, and the Theosophists made attacks as scathing as anything launched by the spiritualists, directed particularly at organized religion. In the May, 1925, issue of the *Theosophist*, a "Member of the League of the Church Militant" accused the male priesthood of the world's religions of keeping women from spiritual equality: "The priesthood of the *Churches* of all religions has looked on all womanhood as Magdalen, the creature of sin, the polluted, unclean, the temptress, the unworthy. Why? Because of her sex current, because of a function of the physical body, because of a quality of the rājasic body, because of an attractive quality of the desire body. The masculine priesthood was afraid of these."[29] This excerpt reveals all the bitterness found in the contemporary feminist movement that women's bodies have been used and reviled—that woman's sexuality has been used against her to keep her from positions of authority, not through any fault of her own but because the priests "recognized their own weakness, and instead of facing their foe—their own lower nature—fair and square in the face and conquering it, they acknowledged and acquiesced in their moral weakness but maintained the innocence and purity necessary to their office . . . by arrogating to themselves occult spiritual power and banishing from their environment possible excitements of sex."[30]

The Theosophists were not naive, then, about many of the causes of women's oppressions, but they were more likely to express them in broader terms than is the case above and to express in the same general way their optimism that women's rights would triumph over a corrupt society. The "remarkable coincidence" that Charlotte Despard saw "between the uprising of woman . . . all over the world and the rise and growth of Theosophy" convinced her that "the Woman's Cause is bound to triumph, because there is an irresistible force behind it."[31] In the occult world view of the Theosophists it was not only desirable that the feminine principle assert itself by an increase in women's rights, it was a cosmic necessity.

Theosophy's understanding of the essence of the feminine nature was founded on another aspect of its occult world view: the importance of the Mother Goddess in the Theosophical system. Helen Knothe quotes from Blavatsky's *Secret Doctrine* in support of her contention that the Mother in ancient religions predates the Father: "The higher gods of antiquity are all 'Sons of the Mother' before they become 'Sons of the Father.' . . . All these, the upper and the lower Hierarchies included, emanate from the Heavenly or Celestial Virgin, the Great Mother in all religions, the Androgyne, the Sephira Adam Kadmon."[32] Knothe uses the *Secret Doctrine* to argue the need for recognition of the feminine manifestation of the divine, which will in turn assure the acceptance of the divine aspect of woman. Knothe sees "maternity" as the essential quality of the feminine principle and as necessary for the spiritual fulfillment of women. This maternity may be figurative rather than literal: "Whether child-bearing or not, woman is essentially maternal, and only fully enters her kingdom when she becomes a mother." Knothe speaks of motherhood in occult terms as "an initiation into a divine experience, generating and giving birth to form."[33]

But the maternal aspect of the feminine has implications beyond the experience of the individual. Writing just before Knothe, W. K. Heyting laments that women in politics seem merely to imitate men and predicts for women that "their supposed freedom in being able to hold these positions will be nothing but a burden."[34] Heyting asks whether women have "nothing to give to the body politic which is peculiarly and undeniably theirs by right of their womanhood, something that men cannot contribute so effectively?" He suggests that the answer lies in woman's capacity to "mother," to be "guided by that personal love for humanity which men lack. . . ."[35]

Another spokesperson for what appears to be a traditional interpretation of women's roles coming out of a radical religious stance was Katherine Tingley, leader of the Point Loma Theosophical community in California until her death in 1929. In a series of lectures on Woman's Mission by women leaders at Point Loma in 1915, Tingley said, "I believe in the equality of the sexes, but I hold that man has a mission and that woman has also a mission, and that these missions are not the same; the difference is due in part to lines of evolution." Tingley urges that the balance of the sexes must prevail: "If a woman is to understand the duties of real wifehood and motherhood, and to reach the dignity of ideal womanhood, she must cultivate her femininity. She was born a woman and she must *be* a woman in the truest sense; and the contrast between men and women exists in life."[36] These are interesting words from a strong woman leader of a large group of people (500 at its maximum), who lived in a community in the company of other strong women, among them Gertrude Van Pelt, a physician, and Grace Knoche, mother of the present head of the Theosophical Society International. Tingley does echo the general cultural perception of woman's nature as more "spiritual" than man's: "Woman is more mystical than man; she lives more in the heart. Her emotional nature, however, becomes a source of weakness if not governed understandingly."[37] While that sounds very traditional, Tingley cautions women that they must live out their nature within the framework of the "higher life" of Theosophy, that unless they do they will always "be imposed upon. They are forever sacrificing their lives to no beneficial result, forever bearing children in disharmony, who must later suffer just as they have done. For there is no balance in their lives, no justice."[38] If the balance of male and female is maintained in a society, then woman finds fulfillment rather than exploitation in her role as mother and nurturer, for she mirrors the Mother Goddess.

Reality for the woman—and the man—Theosophist was composed not only of matter but of a mystic center in nature, of forces and principles, of higher levels of being and knowing than those apparent in the earthly sphere. The woman's power over that reality arose from her cultivated understanding that she participated in divinity and that since "sin does not consist in fulfilling any of the functions of nature,"[39] the incidence of her gender would not keep her from exercising that power.

By contrast with both spiritualism and Theosophy, whose memberships were both male and female and whose feminism was one among other concerns, feminist witchcraft is a separatist movement, drawing its energy from women alone and seeing itself in opposition to male society and male values. Feminist witchcraft considers itself as practicing the Dianic tradition and, in fact, sets itself apart from the Craft, the contemporary, neo-pagan witchcraft described by Margot

Adler in *Drawing Down the Moon*. Adler says that "a number of feminists have stated that women are Witches by right of the fact that they are women, that nothing else is needed, and feminist Witch Z. Budapest has at times declared the Craft to be 'Wimmins Religion,' a religion not open to men."[40]

As a product of the counterculture revolution of the 1960s and the contemporary feminist movement, feminist witchcraft rejects both technocracy and the revelations of traditional Christianity and Judaism. It seeks truth in the depths of the female psyche and finds its energy in the worship of "the goddess." Any hint of the supernatural is missing from feminist witchcraft, but neither does the movement accept the "merely" natural universe of the materialist. Like the Theosophist, the feminist witch articulates an understanding of the feminine principle, but, as will become evident, it takes a different twist from the cosmic to the personal. Z. Budapest says that "feminist witches are wimmin who search within themselves for the female principle of the universe and who relate as daughters to the Creatrix. We believe that just as it is time to fight for the right to control our bodies, it is also time to fight for our sweet womon souls."[41]

The breadth of the criticisms against contemporary society by feminist witches in some ways resembles that of the nineteenth-century spiritualists. In fact, Z. Budapest's *The Holy Book of Women's Mysteries* has sections on alternative medicine and astrological birth control that echo the ads in the nineteenth-century *Banner of Light*. But the basis for the criticisms is different. Spiritualist feminism embraced the scientific and insisted that traditional religion was not rational enough. Feminist witchcraft criticizes society because its institutions, particularly religion, are too rational, too falsely coherent. According to one feminist witch, the basis for a new woman's spirituality will arise out of a variety of struggles: "Feminist spirituality has taken form in Sisterhood—in our solidarity based on a vision of personal freedom, self-definition, and in our struggle together for social and political change. The contemporary women's movement has created space for women to begin to perceive reality with a clarity that seeks to encompass many complexities. This perception has been trivialized by male dominated cultures that present the world in primarily rational terms."[42] The feminist witch seeks not just reform of social institutions but, rather, "fundamental change in cultural beliefs, society's institutions, and human relationships—beginning with the rejoining of woman to woman."[43]

For feminist witches, criticism of society implies an interdependence of spirituality and politics, which, as Margot Adler points out, is a distinguishing mark setting them apart from other practitioners of the Craft. This does not necessarily mean that feminist witches advocate violent revolution; for most of them the combining of spirituality and politics has meant the redefining of "politics." "Traditionally," says Dorothy Riddle, "spirituality has had to do with loving, and politics has had to do with power. We have seen them as unrelated because we have experienced our personal lives and relationships as separate from our work and institutional involvements."[44] For the feminist witch who advocates a holistic view of life over a compartmentalized view, every aspect of a woman's being has political import: "One important contribution of feminism is our dawning recognition that our lives are a whole, that the personal is political and the political is personal, that how we are with ourselves and each other *is* the revolution."[45]

This understanding of the interconnectedness of the political and the personal stems from an occult view that is natural rather than supernatural in its underpinnings. Starhawk, a feminist witch, speaks of her belief as "earth religion. . . . There is no dichotomy between spirit and flesh. . . . The Goddess is manifest in the world; she brings life into being, *is* nature, *is* flesh. . . . Spiritual union is found in life, with nature, passion, sensuality—through being fully human, fully one's self."[46] In *Changing of the Gods*, Naomi Goldenberg sees feminist witchcraft as creating a "powerful new religion" that is earth-bound in its worship of the goddess. Their understanding of the occult doctrine, "as above, so below," leads feminist witches to reject a male God in a faraway heaven so that women will have the strength to reject male rule on earth. This creation is an indictment of "a civilization in which males in high places imitate a male god in heaven—both think themselves above the petty concerns of simple nurture and delight in generative life."[47]

Feminist witches make use of ritual worship of the goddess in order to strengthen woman's identification with the divine feminine in herself, and they make use of the "occult sciences," such as astrology and the reading of Tarot cards, as ways of practicing what they call a prepatriarchal understanding of the self and its connections with the cycles of the universe. Carol Christ suggests further that women, not only feminist witches, find in the Tarot cards "a prepatriarchal set of images that can be more useful in charting their spiritual journeys than Biblical symbolism."[48] While many of the rituals and practices are communal in nature and designed to stress not only cosmic rootedness but also sisterhood, others are performed by the individual. One of them is a "Self-Blessing Ritual," which Z. Budapest describes as a way of "exorcising the patriarchal policeman, cleansing the deep mind, and filling it with positive images of the strength and beauty of women."[49] Another is a kind of "Morning Offering," with a poignant earth-bound theme said each morning by a Minneapolis witch, Carol Wisewomoon: "I get up and thank the night, give blessing to creatures who live at night and are going to bed, look at the sun and say good morning to her; ring my bell which gives new dimensions to the air, breathe the sound the bell sends across the room, light the candle and feel the heat of the flame. I ask 'the women' for strength, wisdom and serenity and surrender the results of that day."[50]

Feminist witchcraft sees woman's nature as inherently divine, as not merely reflecting the goddess but, as Mary Daly says, being the Goddess.[51] Like spiritualism and Theosophy, feminist witchcraft denies human depravity and affirms the essential goodness of the human person, but because of its separatist tendencies, feminist witchcraft elevates woman's nature above man's in its life-giving abilities. Z. Budapest claims that men cannot be considered equal to women in divinity.[52] Whereas spiritualism stressed woman's passive nature as particularly conducive to spirit communication and Theosophy considered woman's maternal nature as essential to balance and wholeness in the cosmos and society, feminist witches speak of the necessity of women's ascendency over men: "We believe that female control of the death (male) principle yields human evolution."[53] Feminist witches do not deny the reality, or even the importance, of the male principle, but they claim that balance of the male and female principles can be cultivated within the individual. Margot Adler sees in feminist witchcraft a tendency toward dogmatism, a "substituting 'Big Mama' for 'Big Daddy,'" but many feminist witches see themselves as trying to overcome the dualism inherent in Western culture that has so distinguished the characteristics of male and female from each other that it is impossible for one person to achieve any kind of balance of both. Feminist witches describe themselves as committing a "political act" when they replace the Father with the Mother: "The image of the Mother does not lose its old connotations of earth, intuition, nature, the body, the emotions, the unconscious, etc. But it also lays claim to many of the connotations previously attributed to the father symbol: beauty, light, goodness, authority, activity, etc."[54] The feminist witch claims both sun and moon, both heaven and earth, and she invokes the goddess in herself and in other women in her efforts to make it possible.

For the feminist witch the only reality is the physical universe, but it is a reality that is inherently sacred, full of psychic energy that she can tap as she understands her own nature as participating in that of the goddess. For the feminist witch this power is not manipulative but, rather, "the psychic power with which our spiritual awareness brings us in touch . . . the power to generate new visions and the power to end or shield ourselves from old habits or old ways of being."[55]

In contrast with the women who have sought religious fulfillment in marginal religious groups such as spiritualism, Theosophy, and feminist witchcraft, many thousands of women have been content to participate in mainstream Christianity and Judaism. As historians like Nancy Cott have pointed out, their functions—centered around charitable and missionary societies, nonclerical teaching, and the safeguarding of home and family—provided a source of strength and identity as well as the feeling of sisterhood.[56] But for those women who felt, perhaps with a different intensity, their deprivation of the kind of spiritual equality that could lead to ordination, religious fulfillment and the development of a feminine spirituality would have to come from without the system. For within the system, both the affirmation of the churches as well as their negative judgments bespoke the relegation of women to a lower spiritual order.

In 1853, when Antoinette Brown was ordained as the first Congregational minister in America, the male minister who preached at her ordination ceremony defended women ministers in a way that was enlightened for the time, but exemplified the kind of tortured exegesis that has accompanied much theological reflection on whether there is scriptural basis for the ordination of women. The Reverend Luther Lee contended that Paul's admonition that women keep silent in church extended only to married women; further, if a married woman's husband gave his permission, she, too, might be ordained.[57] In 1976, when the Sacred Congregation for the Doctrine of the Faith of the Roman Catholic Church made its pronouncement on the question of women's ordination, Franjo Cardinal Seper, speaking for the congregation and with the approval of Paul VI, explained that "the problems of sacramental theology, especially when they concern the ministerial priesthood . . . cannot be solved except in the light of Revelation." According to the Church, revelation had made clear that the maleness of Jesus must be reflected in the priesthood: "When Christ's role in the Eucharist is to be expressed sacramentally, there would not be this 'natural resemblance' which must exist between Christ and his minister if the role of Christ were not taken by a man."[58] According to Sister Elizabeth Carroll, this statement says that "woman . . . has no 'imaging' power of Christ in this world or the next."[59]

While the examples above deal specifically with women's ordination, the questions they raise are broader and deal with the effect of a "closed" revelation on women's position in the churches, the churches' attitude toward woman's gender and sexuality, her relationship to the numinous, and her subjection to male authority.

At least three occult movements in American history have provided an arena where women have addressed these issues, protested against the prevailing structures, and worked to create an alternate reality based on a new revelation that would be more affirming both of woman's sexuality and her spirituality.[60] For the spiritualists and the Theosophists the new revelation had exterior bases, that of the spirits and the Mahatmas. For feminist witches it has been an interior phenomenon: "I am constantly being revealed to myself, I am constantly reaching new understandings of how to be myself-Source on Earth."[61] The power of participation in the divine that came with the new revelation and the new reality was a power that adhered within and could be developed by the individual, leaving her free to define and create her own kind of spirituality beyond what she considered to be the strictures of church and society.

NOTES

1. Kirsten Grimstad and Susan Rennie, "Spiritual Explorations Cross-Country," *Quest*, 1 (1975) :50.

2. Ibid., pp. 50–51.

3. W. J. Colville, *Ancient Mysteries and Modern Revelations* (New York: R. F. Fenno, 1910), p. 342. The spiritualists were by no means the first to articulate the connection between a male-dominated religion and woman's oppression. Shaker Elder Frederick Evans held the "lost and fallen world" responsible for the *"degradation* and *oppression* of WOMAN": "Thus it appears that those who reject their Heavenly Mother, do thereby reject *true wisdom.* And this accounts for self evident want of *wisdom* in all human governments and societies, civil and religious." See *A Short Treatise on the Second Appearing of Christ in and through the Order of the Female* (Boston: Bazin and Chandler, 1853), p. 14. Nor is the connection perceived only by those in occult groups. Carol Christ, a feminist theologian who has done a great deal of work on "the goddess," says that "religions centered on the worship of a male God create 'moods' and 'motivations' that keep women in a state of psychological dependence on men and male authority, while at the same time legitimating the *political* and *social* authority of fathers and sons in the institutions of society." See "Why Women Need the Goddess," in Carol P. Christ and Judith Plaskow, eds., *Womanspirit Rising: A Feminist Reader in Religion* (San Francisco: Harper and Row, 1979), p. 275.

4. Helen Knothe, "The Woman-Aspect of Divinity," *Theosophist*, 49 (1928) :454.

5. Z. Budapest, *The Holy Book of Women's Mysteries, Part I* (Los Angeles: Susan B. Anthony Coven no. 1, 1979), pp. 10–11.

6. R. Laurence Moore, *In Search of White Crows: Spiritualism, Parapsychology, and American Culture* (New York: Oxford University Press, 1977), p. 83.

7. R, "Review—'Reichenbach's Dynamics,'" *Shekinah*, 1 (1852) :197–99.

8. Moore, *In Search of White Crows*, p. 224.

9. See Howard Kerr's analysis of *The Bostonians* in *Mediums, and Spirit-Rappers, and Roaring Radicals: Spiritualism in American Literature, 1850–1900* (Urbana: University of Illinois Press, 1972).

10. Robert Riegel, *American Feminists* (Lawrence: University of Kansas Press, 1963), p. 191.

11. Moore, *In Search of White Crows*, p. 226.

12. *Banner of Light*, May 13, 1876.

13. A typical accusation against the clergy appears in a list of resolutions passed by the Northern Wisconsin Association of Spiritualists in 1874: "Resolved, that the 50,000 ministers of the United States furnish a greater ration of criminals in our prisons than do the 5,000,000 Spiritualists, particularly in their infidelity to marriage and terrible record of adultery in every community around us. . . ." See *Milwaukee Journal*, Jan. 13, 1874.

14. *Banner of Light*, July 16, 1857.

15. Ibid., May 13, 1876.

16. Harrison D. Barrett, *Life Work of Mrs. Cora L. V. Richmond* (Chicago: Hack & Anderson, 1895), pp. 8–9.

17. *Spiritualist*, July, 1868.

18. See Mary Farrell Bednarowski, "Outside the Mainstream: Women's Religion and Women Religious Leaders in Nineteenth Century America," *Journal of the American Academy of Religion*, 48 (1980) :207–31, for a discussion of the characteristics of Shakerism, spiritualism, Christian Science, and Theosophy that made them particularly attractive to women.

19. Lizzie Doten, *Poems of Progress* (Boston: Colby and Rich, 1870), pp. 7–8.

20. Lizzie Doten, *Free Love and Affinity: A Discourse Delivered under Spirit Influence at the Melodean, Boston* (Boston, 1867), p. 5.

21. *Milwaukee Journal*, May 13, 1874, a further excerpt from the proceedings of the Northern Wisconsin Association of Spiritualists.

22. William Hepworth Dixon, *Spiritual Wives*, 2d ed. (Philadelphia: Lippincott, 1868), p. 385.

23. See ch. 4, "The Medium and Her Message: A Case of Female Professionalism," in Moore, *In Search of White Crows*, pp. 102–32.

24. Doten, "Free Love and Affinity," p. 6.

25. *Woman* (New York: Agni Yoga Society, 1958). The quotation is taken from the Foreword, which is an excerpt from the *Letters of Helena Roerich*, 1:409. Other publication information not given.

26. Charlotte Despard, *Theosophy and the Woman's Movement* (London: Theosophical Publishing Society, 1913), p. 27.

27. Bill Quinn, "The Feminine Principle," *American Theosophist*, 64 (1976) :102–3.

28. Ibid.

29. "Woman and Holy Orders by a Member of the League of the Church Militant," *Theosophist*, 46–2 (1925) :203–4.

30. Ibid., p. 204.

31. Despard, *Theosophy and the Woman's Movement*, pp. 43–44.

32. Helen Knothe, "Woman-Aspect of Divinity," p. 452. Knothe does not mention the possibility of "Daughters" of the Mother.

33. Ibid., pp. 453–54.

34. W. J. Heyting, "Woman's Place in Politics," *Theosophist*, 47 (1926) :403–4. The tone of the article strikes an ominous note with the contemporary ready, since it seems to be advocating a kind of selective breeding.

35. Ibid., p. 409.

36. Katherine Tingley et al., *Woman's Mission: Short Addresses by Katherine Tingley and Other Officials of the Woman's International Theosophical League, . . .* February 7, 1915 (Point Loma, Calif.: Woman's Theosophical League, 1915), pp. 24–25. Emmett Greenwalt mentions, in *California Utopia: Point Loma, 1892–1942,* 2d rev. ed. (San Diego: Point Loma Publications, 1973), p. 168n, that Tingley was opposed to the suffragette movement. But John and Kirby Van Mater, of the Theosophical University Library in Pasadena, both of whom lived at Point Loma, told me in Apr., 1980, that they find that allegation very puzzling. John Van Mater was particularly gracious in helping me find material related to women in the Theosophical Society International, as were Mary Jo Schneider and Wayne Montgomery with their assistance at the Olcott Library of the Theosophical Society in America, Wheaton, Ill.

37. Katherine Tingley, *Theosophy the Path of the Mystic,* comp. Grace Knoche (Point Loma, Calif.: Woman's International Theosophical League, 1922), p. 130.

38. Ibid., p. 125. This excerpt is taken from sec. IV, "Woman and the Theosophic Home."

39. "Woman and Holy Orders, etc.," p. 204.

40. Margot Adler, *Drawing Down the Moon* (New York: Viking, 1979), p. 173. Z. Budapest states very directly in *The Holy Book of Women's Mysteries, Part I,* "We are opposed to teaching our magic and our craft to men until equality of the sexes is reality" (p. 10). Morgan McFarland, on the other hand, says that there may be men at a coven if they do not outnumber the women, but her Dianic tradition "condones and even encourages all-female circles and covens." See "Witchcraft: The Art of Remembering," *Quest,* 1 (1975) :46.

41. Budapest, *Holy Book of Women's Mysteries, Part I,* p. 9. The spelling of "womon" indicates an avoidance of "man."

42. Judy Davis and Juanita Weaver, "Dimensions of Spirituality," *Quest,* 1 (1975) :2.

43. Ibid., p. 3.

44. Dorothy Riddle, "New Visions of Spiritual Power," *Quest,* 1 (1975) :7.

45. Ibid.

46. Starhawk, "Witchcraft and Women's Culture," in Christ and Plaskow, eds., *Womanspirit Rising,* p. 263.

47. Naomi Goldenberg, *Changing of the Gods: Feminism and the End of Traditional Religions* (Boston: Beacon Press, 1979), p. 90.

48. Carol P. Christ, *Diving Deep and Surfacing: Women Writers on Spiritual Quest* (Boston: Beacon Press, 1980), p. 94.

49. Z. Budapest, "Self-Blessing Ritual," in Christ and Plaskow, eds., *Womanspirit Rising,* p. 272.

50. Carol Wisewomoon, "I'm a lesbian, I'm a witch," *Minneapolis Tribune,* May 10, 1980, interview by Ruth Hammond.

51. Mary Daly, *Gyn/Ecology: The Metaethics of Radical Feminism* (Boston: Beacon Press, 1978). Daly makes use of words like "hag" and "crone" in what she calls a transvaluated sense to denote women of strength, courage, and wisdom.

52. Goldenberg, *Changing of the Gods,* p. 103.

53. Budapest, *Holy Book of Women's Mysteries, Part I*, p. 9.

54. Barbara Starret, "I Dream in Female: The Metaphysics of Evolution," *Amazon Quarterly*, 3 (1974) :24–25, quoted in Adler, *Drawing Down the Moon*, p. 214.

55. Riddle, "New Visions of Spiritual Power," p. 8.

56. Nancy Cott, *The Bonds of Womanhood: "Woman's Sphere" in New England, 1780–1835* (New Haven, Conn.: Yale University Press, 1977).

57. Luther Lee, *Woman's Right to Preach the Gospel: A Sermon Preached at the Ordination of the Rev. Miss Antoinette L. Brown at South Butler, Wayne County, N.Y., Sept. 15, 1853* (Syracuse, N.Y.: Lee, 1853), p. 21.

58. Franjo Cardinal Seper, *Declaration on the Question of the Admission of Women to the Ministerial Priesthood* (Rome: Sacred Congregation for the Doctrine of the Faith, 1976), p. 6.

59. Sister Elizabeth Carroll, RSM, *Women's Ordination and the Catholic Church* (Washington, D.C.: Center of Concern—Focus: Toward a World That Is Human, 1977), p. 4.

60. Of course, an occult movement is not without its own traps for women. Carol Christ was speaking of contemporary goddess worship when she stated optimistically, "This view will not be a new monism in which differences between the body and mind and nature are denied, but it will be a more integrated view in which the differences are not viewed in hierarchical and oppositional ways." *Diving Deep and Surfacing*, p. 129. Nineteenth-century spiritualists might have heeded that description as they imposed a kind of tyranny of the scientific method on the universe. The Theosophists could have benefited from an admonition to keep the understanding of the male and female principles from reifying into a description of the sex roles that already prevailed in the dominant culture. Finally, as mentioned above, some feminist witches have begun to perceive that "Big Mama" can be just as restricting as "Big Daddy."

61. Riddle, "New Visions of Spiritual Power," p. 11.

CHAPTER
13

Indians, Missions, and Cultural Conflict

From first contact, Christianization was a major motive of the European conquerors. Whether Spanish missionaries to the South, French Jesuits in Canada, or English Protestants on the Atlantic seaboard, missionaries sought to convert the native
peoples to the white man's god. Oftentimes they were successful, but at tragic costs
to the Native American populations. As one reads through the records of prose-lytiza-
tion there is hardly any evidence that white interactions with Indian religions affected white beliefs or practices. But reverse influences can be perceived everywhere.

In creative but tragic ways, Native American Indians had to adjust, first to
widespread European settlement on their shores, and second to the creation of a
continent-wide federal union that excluded them from full citizenship. Raymond J.
DeMallie's superb general account of the Lakota Ghost Dance explains the background and character of the Ghost Dance, the causes of Christian opposition to it,
and the deep tensions its appearance created between American Indians and Christian missionaries on the government reservations. In his subtitle, DeMallie terms his
analysis "an ethnohistorical account." What does he mean by this term? What is the
difference between a historian and an anthropologist? How does method affect the
histories we write? Are interdisciplinary studies the best route toward a truly holistic
history?

Additional Reading: Dennis Tedlock and Barbara Tedlock, eds., *Teachings from the
American Earth: Indian Religion and Philosophy* (New York, 1975) offers original
readings in Native American religion. John D. Loftin, *Religion and Hopi Life in
the Twentieth Century* (Bloomington, 1994) and Raymond J. DeMallie and Douglas
R. Parks, eds., *Sioux Indian Religion: Tradition and Innovation* (Norman, 1987) describe religion in two different modern Indian cultures. Henry Warner Bowden,
American Indians and Christian Missions: Studies in Cultural Conflict (Chicago,
1981) offers a general history of Christian missions to American Indians, and two

books by Francis P. Prucha, *American Indian Policy in Crisis: Christian Reformers and the Indian, 1865–1900* (Norman, 1976) and *The Churches and the Indian Schools, 1888–1912* (Lincoln, 1979), describe the history of missions in the late nineteenth and early twentieth centuries.

Raymond J. DeMallie[1] # The Lakota Ghost Dance: An Ethnohistorical Account

The Lakota Ghost dance (*wanáǧi wacipi*)[2] has been the subject of extensive study, first by newspapermen, who made it a true media event, and later by anthropologists and historians. The chronology of the contextual events in Lakota history— the 1888 and 1889 land cession commissions and their subsequent delegations to Washington, the beef ration cuts at the agencies, the spread of the ghost dance ritual among the Lakotas in 1890, the death of Sitting Bull, the calling in of U.S. troops, the flight of Lakota camps to the badlands, the blundering massacre at Wounded Knee, and the eventual restoration of peace under U.S. army control of the Sioux agencies—is voluminously detailed in the printed literature.[3]

The historiography of the Lakota ghost dance period begins with two contemporary works drawn primarily from newspaper sources. James P. Boyd's *Recent Indian Wars* (1891) and W. Fletcher Johnson's *Life of Sitting Bull and History of the Indian War of 1890–91* (1891). Despite the sensationalist tone, both volumes compiled a substantial body of important historical material. James Mooney, in his anthropological classic, *The Ghost-Dance Religion and the Sioux Outbreak of 1890* (1896), included a balanced historical discussion based on unpublished government records, newspaper accounts, and interviews with Indians. Mooney stressed the revivalistic aspects of the ghost dance and the hope it offered for regeneration of Indian culture. Subsequently there have been numerous historical studies of the Lakota ghost dance, most of which are partisan, focusing either on the Indian or military point of view. George E. Hyde's *A Sioux Chronicle* (1956) attempted to reconcile both perspectives and present the ghost dance in its political and economic context. The definitive modern historical study is Robert M. Utley's *The Last Days of the Sioux Nation* (1963), the best presentation of the military perspective.[4]

The so-called "Sioux Outbreak" with the associated troop maneuvers and the resultant Wounded Knee massacre were, from the moment they began, linked with the ghost dance. This new religion had come into Sioux country from the West, originating with Jack Wilson (Wovoka), a Paiute prophet living in Nevada. Lakota acceptance of the ritual has been interpreted as a response to the stress caused by military defeat, the disappearance of the buffalo, and confinement on a

Reprinted from *Pacific Historical Review*, Vol. 51, No. 4, (Nov. 1982), 385–405, by permission. Copyright © 1982 by Pacific Coast Branch, American Historical Association.

reservation. The ghost dance religion itself has been seen as an epiphenomenon of social and political unrest. As the redoubtable Dr. Valentine T. McGillycuddy, the former dictatorial agent of Pine Ridge, diagnosed the situation in January 1891: "As for the ghost dance, too much attention has been paid to it. It was only the symptom or surface indication of deep-rooted, long-existing difficulty. . . ."[5]

Such an analysis has become standard in the writings of both historians and anthropologists. Mooney wrote that among the Sioux, "already restless under both old and new grievances, and more lately brought to the edge of starvation by a reduction of rations, the doctrine speedily assumed a hostile meaning."[6] Similarly, Robert H. Lowie asserted in *Indians of the Plains* (1954), a standard text: "Goaded into fury by their grievances, the disciplines of Wovoka in the Plains substituted for his policy of amity a holy war in which the Whites were to be exterminated."[7] However, this consensual interpretation of the ghost dance has not gone unchallenged. For example, in an anthropological overview, Omer C. Stewart explicitly rejected the characterization of the ghost dance as a violent, warlike movement.[8] Nonetheless, this is a minority viewpoint in the literature.

Reevaluation of the ghost dance starts with an examination of the consensual interpretation exemplified in Robert M. Utley's work. He wrote:

> Wovoka preached a peaceful doctrine, blending elements of Christianity with the old native religion. . . . The Ghost Dance gripped most of the western tribes without losing this peaceful focus. Among the Teton Sioux, however, it took on militant overtones. . . . In their bitterness and despair, the Sioux let the Ghost Dance apostles, Short Bull and Kicking Bear, persuade them that the millennium prophesied by Wovoka might be facilitated by destroying the white people. Wearing "ghost shirts" that the priests assured them would turn the white man's bullets, the Sioux threw themselves wholeheartedly into a badly perverted version of the Ghost Dance.[9]

Before this analysis can be evaluated, a number of fundamental assumptions underlying it must be made more explicit. First, the statement that Wovoka's doctrine blended Christianity with "the native religion" implies that there was some fundamental similarity between the native religions of the Paiutes and the Lakotas. This assumption underestimates the significance of the vast cultural differences between these two tribes.

Second, the analysis asserts that the Lakotas perverted a doctrine of peace into one of war. This assertion incorrectly implies that the Lakota ghost dance religion was characterized by a unified body of doctrinal teaching. Lakota accounts of visits to the prophet clearly show that his teachings were not formulated into a creed; each man went away from meeting Wovoka with a personal interpretation of the ghost dance religion. For the Lakotas, this behavior was very much in accord with traditional religious practices, which defined loci of power (*wakan*) in the universe and devised rituals to tap this power, but which left each individual free to contribute to the understanding of the totality of the power (*Wakan Tanka*) through his own individual experiences.[10] Within the context of a nondoctrinal religion, there can be no heretics, only believers and nonbelievers.

Third, the analysis asserts that the leaders of the ghost dance misled their followers for political reasons, even to the point of making false claims that their sacred shirts would ward off bullets. This assertion assumes *a priori* that to its leaders the ghost dance was a political movement merely masquerading as religion.

Fourth, the claims that the ghost dance "gripped" the tribes and that "the Sioux threw themselves wholeheartedly into" the ritual suggests irrational fanaticism. But the historical record makes it clear that the period of Lakota participation in the ghost dance was basically confined to the fall and early winter of 1890 and that the majority of the Lakota people in the ghost dance camps had only gone to them because they feared that an attack from the U.S. army was imminent. This factor explains why these camps fled to the safety of the badlands.

The standard historical interpretation of the Lakota ghost dance takes too narrow a perspective. It treats the ghost dance as an isolated phenomenon, as though it were divorced from the rest of Lakota culture. It also refuses to accept the basic religious nature of the movement. The so-called ghost dance outbreak has broader implications and interconnections than historical studies have indicated. To dismiss the ghost dance as only a reaction to land loss and hunger does not do it justice; to dismiss it as merely a desperate attempt to revitalize a dead or dying culture is equally unsatisfactory. Even though it was borrowed from outside sources, the ghost dance needs to be seen as part of the integral, ongoing whole of Lakota culture and its suppression as part of the historical process of religious persecution led by Indian agents and missionaries against the Lakotas living on the Great Sioux Reservation.

The primary reasons why previous historical analyses of the Lakota ghost dance have been inadequate lie in our reluctance to consider seriously the symbolic content of Indian cultures—in this instance, to allow the Lakotas their own legitimate perspective. Instead, empathetic writers have characterized the Lakotas as though they were either uncomprehending children or were motivated by precisely the same political and economic drives as white men. Both attitudes are as demeaning as they are misleading, and they fail to treat Indian culture with the same serious consideration afforded other cultures.

Writing history that deals with the meanings and conflicts of peoples with different cultural systems is a complex task. In recent years historians of the American Indian have turned to ethnohistory to provide methods for understanding the complexities of interactions between participants coming from totally different cultures. In a discussion of the new perspectives available from political, ecological, economic, and psychological anthropology, Calvin Martin has demonstrated the utility and contributions of each to the writing of ethnohistory.[11] Within the discipline of anthropology, however, there is a more general theoretical perspective that may profitably be applied to ethnohistorical study—namely, symbolic anthropology. This method attempts to isolate differing significant symbols—units of meaning—that define perspectives on reality within different cultural systems.[12] In the context of ethnohistory, it attempts to compare epistemological and philosophical bases for action from the perspective of the different cultures involved. Its focus is on ideas systematically reconstructed for each cultural system. It does not reduce history to ideological conflicts, but uses ideology to understand the motivation that underlies behavior.[13]

It must not be assumed that the intention of a symbolic approach to ethnohistory is to penetrate the minds of individuals in the past. Psychological approaches to history are necessarily highly speculative, and any claim to intersubjectivity is no more possible with individuals in the past than with those of the present. Rather, the symbolic approach attempts to delineate collective understandings from each of the cultural perspectives involved, and thus to describe the cognitive worlds of the participants in the events under study. Using this as background, the ethnohistorian has a basis for ascribing motives and meanings to past actions. Robert Berkhofer expressed it well when he wrote: "Historical study, then, in my view, is the combination of the actors' and observers' levels of analysis into a unified representation of past reality."[14]

In attempting to reconcile and combine both Lakota and white perspectives on the ghost dance, it is essential to compare causal notions of change as understood by the two cultures. During the late nineteenth century the basic issues on the Great Sioux Reservation were what kinds of change would occur in Indian culture and social life and who would direct this change. Whites assumed that Indian culture was stagnant and that the Indians could be transformed for the better only by the imposition of Western civilization. Indians, on the other hand, sought to control the process of change themselves.

For the Lakota people, the nineteenth century had been a period of continual changes: further explorations on the Plains, the complete integration of the horse into their culture, the flourishing of the sun dance as the focal point of ritual activity, the slow take over of their country by the whites, the disappearance of the buffalo, and finally the adjustment to reservation life. A discussion of the Lakotas view of the relationship between mankind and the natural world, particularly the buffalo, can help us begin to understand these changes from the Lakotas' perspective.

During the 1860s, when commissioners traveled up the Missouri River to sign treaties with the Indians, they found the attitude of the Lakotas toward the buffalo to be particularly unrealistic. To the commissioners it was evident that the buffalo were being exterminated and would soon be gone from the region. To the Indians this decline did not appear to be an irreversible process. For example, the chiefs told the commissioners that they hoped the whites would take away the roads and steamboats and "return us all the buffalo as it used to be."[15] Baffled at this illogic, the commissioners reported that the Indians "are only too much inclined to regard us possessed of supernatural powers."[16] This complete failure to communicate stemmed from the commissioners' assumption that the facts of the natural world must have appeared the same to the Indians as they did to the whites. Yet the Indians themselves recorded testimony which showed dramatically that the Lakotas thought of the land, the animals, and the people as a single system, no part of which could change without affecting the others. Thus when the commissioners asked if the Indians would consent to live on the Missouri River, they were told: "When the buffalo come close to the river, we come close to it. When the buffaloes go off, we go off after them."[17] The Indians, the animals, and the land were one; while the people lived, talk of buffalo extinction was without meaning. Much later, Black Elk expressed the same attitude when he commented to poet John G. Neihardt: "Perhaps when the wild animals are gone, the Indians will be gone too."[18]

To understand this interrelatedness of man, land, and animals—particularly the buffalo—it is necessary to understand the Lakota view of their origins. During the early twentieth century, the old holy men at Pine Ridge instructed Dr. James R. Walker, the agency physician, in the fundamentals of their religion. A cornerstone of their belief was that both mankind and the buffalo had originated within the earth before they emerged on the surface.[19] When the buffalo became scarce, it was believed that they went back inside the earth because they had been offended, either by Indians or whites. At any given time, this explanation accounted for the scarcity of buffalo. Later, Black Elk told Neihardt about a holy man named Drinks Water who had foretold during the mid-nineteenth century that "the four-leggeds were going back into the earth."[20] But this explanation also allowed for the return of the buffalo. The ghost dance Messiah's promise of a new earth, well stocked with buffalo, was completely consistent with the old Lakota system of cause and effect by which they comprehended the ecology. If the buffalo had been driven back into the earth by the white man, they could be released again by the Messiah.

The Lakotas' casual model of change was vastly different from the white man's. The Lakota world was a constant, with relationships among its parts varying according to external pressures. As the nineteenth century wore on, these pressures came more and more from the whites. But these pressures were not conceived of by the Lakotas as cumulative or developmental. All that *was* existed in its potentiality before the whites intruded; if they would leave, the world could be again as it had been. From the 1850s through the 1870s the Lakotas tried to get rid of the whites by war; in 1890 they tried ritual dancing and prayer. The white view, of course, was diametrically opposed. This was the age of the developmental social philosophers preaching the doctrine of individual competition for the evolution of humanity. The history of mankind was religiously believed to be progressive; changes were accepted as good and cumulative, leading from earlier stages of savagery and barbarism (in which the Indians still lived) to civilization, which was believed to be becoming progressively better, not only technologically, but morally as well.

It is within this general context of cross-cultural misunderstanding that a symbolic approach can contribute to an analysis of the Lakota ghost dance and subsequent military action. The dance itself, the actual ritual, became the focus of misunderstanding between Indians and whites. Most importantly, dance was a highly charged symbol. For the Lakotas the dance was a symbol of religion, a ritual means to spiritual and physical betterment. Even Lakota nonbelievers accepted the religious motivation of the ghost dance. For the whites, on the other hand, Indians dancing symbolized impending war. Similarly, Indian and white conceptions of ghosts were different. For the Lakotas, the ghost dance promised a reunion with the souls of their dead relations. For the whites it suggested that the Indians were expecting to die, caught up in a frenzy of reckless fatalism.

This clash over the meaning of the ghost dance is fully documented in the literature. For example, in 1890, according to James Boyd's *Recent Indian Wars*:

> The Indians mingled tales of their hard treatment with their religious songs,
> and their religious dances assumed more and more the form of war dances.
> . . . The spirit of fatalism spread and they courted death at the hands of white
> men, believing that it would be a speedy transport to a happier sphere.[21]

However, Boyd's sources—both Indian and white—do not provide factual support for his interpretation. Nonetheless, this seems to have been the general opinion held by whites living on the frontiers of the Great Sioux Reservation. Boyd wrote:

> Older residents, and those acquainted with Indian warfare, knew well that an
> outbreak was always preceded by a series of dances. While these men were
> quite familiar with Indian nature, they failed to discern between a religious
> ceremony and a war dance.[22]

Boyd reviewed the progress the Sioux had made in Christianity, home building, farming, and ranching, and he raised the question of why they would wish to precipitate war. One possible answer came from Red Cloud, who said in an interview:

> We felt that we were mocked in our misery. . . . There was no hope on earth,
> and God seemed to have forgotten us. Someone had again been talking of the
> Son of God, and said He had come. The people did not know; they did not
> care. They snatched at the hope. They screamed like crazy men to Him for
> mercy. They caught at the promises they heard He had made.[23]

Towards the end of the book, Boyd revealed his personal interpretation of the cause of the trouble: "The Indians are practically a doomed race, and none realize it better than themselves."[24]

Doubtlessly, some individual Lakotas shared this sense of despair. There were no buffalo; the government systematically broke its promises to support the Sioux until they could provide for themselves; and the Indians were starving. The ghost dance, arising at this opportune time, held out hope for the Lakotas. But if the Lakotas truly had believed themselves to be a doomed people, they would have paid no attention to the ghost dance. The religion was powerful because it nurtured cultural roots that were very much alive—temporarily dormant, perhaps, but not dying.

Is it reasonable to dismiss the Lakota ghost dance as insignificant, the mere "symptom" of other troubles, to use McGillycuddy's medical metaphor? This depiction does not explain the popularity of the ghost dance as a religious movement among other tribes. Perhaps it could be used to explain the warlike twist that the ghost dance took among the Lakotas. But when the record is evaluated objectively, it seems clear that the Lakota ghost dance did not have warlike intentions. Hostility was provoked only when Indian agents demanded that the dance be stopped, and violence came only after extreme provocation—the assassination of Sitting Bull by the Standing Rock Indian Police and the calling in of the army. For all intents and purposes, Sitting Bull's death was unrelated to the ghost dance.

Agent McLaughlin had been clamoring for the old chief's arrest and removal from the reservation for some time, ever since Sitting Bull had refused to take up farming and be a model "progressive" Indian, to use McLaughlin's own term.[25]

Lakota ghost dancers were enjoined to put away whatever they could of the white man's manufacture, especially metal objects. George Sword, captain of the Pine Ridge Indian Police, noted that some of the ghost dancers did have guns.[26] When the agent demanded that the dance at No Water's camp cease, he was threatened with guns and retreated to the agency.[27] Apparently, the purpose of the weapons was to ward off outside interference with the ritual. However, Boyd quoted a ghost dancer named Weasel: "We did not carry our guns nor any weapon, but turned to the Great Spirit to destroy the soldiers." This statement was made after troops had arrived at Pine Ridge. Weasel related: "The priests called upon the young men at this juncture not to become angry but to continue the dance, but have horses ready so that all could flee were the military to charge the village."[28] However, even this precaution was not considered necessary by fervent believers. Short Bull, one of the ghost dance leaders, assured his people that they would be safe from the white soldiers:

> If the soldiers surround you four deep, three of you, on whom I have put holy shirts, will sing a song, which I have taught you, around them, when some of them will drop dead. Then the rest will start to run, but their horses will sink into the earth. The riders will jump from their horses, but they will sink into the earth also. Then you can do as you desire with them. Now you must know this, that all the soldiers and that race will be dead.[29]

Historical sources provide more information about the ghost dance from Short Bull than from any other of the leaders. Talking to Walker, he outlined his understanding of the prophet's teachings: "It was told that a woman gave birth to a child and this was known in heaven."[30] Short Bull went to meet him. "This man professed to be a great man, next to God." The prophet told Short Bull and the other Lakotas "that he wished to be their intermediator. He said 'Do nothing wrong.'" On another occasion Short Bull said:

> Who would have thought that dancing could have made such trouble? We had no wish to make trouble, nor did we cause it of ourselves. . . . We had no thought of fighting. . . . We went unarmed to the dance. How could we have held weapons? For thus we danced, in a circle, hand in hand, each man's fingers linked in those of his neighbor. . . . The message that I brought was peace.[31]

The messianic and strongly Christian nature of the ghost dance is very clear in Short Bull's teachings:

> The Father had commanded all the world to dance, and we gave the dance to the people as we had been bidden. When they danced they fell dead and went to the spirit-camp and saw those who had died, those whom they had loved. . . .

In this world the Great Father has given to the white man everything and to the Indian nothing. But it will not always be thus. In another world the Indian shall be as the white man and the white man as the Indian. To the Indian will be given wisdom and power, and the white man shall be helpless and unknowing with only the bow and arrow. For ere long this world will be consumed in flame and pass away. Then, in the life after this, to the Indian shall all be given.[32]

Through the teachings of the ghost dance, and statements about it by Lakotas recorded from 1889 until about 1910, it is possible to proliferate evidence to demonstrate the peaceful intentions of the leaders of the ghost dance. The historical record does not support the accusation that the Sioux "perverted" the ghost dance doctrine of peace to one of war.

Simple refutation of the consensual historical interpretation does little to advance an understanding of the ghost dance. Since it had a short life among the Lakotas, at least as far as active performance of the ritual, perhaps it might be dismissed as an isolated reaction to social stress, a revitalization movement that failed. After all, Mooney estimated that only half of the Sioux were affected by the ghost dance and his sources suggest that of these, only a small number were real believers in the religion.[33] But this conclusion ignores the extreme importance that the Lakotas of 1890 placed on the dance, as well as the extent to which its suppression has served in later years as a symbol of white oppression. When Mooney visited Pine Ridge in 1891 as part of his comparative study of the ghost dance, he found the Lakotas uncooperative. He wrote: "To my questions the answer almost invariably was, 'The dance was our religion, but the government sent soldiers to kill us on account of it. We will not talk more about it.'"[34]

The study of Lakota history from 1880 to 1890 suggests that it is a mistake to treat the ghost dance as an isolated phenomenon. Its prohibition was only another step in the systematic suppression of native religious practices that formed an integral part of the U.S. government's program of Indian civilization. Missionary observers felt that the ghost dance was only one more eruption of the "heathenism" that necessarily underlay the Indian psyche, a heathenism to be conquered and dispatched when Indians, as individuals, raised themselves from barbarism to civilization. The evolutionary social theory of the times held sway in the rhetoric of Indian policy.[35] *The Word Carrier,* a Protestant missionary newspaper published at the Santee Agency in Nebraska, argued in 1890 (before Wounded Knee) that it was the government's responsibility to end the ghost dancing because of its political potential. The argument was an insidious one, expressed as follows:

Their war dances have been suppressed simply as a political measure. The sun dance was forbidden in the name of humanity, as cruel and degrading. The Omaha dances should be summarily suppressed in the name of morality. But all of these alike, as well as all other of their heathen dances, should be prevented as far and as fast as possible until utterly eradicated, because they are potentially dangerous. We ought not to touch them as religious ceremonials, but, as breeders of riot and rebellion, we must.[36]

The callousness of missionary zeal for the suppression of heathenism is nowhere more dramatically revealed than in *The Word Carrier's* editorial on the Wounded Knee massacre printed in the January 1891 issue:

> The slaughter of a whole tribe of Indians at Wounded Knee was an affair which looks worse the more it is investigated. But aside from the question of culpability there is a providential aspect which demands notice. Taking it in its bearings on the whole condition of things among the rebellious Titon [*sic*] Sioux it was a blessing. It was needful that these people should feel in some sharp terrible way the just consequences of their actions, and be held in wholesome fear from further folly.[37]

Commentary is perhaps unnecessary, but we can suggest that the fanaticism of Christian missionaries was no less than that of the ghost dancers themselves. Stanley Vestal, in his biography of Sitting Bull, takes the Christian aspects of the ghost dance at face value and seizes the opportunity to comment on the missionaries:

> The Ghost dance was entirely Christian—except for the difference in rituals. However, it taught nonresistance and brotherly love in ways that had far more significance for Indians than any the missionaries could offer. No wonder the missionaries became alarmed; they were no longer sure of their converts.[38]

However, the dominant interpretation of the ghost dance, contemporarily and historically, places little significance on Christian parallels.

Some contemporary observers felt that the ghost dance showed striking resemblances to the sun dance, a suggestion that seems at first unfounded, but which gains credibility by reading descriptions of the ritual. Mary Collins, a missionary, witnessed the ghost dance in Sitting Bull's camp and recorded the following description:

> I watched all the performance, and I came to the conclusion that the "ghost dance" is nothing more than the sun dance revived. They all looked at the sun as they danced. They stopped going round now and then, and all faced the sun, with uplifted faces and outstretched arms, standing in straight lines and moaning a most horrible sound. Then they raised themselves on the toes, and then lowered themselves, raising and lowering their bodies in this way, and groaning dismally, then joined hands with heads strained backwards, watching the sun and praying to it until, with dizziness and weariness, one after another fell down, some of them wallowing and rolling on the ground and frothing at the mouth, others throwing their arms and running around and whooping like mad men, and all the time, as much as possible, still gazing sunward. They have not yet cut themselves, as in the old sun dance, but yesterday I heard this talk: Some said, "If one cuts himself, he is more 'wakan,' and can see and talk with the Messiah."[39]

These similarities to the sun dance—gazing sunward and the dance step of the sun dance—are aggressive. Also, Mooney notes that of all the tribes who adopted the ghost dance, the Sioux were one of the few to dance around a sacred tree (or pole), the structural form of the old sun dance.[40] This element may be superficial, serving only to indicate that when people borrow new ideas, they adapt them to older cultural forms as closely as possible. However, it reinforces the Lakotas' sense of religious loss and their deep felt need to establish continuity with their past. It seems that the new religion, believed to come from a reincarnated Christ wearied of the faithlessness of the whites and ready to aid his Indian children, was incorporated in a ritual form that merged the circle dance of the Paiutes (in which men and women danced together in a circle, holding hands—an innovation for the Lakotas) with the sacred dance circle and center pole of the traditional Lakota sun dance.

A speech by Short Bull to his people on October 31, 1890, points out the importance of the tree or center pole as defining the sacred space for the ghost dance ritual: "Now, there will be a tree sprout up, and there all the members of our religion and the tribe must gather together. That will be the place where we will see our dead relations." Short Bull's ghost dance preachings incorporated traditional Lakota symbolism of the four directions to suggest the unifying effects of the ghost dance on all Indian tribes. "Our father in heaven has placed a mark at each point of the four winds," indicating a great circle around the central tree. To the west was a pipe, representing the Lakotas; to the north, an arrow, representing the Cheyennes; to the east, hail, representing the Arapahoes; and to the south, a pipe and feather, representing the Crows. "My father has shown me these things, therefore we must continue this dance." He promised that the ghost dance shirts would protect them from the soldiers. "Now, we must gather at Pass Creek where the tree is sprouting. There we will go among our dead relations."[41] Many years later one Lakota who had participated in the ghost dance as a boy commented: "That part about the dead returning was what appealed to me."[42]

In practice, the millenialism of the ghost dance was merged with the symbols of the old religion. The tree, which had symbolized the body of an enemy in the old sun dance, became in the ghost dance symbolic of the Indian people themselves; this tree was dormant, but it was about to sprout and bloom. The tree symbol is best known from Black Elk, who found the outward symbols of the ghost dance so strikingly similar to his own vision during childhood that he was immediately caught up in the new religion. He felt it as a personal call, a reminder that he had not yet begun the work assigned him by his vision. "I was to be intercessor for my people and yet I was not doing my duty. Perhaps it was the Messiah that had appointed me and he might have sent this to remind me to get to work again to bring my people back into the hoop and the old religion."[43]

It seems clear in Black Elk's case that the ghost dance, while seen as a new ritual, inaugurated by a new prophet—perhaps Christ himself—was in no way felt to be a sharp break with the old religion. It was rather a means to bring the old religion to fulfillment. There is no denial that this new hope for religious fulfillment was born of frustration and unhappiness bordering on despair. The ghost dance was to bring about the transformation to a new life on a rejuvenated earth filled with all the Lakota people who had ever lived before—living again in the old ways, hunting buffalo unfettered by the demands of whites, and freed from the cares of the old earth. Years later, one ghost dancer recalled the wonderful promise of the ghost dance visions:

> Waking to the drab and wretched present after such a glowing vision, it was little wonder that they wailed as if their poor hearts would break in two with disillusionment. The people went on and on and could not stop, day or night, hoping perhaps to get a vision of their dead, or at least to hear of the visions of others. They preferred that to rest or food or sleep. And I suppose the authorities did think they were crazy—but they weren't. They were only terribly unhappy.[44]

In order to put the ghost dance in its proper perspective in Lakota religious history, it is imperative to review the process of religious persecution that marked the Lakota experience during the 1880s. At Pine Ridge, from the beginning of the decade, Agent McGillycuddy preached against the evils of the sun dance. Finally, in his annual report for 1884, he wrote that "for the first time in the history of the Ogalalla Sioux and Northern Cheyennes" the sun dance was not held.[45] Though McGillycuddy did not fully understand the reasons why, the prohibition of the sun dance was indeed a drastic blow. As a public festival it brought together Lakotas from all the agencies into old-time encampments, with opportunities for courting and fun. In addition to the actual ritual of the ceremony, the sun dance provided the time and place for many additional rituals, including the acting out of visions, dances by groups of people with shared vision experiences, demonstrations of the powers of medicine men (healers), the piercing of babies' ears (essential for identity as a Lakota), and lavish giveaways. Camped around the sacred circle with the sacred tree at its center, the occasion of the sun dance was a real affirmation of Lakota identity and power, in both physical and spiritual senses. In the words of Little Wound, American Horse, and Lone Star, as they explained their traditional religion to Dr. James R. Walker in 1896: "The Sun Dance is the greatest ceremony that the Oglalas do. It is a sacred ceremony in which all the people have a part. . . . The ceremony of the Sun Dance may embrace all the ceremonies of any kind that are relative to the Gods."[46]

In 1888, as the Oglala winter counts—native pictographic calendars—record, a further government prohibition was enforced on the Lakotas: "Bundles were forbidden."[47] It had been the custom when a beloved person died to cut a lock of his or her hair and save it in a ritual bundle for a year, thus causing the spirit (*wanaǧi*) to remain with the people. At the end of the period, the spirit was released, and a great giveaway was held; throughout the year goods were amassed to give away in honor of the departed one. In some cases, as upon the death of a first-born son, the parents gave away everything they owned, although, according to tribal customs of sharing, they would in return be given the necessities of life and thus reestablished in a new home to help put the past out of their minds. Agent H. D. Gallagher at Pine Ridge decided in 1888 that although this custom had been allowed unchecked by his predecessors, he would put an immediate stop to it. Yet, he wrote in his annual report, "I found myself opposed by every Indian upon the reservation."[48] To the Lakotas it was a final horror: not even in death was there escape from the white man's restrictions. The giveaway after death was prohibited and became an offense punishable by arrest. Ten years later, in 1898, Short Bull, in his capacity as religious leader, sent a plea to the agent begging for understanding:

> The white people made war on the Lakotas to keep them from practicing their religion. Now the white people wish to make us cause the spirits of our dead to be ashamed. They wish us to be a stingy people and send our spirits to the spirit world as if they had been conquered and robbed by the enemy. They wish us to send our spirits on the spirit trail with nothing so that when they come to the spirit world, they will be like beggars. . . . Tell this to the agent and maybe he will not cause us to make our spirits ashamed.[49]

Such requests fell on deaf ears. From the agents' point of view, every vestige of heathen religion had to be eliminated before civilization could take firm root. The powers of the agents were dictatorial in the matter.

Following the prohibition of public rituals surrounding the sun dance, as well as the rituals of death and mourning, came the prohibition in 1890 against the new ritual of the ghost dance. Then came the murder of Sitting Bull and the massacre at Wounded Knee. It was a period of grave crisis for the Lakota people, physically and emotionally. Their religion had been effective before the whites came, but now the *Wakan Tanka* seemed no longer to hear their prayers. Under the restraints of reservation life, traditional customs relating to war and hunting were abandoned. For spiritual renewal there were only two places to turn: secret rituals of the purification lodge, vision quest, *yuwipi*, and attenuated versions of the sun dance, or alternatively to the various Christian churches which were clamoring for converts.

But the years immediately following the ghost dance were bad ones for missionaries to make new converts. According to Agent Charles G. Penney, in his annual report for 1891, there were yet "a considerable number of very conservative Indians, medicine men and others, who still insist upon a revival of the Messiah craze and the ghost dancing."[50] The following year the missionary John P. Williamson, a perceptive observer, reported from Pine Ridge that "the effect of the ghost dances in the former years was very deleterious to Christianity, and is still felt among the Ogalallas. The excitement of a false religion has left a dead, indifferent feeling about religion."[51]

The Lakota religious leaders at Pine Ridge who shared their thoughts with Dr. Walker at the beginning of the twentieth century were disappointed, but not defeated. Little Wound, after revealing the sacred secrets of the *Hunka* ceremony, said to Walker:

> My friend, I have told you the secrets of the *Hunkayapi*. I fear that I have done wrong. But the spirits of old times do not come to me anymore. Another spirit has come, the Great Spirit of the white man. I do not know him. I do not know how to call him to help me. I have done him no harm, and he should do me no harm. The old life is gone, and I cannot be young again.[52]

Afraid of Bear commented: "The spirits do not come and help us now. The white men have driven them away."[53] Ringing Shield stated: "Now the spirits will not come. This is because the white men have offended the spirits."[54]

One of the most eloquent testimonies comes from a speech by Red Cloud, recorded by Walker, in which he outlined his understanding of the Lakota *Wakan Tanka.* Then he added:

> When the Lakotas believed these things they lived happy and they died satis-
> fied. What more than this can that which the white man offers us give? . . . .
> *Taku Skanskan* [Lakotas' most powerful god] is familiar with my spirit (*nagi*)
> and when I die I will go with him. Then I will be with my forefathers. If this is
> not in the heaven of the white man, I shall be satisfied. *Wi* [Sun] is my father.
> The *Wakan Tanka* of the white man has overcome him. But I shall remain true to
> him.[55]

Outwardly, the white man's victory over Lakota religion was nearly complete. In-wardly, even among those who—like Red Cloud—accepted Christianity for what it was worth, the recognition of the existence of *wakan* in the life forms of the universe provided foci of belief and hope.

Any meaningful understanding of the Lakota ghost dance period must begin with an analysis of the foundations for cultural conflict. Lakotas and white men operated under radically different epistemologies; what seemed illogical to one was sensible to the other and vice versa. Objects in the natural world symbolized totally different realms of meaning in the two cultures. This difference has impor-tant implications for the writing of history. For example, Utley suggests that "when the hostile Sioux came to the reservation, they doubtless understood that the life of the future would differ from that of the past."[56] But we can raise a rea-sonable doubt that this statement truly characterized the Lakota point of view. When Utley writes: "That the vanishing herds symbolized their own vanishing ways of life cannot have escaped the Sioux,"[57] we must deny the assertion. This is the unbeliever's attitude, totally dependent on acceptance of western philosophy. Similarly, it is necessary to take issue with Utley's claim that "after Wounded Knee . . . the reality of the conquest descended upon the entire Nation with such overwhelming force that it shattered all illusions."[58] This is political rhetoric to justify the defeat of the Indians, not reasoned historical assessment.

The vast differences between the rhetoric of whites and Indians gives special significance to the ghost dance as the last step in a decade-long series of events aimed at crushing every outward expression of Lakota spirituality. From the be-liever's standpoint, the social and political problems—the so-called outbreak and the Wounded Knee massacre—were but epiphenomena of religious crisis. The ghost dance was inextricably bound to the whole of Lakota culture and to ongo-ing historical processes in Lakota society. Although it was introduced from the outside, it was rapidly assimilated to the Lakota system of values and ideas, espe-cially because it promised resolution to the grave problems that beset the people. To recognize it as a religious movement in its own right does not deny its inter-connection with all other aspects of Lakota life or negate its intended practical consequence to free the Lakotas from white domination. However, such recogni-

tion does retain the Lakotas' own focus on the ghost dance as a fundamentally religious movement which was to bring about radical transformation completely
through religious means. Virtually all historical data point to the non-violent intentions of the ghost dance religion and the commitment of the believers to
achieving their ends non-violently. It was the explicit command of the Messiah. In
a cultural sense, this understanding of the ghost dance was shared by all Lakotas,
believers and nonbelievers alike.

The importance of the ghost dance is not to be measured in the simple number of participants or in the unhappiness or despair that it reflected, but rather as
part of the religious history of the Lakota people. For a time it held out such hope
to the Lakotas that its ultimate failure, symbolized by the tragic deaths of the believers at Wounded Knee, generated a renewed religious crisis that forced a final
realization that the old ways, with the hunting of the buffalo, were actually gone
forever. Out of this religious collapse, new beliefs, new philosophies, eventually
developed that would entail a major intellectual reworking of the epistemological
foundations of Lakota culture.

Among the writers on the Lakota ghost dance, only John G. Neihardt accepted it as a legitimate religious movement and saw it as an attempt by the holy
men of the Lakotas to use sacred means to better the condition of their people.[59] A
symbolic approach forces examination of the religious aspects of the ghost dance,
not only because it *was* primarily religious from the Lakotas' perspective, but also
because at least some contemporary white observers—the missionaries—understood that the ritual's true power lay in its religious nature. To the white men the
ghost dance was seen as the last gasp of heathenism; to the Indians it offered renewed access to spiritual power.

The ghost dance ritual itself was a powerful symbol, but one on whose meanings the whites and Lakotas were incapable of communicating. They shared no
common understandings. That the ghost dance could be a valid religion was incomprehensible to the whites, just as the whites' evolutionary perspective on
Lakota destiny—that the barbaric must develop into the civilized—was incomprehensible to the Lakotas. Religion, dancing, g

hosts, the processes of social change, and animal ecology were all important
symbols to both whites and Indians, but the meanings of these symbols in the two
cultures were diametrically opposed. By focusing on these symbols it is possible
for the ethnohistorian to reconstruct the meanings of events from the perspective
of the participants and to arrive at an analysis that has both relevance and insight,
and which contributes to an understanding of the historical realities of the Lakota
ghost dance.

NOTES

1. The author is a member of the anthropology department in Indiana University.

2. Literally, "spirit dance." The term *wanaǧi* refers to the immortal spirit of a human and
may be translated as "spirit," "ghost," or "soul." See James R. Walker, *Lakota Belief and
Ritual*, ed. by Raymond J. DeMallie and Elaine A. Jahner (Lincoln, 1980), 70–71.

3. For a historiographical survey of the literature on the Lakota ghost dance, see Michael A. Sievers, "The Historiography of 'The Bloody Field . . . That Kept the Secret of the Everlasting Word': Wounded Knee," *South Dakota History*, VI (1975), 33–54.

4. James P. Boyd, *Recent Indian Wars, Under the Lead of Sitting Bull, and Other Chiefs; with A full Account of the Messiah Craze, and Ghost Dances* (Philadelphia, 1891); W. Fletcher Johnson, *Life of Sitting Bull and History of the Indian War of 1890–'91* (Philadelphia, 1891); James Mooney, *The Ghost-Dance Religion and the Sioux Outbreak of 1890*, Bureau of American Ethnology Annual Report 14, pt. 2 (Washington, D.C., 1896); George E. Hyde, *A Sioux Chronicle* (Norman, 1956); Robert M. Utley, *The Last Days of the Sioux Nation* (New Haven, 1963).

5. Mooney, *Ghost-Dance Religion*, 833.

6. *Ibid.*, 787.

7. Robert H. Lowie, *Indians of the Plains* (New York, 1954), 181.

8. Omer C. Stewart, "The Ghost Dance," in W. Raymond Wood and Margot Liberty, eds., *Anthropology on the Great Plains* (Lincoln, 1980), 184.

9. Robert M. Utley, *Frontier Regulars: The United States Army and the Indian, 1866–1890* (New York, 1973), 402–403.

10. See Walker, *Lakota Belief and Ritual*, 68–73; Raymond J. DeMallie and Robert H. Lavenda, "Wakan: Plains Siouan Concepts of Power," in Richard Adams and Raymond D. Fogelson, eds., *The Anthropology of Power: Ethnographic Studies from Asia, Oceania and the New World* (New York, 1977), 154–165.

11. Calvin Martin, "Ethnohistory: A Better Way to Write Indian History," *Western Historical Quarterly*, IX (1978), 41–56.

12. For an introduction to the field, see Janet L. Dolgin, David S. Kemnitzer, and David M. Schneider, eds., *Symbolic Anthropology: A Reader in the Study of Symbols and Meanings* (New York, 1977) and Clifford Geertz, *The Interpretation of Cultures* (New York, 1973).

13. See, for example, DeMallie, "Touching the Pen: Plains Indian Treaty Councils in Ethnohistorical Perspective," in Frederick C. Luebke, ed., *Ethnicity on the Great Plains* (Lincoln, 1980), 38–53.

14. Robert E. Berkhofer, Jr., *A Behavioral Approach to Historical Analysis* (New York, 1969), 73.

15. *Proceedings of a Board of Commissioners to Negotiate a Treaty or Treaties with the Hostile Indians of the Upper Missouri* (Washington, D.C., 1865), 104.

16. Indian Peace Commission, in *Annual Report of the Commissioner of Indian Affairs* (1866), 169.

17. *Proceedings of A Board of Commissioners*, 34.

18. Transcript of interviews of Black Elk by John G. Neihardt, 1931, pp. 3–4, Western History Manuscripts Collection, University of Missouri, Columbia.

19. Walker, *Lakota Belief and Ritual*, 124, 144.

20. Black Elk interview transcripts, 161.

21. Boyd, *Recent Indian Wars*, 198.

22. *Ibid.*, 180.

23. *Ibid.*, 181.

24. *Ibid.*, 289.

25. A good analysis is provided by Stephen D. Youngkin, "Sitting Bull and McLaughlin: Chieftainship Under Siege," unpublished M.A. thesis, University of Wyoming, 1978.

26. Mooney, *Ghost-Dance Religion*, 798.

27. *Ibid.*, 847.

28. Boyd, *Recent Indian Wars*, 194–195.

29. Mooney, *Ghost-Dance Religion*, 789.

30. Walker, *Lakota Belief and Ritual*, 142.

31. Natalie Curtis, *The Indians' Book* (New York, 1935), 45.

32. *Ibid.*, 46–47.

33. Mooney, *Ghost-Dance Religion*, 917, 927.

34. *Ibid.*, 1060.

35. See Francis Paul Prucha, *American Indian Policy in Crisis: Christian Reformers and the Indian, 1865–1900* (Norman, 1976), 155–158.

36. *The Word Carrier*, XIX, no. 12 (Dec. 1890), 34.

37. *Ibid.*, XX, no. 1 (Jan. 1891), 1.

38. Stanley Vestal, *Sitting Bull: Champion of the Sioux* (new ed., Norman, 1957), 272.

39. *The Word Carrier*, XIX, no. 11 (Nov. 1890), 30.

40. Mooney, *Ghost-Dance Religion*, 823.

41. *Ibid.*, 788–789.

42. Ella C. Deloria, *Speaking of Indians* (New York, 1944), 83.

43. Black Elk interview transcripts, 182.

44. Deloria, *Speaking of Indians*, 83.

45. Valentine T. McGillycuddy, in *Annual Report of the Commissioners of Indian Affairs* (1884), 37.

46. Walker, *Lakota Belief and Ritual*, 179–180.

47. James R. Walker, *Lakota Society*, ed. by Raymond J. DeMallie (Lincoln, 1982), 151.

48. H. D. Gallagher, in *Annual Report of the Commissioner of Indian Affairs* (1888), 49.

49. Walker, *Lakota Belief and Ritual*, 141.

50. Charles G. Penney, in *Annual Report of the Commissioner of Indian Affairs* (1891), 410.

51. John P. Williamson, in *ibid.* (1892), 459.

52. Walker, *Lakota Belief and Ritual*, 198.

53. *Ibid.*, 202.

54. *Ibid.*, 206.

55. *Ibid.*, 140.

56. Utley, *Last Days of the Sioux Nation*, 22.

57. *Ibid.*

58. *Ibid.*, 5.

59. John G. Neihardt, *The Song of the Messiah* (New York, 1935).

CHAPTER
14

Religion and Politics

Even as the "New Social History" redirected religious historians' attentions to "ordinary people" and "religious outsiders," so also did it expose historians to new, computer-assisted quantitative techniques and methods of statistical analysis. When these methods were applied to political behavior in nineteenth-century America, the "quantifiers" made a startling discovery. In charting the key variables that could predict how an individual might vote, the strongest predictors are not class or gender or region, but religion. Irish Catholics, for example, voted Democratic, whether they were rich or poor, while New England Protestants tended to be Whigs. All of this confirmed how, in a voluntaristic society, religion and ethnicity proved to be the glue holding groups of American citizens together.

In the article to follow, Robert P. Swierenga charts the rise of "Ethnocultural" historiography and summarizes some of the major findings to emerge in the past twenty years. When read together with Jay Dolan's essay on "The Immigrants and their Gods," some of the same questions emerge. How significant is religion in American political life? Is it possible to separate out what is "ethnic" in politics and what is "religious"? Finally, does the ethnocultural paradigm continue to characterize political behavior in the twentieth century?

Additional Reading: Two good general surveys of voting studies are: Joel H. Silbey, Allan G. Bogue, William H. Flanigan, (eds.), *The History of American Electoral Behavior* (Princeton, 1978), and Richard L. McCormick, "Ethnocultural Interpretations of Nineteenth Century American Voting Behavior," in Richard L. McCormick, *The Party Period and Public Policy* (New York, 1986), 29–63. Among the best "case studies" of voting behavior are: Paul Kleppner, *The Cross of Culture: A Social Analysis of Midwestern Politics, 1850–1900* (New York, 1970); Richard J. Jensen, *The Winning of the Midwest: Social and Political Conflict, 1888–1896* (Chicago, 1971); Wm. Ray Heitzmann, *American Jewish Voting Behavior: A History and Analysis* (San Francisco, 1975); and Ronald P. Formisano, *The Transformation of Political Culture: Massachusetts Parties, 1790s–1840s* (New York, 1983).

Robert P. Swierenga

Ethnoreligious Political Behavior in the Mid-Nineteenth Century: Voting, Values, Cultures

The most exciting development in American political history in the last twenty years is the recognition that religion was the key variable in voting behavior until at least the Great Depression. The move to restore religion to political analysis gained momentum slowly in the 1940s and 1950s through the work of the eminent scholars Paul Lazarsfeld, Samuel Lubell, and Seymour Martin Lipset, and it culminated in the 1960s when historians Lee Benson and Samuel Hays brought the new perspective to a generation of graduate students.[1] By the 1970s this so-called ethnocultural (or ethnoreligious[2]) interpretation of voting behavior had become the reigning orthodoxy, having supplanted the populist-progressive paradigm that "economics explains the mostest," to quote Charles Beard.[3] In recent years, a resurgent neoprogressive, or "new left," historiography, led by cultural Marxists, has challenged the ethnoreligious interpretation, but the edifice, which stands on solid research at the grass roots, remains largely intact.[4]

This essay summarizes the accumulated evidence in support of the thesis that religion was the salient factor in nineteenth-century voting behavior. How and why religion was at the center is extremely complex, as are the related issues of documentation and measurement. There were also regional and temporal variations in the role of religion in politics. Nevertheless, despite its limitations, a theological interpretation of voting behavior offers a refreshing new angle to our understanding of political culture in the eras of Andrew Jackson and Abraham Lincoln.

THE REDISCOVERY OF RELIGION

The revolution in American political history began when Lazarsfeld and his associates at the Bureau of Applied Social Research at Columbia University systematically surveyed voters during the 1940 presidential election campaign in Erie County, Ohio. To their surprise they found that voters were most influenced by their churches, or, in sociological jargon, their "social reference groups." Protestants and Catholics clearly differed in voting and party identification, even when

From *Religion and American Politics: From the Colonial Period to the 1980s,* edited by Mark A. Noll (New York: Oxford University Press, 1990). Reprinted by permission of Oxford University Press.

"controlling" for socioeconomic factors.[5] In one giant step, Lazarsfeld and associates had brought into political analysis the religious variable that had been jettisoned by the first generation of professional historians and political scientists in the late nineteenth century. The prevailing wisdom was encapsulated in James Bryce's terse assertion in 1894: "Religion comes very little into the American party."[6] Sectional economic rivalries, class conflicts, and melting pot doctrines were the reigning orthodoxies following the influential historians Frederick Jackson Turner and Charles Beard. Why the rising professoriate was blind to expressions of religious values in politics is complex. Put simply, they were highly secularized and believed religion should be privatized and church and state kept totally separate. The doctrine of the melting pot, then dominant, also held that ethnic and religious differences were narrowing in society and politics.

So strong was this thinking in the twentieth century that political pollsters of the modern era never considered religious questions when gathering data on voting behavior. George Gallup, the first professional pollster and himself a Protestant churchgoer, did not ask respondents for their church affiliation until after Lazarsfeld published his 1940 study, *The People's Choice,* in 1944. Indeed, when Lazarsfeld told Gallup of his startling finding, Gallup expressed disbelief.[7] As late as 1959, during the Kennedy-Nixon presidential race, Elmo Roper, another leading pollster, challenged the "myth of the Catholic vote" and denied any connection between religion and voting.[8] The pollsters' skepticism gave way when Lipset, the prestigious director of the Institute of International Studies at the University of California, Berkeley, further documented the place of religion in American culture and politics. But Lipset still deferred to the long-dominant neo-Marxist paradigm then in its declension. Religion did not "explain everything," he allowed; class position was equally determinative.[9]

The next challenge to the liberal paradigm carried the day. In 1961 Lee Benson, a young historian who had studied nineteenth-century voting patterns at Lazarsfeld's Bureau in the mid-1950s, published one of the most significant books in American political history, *The Concept of Jacksonian Democracy: New York as a Test Case.* Benson began his research as a convinced economic determinant, but his analysis of group voting behavior led him to develop a sociological-psychological model based on ethnoreligious conflict. His key conclusion is the now classic statement: "At least since the 1820s, when manhood suffrage became widespread, ethnic and religious differences have tended to be *relatively* the most important source of political differences in the United States." Benson made no attempt to "prove" his proposition other than to demonstrate its validity in the 1844 presidential election in New York State. Intuitively, he felt that this theory conformed to common sense. "Since the United States is highly heterogeneous, and has high social mobility," he reasoned, "I assume that men tend to . . . be more influenced by their ethnic and religious group membership then by their membership in economic classes or groups."[10]

Within a decade, a host of historians led by Benson and Hays completed additional research for various Northern states that generally confirmed the religious dimension. These publications, which employed quantitative and social science methods and theories, demonstrated that religion and ethnicity were basic to

American voting patterns.[11] This finding should not have been surprising. Foreign observers of America in the nineteenth century, such as Alexis de Tocqueville, had remarked often about the high religiosity of American society, especially after the Second Great Awakening filled empty churches with new converts. As Richard Jensen has stated: "The most revolutionary change in nineteenth century America was the conversion of the nation from a largely dechristianized land in 1789 to a stronghold of Protestantism by mid-century. The revivals did it." By 1890, church affiliation was above 70 percent in the Midwest, with the new revivalist sects and churches claiming over half. The revivals sparked confrontation in every denomination. Again quoting Jensen: "Until the mid-1890s the conflict between pietists and liturgicals was not only the noisiest product of American religion, it was also the force which channeled religious enthusiasm and religious conflicts into the political arena."[12] This was all the more true because the militant Evangelicals sought to link Christian reform and Republicanism into an unofficial Protestant establishment that virtually equated the Kingdom of God with the nation.[13]

FROM RELIGION TO POLITICS: VALUES AND CULTURE

The mechanism for translating religion into political preferences is complicated and much disputed. Lazarsfeld, Lipset, Lubell, Benson, and Hays all stressed the socialization process.[14] Individuals learned attitudes and values early in life from family, church, and community, which then shaped their perception of the larger world and gave them ethical values to live by. Persons, if you will, absorbed voting habits with their mother's milk, and these subconscious dispositions were later reinforced by the parson's sermons and the wisdom of the brethren. One political party was "right," the other "wrong." Parties were bound to conflict in a society flooded by wave after wave of immigrants. Each ethnoreligious group had its own social character, historical experience, and theological beliefs. Each had its friends and enemies, or, in Robert K. Merton's words, its positive and negative reference groups.[15] Irish Catholics, for example, reacted against hostile New England Protestants, who tended to be Whigs, by joining the Democratic party. Then, new British immigrants voted Whig because Irish Catholics voted Democratic, and so on.

The ethnoreligious thesis, on one level, shifted the focus from national to local issues and from elites to the behavior of voters at the grass roots. At a deeper level, it substituted religious culture for class conflict and sectionalism as a significant independent variable in voting choices. As Hays explained simply: "Party differences in voting patterns were cultural, not economic." "Ethnocultural issues were far more important to voters than were tariffs, trusts, and railroads. They touched lives directly and moved people deeply."[16] Instead of battles in Washington and statehouses over economic benefits and favors, ethnoreligionists stress fights over prohibition of alcohol, abolition of slavery, Sunday closing laws, parochial-school funding, foreign-language and Bible usage in public schools, anti-Catholic nativism and alien suffrage, sexual conformity and capital punishment, and a host of lesser crusades. The point of the new view is that moral rather than economic issues impelled nineteenth-century voters and produced the major political conflicts. Instead of being assimilated, ethnoreligious groups clung to their customs, beliefs, and identities for generations, and as they clashed over public policy at the polls, their values and attitudes were hardened, reshaped, or mellowed, depending on changing historical circumstances. Nevertheless, these structural differences remained deep-rooted. As Lipset noted, this made "religious variation a matter of political significance in America."[17]

Political socialization of individuals and structural conflict among social groups may explain how voters absorbed their values and prejudices and had them reinforced as groups fought to defend or advance their interests in the political arena; but this does not explain why particular ethnoreligious groups voted as they did. Why were Irish Catholics Democrats and New England Congregationalists Whig and Republican?

Ethnoreligionists have offered at least three distinct but often intertwined theories to explain how religious group impulses became political ones. Benson emphasized reference group theory, especially negative reactions. While valid in limited historical settings, such as Boston in the 1840s when Irish Catholic immigrants overran this Anglo-Protestant center, reference group theory is rather limited and simplistic, especially the notion that group members merely "absorb" political ideas and "react" to other groups. Hays added a refinement, that of group hegemonic goals, which he called the "social analysis of politics."[18] Ethnoreligious groups use political means to try to extend the domain of their cultural practices or, conversely, to protect themselves from legal or legislative attacks. As Catholic Irish and German immigrants seemed to inundate the United States, for example, native-born Protestants turned to nativist laws to keep Catholic Sabbath desecration or beer drinking in check. Again, this social approach begs the question of the sources of differing lifestyles. If groups clashed because of historic antagonisms and conflicting cultural traditions, it was because their religious roots differed.[19]

This led to the third theory, that "theology rather than language, customs, or heritage, was the foundation of cultural and political sub-groups in America," to quote Richard Jensen.[20] "Political choices were thus derived from beliefs about God, human nature, the family, and government. Citizens were not robots, but reflective beings whose value system had been 'sanctified' by their family, friends, and congregations."[21] Different ways of living and voting derive from different ways of believing. Moral decision-making rests on religious values, theological distinctions, or, more broadly, worldviews.[22]

Kleppner cogently explained the nature of belief. Religion "involves a rationale for existence, a view of the world, a perspective for the organization of experience; it is a cognitive framework consisting of a matrix within which the human actor perceives his environment." Although it is not the only perspective, it "penetrates all partial and fragmentary social worlds in which men participate; it organizes and defines how they perceive and relate to society in general." Religiosity, Kleppner continues, comprises five core dimensions: belief, knowledge, practice, experience, and consequences. Various denominations emphasize different dimensions and their linkages, and out of this come behavioral differences. Historically, the two broad clusters of denominations were the pietists, who went from belief to experience and consequences, and the liturgicals, who tied belief to knowledge and practice.[23]

It must be admitted that any attempt to explain voting behavior on the basis of Christian theology, liturgy, or lifestyle is a sticky wicket. Voters, because their minds and wills are innately flawed, do not *always* act consistently with their ultimate beliefs. They may be cross-pressured by competing and conflicting religious "oughts." Finney evangelicals, for example, worked to free slaves but not women. Voters may delude themselves and vote their pocketbook while claiming to follow ethnical principles. Churches and historical issues and pressures also changed over time, and generalizations are thus necessarily limited in time and place.[24] Scholars have also struggled with theological typologies that can adequately categorize the many denominations according to their various belief systems.

THE LITURGICAL-PIETIST CONTINUUM

Kleppner and Jensen offered the first sophisticated religious theory of American voting in the nineteenth century. Based on a wide reading in the sociology of religion and the history of individual denominations and groups, they developed the ritualist-pietist, or liturgical-pietist, continuum, which locates ethnoreligious groups and denominations along a single dimension based on the central tendency of their theological orientation.[25] On the one side were ecclesiastical, ritualistic, and liturgically oriented groups; and on the other were the sectlike evangelicals or pietists who stressed a living, biblical faith and the imminent return and rule of the Messiah. The liturgical churches (such as the Roman Catholic, Episcopal, and various Lutheran synods) were credally based, sacerdotal, hierarchical, nonmillenial, and particularistic. These ecclesiasticals were ever vigilant against state encroachment on their churches, parochial schools, and the moral lives of their members. God's kingdom was other-worldly, and human programs of conversion or social reform could not usher in the millennium. God would restore this inscrutable, fallen world in His own good time and in His own mighty power.

The pietists (Baptists, Methodists, Disciples, Congregationalists, Quakers) were New Testament-oriented, antiritualist, congregational in governance, active in parachurch organizations, and committed to individual conversion and societal reform in order to usher in the millennial reign of Jesus Christ. Pietists did not compartmentalize religion and civil government. Right belief and right behavior were two sides of the same spiritual coin. The liturgicals excommunicated heretics, the pietists expelled or shunned sinners.

These theological differences directly affected politics in the Jacksonian era because the Yankee pietists launched a crusade to Christianize America and the liturgicals resisted what they viewed as an enforced Anglo-conformity.[26] The pietists staged a two-pronged public program. First they created the "benevolent empire" in the 1810s to spread the gospel and teach the Bible. Then, in the 1820s, they established reform societies to eradicate slavery, saloons, Sabbath desecration, and other social ills. Finally, in the 1830s, they entered the political mainstream by joining the new Whig party coalition against the Jacksonian Democrats. By the 1840s, in fear of the growing Catholic immigrant menace, they added nativist legislation to their agenda, especially extending the naturalization period from five to fourteen years. As the reformed-minded Yankees threatened to gain control of the federal and state governments through the Whig party and, after 1854, the Republican party, the liturgicals, who were mainly immigrants, fought back through the Democratic party.

Why the liturgicals joined the Democracy and the more pietist Christians gravitated to the Whig and Republican parties requires a brief explanation of party ideologies and programs. With Thomas Jefferson as its patron saint and Andrew Jackson as its titular head, the Democratic party from its inception in the 1820s espoused egalitarian, libertarian, and secularist goals.[27] The Democrats were social levelers who believed in a limited, populistic government and a society rooted in self-interest and individual autonomy. They sought a secular state that did not try to legislate social behavior and was free of church control.[28] An editorial in an Ohio Democratic newspaper condemned all reform movements that were motivated by "ascetic law, force, terror, or violence," and a Michigan editor declared: "We regard a man's religious belief as concerning only himself and his Maker." Government must thus restrain all economic power brokers and promote a laissez-faire society. Democratic theorists like George Bancroft believed that "the voice of the people is the voice of God."[29] The highest good was universal manhood suffrage, majoritarian rule, a nonexploitative society, and a government that granted no undue favors. The Democrats easily attracted immigrants from the beginning and always stood for cultural and ethnic diversity.[30]

The opposition Whig party was more elitist, paternalistic, cosmopolitan, entrepreneurial, and legalistic.[31] This "Yankee Party" viewed government positively, trusted the governors more than the governed, and believed in absolute law based on external verities. The goal of the Northern Whigs was to enlist all Christians and their clerical leaders who sought collectively to promote moral behavior and social harmony.[32] The Whigs, said Robert Kelley, were "the party of decency and respectability, the guardians of piety, sober living, proper manners, thrift, steady habits, and book learning."[33] The Whig agenda of building a "righteous empire" (to use the apt title of Martin Marty's book) received a tremendous boost initially from the Second Great Awakening. Indeed, without the spiritual revivals, the Whig leaders could not have built a viable mass party. Later in the 1840s the backlash against mass immigration and the perceived Irish menace further strengthened the Anglo-Whig party. When Bishop John Hughes of New York City objected to the reading of the King James Bible in the public schools as an attempt to proselytize Catholic children, and tried to obtain public funding for Catholic schools, Protestant leaders became alarmed and worked through the Whig party to enact nativist laws to weaken or contain the Catholic threat.[34] To Yankees, the Irish were English "blacks," social pariahs who were now infesting Protestant America.[35]

Given these opposing ethnoreligious groups, it is not surprising that historians find many links between religion and politics. Liturgicals demanded maximum personal freedom and state neutrality regarding personal behavior. They tended to find a congenial home in the Democratic party. But pietists, who felt an obligation to "reach out and purge the world of sin," found in the Whigs a vehicle to accomplish this.[36] Paul Kleppner's generalization is the standard summary of the ethnoreligious thesis: "The more ritualistic the religious orientation of the group, the more likely it was to support the Democracy; conversely, the more pietist the group's outlook the more intensely Republican its partisan affiliation."[37] In short, "the primary cleavage line of party oppositions . . . pitted evangelical pietistics against ritualistic religious groups."[38]

Was this political and social conflict between religious groups rooted in simple ethnic and religious prejudices and differing lifestyles, or did a theological cleavage underlay the behavioral distinctions? Some scholars (Benson and Formisano, for example) stress the clash of cultures, the historic reference group hatreds and prejudices, the group defenses and hegemonic goals. Although there is no dearth of historical evidence for such a pattern of brokenness in American history, it does not mean that human behavior is usually (or always) unthinking, reactive, and culturally determined. As noted earlier, to explain that German Catholics supported the Democrats because the party opposed prohibition and Quakers voted Whig and Republican because that party favored prohibition is not to explain the behavior at all. To claim that Irish Catholics voted Democratic because they hated Yankee Whigs does not explain the source of the prejudice. The reason that people voted this way ultimately lies deeper than symbols or culture; it is rooted in religious worldviews.[39] People act politically, economically, and socially in keeping with their ultimate beliefs. Their values, mores, and actions, whether in the polling booth, on the job, or at home, are an outgrowth of the god or gods they hold at the center of their being.

In a nation of immigrants, where members of ethnoreligious groups often lived out their daily lives together in churches, schools, societies and clubs, work and play, and in marriage and family life, group norms were readily passed from parents to children, along with a strong sense of identity and a commitment to their political and social goals. Such groups were understandably ready to promote or defend their beliefs when public policy issues arose that touched their lives directly. Religious issues, more than social class, status, or sectional interests, were at the crux. As Kleppner asserts: "Attachments to ethnoreligious groups were *relatively* more important as determinants of nineteenth-century social-group cohesiveness and party oppositions than were economic attributes or social status." Notice the word "relatively." Ethnoculturalists have not claimed that their findings *exclusively* explain mass voting patterns, only that differing religious beliefs *best* explain that behavior.[40] They also recognize that in the South the race issue was paramount.

Ethnoculturalists also recognize that cross-pressures and particular historic contexts may change patterns or create unique situations.[41] The Pella (Iowa) Dutch pietists continued to vote Democratic after the Civil War when other Dutch Reformed colonies in the Midwest switched en masse to the Republicans. The nativist attacks on the community in the 1850s had been too strong and bitter to forget.[42]

MEASUREMENT PROBLEMS

Having explained the religious roots of voting behavior, I now turn to the pithy question Lee Benson first posed in 1957: "Who voted for whom, when?"[43] How ethnoreligious group members voted is a factual question that requires an empirical answer.[44] While the question is straightforward, finding the answers have been very difficult. Two basic measurement problems keep cropping up. The first is to determine the religious affiliation of party members and voters, and the second is to measure the extent to which religious values acted in conjunction with socioeconomic and other factors to determine voting behavior.

Identifying the religion of voters is by far the more difficult problem. Federal census publications did not report the number of church members or communicants until the 1890 census. Beginning in 1850, however, the census enumerated church seating capacity per community. Since "sittings" were not directly proportionate with membership, particularly in the Catholic church, some scholars estimated pre-1890 membership by assuming that the 1890 ratio of members to sittings was a reasonable approximation of the earlier ratio.[45] Some scholars simply used sittings, or an even cruder measure, the number of church buildings.[46] It is also recognized that church attendance consistently exceeded membership, but nominal and occasional members likely shared the values and worldviews of full members.[47]

In some areas, local sources such as county biographical directories occasionally state the religious affiliation of family heads.[48] But one had to pay to be listed in these "mug books," so they do not include all potential voters. Poll books of active voters survive in some counties and when they are collated with church membership records, it is possible to determine precisely the religion of voters.[49] Such individual-level data are ideal, but rare. One scholar estimated Catholic strength in minor civil divisions by collating the names of fathers and godfathers listed in baptism records with names in federal census records, multiplying by the ratio of births per adult member (15:1 in 1860), and thus determining the Catholic population per ward.[50]

Another common method of estimating religion was to note the state or country of birth in the manuscript censuses (recorded from 1850 on) as a proxy for ethnoreligious identity, and then to locate "homogeneous" counties or preferably townships and wards, that is, communities that were predominantly German Lutheran, Dutch Reformed, Swedish Lutheran, New England Yankee, and so on. The voting behavior in these homogeneous townships is then taken to represent the voting of the entire group in a state or region.[51] Critics charged that such communities were atypical, because group pressures would be unduly strong there. Would a German Lutheran living in a largely German village in Wisconsin vote differently than a fellow church member who was living among Irish Catholics in Chicago?

The alternative to finding homogeneous areas is to estimate the relative proportion of ethnoreligious groups per county for an entire state or section of the country, either in whole or by sampling. The ideal, which no one has yet attempted, is to draw a random township and ward sample of the northeastern United States, compile township-level aggregate data on religion, ethnicity, occupation, wealth, and other pertinent variables in the period 1850–1900, and then, using multiple regression analysis, determine the relative relationships between religion and voting, taking into account the effects of all of the other variables.[52] Until such a large project is undertaken, we must rely upon the several dozen case studies at the state and local level completed in the last twenty years. These studies cover the years from 1820 to 1900 in the Northeastern and Midwestern states.[53]

ETHNORELIGIOUS GROUPS

Although regional variations existed, the findings generally agree in the political categorization of the major ethnoreligious groups. The various groups can best be arranged in four categories: strongly Democrat (75+ percent), moderately Democratic (50–75 percent), moderately Whig or Republican (50–75 percent), and strongly Whig or Republican (75+ percent) (see Table 1). Strongly Democratic

Table 1. Political Orientation of Major Ethnoreligious Groups, 1830–1890

Strongly Whig/Republican 75–100%	Moderately Whig/Republican 50–75%
Quaker	Christian Church - Disciples
Scotch-Irish Presbyterian	Missionary Baptist
Free Will Baptist	Regular Baptist
Congregationalist	Universalist (Midwestern)
New School Presbyterian	Old School Presbyterian
Unitarian	New German Lutheran
Northern Methodist	Danish Lutheran
Irish Methodist	German Pietist Groups
Cornish Methodist	Amish
Welsh Methodist	Brethren
Swedish Lutheran	Mennonite
Norwegian Lutheran	Moravian
Haugean Norwegian	New Dutch Christian Reformed
English Episcopal	
Canadian English Episcopal	
New Dutch Reformed	
French Huguenot	
Black Protestants	

Strongly Democratic 75–100%	Moderately Democratic 50–75%
Irish Catholic	Old British Episcopal
German Catholic	Southern Presbyterian
French Catholic	Universalist (New England)
Bohemian Catholic	Southern Disciples of Christ
French Canadian	Old German Lutheran
French	Old German Reformed
Southern Baptist	Old Dutch Reformed
Southern Methodist	

Source: Works cited in notes 11 and 45, especially Kleppner, *Cross* and *Third;* Jensen, *Winning;* and Formisano, *Birth.*

groups were all Catholics (Irish, German, French, French Canadian, Belgian, Bohemian, etc.), and Southern Baptists and Southern Methodists. Moderately Democratic groups were Old (i.e., colonial) German Lutheran, Old German and Old Dutch Reformed, Old British Episcopalians, New England Universalists, and Southern Presbyterians and Disciples of Christ. Moderately Whig and Republican in their voting were the German pietist sects (Brethren, Mennonites, Moravians, Amish), New German and Danish Lutheran, New Dutch Christian Reformed, Old School Presbyterians, Regular and Missionary Baptists, Midwestern Universalists, and the Christian Church. Strongly Whig and Republican were Northern Methodists (including Irish and Cornish Methodists), Free Will Baptists, Congregationalists, New School Presbyterians, Unitarians, Quakers, French Huguenots, Swedish and Norwegian Lutherans, Haugean Norwegians, New Dutch Reformed, Canadian English and New England Episcopalians, and blacks. (Groups designated "Old" immigrated prior to the American Revolution; "New" arrived afterwards.)

The ethnoreligious specialists deserve credit for discovering these group voting patterns. Some distinctions are extremely subtle. For example, among Michigan's Dutch Calvinist immigrants of the mid-nineteenth century, the majority group affiliated with the largely Americanized Old Dutch Reformed Church in the East in 1850, but a minority opposed the union, seceded, and formed an independent immigrant church, the Christian Reformed Church. One of the major doctrinal issues in the split was the conviction of the seceders that the Dutch Reformed espoused a revivalist free-will theology and used evangelical hymns and other "tainted" aspects of Yankee pietism.[54] In their politics, Kleppner found that the Dutch Reformed after the Civil War consistently voted Republican more strongly than did the Christian Reformed (66 percent versus 59 percent).[55] Even among a homogeneous immigrant group like the Dutch Calvinists, the inroads of revivalism strengthened commitments to the Yankee political party.

RELIGION AND POLITICS

Not only for the Dutch Calvinists but for all ethnoreligious groups, revivalism was the "engine" of political agitation.[56] Evangelist Charles G. Finney began preaching revival in the mid-1820s throughout New England and its Yankee colonies in western New York. By 1831 religious enthusiasm had reached a fever pitch in Yankeedom and mass conversions swept town after town. Church membership doubled and tripled and large portions of the populace were reclaimed for Protestantism. Finney challenged his followers to pursue "entire sanctification" or perfectionism and to become Christian social activists. The converts first entered politics in the anti-Masonic movement in New York in 1826–27. By the mid-1830s the evangelicals entered national politics by opposing slavery, alcohol, and other social ills that they believed the Jackson administration condoned. Converts such as Theodore Dwight Weld became leaders in the antislavery movement. And in the 1840s and 1850s, revivalist regions of the country developed strong anti-slavery societies and voted Liberty, Whig, and later Republican.[57] Ultimately, the allegiance of pietists to the Whig party led to its demise because the pietists put ethical goals, such as abolition of slavery, above party loyalty. The idea of a party system built on patronage and discipline was much stronger in Democrat than in Whig ranks. Evangelicals had a disproportionate share of antiparty men. In their estimation, Popery, Masonry, and Party were all threats to freedom of conscience and Christian principles.[58]

The disintegration of the Whig party in the early 1850s, followed by the brief appearance of the Know-Nothings and then of the new Republican party, and the fissure of the Democratic party in 1860 were the main components of the political realignment of the decade. The Second Electoral System gave way to the Third System. But "Yankee-cultural imperialism" now expressed through the Republican party continued as the dynamic force, carrying out God's will against racists and other sinners in the Democratic party. Broadly speaking, in the third electoral era pietist religious groups, both native-born and immigrant, led the Republican party against antipietist Democrats.[59]

The 1860 presidential election signaled the future direction of the social bases of partisanship. Catholic voter groups of all ethnic backgrounds and across all status levels voted more solidly Democratic than ever before. Meanwhile some former Democrats moved toward the Republicans, notably Yankee Methodists and Baptists, and pietistic Norwegians, Dutch Reformed, and Germans.[60] The increasingly Catholic character of the Democracy, as well as that party's presumed responsibility for the Civil War, drove these Protestants away.

The impact of religious conflict on voting behavior in the 1860 Lincoln-Douglas election is illustrated in Cleveland, Ohio, in a study by Thomas Kremm.[61] Although founded by New England Yankees, Cleveland lay astride the immigrant route from New York to points west, and by 1860 the majority of the population was foreign-born. Roman Catholic immigrants, mainly German and Irish, comprised 30 percent of the population in 1860. Catholics numbered more than half the population in two wards (out of eleven in the city) and just under half in another ward.

The influx of Catholics in the 1840s and 1850s led to a nativist backlash. To the Protestant majority, Catholics were un-American; they rejected the "public religion" of the republic. Moreover, the Catholic church was an "undemocratic engine of oppression." As the editor of the Cleveland *Express* declared: "Roman Catholics, whose consciences are enslaved, . . . regard the King of Rome—the Pope—as the depository of all authority."[62] Religious tensions were also stirred by Catholic opposition to public-school tax levies, by their "European" use of the Sabbath for recreation, and by their consistent bloc voting for the Democrats. Irish Catholics, charged the editors of the Cleveland *Leader*, "were sots and bums who crawled out of their 'rotten nests of filth' on election days to cast 'ignorant' ballots for the candidates of the 'slavocracy.' These 'cattle' lured to the polls by huge quantities of whisky, worshipped the three deities of the Ruffian Party—the Pope, a whisky barrel, and a nigger driver."[63]

This level of invective suggests that the Cleveland electorate divided along Catholic versus non-Catholic lines, rather than over slavery extension. Voting analysis of the 1860 election proves this. The percentage of Catholic voters per ward and the Douglas vote were almost perfectly correlated. Similarly, the percentage of non-Catholic voters and the Lincoln vote were almost perfectly correlated. Even when removing the effects of ethnicity, occupation, and wealth, religion explains over 80 percent of the variation across wards in the Republican and Democratic percentages. Religion, Kremm concluded, was the "real issue," the "overriding factor determining party preference in 1860." Catholics voted for the Democratic candidate, Stephen Douglas, and non-Catholics, irrespective of other socioeconomic factors, voted for Lincoln.[64]

The rise of the Republican party in Pittsburgh in the 1850s is similar to the Cleveland story. As Michael Holt discovered, the Republican coalition rose on a wave of anti-Catholic sentiment among native-born Protestants, which flared on issues of Sabbatarian laws and parochial schools. The growing Irish and German Catholic population increasingly voted the Democratic ticket. Holt's careful statistical correlations between voting patterns and ethnoreligious and economic characteristics of the city's wards revealed that "economic issues made no discernible contribution to Republican strength. . . . Instead, social, ethnic, and religious considerations often determined who voted for whom between 1848 and 1861. Divisions between native-born Americans and immigrants and between Protestants and Catholics, rather than differences of opinion about the tariff or the morality of slavery, distinguished Whigs and Republicans from Democrats."[65]

The temperance issue and other social concerns, except abolition of slavery, lessened during the war years, but in the early 1870s legal moves against alcohol and saloons resurfaced. The Republicans, who were generally supportive, lost voting support over temperance agitation. The Yankee party also had a negative fallout from the economic depression set off by the financial panic of 1873.[66] The Democrats, meanwhile, benefited from the Catholic fertility "time bomb" that exploded in the 1870s. The relative strength of the ritualists thus grew at the expense of the pietists. In 1860, pietists outnumbered ritualists nationwide by 21 percentage points (50 to 29 percent), but by 1890 pietists led by only 5 percent (40 to 35). The population increase among pietist groups averaged 2.4 percent per year, compared with 5.3 percent among liturgicals (and 6.2 percent among Catholics).[67]

Out of political desperation, as well as concern for the moral decline in American society, the Republican pietists in the 1870s and 1880s revived the "politics of righteousness"—Sabbatarian and temperance laws, anti-Catholic propaganda, and defense of Protestant public schools and English-only language instruction. Despite these efforts, the Democrats, bolstered by the "solid South," surged after 1876, winning three of four presidential elections by close margins. In effect, the Northern supporting groups held steady in both camps for several decades until the major realignment of the 1890s caused a "cross of culture." In the political upheaval of the nineties, William Jennings Bryan molded the old Democracy into a new "party of reform" and William McKinley redirected the Republicans into a middle-of-the-road position that fought against silver coinage rather than alcoholic beverages.[68]

CONTRIBUTIONS AND CRITIQUE

There are many positive results of the ethnoreligious interpretation of American voting behavior. Most important is the realization that religious beliefs significantly affected mass voting behavior. Religious groups and political parties had a symbiotic relationship. Churches influenced political agenda by determining that slavery or alcohol or some other moral problem required legislative action.[69] Parties, in turn, built constituencies from various religious groups whose worldviews jibed with the party's programs and goals. The relationship between religion and politics was so close in the nineteenth century that Kleppner rightly calls the parties "political churches" and their ideologies "political confessionalism."[70]

The ethnoreligionists had made their case convincingly, even to the point of "boredom and hostility," in the words of a Marxist reviewer. By 1970 religion had become the new orthodoxy in voting studies. As critic James Wright admitted, the new school had "done their work well. It is virtually impossible to avoid their frame of reference."[71] Since the mid-1970s political historians have had to *disprove* the salience of religion and culture as major explanations of voting patterns. Even the cultural Marxists have factored religious forces into their economic models.[72]

Second, the ethnoreligious research shifted attention from the national to the local level, from political elites to voters at the grass roots. The radically different perspective, working "from the bottom up," brought great excitement to the new political history in the 1960s and 1970s and sparked many new studies.[73]

Unfortunately, the momentum slipped in the 1980s. There has been no major research study since Kleppner's *Third Electoral System* appeared in 1979 and Formisano's *Transformation of Political Culture* in 1983. Must we agree with Jean Baker that "the limits have been reached," or with Richard McCormick that ethnoreligious political analysis "as originally conceived, was at a dead end" by the late 1970s?[74] I think not, and neither does McCormick, who has been a cogent critic. The ethnocultural interpretation received a boost from new scholarship in the 1980s, which blended the political ideology of republicanism and the rising forces of capitalism with the social analysis of politics.[75] Moreover, the best work since the mid-1970s has incorporated more sophisticated statistical techniques (multivariate correlation and regression analysis, partialing, path analysis) that explain the relationship between voting choices and occupation, wealth, status, religion, and ethnicity. These studies proved again that the politics of "'Amens' and 'Hallelujahs'" determined voting more than class and status variables.[76]

Critics have leveled against the ethnoreligionists many charges, a few of which are valid but most are not. Unsubstantiated charges are that they are mono-causalists who have exaggerated the religious variable to the point of "religious determinism," that they have a "fixation" with vague "symbolic" aspects of politics while ignoring concrete issues, that they are ahistorical in treating religion independently of time and place, that they ignored the unchurched or nominally churched half of the population, that their statistical methods were weak and misguided, and that their case study approach was not representative of the nation at large.[77] The cultural Marxists have also reiterated their a priori assumptions about the centrality of economic factors.[78]

There are two valid criticisms—one relates to the religious model and the other involves research design. Most important is the pietist-liturgical continuum, which predicted how doctrinal beliefs were translated into voting patterns. It is inadequate not because religious beliefs were "seldom dominant" in voting decisions, as one critic charged, but because ultimate values and beliefs, which are always dominant in human decision-making, are too complex for a one-dimensional, "either-or" scale. In his 1979 book Kleppner offered a more complex model that treated the pietistic and ritualistic perspectives as "more-or-less" characteristic of the various denominations rather than divided into two mutually exclusive types. He also drew distinctions among pietists between Northern "evangelicals" and Southern "salvationists," and among ritualists between Lutherans and Catholics, centering on the extent to which these groups compartmentalized the sacred from the secular. The sharper the division, the less moral legislation.[79]

But this more sophisticated model still fails to incorporate necessary distinctions among Northern evangelical pietists between mainline denominations such as Congregationalists, perfectionist denominations such as Wesleyan Methodists, primitivist denominations such as the Churches of Christ, and separatists such as the Amish.[80] Issues of theology, polity, and praxis separated these groups, and we still need a model that incorporates these complexities and yet is sufficiently simple to be useful in research (the jargon word is "operational"). Kleppner's newer model points in the right direction. The relationship of the church to the world is crucial, as H. Richard Niebuhr explained in his book *Christ and Culture*.[81] Niebuhr identified five historic views: Christ *against* culture, Christ in *agreement* with culture, Christ *above* culture, Christ in *tension* with culture, and Christ *transforming* culture. While Niebuhr's categories need revision, especially since the current religious Right has made a shambles of the opposition view which stressed separation from culture, yet the key issue remains: how do persons of faith relate to the political world? Specialists in American religious history could make a major contribution to political history by developing a usable theological topology.

The other challenge is for energetic political historians with good statistical skills to undertake the massive study Kousser called for in 1979.[82] This is to validate the ethnoreligious interpretation by drawing random areal samples of rural townships and city wards, gathering all relevant socioeconomic facts for several decennial census years in the nineteenth century for these areas, and then making multivariate statistical tests to uncover the key determinants of voting behavior. Such a study might well yield a more generalized model of American voting behavior. It might even convince skeptics that religious institutions and values counted heavily in American politics and American history generally.

Religion, we now know, was the "stuff of political choice" in the last century, shaping the issues and rhetoric and determining party alignments.[83] Churches were primary value-generating institutions and religious beliefs inevitably affected political choices and goals. Voters responded to the theological outlook toward culture of their particular denominations, encouraged by in-group pressures and the influence of pastors and teachers. For opening this long-overlooked component of American political history, the ethnoreligious scholars deserve accolades. Until proven otherwise by new research, the legacy of their work stands.

NOTES

1. Joel H. Silbey, Allan G. Bogue, William H. Flanigan, eds., *The History of American Electoral Behavior* (Princeton, NJ: Princeton University Press, 1978), 3–27, and references cited therein; Allan G. Bogue, "The New Political History of the 1970s," in Bogue, *Clio and the Bitch Goddess: Quantification in American Political History* (Beverly Hills: Sage, 1983), 113–135. See also Bogue, "Inside the 'Iowa School'," in ibid., 19–50, esp. 22–24; Seymour Martin Lipset, "Religion and Politics in the American Past and Present," in Robert Lee and Martin E. Marty, eds., *Religion and Social Conflict* (New York: Oxford University Press, 1964), 69–126; Samuel Lubell, *The Future of American Politics* (Garden City, NY: Doubleday Anchor, 1956), 129–157; Lee Benson, "Research Problems in American Political Historiography," in Mira Komarovsky, ed., *Common Frontiers of the Social Sciences* (Glencoe, IL: Free Press, 1957), 113–183; Benson, *The Concept of Jacksonian Democracy: New York as a Test Case* (Princeton, NJ: Princeton University Press, 1961); Samuel P. Hays, "History as Human Behavior" [1959] and "New Possibilities for American Political History: The Social Analysis of Political Life: [1964], reprinted in Samuel P. Hays, *American Political History as Social Analysis* (Knoxville: University of Tennessee Press, 1980), 51–65, 87–132; Richard L. McCormick, "Ethnocultural Interpretations of Nineteenth Century American Voting Behavior" [1974], in Richard L. McCormick, *The Party Period and Public Policy: American Politics from the Age of Jackson to the Progressive Era* (New York: Oxford University Press, 1986), 29–63.

2. Lawrence H. Fuchs coined the term "ethnoreligious" in 1956 because of its "inclusive quality"; it incorporated ethnic groups such as the Irish, religious groups such as Jews and Quakers, and even racial groups such as blacks. See Fuchs, *The Political Behavior of American Jews* (Glencoe, IL: Free Press, 1956), 13. Another early analysis of the influence of religion in American voting is Benton Johnson, "Ascetic Protestantism and Political Preference," *Political Science Quarterly* 26 (Spring 1962): 35–46.

3. Silbey et al., *American Electoral Behavior,* 20, 253–262; Robert P. Swierenga, "Ethnocultural Political Analysis: A New Approach to American Ethnic Studies," *Journal of American Studies* 5 (April 1971): 59–79; Samuel T. McSeveney, "Ethnic Groups, Ethnic Conflicts, and Recent Quantitative Research in American Political History," *International Migration Review* 7 (Spring 1973): 14–33; McCormick, "Ethnocultural Interpretations." A perceptive analysis of the evolving ethnic component of religion is Harry S. Stout, "Ethnicity: The Vital Center of Religion in America," *Ethnicity* (April 1975): 204–224.

4. The best summary of the literature is Richard L. McCormick, "The Social Analysis of American Political History—After Twenty Years," in McCormick, *Party Period,* 89–140.

5. Lipset, "Religion and Politics," 70; Silbey et al., *American Electoral Behavior,* 12–13.

6. Quoted in Richard Jensen, "The Religious and Occupational Roots of Party Identification: Illinois and Indiana in the 1870s," *Civil War History* 16 (December 1970): 325.

7. Lipset, "Religion and Politics," 120, n. 2.

8. Elmo Roper, "The Myth of the Catholic Vote," *Saturday Review of Literature,* October 31, 1959, p. 22.

9. Lipset, "Religion and Politics," 71, 120–121.

10. Benson, *Concept,* 165.

11. The core studies are: Paul Kleppner, *The Cross of Culture: A Social Analysis of Midwestern Politics, 1850–1900* (New York: Free Press, 1970); Richard J. Jensen, *The Winning of the Midwest: Social and Political Conflict, 1888–96* (Chicago: University of Chicago Press, 1971); and Ronald P. Formisano, *The Birth of Mass Political Parties: Michigan, 1827–1861* (Princeton, NJ: Princeton University Press, 1971). Recent major additions are: Paul Kleppner, *The Third Electoral System, 1853–1892: Parties, Voters, and Political Cultures* (Chapel Hill: University of North Carolina Press, 1979); and Ronald P. Formisano, *The Transformation of Political Cul-*

ture: Massachusetts Parties, 1790s–1840s (New York: Oxford University Press, 1983). Although omitted in this paper, Jews also had block voting for Jeffersonian Republicans and Jacksonian Democrats in the early republic, and after the 1840s they switched and became solidly Republican until the New Deal. See Wm. Ray Heitzmann, *American Jewish Voting Behavior: A History and Analysis* (San Francisco: R & E Research Associates, 1975).

12. Jensen, *Winning*, 62, 63–64. The exceptional religiosity of American life is also described in Seymour Martin Lipset, *The First New Nation* (New York: Basic Books, 1963), ch. 4, "Religion and American Values," 140–169.

13. George M. Marsden, *The Evangelical Mind and the New School Experience* (New Haven: Yale University Press, 1970), 239–242, relying on Perry Miller.

14. Benson, *Concept*, 281–287; Hays, "New Possibilities," 104–116; Hays, *American Political History*, 13–36, 132–156; Lipset, "Religion and Politics," 21, 111–120.

15. Derived from Merton's observation that "men frequently orient themselves to groups *other than their own* in shaping their behavior and evaluations," in *Social Theory and Social Structure* (Glencoe, IL: Free Press, 1957), 288.

16. Hays, "History as Human Behavior" [1959], in Hays, *American Political History*, 54; and Hays, "Political Parties and the Community—Society Continuum" [1967], in ibid., 300.

17. Lipset, "Religion and Politics," 71.

18. Benson, *Concept*, 27, 281–287; Hays, "History," in Hays, *American Political History*, 66, 87, and passim.

19. McCormick, "Ethnocultural Interpretations," 39–47, perceptively explains that the ethnocultural scholars somewhat carelessly intermixed these three theories.

20. Jensen, *Winning*, 82, 89.

21. Kleppner, *Cross*, 37, 75; Kleppner, *Third*, 183–197; Formisano, *Birth*, 102, 55; Jensen, *Winning*, 58, 88.

22. Kleppner, *Third*, 183, following Milton Rokeach, J. Milton Yinger, Rodney Stark, Charles Glock, Peter Berger, and other psychologists and sociologists of religion. While acknowledging religious values, some scholars believe that political parties took shape independently and then they either attracted or repelled religious groups, depending on their platforms and programs. This is only a variant on the interest group interpretation. See John Ashworth, *'Agrarians' and 'Aristocrats': Party Political Ideology in the United States, 1837–1846* (London: Royal Historical Society, 1983), 219–221. Churches preceded parties in America and it is also logical to assume that religious preference preceded partisan preference. Cf. Jensen, *Winning*, 59.

23. Kleppner, *Third*, 183–185.

24. Kleppner, makes this point forcefully in ibid., 357–382.

25. Kleppner, *Cross*, 71–72; Kleppner, *Third*, 185–189; Jensen, *Winning*, 63–67. A contemporary scholar, Robert Baird, in *Religion in America* (New York: Harper & Row, 1844), divided all denominations into "Evangelical" and "Unevangelical" (p. 220). Scholars have struggled with other terms to identify the same distinction: Benson, puritan/nonpuritan (*Concept*, 198); Formisano, evangelical/anti-evangelical (*Birth*, 138) and center/periphery (*Transformation*, 5–7, passim); Philip R. VanderMeer, church/sect ("Religion, Society, and Politics: A Classification of American Religious Groups," *Social Science History* 5 [February 1981]: 3–24); Roger D. Peterson, traditionalist/pietist ("The Reaction to a Heterogeneous Society: A Behavioral and Quantitative Analysis of Northern Voting Behavior, 1845–1870, Pennsylvania a Test Case" [Ph.D. diss., University of Pittsburgh, 1970]; Edward R. Kantowitz, insider/outsider and dogmatist/pietist ("Politics," in Stephan Thernstrom, Ann Orlov, and Oscar Handlin, eds., *Harvard Encyclopedia of American Ethnic Groups* [Cambridge, MA: Harvard University Press, 1980], 803–804). Benson and Formisano are more reluctant than the other scholars cited to associate liturgical and pietist values with theology rather than to offer sociological explanations. See McCormick, *Party Period*, 48.

26. Alternatively, some have argued that the Jacksonians were rationalistic, republican nation-builders who enlisted Protestant imagery and symbols in order to legitimate and unify the "new experiment in self-government" and create a "public religion," to use Benjamin Franklin's phrase. Sidney Mead argues that in the second half of the nineteenth century, Protestantism was amalgamated with "Americanism" to form an all-encompassing "civil religion," the "Religion of the Republic." See Martin E. Marty, *Pilgrims in Their Own Land: Five Hundred Years of Religion in America* (New York: Viking Penguin, 1984), 154–166; Sidney E. Mead, *The Lively Experiment: The Shaping of Christianity in America* (New York: Harper & Row, 1963), 134–187; and Marsden, *Evangelical Mind*, 239–241.

27. This paragraph and the following rely heavily on Robert Kelley, *The Cultural Pattern in American Politics: The First Century* (New York: Knopf, 1979), ch. 5–8, esp. 160–170, 223–227; and Ashworth, 'Agrarians'.

28. Georgetown *Democratic Standard*, September 12, 1843, as quoted in Stephen C. Fox, "The Bank Wars, The Idea of 'Party,' and the Division of the Electorate in Jacksonian Ohio," *Ohio History* 88 (Summer 1979): 257; Ann Arbor *Michigan Argus*, February 1, 1843, quoted in Formisano, *Birth*, 110.

29. See Bancroft, "The Office of the People in Art, Government and Religion," *Literary and Historical Miscellanies* (New York, 1855), 408–435, excerpted in Joseph L. Blau, *Social Theories of Jacksonian Democracy: Representative Writings of the Period, 1825–1850* (Indianapolis: Bobbs-Merrill, 1954), 263–273; and quotes in Arthur M. Schlesinger, Jr., *The Age of Jackson* (Boston: Little, Brown, 1945), 419.

30. Kelley, *Cultural Patterns*, 147; Ashworth, 'Agrarians', 178.

31. The best analysis of Whig culture and ideology is Daniel Walker Howe, *The Political Culture of the American Whigs* (Chicago and London: University of Chicago Press, 1979).

32. The Reverend Ezra Stiles Ely, pastor of Philadelphia's Third Presbyterian Church, was one such cleric who called for a Christian citizens movement, a loosely organized "Christian party in politics," to influence Christians to vote for avowed Christian candidates. Ezra S. Ely, *The Duty of Christian Freeman to Elect Christian Rulers* (Philadelphia, 1827), cited in John R. Bodo, *The Protestant Clergy and Public Issues, 1812–1848* (Princeton: Princeton University Press, 1954). See also Benson, *Jacksonian Democracy*, 199–200.

33. Kelley, *Cultural Patterns*, 160–169.

34. Sydney E. Ahlstrom, *A Religious History of the American People* (New Haven: Yale University Press, 1972), 559–563.

35. Kelley, *Cultural Patterns*, 172.

36. Jensen, *Winning*, 67–68.

37. Kleppner, *Cross*, 72–75; and *Third*, 74, 360–363; cf. Jensen, *Winning*, 69; Formisano, *Birth*, 128, 324, 330; and Benson, *Concept*, 198–207.

38. Kleppner, *Third*, 363.

39. Ibid., 363–364. McCormick allows that religious beliefs explain the political behavior of pietists but not liturgicals, who simply acted in self-defense. Their worldview, says McCormick, had "no political significance until they were assaulted by pietists" (*Party Period*, 367). But it is illogical to hold that pietist theology was intrinsically political and liturgical theology was intrinsically apolitical. Liturgicals were on the defensive in the antebellum era because the Great Awakening impelled revivalists toward social activism. In the progressive era, however, pietist fundamentalists made the "great reversal" and withdrew from political life, while the liturgicals launched the social gospel movement. See David O. Moberg, *The Great Reversal: Evangelicalism versus Social Concern* (Philadelphia: Lippincott, 1972).

40. Kleppner, *Third*, 371, 359–361. Kelley, *Cultural Patterns*, 164, speaks of a "marginal preponderance."

41. Kleppner, *Third*, 363.

42. Ibid., 363–371, 167–168; Robert P. Swierenga, "The Ethnic Voter and the First Lincoln Election," *Civil War History* 11 (March 1965): 27–43; reprinted in Frederick C. Luebke, ed., *Ethnic Voters and the Election of Lincoln* (Lincoln: University of Nebraska Press, 1971), 129–150.

43. Benson, "Research Problems," 122.

44. See Kleppner, *Third*, 9–15, 322–331, 355–373, and passim for a discussion of the concept of social group.

45. Kleppner, *Third*, 204–205; Jensen, *Winning*, 85–87. Dale Baum, "The 'Irish Vote' and Party Politics in Massachusetts, 1860–1976," *Civil War History* 26 (June 1980): 120, argues that systematic underenumeration in counting "seats," especially for Catholic churches, which served several groups of parishioners, would "make no difference" in statistical analyses. Formisano is unduly pessimistic when he says: "religion counted for very much in politics, [but] it is almost impossible to measure precisely religious affiliation among the electorate" (*Transformation*, 289–290). Formisano was more favorable earlier. See his "Analyzing American Voting, 1830–1860: Methods," *Historical Methods Newsletter* 2 (March 1969): 1–12. The censuses of "Social Statistics" from 1850 list each church by denomination in every town and give the number of "accommodations" or "seats" in each building. The percentage of each denomination's seats of the total seats indicates the "religious preferences" of each township.

46. Peterson, "Reaction."

47. Lipset, "Religion and Politics," 101–102.

48. Jensen, "Religious and Occupational Roots," 168–169; Jensen, *Winning*, 325; Peterson, "Reaction," 263–269.

49. Formisano, *Birth*, 297–298, 318–323, 346–348, found voter lists for Lansing, Detroit, and Ingham County in the 1850s. Melvyn Hammarberg, *The Indiana Voter: The Historical Dynamics of Party Allegiance During the 1870s* (Chicago: University of Chicago Press, 1977), 107–108, found *People's Guides* in Indiana in the 1870s that specified religion. See also: Kenneth J. Winkle, "A Social Analysis of Voter Turnout in Ohio, 1850–1860," *Journal of Interdisciplinary History* 13 (Winter 1983): 411–435; Paul F. Bourke and Donald A. DeBats, "Individuals and Aggregates: A Note on Historical Data and Assumptions," *Social Science History* 4 (May 1980): 229–250; John M. Rozett, "Racism and Republican Emergence in Illinois, 1848–1860: A Re-Evaluation of Republican Negrophobia," *Civil War History* 22 (June 1976): 101–115, based on Rozett, "The Social Bases of Party Conflict in the Age of Jackson: Individual Voting Behavior in Greene County, Illinois, 1838–1848" (Ph.D. diss., University of Michigan, 1974); David H. Bohmer, "The Maryland Electorate and the Concept of a Party System in the Early National Period," in Silbey et al., *History of American Electoral Behavior*, 146–173.

50. Thomas A. Kremm, "Cleveland and the First Lincoln Election: The Ethnic Response to Nativism," *Journal of Interdisciplinary History* 8 (Summer 1977): 77–78. This article is based on Kremm, "The Rise of the Republican Party in Cleveland, 1848–1860" (Ph.D. diss., Kent State University, 1974).

51. Lee Benson and Samuel Hays pioneered this technique. See Benson, *Concept* (paperback ed., 1963), ix–x, 165–207; and Hays, *American Political Analysis*, 10–12. J. Morgan Kousser, "The 'New Political History': A Methodological Critique," *Reviews in American History* 4 (March 1976): 1–14, harshly castigates this as "gestalt correlation," and "proving correlation by intimidation" (5–6). McCormick is also critical; see "Ethnocultural Interpretations," 41.

52. Kousser, "'New Political History,'" 10–11.

53. In addition to the studies already cited, see: Michael F. Holt, *Forging a Majority: The Formation of the Republican Party in Pittsburgh 1848–1860* (New Haven: Yale University Press, 1969); William E. Giennap, *The Origins of the Republican Party, 1852–1856* (New York: Oxford

University Press, 1987); William G. Shade, *Banks or No Banks: The Money Issue in Western Politics* (Detroit: Wayne State University Press, 1972); Samuel McSeveney, *The Politics of Depression: Political Behavior in the Northeast, 1893–1896* (New York: Oxford University Press, 1972); John L. Hammond, *The Politics of Benevolence: Revival Religion and American Voting Behavior* (Norwood, NJ: Abbey, 1979); Frederick C. Luebke, *Immigrants and Politics: The Germans of Nebraska, 1880–1900* (Lincoln: University of Nebraska Press, 1969); Philip R. VanderMeer, *The Hoosier Politician: Officeholding and Political Culture in Indiana 1896–1920* (Urbana: University of Illinois Press, 1985); Dale Baum, *The Civil War Party System: The Case of Massachusetts, 1848–1876* (Chapel Hill: University of North Carolina Press, 1984); Joel H. Silbey, *The Transformation of American Politics* (Englewood Cliffs, NJ: Prentice-Hall, 1967); Jed Dannenbaum, *Drink and Disorder: Temperance Reform in Cincinnati from the Washingtonian Revival to the WCTU* (Urbana: University of Illinois Press, 1984); Walter D. Kamphoefner, "Dreissiger and Forty-Eighter: The Political Influence of Two Generations of German Political Exiles," in Hans L. Trefousse, ed., *Germany and America: Essays on Problems of International Relations and Immigration* (New York: Brooklyn College Press, 1980), 89–102; Stephen C. Fox, "The Group Bases of Ohio Political Behavior, 1803–1848" (Ph.D. diss., University of Cincinnati, 1973); Fox, "Politicians, Issues, and Voter Preference in Jacksonian Ohio: A Critique of an Interpretation," *Ohio History* 86 (Summer 1977): 155–170; Robert E. Wyman, "Wisconsin Ethnic Groups and the Election of 1890," *Wisconsin Magazine of History* 51 (Summer 1968): 269–293, reprinted in Robert P. Swierenga, ed., *Quantification in American History: Theory and Research* (New York: Atheneum, 1970), 239–266.

54. The leader of the Holland colony, Albertus C. Van Raalte, who had led the affiliation with the Reformed Church in the East, was accused of promoting the Arminian theology of the Reverend Richard Baxter, found in his booklet "Call to the Unconverted." See *Classis Holland Minutes, 1843–1858* (Grand Rapids: Eerdmans, 1950), 144–145, 181–182, 227–228, 240–243, 246.

55. Kleppner, *Third*, 166–169.

56. Formisano, *Birth*, 104.

57. Hammond, *Politics*, ch. 4–5, esp. 75–76, 124–133.

58. Formisano, *Birth*, 58, 79.

59. Kleppner, *Third*, 59, 73, citing Richard L. Power, *Planting Cornbelt Culture* (Indianapolis: Indiana Historical Society, 1953).

60. Ibid., 74.

61. Kremm, "First Lincoln Election," 69–86.

62. Ibid., 82, citing the January 30, 1855, issue of the Cleveland *Express*.

63. Ibid., 83–85, quote on 85, citing various articles of the Cleveland *Leader*.

64. Ibid., Table 6, 76, 80–81.

65. Holt, *Forging*, 218, quote on 7, 9.

66. Kleppner, *Third*, 136–140.

67. Ibid., Table 6.3, 205–206.

68. Kleppner, *Cross*, 316–368.

69. VanderMeer, "Religion," 18. Other positive comments are in VanderMeer, "The New Political History: Progress and Prospects," *Computers and the Humanities* 11 (September–October, 1977): 267.

70. Kleppner, *Third*, 196.

71. Sean Wilentz, "On Class and Politics in Jacksonian America," *Reviews in American History* 10 (December 1982): 47–48; James E. Wright, "The Ethnocultural Model of Voting: A Behavioral and Historical Critique," in Allan G. Bogue, ed., *Emerging Theoretical Models in Social and Political History* (Beverly Hills: Sage, 1973), 40.

72. See, for example, Paul E. Johnson, *A Shopkeeper's Millennium: Society and Revivals in Rochester, New York, 1815–1837* (New York: Hill and Wang, 1978). An excellent review of the Marxist social historians of American politics is McCormick, "Social Analysis," 98–115.

73. Allan G. Bogue, "The New Political History in the 1970s," in Bogue, *Clio and the Bitch Goddess*, 116.

74. Jean H. Baker, *Affairs of Party: The Political Culture of Northern Democrats in the Mid-Nineteenth Century* (Ithaca: Cornell University Press, 1983), 11; McCormick, "Social Analysis," 95.

75. McCormick, "Social Analysis," 96–97.

76. Kleppner, *Third*, 326–328, 361–363.

77. Allan G. Bogue, "The New Political History," *American Behavioral Scientist* 21 (November–December 1977), 203 (but Bogue withdraws the charge of monocausality in "New Political History in the 1970s," 122); Richard B. Latner and Peter Levine, "Perspective on Antebellum Pietistic Politics," *Reviews in American History* 4 (March 1976): 19, and Eric Foner, "The Causes of the American Civil War: Recent Interpretations and New Directions," *Civil War History* 20 (September 1974): 200, make the charge of religious determinism; Edward Pessen, review of Kelley, *Cultural Pattern*, in *Civil War History* 25 (September 1979): 281, for the fixation charge; Latner and Levine, "Perspectives," 17, Foner, "Causes," 200, and Wright, "Ethnocultural," 46, for the ahistorical charge; Hammarberg, *Indiana Voter*, 116, for ignoring unchurched; Krousser, "'New Political History,'" 1–14, and A. J. Lichtman and L. I. Langbein, "Ecological Regression Versus Homogeneous Units: A Specification Analysis," *Social Science History* 2 (Winter 1978): 172–193, for methodological critiques (but for a rebuttal, see William G. Shade, "Banner Units and Counties: An Empirical Comparison of Two Approaches," unpublished paper); Bogue, "New Political History," 209, for the case approach comment.

78. Kleppner, *Third*, 376; McCormick, "Social Analysis," 98–115. The strongest voting study from an economic perspective is Baum, *The Civil War Party System*.

79. Kleppner, *Third*, 186–188.

80. VanderMeer, "Religion," 10–16.

81. Niebuhr, *Christ and Culture* (New York: Harper, 1951), 39–44.

82. Kousser, "'New Political History,'" 10–11.

83. Silbey et al., *American Political Behavior*, 23.

15

The Creation of an African-American Preaching Style

A revolution transformed Christian worship in the old Confederate states between 1863 and 1900. From the colonial period to the Civil War, relatively few slaves had been formally Christianized and almost all who participated in public Christian worship did so in white congregations, where they listened to white clergymen, sat with their owners or in segregated seating at the back of the auditorium or in the balcony, and did not participate in church governance. The reason was simple: white slaveholders feared independence among slaves and in religion especially.

Between 1863 and 1900, enormous numbers of freed slaves fled these white congregations to organize congregations they would manage themselves. The result was an extraordinary, mountainous rise in African-American church membership, for the new congregations not only attracted worshipers from the old white-dominated congregations but found themselves inundated by hundreds of thousands of former slaves who never joined a Christian congregation under slavery. By 1900 the new independent African-American congregations in the Southern states counted almost 3,000,000 members, although probably no more than 400,000 slaves belonged to Christian congregations in 1860; the white-dominated Methodist Episcopal Church South counted about 200,000 slaves as members in 1860 but had lost almost all its African-American members by 1870.

Nothing in the previous history of religion in America compared with the revolution in African-American religious affiliation between 1865 and 1900. The African Methodist Episcopal Church grew from 20,000 members to about 400,000 members between 1865 and 1884, the African Methodist Episcopal Church Zion grew from 6,000 members to 300,000 members, and African-American Baptist congregations expanded from about 20,000 members in 1865 to 900,000 members by 1884. Between 1865 and 1900 African Americans constructed several thousand new church buildings in the South, formed many new denominations, worked with some Northern missionaries, especially from the Northern white Methodist Episcopal Church, to create new African-American congregations, and founded colleges and seminaries to provide leadership for a free, religious people.

William E. Montgomery's essay, taken from his superb study of African-American religious life after the Civil War, *Under Their Own Vine and Fig Tree*, explores one of the most fascinating aspects of this process—the creation of a new preaching elite among freed slaves. Prior to the Civil War, whites had allowed very few African Americans, free or slave, to preach in the South and usually only under carefully controlled conditions. But after the Civil War, the number of African-American preachers skyrocketed, and they evolved preaching styles that would have dramatic impact on African-American Christianity well into the twentieth century.

What explains the freed slaves' overwhelming eagerness to form and join Christian congregations when slaveholders had used Christianity to support slavery for over a century, as the earlier reading by George Armstrong demonstrates? What was distinctive about African-American preaching? What role did women play in African-American preaching?

Additional Reading: The classic work on antebellum slave religion is Albert J. Raboteau, *Slave Religion: The "Invisible Institution" in the Antebellum South* (New York, 1978). In addition, readers should see Eugene Genovese, *Roll, Jordan, Roll: The World the Slaves Made* (New York, 1975) and Lawrence Levine, *Black Culture and Black Consciousness: Afro-American Folk Thought from Slavery to Freedom* (New York, 1971). Studies of postbellum African-American religion are much more sparse. Reginald F. Hildebrand, *The Times were Strange and Stirring: Methodist Preachers and the Crisis of Emancipation* (Durham, 1995) examines Methodist preaching after the Civil War. Stephen W. Angell, *Bishop Henry McNeal Turner and African-American Religion in the South* (Knoxville, 1992) discusses the most important postbellum leader of the African Methodist Episcopal Church, though many equally important figures, such as the A.M.E. bishop, Daniel Payne, have no modern biographies. Evelyn Brooks Higginbotham, *Righteous Discontent: The Women's Movement in the Black Baptist Church, 1880–1920* (Cambridge, Mass., 1993) offers a unique view of women in the postbellum Baptist denominations.

William E. Montgomery The Preachers

In July, 1867, Enoch K. Miller, an American Missionary Association minister who was frustrated by local preachers' opposition to his missionary work, wrote from Napoleon, Arkansas, that there was a class of men who exercised great influence among the freedmen and monopolized their attention: "I refer to their preachers." A few years later T. Thomas Fortune, writing from an altogether different perspective, made a similar observation: "No class of men wield more influence, for good or evil, among Afro-Americans than the preachers." And at the turn of the century, William E. B. Du Bois wrote in *Souls of Black Folk*, "The Preacher is the most unique personality developed by the Negro on American soil." All three of these commentators acknowledged not only the great power that black preachers wielded in the religious affairs of black men and women but also their role in shaping the people's social and political relationships. Through the immediate postemancipation period, preachers were almost universally esteemed by the freed and the freeborn population alike and were recognized as the social and political leaders of the black community. They were the only group of leaders who crossed the lines between the political, religious, and social realms and who represented the status and economic elites on one hand and the masses of poor and illiterate freedmen on the other. But as both Miller and Fortune implied, the preachers had their critics, and by the close of the century the voices of dissatisfaction reverberated through the black community, emanating from women within the churches and especially from the educated and economically well-to-do members of the upper classes who were asserting their leadership of the race.[1]

Despite the dependence on their masters imposed by slavery and the slaves' inability to control any part of their external lives, the bondsmen had produced their own leaders. Among these were their preachers. The profile and the functions of leaders among slaves differed somewhat from those in a free society, primarily because ultimate authority in the slave system rested in the hands of the white masters. As chattel, the slaves were unable to acquire wealth, education, and high status, qualities that the larger American society valued and that both whites and blacks attributed to leaders. Furthermore, nobody could relieve the slaves of their burden of work, or protect them from punishment, or secure better housing or food or clothing for them if doing so was at variance with the master's will. Leaders among the slaves usually had to accommodate the needs of the slaves with the indomitable will of the masters. The role of the preachers on plantations was thus very difficult. Though often illiterate and frequently subservient to their masters, they were popular and influential among plantation slaves. They enjoyed status not so much because of their relationship with the plantation's power structure as because of their relationship with the power structure of the spiritual world. Their main purpose was to make their people feel good about themselves in spite of the cruel realities of their lives and about their prospects for salvation at some time in the future.[2]

After emancipation, the former slaves naturally looked to the preachers—both the old slave preachers and the northern missionaries—for guidance in spiritual matters, but they also looked to them for help in dealing with the manifold problems and challenges that confronted them. The preachers were not always well-equipped to assist the freed people, but there were few others to whom the freedmen could turn or who could relate to them and their needs in ways that produced confidence. Commentators reported frequently on the preachers and noted their vital role in helping the freedmen adjust to their new lives. A report to the American Baptist Home Mission Society in 1866 explained that preachers were "a class of men who . . . have won the confidence, love, and respect of their people." Another observer noted that "within his own parish he is practically priest and pope." The scope of the preachers' influence stretched far beyond the pulpit and the congregation. Du Bois described the powerful political role of the black preacher as "a leader, a politician, an orator, a 'boss,' an intriguer, and idealist." Episcopal bishop John F. Young compared black preachers to the chiefs of primitive tribes, implying a joining of political and religious functions similar to that among the native people of West Africa. Other contemporaries and later historians have echoed and amplified that characterization, suggesting that the role of the preacher in African-American society, mediating between two worlds and combining spiritual and political leadership, followed a pattern carried over from traditional West African societies. In the postwar period, the preachers looked after the freed people's welfare, helping to build an institutional infrastructure that provided a variety of social services ranging from education to burial insurance. The preachers' all-encompassing role gave them visibility and high status in many communities. To the British traveler Sir George Campbell preachers appeared to be a "sort of Christian Brahmins."[3]

John Jasper's career illustrates the evolution of the position of the preacher from slavery into postwar black society and how former slave preachers retained the support of many freedmen by responding to their needs in ways they could appreciate, although they antagonized the growing number of educated and prosperous southern blacks who did not understand at all. Born a slave in Fluvanna County, Virginia, Jasper grew up around tobacco and worked in a tobacco factory in Richmond as a stemmer. He felt the power of God strike him one day while pulling the stems off of tobacco leaves and was converted to Christianity. He felt not only the transforming power of the Holy Spirit but a call to preach God's word to the people as well. He became a member of the First African Baptist Church, one of the few regular black congregations in the antebellum South. It was under the pastoral care of a white minister, Robert Ryland, but Jasper wanted to preach, and he did, although apparently not to that congregation. He earned a widespread reputation for his funeral sermons. Slaves from neighboring plantations often requested that he be allowed to preside over their funeral services. Through these sermons he gained fame as a preacher to slave audiences. During the Civil War, he preached to wounded soldiers in Richmond hospitals. When freedom finally came, he was about fifty years old, thrust on his own, and with a family but no job and no church to preach to. He found work making bricks and set about building a church of his own among the freedmen. Nine people initially gathered on a small island in the middle of the James River and formed his first congregation. The tiny group worshiped for a while in a house on the island or in a deserted stable, it is not clear which, but the number of worshipers grew, and eventually they purchased from a Presbyterian church a building located in a growing black neighborhood on the north side of the city. This group became the Sixth Mount Zion Baptist Church. The congregation, numbering in the hundreds, outgrew that building, and they and Jasper soon constructed a new one. Ultimately, the church's membership reached two thousand.

According to William E. Hatcher, who knew Jasper and visited his church from time to time, he did not change his preaching style much after emancipation.

Continuing in the same manner that had made him popular among slaves, he drew his texts from the Old Testament, created vivid word pictures, and spoke simply and in the dialect of the freedmen. Educated blacks scoffed at both the substance and the style of his sermons, but that did not seem to bother him or his congregation. Indeed, the people came in droves to hear him preach. Nor did his attitude toward whites change very much. In Hatcher's view, Jasper's warm and kindly "allusions to his old master were in keeping with his kindly and conciliatory tone in all that he had to say about the white people after the emancipation of the slaves." There is no record of his sermons taking on an overtly political character or of his being involved in political activity. His fame and his role in the black community of Richmond was as a gospel preacher. At the time of his death, at the age of eighty-nine, he enjoyed the love of his congregation but bore the ridicule of educated blacks for his folksy way of preaching to his people.[4]

Morris Henderson, another Baptist preacher, emerged from the shadows of slavery very much as Jasper had done to become a member of the leadership elite in post–Civil War Memphis. He was born in Virginia in 1802 and brought by his master to Shelby County at the age of forty-seven. Dark in color, short in stature, and unable to read or write, Henderson preached to blacks under close white supervision until freedom came to him and the other slaves in the country early in 1865. He then led his followers out of the white-controlled Baptist church and formed an independent congregation in a brush arbor. With the assistance of the women of the church, Henderson made a down payment on a building site on Beale Street, and the congregation erected a wood-frame building. The membership of Beale Street Baptist Church multiplied and soon reached several hundred. Active in Reconstruction politics, organizing programs to feed and educate the thousands of freedmen from the surrounding countryside who swarmed into Memphis looking for work, and launching plans to build a fine new church, Henderson was one of the most visible and influential people in the city's black community, and his church, with its twenty-five hundred members, was the largest black church in the city. There were so many members that worshipers were asked to attend only one of the three regular Sunday services so as to make room for all who wanted to attend. After involving himself in political activity during the first few years of freedom, Henderson closed the church to political meetings in 1872, no doubt, as the *Daily Appeal* noted, winning "for him the respect and confidence of the white people." When he died in 1877, five thousand people came to celebrate his life. The *Daily Avalanche* reported that he "has for years been the most influential man of his race in the city of Memphis." It claimed that people "who possessed a hundred times more education looked up to the little man with reverence and respect. On the sincerity of his religion, in the good common sense with which Nature had endowed him, he commanded the esteem of all who met him."[5]

Apart from the religious symbolism inherent in the ministry as an emblem of individual faith, it was a very popular occupation among the freedmen. It was one of the few that were accessible to blacks, and it offered high status, two very important considerations for people trying to advance upward from slavery. In the years following emancipation, preachers were probably the most numerous of all black professionals. It is impossible to know exactly how many there were because preaching was frequently not a full-time occupation, especially in the early years of freedom. The precise number of people who worked on farms or in other jobs during most of the week and preached to congregations on Sunday probably cannot be gleaned from regular census reports. By the turn of the century, however, when census of religious organizations began to record such data, the number was considerable. The black church in 1906 had 31,624 ordained ministers. That was 231 more ministers than reported congregations. Most of those ministers, 17,117 in all, were Baptists. The AME church had 6,200 ministers, the AME Zion had slightly over 3,000, and the CME church had almost 2,700. And in addition to ordained ministers, there were countless numbers of licentiates, exhorters, and informal preachers who were not included in those enumerations. In addition, there were in the neighborhood of 400 Presbyterian ministers (counting those in the Colored Cumberland Presbyterian church and the Afro-American Presbyterian Synod), and several small sects reported another 563 ministers. The Catholic church, which stubbornly resisted the creation of an African-American clergy, ordained only 5 black priests between 1866 and 1900. This was far less than the Episcopal church, which had been more liberal than the Catholics in admitting blacks to the ministry. Early in the twentieth century there were 178 black Episcopal ministers, 99 of whom were in charge of southern churches.[6]

The churches' central position in community life combined with a strong desire on the part of blacks to have preachers of their own race in their pulpits, and the high status that preachers generally enjoyed, especially in ritual society, led many to aspire to the ministry from the time they were youngsters. As young boys, both Booker T. Washington and Paul Laurence Dunbar were drawn to the ministry, although neither was ever ordained and both later became outspoken critics of the clergy. Charley White, who grew up in the piney woods of east Texas during the 1880s, played preacher the way later generations of children acted out their fantasies by playing everything from soldiers to astronauts. His playmates acted as members of White's congregation, and he preached earnestly and frequently to them. The youthful Wesley J. Gaines preached many funeral sermons for birds, dogs, and barnyard animals that died on the farm. The dreams and aspirations of many of these young boys were fulfilled owing to the great number of congregations scattered across the South and the demand from black folk for preachers.[7]

The church accepted virtually any candidate who asked to be licensed. Requirements for entering the ministry varied from one denomination and regional ordaining authority to another, but the universal and usually the sufficient prerequisite was a call from God to preach the gospel. There was no common understanding, however, of what precisely constituted a call, although among freedmen it included a mystical spiritual experience akin to the conversion experience. One old preacher recalled that the first impulse he had after his conversion experience was to go out and preach God's word. Not long afterward he preached his first sermon. The call came to many others in very much the same way. Booker T. Washington wrote that "usually the 'call' came when the individual was sitting upon the floor as if struck by a bullet, and would lie there for hours, speechless and motionless."[8]

Whether the call was true or spurious mattered both to the individual and to a congregation that might receive him as their preacher and spiritual leader, but there was no absolute, objective evaluation that could be made of it. In one sense, the individual himself was the only one who knew for certain that God had called him to preach. The more dramatic the circumstances surrounding it, the more persuasive he might be in trying to prove to others that it was genuine. But ultimately, it was for the congregation to decide by whether they hired him to preach. Emanuel K. Love, the Georgia Baptist and pastor of Savannah's First African Church, attempted to define a true call and its manifestations: "When the candidate has a desire, of which I'll repeat, he is the judge, and the church finds him qualified by moral character, and other requirements, among them the ability to teach, where the church can approve him as a good man and capable of instructing men in the way of salvation, and the judgment of the church and his convictions of duty coincide, I think that may be regarded as a call to the ministry."[9]

Along with having been called by God to preach the gospel, preachers were expected to exhibit moral uprightness, familiarity with the Scriptures, and knowledge of denominational doctrine that epitomized the evangelical standard of Christian behavior. Sins of sexual impropriety and drunkenness were among the un-Christian behaviors church authorities most commonly guarded against, and although other offenses carried sanctions, these were the ones that were most often cited in the criteria for ordination and for defrocking a minister. Ordaining agencies set down specific standards against which they measured candidates' qualifications. Cedar Grove Baptist Association in North Carolina, for example, ruled that "no minister dealing in ardent spirits or malt liquors, or having an interest in any firm, saloon, groggery or jug tavern, trafficking in alcoholic drinks, shall be recognized by this Association." Being educated was not always a prerequisite for entering the ministry, nor was it indicative of how successful a person might be in the profession, but more and more toward the close of the nineteenth century church authorities and laypeople in the congregations demanded an educated ministry. One former slave, who many years later talked about how he had come to be a preacher, said that he could not remember exactly but felt that he "had been ordained of god to preach the gospel even though I couldn't read and write." But the Cedar Grove Association, like most other regional organizations among Baptists and Methodists, established modest though surprisingly high standards that reflected the people's appreciation for education and an educated ministry. "No candidate shall be ordained to the ministry within our bounds," the association resolved, "unless he is competent of mastering the English correctly, and also have a complete knowledge of mathematics."[10]

The effectiveness of procedures for screening candidates was undermined by the congregational polity of most black churches and, particularly during the years immediately after emancipation, the compelling demand for black ministers. Given the poor educational backgrounds of most freedmen, strict enforcement of educational standards would have been too exclusionary to allow adequate numbers of blacks into the ministry. In attempting to weigh the importance of setting high standards against the need for ordained ministers, the more practical consideration of having ministers in the pulpits prevailed over the ideal of a learned and articulate clergy. Many ordaining agencies wanted to set high educational standards but usually ordained all but the most woefully deficient candidates who came before them and hoped for the best. When the Missouri Annual Conference of the AME church met in New Orleans in 1865, a committee on admissions and orders reported that one group of men was "considerably deficient" in studies prescribed by the church discipline, but the committee candidly confessed that the church's need for ordained ministers surpassed its desire for a learned clergy. Candidates who promised to pursue theological studies often received ordination. The examination committee of the Northern Neck Baptist Association of Virginia instructed one person to attend school and prepare himself more fully for the work but nevertheless recommended his immediate ordination.[11]

Even though educational attainments were stated requirements for ordination and the people in the congregations had a high regard for education, black folk did not always consider education a qualification for preachers. Many preachers concurred in that opinion. As one minister put it, preachers were "called by God" and not "made by education." The prophets and Jesus' disciples, another minister argued, came to their work with a sense of mission and not as an intellectual pursuit. There was nothing "stated or inferred in the Bible, nor suggested by reason to cause one to conclude that the Almighty has ever changed His method of bringing into service those who are to proclaim and to interpret His word." Many freedmen did not respond to the scholarly discourses that some ministers passed off as sermons. More than a few people thought too much education actually detracted from good preaching. Even late in the century, when there were significant numbers of educated clergymen in the South, sermons were marked by emotional rather than intellectual stimulation and congregations judged their preachers by their ability to get them "in the spirit."[12]

The level of education in the black community between emancipation and the end of the century and the people's attitude about an educated clergy were reflected in the educational attainments of black preachers. Most of the first generation of freedmen preachers were uneducated—even in scriptural principles—and only marginally literate. An officer of the Methodist Freedmen's Aid Society later recalled that hundreds of men who could not read had received ordination as ministers. He had seen one preacher who was supposedly reading from a hymnal but was holding it upside down. James Redpath, a white newspaperman, found a "majority of them illiterate." Isaac Brinckerhoff, a northern teacher who worked among the freedmen in South Carolina, Georgia, and Florida during the 1860s, noted in his journal that many preachers in the rural districts scarcely possessed "the first rudiments of knowledge." Even by the end of the nineteenth century, many ministers were barely literate and mostly uneducated in standard denominational doctrine, as William E. B. Du Bois and his Atlanta University students discovered in their study of black churches.[13]

By no means, though, were all black preachers entirely—or even largely—uneducated or illiterate. The image of an ignorant exhorter reflects only one facet of the black clergy. The missionaries who came into the South at the close of the Civil War were generally well-trained and often college-educated. The seminaries and ministers' institutes that northern denominations and black churches established provided training for students who hoped to enter or were already practicing the ministry. By the close of the nineteenth century, thousands of students had received significant formal theological instruction. An observer at that time noted that "forty years ago the minister who could read was the exception; now the exception is the one who cannot."[14]

The formal theological training that black ministers received was limited and rudimentary. Hosts of ministerial students were unable to gain the maximum benefit from their school or seminary experiences because they failed to complete the courses or had to work at tiring jobs to earn the cost of room, board, and tuition. A serious handicap in many instances was the student's utter lack of preparation for collegiate or seminary instruction. One northern teacher reported to the American Baptist Home Mission Society in 1868 that "when they commence study they are as ignorant of the world outside of the very narrow circle in which they have moved, as if they had but lately arrived from the moon." For those who did posses both the willingness and the ability to learn, the training they received was often restricted by the inadequacies of the faculties and the facilities of the schools they attended. Not all of the schools were poor, but many were.[15]

Yet many congregations, especially in Presbyterian and Episcopal churches, placed great value on learning and demanded and got ministers who had impressive academic credentials. William H. Franklin, for example, a Presbyterian minister, was the son of a brickmason in Knoxville and received an elementary education before the Civil War. Afterward he attended Knoxville College, a Presbyterian school, and then a Presbyterian seminary before entering the ministry in Rogersville, Tennessee, where he distinguished himself and became esteemed as a minister and a teacher. Jonathan Gibbs was born in the North and received his ordination from Presbyterian authorities before the Civil War. He attended Dartmouth College and Princeton Seminary and came to South Carolina and Florida as a missionary during Reconstruction. The most outstanding Presbyterian minister of the period was Francis J. Grimké, the mulatto son of a white Charleston father and a slave mother, who attended Lincoln University and graduated from Princeton in 1878. Alexander Crummell, another college-educated minister, attended Beriah Green's Oneida Institute in the 1830s, a school widely known for nurturing anti-slavery convictions and for educating blacks. After leaving Oneida, Crummell was denied admission to the General Theological Seminary of the Protestant Episcopal church because of his race. Nevertheless, he was ordained and appointed to a pastorate. Continually frustrated and often humiliated by racial bigotry both inside and outside of the church, he left the United States and continued his formal education in England, receiving a degree from Cambridge University in 1853. After successfully ministering to blacks in Africa, Crummell returned to the United States in 1871 and became rector of St. Luke's Protestant Episcopal Church in Washington.[16]

Congregations of educated Baptists and Methodists demanded and got educated ministers. William H. McAlpine, an Alabama Baptist, had learned to read and write from his master's children during slavery, was a pupil at a freedmen's school after emancipation, and then attended Talladega College. He became a missionary in Alabama and president of the Alabama Baptist State Convention. He also was a major fund-raiser for Selma University, which the state convention founded and operated, and served on the board of trustees of Lincoln Normal University in Marion, Alabama. J. Francis Robinson was another respected Baptist minister. Early in 1871, T. Thomas Fortune paused in Charlottesville during a trip through the South and took note of Robinson, who was then pastor of Mt. Zion Baptist Church. Fortune was surprised by the universal respect the people accorded him "and the heroic manner in which they held up his hands in the important and necessary religious and educational work he is doing." Born in Winchester, Virginia, in 1862, Robinson attended private and public schools after the war until he was twelve years old, when he moved to New York with his mother. When he was a few weeks short of graduating from a public grammar school there, his mother's illness forced him to quit school and take a job. Shortly after reaching the age of sixteen, Robinson, then a member of a Methodist Episcopal congregation, obtained a license to preach and entered Centenary Biblical Institute, later Morgan College, in Baltimore. Upon completing the theological course, he was assigned to a church in Norwich, New York. Sometime later he forsook the Methodist church and joined the Baptist ministry in Charlottesville. Fortune described him as "an exceedingly progressive young man, an earnest minister, a successful financier, and an effective organizer." Also prominent among the educated clergy were Daniel A. Payne, Richard H. Cain, James Lynch, Hiram Revels, Henry M. Turner, Levi J. Coppin, Reverdy Ransom, Benjamin T. Tanner, Charles H. Phillips, Charles Pearce, and Anthony Binga. A white teacher who attended the Florida Annual Conference of the AME church in 1874 noted that "many of the delegates were educated men, and all were interested in education." By the turn of the century, most black ministers probably fell in between the categories of illiterate country preachers and the still fairly small group of college-educated and seminary-trained clerics. The type which one of Du Bois' Atlanta University students found to be prevalent in Atlanta was common in the small towns and cities of the New South: "They are not usually highly educated men, although they are by no means illiterate."[17]

The rising level of education among the clergy reflected the deepening social class divisions within the black community. The better-educated ministers were usually very critical of the emotionalism that appealed so strongly to the uneducated masses and attempted to reform their profession. Those clergymen were keenly aware of the images that their less sophisticated colleagues implanted or reinforced in the minds of prejudiced whites. They wanted blacks to make the best possible impression on whites, especially those who criticized blacks and challenged the principle of racial equality on the basis of white superiority. Accordingly, they vigorously agitated for higher levels of learning for preachers. "The indispensable need of ministerial education can't be too much emphasized," one minister mused. Preachers whose congregations included members of the young, educated black elite were particularly vulnerable to pressure to alter their style or vacate the pulpit. Thomas Fuller believed that advances in education among blacks would put many of the older generation of preachers in jeopardy. The "ministers of today must be educated," he insisted, "or they will be forced from their pulpits by the rising pews." In some cities ministers formed societies to inculcate greater respect for high educational standards among members of their profession.[18]

Not only the educational but also the moral standards of black preachers were being challenged by elite blacks by the close of the nineteenth century. Laypeople often criticized the folk ministry. There always were unflattering rumors and stories about individual preachers. Regardless of their truth, they caused the ministry to suffer suspicion and ridicule. The names of preachers occasionally found their way onto the rolls of jailed criminals, although serious transgressions such as larceny or acts of violence do not appear to have been frequent. The moral frailties of black preachers usually took the form of less damnable vices. Most preachers were common people who were neither more nor less upright than their congregants; very often black ministers reflected the values of their neighbors. "The black preacher," Alexander Crummell explained, "is the creation of the people." Black folk were remarkably tolerant of their preachers' behavior. Few labored under illusions about the moral character of their preachers. They imposed higher standards of conduct on them than they did on themselves but did not always expect those standards to be met. This realistic outlook is revealed in a folktale in which the narrator explains: "This ain't no different from nobody else. They mouth is cut cross ways ain't it? Well, long as you don't see no man wid they mouth cut up and down, you know they'll lie jus' like de rest of us." Those who disapproved of a preacher's conduct could do little to change it. They might dismiss him from their church, but there was no way of preventing him from preaching to anybody who wanted to hear him.[19]

What otherwise was virtually an open door to the ministry was generally closed fast against women. The laity was predominantly female, but the pulpit was almost exclusively a male domain. Females enjoyed power and high status in African-American society, but the basis for both was familial and domestic. Some professions were open to women, particularly teaching, and women were prominent in the supernatural realm of magic and conjuring, but the Christian ministry was largely closed to them. The men's protectiveness of their territory was evident in the assertion of one minister that God had made woman "to be a help meet for man, but not his head." He believed that "she was never made or created to be his High Priest and Ruler in the Church of God." Thomas Fuller, a Tennessee minister, wrote that although no church program could succeed without the women's acquiescence and assistance, their proper role was auxiliary to that of male leaders. "The Baptists of Tennessee and in the South do not take kindly to women preaching," he stated. The field for women was "large enough for the exercise of all their gifts and powers" without their becoming involved in areas already the province of men. Not all women accepted their assigned position in the church organization. One Alabama woman, noting that the ministers did not do much to help in community service work, told the Baptist state convention that "it is no more our duty to help them than it is theirs to help us." And a female teacher in Memphis complained that it was strange that men should "suffer women to do all the drudgery work, plow, plant, cultivate and gather the crop, draw water and split rails," but when it came to mental or spiritual work they acted as if "women had all the muscular strength and they had all the brains and thinking power." A few women did enter the regular ministry, including Sarah Hughes, an educated mulatto whom Bishop Henry M. Turner of the AME church ordained in 1886, and as missionaries both at home and abroad, they carried the gospel to large numbers of Christians and pagans alike. But as a rule women exercised their considerable powers in the church from the pew and from their auxiliary organizations.[20]

Women seldom challenged male ministers for positions in the pulpit, but if they accepted their auxiliary status without too much complaint they were not timid about expressing their opinions about how the preachers led the churches. They knew full well that the churches—and the preachers—depended heavily on them and the money they raised for support, and that dependence gave them considerable leverage in influencing church policy. Many educated women believed that uneducated preachers with their pie-in-the-sky sermons were doing very little to help their people. Indeed, the worst of them were exploiting the people with constant demands for money and were living off them like shameless parasites. They complained about preachers who were not keen on social service. In the years after emancipation, especially as the black urban population increased in size, women became concerned about the problems of poverty, disease, and demoralization that afflicted the people. Relating the conditions of life to spiritual salvation, an idea that was gaining popularity in urban Christianity during the latter part of the nineteenth century and was known as the Social Gospel, many church women registered their impatience with the "otherworldliness" and backwardness of the uneducated ministry. Many women in the church agreed with Nannie M. Burroughs, who headed the Baptists' National Training School for women, when she criticized those who preached "too much Heaven and too little practical Christian living." Some of the more vocal and radical women charged the ministry with sexism by refusing to support training institutes and scholarships for women and girls, programs aimed at enriching their lives. "But our churches find a way to help the men who want to go away to study theology or medicine."[21]

The ministers, educated and unlettered alike, regarded preaching as their primary function but not the only one. When Elias C. Morris, president of the National Baptist Convention, told his fellow Baptists that "ministers are expected to stand for the people in nearly every avenue of life," he was not exaggerating. The older generation of preachers followed the model of the paternalistic master in their relationships with their congregations. Their lack of education and the poverty of their followers severely limited their ability to give material help, but along with communicating their faith and delivering rousing sermons they coached their congregants in everything from relating to God to coping with the mundane minutia of daily life. As a Baptist clergyman told the South Carolina state convention, the preacher must know "the best remedy for teething infants—and preachers generally have much experience on this line; he must be a horse doctor, weather prophet, must attend the living, bury the dead, tell the farmers when to plant, act as bondsman for all his people; in short, he must know as nearly as possible everything under the sun as it is possible for the human mind to know." If he was successful, he commanded the complete loyalty of his congregation and became its patriarch. T. Thomas Fortune remarked in 1883 that "to speak in damaging terms of one of our ministers, even when he is guilty of the offense charged, is to arouse his congregation to a frenzy." Indeed, he added, preachers frequently enjoyed their congregations' support regardless of their behavior.[22]

But a preacher could not behave arrogantly or arbitrarily and get away with it. Black folk knew how to suffer external oppression, but they had no tolerance for tyrants among their preachers. "The people like to have a large voice in all their religious affairs," commented one observer. "Takin' it all and all," explained John Harris, a Georgia Baptist preacher, "you're only at a church as long as you'n the members agree on everything. Just let something come up in the church where the pastor don't see things just the way all his members wants him to, and right then they'll throw him out for sho, before he know's what's happenin'." The respect and allegiance that most preachers enjoyed grew out of the love and mutual support the evangelical church promoted among members of the community of true believers. Successful preachers carefully cultivated their congregations for sympathy and support, emphasizing the necessity for clergy and laity to help one another live in accordance with God's law. The career of Emanuel K. Love, a Baptist minister in Savannah, serves as an example of how successful preachers plotted their course so as to gain the confidence of their congregations. Love resigned his position as a representative of the American Baptist Publication Society in 1885 to accept a call to the pastorate of the First African Baptist Church in Savannah. On his arrival there, he set about placing himself firmly in control of the congregation. He instructed them that the first thing they must do was trust him. "For in order that we may follow one we must first have faith in such an one." The second requirement was that they love him, "for there will be times when you will be called upon to bear very much with your leader, and if you don't love him you can't bear the burdens that may be put upon you." The third commandment was that they obey him, "for the good book informs you that obedience is better than sacrifice." At the same time, Love warned the congregation that they must not be disrespectful, critical, or complaining. They should commend him when he preached a good sermon, and when he did not preach well, they should not complain but instead help him to do better the next time. Maybe not all preachers were so explicit in stating what they expected from their congregations, and certainly not all of them succeeded in getting it, but the good ones did. The bonds that were formed between preacher and congregation were the strongest ones outside of the family that existed within the black community, and one must believe they were far stronger than typically existed within the white churches.[23]

The generation of freedmen in the postwar black community respected, loved, and often venerated their preachers, but it was a rare preacher who went totally unscathed by criticism. The stress that black clergymen placed on raising money from their congregations often caused them to appear avaricious, conniving, and self-serving and to gain reputations for taking advantage of their congregations. The people may have loved them, but they had to keep watch on them too. "Everything," Francis Grimké noted, "seems to be arranged with reference to the collection. The great objective point seems to be to reach the pocketbooks of the people." Black folk seemed to be less offended by the antics of their preachers, real or legendary. They saw their preachers as fallible human beings and accepted them as such. The preacher's foolishness was the subject of many jokes, or "lies," told by black folk. The tone of these tales suggests not only that the people could be critical of their preachers but also that they did not always take their preachers as seriously as the preachers sometimes took themselves. According to one folktale, the "haid deacon of de Mt. Zion Baptis' Chu'ch up at Rocky Hill" had a son named John, "de black sheep of de family, de baby boy." John usually became offensive when his father entertained the local preacher for a Sunday chicken dinner. The reason for John's attitude was that the preacher "lack de same paa't of de chicken dat li'l John lack, an' he tuck de drumsticks offen de platter an' put 'em on his plate." Presently the hot-tempered boy shouted: "Ah done tole y'all Ah'm gittin tiahed of dese damn preachuhs eaten' up mah paa't of de chicken." When on one occasion the preacher encountered John alone he asked where the boy had been. John replied that he had been in Hell, where his father had told him he was bound if he did not stop being disrespectful to the preacher. "Well, how is things down dere?" the preacher inquired. "Jes' lack dey is heah," John answered, "so many damn preachuhs 'roun de fiah till you cain't git to hit."[24]

As public servants, ministers needed community support. A successful preacher was one who could raise money for church buildings and activities as well as for his own salary and accommodations. The AME *Christian Recorder* suggested that clergymen who experienced difficulty with fund-raising should endeavor to get the congregation "spiritually alive," in other words, work on their emotions until they were responsive to a persuasive appeal. Finances might take care of themselves, but "we do say that the burden of church financiering will be immeasurably lightened." Bishop Jabez P. Campbell's secret was not to permit the fervor of converts to grow cold, "for they do better at this time than any other."[25]

Preachers' salaries varied widely depending on individual congregations' ability to pay and the preachers' ability to elicit contributions. By the end of the nineteenth century in rural and small-town churches, especially those that recognized and accepted a professional ministry, salaries generally ranged from $250 to $350 per year, averaging $316 for CME, $315 for AME, $313 for AME Zion, and $227 for Baptist clergymen. Two preachers in Farmville, Virginia, however, received $480 and $600 respectively in 1898. Both were young members of the progressive element of the clergy that stressed education and were graduates of theological schools. In about 1900, a black minister in Sandy Spring, Maryland, who was pastor of three churches, one of them some distance from the other two, received a combined income of $600. In cities and larger towns average salaries were somewhat higher. According to census figures, urban salaries averaged $835 for AME ministers, $698 for AME Zion, $605 for Baptist, and $350 for CME ministers. By comparison, the average white minister earned about $1,000. Those figures provide a good indication not only of the earnings of urban ministers but also of the relative wealth of congregations in those denominations. Individual salaries, however, did not always conform to those averages. Some urban ministers earned far less while some, especially Episcopalian and Presbyterian ministers and Methodist hierarchs, received annual salaries of up to $1,500. Preachers in denominations or sects that did not believe in a professional ministry received no income at all. Most ministers who supported themselves outside of the pulpit were farmers; others worked as laborers or teachers or at some other occupation. John Harris rented a farm and worked at other odd jobs to supplement his farm and ministerial income. His congregation did not like his working outside of the church, which evidently created a problem. "My members never wanted me to keep no other job," he told an interviewer, "but just to preach for 'em and visit 'round 'mongst the disabled members." But Harris had a family to support and rent to pay, and he did not trust his church income. "I needed my daily wages too bad to depend on a church salary." Consequently, "I worked every day when I was pastorin' churches."[26]

Preachers often endured considerable hardships in fulfilling their ministerial duties. The poor went hungry, and itinerants spent nights in uncomfortable places. Circuit riders covered hundreds of miles each month, preaching to different congregations each Sunday. Ministers sometimes experienced great difficulty in obtaining their salaries, small as they were. Bishop Jabez P. Campbell of the AME church told the General Conference in 1880 that some preachers and their families had endured much suffering because of unpaid salaries. An officer of the Cedar Grove Baptist Association of North Carolina maintained that a church must never "promise more than it is able to pay" but should always pay "what it promises promptly, timely and uncomplainingly." According to the "law of Christ," a preacher "shall have a proper return from those whom he serves." The pastor required to labor without food, clothing, or a place to shelter himself and his family could "neither preach nor discharge any of the claims" of his office. In 1902 a minister in Thomas County, Georgia, charged that 75 percent of the churches there were in debt to their former preachers.[27]

During the troublesome years that followed the Civil War, preachers who took part in political activities sometimes suffered reprisals from angry whites. Conservative whites used intimidation to discourage black political leaders from organizing Union League and Republican party groups and from voting and campaigning for public office, and preachers were not exempted from such treatment. More than one preacher was attacked or felt the threat of bodily injury or was arrested by white authorities, and more than one church was set afire by night riders. Even after the collapse of the Republican state governments in the South, many black preachers who challenged white supremacy found themselves in mortal danger.[28]

Attacks on black preachers did not come only from whites. Ministers, though supposedly men of peace and goodwill, occasionally became the objects of bitter animosity within their own communities, as an incident reported in a church in 1890 illustrates. There were several aspirants for a vacant pastorate. One of the candidates, favored by the women of the congregation but strongly opposed by some of the men, had to hide because of threats made against him. Charley White, an east Texas minister, once attempted to escort from his church a woman who had come inside in an inebriated condition and inappropriately dressed. The woman suddenly drew a knife on him and threatened to stab him if he did not leave her alone. On another occasion a drunken husband threatened to shoot up

White's church if the man's wife did not come out of the building immediately. She walked out and thus averted a possible disaster, but the threat of violence was so great that another female church member offered her services as White's armed bodyguard. Thomas Fuller, writing in 1938 about earlier events, told of three ministers who had been shot to death in Memphis during the previous quarter-century, one who was ambushed on his way home, another attacked while he was inside his church at the end of a service, and the third killed as he visited people in the neighborhood. For some preachers the rewards of their calling were indeed hard-earned.[29]

By the close of the nineteenth century the status of the preacher was showing signs of decline. It was a development that the American Baptist Home Mission Society had predicted in 1866, when it concluded that "if we devote ourselves to educating the youth, neglecting the education of their preachers, we elevate the youth to an intellectual plane from which they shall look down upon the meager attainments of their present religious leaders." The ministers greatly influenced the attitudes of the people. The Chicago *Defender* described ministers as occupying positions of "moral, spiritual and, in a sense, the social leadership of the Race. They have the ear of the people even more than a newspaper, for they reach a multitude of people who neither read nor think." But in 1903 Du Bois noted that "the old leaders of Negro opinion . . . are being replaced by new." The old preachers did not command the respect they once elicited, and the younger ones did not enjoy the loyalty the old generation had had because they were not patriarchal figures.[30]

The increasingly frequent criticisms directed at the ministry also explained the change in preachers' status. The generation of educated blacks who had grown up since the Civil War refused to accept the old preachers, whom they regarded as superstitious and backward, as leaders. The critics were not irreligious; they were disgusted by the emotionalism, ignorance, and occasional moral lapses of the churches' old leaders. They preferred ministers who "did not indulge in moaning, running around the sanctuary, and condemning all religious denominations but their own." They wanted preachers who would address contemporary social problems as well as the hereafter. T. Thomas Fortune demanded that ministers "preach less about the hell beyond the Jordan and more about the one, ever present, on this side of the river." He advised them to "make religion attractive. Let Daniel remain in the lion's den, and tell us about the sins of gamblers, stock jobbers, thieves in the temple; you will find plenty of Biblical philosophy to back you up." Ida B. Wells, one of the new generation of blacks who were intensely anxious to improve the condition of the race, condemned the black ministry's failure to provide "practical talks" and guidance in worldly matters. The poet Paul Laurence Dunbar, who once aspired to the ministry, wrote disparagingly:

> I am no priest of crooks nor creeds,
> For human wants and human needs
> Are more to me than prophets' deeds;
> And human tears and human cares
> Affect me more than human prayers.

Go, cease your wail, lugubrious saint;
You fret high Heaven with your plaint,
Is this the "Christian's Joy" you paint?
Is this the Christian's boasted bliss?
Avails your faith no more than this?

Take up your arms, come out with me,
Let Heaven alone; humanity
Needs more and Heaven less from thee,
With pity for mankind look 'round
Help them rise—and Heaven is found.

Booker T. Washington, who understood the influence of the churches among black folk as fully as anyone and who, as a race leader, worked closely with the churches and church leaders, could not have agreed more with Dunbar's sentiments. Washington thought the ministry not only irrelevant but also unfit mentally and morally to lead the people. In a widely quoted article that appeared in the New York *Christian Union* in 1890, he asserted that "three-fourths of the Baptist ministers and two-thirds of the Methodist are unfit, either mentally or morally, or both, to preach the Gospel to any one or to attempt to lead any one. . . . There is no use mincing matters. Every bishop, every presiding elder, every leading man who comes into contact with the ministry knows exactly what we are talking about." The critics also blamed church indebtedness and the slow economic advancement of African Americans on ministers. "It is a lamentable fact," Fortune wrote, "that our churches are always head and ears in debt, and if a pastor happens to come to a church and finds it free from debt, he is unhappy until he gets his church ten, fifteen, or twenty thousand dollars in debt." That was an exaggeration. The average indebtedness was only a few hundred dollars, and three-quarters of the churches reported no debt on their property. But it was a powerful accusation that revealed the impression that many people in the community had of the preachers, an attitude manifested in a folk rhyme: "Preacher in de pulpit preachin' mighty well; But when he gits the money yo' ken go to hell."[31]

Washington and the other detractors drew a mixed response from the preachers to the criticisms directed at them. Some ministers defended themselves and their profession. The Eufaula Baptist Association in Alabama announced a boycott of Tuskegee Institute in reaction to Washington's article, and the Alabama state convention declared that his allegations regarding the ministers' fitness to preach had been "made at the expense of the truth." Yet Daniel A. Payne was probably closer to the truth than the Alabama Baptists when he agreed in an open letter to Washington that the clergy did not measure up to the standards imposed by the educated and upwardly mobile segment of the black community. He averred that "in regard to the moral qualifications of the Methodist and Baptist ministers, so far as I have seen and known them by personal contact, I believe that you have not overstated, but rather understated the facts. I say, emphatically, in the presence of the great Head of the Church, that not more than one-third of the ministers, Baptist or Methodist, in the South are morally and intellectually qualified." Francis Grimké too was disturbed by the number of clergymen who were "ignorant men—men who can scarcely do more than read and write. Some of them can hardly do that."[32]

The rising volume of criticism directed at ministers thrust the churches into deep and serious division over the proper character of the ministry and the need for reforms. Frederick Douglass, one of the churches' leading antagonists, had said as early as 1883 that the younger generation "demand an educated, chaste, and upright ministry. . . . These old-fashioned preachers minister to passion, decry the intellect, and induce contentment in ignorance and stupidity, and are hence a hindrance to progress." Charles Tanner, the son of Methodist bishop Benjamin T. Tanner, wrote in the New York *Age* in 1888, "We are . . . divided into two classes religiously, the old church folks and the model church. Yet we worship in the same church." A little Baptist church in Palatka, Florida, exemplified the situation that Tanner alluded to. In 1888 some of the younger members claimed that the pastor, who had been at his post almost twenty years, was not keeping pace with the intellectual progress of the race and was thus incapable of providing effective leadership. The older element maintained that because the preacher had guided the church through many hard times and the construction of a new building he should be allowed to remain in the pulpit for as long as he wished. After the insurgents lost an election on the question, they withdrew and established a new church. It was perhaps a wish to avoid such a division that prompted Levi Thornton, a Baptist minister, to make a poignant appeal to the younger members of the First African Baptist Church of Savannah to be patient with the old preachers: "Deal tenderly with them, you men. Do not run over them because you are educated, young and strong. Notwithstanding their superstition, the people are living in them."[33]

The churches depended on the people for their existence, and the spirit of the people truly lived in the preachers. The old-time preachers and their style of ministry were still well liked by many churchgoing blacks at the close of the nineteenth century. There was truth in the statement that "the church which does not have its shouting, the church which does not measure the abilities of a preacher by the 'rousement of his sermons, and indeed does not tacitly demand of its minister the shout-producing discourse, is an exception to the rule." Education, however, was lifting some ministers "out of sympathy" with their congregations, and as people acquired education and respectability they became less tolerant of the older generation of emotional preachers. Perhaps the traditional preacher was a dubious leader, but he, as well as the younger generation of ministers, "fairly represented those whom they lead."[34]

NOTES

1. Enoch K. Miller to William M. Colby, July 31, 1867, in Records of the Superintendent of Education for the State of Arkansas, U.S. Bureau of Refugees, Freedmen, and Abandoned Lands, Record Group 105, National Archives (hereinafter cited as Freedmen's Bureau Records); New York *Age*, September 6, 1890.

2. Eugene D. Genovese, "Black Plantation Preachers in the Slave South," *Louisiana Studies,*

11 (1972), 188–214; Albert J. Raboteau, *Slave Religion: The "Invisible Institution" in the Antebellum South* (New York, 1978), 231–39.

3. American Baptist Home Mission Society, "Report of the Thirty-fourth Annual Meeting of the Executive Board," in *Thirty-fourth Annual Report of the American Baptist Home Mission Society . . . 1866* (New York, 1866), 17; New York *Globe,* November 24, 1883; William E. B. Du Bois, *The Souls of Black Folk: Essays and Sketches* (Chicago, 1909), 190; Joe M. Richardson, *The Negro in the Reconstruction of Florida, 1865–1877* (Tallahassee, 1965), 94; Sterling Stuckey, *Slave Culture: Nationalist Theory and the Foundations of Black America* (New York, 1987), 255; Sir George Campbell, *White and Black: The Outcome of a Visit to the United States* (New York, 1879), 344; Armstead L. Robinson, "Plans Dat Comed from God: Institution Building and the Emergence of Black Leadership in Reconstruction Memphis," in *Toward a New South? Studies in Post–Civil War Southern Communities,* ed. Orville Vernon Burton and Robert C. McMath, Jr. (Westport, 1982), 71–102.

4. William E. Hatcher, *John Jasper: The Unmatched Negro Philosopher and Preacher* (London, 1908), 23–29, 38, 58–62, 74, 94–105.

5. David M. Tucker, *Black Pastors and Leaders: Memphis, 1819–1972* (Memphis, 1975), 8–14; Robinson, "Plans Dat Comed from God," 73–75, 92.

6. *Census of Religious Bodies: 1906* (2 vols., Washington, D.C., 1909), I, 146: Andrew E. Murray, *Presbyterians and the Negro—A History* (Philadelphia, 1966), 150–51; Stephen J. Ochs, *Desegregating the Altar: The Josephites and the Struggle for Black Priests, 1871–1960* (Baton Rouge, 1990), 36–18; George F. Bragg, *History of the Afro-American Group of the Episcopal Church* (Baltimore, 1922), 285–92.

7. John L. Bell, "Baptists and the Negro in North Carolina During Reconstruction," *North Carolina Historical Review,* XLII (1965), 403; Louis R. Harlan, *Booker T. Washington: The Making of a Black Leader, 1865–1910* (New York, 1972), 62–80; Benjamin E. Mays, *The Negro's God as Reflected in His Literature* (1938; rpr. New York, 1968), 134; Charley C. White, *No Quittin' Sense* (Austin, 1969), 3–5; *A.M.E. Church Review,* V (October, 1888), 69–71; New York *Age,* November 29, 1890.

8. Clifton H. Johnson, ed., *God Struck Me Dead: Religious Conversion Experiences and Autobiographies of Ex-Slaves* (Philadelphia, 1969), 74; Booker T. Washington, *Up from Slavery: An Autobiography* (Garden City, 1949), 81–83.

9. Emanuel K. Love, *A History of the First African Baptist Church of Savannah from its Organization, January 20th, 1788, to July 1st, 1888* (Savannah, 1888), 239–45.

10. Johnson, ed., *God Struck Me Dead,* 84–85; Cedar Grove Missionary Baptist Association (North Carolina), *Minutes of the Eighth Annual Session of the Cedar Grove Missionary Baptist Association . . . 1875* (Raleigh, 1875), 13–17; Berean Valley Baptist Association (Virginia), *Minutes of the Fourteenth Annual Session of the Berean Valley Baptist Association . . . 1896* (Washington, D.C., n.d.), 9.

11. Charles S. Smith, *A History of the African Methodist Episcopal Church* (1922; rpr. New York, 1968), 935; Northern Neck Baptist Association (Virginia), *Minutes of the Twentieth Annual Session of the Northern Neck Baptist Association . . . 1897* (Washington, D.C., 1897), 13–14.

12. Lillie B. Chace Wyman, "Colored Churches and Schools in the South," *New England Magazine,* III (February, 1891), 786: Levi J. Coppin, *Unwritten History* (1919; rpr. New York, 1968), 211–12; William E. B. Du Bois, ed., *The Negro Church: Report of a Social Study Made Under the Direction of Atlanta University* (Atlanta, 1903), 84–85; Charles S. Johnson, *The Shadow of the Plantation* (Chicago, 1934), 157.

13. Alexander Crummell, Sermon No. 32 (MS in Schomburg Collection, New York Public Library); James Redpath, "Special Report to M. Pleiance, Secretary of State of the Republic of Hayti, October 1, 1861" (MS in Manuscripts Division, Library of Congress); Isaac W. Brinckerhoff, "Thirty Years Among Freedmen: Mission Work Among the Freedmen, Beau-

fort, S. Carolina, St. Augustine, Florida, Savannah, Georgia, 1862–1894" (MS in American Baptist Historical Society, Rochester, New York); Du Bois, ed., *Negro Church,* 58–59.

14. Du Bois, ed., *Negro Church,* 96, 122–23.

15. *A.M.E. Church Review,* V (January, 1889), 325–26; American Baptist Home Mission Society, *Thirty-sixth Annual Report of the American Baptist Home Mission Society . . . 1868* (New York, 1868), 11; Ray Stannard Baker, *Following the Color Line: American Negro Citizenship in the Progressive Era* (2nd ed.; New York, 1964), 53.

16. New York *Freeman,* May 23, 1885; Richardson, *Negro in the Reconstruction of Florida,* 154; Du Bois, *Souls of Black Folk,* 215–27; Wilson Jeremiah Moses, *Alexander Crummell: A Study of Civilization and Discontent* (New York, 1989), 11–195.

17. Justus N. Brown to E. M. Cravath, October 20, 1870, in American Missionary Association Archives, Amistad Research Center, Tulane University; New York *Age,* April 18, 1891; Richardson, *Negro in the Reconstruction of Florida,* 93; Du Bois, ed., *Negro Church,* 79.

18. Du Bois, ed., *Negro Church,* 229–49; Love, *History of the First African Baptist Church,* 249, 273–74; Thomas O. Fuller, *History of the Negro Baptists of Tennessee* (Memphis, 1936), 236.

19. Zura Neale Hurston, *Males and Men: Negro Folktales and Voodoo Practices in the South* (1935; rpr. New York, 1970), 37–38; Cedar Grove Missionary Baptist Association, *Minutes of the Eighteenth Annual Session of the Cedar Grove Missionary Baptist Association . . . 1885* (Danville, Va., 1885), 12–13; Baptist State Convention of North Carolina, *Minutes of the Sixteenth Annual Session of the Baptist State Convention of North Carolina . . . 1882* (Raleigh, 1883), 16; Northern Neck Baptist Association, *Minutes of the Twentieth Annual Session of the Northern Neck Baptist Association . . . 1897,* 8; *Christian Recorder,* September 3, 1864; Crummell, Sermon No. 32.

20. J. P. Campbell, "The Ordination of Women: What Authority for it," *A.M.E. Church Review,* II (April, 1886), 351–54; Wesley J. Gaines, *African Methodism in the South: or, Twenty-Five Years of Freedom* (Atlanta, 1890), 65–66; Evelyn Brooks, "The Women's Movement in the Black Baptist Church, 1880–1920" (Ph.D. dissertation, University of Rochester, 1984), 99–100, 109–10, Fuller, *Negro Baptists of Tennessee,* 238–39; Virginia W. Broughton, "Woman's Work," *National Baptist Magazine,* 1 (January, 1894), 34.

21. Brooks, "Women's Movement in the Black Baptist Church," 98–101, 216–17, 294–95.

22. National Baptist Convention, *Journal of the Twenty-first Annual Session of the National Baptist Convention . . . 1901* (Nashville, 1901), 26–28; *Christian Recorder,* March 4, 1865: Baptist Educational Missionary and Sunday School Convention (South Carolina), *Minutes of the Seventeenth Anniversary of the Educational, Missionary and Sunday School Convention of the Colored Baptists of South Carolina . . . 1893* (Columbia, 1893), 57; New York *Globe,* June 30, 1883.

23. New York *Age,* September 15, October 27, 1888; Campbell, *White and Black,* 344; George P. Rawick, ed., *Georgia Narratives* (Westport, 1977), Pt. 1, p. 294, Vol. III of Rawick, ed., *The American Slave: A Composite Autobiography Supplement Series 1,* 12 vols.; Love, *History of the First African Baptist Church,* 94–96.

24. Huntsville *Gazette,* April 14, 1883; Charles Dudley Warner, *On Horseback: A Tour in Virginia, North Carolina, and Tennessee* (Boston, 1889), 9–10; Wyman, "Colored Churches and Schools in the South," 788; Francis J. Grimké, *The Afro-American Pulpit in Relation to Race Elevation* (Washington, D.C., 1893), 7; Hurston, *Mules and Men,* 37–38; J. Mason Brewer, ed., *The Word on the Brazos: Negro Preacher Tales from the Brazos River Bottoms of Texas* (Austin, 1953), 92.

25. *Christian Recorder,* July 20, 1899; Edward W. Lampton, *Digest of Rulings and Decisions of the Bishops of the African Methodist Episcopal Church from 1847 to 1907* (Washington, D.C., 1907), 254.

26. *Census of Religious Bodies: 1906,* I, 94–97; W. E. B. Du Bois, "The Negroes of Farmville, Virginia: A Social Study," *Bulletin of the Department of Labor,* III (January, 1898), 16–17;

William Taylor Thom, "The Negroes of Sandy Spring, Maryland: A Social Study," *Bulletin of the Department of Labor,* VI (January, 1901), 72; Rawick, ed., *Georgia Narratives,* 276–304.

27. North Mississippi Conference (AME), *Journal of the Thirtieth Session of the North Mississippi Annual Conference of the A.M.E. Church . . . 1906* (Jackson, 1906), 8; Hightower T. Kealing, *History of African Methodism in Texas* (Waco, 1885), 36–37; Smith, *History of the African Methodist Episcopal Church,* 129; Cedar Grove Missionary Baptist Association, *Minutes of the Eighth Annual Session of the Cedar Grove Missionary Baptist Association . . . 1875* (Raleigh, 1875), 17; *ibid., 1889* (Raleigh, 1889), 10; Du Bois, ed., *Negro Church,* 60.

28. Peter Kolchin, *First Freedom: The Response of Alabama's Blacks to Emancipation and Reconstruction* (Westport, 1972), 121; Edmund L. Drago, *Black Politicians and Reconstruction in Georgia: A Splendid Failure* (Baton Rouge, 1982), 164–71.

29. Washington *Bee,* November 8, 1890; White, *No Quittin' Sense,* 149–51; Thomas O. Fuller, *The Story of the Church Life Among Negroes in Memphis, Tennessee, for Students and Workers, 1900–1938* (Memphis, 1938), 16.

30. F. M. Gaebel to G. L. Eberhart, May 25, 1867, in Freedmen's Bureau Records; Washington *Bee,* November 2, 1889; Benjamin P. Mays and Joseph W. Nicholson, *The Negro's Church* (New York, 1933), 50–51; Robert T. Kerlin, ed., *The Voice of the Negro, 1919* (New York, 1968), 176; Du Bois, *Souls of Black Folk,* 80; *Census of Religious Bodies: 1906,* 1, 91–92; *Christian Recorder,* October 15, 1870; Emma Lou Thornbrough, *T. Thomas Fortune: Militant Journalist* (Chicago, 1972), 25, 56; Benjamin E. Mays, *The Negro's God as Reflected in His Literature* (1938; rpr. New York, 1968), 128–55; New York *Freeman,* June 25, 1887, February 9, 1889; Ida B. Wells, *Crusade for Justice: The Autobiography of Ida B. Wells* (Chicago, 1970), 22; New York *Age,* September 6, November 29, 1890.

31. New York *Age,* February 9, 1889, July 10, 1891; Mays, *Negro's God,* 134: New York *Globe,* May 12, 1883: New York *Freeman,* June 25, 1887; Ida B. Wells, *Crusade for Justice: The Autobiography of Ida B. Wells* (Chicago, 1970), 22; *Census of Religious Bodies: 1906,* I, 143; J. Mason Brewer, ed., *American Negro Folklore* (Chicago, 1968), 336.

32. New York *Age,* November 29, December 6, 1890; Alabama Baptist State Convention, *Proceedings of the Twenty-third Annual Session of the Alabama Baptist State Convention . . . 1890* (Montgomery, 1890), 21; Grimké, *Afro-American Pulpit,* 4; Love, *History of The First African Baptist Church,* 274; George W. Clinton, "The Pulpit and the School Room," *A.M.E. Church Reviews,* V (April, 1889), 395; Wesley J. Gaines, *The Negro and the White Man* (Philadelphia, 1897), 129–30; *Christian Recorder,* October 15, 1870.

33. Frederick Douglass, "The Condition of the Negro," on *The Life and Writings of Frederick Douglass,* ed. Philip S. Foner (4 vols; New York, 1950–58), IV, 405–406; New York *Age,* June 30, October 20, 1888; Love, *History of the First African Baptist Church,* 238.

34. Du Bois, ed., *Negro Church,* 58, 64; New York *Globe,* November 20, 1883; Richardson, *Negro in the Reconstruction of Florida,* 91; Johnson, *Shadow of the Plantation,* 170–79.

CHAPTER
16

The Rise of American Fundamentalism

Following the Civil War, American society and intellectual life moved increasingly in "modern" directions. It became urban, not rural; men and women worked for large corporations or in massive factories rather than on small farms; and the rise of modern "science" seemed to denigrate traditional understanding of God and the universe.

These changes were unequal, however, and strong entrenched interests resisted. One was the group of believers later called the "fundamentalists." As new religious groups proliferated and older "mainline" groups like Episcopalians, Congregationists, and many Baptists and Presbyterians eagerly accepted modern society without hesitation, more conservative evangelical Protestants became increasingly isolated and formed separatist "fundamentalist" movements directed against "modernism" in all its variegated forms.

In this essay, George Marsden contrasts Fundamentalism in Britain and America to determine what was uniquely "American" about American fundamentalism. What evidence does Professor Marsden rely on? Is it possible that he exaggerates American uniqueness? Who is he responding to in this article? Fundamentalists were always eager to employ technological innovations in print and communications to spread their message. How do we reconcile their eagerness for new technology with their "anti-modernism"?

Additional Reading: After decades of inattention, historians have produced major new studies of American fundamentalism and evangelicalism since the mid-1970s. George Marsden, *Fundamentalism and American Culture: The Shaping of Twentieth-Century Evangelicalism, 1870–1925* (New York, 1980) and Ernest R. Sandeen, *The Roots of Fundamentalism: British and American Millenarianism* (Chicago, 1970) offer broad-ranging studies of both fundamentalism and evangelicalism. Edith Blumhofer's biography, *Aimee Semple McPherson: Everybody's Sister* (Grand Rapids, 1993) describes the history of the twentieth century's most famous female evangelist, and Blumhofer's *Restoring the Faith: The Assemblies of God, Pentecostalism, and American Culture* (Urbana, 1993) traces the history of the nation's major Pentecostal denomination. Betty A. DeBerg, *Ungodly Women: Gender and the First Ways of American Fundamentalism* (Minneapolis, 1990) describes women's experience as fundamentalism emerged. An international, comparative history of "fundamentalism" in world religions can be found in Martin E. Marty and R. Scott Appleby, (eds.), *Fundamentalisms Observed* (Chicago, 1991).

George Marsden

Fundamentalism as an American Phenomenon, A Comparison with English Evangelicalism

"Fundamentalism" is used in so many ways that a definition is the only place to begin. As I here use the term, "fundamentalism" refers to a twentieth-century movement closely tied to the revivalist tradition of mainstream evangelical Protestantism that militantly opposed modernist theology and the cultural change associated with it. Fundamentalism shares traits with many other movements to which it has been related (such as pietism, evangelicalism, revivalism, conservatism, confessionalism, millenarianism, and the holiness and pentecostal movements), but it has been distinguished most clearly from these by its militancy in opposition to modernism. This militancy has typically been expressed in terms of certain characteristic theological or intellectual emphases: whereas modernism or liberal theology tended to explain life and much of religion in terms of natural developments, fundamentalists stressed the supernatural. Accordingly, their most distinctive doctrines (although not all have been held by everyone in the movement)[1] were the divinely guaranteed verbal inerrancy of Scripture, divine creation as opposed to biological evolution, and a dispensational-premillennial scheme that explained historical change in terms of divine control. In America, where fundamentalism originated, adherence to the first of these teachings became a test for the purity of denominations, the second a symbol for efforts to preserve the Christian character of the culture, and the third a basis for fellowship among fundamentalists themselves.

During the 1920s, fundamentalists in America engaged in furious and sensational battles to control the denominations and the wider culture. When these efforts failed they became increasingly separatist, often leaving major denominations and flourishing in independent churches and agencies.[2] They continued however to have an impact on large areas of American Protestantism and most of

Reprinted with permission from *Church History* 46 (June 1977), 215–32.

the pietistic or conservative movements with which they had contact took on some fundamentalist traits.

The phenomenon that I have defined as "fundamentalism" was overwhelmingly American in the sense that almost nowhere else did this type of Protestant response to modernity have such a conspicuous and pervasive role both in the churches and in the national culture.[3] An examination of fundamentalism should reveal some significant traits of American culture and, conversely, the American context will provide a key for understanding fundamentalism.

The crucial variables in the American environment can best be identified by comparing the American development of fundamentalism with its closest counterpart, English evangelicalism. The approach is particularly revealing since from the time of the Puritans down through the awakenings to the end of the nineteenth century British and American evangelicalism had been in many respects parts of a single transatlantic movement. Ernest R. Sandeen has even argued (although too simplistically) that on the basis of one of the many connections—millenarianism—the origins of fundamentalism were essentially British.[4] In any case, British-American ties were taken for granted even as late as the beginnings of the organized fundamentalist crusade; in *The Fundamentals*, published from 1910 to 1915, one-fourth of the authors were British.[5] Yet, strikingly, by the 1920s when the American fundamentalists were engaged in intense spiritual warfare, there were few on the English front willing to sound the battle cry.

As will be seen, a number of English evangelicals during the 1920s firmly resisted the almost overwhelming trend to accept liberal theology; yet, despite their similarity to American fundamentalism, most of their efforts lacked its aggressiveness and militancy and certainly had no comparable role in the culture and the churches. For Englishmen the Scopes trial, for instance, was totally foreign to their own experience and almost inconceivable. "Perhaps no recent event in America stands more in need of explanation . . ." wrote one British observer in 1925.[6] Even those who closely followed English church life saw no counterpart to militant fundamentalism. "Perhaps it was [his] greatest service," observed the *Times* of London in 1929 concerning A. S. Peake, a moderate British evangelical who had done much to introduce the public to biblical criticism, ". . . that he helped to save us from a fundamentalist controversy such as that which has devastated large sections of the church in America."[7]

There had been, of course, considerable controversy when the new evolutionary and higher critical views were first publicized in Great Britain, but it never grew to the proportions of the American reaction. In fact, one of the striking differences between the patterns of reactions is that, while in America the controversies intensified from the 1860s to the 1920s, in England the peak of popular furor had been reached already by the 1860s. Initial reactions in English churches to *Origin of Species* (1859), *Essays and Reviews* (1860), and the first volume of Bishop John Colenso's *The Pentateuch and Book of Joshua Critically Examined* (1862–1879) were largely negative. Yet the sensational and emotional aspects of the controversies had already largely passed by the end of the 1860s.[8] After that, biological evolution never became a divisive issue of nearly the proportions reached in

America.[9] The question of the nature of Scripture was more difficult to resolve; but in general, once moderate historical-critical ideas were advanced by evangelicals known as reverent defenders of the faith, the new attitudes were accepted with remarkable swiftness. By the 1890s most of the clergy had abandoned traditional assumptions concerning the full historical accuracy of Scripture for some form of higher criticism.[10] Considerable numbers of church members still did not accept the newer ideas;[11] but most were at least familiar with the major issues so that there was little potential for an outbreak of public alarm after that time. In all, this rather peaceful development suggests that nineteenth-century British evangelical religion, like British politics, was closer in style to Edmund Burke than to Oliver Cromwell.

What accounts for the relatively smooth and rapid acceptance in England of the same views that caused so much turmoil in America? Both a strong tradition of theological latitude dating back to the Elizabethan settlement and a policy of toleration since at least the Act of Toleration of 1689 were major factors. These policies, however, were at least officially parts of the American religious heritage, and in fact Americans since the Revolution had been proud of their country's unusual degree of religious liberty and tolerance. The fact that often in American religious life there was not the degree of toleration that the popular mythology proclaimed is in part the phenomenon that needs to be explained.

Given the generally greater tolerance among evangelicals in nineteenth-century England, other factors are still needed to explain why the revolutionary new views concerning higher criticism and evolution did not foment a long and major controversy in England. Clearly the English were prepared in some way for the new ideas, but the initially strong opposition of the 1860s indicates that this preparation was not one of direct familiarity. English theologians seem not to have had, for instance, a great deal more of sympathetic contact with the earlier German higher criticism than did their American counterparts. More basic than any specific preparation seems to have been a general intellectual climate—that is, the concepts of natural and historical development on which both Darwinism and higher criticism were based were closely akin to trends that had been developing in British thought for some time.[12] The whole English constitutional system (in contrast to America, where newness demanded written and rational definition) reflects a sense of gradually developing tradition that appears characteristic of English thought generally. Regarding the acceptance of higher criticism in nineteenth-century England, Willis Glover in his careful study of the Nonconformists correctly makes much of this point. He says:

> But the most essential presuppositions of criticism, such as the unity and continuity of history, were a part of the general climate of opinion shared by traditionalists and critics alike. The historical sense of the century was so strong that the defenders of tradition found it extremely difficult to deny higher criticism in principle. In the last quarter of the century even those who upheld tradition against the critics on every count were often ready and even anxious to make it clear that they did not oppose the critical and historical study of the Bible but merely the conclusions of "rationalistic" critics.[13]

This estimate of Glover applies well, for instance, to the work of James Orr of Scotland, the leading British theological critic of liberalism around the turn of the century. Because of his reputation as a defender of the faith, Orr had close and cordial relations with the American revivalists who organized *The Fundamentals* and was a major contributor to that series. Yet unlike the American leaders of the emerging fundamentalist movement, Orr not only was amenable to limited forms of biological evolution but also accepted historical criticism of Scripture in principle, even while vigorously attacking most of its usual applications. The attempt to defend the faith on the basis of "inerrancy," said Orr, was simply "suicidal."[14]

While most British evangelicals in the twentieth century were moving much further than James Orr,[15] and few were doctrinally militant, some conserved traditional views chiefly through vigorous piety. Outstanding in this respect was the Keswick Convention, founded in 1875 in the wake of the Moody revivals. The Keswick summer conferences became the informal meetingplace for British conservative evangelicals and its emphases on Bible study, evangelism, missions, personal piety, and "victory over sin" had wide influence. Like Moody, Keswick teaching took for granted a conservative view of Scripture, yet explicitly avoided any controversy.

This non-controversialist stance gave Keswick and much of the British conservative evangelicalism that it nourished an emphasis rather different from twentieth-century American fundamentalism. While many American fundamentalists adhered to Keswick teaching concerning the "victorious life," its irenic emphases were overshadowed in the early decades of the twentieth century by anti-liberal militancy. By the 1920s Keswick was becoming suspect even to fundamentalist leaders. After a visit in 1928, William B. Riley, president of the World Christian Fundamentals Association, criticized Keswick for "carelessness" in tolerating doctrinal error and noted, no doubt in reference to himself, that "'a controversialist' could never be on its platform."[16]

While in England enthusiasm for controversy was hardly considered evidence of true faith, some British conservative evangelicals more or less in the Keswick tradition responded to the threats of liberalism by maintaining doctrinal purity and a degree of separateness.[17] Prominent among such efforts was the Inter-Varsity Fellowship organized in 1928 among university student groups that had been steering a course separate from the more liberal Student Christian Movement. The constitution of IVF affirmed "the fundamental truths of Christianity," including the infallibility of Scripture, and decreed its continued non-cooperation with liberals. Despite these fundamentalist resemblances IVF placed far more emphasis on the personal piety and evangelism reminiscent of the Moody-Keswick era (when its progenitor the Cambridge Inter-Collegiate Christian Union had originated) than on the doctrinal militancy of the fundamentalist era.[18] Its ties to America were confined largely to the moderate variety of fundamentalism eventually known as "neo-evangelicalism."[19]

A similar development was the split in 1922 of the Church Missionary Society, the missions agency of the evangelical party in the Church of England. A rather distinguished group of conservatives, who made the historical trustworthiness of Scripture a doctrinal test, withdrew in protest over inclusivist tendencies and formed the Bible Churchmen's Missionary Society. This move closely paralleled American controversies concerning missions following World War I, yet it was effected without prolonged dispute;[20] questions of separation and independent action could readily be resolved within the wider spirit of Anglican comprehension. Within the Bible Churchmen's Missionary Society and in numerous older agencies,[21] evangelicals felt free to operate without purging established ecclesiastical structures.

Although the foregoing examples illustrate that uncompromising conservative evangelicalism survived in England, the contrast to America becomes apparent when we consider the fragmentary scope of English attempts to organize something like a militant anti-liberal crusade. The prototype of such efforts was the separation of Charles Haddon Spurgeon from the Baptist Union in the "Downgrade controversy" of 1887. This action near the end of the career of this illustrious London preacher seems to have had little wider impact.[22] It was not that no effort was made to carry on his controversialist work, for A. C. Dixon, one of the editors of *The Fundamentals,* came from America in 1911 to serve as pastor of Spurgeon's Metropolitan Temple but departed again in 1919 without leaving any substantial fundamentalist organization behind him.[23] Slightly more successful in organizing a full-fledged controversialist fundamentalist movement in England[24] was E. J. Poole-Connor, who also thought he was carrying on Spurgeon's cause. Poole-Connor opposed any cooperation with or tolerance for theological liberalism, and in 1922 he founded the Fellowship of Independent Churches which he described in 1925 as having "a strongly fundamentalist credal basis."[25] The organization remained quite small (perhaps 100 to 150 congregations and six to seven thousand members in its first twenty years)[26] and Poole-Connor himself compared the non-militant stance of most conservative evangelicalism in England unfavorably to American fundamentalism.[27] The general extent of Poole-Connor's influence in English church life is revealed by the remark of his admiring biographer, "Truly he was a prophet 'without honour.'"[28]

Paradoxically one factor contributing to this notable lack of success of such separatist fundamentalist efforts was the significant presence in England of the Plymouth Brethren. The Brethren had many of the same traits as American fundamentalists, and no doubt attracted some persons who in the American context might have become involved in wider denominational struggles. Between 1910 and 1960 the principal (Open) Brethren group increased in adherents by roughly half, reaching a total of perhaps ninety thousand.[29] However, by the nature of the case, Brethren separatism left them with little ecclesiastical influence outside their own circles. Even among other conservative evangelicals they were viewed with some suspicion and regarded as operating too much like a secret society.[30] In all, Brethren influence in England was much like a religious underground and did not gain the role in the churches and the culture that fundamentalism had in America.

In conclusion it appears that the English conservative evangelicals differed from their American counterparts in two major respects: (1) a lack of widespread militancy, but instead Keswick-type emphases on non-controversialist piety; (2) a lack of general impact on the churches and the culture.[31]

AMERICA

Compared to the English, what in the American situation fostered militant fundamentalism as a major and sometimes influential religious force? The answers to this intriguing question inevitably will be rather speculative. The most significant factors on the American scene can be broken down conveniently into three interrelated categories, the social, the religious, and the intellectual.

Social Factors

Although a number of social factors might be explored, the most apparent involves the communication of ideas. Every observer has noticed, for instance, that fundamentalism sometimes flourished in isolated rural areas. Such cases suggest that in a very large, recently settled, and rapidly changing country, cultural pockets developed that were effectively insulated from the central intellectual life. The importance of this phenomenon can be seen more clearly by comparison with England. English intellectual and cultural life is relatively centralized. Ancient and well-established channels of communication made it difficult for an issue to be discussed in the universities, for instance, without soon being well-known throughout the parishes. Although there might have been a few "backward" areas,[32] the dissemination of new trends seemed to proceed at a relatively even pace.

In America there were great lags in communication. These resulted primarily from sociological, ethnic, and geographical factors, but were also reinforced by denominational differences. Congregationalists, Presbyterians, and Baptists, for instances, became familiar with the novel ideas at differing times. Within these groups, Northerners and Southerners, or Easterners and Westerners, might seriously encounter the ideas as much as generations apart.[33] Theological discussion could proceed in one section of the country, in one denomination, or among the educated elite while many people in other areas were virtually oblivious. In a period of rapid intellectual change, the potential for theological warfare once these diverse groups discovered each other was immense. In fact, the principal moment of discovery came just following World War I, when a general sense of cultural alarm heightened the intensity of fundamentalist reactions.

Although during the controversies of the 1920s fundamentalism appeared to many as primarily a social phenomenon, especially related to rural-urban tensions, such factors, while very important, only partially explain its development.[34] First of all (as Ernest Sandeen has pointed out), fundamentalism was not necessarily rural; its principal centers were initially urban and Northern. Furthermore (as Sandeen has also argued), if fundamentalism were to be adequately explained by social tensions, rural-urban themes, problems of communication and the like, then fundamentalism should have generally disappeared, as many in the 1920s predicted it would, once the crises of social transitions were past. Since in fact fundamentalism survived the 1920s and continued to flourish, its roots must have been considerably deeper. Sandeen finds these deep roots particularly in the millenarian movement.[35] It remains to be explained why they took their strongest hold in America, and not in England where the fundamentalist forms of millenarianism in fact originated. The lasting appeal of fundamentalism must be explained by elements deep in the American religious and cultural traditions themselves.

Religious Traditions

The primary force in the American religious experience that prepared the way for fundamentalism is what can be called "the dynamics of unopposed revivalism."[36] Although revivalism has flourished in many other countries since the eighteenth century, in America it came to be almost unchallenged by other formidable traditions and institutions. The comparison with England is again instructive. While revivalism was long a transatlantic phenomenon, in England the universities, the established church, and the pre-revivalist traditions of most of the Nonconformist groups were among the venerable forces promoting moderation and restraint. Tradition in general was much stronger in England than in America. The strength of resurgent evangelicalism in early nineteenth-century England, for instance, as a force for theological conservatism was substantially offset toward the middle of the century by the High Church movement which made even stronger claims upon traditionalist sentiments.[37]

In America such forces either were absent or had little effect, thus leaving revivalism an almost open field for determining the distinctive characteristics of American religious life.[38] Many of these traits (such as individualism, Biblicism, and primitivism) are conspicuous both in the mainstream of nineteenth-century American Protestantism and in twentieth-century fundamentalism. Such continuities suggest that fundamentalism can best be understood not primarily as an outgrowth of the movements promoting millenarianism and inerrancy (as Sandeen suggests), but rather to a large extent as a sub-species of revivalism in which certain types of new emphases became popular as part of the anti-modernist reaction.

Unopposed revivalism often fostered anti-intellectualism, as Richard Hofstadter has described,[39] yet perhaps even more important for the development of fundamentalism was the revivalists' tendency to promote and reinforce a particular type of intellectual emphasis—that is, a tendency to think in terms of simple dichotomies. The universe was divided between the realm of God and the realm of Satan; the supernatural was sharply separated from the natural; righteousness could have nothing to do with sin. The central impulse of revivalism was to rescue the saved from among the lost, and its whole way of conceiving reality was built around this central antithesis. In such a dichotomized view of things, ambiguities were rare. Like the conversion experience itself, transitions were not gradual, but were radical transformations from one state to its opposite.

Such intellectual categories left almost no room for the motifs of thought that were characteristic of liberal theology and scientific naturalism in the later nineteenth century. Both Darwinism and higher criticism emphasized gradual natural development, and the new theology saw God working through such means, emphasizing the synthesis of the natural and the supernatural rather than the antithesis. Wherever revivalism had been relatively unopposed in American religious life, there was virtually no preparation for the acceptance of the new categories—indeed there was hardly a way to discuss them. The reaction of many American Protestants, then, was not only to reject them outright as antithetical to the faith, but to assert the antitheses even more decisively. In reaction to naturalism, the supernatural aspects of the faith, such as the Virgin Birth, were emphasized in lists of fundamental doctrine. The three most distinctive doctrines of fundamentalism itself, inerrancy, opposition to evolution, and the premillenial return of Christ, all uncompromisingly accentuated the supernatural in the way God works, drawing the sharpest lines against any naturalistic or developmental explanations.

Although the dynamics of revivalism appear central to understanding the popularity of militant defenses of such doctrines in America, much of American revivalism and more broadly, pietism, had developed in the context of one other major religious tradition—that of Calvinism. From the beginning, Calvinism in America supported a tendency to demand, among other things, intellectual assent to precisely formulated statements of religious truth in opposition to all error.[40] Revivalists often modified and simplified the doctrines involved, yet many of them preserved both the emphasis on antitheses and the general point the assent to rightly-stated doctrine could be of eternal significance.

This tradition helps explain the paradox between Americans' reputation for religious tolerance and the actual intolerance in most of their ecclesiastical life. Both Calvinists and their revivalist heirs accepted and even endorsed civil tolerance of religious diversity by the eighteenth century, but civil tolerance was quite different from intellectual tolerance. One might allow Quakers or Roman Catholics full political equality and yet consider semi-Pelagianism to be legitimate grounds for fierce theological debate and separation. For Calvinists, separation of church and state often meant, among other things, that toleration did not have to extend to the churches.

Such tendencies, initiated in Calvinism, were preserved to some extent in American revivalism and hence continued into twentieth-century fundamentalism. This point is confirmed by the fact that fundamentalism appeared primarily among groups with Reformed origins, such as Baptists and Presbyterians, but was rather rare on the side of American revivalism with Methodist origins where ethical rather than intellectual aspects of Christianity tended to be emphasized.[41] Furthermore, in the late nineteenth and early twentieth centuries, the most natural allies of the revivalist fundamentalists were the Princeton theologians who for generations had been firing heavy theological artillery at every idea that moved and who were almost indecently astute at distinguishing Biblical and Reformed truth from all error.

Intellectual Factors

The wider fundamentalist battle against the new ideas was fought with materials drawn from both the Bible and the common stockpile of American assumptions and concepts. The relative popularity of the fundamentalist account of things reveals something, therefore, about the character of American intellectual life generally. Continuing the comparison with England, it appears that the historical sensitivities of the mid-nineteenth century had inclined Englishmen toward a rather ready acceptance of new and sometimes startling ideas concerning biological evolution and the historical development of the Bible. Much of the same might be said of some portions of America (such as New England) where many people were well-prepared to accept the new ideas; yet there were important countervailing forces as well.

Perhaps the best way to describe the difference on this point between America and Europe is to say that in America the romantic era was truncated. America came of age during the Enlightenment and remained generally content with mid-eighteenth-century modes of thought long after these had gone out of style in Europe. The American intellectual community remained rather isolated during the early national period; well into the second half of the nineteenth century the type of philosophy taught in almost all American colleges was the "common sense realism" of the Scottish Enlightenment. Although this philosophy was susceptible to a romantic interpretation in which persons could intuit truth, the truths involved were basically fixed aspects of reality from which could be derived rather definite law, so that there was little concept of development. Although it is difficult to document, a version of this common sense approach to reality appears to have been strong in shaping the popular philosophy nineteenth-century America as well.

By the mid-century, of course, there were many manifestations of romanticism on the American philosophical, religious, and artistic scenes, yet even at that time these had to contend with strong counterforces that still embodied Enlightenment categories. Among evangelicals, who controlled most of American higher education, the tension between these two tendencies was far from resolved at mid-century. Theologians such as Horace Bushnell, Henry B. Smith, and John Nevin were just emerging, and those closer to the eighteenth-century tradition such as Charles Hodge or Nathaniel William Taylor were still strong influences.[42] Revivalism did provide a popular romanticism emphasizing personal sentiment and piety, but this had little if anything to do with the sort of romanticism that since before the beginning of the nineteenth century had been fostering among Europeans a sensitivity to the dynamics of change and a suspicion of rational and fixed definitions of experience.[43]

The result was that in the second half of the nineteenth century many Americans were only just beginning romantic explorations when the second scientific revolution, associated with Darwinism, demanded that the new historical and developmental views be placed on the theological agenda. Even the intellectual community, then, was not always thoroughly prepared for the post-romantic modes of thought. As a result some rather well-educated Americans were among those who met naturalist challenges with pre-romantic rationalistic defenses. Emerging fundamentalism at the popular level accordingly did not entirely lack intellectual leadership, especially from a number of older theological institutions. Its modes of thought were not simply shaped to revivalist eccentricities, but by the substantial pre-romantic and rather rationalistic intellectual trends that survived in the American academic and theological communities.

The fundamentalist response to Darwinism, for instance, generally was not an anti-intellectualistic one framed in terms of the incompatibility of science and religion. It was an objection rather to a *type* of science—a developmental type— which they almost always branded as "unscientific."[44] Seldom did they denounce science in principle. Fundamentalist theology likewise reflected high esteem for being "scientific" in the sense of organizing, classifying, and rationally ordering data.[45] Similarly their view of Scripture tended to be positivistic: the Bible contained only firm evidence and no error.[46]

There is in fact little reason to suppose that many Americans would be inclined to reject science outright as an authority. The opposite would be more likely in a highly technological society with strong Enlightenment roots. The fundamentalist view of science was thus not wholly incompatible with the American intellectual climate.

Perhaps even more striking in suggesting American cultural traits is the attitude toward history found in fundamentalism. Here the contrast to English evangelicalism is particularly instructive. The characteristic view of history among fundamentalists has been dispensational-premillenialism (although not every fundamentalist, especially in the 1920s, held this position). Dispensational-premillennialism originated in England in the early nineteenth century. Yet in the twentieth century it apparently has had relatively few adherents in England except among Plymouth Brethren while in America it remains tremendously popular.[47] What, then, accounts for the remarkable popularity in America of this imported British view?

Dispensationalism is essentially an anti-developmental and anti-naturalistic way of explaining historical change. History is divided into seven "dispensations," each representing "some change in God's method of dealing with mankind," and each involving "a new test of the natural man." Man fails these tests, so that each dispensation ends in judgement and catastrophe.[48]

Two general tendencies found in fundamentalist thought are particularly evident in this scheme. First is a fascination with dividing and classifying.[49] The second is a heightened supernaturalism. Human efforts and natural forces have almost nothing to do with historical change. Instead, God periodically intervenes with a series of spectacular supernatural events that suddenly transform one age into another. In fact, God and Satan are virtually the only significant historical forces, and they are armed forces at that. In contrast to any romantic and developmental interpretations, dispensationalism explains history as a series of supernatural impositions of highly abstract, logical, and almost legalistic principles that humans might either accept or reject.[50]

The popularity of such views in twentieth-century America reveal an important American thought pattern—that in comparison with other Western countries many Americans lacked certain typically modern concepts of history. In the views of history popular in America the elements that were missing were precisely the assumptions central to most modern historical scholarship. These were the assumption that history is a natural evolutionary development and the corollary that the present can be understood best as a product of developing natural forces from the past. American historiography had long been dominated by supernatural, or at least providential, interpretations.[51] Furthermore, even the secular histories frequently emphasized the newness of America, dwelling on the past only to accentuate progress and the future. To Americans, who had relatively little history of their own, their national experience often seemed like a new dispensation, discontinuous with the past.

This widespread absence of a sense of gradual or natural historical change had been reinforced and partly created by the revivalist tradition, and in many places preserved from encounters with developmental ideas by social and geographical factors. These influences combined to dispose many persons to declare every aspect of the new views to be anathema and to oppose them with various non-negotiable logical antitheses. The greater the claims and the greater the influence of the naturalistic developmental views, the more firmly the fundamentalists stressed the opposing paradigms.[52]

This observation should not be interpreted to mean that because modern developmental paradigms were newer they were for that reason necessarily superior to fundamentalist emphases on antitheses. Furthermore, it seems to me incorrect, at least as far as Christian thought is concerned, to regard antithesis and natural historical development as incompatible categories, since central to Christianity itself is the wholly-other God revealing himself and acting in history. In America in the early twentieth century both fundamentalists and liberals tended to oversimplify the issue on this point. Fundamentalists, seeing clearly that the Bible spoke of antitheses, would hear almost nothing of natural development; liberals, enamored of historical and developmental explanation, proclaimed that the old antitheses must be abandoned. Perhaps in part because of the novelty in America of the modes of thought associated with modernism, both sides oversimplified the issues and each overestimated the degree to which recognition of historical development necessitated the abandonment of traditional Christian teaching.

NOTES

1. Fundamentalism especially in the 1920s was a coalition of rather diverse co-belligerents. For helpful accounts of some varieties within the leadership see the essays of C. Allyn Russell collected in *Voices of American Fundamentalism: Seven Biographical Studies* (Philadelphia, 1976).

2. In "From Fundamentalism to Evangelicalism: An Historical Analysis," *The Evangelicals*, ed. David Wells and John Woodbridge, (Nashville, 1975) I have discussed the changes in the character of fundamentalism since the 1920s. Among those close to the movement the meaning of the term, "fundamentalist," has narrowed in recent decades to include almost

solely doctrinally-militant premillennialist revivalists. Cf. George W. Dollar, *A History of Fundamentalism in America* (Greenville, S.C., 1973).

3. Ulster appears to be an exception—one that would offer another illustration of the relationship of fundamentalism to relatively unique cultural experiences. Canada has some fundamentalism, although I have the United States primarily in mind in the "American" comparison. In many nations, confessionalists and churchly conservatives survived and in some, such as the Netherlands, they had considerable influence; but these lacked the revivalist ties and some of the intellectual emphases characteristic of fundamentalists. Evangelical or pietist revivalism, sometimes with genuinely fundamentalist traits, could be found throughout the world in the twentieth century, but even if vigorous, as scattered minorities often operating with an aspect of a religious underground.

4. *The Roots of Fundamentalism: British and American Millenarianism 1800–1930* (Chicago, 1970). My criticisms are found in a review article, "Defining Fundamentalism," *Christian Scholar's Review* I:2 (Winter, 1971): 141–151; see Sandeen's reply, 1, 3 (Spring, 1971): 227–233. See also LeRoy Moore, Jr., "Another Look at Fundamentalism: A Response to Ernest R. Sandeen," *Church History* 37 (June, 1968): 195–202.

5. A number of the British authors, however, were no longer living.

6. S. K. Ratcliffe, "America and Fundamentalism," *Contemporary Review* 128 (September, 1925); now in *Controversy in the Twenties: Fundamentalism, Modernism, and Evolution*, ed. Willard B. Gatewood, Jr., (Nashville, 1969), p. 414. Other British commentators seem to have agreed that fundamentalism was peculiarly American; see Gatewood in ibid., pp. 409–412.

7. August 20, 1929, obituary of Dr. Arthur Samuel Peake, quoted in David G. Fountain, *E. J. Poole-Connor (1872–1962): "Contender for the Faith,"* (London, 1966), p. 91.

8. This interpretation and that immediately below follow that of Willis B. Glover, *Evangelical Nonconformists and Higher Criticism in the Nineteenth Century* (London, 1954). Owen Chadwick, *The Victorian Church: Part II*, 2d ed. (London, 1972) provides a similar account of Anglican reactions to *Essays and Reviews* (pp. 75–90) and Colenso (pp. 90–97). A recent general account of British reaction to Darwinism in the 1860s is M. J. S. Hodge, "England," in *The Comparative Reception of Darwinism*, ed. Thomas F. Glick, (Austin, Texas, 1972). See Edward J. Pfeifer's interesting essay, "United States," in ibid.

9. Chadwick, *op. cit.*, p. 23, says that evolution was fully accepted and respectable among clergymen by 1896. G. Stephen Spinks, "Victorian Background," in Spinks *et al.*, *Religion in Britain since 1900* (London, 1952) remarks that it was easier for the British to come to terms with the new biology than with Biblical criticism, p. 20.

10. Glover, *op. cit.*, pp. 71–90, 109–110. On Anglican parallel see p. 9 and Chadwick, *op. cit.*, pp. 1–111. Cf. H. D. McDonald, *Theories of Revelation: An Historical Study 1860–1960* (London, 1963), pp. 101–118. By 1900, English champions of higher criticism thought "the battle was won" and that higher criticism had already "penetrated to the country clergymen," p. 116. McDonald, however, shows that at least the former of these statements was an overestimate since a few conservative attacks continued, pp. 118–136, 203–217. Already by the time of *Lux Mundi* (1889) which helped promote higher criticism among Anglicans, all the bishops except J. C. Ryle of Liverpool (a rather tolerant conservative) reportedly accepted the new ideas. See Marcus L. Loune, *John Charles Ryle 1816–1900: A Short Biography* (London, 1953), pp. 47–48, 56–57. Anti-evolution does not seem to have been a major issue even for the most conservative twentieth-century English evangelicals cited below.

11. Chadwick, *op. cit.*, p. 24, says that "for a decade or two after 1896 some members of the Church of England, especially among the evangelicals . . . and most of the simple worshippers among the chapels of the poor, continued to know nothing of evolution or to refuse to accept it on religious grounds. . . ." This estimate would still place the general popular acceptance by World War I. Cf. Glover, *op. cit.*, p. 217 for a similar observation regarding acceptance of higher criticism.

12. Darwinism quite evidently reflected tendencies developing in the British intellectual climate for some time. The sense of history as "a natural and organic development" was commonplace by the mid-nineteenth century. See, for example, the account in Walter E. Houghton, *The Victorian Frame of Mind: 1830–1870* (New Haven, 1957), pp. 29–31, and *passim*. Romanticism, which had been a major force in England since before 1800, also encouraged emphasis on process rather than on fixed or static truth. (Cf. note 43, below.)

13. Glover, *op cit.*, p. 25. Cf. Chadwick, *op. cit.*, p. 59, who attributes the widespread agreement on new views of the Old Testament ". . . not only to German criticism and to English scholarship but to the general growth of historical consciousness. . . ." Cf. p. 462.

14. Orr, *Revelation and Inspiration* (New York, 1910), p. 198; cf. 209–210, 214–215. Orr was critical of the emphasis of the Princeton theologians on inerrancy although he thought he had much in common with them regarding Scripture. On evolution see Orr, "Science and the Christian Faith," in *The Fundamentals: A Testimony to the Truth* (Chicago, 1910–1915), 4:91–104. The inclusion of Orr's moderate statement on evolution in *The Fundamentals* indicates that the lines had not yet firmly hardened on this point among the American revivalists.

15. Even some evangelicals who protested against the more liberal trends were rather progressive themselves. Charles H. Vine, ed., *The Old Faith and the New Theology: A Series of Sermons and Essays on Some Truths Held by Evangelical Christians* (New York, 1907), being protests by British Congregationalists against the "new theology," and B. Herklots, *The Future of the Evangelical Party in the Church of England* (London, 1913) both parallel fundamentalist concerns over questions such as miracles yet assume a tolerance toward higher criticism not found among American fundamentalists. See, e.g., Vine, *op. cit.*, pp. 225 and 227; Herklots *op. cit.*, pp. v, 57–68, 107, 113. Cf. general accounts by E. L. Allen, "The Acids of Modernity," in Spinks, *Religion in Britain*, pp. 49–64 and John Kenneth Mozley, *Some Tendencies in British Theology from the Publication of* Lux Mundi *to the Present Day* (London, 1951), p. 24–46.

16. *The Christian Fundamentalist*, 2 (1928): 7, 17. General accounts of Keswick are found in Bruce Shelley, "Sources in Pietistic Fundamentalism," *Fides et Historia* 5 (1973): 68–78 and Steven Barabas, *So Great Salvation: The History and Message of the Keswick Convention* (Westwood, N.J., 1952). At this same time Riley was engaged in an all-out attack on the well-known conservative-evangelical British preacher, G. Campbell Morgan, sometimes also associated with Keswick, and a contributor to *The Fundamentals.* Morgan, concluding a brief and stormy stay at the Bible Institute of Los Angeles, described as "frankly impossible" the attitude of fundamentalists. "They separate themselves, not only from those who accept evolutionary theory, but from those who deny the liberal inerrancy of Scripture." Quoted from *The British Weekly in The Christian Fundamentalist* 2 (1928): 14.

17. I am very greatly indebted to Ian S. Rennie of Regent College, Vancouver, for pointing me toward much of the information used in the following sections on English evangelicalism. In two very extensive critiques of an earlier version of this essay he argues that there was "an identifiable movement known as English Fundamentalism" and that "its controversies were only different in the fact that England provided a somewhat different context." While I am impressed by the evidence used to support this conclusion, and hope that Professor Rennie will publish his own account of it, I nevertheless remain convinced that the English movement differed significantly from American fundamentalism. However, I do not object strongly to calling the British movement (as Rennie does) "fundamentalist," which I think is consistent with British parlance. With such a broader definition, my thesis would be that there is a qualitative difference between British and American fundamentalism as well as a difference in impact on the churches and the culture.

18. J. C. Pollock, *A Cambridge Movement* (London, 1953) gives a very complete account of the background and origins of I.V.F. His work may be supplemented by broader accounts in Frederick Donald Coggan (ed.), *Christ and the Colleges: A History of the Inter-Varsity Fellowship of Evangelical Unions* (London, 1934), which contains the constitution, and Douglas Johnson (ed.), *A Brief History of the International Fellowship of Evangelical Students* (Lausanne, 1964).

19. George W. Dollar in his militantly fundamentalist *A History of Fundamentalism in America* (Greenville, S.C., 1973) includes I.V.F. in "An Enemy Within: New Evangelicalism," p. 205; cf. p. 258. On the other hand more liberal critics in England called I.V.F. "fundamentalist" in the 1950s, e.g., Gabriel Hebert, *Fundamentalism and the Church of God* (London, 1957); cf. J. I. Packer's defense, *"Fundamentalism," and the Word of God* (London, 1958). The "fundamentalism" in these debates is more sophisticated, scholarly, and flexible than all but a very small portion of American fundamentalism.

20. Complementary accounts of this dispute are found in Gordon Hewitt, *The Problems of Success: A History of the Church Missionary Society 1910–1942* (London, 1971) and in G. W. Bromiley's sympathetic biography of the leader of the conservatives, *Daniel Henry Charles Bartlett: A Memoir* (Burnham-on-Sea, Somerset, Eng., 1959).

21. Ian Rennie points out that there was a substantial infra-structure of such agencies. Among those he mentions are: the Church Pastoral-Aid Society, the South American Missionary Society, the (now-named) Commonwealth and Continental Missionary Society, and the Church's Ministry to the Jews (all Anglican), the Scripture Union and Children's Special Service Mission, the Christian Alliance of Women and Girls (a secession in 1919 from the YWCA), the Bible League, and the Victoria Institute (a center for anti-evolution thought); among theological schools, Tyndale, Clifton, Oak Hill, and to some extent St. John's Highbury, a few Bible colleges, but no colleges at the universities; publications, *The Christian, The Life of Faith* and the annual *Keswick Week*. Correspondence with author.

22. Ian Murray, *The Forgotten Spurgeon* (London, 1966), whose title is revealing, documents a sympathetic account of Spurgeon's role as a controversialist in Downgrade, pp. 145–206. Willis B. Glover, "English Baptists at the Time of the Downgrade Controversy," *Foundations* 1 (1958): 46, goes so far as to conclude of Downgrade, "its chief interest is the fact that it has so few long-range effects."

23. Among the Baptists, however, a "Baptist Bible Union" was organized by the 1920s. See a report on its fundamentalist activities by its founder, John W. Thomas, "Modernism and Fundamentalism in Great Britain," *The King's Business* 14 (1923): 817–821. The impact, however, appears to have been slight. E. J. Poole-Connor, *Evangelicalism in England*, rev. ed. (London 1965 [1951]), p. 249, laments that modernism had triumphed almost completely among British Baptists by 1925. Arthur H. Carter, in "Modernism: the Outlook in Great Britain," *The King's Business* 15 (1924): 691, remarks: "But the saddest aspect of the situation lies in the fact that the entire body of English Nonconformity accepts their theological position, and, save in a few isolated cases, the whole body of the Free Churches has gone *holus bolus* over to the ranks of Modernism." No doubt more non-militant Biblicism survived among Nonconformists than these estimates would allow. Yet contrast American fundamentalists at this time who often claimed to represent the majority of American church members, e.g., "A Divided House," *The King's Business* 15 (1925): 347.

24. Another Englishman who qualified as a full-fledged fundamentalist was W. H. Griffith Thomas (1861–1924). He was associated with *The Fundamentals*, Keswick, dispensationalism, and the founding of Dallas Theological Seminary. However, he left a position as principal at Wycliffe Hall, Oxford, in 1910 to become professor of Old Testament at Wycliffe College, Toronto, hence reducing his influence in England. C. G. Thorne, Jr., "William Henry Griffith Thomas," *The New International Dictionary of The Christian Church*, ed. J. D. Douglas (Grand Rapids, 1974), p. 972.

25. Quoted in Fountain, *E. J. Poole-Connor*, p. 126.

26. The statistics are approximations, Fountain, *Poole-Connor*, p. 18. Nearly three hundred congregations were claimed by the time of Poole-Connor's death in 1962, p. 211.

27. Fountain, *Poole-Connor*, pp. 34, 44, 131–134. Fountain, p. 119 observes, "In the United States the conflict was sharper than in this country for two reasons. The Liberals were more extreme and the Evangelicals more faithful and more able."

28. Fountain, *Poole-Connor*, p. 134. Conservative evangelical scholarship also seems to have been at its nadir during the period between the wars. H. D. McDonald, *Theories of Revelation*, in a very sympathetic account remarks nevertheless on this era that "There was, on the whole, however, no serious conflict, because, not only were other interests uppermost, but evangelicals were in the backwood as far as convincing Biblical scholarship was concerned," p. 208; cf. pp. 280–282. The founding of the *Evangelical Quarterly* in 1929 signaled the reversal of this trend.

29. F. Roy Coad., *A History of the Brethren Movement* (London, 1968), p. 185. The figures are for the entire British Isles.

30. Coad., ibid., p. 284. They included, nonetheless, notable elements from higher economic and social standing. Rennie correspondence with author.

With respect to the possibility of a more general social factor, Rennie, noting a variety of evidences, observes, "Thus a significant difference does appear—English Fundamentalism often seems upper middle class while its American counterpart is usually much more plebian."

31. These conclusions may be compared to those of William R. Hutchison, "The Americanness of the Social Gospel; An Inquiry in Comparative History," *Church History* 44 (1975): 367–381, who stresses the essential similarities between British and American social gospel. Hutchison does find American liberals to have been more optimistic in their humanism and affirmations of the present age than were their British counterparts. It might be added that by the 1920s liberalism appeared to have triumphed far more completely in British churches (cf. note 23 above).

32. The fact that the industrial revolution was earlier in England than America and hence the transitions from rural to urban cultural patterns more nearly completed by the late nineteenth century helped also to reduce such cultural pockets. Cf. Harold Perkin, *The Origins of Modern English Society 1780–1880* (London, 1969).

33. Albert H. Newman, "Recent Changes in Theology of Baptists," *The American Journal of Theology* 10 (1906): 600–609, made essentially this point at the time.

34. The classic statement of this interpretation is Stewart G. Cole, *History of Fundamentalism* (New York, 1931). In "From Fundamentalism to Evangelicalism," *The Evangelicals*, I have attempted to explain some social factors by suggesting that fundamentalism might involve a White Anglo-Saxon Protestant experience analogous to that of elements in immigrant groups.

35. Sandeen, *Roots*, esp. pp. ix–xix, and his "Fundamentalism and American Identity," *The Annals of the American Academy of Political and Social Science* 387 (January, 1970): 56–65. Paul A. Carter, "The Fundamentalist Defense of the Faith," in *Change and Continuity in Twentieth Century America: The 1920s*, ed. John Braeman *et al.*, also offers an effective critique of primarily social and social-economic or political interpretations of fundamentalism, which he himself had endorsed in his earlier work.

36. This phrase is borrowed in part from Stanley Elkins, *Slavery: A Problem in American Institutional and Intellectual Life* (Chicago, 1959) who refers to "the dynamics of unopposed capitalism."

37. Cf. Poole-Connor, *Evangelicalism*, p. 220. Well into the twentieth century Anglican conservative evangelicals had to deal with two fronts—the liberals and the High Church party.

38. Cf. Donald G. Mathews, "The Second Great Awakening as an Organizing Process 1780–1830: An Hypothesis," *American Quarterly* 21 (1969): 23–43. See also William G. McLoughlin, "Revivalism," in *The Rise of Adventism: Religion and Society in Mid-Nineteenth-Century America*, ed. Edwin S. Gaustad, pp. 119–154, who goes so far as to suggest that revivalism is the key to understanding American life generally.

39. *Anti-Intellectualism in American Life* (New York, 1962). Cf. *The Paranoid Style of American Politics and Other Essays* (New York, 1965). Hofstadter is correct in seeing anti-intellectual-

ism as an important component of fundamentalism, although this single emphasis obscures many other aspects.

40. Seventeenth-century Puritans, for instance, were fascinated by dichotomies and antitheses as the popularity of the Ramist method and their concerns over precisely distinguishing between the regenerate and the unregenerate indicate.

41. Pentecostalism is the movement of this tradition that parallels fundamentalism. Pentecostals also rejected modern culture but more in terms of intense personal piety that separated individuals from the world, rather than in terms of doctrinal warfare. The two movements should be kept distinct, I think, even though they sometimes overlapped and had some common origins in American revivalism and hence many common traits. W. J. Hollenweger, *The Pentecostals* (Minneapolis, 1972), comments on fundamentalist traits in Pentecostalism, p. 9 and elsewhere. Various holiness teachings are likewise found among fundamentalists.

42. The above generalizations about nineteenth-century American evangelicals are illustrated (among other places) in Marsden, *The Evangelical Mind and the New School Presbyterian Experience* (New Haven, 1970).

43. It is common practice to set the peak of European (including English) romanticism in the period from 1780 to 1830; e.g., Arthur O. Lovejoy, "The Meaning of Romanticism for the Historian of Ideas," *Journal of the History of Ideas*, 2 (June, 1941): 260–261 and Jacques Barzun, *Romanticism and the Modern Age* (Boston, 1943), pp. 134–139. The tiny Mercersburg movement in America compared to the Anglo-Catholic movement in England during the same era suggests something of the contrast in the strength of romanticism in the religious life of the two countries; cf. James Hastings Nichols, *Romanticism in American Theology: Nevin and Schaff at Mercersburg* (Chicago, 1961).

44. For examples, John Horsh, "The Failure of Modernism," (Chicago, 1925) (pamphlet), pp. 22–23 says "The science with which Scripture conflicts is unproved theory; it is science falsely so-called." William B. Riley defines science as "knowledge gained and verified by exact observation and correct thinking; especially as methodologically arranged in a rational system," which he takes to exclude "theory," "hypothesis," and "assumptions," p. 5, "Are the Scriptures Scientific?" (Minneapolis, n. d.) (pamphlet).

45. A good example is Reuben A. Torrey, *What the Bible Teaches*, 17th ed., (New York, 1933 [1898]), which he describes as ". . . simply an attempt at a careful, unbiased, systematic, thorough-going, *inductive* study and statement of Bible truth. . . . The methods of modern science are applied to Bible study—through analysis followed by careful synthesis," p. 1.

46. Cf. John Opie, "The Modernity of Fundamentalism," *Christian Century*, May 12, 1965, pp. 608–611.

47. One example is the popularity of Hal Lindsey, *The Late Great Planet Earth* (Grand Rapids, 1970). As of the July 1974 printing the publisher claimed 4,300,000 copies in print.

48. These dispensations are 1) "Innocence," ending with the Fall; 2) "Conscience," ending with the Flood; 3) "Human Government," ending with Babel; 4) "Promise," ending in the bondage in Egypt; 5) "Law," ending with the death of Christ; 6) "Grace," which will end with a period of great tribulation, immediately followed by Christ's return to earth, victory at Armageddon; and 7) the millennium or personal reign of Christ, ending with Satan "loosed a little season" but quickly defeated. After the millennium is the "new heavens and new earth" of eternity. C. I. Scofield, *"Rightly Dividing the World of Truth"* (Revell paper edition, New York, n.d. [1896]), pp. 12–16.

49. Scofield says, "The Word of Truth . . . has right divisions . . . so *any study* of that Word which ignores these divisions must be in large measure profitless and confusion." Ibid., p. 3.

50. C. Norman Kraus, *Dispensationalism in America* (Richmond, 1958), pp. 66–67 and 125–126 comments perceptively on this point.

51. Ernest Lee Tuveson, *Redeemer Nation: The Idea of America's Millennial Role* (Chicago, 1968) gives many examples of this point.

52. The total lack of communication between fundamentalists and modernists concerning both history and science fits well the now-familiar patterns of paradigm conflict described in Thomas S. Kuhn, *The Structure of Scientific Revolutions* (Chicago, 1962).

THE TWENTIETH CENTURY

In the 1880s and 1890s, most American religious leaders, at least Protestant religious leaders, looked only with gloom at the approach of the next century. In their minds, Christianity generally, and Protestantism specifically, seemed doomed to failure. If the "rise of science" did not remove the intellectual justification for a belief in God, urbanization and industrialism seemed to be removing the social milieu that had long underwritten traditional religious activity.

Yet in America, at least, the twentieth century appears to be ending on an extraordinarily positive note for organized religion. Religious membership and activity were higher from 1955 to 1990 than at any other point in American history, except the Puritan experiment in New England from 1630 to 1660, and religion dramatically affected American politics from the 1960s to the 1990s.

The history of religion in twentieth-century America demonstrates the complexity and breadth of this outcome. The commercialization of American culture so often feared by religious leaders may have developed in ways that actually supported religion, even while changing it. Amidst the challenge of the depression, some religious groups laid the foundation for future success. A wide variety of immigrant groups adapted to American circumstances in astonishing ways. A belief in the miraculous, rather than fading, not only persevered but may have strengthened. Religious rhetoric underwrote idealism of many kinds, and religion's involvement in politics took so many different turns that it was impossible to tag "religion" as supporting only one kind of political and social activism. In the end, it might be said that the twentieth century has proved to be *the* century of religion" in American history, rather than the century in which religion disappeared.

CHAPTER
17

Religion and Sociology

Historians and sociologists have long pursued similar themes from different vantage points. Beginning in the 1970s, social historians regularly consulted sociological theories and sought to test them with reference to historical case studies. Mobility and migration methodology, demographic analysis of vital records, and modernization theory represented the chief intersections of the two disciplines.

In terms of the impact of sociological theory on American religious history, nothing has engaged historians more than debates over "secularization." We place that term in quotation marks because a good deal of recent scholarship in American religious history questions whether secularization is the inevitable consequence of modernization that sociologists from Max Weber on had assumed. In the language of the social sciences, secularization is now more of a "problématique" to be explored than a "paradigm" or model to be followed. In the following essay by Professor Bryan Wilson we see one definition of secularization by a sociologist. What does Professor Wilson rely upon for evidence? How do we reconcile models of secularization with public opinion surveys that find that modern Americans have never been more widely Christianized, and that in all religious traditions there is a marked return to "tradition," and "orthodoxy"?

Additional Reading: Any understanding of the problem of "secularization," should begin with the two most famous books ever written on the sociology of religion: Max Weber, *The Sociology of Religion,* translated by Talcot Parsons (London, 1992), and Emile Durkheim, *The Elementary Forms of the Religious Life,* translated by Joseph W. Swain (London, 1915). The perspectives of historians and sociologists are contrasted in Steve Bruce, (ed.), *Religion and Modernization: Sociologists and Historians Debate the Secularization Thesis* (Oxford, 1992). Sabino S. Acquaviva, *The Decline of the Sacred in Industrial Society,* translated by Patricia Lipscomb (Oxford, 1979), is an important study of secularization in twentieth-century Europe, while Bryan Wilson, *Religion in Secular Society* (London, 1966) studies the subject in

Britain. George M. Marsden and Bradley J. Longfield, (eds.), *The Secularization of the Academy* (New York, 1992) discusses the secularization of American universities. Two important and still valuable books challenged the "secularization thesis" after World War II: Will Herberg, *Protestant-Catholic-Jew: An Essay in American Religious Sociology* (Garden City, 1955) and Gerhard Lenski, *The Religious Factor: A Sociological Study of Religion's Impact on Politics* (New York, 1961).

Bryan Wilson

Secularization: The Inherited Model

August Comte is not now much remembered, even by sociologists, whose discipline he both shaped and named. Sociologists of religion, however, have special reason to remember him, and with him his immediate precursor, Saint-Simon, since they defined the new science of society with specific reference to, and in direct contrast with, the previously existing body of social knowledge. Man, society, and the world were, hitherto, explained—in the Western tradition, but perhaps in all traditions—by reference to transcendent laws, states, or beings. As a methodology for interpreting society, sociology was, from its first enunciation, directly set over against theology. Quite explicitly, Comte indicated the contrast between theological and (social) scientific ways of knowing. Although he did not use the term, and his interests were certainly broader, Comte provided a comprehensive account—its many factual errors notwithstanding—of a process of secularization. Sociology's charter as a discipline implied from the outset that it was to be an empirical, man-centered, this-worldly, matter-of-fact explanation of human organization and development. The work of Comte's major successors, beginning from different starting points, using different terms, and within different frameworks of argument, reinforced this general orientation: Marx's emphasis on materialism; Weber's *Entzauberung;* Durkheim's pursuit of a rational ethnic; Veblen's "matter-of-fact" thinking. Sociology documented a secularizing process.

The deep-laid ambiguity in sociology, and its central epistemological problem, is evident in the fact that sociology was not merely a commentary on a process of secularization; it was also—as Comte claimed it to be—a value-free, positivistic discipline, as objective and neutral as the natural sciences. (Marx, too, saw his own system of explanation as managing to transcend the riddle of the relativism implicit in a sociology of knowledge; Marxism, although issuing from the world view of the proletariat, would also be established as an objective science.) Sociology began as a contradiction of theology, rejecting theological explanations because they were conditioned by the limited range of social experience of their

From *The Sacred in a Secular Age: Toward Revision in the Scientific Study of Religion* (Berkeley, 1985). Reprinted by permission of the Regents of the University of California and the University of California Press.

proponents and by evaluative and emotional impediments to proper cognitive understanding. There was, then, a commitment to ethically neutral and objective procedures and, simultaneously, an explicit rejection of the various assumptions embodied in the earlier way of interpreting the world. Sociology was a new methodology to explain society. Understandably, its rejection of theological assumptions and assertions was taken not merely as a transfer from one methodology and one philosophy to another but as an onslaught against the theological, and against the supernatural entities (beings, laws, events, places, and actions) which religion projected as of real, determining importance in man's affairs.

The theological world view was committed not only to the proposition of a purportedly factual account of society, history, psychology, and the future but also to the active and vigorous advocacy of that world view and of certain epistemological and moral commitments thought to be implicit within it. Given this confusion of fact and value, it was thus not possible—at least at that time—for the theologically committed to see sociology merely as a change of perspective, as an alternative set of assumptions about history and society. It was seen as an assault on truth, as a heresy—it was seen, in short, as all previous alternative (inevitably theological) systems of knowing had been seen, as an evil conspiracy against the supernatural entities which the theologian not only projected as causal agencies but towards which he also sought to inspire universal devotion. The theologians were caught in a system in which the world was not merely factually known (insofar as their assumptions allowed it to be accurately known) but in which it was also evaluatively interpreted. In accord with their evaluative procedures, they had to categorize the new method of knowing in terms of praise and blame; this was their métier. Despite its formal espousal of ethical neutrality, then, sociology was compromised by the animosity engendered among the theologically minded by its very different explanation of society—and of religion. To the theologians, in the light of the prevailing conventional body of knowledge and "way of knowing," the radical methodological premises of sociology were incomprehensible.

The confrontation is here depicted schematically as a philosophic divergence, but historical evidence could be adduced to illustrate it, occluded as it was by the more dramatic challenge to the theocentric view of the world arising from the natural sciences. With sociology, the battle was, if at first more muted, eventually more disturbing for the supernaturalist *Weltanschauung*. The natural sciences touched only the facts of nature, and even though, in Christianity at least, these were purportedly set forth in ancient revelations couched in terms supposedly timelessly true, it was eventually easier for the entrenched intellectual establishment to abandon these so-called facts about nature than to admit the possibility of an alternative methodology for the interpretation of facts about society, man's history, and the meaning of morality.

With the decline of strong forms of theocentric or supernaturalist views of the world, the diametrically opposite approaches of these two intellectual systems have regularly been forgotten or ignored. But suspicion has remained, and it has been echoed in misunderstandings particularly on the subject of secularization. The discussion of secularization, although acknowledged in everyday terms by many clerics, is often seen as in itself an aggressive commentary on religion. Committed religionists still confuse the evaluative and the analytic; they regularly mistake "secularization"—the process occurring within the social structure—for "secularism"—the ideology of those who wish to promote the decline of religion and to hasten the process of secularization. Hence the frequent assumption that those who seek to describe a process of secularization must favour that process, and may well be advocating a Marxist organization of society. The secularization thesis, despite the hostility it provoked toward sociologists who, in some form or another, propounded it, can be set forth (and the sociological intention is to set it forth) in entirely neutral terms, as a description of a process that can be traced in the course of social development.

The inherited model of secularization has lacked formal specification. It has frequently been used in diverse ways, encompassing a very wide range of phenomena. It has been appropriately referred to as a multidimensional concept. In essence, it relates to a process of transfer of property, power, activities, and both manifest and latent functions, from institutions with a supernaturalist frame of reference to (often new) institutions operating according to empirical, rational, pragmatic criteria. That process can be demonstrated as having occurred extensively, if unevenly, over a long historical period, and to have done so notwithstanding the spasmodic countervailing occurrence of resacralization in certain areas and instances of cultural revitalization exemplified in the emergence of charismatic leaders and prophets.

In particular, the secularization model has been taken as referring to the shift in the location of decision making in human groups from elites claiming special access to supernatural ordinances to elites legitimating their authority by reference to other bases of power. Political authority is, however, only the most conspicuous arena in which this transfer from agencies representing the supernatural has occurred. Perhaps more basic has been the transformation of work activities by the development of new economic techniques and procedures that are increasingly dictated by more and more rational application of scarce resources and which, in consequence, more regularly ignore or abrogate rules of sacrality. To contrast North American Indian attitudes to the soil and agriculture with those of white men, or medieval codes of moral economic behavior with those of subsequent times, illustrates the steady transcendence of rational methods. Consequent on changes such as these, the reward structures of society change in commensurate ways, with diminished rewards and status accorded to those who manipulate supernatural "explanations" and legitimations, and increased rewards to those whose work is directed to materialistic, empirically validated productivity. Human ecology and population distribution, following changes in economic technique and (to some extent) political organization, have further secularizing implications. Religion had its basis in the local social group and in the solemnization and sacralization of interpersonal relationships. New methods of social organization and economic activity permitted, and at times necessitated, a new distribution of wealth and of people, as the surplus productivity of the countryside facilitated consumption in cities, the growth of tertiary industry, and perhaps now—with the growth of entertainment—one might say in quaternary industry.

The increasing awareness that rules were not absolute and heaven-sent but were amenable to changing need, and that even the most sacred norms of society could be renegotiated, altered, and perhaps even superseded, challenged assumptions about the will of higher beings in favour of the more conscious purposes of man himself. The shift, which might be most dramatically documented in the area of law, led to the steady modification of those absolute decrees and transcendent social norms in which individual well-being was always sacrificed to community cohesion. The steady accumulation of empirical knowledge, the increasing application of logic, and the rational coordination of human purposes established an alternative vision and interpretation of life. Steadily, the good man displaced what was once seen as the "will of providence" (or such other supernatural categories) and, in such areas as health, the dispositions of the supernatural were no longer regarded as adequate explanation for man's experience. Sanitation, diet, and experimental pharmacology displaced prayer, supplication, and resignation as the appropriate responses to disease and death. Man ceased to be solely at the disposition of the gods. Change in the character of knowledge implied change in the method of its transmission, and the consequent amendment of the institutions concerned with the socialization and education of the young. And, finally, the shifting awareness of man's potential—and thus his freedom—diminished the sense of the need for responsibility and, indeed, responsiveness toward superhuman agencies. Man acquired greater control of wide areas of his own experience; mankind attained a sense of self-determination, and employed new criteria of human happiness—the latter particularly in the use of leisure time.

All of the foregoing processes have been documented, in varying terms, by sociologists, whether they explicitly recognized them as aspects of secularization or not. Most conspicuously in Weber's documentation of the processes of rationalization, the political and economic changes are discussed, while Marx sets forth the economic causes of change in social stratification. Toennie's analysis of basic transformations in social organization, following from changing distributive and ecological patterns of human population, has strong implications for man's conception of the sacred. Durkheim documented the difference between retributive and restitutive justice, even though he only gradually perceived the implications for the character of moral norms, and even though the consequential shift in the basis of social cohesion was more radical than he recognized. Comte had already indicated the methodology of the natural sciences as the model for a new methodology in interpreting society. Hobhouse, among others, saw the possibilities for the growth of self-determining societies, and Freud provided a mode of analysis which related man's irrational psychology to his supernaturalist predispositions and which promised new conceptions of moral judgment and individual responsibility.

The shift from primary preoccupation with the superempirical to the empirical; from transcendent entities to naturalism; from other-worldly goals to this-worldly possibilities; from an orientation to the past as a determining power in life to increasing preoccupation with a planned and determined future; from speculative and "revealed" knowledge to practical concerns, and from dogmas to falsifiable propositions; from the acceptance of the incidental, spasmodic, random, and charismatic manifestations of the divine to the systematic, structured, planned, and routinized management of the human—all of these are implicit in the model of secularization which, in various strands, constitute the inheritance not only of the sociology of religion but of sociology per se.

This is not to say that the concept of secularization embraces all aspects of social change, of course, but rather to say that in the long-run course of such change, secularization has been a significant element. Since sacrality powerfully influenced so many of man's concerns in traditional society, the shift from the traditional to the innovatory affects conceptions of the sacred in all these departments. Nor is this to say that the sacred always gives way in equal measure as change occurs. The model does not specify the pace or the details of each aspect of the process. In institutions that remain locally organized—for example in the family, which is highly localized even in the more attenuated, or volatile, and increasingly mobile form that it has acquired—conceptions of the sacred may endure more easily than in politics. Similarly, education, which resists "massification," may for some time persist as a better vehicle for supernaturalism than, say, the economy. Nor does the model predicate the disappearance of religiosity, nor even of organized religion; it merely indicates the decline in the significance of religion in the operation of the social system, its diminished significance in social consciousness, and its reduced command over the resources (time, energy, skill, intellect, imagination, and accumulated wealth) of mankind.

An alternative way of formulating the implications of the secularizing process to the one already given is to indicate the loss of functionality of religion, in the process of the structural differentiation of society. There is no need here to set forth in these, somewhat different, terms the points already made with respect to various social institutions. All that need be said is that—whereas legitimate authority once depended on religious sanctions; whereas social control once relied heavily on religiously defined rewards and punishments; whereas social policies, conspicuously including warfare, at one time needed supernatural endorsement, or at least the endorsement of those who were recognized as the agents of the supernatural; and whereas revealed faith once specified the boundaries of true learning—now, all of these functions have been superseded. Authority is now established by constitutions. Social control is increasingly a matter for law rather than for a consensual moral code, and law becomes increasingly technical and decreasingly moral (even theologians now draw a sharp line between sin and crime), while effective sanctions are physical and fiscal rather than threats or blandishments about the afterlife. Social policies increasingly require the approval of an electorate, which endorses a manifesto. Revelation is a distrusted source of knowledge, and the methodology of modern learning puts a premium on doubt rather than on faith, on critical scepticism rather than on unquestioning belief. The erstwhile functions of religion have been superseded, and this constitutes a process of the secularization of society. Religion has lost its presidency over other institutions.

It is sometimes argued—and particularly so by Christian apologists—that this diminution of the role of religion is an evidence not of secularization but of religion's having been purged of extraneous social involvements which were, at best, a distraction from religion's true purpose and, at worst, a corruption of the spirit by the world. This argument, however, is in itself inconsequential for the secularization thesis. It is not the sociologist's concern to decide whether religion is purer now, in a secularized world where it has diminished power, than it was in a sacralized world, where it (or its agents) exerted considerable influence. It suffices to say that the influence of religion has declined. The argument is also heavily predicated on the specifically Christian case; its exponents, when they say "religion," clearly allude only to "Christianity," and their spectrum for secularization in all probability extends no further back than, perhaps, the age of faith of Innocent III. They forget that religion, in the wide sense, was more pervasive in society before it acquired its roles in the increasingly differentiated political, juridical, economical, educational, and status systems of the Middle Ages, and that this pervasive influence was "what religion was for"—this was its utility for man, and the reason for which he subscribed to it, long before its incorporation into the rules, roles, and procedures of medieval society.

It would follow from such an argument that, for those who espouse it, secularization is seen as in itself a not undesirable phenomenon—a purification agency for religion. That case could be made out, of course, only after a precise specification has been given of what a religion "should be like," and that is not a sociological concern. The process of secularization, however, may be seen as extending over the very long term—evident, according to Max Weber, particularly in Judaism in its elimination of the diverse, localized, immanentist magical cults of Palestine. To the extent that they disciplined, unified, and systematized conceptions of the supernatural, other major religions were also agencies of secularization, reducing, regulating, and circumscribing the operation of the sacred. But none of them—even the rigorous monotheism of Islam notwithstanding—has been so radically effective in this process as Judaism and Christianity (especially in its Protestant form), and some of them have not even been exclusivistic, but have tolerated, accommodated, or incorporated alien indigenous manifestations of magic and local religious cults.

It is not, however, to be assumed that the secularization thesis is merely a commentary specifically on Christian history. The model is intended to have general validity. Were it to be stated in sufficiently abstract terms, there would be no reason why it should not be applied in any context. In practice, because we are dealing with "historical individuals" on a grand scale, because of the uneven pace of economic and social development of different cultures, and because of the fullest availability of documentation in the Western case, secularization is sometimes discussed as if it were specific to Christianity. There is reason for this, since there are distinct differences among religions. Certain characteristics, embraced more fully or explicitly in some traditions than in others, directly favor the process of secularization. Exclusivity has already been mentioned. Commitment to intellectual coherence and formal logic—both agencies of secularization—are also more markedly evident in the case of Christianity than in other world religions. Christianity has influenced social development, but it has also been receptive to change in economy and polity that have made Christianity an obvious religious locus of secularizing dispositions. As the degree of technical, economic, and political changes occurring in Western societies is experienced elsewhere and comes to characterize other cultures, we can expect to see a recession of the influence of religion there, even though indigenous religious traditions may themselves have been less directly responsible for encouraging or accommodating social change than Christianity has been. The course of social change generally has been toward the diminution of religious influence on social organization. These trends occurred earlier, more extensively, and more pervasively, in the West than elsewhere and were first adumbrated within existing religious traditions among dominant intellectual elites who, historically, were necessarily religious or religiously informed elites. The source of change must now differ from one context to another because of the multiplicity and increased intensity of influences operative in societies of Asia, Africa, Latin America, and Oceania, including, specifically, influences from the West.

It may also be asked whether, given the very long term over which the inherited model posits the process of secularization as taking place, there may not also have been occasions, or even epochs, of "resacralization," which would account for the slowness of the process of secularization. Certainly, it is an open question whether secularization is reversible. It would be difficult to demonstrate that any such reversals have ever occurred. Mere processes of religious change, however, such as occurred as Christianity was transplanted throughout Europe, are not, in a sociological view, a resacralization; indeed, given the exclusivity that Christianity embraced from its origins, and the rationalizing disposition that Christianity eventually acquired, this diffusion of Christian faith may be said to have been the beginning of a secularization process that disciplined and partially absorbed and partially evacuated the religiosity of indigenous populations, eventually virtually eradicating its earlier manifestations. The process, nearly complete in Europe, continues, perhaps at a different pace, in Latin America and the Christianized parts of Africa.

At a less than societal level, periodic reform and revivalism might also appear to be reversals of the process of secularization. Closer examination of such relatively sudden upsurges in religious activity, however, are interpreted according to the secularization thesis as revealing the long-term effect of revitalization movements—not so much a restoration of the past as an accommodation of the pressing claims of the present. The Reformation is readily interpreted as a movement of secularization reducing the institutional power of religion and circumscribing the sacerdotalism and sacramentalism of the past. Processes of laicization accompanied subsequent revivalism, from Methodism to Pentecostalism, and even though the intensified religious commitment amounted to a resocialization of hitherto unaccommodated social groups, inducing work commitment and reinforcing social control, they nonetheless did not bring concepts of the sacred back to a central place in the social system. After a time, their effects weakened, the religiosity waned, even when new standards of duty and decency were disseminated. Once again, the magical and the emotional elements receded, and what was left—for as long as it lasted—was an ethical deposit. These inchoate moral dispositions, which were once religiously charged, were, for the remainder of their existence, effectively secularized. The new movements came to impose their own discipline which, in the Christian case, was eventually valuable as a social attribute facilitating the operation of a social system that functions without recourse to concepts of the supernatural.

The secularization process is recognized in the inherited model as being slow because religious dispositions are deep-laid in man's essential irrationality, which resists the rationalization of the external social order. The fears, hopes, fantasies, the search for meaning and wish fulfillment, and the encapsulation of these tendencies in folklore and local custom have provided religion with source materials. Local groups, and their ethnic, national, and class extensions, have had their identities sanctified and have acquired transcendent legitimation from religious formulations. At least for some, purpose, meaning, and motivation continue today to be enhanced by religious legitimation, and to be reinforced by religious supplication. Traditionally, religion supplied total and final explanations, not so much for intellectual and technical as for emotional and moral problems. It is the increasing dominance of the intellectual, scientific, technical, and practical over the emotional and the moral which is the basic premise of the inherited model of secularization. The secularization thesis acknowledges the unevenness of the decline in the significance of religion, and recognizes that this decline presents problems for the socializing and motivating of men, and the diffusion of dispositions conducive to public order.

Religious institutions are also slow to succumb entirely to the rationalizing tendencies of contemporary social systems, even though there is a process of internal secularization in religious institutions. These institutions fulfill other functions, some of which are quite specific to particular societies in particular historical periods, besides their functions in maintaining conceptions of the supernatural and stimulating the service and worship of it, and these other functions facilitate their endurance. The rhetoric (sometimes including liturgies) of past religion persists in these institutions, even though it is not always entertained with due intellectual seriousness. Even in the very attenuated religiosity of contemporary "liberal" churches, there is thus still reference to ultimate values, and still the canvas of religiously inspired moral dispositions and emotional orientations. Religion still facilitates communal expression, particularly when there is moral crisis, and no other agency claims the transcendent legitimacy which religious institutions still claim. More regularly, religion still provides occasions and opportunities for the private expression of emotions and aspirations, providing a language in terms of which individuals may choose to interpret their human experience. The secularization of the social system does not at once displace these attributes of religiosity; the native dispositions of man himself resist, in various aspects of experience, the rationalization that increasingly characterizes social systems.

Basically, the inherited model of secularization is concerned with the operation of the social system. It is the *system* that becomes secularized. Conceptions of the supernatural may not disappear, either as rhetorical public expressions or as private predilections, but they cease to be the determinants of social action. The system no longer functions, even notionally, to fulfill the will of God. Neither institutions nor individuals operate primarily to attain supernatural ends. As Comte predicted, and in ways that Max Weber indicated, rational planning and the deployment of new technology invoke as their justification the goal of human well-being, not the greater glory of God. Human consciousness is itself depicted as changing in response to the increasingly rational patterns of social organization and the imposition on man of increasingly abstract patterns of role playing. Men learn to regulate their behavior to conform to the rational premises built into the social order; action must be calculated, systematic, regulated, and routinized. In their private lives, men do not abandon their evaluative, emotional dispositions, and they may continue to resort to the supernatural for private gratification, but such dispositions are allowed to affect the public sphere to only a limited and decreasing extent. In his public roles, irrational man even contributes to the increasingly rational character of external order in an environment that is increasingly man-made. The secularization thesis implies the privatization of religion; its continuing operation in the public domain becomes confined to a lingering rhetorical invocation in support of conventional morality and human decency and dignity—as a cry of despair in the face of moral panic.

Various aspects of religious behavior may, at least for some time, remain independent of the major processes of secularization of the social system. Thus, although religious observance ceases to be obligatory (itself an evidence of the increasingly secularity of society), it continues as a much commended voluntaristic exercise. Even so, churchgoing and other patterns of religious observance are activities that carry many extrareligious connotations: they express cultural conservatism, conventionality, attachment to custom, and claims to social status, according to the specific historical and psychological features of each society. Even apparent manifestations of religiosity are, then, not always what they seem. And despite some persistence of religious observance, there are intrinsic changes in religious ideology and procedures, mostly in a secularizing direction. The inherited model of secularization does not predict the eventual total eclipse of all religion, however. In this private sphere, religion often continues, and even acquires new forms of expression, many of them much less related to other aspects of culture than were the religions of the past. (This lack of relation is also an evidence of the inconsequentiality of religion for the social system.) Yet, the very rationalization of society's operation and its dessicating effect on everyday life may provide their own inducement for individuals privately to take up the vestiges of ancient myths and arcane lore and ceremonies, in the search for authentic fantasy, power, possibilities of manipulation, and alternative sources of private gratification. In this sense, religion remains an alternative culture, observed as unthreatening to the modern social system, in much the same way that entertainment is seen as unthreatening. It offers another world to explore as an escape from the rigors of technological order and the ennui that is the incidental by-product of an increasingly programmed world.

C H A P T E R
18

Commercial Culture and American Christianity

Twentieth-century Americans are notoriously a nation of consumers. As any tel-evangelist show confirms, this includes religion. But long before the twentieth cen-tury, religious movements learned they would have to compete in the marketplace if they were to gain "market share" for their faith or denomination. This meant they would have to entertain. The eighteenth-century revivalist George Whitefield inau-gurated a tradition of highly entertaining, theatrical revivals to bring listeners into his evangelical camp. Since then American audiences have never looked back. If Ameri-can religion is voluntary, edifying, and conversionist, it is also entertaining. Whether by word-of-mouth, pamphlet, radio, television or, around the corner, CD-ROM, reli-gious entrepreneurs have stopped at nothing to publicize the truths they proclaim.

This article by Leigh Eric Schmidt suggests that the continuing rise in religious interest and affiliation in late nineteenth- and early twentieth-century America may come from Christianity's increasing commercialization, not just from traditional church activities. Thus, according to Schmidt, organized religion probably profited from the sophistication of American retailers, who eagerly incorporated religious themes in their commercial enterprises, from the "Easter Parade" to Christmas. Are there equivalents to the Easter parade today? Why do retailers find in religion such a compelling theme? Does this suggest new connections between religion and capi-talism? Is the retailing of religion a "bad thing"?

Additional Reading: An important overview of American religion and the market-place is R. Laurence Moore, *Selling God: American Religion in the Marketplace of Culture* (New York, 1994). A recent and controversial study by two sociologists de-scribes American religion as a "religious economy." See Roger Finke and Rodney Stark, *The Church of America, 1776–1990: Winners and Losers in Our Religious Economy* (New Brunswick, 1992). On religion and holidays see: Leigh Eric Schmidt, *Consumer Rites: The Buying and Selling of American Holidays* (Princeton, 1995); M. Golby and A. W. Purdue, *The Making of the Modern Christmas* (Athens, Ga.,

1986); and Clement A. Miles, *Christmas in Ritual and Tradition, Christian and Pagan* (London, 1912). Recent studies on religion and mass media include: Steve Bruce, *Televangelism in America* (London, 1990); Jeffrey Hadden and Anson Shupe, *Televangelism, Power, and Politics on God's Frontier* (New York, 1988); Peter Horsfield, *Religious Television: The American Experience* (New York, 1984); Gregor T. Goethals, *The Electronic Golden Calf: Images, Religion, and the Making of Meaning* (Cambridge, 1990); and Tyron Inbody, (ed.), *Changing Channels: The Church and the Television Revolution* (Dayton, 1990).

Leigh Eric Schmidt   # The Easter Parade: Piety, Fashion, and Display

Irving Berlin's popular musical of 1948, *Easter Parade,* starring Fred Astaire and Judy Garland, opens with a wonderful shopping scene. It is the day before Easter, 1911. Astaire's character, Don Hewes, sings and dances his way along the streets of New York past a dry-goods store and through millinery, florist, and toy shops. "Me, oh, my," he sings, "there's a lot to buy. There is shopping I must do. Happy Easter to you." In the millinery store saleswomen model elaborate Easter bonnets and mellifluously offer their wares: "Here's a hat that you must take home. Happy Easter. . . . This was made for the hat parade on the well-known avenue. This one's nice and it's worth the price. Happy Easter to you." Everywhere Hewes goes he buys things—a bonnet, a large pot of lilies, a toy bunny. By the time he leaves the florist, he has purchased so many gifts that he is followed by three attendants who help carry all the packages. Don Hewes is a consumer on a spree, and Easter is the occasion for it.[1]

With a boyish exuberance, Hewes prepares for Easter by shopping. His efforts are aimed not at readying himself for church or sacrament but at insuring that his companion will make a fine appearance in New York's fashion parade. The opening chorus chirrups this theme: "In your Easter bonnet with all the frills upon it, you'll be the grandest lady in the Easter parade. I'll be all in clover, and when they look you over, I'll be the proudest fellow in the Easter parade." Fulfillment consists of having his consort admired with envious gazes. When Hewes and his new dance partner, a humble show girl who doubles as a barmaid, actually encounter the promenade the next day, she is overawed. "I can't believe I'm really here," she gasps. "You know, I used to read about the Easter parade in New York, and then I'd look at the pictures of the women in their lovely clothes and dream that maybe someday I'd . . ." Her voice trails off in wonder and dreamy aspiration. The only religious image in the film appears in the last scene when the Easter parade has returned for another year. A Gothic church looms as a dim backdrop for the fancily dressed couples who stroll by in a streaming concourse of affluence.

Reprinted from *Religion and American Culture,* vol. 4, no. 2, by permission of Indiana University Press.

The film is not primarily about Easter, of course, but about Astaire and Garland and their marvelous dancing and singing. But the movie and Berlin's popular theme song are illuminating texts about the American Easter all the same. From at least the 1800's through 1950's, this dress parade was one of the primary cultural expressions of Easter in the United States, one of the fundamental ways that the occasion was identified and celebrated. The holy day blossomed in the late nineteenth century into a cultural rite of spring with elaborate floral decorations, new clothes, fancy millinery, chocolate bunnies, greeting cards, and other gifts. The movie, like the Easter parade itself, embodied an expansive public faith in American abundance, a gospel of wealth, self-gratification, and prosperity: "Everything seems to come your way," the chorus lilts, "Happy Easter!"

In his recent novel *Operation Shylock,* Philip Roth celebrates Irving Berlin's *Easter Parade* for its creative de-Christianization of the festival, for its promotion of a "schlockified Christianity" in which the bonnet overthrows the cross.[2] But, in many ways, Berlin was merely offering a catchy, hummable benediction for the fashionable modern festival that American Christians had been busily creating for themselves over the previous century. This consumer-oriented Easter actually had deep religious wellsprings, and the juxtapositions of Christian devotion and lavish display were as richly polychromatic as the holiday flowers and fashions themselves. Fathoming the growing significance attached to church decoration in the second half of the nineteenth century is of first importance in making sense of this modern Easter. These religious patterns of embellishment, in turn, fed commercial holiday displays and spectacles of Easter merchandising. Lushly adorned churches provided the backdrop for finely appareled congregants and for the efflorescence of the Easter parade in New York City and elsewhere. All along, this Easter fanfare elicited sharp criticism from devotees of simplicity and plainness; that is, from those who were alienated from this faith of comfortable materialism, an estrangement that was often etched in sharply gendered terms. A complementary yet contested relationship between American Christianity and the modern consumer culture became increasingly evident in the second half of the nineteenth century, and that conjunction found performance in the Easter festival.

THE ART OF CHURCH DECORATION AND THE ART OF WINDOW DISPLAY

The Gothic church that flickers in the last frames of *Easter Parade* stands very much in the background, perhaps a nostalgic image—distant, unobtrusive, evanescent. Yet, to understand the development of the Easter parade as a cultural and religious event, this neo-Gothic edifice and others like it have to be brought into the foreground. Churches such as Trinity Episcopal Church, St. Patrick's Cathedral, and St. Thomas's Episcopal Church in New York City, with their rich Gothic ornament, are central, not peripheral, to this story. The elaborate decorations that these splendid urban churches created for ecclesiastical festivals such as Christmas and Easter are crucial for fathoming the emergence of a fashionable Easter in the second half of the nineteenth century. The newly cultivated art of church decoration, in turn, helped inspire inventive window trimmers and interior designers in their creation of holiday spectacles for merchandising purposes.

Easter, even more than Christmas, remained under a Puritan and evangelical cloud in the antebellum United States. Though various denominations all along preserved the holiday—most prominently Episcopalians, Roman Catholics, Lutherans, and Moravians—their celebrations were, until mid-century, localistic, parochial, and disparate. The festival became a well-nigh ubiquitous cultural event only in the decades after 1860 as low-church Protestant resistance or indifference gave way to approbation and as Episcopalian, Roman Catholic, and new immigrant observances became ever more prominent. Middle-class Victorians, fascinated with the recovery of fading holiday traditions and the cultivation of new home-centered festivities, discovered lush possibilities in this spring rite. The *New York Herald,* in a report on "Eastertide" in 1881, proclaimed that "A few years ago and Easter as a holiday was scarcely thought of, except by the devout; now all are eager to join in the celebration." Between about 1860 and 1890, Easter took distinctive religious and cultural shape as an American holiday.[3]

In an 1863 article on Easter, *Harper's New Monthly Magazine* suggested the growing embrace of the feast in American culture. "It is one of the obvious marks of our American religion," the article related, "that we are noticing more habitually and affectionately the ancient days and seasons of the Christian Church." Easter, following Christmas's rising popularity, showed "unmistakable signs that it is fast gaining upon the religious affection and public regard of our people." "We have carefully noted the gradual increase of observance of the day," the journal continued, "and can remember when it was a somewhat memorable thing for a minister, not Catholic or Episcopal, to preach an Easter sermon." What the magazine found most revealing of "this new love for Easter," however, was the increasing use of elaborate floral decorations for the festival. "Easter flowers are making their way into churches of all persuasions," the magazine applauded. "One of our chief Presbyterian churches near by decked its communion-table and pulpit with flowers for the third time this Easter season." The writer praised Easter floral displays for their artistic taste and devotional symbolism—their "ministry of the beautiful." The splendor of Easter flowers embodied the new compelling allure of the festival.[4]

In lauding Easter flowers, the *Harper's* piece was celebrating the expanding art of church decoration. As a liturgical movement, this art effloresced in England and the United States in the middle decades of the nineteenth century. An outgrowth of the ritualist or Catholic turn within Angelican and Episcopalian circles, the new forms of church decoration meshed with the Gothic revival in Victorian church architecture and ornament. English writers such as William A. Barrett and Ernest Geldart led the way in formalizing the rubrics of modern church decoration in a number of handbooks that helped foster and guide the burgeoning art on both sides of the Atlantic. These writers codified a new aesthetic for church adornment, nostalgically medieval and Gothic in its vision but decidedly Victorian and modern in its elaboration. They cultivated what T. J. Jackson Lears has called "the religion of beauty"—a devotional love of liturgical drama, material symbolism, polychromatic color, sumptuous music, and graceful ornament. They wanted to fill the churches, as one handbook attested, with "sermons in stones, in glass, in wood, in flowers, and fruits, and leaves."[5]

Much of this ritual adornment focused on the high holy days of Christmas and Easter. Festooning the interior of churches with evergreens, flowers, vines, mosses, berries, leaves, wreaths, illuminated texts, emblems, tracery, and other devices became holiday staples. Indeed, such festal decorations reached modish proportions among Victorian churchgoers. "Few fashions," Edward L. Cutts commented in 1868 in the third edition of his handbook on church decoration, "have made such rapid progress within the last few years as the improved fashion of Decorating our Churches with evergreens and flowers for the great Church festivals." By 1882, another leading advocate of the "new fashion," Ernest Geldart, could remark that "it requires an effort of memory to recall the days when, save a few ill-set sprigs of holly at Christmas, none of these things were known."[6]

Christmas initially led the way in church decoration, but Easter soon came to rival, if not surpass, the winter feast for special adornment. Ernest R. Suffling commented on Easter's ascent in his manual *Church Festival Decorations:*

> Decorating the church at Easter, which a generation ago was but feebly carried out, has now become a recognized and general institution, and at no season of the year is it more appropriate. The joy of our hearts at the Resurrection of our Saviour—the seal of the completion of His work on earth—must surely be even greater than on the festival of His birth. The festival, coming as it does in early spring, is best commemorated by the use of as many flowers as possible.[7]

Weaving garlands around pillars, covering fonts and reading desks with fresh blooms, hanging wreaths from arches and rails, erecting floral crosses on the altar or communion table, filling windowsills with bouquets, setting up vine-covered trellises, and creating pyramids of lilies—in short, putting flowers everywhere—became an Easter vogue of dazzling proportions.

One way to render specific the rising importance of floral decorations at Easter is through diaries. The journal of Henry Dana Ward, rector of St. Jude's Episcopal Church in New York City, survives for the years 1850 to 1857, and it suggests the budding interest in Easter flowers. He mentioned no special floral displays for his Easter services from 1850 to 1854, but, in 1855, he noted that "the recess behind the Table was furnished with three pots of flowers in full bloom and the Font with the same in partial bloom." Ward thought that the flowers, all "Egyptian lilies," were pretty and pleasing, adding to the solemnity of the service. Of these decorations, as well as new coverings for the communion table and the pulpit, he took comfort that "no one was offended by these small novelties." He also made clear that his forays into festal decoration were tame compared to those of some other Episcopal churches. Visiting an afternoon Easter service at Trinity in 1857, he found the ritualism and decorations excessive: "They make *too much* of a good thing—chant the Anthems to death—and make a show of flowers on the Font & the reading Desk."[8] Decades before "the concept of show invaded the domain of culture" in the form of showplaces, showrooms, and fashion shows, churches like Trinity were cultivating a festive, luxuriant, and dramatic religious world through the increasingly ornate art of church decoration.[9] This sense of Easter decorations as a show or spectacle would become all the more evident in the decades after the Civil War.

The diary of a young man who worked as a clerk for Tiffany's in New York City in the early 1870's suggests the dramatic impression that Easter decorations made. For Easter 1873, he went to a morning service at Christ Church and an afternoon service at St. Stephen's, both of which he found "magnificent," if fearfully crowded. The two churches, "well trimmed with beautiful flowers," were stunning in their decorations. He continued:

> At Christs Church the burning star they had Christmas was over the alter [*sic*] besides the decorations of flowers. At St Stephens was arranged in the same manner—gas jets[.] Over the alter [*sic*] (as if it was there without anything to keep it there) was suspended a cross and above over it a crown. The effect was very good[,] the flaming of the gas making it so brilliant.[10]

The decorations clearly made a lasting impression on this young man (here at Easter he still remembers the blazing star from the previous Christmas). Indeed, he seemed far more overawed by the decorations that he saw in New York's Episcopal and Catholic churches than anything he came across in New York's stores. For theatrical effect, the stores in the 1870's still had much to learn from the churches.

The special floral decorations for Easter received particular attention in women's diaries. An active Baptist laywoman in New York City, Sarah Todd, commented in her diary on a visit to an Episcopal church for an Easter service in 1867: "Being Easter Sunday the Church was handsomely dressed with flowers." Likewise, in her diary, New Yorker Elizabeth Merchant often made note of the Easter display of flowers: "Our church was beautifully dressed with flowers," she wrote of Easter 1883; "The church was lovely with flowers," she recalled of Easter worship in 1886; "Flowers perfectly beautiful & Mr Brooks splendid," she eulogized of two Easter services at Trinity Episcopal that she and her son enjoyed in 1887. Another New York woman made similar notations about Easter in her diary, writing in 1888: "Easter Day, Communion Sunday. Flowers in church. Alice & I took the children to the Church to see the flowers." Decorations seen, as much as sermons heard or eucharistic elements received, stood out in the memories that these women recorded. Perhaps for women especially, who often took charge of these floral displays, Easter in the churches became preeminently a time of flowers.[11]

The implications and consequences of the new fascination with Easter decorations were manifold. Certainly, and perhaps quintessentially, this art constituted an important new medium for religious expression. The decorations were devotional; their "double purpose" was to glorify God and edify wayfaring Christians. At Trinity Episcopal in 1861, the *New York Sun* reported, the Easter floral decorations were "in fine taste": "Flowers suggestive of the fundamental doctrines of Christianity composed the ornaments, and were so grouped as to indicate the cardinal truths of religion. In the centre of the altar was a floral globe mounted by a cross, and expressive of the redemption of the world." Floral decorations, testifying to the promise of new life, became for Victorians one of the dominant ways of communicating the Christian message of resurrection. To make certain that the devotional significance of the decorations remained clear, the churches often prominently displayed illuminated scriptural texts, usually drawn in intricate Gothic lettering. Arches and altars, chancels and choirs, brimmed with monumental affirmations: "He is risen"; "I am the Resurrection and the Life"; "Now is Christ risen from the dead, the first-fruits of them that slept"; "O death, where is thy sting? O grave, where is thy victory?" Easter decorations were a form of popular piety that evoked the ancient coalescence of the rebirth of spring and the resurrection of Christ.[12]

In their devotional dimensions, Easter decorations also suggested a sentimental and domestic version of Christian piety. Easter, *Harper's* said, was "winning our household feeling as well as our religious respect"; it served as a liturgical affirmation of the eternality of "family affections," as a celebration of "the great sentiment of home love." This domestic tenor was evident in the increasing overlap of church and home decorations: lilies, floral crosses, and distinctive Easter bouquets, for example, all ornamented Victorian altars and parlors alike. The decorative result was to join the church and the home in a shared, overarching design—"the House Beautiful."[13] Moreover, flowers suggested how Easter was becoming preeminently "the festival of sacred remembrance." Easter blooms, lilies especially, were presented in the churches as personal memorials for "departed kindred and friends"; they were hopeful, powerful tokens of the restored wholeness of familial circles. Indeed, the new love of Easter flowers was at one level the liturgical counterpart to Elizabeth Stuart Phelp's Victorian best-seller *The Gates Ajar*—a sentimental, consoling portrayal of heaven in terms of home, family, and friends. The new Easter helped reinforce the Victorian predilection for picturing heaven more as a place of human relationships and domestic reunions than as a God-centered realm of divine praise, light, and glory.[14]

The new passion for floral decoration clearly carried consequences that were not only devotional and domestic. For one thing, issues of competition and emulation crept into the Easter displays. The handbooks warned against the tendencies toward extravagance and rivalry: "Never try to beat the record," Ernest Geldart instructed. "Pray don't let it be your ambition that prompts you to 'beat' anything you have ever done, and above all, don't try to beat your neighbour's efforts." Admonitions notwithstanding, competition became an acknowledged undercurrent in holiday decoration. Who would have the most beautiful and extensive floral displays? Who would have the most inspiring music, the most solemn, dramatic, and crowded services? As the *New York Herald* observed in 1881, "The Catholics and Episcopalians are, of course, the foremost in the observance of the season, but other denominations are not far behind, and all vie with each other to make their house the most attractive to the worshipper." In America's free-market religious culture, church decoration became another way of attracting parishioners and gaining attention. Less ritualistic denominations—Presbyterians, Methodists, and even Baptists—learned to emulate Episcopalian and Catholic forms of holiday celebration in order to hold the allegiance of their people at these seasons of the year. Thorstein Veblen was wrong to view the "devout consump-

tion" of the churches in the 1890's—their increasingly elaborate "ceremonial para-
phernalia"—simply in terms of "status" and "conspicuous waste" (such an interpretation was irredeemably monochromatic and reductionistic.) But he was right
to see competition and emulation as component parts of Victorian church furnish-
ing and decoration.[15]

Another unintended consequence of holiday church decoration was how it
fostered modishness and exoticism. In 1867, the *New York Herald,* in commenting
on the "elaborate floral decorations" for Easter at St. John the Baptist Episcopal
Church, noted that the display included "one of the only three genuine palms
known to exist in the United States." Similarly, the *Herald's* 1873 report on the
Easter decorations in the Church of the Divine Paternity struck the same chord of
rarity: "Surmounting the reredos was a magnificent cross made of lilies, on either
side of which were two recumbent beds of roses. The altar was profusely covered
with the rarest of exotics." Ernest Suffling, summarizing this trend toward floral
exoticism—if not colonialist rampage—observed that where a few "indigenous
evergreens" had formerly satisfied the church decorator, now "we ransack the
whole world, for our grasses, flowers, and palms, or fruits and mosses." There
was little that was traditional, antimodern, or medieval, the *New York Sun* declared, in searching out "rare evergreens," "choice tropicals," or "calla lilies of remarkable size and beauty, sent hermetically sealed from California." Style, taste,
abundance, and novelty—the very values of the burgeoning consumer culture—
became defining features of Easter decorations in the churches. The fashionable
Easter given expression in the Easter parade and in turn-of-the-century department stores had its roots in the religious culture, which itself was becoming progressively more consumerist in its modes of celebration. At Easter, devout consumption fed its more worldly counterpart.[16]

A final, portentous consequence of the new art of church decoration was that
it provided a model or repertory for holiday displays outside the churches in the
marketplace. With Easter, even more than with Christmas, the commercial culture
built its enterprise very directly on the religious culture—on Christian patterns of
decoration, display, and celebration. Church music, flowers, ornaments, banners,
and other decorations all found their way into show windows and interior displays in late-nineteenth- and early twentieth-century department stores. Easter
decorations were clearly very attractive for commercial appropriation; their associations with the church, with women and the home, with fashion and affluence,
were all useful connections for merchandising. With multiple layers of meaning,
Easter emblems, popularized through church decoration, provided retailers with
rich and redolent symbols. More broadly, the art of church decoration offered a
useful aesthetic for the art of store decoration. Church decorators, like their commercial counterparts after them, stressed the power of visual representation, the
importance of harmonizing form and color, the careful planning of designs, and
the expressive potentialities of lighting and glass. Church decorators also provided a principle of innovation, regularly experimenting with new decorative materials and warning against "sameness," "feeble repetition," and "distasteful mo-
notony" in beautifying the sanctuary. This outlook intermeshed with the
mounting desire of window trimmers and store decorators to bring seasonal

variety and originality to their display of goods. Thus, in surprising and hitherto little seen ways, the art of church decoration helped generate what William Leach has called "the display aesthetic" that came to characterize the modern consumer culture.[17]

Irving Berlin's *Easter Parade* in itself suggests the migration of church decoration into the marketplace: Don Hewes passes the show window of a dry-goods store that is trimmed with Easter lilies, as is the interior of the millinery shop he patronizes. The transformation of church decorations into store embellishments was evident as early as the 1880's and 1890's. "Make a gala week of the week before Easter," the *Dry Goods Chronicle* exhorted in 1898. "Tog your store out until it shines with the Easter spirit. . . . Blossom with the Easter lily, give your store a dress in keeping with this Easter festival." This kind of advice was regularly put into practice. "The store is in harmony with the occasion," Wanamaker's Easter catalog boasted in 1893; "Easter Symbols are everywhere in the decorations. . . . Easter merchandise is all over the store." By the turn of the century, such Easter displays and embellishments had become standard trade preparations: lavish store decorations were considered essential for imparting and evoking the Easter spirit and for attracting holiday shoppers.[18]

All along, trimming a store for Easter meant a profusion of seasonal folk symbols such as rabbits, chicks, and eggs. It also meant a surplus of Christian iconography—miniature churches, choirs, pipe organs, stained glass, crosses, lilies, religious banners, and devotional mottoes. The *American Advertiser* offered this description of a "delicate and pleasing" Easter window in a Chicago jewelry store in 1890:

> The window floor was covered with white jeweler's cotton in sheets, looking pure as snow. A cross of similar material and whiteness was slightly raised above the level of the window-floor, in the middle rear part of the window. On each side of the window was a calla lily blossom, the flower being cut short off below the bloom. Inside the lily, like a drop of purest dew, sparkled a diamond—just one on each lily. The cross was slightly twined with smilax, which also bordered the back of the window. A white rose was scattered here and there, and on the cross and on the white window floor were displayed a few gems and trinkets,—not enough to distract the attention or give the appearance of crowding. . . . Taken altogether the display was the perfection of good taste and artistic skill.

The cross and lilies, staples of church decoration, became mainstays of the window dresser's art—repeated centerpieces for the display of goods, whether millinery, greeting cards, or even groceries. In this case, jewelry and other items were actually attached to the lilies and the cross, making their linkage direct and tangible.[19]

Designs for show windows also played upon the sentimental, domestic dimensions of Victorian Easter piety. One window trimmer bragged in 1896 of a crowd-shopping Easter display that proved pleasing to patrons and proprietor alike. Entitled "Gates Ajar," the window was trimmed from floor to ceiling "with spotless white silk handkerchiefs entwined with ferns and smilax from the millinery stock and plants from the hot-house." The focal point of the window was "a flight of five steps, at the head of which was a large double gate, partially opened, so as to show one large figure in white silk and pretty little cherubs (dolls with wings of gold and silver paper) as if in the act of flying." This show-window glimpse of silky white seraphs and everlasting life dovetailed with the alluring domestic heaven depicted in Elizabeth Stuart Phelps's *Gates Ajar* and its sequels. In *The Feminization of American Culture,* Ann Douglas wryly comments that reading Phelps's novels about heaven with all their luminous detail about domestic furnishings and possessions "is somewhat like window-shopping outside the fanciest stores on Fifth Avenue." Window trimmers and store decorators had the same intuition. In their appropriation of Phelps's themes, they made explicit the otherwise implicit interconnections between this domestic piety and consumerist ideals.[20]

Store decorations for Easter were often more elaborate than such relatively modest show windows and sometimes rivaled the churches in what one window trimmer called "cathedral effect[s]." This decorative intricacy was epitomized in the Easter adornment in Wanamaker's in Philadelphia. As was the case at Christmas, Wanamaker's Grand Court was transformed at Easter into a religious spectacle. Statues of angels, thousands of lilies and ferns, displays of ornate ecclesiastical vestaments, religious banners and tapestries, and mottoes proclaiming "He is Risen!" and "Alleluia!" all found place in Wanamaker's during the Easter season in the early decades of this century. The store's grandest Easter spectacle, however, was the annual display, beginning in the mid-1920's, of two monumental canvases by the Hungarian artist Michael de Munkacsy—one painting (20' 8" by 13' 6"), entitled *Christ before Pilate,* and the other (23' 4" by 14' 2"), entitled *Christ on Calvary.* Painted respectively in 1881 and 1884, these works had been widely exhibited and heralded in this country and had achieved international repute in their day as grand masterpieces. Purchased by John Wanamaker as favored treasures for his own impressive collection of art, the paintings were eventually put on display in the Grand Court each year during Lent and Easter. The exhibition of paintings with this level of acclaim was something that the churches could rarely match or duplicate. Easter displays like these brought into sharp relief the dynamic interplay of art, piety, and commerce in the American marketplace. Easter in Wanamaker's epitomized the translation of the Gothic revival and the art of church decoration into a commercial idiom.[21]

Discerning the meaning and significance of the varied Christian emblems that found their way into show windows and department stores is no easy task. What did religious symbols—such as the cross, lilies, church replicas, or the Agnus Dei—come to symbolize when placed within the context of Easter displays? In the ersatz, artful, and cunning world of the marketplace, the meanings of symbols were particularly unstable, uncertain, and slippery. Perhaps such religious emblems became quite literally so much window dressing, that is, artificial, distracting, and illusory fluff, little more than splashes of color and attractive packaging, a vapid and insincere mimicry of liturgical art. Certainly, the employment of religious symbols as merchandising icons carried an undeniable artifice and doubleness, a sharp edge of deception. In their intramural discussions of display techniques, window trimmers were often quite candid about their purposes. L. Frank Baum, who started in the fantasy world of show windows before moving on to the *Wizard of Oz*, commented matter-of-factly on the place of the cross in Easter displays: "The cross is the principal emblem of Easter and is used in connection with many displays, being suitable for any line of merchandise. To be most effective it should be a floral cross." The essential object in window dressing was, after all, to sell goods, and religious symbols, as with all display props, were used self-consciously to maximize this effect. Creatively negotiating the borderland between commerce and Christianity was part of the window trimmer's calling, and these Easter icons were, at one level, simply another trick of the trade.[22]

But these displays represented more than commercial artifice. The widespread infusion of religious symbols into the marketplace also suggested the deep hold of Christianity on the culture and indicated anew how "adaptable" American religion was to "popular commercial forms."[23] Far from eschewing Christian emblems, retailers seized the opportunity to consecrate their stores through holiday decorations. Often enough, churchgoing merchants employed these emblems straightforwardly to evoke and affirm the old-time piety; certainly John Wanamaker, YMCA leader and Sunday school titan, understood his cathedral-like decorations and his in-store choir concerts in religious terms. The density of spiritual referents was, after all, what made these symbols so powerful; it is also, of course, what made them so useful. Still, the manipulation, misappropriation, or displacement of Christian symbols was rarely the issue for merchants or customers: in these displays, Christian hopes and consumerist dreams regularly merged into a cohesive cultural whole. Rather than shunting aside the church, the department stores (and the emergent mass culture that these institutions represented) accorded Christianity considerable cultural authority during the holidays. And, in some ways, merchants seemed to be doing exactly what liberal Protestant pundits had been calling for; namely, the wholesale sacralization of the marketplace. Social gospeller George Herron exhorted "the Christian business men of America" to "make the marketplace as sacred as the church." "You can draw the world's trades and traffics within the onsweep of Christ's redemptive purpose," Herron insisted. Wanamaker and other merchants like him were seen by many Protestants as the consummate consecrators of wealth and the market. In the "one undivided Kingdom of God," commerce and Christianity would harmoniously support one another. The turn-of-the-century celebrations of Christmas and Easter in the department stores were the festivals of that liberal cultural faith. Indeed, in some ways, they represented a re-visioning in modern Protestant guise of the "festive marketplace" of the Middle Ages and the Renaissance in which church celebration met the "brimming-over abundance of the fair."[24]

This seemingly happy convergence of Christianity and consumption suggested in itself, however, a profound transformation in the meaning of Christian symbols. The stores all too clearly presented a new prosperity gospel that was far removed from traditional Christian emphases on self-abnegation. "When I survey the wondrous cross on which the Prince of glory died," Isaac Watts had versified in the eighteenth century in lines his Victorian heirs still sang, "My richest gain I count but loss, and pour contempt on all my pride. . . . All the vain things that charm me most, I sacrifice them to his blood." Surveying the wondrous cross within a show window or a department store effectively shifted the foundations of this crucicentric piety from self-denial to self-fulfillment. The very context in which these symbols appeared suggested a substantial revision of the faith—a new image of piety at peace with plenty and at home in the new "dream world" of mass consumption. This was no small subversion. Traditional Christian symbols of self-abnegation had come to legitimate luxury, elegance, and indulgence. The cross itself had become one of the charms of the merchandiser's art, its religious power absorbed into the new magic of modern commodities and advertising.[25]

PIETY, FASHION, AND A SPRING PROMENADE

The vogue for Easter flowers and church decoration intertwined with other Easter fashions—those in clothing and millinery. Of an Easter service at Christ Church, an Episcopal congregation on Fifth Avenue, the *New York Herald* wrote in 1873: "More than one-half of the congregation were ladies, who displayed all the gorgeous and marvelous articles of dress which Dame Fashion has submitted to be the ruling idea of Spring, and the appearance of the body of the church thus vied in effect and magnificence with the pleasant and tasteful array of flowers which decorated the chancel." In a similar vein, a reporter compared "the costumes of the ladies" at St. Patrick's Cathedral for Easter 1871 with "a parterre of flowers." Since spring millinery fashions actually tended to include various flora and fauna, such comparisons were not mere similes. Fashions in flowers and dress, indeed, interpenetrated one another. In 1897, for example, the *New York Times* reported that violets were in greater demand than any other Easter flower "because the violet, in all its various shades, is the predominating color in dress." The very development of the Easter parade along Fifth Avenue was in part connected with the popularity of visiting the different churches to see their elaborate floral decorations. "Many will go to church to-day to see the flowers," the *New York Times* observed in 1889, "and not a few are accustomed to join the parade on Fifth-avenue from church to church, just to look at the beautiful productions of nature." The Victorian love of Easter flowers and church decoration blossomed naturally into the famous promenade of fashions.

Having new clothes for Easter or dressing up in special ways for the festival was never simply about modern fashions or modern forms of consumption and display. The practice had deep roots, or at least resonances, in European religious traditions and folk customs at Easter. Sacred times—baptisms, weddings, funerals, fasts, and feasts—warranted special forms of dress, material markers of holiness and celebration. Uncommon or distinctive garb for Easter, as with the Sunday best of the sabbatarian or the special vestments of priests, had long communicated the solemnity, sacrality, and seriousness of the occasion. The special raiment might be as simple as wearing new gloves, ribbons, or stockings or as stunning as dressing wholly in white. Conventions were localistic and diverse, but the overarching point was captured in an Irish adage: "For Christmas, food

and drink; for Easter, new clothes." A frequently recited maxim from Poor Robin
distilled such holiday expectations into a couplet:

> At Easter let your clothes be new,
> Or else be sure you will it rue.

This old English saying itself became part of the Victorian memory about
Easter, a selective slice of Easter folklore that helped people situate their own in-
terest in new attire for the holiday within the comforting framework of tradition.
As the *New York Herald* noted in 1855, "There is an old proverb that if on Easter
Sunday some part of your dress is not new you will have no good fortune that
year."[26]

The parade of Easter fashions in New York City emerged as a distinct religious and cultural event in the 1870's and 1880's, and the Easter services of the
churches were at the center of it. An account in 1873 in the *New York Herald* of "the
throngs of people" going to and from church suggested the parade's incipient
form:

> They were a gaily dressed crowd of worshippers, and the female portion of it
> seemed to have come out *en masse* in fresh apparel, and dazzled the eye with
> their exhibition of shade and color in the multiudinious and variegated hues of
> their garments. Fifty avenue, from Tenth street to the Central Park, from ten
> o'clock in the morning till late in the afternoon, was one long procession of
> men and women, whose attire and bearing betokened refinement, wealth and
> prosperity, and nearly all these were worshippers of some denomination or an-
> other, as the crowds that poured in and out of the various religious edifices
> along the line of the avenue amply testified.

By the end of the 1870's, the "fashionable promenade" was more clearly defined
in terms of the early afternoon, ensuing at the conclusion of the morning church
services: "In the afternoon," the *Herald* reported in 1879, "Fifth avenue was a brilliant sight when the thronging congregations of the various churches poured out
upon the sidewalks and leisurely journeyed homeward." *Le beau monde* flowed
out of the churches into a vast concourse of style, affluence, and luxury.[27]

In the 1880's, the afternoon promenade of Easter churchgoers became all the
more "the great fashion show of the year." By 1890, the procession had achieved
standing as a recognized marvel on New York's calendar of festivities and had
taken on its enduring designation as *the Easter parade*. As the *New York Times* reported in 1890, "It was the great Easter Sunday parade, which has become such an
established institution in New-York that the curious flock to Fifth-avenue almost
as numerously and enthusiastically as they do to see a circus parade." A spectacle
of new spring fashions, prismatic colors, Easter bouquets and corsages, elaborate
and ever-changing millinery, New York's "great Easter parade" was an occasion
for people "to see and be seen." By the mid-1890's, day-trippers from New Jersey
and Long Island as well as other visitors flocked to the Fifth Avenue pageant to
survey the fashions and to join in the promenade. Thus having begun as a procession of fashionable and privileged churchgoers, the parade quickly became a

jostling, crowded scene—"a kaleidoscope of humanity that changed incessantly and presented a new picture with every change."[28]

The emergence of the Easter parade presented a choice opportunity for dry-goods and millinery establishments. Surprisingly, however, retailers were not overly quick to push the promotional connection between Easter and seasonal fashions. While Christmas was already garnering the advertising attention of New York's emergent dry-goods palaces in the 1840's and 1850's as well as attracting the humbug of smaller shopkeepers even earlier, Easter went unnoticed. Spring openings were a merchandising staple for New York firms by the mid-nineteenth century, yet no advertising efforts were fabricated to link spring bonnets or other spring fashions explicitly to Easter. In the 1850's and 1860's, newspaper advertisements for seasonal apparel remained the same before and after Easter. Through the mid-1870's, few, if any, attempts were made to create a specific market for the holiday, even though the connection between Easter and new spring styles was already apparent in New York's most fashionable churches. Only in the late 1870's did New York's merchants begin to exploit the growing religious linkage between Easter and fashion. According to Ralph M. Hower, Macy's first began to promote goods specifically for Easter in its newspaper advertising in 1878, and this coincides with the early efforts of other retailers. For example, in the *New York Sun* in 1878, E. Ridley & Sons advertised "Trimmed Bonnets and Round Hats, Manufactured for Easter," and Lord & Taylor made a similar pitch. In the 1880's, almost all the leading department stores would join in this kind of advertising, thus bringing spring fashions and the Easter festival into explicit and deepening alliance.[29]

By the 1890's, promotion of Easter within the dry-goods industry was in full swing. There was no bigger event in the trade's calendar. "Easter is pre-eminently the festival of the dry goods trade," the *Dry Goods Economist* concluded in 1894. "Much of the success of the year's business hangs upon the demand experienced during the weeks just preceding Easter." Retailers did all they could to stoke the desire for Easter fashions. "Everything is done during these days to influence the shopper to buy," the *Dry Goods Economist* observed of the Easter season in 1894. "Windows are trimmed with all the art at the dresser's command and with as much study as the Royal Academician gives to a magnificent painting." Merchants had clearly come to see their role in the Easter festival as more than one of simply responding to a demand for seasonal goods. Instead, their goal was to expand the market, to deepen and widen these holiday customs. "Women may be induced to think more and more of something special for Easter by telling insinuations judiciously put in your advertising," the *Dry Goods Chronicle* theorized in 1898. "Women may be induced to forego the satisfying of some actual need in order to gratify an Easter fancy, provided you prod their vanity with suggestive advertising and supplement it with a fetching store display." As was the case with so many other dimensions of the expanding consumer culture, women were condescendingly cast as the arch-consumers at Easter and received most of the attention in its promotion. If merchants had been slow to get on the Easter bandwagon in the 1860's and 1870's, they were among its loudest trumpeters and trombonists by the 1890's. Through their tireless promotions, they helped define Easter as "a time for 'dress parade' and 'full feather.'"[30]

A spectacle of vast proportions, the Easter parade was assuredly a multivalent ritual, a multilayered cultural performance. For the devout, the season's new clothes were part of a synthesis of piety and material culture. As the gray of winter and the darkness of Lent and Good Friday gave way to the rebirth of spring and the Resurrection, the sumptuous hues of Easter fashions reflected these transitions. New Yorker Elizabeth Orr suggested this interplay of themes in her diary entry about Easter in 1871:

> Easter Sunday came in bright and beautiful[,] has been one of the most beautiful Spring days I ever experienced. Every one seemed to be influenced by the weather, bright happy faces. Most every one out in their holiday clothes gotten up for the occasion. Dr Eddy gave us one of his good discourses on the reserection [sic] of Christ and his followers. Oh that I may be one of that number! 'Am I his or Am I not' should be a question with us. I know and feel my sinfulness, and he came to save just such a sinner. I repent every day, and trust I am forgiven. Oh that happy day when we will have no more sin to repent of, but constantly [be] in the presence of our Lord and Master.[31]

In her recollections of the day's activities, the beautiful spring weather led naturally to promenading in holiday clothes, which connected seamlessly, in turn, with pious reflections on sin, repentance, and resurrection. Easter devotion was part of a rich mix or jumble of experiences in which impressions of clothes and sunshine and smiles flitted alongside the ringing words of the pastor's sermon.

Elizabeth Merchant's diary entries for Easter displayed the same sort of tangled synthesis of seasonal rejoicing, new clothes, and resurrection. The Saturday before Easter in 1881, she noted: "Went to town looking for Easter cards & buying myself a dress . . . with linings &c. [T]hen went to Bible class & heard a lovely lecture from Dr. Hall on the resurrection." In another passage she waxed eloquent on the interconnections between the new life of Easter and the vernal revival:

> Oh! Such a perfect day! trees budding birds singing—grass is green & sky so beautiful with its fleecy clouds. All the air full of sweet Spring sounds. I long to be out Enjoying every Moment at this season of so much beauty. There is an immense Robin red breast hopping and flying over the lawn! Oh God will the resurrection of our frail bodies be glorious like this waking of nature from the cold death of Winter?

Elizabeth Merchant readily combined the simple satisfactions of Easter shopping with the deeper mysteries of Christianity and nature. The same overlay of experiences was captured in Clara Pardee's clipped entry for Easter 1883: "A lovely Easter day—Out to church & walked up 5th Ave. Crowds of people—spring hats." Marjorie Reynolds was similarly terse in her notes about Easter in 1912: "Robed in new white corduroy. To the Brick [Church] with Oliver & a bunch of flowers. I don't know [what] I enjoyed more . . . a packed church . . . beautiful music & a good sermon . . . on the Av. afterwards w[ith] O[liver] & Mr. M[iddle] up to 59th St." The clear reconfiguring of Easter by the burgeoning consumer culture did not necessarily lessen the feast's religious power; instead it added to its sensuous richness and complexity. In these women's diaries, there was no necessary movement away from salvation to self-fulfillment, no hard-and-fast opposition between Christian soteriology and cosmopolitan display. For religious and cultural critics, it would prove all too easy to associate the feminized domains of church decoration and Easter fashion with vanity and immodesty (one trade writer tellingly spoke of the "masculine contempt" for dress and millinery). In these women's jottings, however, church and parade, fashion and festival, coalesced into an undivided whole.[32]

As Irving Berlin's movie suggests, not all the spring promenaders and curious onlookers cared about this synthesis of piety and materiality. As with any festival, a wide range of motivations and expectations animated those in attendance. Thousands and eventually hundreds of thousands clogged New York's fashionable thoroughfares for the Easter parade, and people took their bearings from various sources, sometimes divergent, often overlapping. Some went forth from the churches on errands of benevolence, making their way to hospitals and orphanages with flowers to brighten up the holiday for others. Others were abroad mostly to court and flirt and ogle; almost all were seeking diversion and entertainment of one kind or another. Not a few came out to work the milling crowds: thieves and pickpockets with fleet hands, hucksters and hawkers with various wares. At the same time, many of Veblen's leisure class graced the avenue, showcasing their status, urbanity, and importance, perhaps most interested in the occasion as a theater of social prestige. Also, many who were frankly indifferent to religion joined in the procession—those, as the *New York Herald* groused in 1890, who had heard "no Easter benediction" and whose holiday glow "came from a brandy cocktail with a dash of absinthe in it." In all the parade presented a pluralistic mélange of characters who processed to various rhythms.[33]

Certainly among the loudest drummers was fashion: lovers of new spring apparel and millinery, devotees of the latest style and vogue, peopled Fifth Avenue. The Easter parade, as Irving Berlin's movie highlighted, was indeed a celebration of the consumer culture—its capitalistic abundance, its unfettered choices, its constantly changing styles. If there was ever a holiday spectacle that apotheosized the American Way of Life, this was it. New York's dress parade was a tableau of American prosperity. Eventually, it even came to be seen as a parable about the bounties of American enterprise that contrasted sharply with the failures of Soviet communism. "Fifth Avenue on Easter Sunday," a *New York Times* columnist wrote in 1949, "would probably irritate Stalin more than he is already exasperated with the United States. . . . It will take a long series of five-year plans before the Soviet woman can buy a dress, a hat or a pair of shoes for anything near the price a New York working girl paid for her Easter outfit."[34] In 1955, the *Saturday Evening Post* was even more blunt about the parade's cultural meaning: New York's springtime pageant stood as "a reflection of the American Dream—that a person is as good as the clothes, car and home he is able to buy." In this writer's reckoning, the church's celebration of Easter was "incidental" to this wider public affirmation of American abundance and prosperity. The Easter parade's essential trademark was, to be sure, a gospel of wealth.[35]

Still, the parade remained all along a polysemous event, hardly reducible to a surface of fashion, respectability, and buttoned-up conventionality. Beneath its consumerist credo were carnivalesque tinges reminiscent of old Easter Monday traditions of mummery, which, as at New Year's, included outlandish costumes and boisterous conviviality. (How else but in terms of the fantastical and improvisational could one explain the large hat worn by one woman in 1953 that contained both a replica of the Last Supper and a live bird in a cage?) In many ways, the Easter parade was an unstructured, boundless, liminal event; there was "no apparent beginning, ending, organization or purpose." People flowed in and out of it—something of a leisurely free-for-all where fashionable promenaders, idle spectators, and publicity mongers merged into a closely commingled throng. The Easter parade may have begun in the 1870's as a parade of refinement—a middle- and upper-class staging of gentility, a sort of ritual primer for immigrants and the working class on the accoutrements of respectability—but by the turn of the century it had far more of the crowded, unpredictable energy of a street fair in which both Lenten and bourgeois strictures often melted into Easter laughter. Certainly, the residual form of the parade that survives today in New York City is more masked frolic than fashion show.[36]

The creative, playful possibilities were also seen in the role women assumed in this public performance. With their elaborate dresses and millinery, they took center stage. In a culture in which men and their civic associations had long dominated formal street parades and in a culture in which rowdy male youths had long made carnivalesque festivity and masking their special domain, the Easter parade was decidedly different. In contrast to the home-centered celebrations that so often prevailed among middle-class Victorian women and in contrast to the commonly minimal role of women as spectators on the edges of civic ceremony, Easter was about women in public procession. Whereas most nineteenth-century parades revolved quite literally around the *man* in the street, the Easter parade turned this convention on its head. Also, women's parading in Easter millinery served as a subversion of Pauline (and evangelical Protestant) views about head-coverings as emblematic of female modesty and meekness. The new world of Easter millinery was, in part, about the assertion of the self; about a world of mirrors and studied appearances ("You cannot have too many mirrors," one book on the art of millinery advised); about self-transformation through bewitching lines, fabrics, and colors; about the fashioning of the self in a parade of protean styles.[37]

Among the most far-reaching consequences of New York's dress parade was that it became a cultural model for spin-off observances around the country. Parallel events cropped up in other major cities, such as Philadelphia and Boston, and appeared in smaller towns as well. The cultural diffusion of New York's great Easter procession became especially evident in satellite resorts such as Coney Island, Asbury Park, and Atlantic City, where the entrepreneurs of commercialized leisure reproduced facsimiles for their own purposes. In these places the Easter parade was transformed into an excursion, a tourist attraction. At Coney Island in 1925, for example, the *New York Herald* reported that the local chamber of commerce had organized, with the help of several manufacturers, "a fashion show and Easter parade." To augment the proceedings the promoters had hired fifty show girls to parade in bathing suits; the crowds were overwhelming. No less hucksterish were the proceedings at Atlantic City, where, by the 1920's, the Easter parade was attracting annual crowds of 200,000 and more. Like Coney Island, Atlantic City was an excursionist's wonderland, and the parade there presented a kaleidoscopic scene of lolling, laughing pleasure-seekers—a Boardwalk carnival of costuming and consumption. Easter, like other American holidays, became a vacation. Begun in an outflow of the churches, the Easter parade climaxed in an amusement for that ultimate consumer, the tourist.[38]

RAINING ON THE EASTER PARADE: PROTEST, SUBVERSION, AND DISQUIET

All the display and fashion of the modern American Easter bewildered various people and inspired recurrent cultural criticism. Distressed commentators presented a wide range of intellectual perspectives from social gospel principles about economic justice to bedrock Puritan and republican convictions about simplicity and plainness. Above all, critics saw this as a cultural contest over the very meaning of Easter. Could the age-old Christian message of redemptive sacrifice and resurrection at the heart of Holy Week shine through the modern fanfare of style, novelty, and affluence? It was a struggle in ritual, liturgy, and performance to define what the values of the nation were and what Christianity demanded of its adherents. Seen from the perspective of the long history of the church, the struggle embodied perennial strains between Christ and culture, Gods and mammon. Viewed from the narrower span of American religious history, the conflict evoked familiar tensions between Puritan theocentrism and Yankee anthropocentrism, between otherworldly hopes of redemption and consumer dreams of material abundance, and between republican notions of male virtue and the corresponding fears of effeminacy and foppery.

Critics worried regularly over Easter extravagance. This "vaunting of personal possessions" in a parade of fashions abraded deep-seated cultural values of simplicity, frugality, and self-denial. If waning in the face of the expanding consumer culture, these principles continued to hold considerable allegiance, and concerns over Easter fashions brought these cultural tensions into sharp relief, perhaps particularly so since, as a religious event, Easter was expected to undergird, not subvert, the traditional values of thrift and moderation. Challenges to Easter indulgence took various forms. One Nazarene minister in Illinois in 1930, for example, gained notice with a bit of evangelical showmanship: he protested the predilection for turning Easter into "a fashion show" and a time of luxury by leading worship "attired in overalls." Likewise a Methodist minister in New Jersey in 1956 made the same point by wearing old clothes to conduct his Easter service. The worldliness of the Easter parade, the swaggering of "supreme ego, self-interest, [and] self-conceit," the searing contrast between Jesus' suffering and humiliation on the road to Calvary and the modern "fanfaronade of women in silks and furs" jarred a writer for the *Christian Century* in 1932. Two decades later another contributor to the same weekly wondered at the Fifth Avenue procession in which all seemed to cry "Look at me!" To its critics, the Easter parade was seen as a giant spectacle of vain self-assertion.[39]

Commentary on the American Easter sometimes cut deep to fundamental issues of social and economic justice. Like the Christmas rush, Easter preparations put huge burdens on workers to meet the surging demand for holiday goods and to satisfy the throng of holiday shoppers. Edwin Markham, poet of the social gospel whose "The Man with the Hoe" (1899) launched him to fame as a prophet against dehumanizing labor, spotlighted the crushing hardships of the holiday seasons in a series of blistering, reform-minded essays on child labor. Fired in part by his understanding of Jesus as a socialistic and progressivist visionary, Markham laid into "this generation of the colossal factory and the multitudinous store and the teeming tenement-house," all of which darkened even the joys of Christmas and Easter. "To thousands of those who depend on . . . the fashion-plate for light and leading," he blasted, "Easter means only a time of changing styles—a date on which to display new spring gowns and bonnets—a sort of national millinery opening. But to the workers in the shadow, . . . it means only a blind rush and tug of work that makes this solemn festival a time of dread and weariness. They might truly say in tears, 'They have taken away my Lord, and I know not where they have laid him.'"[40]

Markham aimed his sharpest attacks at sweatshops where children labored late into the night at piecework wages over artificial flowers for millinery to satisfy "the season's rush." He estimated that three-quarters of those making this product in New York City, the center of the industry, were children under age fourteen. "There is no other Easter preparation," he concluded, "where children are so cruelly overworked as in the making of artificial flowers." These "vampire blossoms" robbed children of education, health, and play:

> I lately visited a factory where a group of girls were making artificial roses. They were working ten hours a day, some of them getting only a dollar and a half a week. . . . Swiftly, rhythmically, the ever-flying fingers darted through the motions, keeping time to the unheard but clamorous metronome of need. Many of the girls had inflamed eyes. . . . The faces were dulled, the gaze was listless. Here was another illustration of the tragedy in our civilization—the work that deadens the worker.

The sweatshop exploitation of women and children, raised to feverish levels during the holiday rush, was, to Markham, "the tragedy behind the flaunting festoons of our Easter Vanity Fair."[41]

With stinging directness, Markham raked the muck on Easter fashions. Writing with a second-person bluntness that indicated again the gendered nature of this contest, he blasted: "Perhaps, last Easter, you, my lady, wore one of those pretty things of lace and chiffon trimmed with shining beads and made at midnight by your starved-down sister."[42] Like Washington Gladden, Walter Rauschenbusch, and other social reformers, Markham pressed the middle class to see their complicity in the suffering of the urban poor, to recognize that their choices as consumers were deeply interwoven with issues of economic justice, and to understand that their festive indulgence and intensified consumption at Christmas and Easter turned the screws on workers in city sweatshops and tenements. But since, in the gendering of consumption, women were seen as the chief devotees of fashion and novelty, these attacks were always directed far more at women than men. In raining on the Easter parade, critics inevitably aimed their sharpest barbs at the supposed vanity and folly of women.

Issues of social justice were also raised within the Easter parade itself as New York's colossal spectacle became the occasion for turning grievance into ritual. Protesters exploited the carnivalesque or fantastical potentialities within the procession to create a platform for various causes. During the Great Depression, groups of the unemployed, for example, paraded in "battered top hats, lumberjack coats, frayed trousers and broken shoes." If their social commentary was not clear enough, some carried placards or banners: "ONE FIFTH AVENUE GOWN EQUALS A YEAR OF RELIEF." Inverting the fashionableness and capitalistic excesses of New York's Easter procession was often used as a tool for labor and socialist protests. The Easter parade as an embodiment of American complacency and abundance called forth protestors and critics who used it as occasion to question the very values that underpinned this rite of spring. The meanings of the festival were thus never univocal, but contested and challenged, always subject to inversion and antithesis. The very modishness of the Easter parade provided the wedge for critics to open up issues of economic fairness and social justice—the lever by which to turn the whole ritual upside down.[43]

It is important, though, to see that these cultural contests over the meaning of Easter were never simply a matter of polarities: anxious critics versus unabashed celebrants; clear-eyed prophets versus profitseeking merchants; ascetics versus sybarites. When people faced consumerist tensions in their own celebrations of Easter, they resolved them variously or simply lived with them. For example, the Reverend Morgan Dix, rector at Trinity Episcopal Church in New York, a parish as fond as any of elaborate floral decorations and the display of Easter finery, found himself wondering in 1880 if festal ornamentation had become too extravagant. Was the church turning into "a hot-house"? One writer in 1883 considered Easter floral adornments in the churches attractive and appropriate, but still questioned whether the churches had, "even without intention, become but poor imitations of the theatre in their efforts at exhibition." The writer praised "simple" floral decorations but rejected costly ones which displayed a "foolish pride and a selfish ambition to out-do all others." Some suggested that Easter flowers should be distributed after church to the poor; still others recommended foregoing them and giving the money to charity. Unresolved tensions, ambiguities, and contradictions were evident also in Edwin Markham's career. At once critic of the "multitude of baubles" and "unmeaning trinkets" of the commercialized Easter—the "flimsy cards," the "glass eggs," the "paste chickens," the "plaster rabbits"—Markham turned around and happily sold his verses for sentiments on greeting cards. Not even the sharpest critics were exempt from the tensions that they highlighted.[44]

Some experienced these polarities and sought self-consciously to harmonize them. Reflecting on the Easter parade in 1905, a writer in *Harper's* recognized the tensions that many felt between mere "outward adornment" and the religious meaning of the festival. "I have known," he reported, "women to say that they avoided springing new frocks on an admiring world on Easter Sunday because they did not wish to intrude so trivial a thing as millinery upon a religious festival of such deep significance." But it "seems to me," he said, "that if one gets the right point of view, all the outward tokens of Easter are harmonious with the inner spiritual meanings of it." The flowers and clothes had sacramental importance; they were "outward manifestations" of Easter's religious solemnity and significance. One minister, writing in 1910, summarized both the tensions and their potential resolution:

> One dislikes the element of fashionable frivolity which has come to mark some people's keeping of the Easter feast; but, apart from that, as the city shops and streets break out into fragrant and beautiful bloom, one realizes the close kinship between heavenly and spiritual things and things material and earthly.

All along this was the corew concern—how to mediate piety and materiality, flesh and spirit, faith and riches, the inward and the outward in a world of proliferating goods.[45]

Easter, even more than Christmas, disclosed the role of the churches in the rise of consumer-oriented celebrations. The enlarging scope of "devout consumption" was seen in the elaborate displays of Easter flowers and other church decorations. The conflux of consumption and Christianity was nowhere more evident than in the streaming parade of Easter fashions as stylish celebrants poured into and out of the churches. Even as the churches helped facilitate this new Easter, cultivating a modern synthesis of piety and display, some critics demonstrated considerable wariness about where this alliance between Christian celebration and the consumer culture was headed. They foresaw the dim outlines of Irving Berlin's *Easter Parade* or Philip Roth's "schlockified Christianity" in which the holiday became a synonym for shopping and abundance, a ritual display of consumerist plenty. But the critics rarely fathomed the complexity of the drama that so disturbed them. They failed to see the hybridized commingling of faith and fashion, renewal and laughter, piety and improvisation that paraded before them.

NOTES

1. These and subsequent quotations have been transcribed from the movie itself, which is widely available on video cassette. I have also consulted a copy of the screenplay at the Lilly Library, Indiana University.

2. Philip Roth, *Operation Shylock: A Confession* (New York: Simon and Schuster, 1993), 157.

3. *New York Herald,* April 16, 1881, 5. Existing secondary literature focuses more on the holiday's folk beliefs and customs than on historical shifts or modern reconfigurations of the festival. See Theodore Caplow and Margaret Holmes Williamson, "Decoding Middletown's Easter Bunny: A Study in American Iconography," *Semiotica* 32 (1980): 221–32; Nada Gray, *Holidays: Victorian Women Celebrate in Pennsylvania* (University Park: Pennsylvania State University Press, 1983), 54–67; Elizabeth Clarke Kieffer, "Easter Customs of Lancaster

County," *Papers of the Lancaster Historical Society* 52 (1948): 49–68; Venetia Newall, *An Egg at Easter: A Folklore Study* (Bloomington: Indiana University Press, 1971); and Alfred L. Shoemaker, *Eastertide in Pennsylvania: A Folk Cultural Study* (Kutztown: Pennsylvania Folklife Society, 1960). For a notable exception, see James H. Barnett, "The Easter Festival: A Study in Cultural Change," *American Sociological Review* 14 (1949): 62–70.

4. "Easter Flowers," *Harper's New Monthly Magazine* 27 (July 1863): 189–94.

5. T. J. Jackson Lears, *No Place of Grace: Antimodernism and the Transformation of American Culture, 1880–1920* (New York: Pantheon, 1981), 183–215; Ernest Geldart, ed., *The Art of Garnishing Churches at Christmas and Other Times: A Manual of Directions* (London: Cox Sons, Buckley and Co., 1882), 12. See also William A. Barrett, *Flowers and Festivals: Or, Directions for the Floral Decoration of Churches* (New York: Pott and Amery, 1868).

6. Edward L. Cutts, *An Essay on the Christmas Decoration of Churches: With an Appendix on the Mode of Decorating Churches for Easter, the School Feast, Harvest Thanksgiving, Confirmation, a Marriage, and a Baptism*, 3rd ed. (London: Horace Cox, 1868), 12; Geldart, ed., *Art of Garnishing Churches*, 11.

7. Ernest R. Suffling, *Church Festival Decorations: Being Full Directions for Garnishing Churches for Christmas, Easter, Whitsuntide, and Harvest*, 2d ed. (New York: Charles Scribner's Sons, 1907), 74.

8. Henry Dana Ward, "Diary," April 8, 1855; March 23, 1856; April 12, 1857, New York Public Library, Rare Books and Manuscripts.

9. On this invasion, see William R. Leach, "Transformations in a Culture of Consumption: Women and Department Stores, 1890–1925," *Journal of American History* 71 (1984): 325.

10. Unidentified Author, "Diary, 1872–1873," April 13, 1873, New-York Historical Society, Manuscripts.

11. Sarah Anne Todd, "Diary," April 21, 1867, New-York Historical Society, Manuscripts; Elizabeth W. Merchant, "Diary," March 25, 1883; April 25, 1886; April 10, 1887, New York Public Library, Rare Books and Manuscripts; Mrs. George Richards, "Diary," April 1, 1888, New-York Historical Society, Manuscripts. For the initiative of women in church decoration, see, for example, "How Some Churches Looked Last Easter," *Ladies' Home Journal* 21 (March 1904): 32–33.

12. Geldart, ed., *Art of Garnishing Churches*, 12, 44; *New York Sun*, April 1, 1861, 2; Suffling, *Church Festival Decorations*, 85–86.

13. "Easter Flowers," 190; Suffling, *Church Festival Decorations*, 2. On this domestic and sentimental piety, see Ann Douglas, *The Feminization of American Culture* (New York: Knopf, 1977); and Colleen McDannell, *The Christian Home in Victorian America, 1840–1900* (Bloomington: Indiana University Press, 1986).

14. "Easter Flowers," 190. On Phelps's novel and "the new domestic heaven," see Douglas, *Feminization of American Culture*, 214–15, 223–26.

15. Ernest Geldart, *A Manual of Church Decoration and Symbolism Containing Directions and Advice to Those Who Desire Worthily to Deck the Church at the Various Seasons of the Year* (Oxford: A. R. Mowbray and Co., 1899), 17–18; *New York Herald*, April 16, 1881, 5; Thorstein Veblen, *The Theory of the Leisure Class: An Economic Study of Institutions* (New York: Macmillan, 1899; repr., New York: Random House, 1934), 199, 307–9. On the narrow limits of Veblen's model, see T. J. Jackson Lears, "Beyond Veblen: Rethinking Consumer Culture in America," in *Consuming Visions: Accumulating and Display of Goods in America, 1880–1920*, ed. Simon J. Bronner (New York: Norton, 1989), 73–97.

16. *New York Herald*, April 21, 1867, 4; April 14, 1873, 4; Suffling, *Church Festival Decorations*, 32–33; *New York Sun*, April 22, 1878, 3. Here I am playing off Lears's argument in *No Place of Grace* about the antimodernism in Anglo-Catholic aesthetics. As Lears suggests, this antimodernist, medievalist stance often had modernist, therapeutic consequences. This was at no point clearer than in the Victorian elaboration of the art of church decoration.

17. Geldart, ed., *Art of Garnishing Churches*, 12, 19; William Leach, "Strategists of Display and the Production of Desire," in Bronner, ed., *Consuming Visions*, 104. Leach's conclusions about this "display aesthetic" are offered in expanded and far more critical form in his *Land of Desire: Merchants, Power, and the Rise of a New American Culture* (New York: Pantheon, 1993).

18. *Dry Goods Chronicle*, March 26, 1898, 19; John Wanamaker (Philadelphia), "Easter, 1893," Dry Goods Scrapbook, Bella Landauer Collection, New-York Historical Society.

19. "News from the Cities," *American Advertiser* 4 (April 1890): unpag. For other examples, see [Charles A. Tracy], *The Art of Decorating Show Windows and Interiors*, 3rd ed. (Chicago: Merchants Record Co., 1906), 199–206, 314–15; Alfred G. Bauer, *The Art of Window Dressing for Grocers* (Chicago: Sprague, Warner & Company, [1902]), 30–32; "Robinson Window," *Greeting Card* 8 (March 1936): 28; "Lilies, a Cross, Lighted Candles," *Greeting Card* 5 (March 1933): 5; and "The Cross Was Illuminated," *Greeting Card* 5 (March 1933), 8.

20. Robert A. Childs, *"The Thoughtful Thinker" on Window-Dressing and Advertising Together with Wholesome Advice for Those in Business and Those about to Start* (Syracuse: United States Window Trimmers' Bureau, [1896]), 21; Douglas, *Feminization of American Culture*, 225.

21. Tracy, *Art of Decorating Show Windows*, 315. For Wanamaker's Easter displays, see box 11B, folders 10 and 23; box 12D, folder 2, Wanamaker Collection, Historical Society of Pennsylvania, Philadelphia. On the paintings of Michael de Munkacsy, see box 55, folder 14; box 63, folder 3, Wanamaker Collection. See also Leach, *Land of Desire*, 213–14, 222–23.

22. L. Frank Baum, *The Art of Decorating Dry Goods Windows and Interiors* (Chicago: Tile Show Window Publishing Co., 1900), unpag. intro., 181, 185. On Baum, see Leach, *Land of Desire*, 55–61.

23. This is R. Laurence Moore's conclusion abut the varied blendings of Protestant values with commercial amusements and popular literature in the first half of the nineteenth-century. See Moore, "Religion, Secularization, and the Shaping of the Culture Industry in Antebellum America," *American Quarterly* 41 (1989): 236.

24. George D. Herron, *The Message of Jesus to Men of Wealth* (New York: Fleming H. Revell Co., 1891), 29–31. The "one undivided Kingdom of God" is a phrase from Washington Gladden, *Things New and Old in Discourses of Christian Truth and Life* (Columbus, Ohio: A. H. Smythe, 1883), 260. On the "festive marketplace," see the classic evocation in Mikhail Bakhtin, *Rabelais and His World*, trans. Helene Iswolsky (Cambridge: M.I.T. Press, 1968), 19, 92. For Wanamaker as the consummate sacralizer of prosperity, see "The Power of Consecrated Wealth: John Wanamaker—What the Rich Can Do," *Christian Recorder*, March 15, 1877, 4–5. On liberal Protestantism and the consumer ethos, see Susan Curtis, *A Consuming Faith: The Social Gospel and Modern American Culture* (Baltimore: Johns Hopkins University Press, 1991).

25. For the Watts hymn within the context of a Victorian Easter service, see Jennie M. Bingham, *Easter Voices* (New York: Hunt and Eaton, 1891), 2. On the consumer culture as a dream world, see Rosalind H. Williams, *Dream Worlds: Mass Consumption in Late Nineteenth-Century France* (Berkeley: University of California Press, 1982). On the new therapeutic gospel, see especially T. J. Jackson Lears, "From Salvation to Self-Realization: Advertising and the Therapeutic Roots of the Consumer Culture, 1880–1930," in *The Culture of Consumption: Critical Essays in American History, 1880–1980*, ed. Richard Wightman Fox and T. J. Jackson Lears (New York: Pantheon, 1983), 3–38. On the wider absorption of religious symbols into modern advertising, see Roland Marchand, *Advertising the American Dream: Making Way for Modernity, 1920–1940* (Berkeley: University of California Press, 1985), 264–84.

26. For the Irish adage, see Francis X. Weiser, *The Easter Book* (New York: Harcourt, Brace and Co., 1954), 159–61. For Poor Robin's maxim, see John Brand and W. Carew Hazlitt, *Popular Antiquities of Great Britain: Comprising Notices of the Moveable and Immovable Feasts, Customs, Superstitions and Amusements Past and Present*, 3 vols. (London: John Russell Smith,

1870), 1:93. On Easter clothes, see A. R. Wright, *British Calendar Customs: England*, 3 vols., ed. T. E. Lones (London: The Folk-Lore Society, 1936–1940), 1:101; and Shoemaker, *Eastertide in Pennsylvania*, 24. For the *Herald's* version of the proverb, see *New York Herald*, April 8, 1855, 1.

27. *New York Herald*, April 14, 1873, 4; April 14, 1879, 8.

28. *New York Herald*, April 26, 1886, 8; *New York Times*, April 7, 1890, 2.

29. Ralph M. Hower, *History of Macy's of New York, 1858–1919: Chapters in the Evolution of the Department Store* (Cambridge: Harvard University Press, 1943), 170, 451n.37; *New York Sun*, April 17, 1878, 4; April 16, 1878, 4. It is important to underline that my analysis of Easter's commercialization is confined to the United States. It is likely that merchants in Paris or London, where the growth of the consumer culture was somewhat ahead of the United States and where Easter traditions were far less encumbered by low-church Protestant sentiments, were significantly in advance of their American counterparts. For a hint of this, see Neil McKendrick, John Brewer, and J. H. Plumb, *The Birth of a Consumer Society: The Commercialization of Eighteenth-Century England* (Bloomington: Indiana University Press, 1982), 74.

30. *Dry Goods Economist*, March 24, 1894, 36, 37; *Dry Goods Chronicle*, March 26, 1898, 19; *Dry Goods Economist*, March 18, 1893, 55.

31. Elizabeth Schuneman Orr, "Diary," April 9, 1871, New York Public Library, Rare Books and Manuscripts.

32. Merchant, "Diary," April 16, 1881; April 21, 1867; Clara Burton Pardee, "Diary," March 25, 1883, New-York Historical Society, Manuscripts; Marjorie R. Reynolds, "Diary," April 7, 1912, New-York Historical Society, Manuscripts; "New York Millinery," *Millinery Trade Review* 7 (April 1882): 56.

33. *New York Herald*, April 7, 1890, 3.

34. Anne O'Hare McCormick, quoted in "The Easter Parade," *Time*, April 25, 1949, 19.

35. Rufus Jarman, "Manhattan's Easter Madness," *Saturday Evening Post*, April 9, 1955, 103.

36. Ibid. On Easter conviviality and costuming, see Shoemaker, *Eastertide in Pennsylvania*, 43–45; and Bakhtin, *Rabelais and His World*, 78–79, 146. For the woman's outlandish hat, see *New York Times*, April 6, 1953, 14.

37. Anna Ben Yûsuf, *The Art of Millinery* (New York: Millinery Trade Publishing Co., 1909), 227. On the male domination of nineteenth-century parades and public ceremonies as well as the efforts of women to gain a foothold in these rituals, see Mary P. Ryan, *Women in Public: Between Banners and Ballots, 1825–1880* (Baltimore: Johns Hopkins University Press, 1990), 19–57; and Susan G. Davis, *Parades and Power: Street Theatre in Nineteenth-Century Philadelphia* (Philadelphia: Temple University Press, 1985; repr., Berkeley: University of California Press, 1986), 47, 149, 157, 190.

38. *New York Herald*, April 13, 1925, 3. For representative accounts of Easter parades in the resorts, see *New York Times*, April 16, 1906, 9; John Steevens, "The Charm of Eastertide at Atlantic City," *Harper's Weekly*, April 18, 1908, 20–22; *New York Times*, April 20, 1908, 3; *New York Herald*, April 8, 1912, 4; and *New York Times*, April 22, 1935, 11. On Coney Island and Atlantic City, see, respectively, John F. Kasson, *Amusing the Million: Coney Island at the Turn of the Century* (New York: Hill and Wang, 1978); and Charles E. Funnell, *By the Beautiful Sea: The Rise and High Times of That Great American Resort* (New York: Alfred A. Knopf, 1975), esp. 46, 89. Barnett noted in 1949 of New York's Easter parade: "The pattern appears to be diffusing as an *American* practice." See Barnett, "Easter Festival," 69.

39. *New York Times*, April 23, 1946, 25; April 19, 1930, 9; April 2, 1956, 14; Raymond Kresensky, "Easter Parade," *Christian Century*, March 23, 1932, 384–85; Dorothy Lee Richardson, "Easter Sunday, Fifth Avenue," *Christian Century*, April 28, 1954, 511.

40. Edwin Markham, "The Blight on the Easter Lilies," *Cosmopolitan* 42 (April 1907): 667–68. Markham's essays on child labor were collected in *Children in Bondage* (New York: Hearst's International, 1914).

41. "Blight on the Easter Lilies," 670–73.

42. Ibid., 669.

43. *New York Times*, March 28, 1932, 1; Jarman, "Manhattan's Easter Madness," 104.

44. *New York Times*, March 28, 1880, 2; "Proper Observance of Easter," *Concert Quarterly* 1 (March 1883): 1; *New York Times*, March 18, 1894, 18; Markham, "Blight on the Easter Lilies," 668; Louis Filler, *The Unknown Edwin Markham: His Mystery and Its Significance* (Yellow Springs, Ohio: Antioch Press, 1966), 140.

45. E. S. Martin, "New York's Easter Parade," *Harper's Weekly*, April 22, 1905, 567; William C. Doane, *The Book of Easter* (New York: Macmillan, 1910), vii.

CHAPTER
19

Debate: 1920–1940—Dark Ages of Modern American Protestantism?

Historians of modern American religion agree that twentieth-century white American Protestantism confronted a loss of mastery. From numerical dominance in the nineteenth century it slipped steadily in overall "churched" population from 85 percent to about 45 percent. For some historians, most notably Professor Robert T. Handy, former president of the American Society of Church History, the decades of the 1920s, 1930s, and 1940s were times of stagnation and "depression," while for historians like Joel Carpenter, these decades signaled periods of "revival" and "awakening." In the following debate, both of these perspectives will be presented. To what extent does denominational focus determine the outcome of this debate? To what extent can any of these traditions stand for or represent a broader "climate of opinion" in America generally?

Additional Reading: The great religious debates of the early twentieth century are traced in Ferenc Morton Szasz, *The Divided Mind of Protestant America, 1880–1930* (New York, 1982). A classic work on fundamentalism is Norman Furniss, *The Fundamentalist Controversy, 1918–1931* (New Haven, 1954), and William R. Hutchison, *The Modernist Impulse in American Protestantism* (New York, 1976) discusses the "modernism" that so angered fundamentalists. William G. McLoughlin, Jr., *Billy Sunday Was His Real Name* (Chicago, 1955) studies one of the best known early twentieth-century evangelists. On millennialism see Timothy P. Webber, *Living in the Shadow of the Second Coming: American Premillennialism 1875–1982* (New York, 1982). Other than Handy's essay, historians have paid little attention to the social and economic problems of churches and synagogues in the 1920s and 1930s, although some of these problems figure in Paul A. Carter, *The Decline and Revival of the Social Gospel: Social and Political Liberalism in American Protestant Churches, 1920–1940* (Ithaca, 1956), and are the subject of a contemporary and famous sociological work, Robert Lynd and Helen Lynd, *Middletown: A Study in Contemporary American Culture* (New York, 1929).

Robert T. Handy   # The American Religious
Depression, 1925–1935

"It is too early to assess the impact of the Great Depression upon American Protestantism," wrote Robert Moats Miller in his recent study of American Protestantism and social issues in the period between the world wars.[1] No doubt it is too early for any overall assessment, yet it is becoming steadily clearer that American religion passed through an important transition in the depression period. If we are to gain a fuller understanding of developments in American Christianity since the 1930's, then serious attention needs to be given to that bleak period. Inasmuch as our understanding of times long past are significantly influenced by our definitions of the present situation, attempts to deal with that particular period of crisis in our recent past may help us more adequately to see the whole story of American religion in fairer perspective. Furthermore, a number of recent dissertations, articles and books have dealt in whole or in part with the period between the wars; they provide guidance for handling the vast array of sources relevant for an understanding of religion in the depression, supply material for at least preliminary interpretations, and point to the need for further analysis. This paper is one effort to suggest some interpretative guide lines for further exploration into an important topic.

I

In approaching the problem, I believe that it is important to distinguish between the economic depression of the 1930's and what may be called the religious depression. That there was an intimate relationship between them I have no doubt, yet they are also distinguishable phenomena. William Kelley Wright, professor of philosophy at Dartmouth College, writing in the heart of the depression period, declared that "today we are passing through a period of religious depression not less severe than the concomitant moral and economic depression."[2] Some months before the stock market crash of October, 1929, William L. Sullivan, a Unitarian writer, prepared an article entitled "Our Spiritual Destitution" in which he noted that the religion of his day was "timorous, unimaginative, quick with comment upon the contemporaneous, but unable in the authentic manner of its great tradition to judge the contemporaneous by categories that are eternal."[3] The effects of religious depression began to be felt by the middle 1920's within Protestantism, then the dominant and of course numerically the largest among the three overall religious groupings into which American religion is familiarly, though too simply, cast.

One sensitive indicator of a religion's vitality is its missionary program. By the middle of the third decade of the present century, Protestantism was becoming

Reprinted with permission from *Church History* 29 (March 1960), 3–16.

aware of a serious decline in missionary enthusiasm and convicion. At the 1926 meeting of the Foreign Missions Conference of North America, there was evident discouragement on the part of missionary leaders concerning the apathy of local churches toward the cause of missions.[4] Even after the disastrous effects of the economic depression had overtaken the missions boards, there was clear recognition that the problem was much more than financial, and that it had predated the economic crisis. "However, we all know that this is not a sufficient explanation of what was happening on the home base," Edmund B. Chafee reported in 1934. "Interest in missions was waning before the depression. All through the decade of the 1920's the foreign missionary enterprise was being questioned and it was failing to attract the vigorous support which it formerly enjoyed."[5] In his sociological study of religion in the economic depression, Samuel C. Kincheloe reported that "even before the depression, missionary funds had begun to decrease."[6] Examination of the income figures of the major mission boards for the later 1920's reveals an irregular pattern but with a generally declining trend—and this in a period of booming prosperity![7] In an article entitled "The Decline of American Protestantism," Charles Stelzle in 1930 reported that according to the United Stewardship Council, per capita gifts for benevolence fell from $5.57 in 1921 to $3.43 in 1929.[8]

There was also a decline in the missionary force in these same years. The number of foreign missionaries in 1929 was less by 4.7 per cent than that for 1923.[9] The steadily waning interest of young people in responding to the missionary challenge was a source of concern at the 1929 meeting of the Foreign Missions Conference of North America, at which it was reported that though 2700 students had volunteered for foreign service in 1920, only 252 had offered themselves in 1928.[10] The decline of the missionary force for China was especially perplexing to missionary leaders, and led Albert W. Beaven to make a statement in 1928 that was in a strange way more prophetic than he could know. "What an absurdity if after one hundred years of service," he exclaimed, "after building up in China $90,000,000 of missionary investments in terms of helpfulness, we were to abandon it, withdrawing our Christian representatives, forsaking the whole enterprise, while at the very same time Russia with all the questionable principles she stands for is eager to offer the Orient men, counsel, money and moral backing."[11] It was the decline in missionary interest that led to the Laymen's Foreign Missions Inquiry in the early 1930's, which itself reflected a questioning of familiar missionary emphases within Protestantism.

The home missions movement also felt the pinch of declining interest and diminishing funds before 1929. Nearly two years before the crash, the executive secretary of the Home Missions Council said:

> Almost all major denominations are now in a period of financial stringency in the conduct of mission work. We are in the days of falling budgets. There has been more or less retrenchment all along the line, and new work has been for several years practically at a standstill.[12]

On the rural church scene there was clear evidence of decline before 1929, both in terms of benevolence contributions and the attendance at services of resident members.[13]

The problem of falling attendance was not limited to the rural scene, of course, for churches in all areas reported difficulties in maintaining attendance levels. A general trend toward the dropping of traditional Sunday evening services, especially in the cities, was observed.[14] Decline in Sunday school enrollment was also evident; C. Luther Fry found in 1930 that "the proportion of young people attending church schools is greater today than in 1906, but less than in 1916."[15] Attempts to plot an "evangelistic index line" for a number of major denominations point to a sharp downturn in the winning of converts and the reception of new members in the 1920's.[16] A somewhat less tangible evidence of Protestant decline was the lowered status of ministers. Paul A. Carter has pointed out that the ministry sank low in public esteem in this period; he quotes a minister of that time who declared that it was "a fairly safe generalization to say that no profession of men is so thoroughly empty of dignity and grace as that of the Proestant minister today."[17]

Many observers have called attention to the slump which overtook the social gospel in the later 1920's; it is referred to in the very title of Carter's book, *The Decline and Revival of the Social Gospel*. But in his recent examination of the period, Robert Moats Miller has found that "social Christianity continued to burn bright enough to warrant future historians in using slightly less somber hues in painting their pictures of the social attitudes of American Protestantism in the Prosperity Decade."[18] I think the apparent contradiction may be resolved by concluding that though proportionately the social emphasis remained strong, the social gospel movement as a whole was caught in Protestantism's overall decline.

Some of the keenest observers of the religious life of the late 1920's recognized that they were in some kind of a religious depression. For example, the Episcopal Bishop of Central New York, Charles Fiske, was convinced in 1928 that he had "evidence of a sad distintegration of American Protestantism."[19] And in his first book, published in 1927, Reinhold Niebuhr remarked that "a psychology of defeat, of which both fundamentalism and modernism are symptoms, has gripped the forces of religion."[20] At least part of the reason for the decline was the penetration into the churches of the prevailing mood of the 1920's. For Protestantism was deeply affected by the general disillusionment of the postwar decade. During the war itself, the American people, with the vigorous support of most religious leaders, maintained a spirit of high optimism. But the tide turned swiftly. As Arthur S. Link has recently reminded us, "the 1920's were a period made almost unique by an extraordinary reaction against idealism and reform."[21] The rapid subsidence of the war spirit, so Walter M. Horton observed in a book written in 1929 but published the following year, led "to a wave of spiritual depression and religious skepticism, widespread and devastating."[22] Protestantism felt the corrosive effects of disillusionment at the very beginning of the decade, for the collapse of the grandiose Interchurch World Movement in 1920 was at least in part caused by the swift change in mood. Winthrop S. Hudson has summarized the swift decline of Protestantism in a vivid way:

> Nothing is more striking than the astonishing reversal in the position occupied by the churches and the role played by religion in American life which took

place before the new century was well under way. By the nineteen twenties, the contagious enthusiasm which had been poured into the Student Volunteer Movement, the Sunday School Movement, the Men and Religion Forward Movement, the Laymen's Missionary Movement, the Interchurch World Movement, and other organized activities of the churches had largely evaporated.[23]

As the decade wore on, scientism, behaviorism, and humanism became more conspicuous in the thought of the time. Religion was often viewed with a negative if not with a hostile eye. In his effort to state the case of "a promethean religion for the modern world," William Pepperell Montague declared in 1930 that "there is today a widespread and increasing belief that the minimum essentials of Christian supernaturalism . . . have been rendered antiquated, false, and absurd by our modern knowledge."[24] More extreme was Joseph Wood Krutch's pessimistic statement of "the modern temper" in 1929. Referring to such classic words as "Sin" and "Love," Krutch wrote that "all the capital letters in the composing-room cannot make the words more than that which they have become—shadows, as essentially unreal as some of the theological dogmas which have been completely forgotten."[25] Criticism of religion and the churches was expressed not only by men like Montague and Krutch, by H. L. Mencken and Sinclair Lewis, but also by many less well-known men. One opinion study showed that although about 78 per cent of the views about traditional Christianity published in 1905 were favorable and only 22 per cent were unfavorable, by 1930 the situation had almost reversed, so that 67 per cent of the opinions published were unfavorable.[26]

Protestantism was deeply penetrated by the disillusionment of the time in part at least because of a long-standing indentification of Protestantism with American culture which left the churches quite exposed to cultural cross-currents. The roots of this identification go far back to the beginnings of American history. As André Siegfried stated the matter in 1927:

> If we wish to understand the real sources of American inspiration, we must go back to the English Puritanism of the seventeenth century, for the civilization of the United States is essentially Protestant. Those who prefer other systems, such as Catholicism, for example, are considered bad Americans and are sure to be frowned on by the purists. Protestantism is the only national religion, and to ignore that fact is to view the country from a false angle.

Siegfried was fully aware of the denominational nature of Protestantism, yet still insisted on his main point: "In order to appreciate the influence of Protestantism in this confusion of sects, we must not look at it as a group of organized churches, for its strength lies in the fact that its spirit is national."[27] Sidney E. Mead has recently shown that the fusion of Protestantism with Americanism was especially evident in the later nineteenth century. He has suggested that "during the second half of the nineteenth century there occurred a virtual identification of the outlook of this denominational Protestantism with 'Americanism' or 'the American way of life' and that we are still living with some of the results of this ideological amalgamation of evangelical Protestantism with Americanism."[28] During and just after the first World War there was an intensification of this synthesis through an emphasis on "Christian Americanization," by which was meant growth toward national democratic and spiritual ideals, of which the churches were the best custodians.[29] One feature of this identification was illustrated in the Lynds' comment following their 1925 study of "Middletown": "In theory, religious beliefs dominate all other activities in Middletown."[30]

The religious education movement, which was at the peak of its influence in the later 1920's, clearly illustrated the theme of the ideological amalgamation of religion and culture. Shailer Mathews pointed to its triumphs in 1927 by declaring that "it commands the same sort of enthusiastic following from idealistic young men and women as did sociology a generation ago. The most generally elected courses in theological seminaries, the greatest activity in churches are in its field." But Mathews warned religious educators that they were tending to neglect the church in their concern for education, insiting that "it is our privilege to teach young people that religion has some other task than that of making good citizens and good neighbors."[31] As H. Shelton Smith was later to document, many religious educators "sought to blend the democratic theory of education and the democratic theory of the Kingdom of God."[32]

In view of this identification, it was inevitable that Protestantism would be deeply and directly influenced by trends within the culture, and that many of them would be accepted and even blessed by the churches. In 1929 the self-styled "puzzled parson," Charles Fiske, indicated that he was not quite as puzzled as he claimed to be when he said:

> America has become almost hopelessly enamoured of a religion that is little more than a sanctified commercialism; it is hard in this day and this land to differentiate between religious aspiration and business prosperity. Our conception of God is that he is a sort of Magnified Rotarian. Sometimes, indeed, one wonders whether the social movement and the uplift in general have not become, among Protestants, a substitute for devotion; worse than that, a substitute for real religion. Efficiency has become the greatest of Christian virtues. I hope I may be forgiven a note of exaggeration that is necessary to make my meaning clear when I say that Protestantism, in America, seems to be degenerating into a sort of Babsonian cult, which cannot distinguish between what is offered to God and what is accomplished for the glory of America and the furtherance of business enterprise.[33]

Edwin Lewis of Drew, reviewing in 1934 the course American Protestantism had taken during the previous twenty years, declared:

> We borrowed our criteria of evaluation from the world about us—a world gone mad in its worship of mere size, a world that had set itself to create bigger ships, bigger aeroplanes, bigger locomotives, bigger buildings, bigger universities, bigger coroporations, bigger banks, bigger everything—except men! . . . And we were guilty of the incredible folly of supposing that "Christ's church was of this world," to be judged by the world's standards, to be modeled on the world's ways, to walk in the world's procession, and to keep step to the crashing discord of its brazen shawms.[34]

In the light of such identification with the culture, Protestantism could hardly avoid a share in the spiritual poverty of the time, or escape wholly from the spirit of disillusionment that swept American life in the 1920's. The American spiritual depression and the decline of Protestantism in the 1920's were intimately correlated.

It was on churches already seriously weakened, already in some decline, that the blow of economic depression fell. When the Lynds returned to Middletown ten years after their first study they found that "the city had been shaken for nearly six years by a catastrophe involving not only people's values but, in the case of many, their very existence. Unlike most socially generated catastrophes, in this case virtually nobody in the community had been cushioned against the blow; the great knife of the depression had cut down impartially through the entire population, cleaving open the lives and hopes of rich as well as poor."[35] The great knife of depression also cut deep into church life. "Outwardly the churches suffered along with the rest of the nation," wrote Robert M. Miller. "Memberships dropped, budgets were slashed, benevolent and missionary enterprises set adrift, ministers fired, and chapels closed. All this can be demonstrated statistically."[36] The evidence need not be summarized here, but a single illustration of the impact of depression may be in order. In 1927 Shailer Mathews had reported the triumph of religious education; less than ten years later, after depression had done its work, Adelaide Teague Case painted a dark picture.

> What shall we say to Christian Education today? Obviously it is in distress. The machinery has broken down. All the denominational boards of education have suffered great losses. The International Council of Religious Education is struggling on with a greatly reduced staff and budget. The Religious Education Association is in abeyance, trying to maintain itself with a handful of volunteers who are holding it together in spite of a staggering debt. Training schools and departments of religious education in universities and seminaries are severely reduced in size; some of them have reorganized or disappeared. The professional leadership is discouraged; directors of religious education are transferring to social work or public education or joining the ranks of the unemployed.[37]

This illustration could be matched by pointing to many other aspects of the churches' programs. Hidden in such a flat statement as "twenty out of thirty-five leading denominations compared in 1934 had reduced their total expenditures by from thirty to fifty per cent and five over fifty per cent" are countless stories of struggles, discouragement, and tragedy.[38]

I believe that this approach to religion in the depression, to distinguish between religious and economic depressions, throws light on many aspects of religious life in the 1930's, but on the following three in particular. First, one of the persistent questions of the depression period was "why no revival of religion?" Some religious leaders, reported Samuel Kincheloe, "actually hailed the depression with rejoicing since they had the idea that previous depressions had 'driven men to God' and felt that the time was overdue for men again to be reminded of the need to let the spiritual dominate the materialistic order."[39] At various times in the American past, depression and revival had been related, classically in 1857–1858. But when the distinction between religious and economic depression is made, it becomes clear that it was an already depressed Protestantism that was overtaken by the economic crisis. Without inner changes it was unable to deal with the needs of the time in a fresh and creative way. The changes that finally came did contribute to conspicuous currents of renewal, but only after the depression itself had passed.

Second, a significant aspect of the religious depression, perplexing to the major denominations, was the mushrooming of the newer and smaller religious groups, the sects. Detailed analyses of particular communities, such as Pope's study of Gastonia, the Lynds' probing of Middletown, and Boisen's samplings of several communities, all document the proliferation of the sects in the depression decade.[40] A number of observers have pointed out that many, probably a majority, of the supporters of sectarian movements were formerly adherents of the older and larger Protestant denominations. That the sects attracted many among the "disinherited" and economically depressed classes has been stated many times.[41] A significant but indirect factor in the rapid growth of the sects in the 1930's would seem to be the internal Protestant depression with its consequent lack of clarity and energy in the churches. Individuals won from older to newer religious bodies often indicated their dissatisfaction with the coldness and formality of the old-line churches.

Third, one of the major shifts of mood which was certainly speeded by the lash of depression was the somewhat precipitous decline of the evangelical liberal theology, which had been so conspicuous a part of Protestant life in the first quarter of the century. There were some signs of the internal disintegration of liberalism even before the first world war.[42] In 1925, Justin Wroe Nixon explained the liberal's dilemma in a forceful article in the *Atlantic*. While the liberals were fighting off the frontal attack of fundamentalism, he declared, they were inadvertently backing toward the humanist position; they were seriously embarrassed by the flank attack of the naturalists and humanists.[43] The latter claimed to speak for a scientifically and naturalistically-minded age far better than the liberals, who were accused of clinging to an unsatisfactorily and unstable compromise, could. By the early 1930's, liberals were finding it increasingly difficult, in terms of their optimistic orientation and idealistic heritage, to deal satisfactorily with the realities of depression, the rise of totalitarianism, and the resurgence of barbarism on the world scene. In his famous article of 1933, "After Liberalism—What?" John C. Bennett said emphatically,

> The most important fact about contemporary American theology is the disintegration of liberalism. Disintegration may seem too strong a word, but I am using it quite literally. It means that as a structure with a high degree of unity theological liberalism is coming to pieces. The liberal preacher has had a coherent pattern of theological assumptions in the background of his message. He has often had the kind of self-confidence which goes with the preaching of an orthodoxy, for liberalism has been a new orthodoxy in many circles. It is that coherent pattern of assumptions, that self-confidence, which are going. Now many of us are left with a feeling of theological homelessness.[44]

Into the vacuum new theological currents immediately flowed, as interpreters of European dialectical theologies appeared.[45] Benson Y. Landis could report in 1933 that "the economic crisis seems to be breeding a theology of crisis."[46] But one must not press too hard the relationship between the depression and the decline of liberalism. It was not the depression alone, however, but the many crises of the 1930's which together weakened the liberal synthesis and made men receptive to new views. When the *Christian Century* published in 1939 its oftquoted series of articles on "How My Mind Has Changed in This Decade," many of America's leading theologicans told how the fateful events of the decade had led them to shift their position to a neoliberalism if not a neo-orthodoxy. A characteristic expression of the impact of the decade on the liberals was penned by E. G. Homrighausen. "I saw evidences of man's lostness: the depression, the constant threat of war, the return to brutality on so vast a scale, the loss of the spiritual substance of life that alone gives society structure, the uncertainty and insecurity of life."[47]

Somewhat paradoxically, for the rise of the social gospel had been intimately related to the earlier success of theological liberalism, there was clearly a resurgence of the social gospel in the 1930's, despite the decay of liberalism. The works of Paul A. Carter and Robert M. Miller, previously cited, document this resurgence of social concern abundantly; a hasty examination of denominational social pronouncements in the bleak decade provides convincing confirmation. Hornell Hart reported some years ago on this aspect of religion in the depression in these words:

> The most striking increase in religious discussion in magazines has been in the field of Christian ethics. *Readers' Guide* entries under this heading and under "Church and Social Problems," "Christian Socialism," and "Christian Sociology" increased from 17 per 100,000 in 1929 to 140 in 1932, and in 1941 they were still more than twice their 1929 level. The rise and recession of this curve is notably similar to the rise and decline in the amount of unemployment and to other indices of the economic depression.[48]

That there was something of a resurgence of the social gospel I do not doubt, but on the whole the resurgence of social interest in the 1930's is perhaps more to be seen as related to a permanent contribution which the social gospel in its creative days earlier in the century had made to the larger Protestant world: a sensitivity to social issues and an awareness of social need. A Protestantism which had been alerted by such a vigorous social movement could not easily be callous to serious social need. Not a few of those who took leadership in movements to the theological right were also conspicuous for their continued attention to social thought and action.

II

I have argued that Protestantism entered the period of religious and economic depression as the dominant American religious tradition, closely identified with the culture. But Protestantism emerged from depression no longer in such a position;

it was challenged by forces outside the Protestant churches and questioned by some within. Siegfried, who identified Protestantism as the national religion as late as 1927, saw the trend of the times: "The worldliness of this Protestantism and its pretensions to be a national religion reserved for the privileged few have antagonized many of its followers as well as its adversaries. They feel that something is lacking, almost the spirit of religion itself; for the ultimate has been reduced until it embraces little more than ethics."[49] And though the Lynds had indicated that *in theory* religious beliefs dominated all other activities in Middletown, they hastened to add that "actually, large regions of Middletown's life appear uncontrolled by them."[50] In this period, the vast rural reservoirs of Protestant strength were rather rapidly being outmatched by the flooding cities. The Protestantism that threw itself so strongly behind prohibition in the 1920's was one in which the rural tradition was still very strong. Indeed, prohibition itself was in one sense part of the struggle of country against city. The legislative superintendent of the Anti-Saloon League recognized in 1917 that the Eighteenth Amendment had to pass before 1920, for with reapportionment would come, as he put it, "forty new wet Congressmen . . . from the great wet centers with their rapidly increasing population."[51] The final failure of prohibition made it clearer to many Protestants that the familiar American culture in which they had flourished and with which they had been so closely identified was going. The comfortable identification with American cultural patterns no longer seemed so relevant or so helpful.

The beginnings of Protestant renewal, which Herbert Wallace Schneider notes as arising in the "dark 30's" and continuing as an "offensive which has grown steadily since then,"[52] developed in part as religious leaders challenged the identification of Protestantism with American culture and summoned the church to recover its own independent standing-ground. In 1935, Harry Emerson Fosdick preached the famous sermon in which he appealed to Protestants to go "beyond modernism." He exclaimed,

> And in that new enterprise the watchword will be not, Accommodate yourself to the prevailing culture! but, Stand out from it and challenge it! For this inescapable fact, which again and again in Christian history has called modernism to its senses, we face: we cannot harmonize Christ himself with modern culture. What Christ does to modern culture is to challenge it.[53]

And in that same year, to cite another example, appeared a book with the revealing title *The Church Against the World*. It vigorously protested the identification of the church with American culture. Francis P. Miller wrote, "The plain fact is that the domestication of the Protestant community in the United States within the framework of the national culture has progesssed as far as in any western land. The degradation of the American Protestant church is as complete as the degradation of any other national Protestant church."[54] What the church should therefore do was stated by H. Richard Niebuhr in these words:

> We live, it is evident, in a time of hostility when the church is imperiled not only by an external worldliness but by one that has established itself within the

Christian camp. Our position is inside a church which has been on the retreat and which has made compromises with the enemy in thought, in organization, and in discipline. Finally, our position is in the midst of that increasing group in the church which has heard the command to halt, to remind itself of its mission, and to await further orders.[55]

As James H. Smylie has analyzed the theological trend of a steadily enlarging group in American Protestantism, it was "a trend from an irrelevant attachment to society toward a relevant detachment to society without becoming irrelevantly detached from society."[56] The "Christ of culture" motif, which had long been of great significance in American Protestantism, was being challenged from within. From a widening circle of Protestants seeking to return again by one route or another to the independent sources of their faith, there came movements of renewal which marked the beginning of the end of the religious depression for Protestants. There were also other sources of renewal, but this one bears an especial relation to our theme.

I have entitled this paper the "American" religious depression because there was a nationally observable spiritual lethargy evident in the 1920's and 1930's, and because the then clearly dominant religious tradition of the country was in decline. Certainly both Judaism and Roman Catholicism were deeply affected by the economic depression; to what extent they were internally affected by spiritual depression the authorities on those bodies must say. Jewish congregations enjoyed a healthy growth in the 1926–36 decade, reporting a 13.7 per cent increase. Roman Catholicism also grew, but considerably more slowly than in the preceding ten year period. The church had then reported an 18.3 per cent growth, which dropped to 7 per cent for 1926–1936.[57] Perhaps this change was influenced both by the cutting off of immigration and by the generally unfriendly attitude toward religion. But neither Judaism or Catholicism was embarrrassed by too close identification with the surrounding culture, for both felt their minority situation rather keenly. When Geroge N. Shuster wrote his widely-read work on the Catholic spirit in America in 1927, he began by noting that "twenty or thirty years ago ambition would have dictated silence about one's mere connection with what is termed the Roman Church. Today prudence still seems to suggest keeping this matter under cover as fully as possible."[58] But during the depression years a significant change took place; Protestantism declined and lost its sense of being the national religion, while Roman Catholicism, reflecting advances made during and after the war years, consolidated by the National Catholic Welfare Conference, rather quickly became more visible on the American scene. It was less than fifteen years from the time that Shuster wrote the words just quoted that the popular historian Theodore Maynard made this claim: "Protestantism—especially American Protestantism—is now so doctrinally decayed as to be incapable of offering any serious oposition to the sharp sword of the Spirit, as soon as we can make up our minds to use it. Except for isolated 'fundamentalists,'—and these are pretty thoroughly discredited and without intellectual leadership—Catholicism could cut through Protestantism as through so much butter."[59] The contrast between the two quotations dramatizes an important religious transition of the depression period. The upshot of that transition which focused in depression years, though it had been long in the making, was summarized by Will Herberg in his book, *Protestant-Catholic-Jew:*

> In net effect, Protestantism today no longer regards itself either as a religious movement sweeping the continent or as a national church representing the religious life of the people; Protestantism understands itself today primarily as one of the three religious communities in which twentieth century America has come to be divided.[60]

During the period of religious and economic depression, then, the "Protestant era" in America was brought to a close; Protestantism emerged no longer as the "national religion." The test of depression was a severe one; it laid bare certain weaknesses in American Protestantism. But the repudiation of the virtual identification of Protestantism with American culture by an able and growing group of religious leaders freed many Protestants to recover in a fresh way their own heritages and their original sources of inspiration. The depression stimulated many Protestants to seek new and deeper understandings of their own religious heritage, though this "positive" contribution of the depression to religion could probably be appreciated only later. The years of religious and economic depression were years of significant transition for the American churches, for in that period trends long in the making were dramatically revealed, and developments important to the future became visible.

NOTES

1. *American Protestantism and Social Issues, 1919–1939* (Chapel Hill: University of North Carolina Press, 1958), p. 63.

2. "The Recovery of the Religious Sentiment," in Vergilius Ferm, ed., *Contemporary American Theology: Theological Autobiographies* (2 vols., New York: Round Table Press, 1932–1933), II, 367.

3. *Atlantic Monthly,* 143 (January–June, 1929), 378.

4. Fennell P. Turner and Frank Knight Sanders, eds., *The Foreign Missions Conference of North America . . . 1926* (New York: Foreign Missions Conference, 1926), pp. 125–47.

5. "Some Conditions in North America that Affect Foreign Missions," in Leslie B. Moss and Mabel H. Brown, eds., *The Foreign Missions Conference of North America . . . 1934* (New York: Foreign Missions Conference, 1934), p. 148.

6. *Research Memorandum on Religion in the Depression* (New York: Social Science Research Council, Bulletin 33, 1937), p. 51.

7. Based on a study of the figures by the Rev. Donald A. Crosby, whose assistance in the research for this paper I acknowledge with thanks.

8. *Current History,* XXXIII (October, 1930), 25.

9. C. Luther Fry, "Changes in Religious Organizations," *Recent Social Trends* (2 vols.; New York: McGraw-Hill, 1933), II, 1046.

10. Stanley High, "The Need for Youth," in Leslie B. Moss, ed., *The Foreign Missions Conference of North America, 1929* (New York: Foreign Missions Conference, 1929), p. 152.

11. "What the Church Has to Say to Business Men About Foreign Missions," in Leslie B. Moss, ed., *The Foreign Missions Conference of North America, 1928* (New York: Foreign Missions Conference, 1928), p. 85.

12. *Home Missions Council Annual Report . . . 1928* (New York: Home Missions Council, 1928), p. 80.

13. Kincheloe, *Research Memorandum,* pp. 133 f.

14. *Ibid.,* p. 51; *Recent Social Trends,* II, 1055.

15. *The U.S. Looks At Its Churches* (New York: Institute of Social and Religious Research, 1930), p. 58.

16. H. C. Weber, *Evangelism: A Graphic Survey* (New York: Macmillan, 1929), pp. 181 f. I have had the opportunity of seeing charts plotting the "evangelistic index" and summarizing membership trends prepared by the Rev. Harold Edgar Martin; in general they all show decline beginning about 1925 and not showing significant upturn until the middle 1930's.

17. *The Decline and Revival of the Social Gospel: Social and Political Liberalism in American Protestant Churches, 1920–1940* (Ithaca: Cornell University Press, 1954), p. 70, quoting Ellis J. Hough, "Terrors of the Protestant Ministry," *Presbyterian Advance,* XL (Jan. 30, 1930), 18.

18. *American Protestantism and Social Issues,* p. 47.

19. *The Confessions of a Puzzled Parson* (New York: Charles Scribner's Sons, 1928), p. 191.

20. *Does Civilization Need Religion? A Study in the Social Resources and Limitations of Religion in Modern Life* (New York: Macmillan, 1927), p. 2.

21. "What Happened to the Progressive Movement in the 1920's," *American Historical Review,* 64 (1959), 833. See also the perceptive article by Henry F. May, "Shifting Perspectives in the 1920's," *Mississippi Valley Historical Review,* 43 (1956), 405–27.

22. *Theism and the Modern Mood* (New York: Harper and Bros., 1930), p. 6.

23. *The Great Tradition of the American Churches* (New York: Harper and Bros., 1953), p. 196.

24. *Belief Unbound: A Promethean Religion for the Modern World* (New Haven: Yale University Press, 1930), p. 20.

25. *The Modern Temper: A Study and A Confession* (New York: Harcourt Brace and Co., 1929), pp. 191 f.

26. Hornell Hart, "Changing social Attitudes and Interests," *Recent Social Trends,* I, 403.

27. *America Comes of Age* (New York: Harcourt, Brace and Co., 1927), trans. by H. H. Hemming and Doris Hemming, pp. 33, 38 f.

28. "American Protestantism Since the Civil War. I. From Denominationalism to Americanism," *Journal of Religion,* XXXVI (1956), 1.

29. Cf. Chap. III, "Christian Americanization," of my *We Witness Together: A History of Cooperative Home Missions* (New York: Friendship Press, 1956), pp. 64–82.

30. Robert S. Lynd and Helen Merrell Lynd, *Middletown: A Study in Contemporary American Culture* (New York: Harcourt, Brace and Co., 1929), p. 406.

31. "Let Religious Education Beware!" *Christian Century,* 44 (1927), 362.

32. *Faith and Nurture* (New York: Charles Scribner's Sons, 1941), p. 41.

33. *Confessions of a Puzzled Parson,* p. 14.

34. *A Christian Manifesto* (New York: Abingdon Press, 1934), p. 202.

35. Robert S. Lynd and Helen Merrell Lynd, *Middletown in Transition: A Study in Cultural Conflicts* (New York: Harcourt, Brace and Co., 1937), p. 295.

36. *American Protestantism and Social Issues*, p. 63.

37. "Christian Education," in Samuel McCrea Cavert and Henry P. Van Dusen, eds., *The Chruch Through Half a Century: Essays in Honor of William Adams Brown* (New York: Charles Scribner's Sons, 1936), pp. 243 f.

38. H. Paul Douglass and Edmund deS. Brunner, *The Protestant Church as a Social Institution* (New York: Harper and Bros., 1935), p. 208.

39. *Research Memorandum*, p. 1.

40. Liston Pope, *Millhands and Preachers: A Study of Gastonia* (New Haven: Yale University Press, 1942), pp. 126, 128; *Middletown in Transition*, p. 297; Anton T. Boisen, "Religion and Hard Times," *Social Action*, V. (March 15, 1939), 8–35.

41. E.g., cf. Boisen, *loc. cit.*; Elmer T. Clark, *The Small Sects in America* (rev. ed.; New York: Abingdon-Cokesbury Press, 1949), pp. 16–20, 218 f., 230.

42. Walter Marshall Horton, *Realistic Theology* (New York: Harper and Bros., 1934), p. 35.

43. "The Evangelicals' Dilemma," *Atlantic Monthly*, 136 (July–December, 1925), 368–74.

44. *Christian Century*, 50 (1933), 1403.

45. Cf. Sydney E. Ahlstrom, "Continental Influence on American Christian Thought Since World War I," *Church History*, XXVII (1958), 256–72.

46. "Organized Religion," *American Journal of Sociology* 38 (July, 1932–May, 1933), 907.

47. "Calm After Storm," *Christian Century*, 56 (1939), 479.

48. "Religion," *American Journal of Sociology*, 47 (July 1941–May, 1942), 894.

49. *America Comes of Age*, p. 46.

50. *Middletown*, p. 406.

51. Wayne Wheeler, as quoted by Paul A. Carter, *The Decline and Revival of the Social Gospel*, p. 37.

52. *Religion in 20th Century America* (Cambridge: Harvard University Press, 1952), p. 18.

53. "Beyond Modernism: A Sermon," *Christian Century*, 52 (1935), 1552.

54. H. Richard Niebuhr, Wilhelm Pauck, and Francis P. Miller, *The Church Against the World* (Chicago: Willett, Clark and Co., 1935), p. 102.

55. *Ibid.*, pp. 1 f.

56. "The American Protestant Churches and the Depression of the 1930's" (Th.M. Thesis, Princeton Theological Siminary, 1950), p. 125.

57. Bureau of the Census, *Religious Bodies: 1936*, I (Washington: U.S. Government Printing Office, 1941), 51.

58. *The Catholic Spirit in America* (New York: Lincoln Mac Veagh, The Dial Press, 1927), p. vii.

59. *The Story of American Catholicism* (New York: Macmillan, 1941), p. 613.

60. *Protestant-Catholic-Jew: An Essay in American Religious Sociology* (Garden City: Doubleday and Co., 1955), pp. 139 f.

Joel A. Carpenter

Fundamentalist Institutions and the Rise of Evangelical Protestantism, 1929–1942

In April of 1952 an article in *Christian Life* magazine proclaimed Chicago "the evangelical capital of the U.S.A."[1] To back this claim, editor Russell T. Hitt cited a host of evangelical agencies in greater Chicago: mission boards, denominational offices, colleges, Bible institutes, seminaries, publishing concerns (including *Christian Life* itself) and youth organizations. In total, the author mentioned over one hundred different agencies such as Youth For Christ International, the Slavic Gospel Association, Scripture Press and the Swedish Covenant Hospital.[2] At first glance, the article appears to present a confusing list of unrelated organizations, but closer inspection reveals a coherent pattern. The agencies in the Chicago area represented the swiftly growing evangelical movement which observers have labelled the third force of American Christianity.[3] Most institutions listed did not belong to the older, more prestigious denominations. The mission boards, such as Wycliffe Bible Translators, the Worldwide Evangelization Crusade and the International Hebrew Christian Alliance were independents. The denominational headquarters, including those of the Conservative Baptist Association, the Evangelical Mission Covenant Church, the North American Baptist General Conference and the General Association of Regular Baptist Churches, represented fundamentalists and other evangelicals. The schools—the Moody Bible Institute, North Park College, Trinity Seminary and Bible College, Wheaton College, the Mennonite Biblical Seminary, the Salvation Army Training College and Emmaus Bible Institute—came from the same source.[4]

Whether or not Chicago was the capital of evangelicalism is not as important as the image the article revealed. Chicago was a regional evangelical stronghold in the 1950s when the evangelicals were leading a revival of popular religious interest. This revival developed largely from the institutional base which evangelicals had established in the previous decades. The fundamentalists were especially prominent in the postwar evangelical revival. This fact might seem surprising to one who supposed that their movement had been crushed twenty years earlier. That was scarcely the case, as we shall see. Fundamentalism was not a defeated party in denominational politics, but a popular religious movement which in the 1930s developed a separate existence from the older denominations as it strengthened its own institutions. By the 1950s, this building phase had paid off and Billy Graham, a fundamentalist favorite son, became the symbol of evangelicalism's new prominence.

As Hitt's article suggests, evangelicalism was not a monolithic fundamentalism but rather a broad mosaic comprised of clusters of denominations and institutions with different ethnic and doctrinal heritages. One of this mosaic's most visible segments is rightly called fundamentalism, a movement of conservative,

Reprinted with permission from *Church History* 49 (March 1980), 62–75.

millenarian evangelicals who came mostly from Presbyterian, Baptist and independent denominations, such as the Evangelical Free Church. Other segments include the Holiness Wesleyans, such as the Church of the Nazarene; the pentecostals, including the Assemblies of God; the immigrant confessional churches, such as the Lutheran Church, Missouri Synod and the Christian Reformed Church; southern-based conservatives, notably the Southern Baptists and the Churches of Christ; peace churches of Anabaptist, Quaker or pietist backgrounds; and black evangelicals of Methodist, Baptist, Holiness and pentecostal denominations.[5] As the twentieth century progressed, the evangelicals cut a progressively wider swath through the ranks of the American churches. By 1960 they comprised an estimated half of the nation's sixty million Protestants.[6]

When the term fundamentalist is used to designate any or all of these churches, it becomes an ambiguous and derogatory term. But by precise and historical definition, fundamentalism is a distinct religious movement which arose in the early twentieth century to defend traditional evangelical orthodoxy and to extend its evangelistic thrust. The movement combined a biblicist, generally Calvinist orthodoxy, an evangelistic spirit, an emphasis on the higher Christian (Holy Spirit directed) life and a millenarian eschatology. Because the urban centers were strongholds of Protestant liberalism and the most challenging home fields for evangelism, they became the principal centers of early fundamentalist activity. The movement drew its name from *The Fundamentals,* a twelve-volume series of articles published by conservative leaders between 1910 and 1915 to affirm and defend those doctrines which they considered essential to the Christian faith, such as the verbal inspiration and infallibility of the Bible and salvation only by faith in the atoning death of Jesus Christ. Fundamentalism was a popular movement, not merely a mentality; it had leaders, institutions and a particular identity. Fundamentalists recognized each other as party members as it were, and distinguished themselves from the other evangelicals listed above.[7]

As a complex aggregate entity, evangelical Protestantism in the twentieth century demands closer attention than it has received. Studies of the 1930s and early 1940s in particular have yielded little understanding of its development. The prevailing opinion among historians is that Protestantism suffered a depression during at least the first half of the 1930s which was relieved only when neo-orthodox theology renewed the vision and vitality of the old-line denominations.[8] Evangelical Protestants fit into this scheme only tangentially. Sydney Ahlstrom noted that "something like a revival took place" among the holiness, fundamentalist and pentecostal churches; and William McLoughlin credited evangelicals with keeping alive the tradition of revivalism during the depression. Other historians, however, viewed the activity of this third force as a symptom of Protestantism's depressed condition rather than a sign of grassroots vitality.[9] The institutional growth in the 1930s of the most vocal and visible evangelicals, the fundamentalists, challenges the widespread notion that popular Protestantism experienced a major decline during that decade. What really transpired was the beginning of a shift of the Protestant mainstream from the older denominations toward the evangelicals.

The older denominations did experience what Robert T. Handy called a "religious depression," beginning in the middle of the 1920s until the late thirties, when their fortunes revived somewhat. For example, membership in the northern Presbyterian and the Protestant Episcopal denominations declined 5.0 and 6.7 percent respectively between 1926 and 1936. The foreign missionary enterprise lost momentum as budgets tightened and many missionaries returned home at mid-career for lack of funds.[10] Social programs also suffered from the loss of contributions as the churches had to cut off the lower end of their priority lists.[11] At the onset of the great depression of the 1930s, many Christians wondered if a revival would descend, bringing with it the return of prosperity. But Samuel C. Kincheloe reported to the Social Science Research Council in 1937 that "the trend over the past thirty years" had been "away from emotional revival services"; and that the depression did "not seem to have produced much variation in this major trend."[12] When Robert and Helen Lynd revisited "Middletown" in 1935, they saw little evidence of a religious awakening. "If the number of revivals is any index of religious interest in the depression," they concluded, "there has been a marked recession."[13] McLoughlin and Ahlstrom recognized, however, that the slight overall growth in Protestant membership in the 1930s stemmed largely from what the Lynds had called "working-class churches."[14]

In singular contrast to the plight of the major denominations, fundamentalists and other evangelicals prospered. During the 1920s, fundamentalists had grown more vocal and apparently more numerous, but the leaders had been publicly defeated in denominational battles, and had made themselves look foolish in the anti-evolution crusade.[15] Adverse publicity from public controversy had discredited fundamentalists and established the Menckenesque image which has dogged them even since.[16] Yet these defeats by no means destroyed the movement. Fundamentalism cannot be understood by studying only its role in headline-making conflicts. Rather, we must examine the growing network of institutions upon which fundamentalists increasingly relied as they became alienated from the old-line denominations.

One of the most important focal points of fundamentalist activity in the thirties was the Bible institute, a relatively new type of institutional structure. The two pioneers of Bible institute education were A. B. Simpson, founder of the Christian and Missionary Alliance, who in 1882 established the Missionary Training Institute in New York City, and Dwight L. Moody, who founded in 1886 what became the Moody Bible Institute of Chicago.[17] The idea of a teaching center for lay Christian workers caught on quickly, and other schools sprang up across the country. By 1930 the fundamentalist weekly *Sunday School Times* endorsed over fifty Bible schools, most of which were in major cities.[18]

The Bible institutes became the major coordinating agencies of the movement by the 1930s, as popular fundamentalist alienation toward the old-line denominations reached new heights. True, most fundamentalists had not left the older denominations, but after the controversies over evolutionary theory and theological liberalism in the 1920s, they were more aware than before of the intellectual attitudes engendered by church-related colleges and seminaries. While the nondenominational Bible institutes had been founded to train lay and paraministerial workers such as Sunday school superintendents and foreign missionaries, now they faced demands for educating pastors and for other services that denominations formerly provided.[19]

Since the Bible institutes had already branched out into activities not directly connected with in-residence instruction, they were well equipped to meet such demands. Some of the schools had extension departments, such as those of the Philadelphia School of the Bible, or the Moody Bible Institute of Chicago. These agencies organized week-long summer and other shorter Bible conferences, supplied staff evangelists for revival meetings and provided churches with guest preachers.[20] Many schools ran publishing and/or distributing ventures, including the Bible Institute of Los Angeles' BIOLA Bookroom, Approved Books of the Philadelphia School of the Bible (PSOB) and the mammoth Bible Institute Colportage Association at Moody.[21] In addition many magazines provided their schools with publicity and the readers with fundamentalist literature and opinion: *The Moody Monthly, The King's Business* of BIOLA, *Serving and Waiting* of PSOB, Northwestern (Minneapolis) Bible and Missionary Training School's *The Pilot* and Denver Bible Institute's *Grace and Truth.*[22] As centers of religious enterprise, the Bible institutes soon saw the potential impact of radio broadcasting both as a religious service opportunity and a way to increase their constituency. BIOLA led the way with its own station, KJS, in 1922. Moody installed WMBI three years later, and, although they did not own stations during the 1930s, Providence (R.I.) Bible Institute, Columbia Bible College in South Carolina and Denver Bible Institute all sponsored radio programs.[23]

With so many services to provide to fundamentalist individuals and small Bible classes and congregations, the Bible schools became regional and national coordinating centers for the movement. Moody Bible Institute (MBI) became the national giant of institutional fundamentalism. The MBI Extension Department held weekend Bible conferences in nearly 500 churches during 1936, more than doubling its exposure of six years earlier. By 1942, WMBI was releasing transcribed programs to 187 different stations, and the radio staff had visited nearly 300 different churches since the stations' inception, returning to many churches several times. The Institute had over 15,000 contributors in 1937 and about the same number enrolled in Correspondence School, while the *Moody Monthly* showed a net increase of 13,000 subscribers over the decade to total 40,000 by 1940.[24] Other schools could not match MBI in scale, but they carried strong regional influence. By the mid-1930s, for instance, Gordon College of Theology and Missions had supplied 100 pastors in greater Boston, and 48 out of the total 96 Baptist pastors in New Hampshire. At one time in the 1930s, every Baptist pastor in Boston proper was either a Gordon alumnus, professor or trustee.[25] In Minnesota, William Bell Riley, the pastor of Minneapolis First Baptist Church, held virtually a fundamentalist bishopric by virtue of the 75 pastors statewide who had attended this Northwestern Bible and Missionary Training School.[26] BIOLA had 180 alumni Christian workers in California by 1939.[27] Considering all the activity Bible institutes engaged in, the influence they wielded through direct contact and alumni, and the support they received, it is no wonder that one confused reader of the *Moody Monthly* asked, "Why don't you publish something on the other denominations once in a while?"[28]

Fundamentalists who desired a Christian liberal arts education for their children in the 1930s sought it for the most part outside the movement proper. The fundamentalists themselves operated only a few such schools, notably Wheaton College near Chicago and Bob Jones College then located in Cleveland, Tennessee, while Gordon College of Missions and Theology in Boston was developing an arts and sciences division. Advertisements in fundamentalist periodicals show, however, that colleges sponsored by other evangelicals, including Taylor University in Upland, Indiana and Grove City College in Pennsylvania, attracted students from fundamentalist congregations.[29] These evangelical colleges prospered during the thirties. A survey of evangelical higher education in 1948 found that the total enrollment of seventy such schools in the United States doubled between 1929 and 1940.[30]

Wheaton College, founded in 1857, provides perhaps the most striking example of the rapid growth of fundamentalist higher education. J. Oliver Buswell, Wheaton's president from 1926–1940, labored to improve its enrollment and academic standing. During his administration the college won a high accreditation rating, and for three years Wheaton led all liberal arts colleges in growth nationwide. By 1941 Wheaton's enrollment of 1100, up from about 400 in 1926, led all liberal arts colleges in Illinois.[31] The school had become the "Harvard of the Bible Belt," a producer of such evangelical leaders as theologian Carl F. H. Henry and Billy Graham.[32]

As millions of Americans motored each summer to popular resorts, a growing number of summer Bible conferences competed with tourist camps and resort hotels for the patronage of vacationing fundamentalists.[33] From the Boardwalk Bible Conference in Atlantic City, and the Montrose Summer Gatherings in the Pennsylvania hills, at Winona Lake in Indiana, at Redfeather Lakes in the Colorado Rockies, and at Mount Hermon, California,[34] Bible conferences offered a unique vacation: a blend of resort style recreation, the old-fashioned camp meeting and biblical teaching from leading fundamentalist pulpiteers.[35] Enrollees might hear Harry A. Ironside of Chicago's Moody Memorial Church, Paul Rood of BIOLA or Martin R. DeHaan of the "Radio Bible Class." The conferences offered different programs so one could choose among sessions featuring missions, young people, the pastorate, Bible study, "Victorious Living," prophecy, sacred music, business men, business women, or Sunday school.[36] The lists of forthcoming conferences published each summer by the *Moody Monthly* grew steadily larger during the thirties, from twenty-seven sites and 88 conference sessions in 1930, to over 200 sessions at more than fifty different locations in 1941.[37]

A report in the Baptist *Watchman-Examiner* of the Bible Conference at Winona Lake, Indiana in 1941 portrays the character of such meetings. Each summer, the whole Winona Lake community became a religious resort with thousands of fundamentalists renting cottages and streaming to the conference grounds. The meetings that capped off the 1941 summer schedule at Winona Lake attracted more than 2,000 enrollees, including some 400 ministers. They were joined by perhaps 2,000 more daily visitors. Participants listened to as many as six sermons a day out of the thirteen to fourteen total sessions scheduled between seven in the morning and ten in the evening. The men on the platform included several fundamentalist celebrities: William Bell Riley of First Baptist Church, Minneapolis; Harold T. Commons, executive director of the Association of Baptists for the Evangelization of the Orient; and evangelists J. C. Massee, Ralph E. Neighbour and J. Hoffman Cohn. The master of ceremonies was Billy Sunday's former partner Homer Rodeheaver, "the leading song director of America."[38] The reporter sensed a brotherhood at the conference which knew no denominational bounds when he saw that

> a Methodist Bishop, a Baptist evangelist, a Presbyterian professor, a Lutheran pastor, a Christian layman and a Rescue Mission superintendent could stand on the same platform and preach the common tenets of the Christian faith while multitudes of believers wept and rejoiced together as if some glorious news had for the first time burst upon their ears.[39]

Such events were a powerful force for cementing the bonds of commitment within the movement. In 1937 the *Sunday School Times* reported a poll taken at a small Bible college which showed that all but fifteen of the 150 students had attended a summer conference. Sixty-five first accepted Christ or made a recommitment to the Christian life there, and sixty-two claimed that they were in Bible college because of a summer conference. According to the editor, the Bible conference had become "one of the most powerful factors in spiritual life of the church."[40]

In the 1930s the rapidly rising commercial radio industry provided the fundamentalists with a new medium through which to send out their "old gospel" to the rest of the nation. The number of radio sets had doubled between 1930 and 1935 to over eighteen million. By 1938 a *Fortune* survey named radio listening the first preference for leisure time entertainment in America. Fundamentalist preachers quickly took to the airwaves. A casual, reader-contributed directory in the January 23, 1932 *Sunday School Times* lists over 400 evangelical programs on eighty different stations nationwide.[41]

Interest in religious broadcasting was not limited to the fundamentalist movement. For a time they and other evangelicals feared restrictive network policies would force them off the airwaves. The Federal Council of Churches, the United Synagogues of America and the National Catholic Welfare Conference cooperated with the Columbia Broadcasting System and the National Broadcasting Corporation to produce nonsectarian programs on free network time. The CBS "Church of the Air" featured such prominent preachers as Harry Emerson Fosdick, Bishop Fulton J. Sheen and Rabbi Stephen S. Wise. This venture reflected the intention of CBS and NBC to limit religious broadcasting to a few hours a week and to "representative" national religious bodies.[42] Father Charles E. Coughlin's controversial radio blasts over the CBS network had led that network to adopt a policy that would insure bland, "safe" religious programming.[43] This change directly affected the evangelical broadcasters, especially the fundamentalists, many of whom had paid for network time. These preachers were often controversial or sectarian in tone and received no place in ecumenical broadcasting schemes. Yet the fundamentalists and friends were by no means driven from the air. The religious programs were too attractive a market for commercial stations to turn down, and hundreds of local stations sold them time, as did the new Mutual Broadcasting System until 1944.[44] Indeed, it became clear by the late thirties that paid programs drew the greater share of popular support. Charles E. Fuller's weekly "Old-Fashioned Revival Hour" became the most popular religious program in the country.[45]

The "Old-Fashioned Revival Hour" climbed rapidly to national prominence. From modest beginnings in 1925, Charles E. Fuller, fundamentalist pastor of Calvary Church in the Los Angeles suburb of Placentia, expanded the work in its early years to include three weekday broadcasts, two Sunday broadcasts from Calvary Church and a Sunday broadcast sponsored by BIOLA over the CBS Pacific Coast network. Fuller left his church for full-time radio ministry in 1933 and soon was heard each Sunday on the Mutual Network. Six years later the "Old-Fashioned Revival Hour" was broadcast weekly coast to coast and overseas to an estimated fifteen to twenty million listeners. Fuller's coverage consisted of 152 stations in 1939 and 456 three years later, the largest single release of any prime time radio broadcast in America.[46]

As a whole fundamentalist forays into national broadcasting were immensely successful. Other programs captured regional and national audiences, most notably Martin R. DeHaan's "Radio Bible Class," Philadelphia Presbyterian Donald Gray Barnhouse's "Bible Study Hour" and the "Miracles and Melodies" series transcribed by Moody Bible Institute's studio. Programs with smaller coverage supplemented them to fill the airwaves with the old-time gospel. More than any other medium, radio kept revivalistic religion before the American public.[47]

Of all the activities pursued by both fundamentalists and major Protestant denominations during the 1930s, their foreign missionary work portrayed most starkly their contrasting fortunes. The great missionary enterprise of the Protestant churches had entered the twentieth century with unbounded hope and zeal; but liberal disillusion with evangelism, inflation and constituents' dislike of liberal programs depleted the denominational mission budgets and stifled enthusiastic young volunteers. For instance, the Northern Baptist Convention experienced an extremely heavy decline in its mission program. Its staff dwindled from 845 in 1930 to 508 in 1940. The year 1936 was particularly disastrous as NBC contributions for missions totaled $2.26 million, down 45 percent from 1920. That year no new missionaries went out, and many in the field came home for lack of money.[48]

Fundamentalists wanted missionaries who preached the old gospel of individual repentance and redemption. They recoiled from the denominational boards because of alleged theological liberalism, social gospel programs and high overhead costs.[49] But fundamentalist interest in missions did not flag. Fundamentalists supported independent, "faith" missions which were not denominationally connected and did not solicit funds directly. They also founded new denominational agencies. While the Laymen's Foreign Missions Inquiry reported in 1932 that evangelism in missions was passé, the fundamentalist-backed missions grew stronger, better financed, more evangelistically aggressive and more successful in recruiting volunteers than ever before.[50] The China Inland Mission (CIM), a giant among the independents, experienced the greatest growth of its history during the thirties. Even though China was then involved in conflict with Japan and suffering internal strife, CIM sent out 629 new missionaries in 1930–1936, for a total force of almost 1400.[51] CIM was but one of a growing group of independent fundamentalist missions. Each year, the *Sunday School Times* published a list of fundamentalist mission agencies, which showed forty-nine in 1931 and seventy-six by 1941. These missions ranged in size from the tiny Layyah Barakat (Syria) Home for Orphan Girls to the Sudan Interior Mission, which received $250,000 in 1937 and doubled its army of missionaries during the decade.[52]

These missions worked in close association with Bible institutes which trained missionaries, housed mission offices and helped raise funds. From the Moody Bible Institute alone came over 550 new missionaries from 1930 to 1941, while BIOLA housed both the Orinoco River Mission and the United Aborigines Mission offices.[53] Unfortunately, we know little about this wave of missionary recruits from the Bible institutes and evangelical colleges. Likewise, we know next to nothing of the collective impact of the independent boards and those of conservative denominations since 1900. Yet this brief glimpse at activities during the 1930s shows that a movement of great proportions was underway. Evangelical fervor for missions generated by the Student Volunteer Movement had not died but rather had changed its institutional base. As a traditional indicator of religious vitality, missionary activity demonstrated the vigor of fundamentalism no less than the movement's other enterprises.

In these four areas of fundamentalist activity—education, summer Bible conferences, radio broadcasting and foreign missions—the evidence shows a growing, dynamic movement. Other activities thrived also: publishing houses such as Fleming H. Revell, Loizeaux Brothers and Moody Press; and seminaries, notably Evangelical Theological College in Dallas, Texas, and Westminster Theological Seminary of Philadelphia, Pennsylvania. Even this brief survey, however, demonstrates that the fundamentalist movement did not decline during the thirties. Rather, there was a shift of emphasis within the movement. Fundamentalist efforts to cleanse the denominations of liberal trends had seemed to fail. Rather than persisting along the 1920s lines of conflict, fundamentalists during the 1930s were developing their own institutional base from which to carry on their major purpose: the proclamation of the evangelical gospel.

Was there an "American Religious Depression" among Protestants during the 1930s? Not among fundamentalists and apparently not among other evangelicals either. Fundamentalist activities mentioned here had parallels. The other evangelical groups grew during the 1930s, some very repidly indeed. The Assemblies of God increased fully fourfold from 47,950 in 1926 to 198,834 members in 1940. The Church of the Nazarene more than doubled its membership from 63,558 to 165,532. The Southern Baptists gained almost 1.5 million members over the same period to total 4,949,174, while the Christian Reformed Church counted 121,755 members in 1940, an increase of 25 percent.[54] Perhaps old-line Protestantism was depressed but popular evangelicalism flourished.

Did the evangelicals provide the impetus for the post–World War II revivals? The fundamentalist community played a leading role. Billy Graham's crusades and other agents of revivalism such as Youth For Christ were not merely throwbacks to the Billy Sunday era. They were the postwar descendants of a continuing revival tradition preserved and transformed by the fundamentalist movement. For instance, Youth For Christ held its first nationwide convention at the Winona Lake Conference in the summer of 1944. Its first president, Torrey Johnson, was a Wheaton College graduate. Of course, Graham was a Wheaton graduate also. His evangelistic team included George Beverly Shea, a former soloist at WMBI, and song leader Cliff Barrows, a Bob Jones College graduate.[55] Revivalism had not died during the depression. Rather, the fundamentalist movement nurtured that tradition, introduced innovations and produced a new generation of revivalists.

The evidence is compelling, therefore: we need a reassessment of the nature and influence of fundamentalism. The revivalistic, millenarian movement that flourished in the urban centers of North America in the late nineteenth and early twentieth centuries continued under the banner of fundamentalism and left no break in the line of succession from Dwight L. Moody to Billy Graham. Fundamentalism bears all the marks of a popular religious movement which drew only part of its identity from opposition to liberal trends in the denominations. The movement had its own ideology and program to pursue. As Ernest R. Sandeen has shown, millenarian eschatology was an important ideological component.[56] Yet fundamentalism's commitment to urban evangelism and foreign missions suggests that the movement was primarily concerned with preaching the evangelical gospel in the twentieth century, both at home and abroad. The evidence shows that it pursued this goal with increasing success during the 1930s.

Once again, as had happened so many times in the past, part of Christianity had taken the form of a vigorous popular movement. Fundamentalists surged out of the bonds of older denominational structures to create flexible, dynamic institutions, such as independent mission agencies, radio programs and Bible schools. Despite or perhaps in part because of opposition, the movement grew. According to anthropologists Luther P. Gerlach and Virginia H. Hine, movements arise to implement changes, to pursue goals that people think the established order is unsuccessful in attaining. Thus, a movement often grows in opposition to the established order from which it came. Because movements are decentralized and based on popular support, they are virtually irrepressible.[57] So it has been with fundamentalism. This widely dispersed network of conservative evangelicals became increasingly at odds with the old-line Protestant establishment. Defeats in the denominational conflicts of the 1920s forced fundamentalists to strengthen their own institutional structures outside of old-line denominations. They responded creatively to the trends in contemporary popular culture and made a lasting place for themselves in American Protestantism. Fundamentalists and other evangelicals prospered. The outlines of a changed Protestant order began to emerge by 1950. However, the task of studying the growth of popular evangelical movements in the context of American cultural history remains. How these movements were involved in the larger process of cultural change has yet to be seen.

NOTES

1. Russell T. Hitt, "Capital of Evangelicalism," *Christian Life* 5 (April 1952):16.

2. Ibid., pp. 16–18, 46–48. *Christian Life* itself was an interesting symbol of a growing evangelical wing of Protestantism. *Christian Life* was formed in 1948 by enterprising young evangelical publishers who wanted a market for a breezy, "Christian" version of *Life* magazine. *Christian Life* 1 (July 1948):3.

3. "The Third Force in Christendom," *Life* (June 9, 1958):113–121; and Henry P. Van Dusen, "The Third Force's Lesson for Others," *Life* (June 9, 1958):122, 125. See also William G. McLoughlin, "Is There a Third Force in Christendom?" *Daedalus* 96 (Winter 1967):43–68; Winthrop S. Hudson, *American Protestantism* (Chicago, 1961), pp. 153–176.

4. Hitt, "Capital of Evangelicalism," pp. 16, 18, 46, 48.

5. Hudson, *American Protestantism*, pp. 155–165. Here I am especially indebted to my colleagues in a research project funded by the National Endowment for the Humanities, "The American Evangelical Mosaic." For information on evangelical groups, see Ernest R. Sandeen, *The Roots of Fundamentalism, British and American Millenarianism, 1800–1930* (Chicago, 1970); Timothy L. Smith, *Called Unto Holiness, The Story of the Nazarenes: The Formative Years* (Kansas City, Mo., 1962); Klaude Kendrick, *The Promise Fulfilled: A History of the Modern Pentecostal Movement* (Springfiled, Mo., 1961); James DeForest Murch, *Christians Only: A History of the Restoration Movement* (Cincinnati, 1962); William Wright Barnes, *History of the Southern Baptist Convention, 1845–1953* (Nashville, 1954); Milton L. Rudnick, *Fundamentalism and the Missouri Synod* (St. Louis, 1966); John Henry Kromminga, *The Christian Reformed Church: A Study in Orthodoxy* (Grand Rapids, 1949); Cornelius J. Dyck, ed., *An Introduction to Mennonite History* (Scottdale, Pa., 1967); E. Franklin Frazier, *The Negro Church in America* (New York, 1964).

6. Hudson, *American Protestantism*, pp. 155, 162.

7. The problem of defining fundamentalism is discussed in Ernest R. Sandeen, "Toward a Historical Interpretation of the Origins of Fundamentalism," *Church History* 36 (March 1967):66–83; LeRoy Moore, Jr., "Another Look at Fundamentalism: A Response to Ernest R. Sandeen," *Church History* 37 (June 1968):195–202; Geroge M. Marsden, "Defining Fundamentalism," *Christian Scholar's Review* 1 (Winter 1971):141–151; Ernest R. Sandeen, "Defining Fundamentalism: A Reply to Professor Marsden," *Christian Scholar's Review* 1 (Spring 1971):227–233; Ernest R. Sandreen, "*The Fundamentals*: The Last Flowering of the Millenarian-Conservative Alliance," *Journal of Presbyterian History* 47 (March 1969):55–73.

8. Martin E. Marty, *Righteous Empire: The Protestant Experience in America* (New York, 1970), pp. 233–243; Robert T. Handy, *A Christian America, Protestant Hopes and Historical Realities* (New York, 1971), pp. 217–219. See also Paul A. Carter, *The Decline and Revival of the Social Gospel* (Ithaca, N.Y., 1954).

9. Sydney E. Ahlstrom, *A Religious History of the American People* (New Haven, 1972), p. 920; William G. McLoughlin, *Modern Revivalism: Charles Grandison Finney to Billy Graham* (New York, 1959), pp. 462–468; Handy, *A Christian America*, p. 203; Marty, *Righteous Empire*, p. 237.

10. Robert T. Handy, "The American Religious Depression, 1926–1935," *Church History* 29 (March 1960):4–5; percentages computed from membership statistics in U.S. Department of Commerce, Bureau of the Census, *Religious Bodies, 1936*, 2 vols., vol. 2 *Denominations* (Washington, D.C., 1941):1386, 1478.

11. Handy, "The American Religious Depression," pp. 5–9.

12. Samuel C. Kincheloe, *Research Memorandum on Religion in the Depression*, Social Science Research Council #17 (New York, 1937), p. 93. See also, "Why No Revival?" *The Christian Century* 52 (Sept. 18, 1935):1168–1170; "Billy Sunday, the Last of His Line," *The Christian Century* 52 (Nov. 20, 1935):1476.

13. Robert S. and Helen M. Lynd, *Middletown in Transition* (New York, 1937), p. 303.

14. Ahlstrom, *A Religious History of the American People,* p. 920; McLoughlin, *Modern Revivalism,* p. 464.

15. Norman F. Furniss, *The Fundamentalist Controversy, 1918–1931* (New Haven, 1954), pp. 103–176; Stewart G. Cole, *The History of Fundamentalism* (New York, 1931), pp. 65–225; Sandeen, *The Roots of Fundamentalism,* pp. 250–264.

16. Furniss, *The Fundamentalist Controversy,* pp. 76–100; Cole, *The History of Fundamentalism,* pp. 259–280.

17. S. A. Witner, *The Bible College Story: Education With Dimension* (Manhasset, N.Y., 1962), pp. 34–37.

18. "Bible Schools That are True to the Faith," *Sunday School Times* 72 (February 1, 1930):63 (hereafter cited as *SST*).

19. Ernest R. Sandeen suggests this development, pointing out in *The Roots of Fundamentalism* (pp. 241–243) that the scope of Bible institute activity was such that the schools functioned as denominational surrogates.

20. Renald E. Showers, "A History of Philadelphia College of Bible," (M.Th. Thesis, Dallas Theological Seminary, 1962), pp. 69, 81, 86; *Brief Facts About the Moody Bible Institute of Chicago* (Chicago, 1928); *Moody Bible Institute Bulletin* 12 (November 1932):14; 16 (November 1936):15.

21. "Institute Items," *The King's Business* 3 (November 1912):295–296; Showers, "Philadelphia College," pp. 69, 89; *A Brief Story of the Bible Institute Colportage Association of Chicago: Forty-five Years of Printed Page Ministry* (Chicago, 1939).

22. "Interdenominational Christian Magazines," *SST* 73 (February 7, 1931):72.

23. Daniel P. Fuller, *Give The Winds A Mighty Voice: The Story of Charles E. Fuller* (Waco, Texas, 1972), pp. 75–77; "WMBI," *Moody Monthly* 30 (January 1930):270; "Radio Station WMBI," *Moody Monthly* 31 (May 1931):480; "The Sunday School Times Radio Directory," *SST* 73 (May 30, 1931):313. Hereafter, *Moody Monthly* is cited as *MM*.

24. *Moody Bible Institute Bulletin* 12 (November 1932):14; 16 (November 1936):15; "Miracles and Melodies," *MM* 42 (April 1942):487. Figures on radio staff itineraries compiled from *Annual Report of the Radio Department of the Moody Bible Institute of Chicago* for the years 1929–1941; "President's Report," *Moody Bible Institute Bulletin* 17 (October 1937):3; typescript table taken from file six, "Enrollment," The Moodyana Collection, Moody Bible Institute; "And Now For 50,000," *MM* 41 (September 1940):4; *N. W. Ayer and Son's Dictionary of Newspapers and Periodicals,* 65th anniversary edition (Philadelphia, 1933).

25. Nathan R. Wood, *A School of Christ* (Boston, 1953), pp. 165–166.

26. "The Sweep of Northwestern Schools," *The Pilot* 17 (January 1937):108.

27. "BIOLA's Workers in the Homelands," *The King's Business* 30 (July 1939):268–270.

28. "A Magazine For All," *MM* 40 (February 1942):249.

29. Several such colleges were advertised in *MM* issues from September 1930 to August 1931.

30. Harry J. Albus, "Christian Education Today," *Christian Life* 1 (September 1948):26, 46, quoted in Louis Gasper, *The Fundamentalist Movement* (The Hague, 1963), p. 104.

31. "The World Is Wondering About Wheaton," *Baptist Bulletin* 3 (March 1938):14; "Wheaton College, 'For Christ and His Kingdom,'" *Baptist Bulletin* 1 (November 1935):5, 11–12; "Dr. Buswell to be President of the National Bible Institute," *SST* 83 (May 24, 1941):434; "Wheaton Annuities," *SST* 79 (September 4, 1937):61; "Wheaton College," *Watchman-Examiner* 29 (October 16, 1941):1067. The survey of higher education in the October 11, 1936 issue of *The New York Times,* section 2, p. 5; confirms the claims for that year.

32. "Wheaton College, Harvard of the Bible Belt," *Change* 6 (March 1974):17–20; McLough-

lin, *Modern Revivalism*, p. 486; Carl F. H. Henry, "Twenty Years a Baptist," *Foundations* 1 (1958):46–47.

33. Dixon Wecter reported that as many as thirty-five million Americans went on vacation trips each summer in the thirties. Wecter, *The Age of the Great Depression, 1924–1941* (New York, 1948), p. 225.

34. "Forthcoming Conferences," *MM* 35 (August 1935):589.

35. "Shall I Go to a Summer Bible Conference?" *SST* 77 (May 18, 1935):337; C. H. Heaton, "The Winona Lake Bible Conference," *Watchman-Examiner* 29 (September 4, 1941):826.

36. "Forthcoming Conferences," *MM* 34 (July 1934):528; "Forthcoming Conferences," *MM* 35 (August 1935):589.

37. "Forthcoming Conferences," *MM* 30 (June 1930):517; "Forthcoming Conferences," *MM* 41 (June 1941):614.

38. C. H. Heaton, "Winona Lake Bible Conference," p. 826.

39. Ibid.

40. "Why Attend A Summer Conference?" *SST* 79 (May 15, 1937):348.

41. Herman S. Hettinger, "Broadcasting in the United States" and Spencer J. Miller, "Radio and Religion," *Annals of the American Academy of Political and Social Sciences* 177 (January 1935):6, 140; "Fortune Survey: Radio Favorites," *Fortune* (January 1938):88; "A Directory of Evangelical Radio Broadcasts," *SST* 74 (January 23, 1932):44–45.

42. Miller, "Radio and Religion," pp. 136–139; Fuller, *Give the Winds a Mighty Voice*, pp. 101–103.

43. "Directory of Evangelical Radio Broadcasts," p. 44; "Another Year of Miracle Gospel Broadcast," *SST* 81 (October 21, 1939):720–722.

44. Fuller, *Give the Winds a Mighty Voice*, pp. 151–157.

45. "Another Year of Miracle Radio Broadcast," p. 720; Fuller, *Give the Winds a Mighty Voice*, pp. 113–122.

46. Untitled listing of radio programs, *SST* 73 (April 12, 1931):184; "The Sunday School Times Radio Directory," *SST* 73 (May 30, 1931):313; Charles E. Fuller File, Baptist Ministers and Missionaries Benefit Board Registry, the Samuel Colgate Library of the American Baptist Historical Society, Rochester, New York; Gasper, *The Fundamentalist Movement*, p. 77; "Another Year of Miracle Gospel Broadcast," p. 720; Fuller, *Give the Winds a Mighty Voice*, p. 140.

47. Gasper, *The Fundamentalist Movement*, pp. 19–20, 76–78; George A. Dollar, *A History of Fundamentalism* (Greenville, S.C., 1973), pp. 255–257; "Hear WMBI Favorites On Your Station," *MM* 41 (September 1940):31.

48. Curtis Lee Laws, "Shall Baptists Go Out of Business?" *Watchman-Examiner* 24 (January 2, 1936):13; "The Tragedy of the Northern Baptist Convention," *Watchman-Examiner* 24 (June 11, 1936):699; "The Tragedy of It All," *Baptist Bulletin* 6 (July 1940):1; *Annual of the Northern Baptist Convention, 1937* (Philadelphia, 1937), p. 28.

49. A classic fundamentalist exposé of the missions situation is in Robert T. Ketcham, *Facts for Baptists To Face* (Chicago, 1937), pp. 5–15. Lewis A. Brown, "A Missionary Speaks Plainly," *Watchman-Examiner* 25 (March 18, 1937):300, and Carey S. Thomas, "Is Non-Cooperation Justifiable?" *Watchman-Examiner* 25 (February 18, 1937):179–181, are lamentations of the nonsupport of conservatives.

50. Handy, *A Christian America*, pp. 190–196. William E. Hocking, ed., *Rethinking Missions* (New York, 1932) is the major report of the findings of the Laymen's Foreign Missions Inquiry.

51. Robert Hall Glover, "What Is a Faith Mission?" *Missionary Review of the World* 58 (September 1935):409–411; "Suggestions for Your Christmas Giving," *SST* 73 (December 26, 1931):737; Ernest Gordon, "A Survey of Religious Life and Thought," *SST* 81 (June 24,

1939):430; Robert Hall Glover, "Decrease in Missions Giving—Its Real Cause and Cure," *Revelation* 7 (June 1937):241.

52. "Suggestions for Your Christmas Giving," *SST* 73 (December 26, 1931):737; "A New Missionary Board for the Old Faith," *SST* 76 (May 5, 1934):287; "The Presbyterian Controversy," *MM* 35 (May 1935):411; "Suggestions for Your Christmas Giving," *SST* 83 (December 6, 1941):1010–1111; Gordon, "A Survey of Religious Life and Thought," p. 430.

53. President's yearly reports, *MBI Bulletin* 12 (November 1932):5; 13 (April 30, 1933):3; 14 (November 1934):4; 16 (November 1936):6; 17 (February 1938):3; 18 (February 1939):3; 19 (February 1940):8; 20 (February 1941):6; 21 (February 1942):5; *The Appeal of the Century* (Chicago, ca. 1937), p. 5.

54. United States Department of Commerce, Bureau of the Census, *Denominations;* Benson Y. Landis, ed., *Yearbook of American Churches, 1941* (New York, 1941); compare Ahlstrom, *A Religious History of the American People,* p. 920.

55. McLoughlin, *Modern Revivalism,* pp. 480–487.

56. Sandeen, *Roots of Fundamentalism,* pp. xviii–xxiii.

57. Luther P. Gerlach and Virginia H. Hine, *People, Power, Change: Movements of Social Transformation* (Indianapolis, 1970), pp. xvi–xix.

CHAPTER
20

Judaism and the American Experience

If Roman Catholics constituted the most significant immigrant group in nineteenth-century America, the Jews would occupy comparable status for the twentieth century. Driven from Europe by economic privation and vicious "pogroms" that severely limited rights of citizenship, Jews found in America a "promised land" of equality and opportunity. At the same time, they encountered American hostility from nativist attempts to limit their immigration and from anti-Semitism that arose in all facets of American life, from industry to colleges and universities.

Persecution did not prevent a process of "Americanization" from taking place, however. The most conspicuous by-product of the European Enlightenment and American republican thought was the numerical triumph of Reform Judaism over the more traditional Orthodox tradition in early and mid-nineteenth-century America. Reform Judaism was, in turn, challenged by an Orthodox tradition strengthened by arriving east European immigrants after 1880, and by a growing Conservative Judaism that occupied a middle place between the Orthodox and Reform traditions in the United States.

Jonathan D. Sarna's essay demonstrates the influence of American democratization and modernization on seating patterns in the American synagogue. Through an imaginative methodology, Sarna shows how something as seemingly innocuous as seating turns out to be a profound social index to patterns of change and continuity in American Judaism.

Additional Reading: Jacob Rader Marcus, *The Colonial American Jew, 1492–1776,* 3 vols. (Detroit, 1970), is the most comprehensive treatment of its subject. Arthur Hertzberg, *The Jews in America: Four Centuries of an Uneasy Encounter: A History* (New York, 1989) and Jonathan D. Sarna (ed.), *The American Jewish Experience: A Reader* (New York, 1986) capture the general history of Jews in America, Two books by Deborah Dash Moore, *At Home in America: Second Generation New York Jews* (New York, 1981) and *To the Golden Cities: Pursuing the American Jewish Dream in*

Miami and L.A. (New York, 1994), describe the Jewish experience on both the east and west coast. Dan A. Oren, *Joining the Club: A History of Jews and Yale* (New Haven, 1985) assesses the history of anti-Semitism in an American university.

Jonathan D. Sarna

Seating and the American Synagogue

One can learn much about the history of the American synagogue by looking at where members of the congregation sat.[1] Seating patterns mirror social patterns. In determining where to sit, people disclose a great deal about themselves, their beliefs, and their relationships to others. Outside of etiquette books, however, seating patterns are rarely written about, much less subjected to rigorous study. Although it is common knowledge that American synagogue-seating patterns have changed greatly over time—sometimes following acrimonious, even violent disputes—we still have no full-scale study of synagogue seating (or church seating, for that matter), certainly none that traces the subject over time. This is unfortunate, for behind wearisome debates over how sanctuary seats should be arranged and allocated lie fundamental disagreements over the kinds of social and religious values that a congregation should project and the proper relationship between a congregation and the larger society that surrounds it. As we shall see, changes in American synagogue-seating patterns reflect far-reaching changes in the nature of the American synagogue itself.

This study of seating patterns focuses on one ramified aspect of American synagogue seating: the allocation of seats and the resulting shift from stratified to free (unassigned) seating. Like the tumultuous debate over mixed seating, the controversy over free seating reflects the impact of American equality and democracy on synagogue life.[2] American society was conflicted with regard to its goals: some considered equality of opportunity the ideal, others looked for equality of condition. Furthermore, egalitarian ideals, however defined, clashed ever more forcefully with the reality of social inequality and the desire of the newly rich to engage in "conspicuous consumption."[3] These disputes—the one a conflict over ideals, the other a clash between ideals and realities—affected religious institutions no less than society at large. Changing synagogue-seating patterns reflected these disputes and provide an illuminating case study of how American religion and society have historically interacted.

The earliest synagogues did not apparently face the problem of where people should sit. Most worshippers either stood wherever there was room or sat on an available floor rug. Some seats have turned up in archeological excavations of

Reprinted from *Belief and Behavior: Essays in the New Religious History,* 1991, by permission of Jonathan D. Sarna.

synagogues, but they are believed to have been reserved for officers, elders, and dignitaries; others could presumably sit where they pleased. To be sure, one rabbi in the Babylonian Talmud teaches the wisdom of setting aside a "fixed place" for one's prayers, but he does not spell out how these places ought to be arranged relative to one another. What we do know is that in order to promote business, the great Alexandrian synagogue, existing even in Second Temple times, arranged seating by occupation ("goldsmiths by themselves, silversmiths by themselves," etc.), making it easier for travelers to find their fellow craftsmen. Rabbi Judah's vivid description of this synagogue suggests that it was unique; the more common practice was for the elders to sit up front while the masses sat "all jumbled together."[4]

Stratified seating found recognition in Jewish legal codes, and in post-Temple times it became the norm in Jewish communities around the world. Sometimes, synagogue officials assigned seats and assessed their occupants depending on what they could pay. At other times, they sold seats for fixed prices or auctioned them off to the highest bidder. Either way, the "best people"—those with the greatest wealth, learning, age, or prestige—ended up occupying the best seats, those along the eastern wall and closest to the front. Those possessing lower status, including the young and the newly arrived in town, occupied seats that were somewhat less choice. The worst seats in the hall were reserved for those who could afford to sit nowhere else. Seating inside the synagogue thus mirrored social realities outside in the community. People worshipped alongside those of their own kind.[5]

When Jews came to America, they found that very similar patterns prevailed among the local churches:

> In the goodly house of worship,
> where in order due and fit,
> As by public vote directed,
> classed and ranked the people sit,
> Mistress first and good wife after,
> clerkly squire before the clown,
> From the brave coat, lace embroidered,
> to the gray frock shading down.[6]

In colonial New England, most town churches assigned a "proper" place to every member of the community based on complicated, controversial, and at times capricious sets of standards that predictably aroused no end of squabbling. "The bulk of criticism . . . ," Robert I. Dinkin observes, "was directed less at the system as a whole than at the specific arrangements made by the various seating committees. Most people did not seem to have disliked the idea of seating as long as they were able to obtain a coveted spot for themselves." Similar patterns of assigning seats appear to have been the rule in other colonies as well, although specific evidence is lacking.[7]

The practice of assigning seats declined only after the American Revolution, being gradually replaced by systems of pew rental and pew sale. This was a bow to republican ideology, for it did away with hereditary privileges and made seats equally available to all who could pay. The new procedure also bespeaks the development in America of a less rigidly defined social order: people no longer had a fixed position in a seating hierarchy. Yet relative stratification based on wealth continued. The house of worship, like the community at large, accepted social inequalities as inevitable, but believed that everyone should have an equal chance to move up.[8]

The earliest American synagogue, New York's congregation Shearith Israel, founded in the seventeenth century, mirrored this church pattern, which also happened to be the method of financing employed by the Sephardic synagogue (Bevis Marks) in London. The congregation carefully allocated a seat to each member, and each seat was assessed a certain membership tax in advance. What happened in 1750 was typical: The minutes recount an agreement "to appoint four proper persons to rate the seats for the year and appoint each person a proper place for which seat he shall now pay to the present parnas [president] the sum annexed to his seat." Members of the wealthy Gomez family enjoyed the most prestigious seats and paid the highest assessments. Others paid less and sat much further away from the holy ark. Considerable revenue was produced by this system, but it also generated a great deal of bad feeling. The congregation's early minutes are strewn with complaints from those dissatisfied with their seats, some of whom, we learn, were "seating themselves in places other than those assigned."[9]

Seating in the women's gallery proved particularly troublesome, perhaps because the gallery held fewer places and the difference between a good and bad seat there was far more pronounced. Interestingly, women did not necessarily sit in the same rank order as their husbands, and sometimes acquired status on their own independent basis. In the minutes of Mickve Israel Congregation in Savannah, Georgia, for example, one woman lay claim to a high-status pew by virtue of being the eldest married woman among the congregants. Front-row seats in the women's gallery of Shearith Israel in New York were similarly reserved for married women, despite vociferous protests from members who were single.[10]

In its constitution of 1805, Shearith Israel, bowing to the demands of American religious voluntarism, abandoned its system of assigned seats and assessments, and committed itself to a system of pew rent. Under this procedure, the trustees assigned different values to different seats and then leased them on a first-come, first-served basis. This allowed for freedom of choice, since a wealthy person could opt to lease a poor seat and a poor person could save up to lease an expensive one. In practice, however, social stratification within the synagogue continued, albeit in less specific and more muted fashion. Where before seats reflected each individual's precise social ranking, now they only offered an approximate picture of the community's economic divisions.[11]

We possess a detailed description from Congregation Mikveh Israel in Philadelphia of how this system of leased pews actually worked. Seats in the synagogue's women's gallery were divided into three categories (termed, quite appropriately, "classes,") from the front seats ("inner range") to the back. In 1851, a

three-year lease to a "first class" seat went for sixty dollars with an additional annual assessment of eight dollars, while second- and third-class seats could be
leased for thirty dollars and twenty dollars with annual assessments of four dollars and three dollars. Leftover seats could be rented on an annual basis for ten,
six, or four dollars. Men's seats were divided into five categories, with a three-
year lease costing one-hundred, sixty, forty, thirty, or twenty-five dollars, depending on the seat's "class," and additional annual assessments of fourteen, nine,
seven, four, or three dollars. Leftover men's seats could be rented at twenty,
twelve, nine, six, or five dollars. Seats in the back ("the sixth and seventh ranges")
were neither leased nor rented "but reserved for strangers or persons unable to
take seats." As non-seatholders, those in the back were separated from everybody
else and marked as outsiders.[12]

The difference here between the price of men's and women's seats is particularly fascinating. Not only were men more socially stratified than women (five
classes as opposed to three), but men of every class level were superior (in terms
of what they paid) to women of their class, and even men with seats in the lowly
fifth class paid more overall than women of the third class. This may reflect real
differences between what men and women earned, but is more likely an indication of women's inferior synagogue status. Since women had to sit upstairs and
were denied synagogue honors, they were charged less than the men were.

Over time, some synagogues experimented with alternative means of allocat-
ing seats. The system pioneered by New York's Temple Emanu-El in 1847
whereby seats were sold in perpetuity—a practice well-known in Europe—
proved particularly popular, for it raised a large fund of capital "up front" to pay
off building debts. In 1854, when Emanu-El moved into its 12th Street Temple, the
sale of seats at auction yielded $31,000. A similar sale fourteen years later, when
the temple moved up to Fifth Avenue and 43rd Street, yielded "100,000 over and
above the cost of the building and the lots." While those with lesser means could
still rent seats at Emanu-El and remain members, only pew owners could serve as
officers. In some other synagogues that sold pews, renters could not be members
at all but were classified as nonvoting seatholders.[13]

Regardless of whether synagogues sold seats or rented them, assigned seats
or not, assessed members once or continually solicited them throughout the year,
they all depended on seat revenues for a large percentage of their upkeep. Survival dictated that the best seats be given to those who supported the synagogue
most liberally. What Edna Ferber found in Appleton, Wisconsin, at the beginning
of the twentieth century was thus true of most synagogues:

> Seating was pretty well regulated by the wealth and prominence of the congre-
> gation. In the rows nearest the pulpit sat the rich old members, their sons and
> daughters and grandchildren. Then came the next richest and most substan-
> tial. Then the middling well-to-do, then the poorest. The last rows were re-
> served for strangers and . . . "Russians."[14]

Some synagogues did set aside a few seats for prominent members (government
officials, scholars, writers, etc.) who lacked means but were felt to merit front-

rank status on account of their social prestige. Others, however, found this to be undemocratic and divisive. One synagogue actually banned the practice in its constitution, declaring that every seat would henceforward be offered for sale, "in order to avoid unnecessary trouble to the Board of Directors and to give more satisfaction to *all* the members of the Congregation." Even here, those too poor to pay for a seat were not completely excluded from synagogue life. As secondary or nonmembers, however, they were expected to know their place. If they sought to occupy vacant pews owned by more affluent congregants, they ran the risk of being forcibly ejected.[15]

Synagogues and churches were hardly to blame for the existence of inequalities in America. Nor were they to blame for the fact that, far too frequently, America's wealthy only made donations of urgently needed funds in return for conspicuous rewards in social status. Still, the intrusion of social and class distinctions into the hallowed domains of sacred institutions troubled many Americans, particularly those who interpreted the country's democratic ideals in egalitarian terms. "As Americans perceive it," James Oliver Robertson has pointed out, "the tendency of American history is toward classlessness. The Revolution was fought to destroy privilege. American reform, since the Jacksonian era, has been motivated by the desire to perfect equality and democracy. . . . In American myth, America *is* a classless society. If it can be shown not to be, then something is wrong and needs to be put right."[16]

Stratified seating so obviously contradicted the goals of egalitarian democracy that opposition to it should not prove surprising. Already in the immediate post-Revolutionary era, when "people on a number of fronts began to speak, write and organize against the authority of mediating elites, of social distinction and of any human tie that did not spring from volitional allegiance," free seating on a first-come, first-served basis became the general rule in many of the new and frontier churches, notably among the Methodists (except in New England) and the Disciples of Christ.[17] Growing experience with "classlessness" both in the public schools, where rich and poor sat side by side, and on the railroads where, in the astonished words of one immigrant Jewish observer, "everyone sits together in one car—for there is only one car of one class for all—rich and poor, master and slave together in one body," made stratified seating in houses of worship seem even more incongruous. Yet at the same time, the realities of economic inequality in America were becoming increasingly profound. Urban geography, clubs, resorts, and the entertainment world all reflected a heightened awareness and acceptance of social and class divisions. In spite of noble ideals and symbolic bows to classlessness, rich and poor in America were actually growing ever further apart.[18]

This paradox—the disjunction between ideal and reality—posed an obvious dilemma for churches and synagogues. Should they maintain the class and status distinctions that many congregants considered proper, or should they champion egalitarian ideals, even at the risk of imperiling their own financial security? The move from assigned seats to sale of seats salved some consciences by opening up pews to anyone with the means to pay for them, but it did nothing about the underlying problems of social inequality itself. Periodically, aggrieved members spoke up on this issue and called for reforms on the frontier church model.[19] However, large-scale changes did not come about until the rise of the Social Gospel movement in the late nineteenth century. Then, concern about the "unchurched" poor, fear of the urban masses, renewed dedication to social justice, and a resulting surge of religious activism lent new weight to the free-pews movement. Free seating won adoption both in many liberal Protestant churches and in many Catholic churches.[20] For the first time, it also won adoption in an American synagogue.

Calls for free seating in the synagogue first rang out early in the Social Gospel era in connection with appeals for more democracy in Jewish life and more aid to the poor and unaffiliated. In 1882, the year that William S. Rainsford originated his free "institutional church" at New York's St. George's Episcopal Church, Myer Stern, secretary of Temple Emanu-El in New York, advocated the creation of a totally free synagogue—all seats unassigned and available without charge—for "those of our faith who are eager to worship with us, but whose circumstances through misfortune and various causes are such as to prevent their hiring pews or seats either in our or any other temple or synagogue."[21] Ray Frank, the remarkable woman preacher whose sermons pricked the consciences of Jews throughout the West, later assailed the whole system of making "stock" of synagogue seats. "If I were a rabbi," she declared in 1890, "I would not sell religion in the form of pews and benches to the highest bidder." She then documented some of the system's worst abuses.[22] Rabbi Isaac Moses of Chicago had come to the same conclusion, and in 1896 attempted to found a congregation based upon this new plan. Attacking the "undemocratic" nature of the synagogue—which, he felt, kept many Jews unaffiliated, and limited the rabbi's independence—he offered full membership to all, "regardless of their annual contributions," with dues payments only "to be such as each individual member feels that he or she is justified in making."[23] Nothing came of this effort, but in 1898 Rabbi William Rosenau of Baltimore, less radical than Moses but equally concerned about the large number of those too poor to afford seats, proposed a different solution: "Every congregation ought to set aside a certain number of pews, not in the rear of the temple, or in the galleries, but in all parts of the auditorium, so that no lines of distinction be drawn between the rich and the poor at least in the house of God."[24]

Since changes in the internal arrangement of a synagogue are easier to propose than to effect, particularly when they have economic implications, assigned seating of one sort or another remained the rule. At Temple Beth El in Detroit, Michigan, however, an unanticipated problem developed. Although a new temple had been erected on Woodward Street in a growing section of town, nobody envisaged that membership would grow as rapidly as it did, increasing at a rate of more than 25 percent a year. The task of assigning seats equitably to all members and their families under these conditions proved impossible. There were enough seats to accommodate those who actually came and worshipped on any given Sabbath, but not enough to accommodate those who had rights to particular seats and wanted them to remain unoccupied even when they themselves were not present. As a result, in September 1903, the congregation voted that seats in the new building would remain temporarily unassigned, available to all on a first-come, first-served basis, while the board of trustees decided what to do. Pragmatic rather than ideological considerations motivated this decision, and nobody expected it to have a lasting effect. But in fact, a historic change had taken place.[25]

Formerly, Beth El had offered members the choice of buying seats, renting them, or having a seat assigned to them from the pool that remained. Those who chose either of the first two options paid both their annual assessment of dues, levied on every member by the board of trustees on a sliding scale based on ability to pay, and an additional sum representing their purchase or rental fee. Everyone else received seats commensurate with their dues assessment. This was a cumbersome and somewhat inequitable system that many members opposed. But the board of trustees finally recommended that it be reinstated in the new synagogue; otherwise, the board feared, the congregation's rapidly rising budget would not be met. The recommendation was greeted with a barrage of criticism and spawned a vigorous congregational debate. Some members wanted all seats sold. Some wanted all seats rented. Some wanted an end to the system of assessments. All agreed to search for a compromise that would seat as many people as possible, as equitably as possible, without threatening the congregation's income. Meeting followed meeting while seats in the new temple remained open and unassigned. Finally, after every other proposal failed to win approval, the new status quo was made permanent. On 27 April 1904, "the unassigned pew system was unanimously concurred in by those present at a large and enthusiastic meeting of the congregation." Higher assessments ensured that the lost revenue from seat income would be more than made up.[26]

Although unassigned seating came to Beth El by accident ("sheer force of circumstances"), and the plan won permanent adoption largely by default, ideological considerations played a significant part both in the debate over the issue and in the justifications that followed it. What began as a practical measure ended up serving a symbolic purpose—a sequence that paralleled what had earlier happened in the movement from separate to mixed seating. In this case, proponents used free seating as evidence of Judaism's concern for "justice, equality and fraternity."[27]

Rabbi Leo Franklin of Beth El, casting himself as the Jewish apostle of free seating, took the lead in trumpeting the system's virtues and defending them against all critics. To him, the system came to be identified as something "essentially Jewish," as "nearly ideal as human institutions can be." "In God's house all must be equal," he maintained, echoing Social Gospel rhetoric: "There must be no aristocracy and no snobocracy." Franklin lambasted as "fundamentally wrong, unjust and unJewish" the contention that those who contributed more to a synagogue deserved disproportionate rewards. He insisted that the finances of the congregation could remain strong without special pews for the rich so long as a graduated dues-assessment system was in effect. He even assured frightened synagogue regulars that "practical experience" demonstrated that most people could "occupy the same seats the year round, even under the unassigned system." As for free seating's benefits, he pointed out that besides equality of opportunity the system encouraged people to come to temple on time and to bring their families. It ended the "abomination of having rented seats unoccupied while perhaps dozens of poor men and women are compelled to stand in the aisles or lobbies." And it made it easier to accommodate guests who no longer had to sit in specially set aside areas, apart from regular members.[28]

Franklin was convinced that free seating's virtues would win it wide acceptance within the American Jewish community, bringing glory to all Jews and introducing a greater degree of "practical idealism" into the synagogue. Even in his own congregation, however, he met with repeated challenges. Various resignations attended the first acceptance of the freeseating plan, including that of Seligman Schloss, one of Beth El's most distinguished members and an ex-president (who later withdrew his resignation). According to one source, "a large percentage" of the other elderly members, including some of the congregations' leading benefactors, were no less adamant in seeking to prevent the plan from ever taking effect.[29] They insisted that status considerations played no part in their opposition, and that they simply wanted some guarantee that they would find a seat somewhere in the sanctuary, even if they came late. They also complained about being forced to scurry around the whole synagogue searching out members of their family who would no longer be found in one place. A proposal to set aside several rows for the elderly did not molify the malcontents. Indeed, "nothing outside of the complete waiver of the principle involved would stisfy them." The fact that opponents used financial leverage to put pressure on the congregation added to the belief that their demands were motivated by more than just disinterested concern for those whom free seating inconvenienced.[30]

Rhetoric aside, it seems apparent that the Beth El dispute actually saw two conflicting and widely accepted American principles colliding head on: belief in equality and recognition of natural inequalities.[31] Rabbi Franklin's supporters recognized inequalities but sought to promote visible equality. They thus both encouraged "religious fellowship," believing that "every man . . . deserves an equal place with every other," and continued to recognize inequalities for purposes of dues assessment.[32] By contrast, opponents of free seating sought one *or* the other. Either all should contribute equally and enjoy equal access to all seats, or all should contribute unequally and be rewarded in the same fashion. While to Rabbi Franklin unassigned seating represented a blow against class divisions and support for the highest values that America and Judaism had to offer, to his opponents the same system exuded injustice and violated the basic principles of equity. At a deep level, the dispute had as much to do with symbols as with substance.

In the end, the two sides compromised. In the congregation, as in the country at large, egalitarian ideas and natural inequalities both won recognition. Free seating thus remained the policy of the congregation alongside the system of dues assessments. At the same time, in return for their agreement to pay their substantial arrears and remain at Beth El, dissident members won the status concessions that they had sought. The three malcontented ex-presidents, for their "long and appreciated services and contributions to the cause of the Temple," each had three seats assigned to them for as long as they lived. Seligman Schloss promptly selected a choice location: "in the easterly row of benches, in the seventh bench from the pulpit, on the western end." The other dissidents won the right to have up to four seats always reserved for them "in the center section of the auditorium" for "up to fifteen minutes after the time set for the commencement of services."[33]

Even before the dispute at Beth El was settled, leading Reform rabbis from around the country had spoken out in favor of free seating as an expression of social justice. Rabbi Emil Hirsch of Chicago, the leading exponent of social justice within the Reform Movement, called it "the ideal plan" for synagogues to adopt. Rabbi Henry Berkowitz of Philadelphia recommended free seating to his own congregation. Others, according to Leo Franklin, wrote to him privately expressing admiration for what he had done. Many promised to watch the experiment carefully.[34]

The rabbi who expressed the greatest immediate interest in free seating was young Stephen Wise, then still at Temple Beth Israel in Portland, Oregon. Wise had taken over the Portland ministry in 1900, and had from the start firmly allied himself with the aims of the Social Gospel movement. He achieved spectacular success, tripled his congregations' membership, and brought the congregation into financial health for the first time, building a surplus of $4,000. Given this financial cushion, he issued, in 1904, his first call for a "free synagogue" in which members could sit where they choose and pay what they choose. As opposed to Beth El, where free seating had come first and justifications later, Wise began with his principles: each man paying what he can afford, all equal in the eyes of the Lord. He also displayed a greater degree of consistency than Rabbi Franklin had, for he attacked both stratified pews and stratified dues at the same time.[35]

Wise's free synagogue experiment, begun in 1905, achieved success. The experiment succeeded again when Wise moved back to New York and opened his Free Synagogue (now the Stephen Wise Free Synagogue) in 1907. There, free seating on a first-come, first-served basis represented a "token and symbol" of other freedoms: freedom from fixed dues, freedom of the pulpit, and freedom of opportunity for all—women included—to become Temple members and officeholders. Drawing (without credit) from the ideas of previous Jewish and Christian critics of stratified seating, Wise established the most compelling case yet for the relationship between free seating, Jewish ideals, and American ideals. He made free seating part of his solution to the twin problems of the fast-waning influence of the synagogue, and the fast-growing number of urban Jews who belonged to no synagogue at all. The values he espoused through synagogue seating were the values he proclaimed to society at large: "freedom, hospitality, inclusiveness, brotherhood, [and] the leveling of the anti-religious bars of caste."[36]

For all of its idealistic appeal, however, the free-synagogue idea failed to take hold nationwide; in the absence of a particularly charismatic rabbi it proved impractical. In Philadelphia, for example, the venerable Sephardic congregation Mikve Israel, after moving into a new synagogue building in 1909, decided to keep its old edifice in the poorer section of town "open all the year around absolutely free to worshippers." But it soon found the cost of this to be prohibitive. When free-will offerings did not reach expectations, the project had to be abandoned. Mickve Israel Congregation in Savannah faced the same problem in 1913: Although it tried to become a free synagogue, economic considerations forced it to abandon the experiment after only one year.[37]

By contrast, free seating combined with some system of required dues posed far less of an economic threat, served as a visible symbol of social-justice ideals, and, in time, did succeed. To take just a few examples, Temple Israel in Memphis instituted free seating in 1918, Rodef Shalom Congregation in Pittsburgh in 1920, Temple Israel in Boston in 1922, and Congregation Beth Israel of Houston in 1927. By 1940, nearly two hundred synagogues had adopted some form of free seating, and many more assigned seats only for the high holidays. The free-seating movement continued to spread, especially during the war years when it was associated with the effort to strengthen democracy at home. By the 1960s, even many old-line synagogues had abandoned assigned seating, replacing it with a new "fair share" system that, by assigning dues on the basis of income rather than seat location, ensured that "democratization" would not result in any loss of revenue from the wealthy. Although statistics are lacking, impressionistic evidence suggests that free seating, while not ubiquitous, is now predominant across the spectrum of American Jewish life, in Reform, Reconstructionist, Conservative, and Orthodox synagogues alike.[38]

If free seating produced more visible equality in the American synagogue, it failed to produce perfect equality. Wealthy congregants were still more likely than their poorer counterparts to be recognized from the pulpit or to serve as synagogue officers, and they soon found alternative means to engage in conspicuous consumption: by leaving their names on synagogue plaques, for instance, or by staging lavish congregational parties to celebrate significant family milestones. Moreover, even with free seating rich and poor did not necessarily sit side by side. Instead, as Samuel Heilman found, synagogue goers naturally tended to sit by their friends, usually people similar in occupation, education, and religious outlook to themselves. As a result, congregational seating patterns often continued to mark status, power, and authority within the synagogue community, albeit far more subtly. "Seating patterns," Heilman concluded, "are not simply physical arrangements but reflect social belongingness."[39]

The rise of free seating is nevertheless a revealing and significant development in American synagogue history. First of all, sheds light on how, under American influence, the synagogue experienced change. Seating by social rank, and later any pattern of assigned seating that emphasized differences based on wealth, became in the eyes of many American Jews an affront to America's democratic ethos. Although stratified seating had characterized synagogues for centuries, American cultural values in this case exerted a much stronger pull. The reason, I think, is that free seating, unlike mixed seating of men and women, was not actually incompatible with Jewish tradition. Furthermore, free seating permitted the synagogue to display a measure of patriotic piety, and had the added advantage of using seats more efficiently. Most important of all, perhaps, experience suggested that the change could be implemented without serious financial loss. As a result, it was hard to oppose. Rabbis like Leo Franklin and Stephen Wise, by investing free seating with deeper Jewish significance, made the process of adjustment even easier. By implementing free seating, congregants could now view themselves not only as better Americans but as better Jews as well.

Second, free seating is significant as an illustration of a noteworthy and little-studied type of Jewish religious innovation that was debated largely on the local congregational level, rather than becoming a major point of contention between the different American Jewish religious movements. Although Reform Jews, who traditionally emphasized social justice, pioneered free seating, I have found no evidence that Orthodox and Conservative Jews were ideologically opposed to it. Moreover, within the Reform Movement itself some leading temples (like Temple Emanu-El of San Francisco and Isaac M. Wise Temple of Cincinnati) maintained traditional patterns of stratified seating long into the twentieth century. Free seating thus spread on a congregation-by-congregation basis, and was decided in each case by balancing egalitarian ideals against pragmatic realities: Would loss of seat income be balanced by increasing dues? Would existing seatholders insist on their property rights? Would wealthy members transfer their membership elsewhere? The answers to such questions had far more to do with whether free seating would be adopted than denominational affiliation did—a reminder that the diversity of American synagogue life cannot be explained on the basis of intra-Jewish politics alone.[40]

Third, free seating demonstrates the impact on American Jewish life of ideas generally associated with the Protestant Social Gospel. Nathan Glazer wrote in *American Judaism* about "the failure of a Jewish 'social gospel' to develop among Reform Jews," and his words have been widely echoed. But in fact, Social Gospel concerns—translated into Jewish terms and stripped of their Christological rhetoric—received considerable attention in American Jewish circles, and influenced not only the Reform movement and synagogue life, but also the whole relationship between American Jews and East European Jewish immigrants. The subject as a whole requires further study and cannot be pursued here. What we do learn from free seating, however, is that even specific Social Gospel causes had their American Jewish analogues.[41]

Finally, free seating is significant for what it teaches us about the ongoing tension between realism and idealism in American Jewish life. Free seating, as its supporters plainly admitted, represented a kind of utopia, an exalted vision of classless democracy where people from different walks of life dwelt harmoniously side by side. Realistically speaking, however, the synagogue could not survive under such conditions; unless wealthier members contributed more than poorer ones, no synagogue could pay its bills. This was the synagogue's version of what Murray Friedman calls the "utopian dilemma," the clash between romantic idealism and pragmatic self-interest. The result, as we have seen, was a compromise.[42]

NOTES

1. Samuel C. Heilman, *Synagogue Life* (Chicago: University of Chicago Press, 1976), 36.
2. Jonathan D. Sarna, "The Debate Over Mixed Seating in the American Synagogue," in

Jack Wertheimer, ed., *The American Synagogue: A Sanctuary Transformed* (New York: Cambridge University Press, 1987), 363–394.

3. The expression, of course, was popularized by Thorstein Veblen in *The Theory of the Leisure Class* (1912; rpt. New York: Mentor, 1953), 60–80. For an illuminating historical analysis of the idea of equality, see R. R. Palmer, "Equality," in *Dictionary of the History of Ideas* (New York: Scribner, 1973), 2:138–148.

4. Samuel Kraus, *Korot Bet HaTefilah BeYisrael* (New York: Ogen, 1955), 251; Babylonian Talmud, Tractate Berakhot, 6b; Tosefta Sukkah 4:6.

5. *Tur*; and see Isserles gloss on *Shulkhan Arukh* OH 150:5; Salo W. Baron, *The Jewish Community: Its History and Structure to the American Revolution* (Philadelphia: Jewish Publication Society, 1945), 2, 130–131; Kraus, *Korot*, 252–256; *Encyclopaedia Judaica* (Jerusalem: Keter Publishing, 1972), 15:593.

6. Quoted in Robert J. Dinkin, "Seating the Meeting House in Early Massachusetts," *New England Quarterly* 43 (1970): 450.

7. Ibid., 459.

8. On stratified seating, see also Ola Elizabeth Winslow, *Meetinghouse Hill, 1630–1783* (New York: W. W. Norton, 1972), 142–149; Peter Benes and Philip D. Zimmerman, *New England Meeting House and Church, 1630–1850* (Boston: Boston University Press, 1979), 55–56; David H. Fischer, *Growing Old in America* (New York: Oxford University Press, 1977), 38–40; and for nineteenth-century Catholicism, Jay P. Dolan, *The Immigrant Church* (Baltimore: Johns Hopkins University Press, 1975), 49–52.

9. *Publications of the American Jewish Historical Society* 21 (1913), 62; see also 81–84, 154–155; 27 (1920): 28; David and Tamar de Sola Pool, *An Old Faith in the New World* (New York: Columbia University Press, 1955), 199, 270–273; and Rachel Wischnitzer, *Synagogue Architecture in the United States* (Philadelphia: Jewish Publication Society, 1955), 12–13.

10. Saul J. Rubin, *Third to None: The Saga of Savannah Jewry 1733–1983* (Savannah, Ga.: Congregation Micke Israel, 1983), 52; Pool, *An Old Faith*, 272.

11. Hyman B. Grinstein, *The Rise of the Jewish Community of New York, 1654–1860* (Philadelphia: Jewish Publication Society, 1945), 479–483; Pool, *An Old Faith*, 299.

12. *At a special meeting of the Board of Managers of K.K.M.I., held on Sunday June 8th, 1851 . . . the following Resolutions were adopted and ordered to be printed* [Broadside] (Philadelphia, 1851), copy in Klau Library, Hebrew Union College, Cincinnati, Ohio. On the traditional position of women in the synagogue, see Carol H. Krinsky, *Synagogues of Europe* (New York: MIT Press, 1985), 28–31.

13. Grinstein, *The Rise of the Jewish Community of New York*, 482–483; *New Era* 4 (1874): 131.

14. Edna Ferber, *A Peculiar Treasure* (New York: Literary Guild, 1939), 74.

15. *Montefiore Congregation Constitution* (Las Vegas, N. Mex.: 1898), 11, copy in American Jewish Archives, Cincinnati, Ohio. For an example of a seating plan where social prestige played a role, see *Canadian Jewish Archives* 1 (August 1955), 16. On the poor, see Pool, *An Old Faith*, 273. Compare Krinsky's description of the London Great Synagogue's "large pew where the poor were kept to prevent their mingling with those who could pay for seats and for building maintenance," *Synagogues of Europe*, 417.

16. James O. Robertson, *American Myth, American Reality* (New York: Hill and Wang, 1980), 259.

17. Nathan O. Hatch, "The Christian Movement and the Demand for a Theology of the People," *Journal of American History* 67 (December 1980): 561; see also *Encyclopedia of World Methodism* (Nashville: United Methodist Publishing House, 1974) s.v. "pew rental"; "Pews," *American Quarterly Church Review* 13 (July 1860): 284–300; and Timothy L. Smith, *Revivalism and Social Reform* (New York: Harper, 1957), 23–24, 164.

18. Leon Horowitz, "Tuv Artsot Habrit," *Rumania Ve'Amerika* (Berlin: 1874), 6; this work

has been translated by Randi Musnitsky, "America's Goodness: An Edited Translation of Leon Horowitz's *Tuv Artsot Habrit*" (Ordination thesis, Hebrew Union College-Jewish Institute of Religion, 1983); for a cultural evaluation of social cleavage during this era, see Neil Harris, ed., *The Land of Contrasts* (New York: George Braziller, 1970), esp. pp. 16–19.

19. Grinstein, *The Rise of the Jewish Community of New York*, 538, n11. See also Solomon Jackson, "Address to Joseph Dreyfous. . . . 1829," reprinted in Solomon Solis-Cohen, "A Unique Jewish Document of a Century Ago," *Jewish Exponent*, 25 (October 1929): 8.

20. Charles Howard Hopkins, *The Rise of the Social Gospel in American Protestantism, 1865–1915* (New Haven: Yale University Press, 1961); Robert D. Cross, ed., *The Church and the City* (Indianapolis: Bobbs-Merrill, 1967); and Ronald C. White and C. Howard Hopkins, *The Social Gospel: Religion and Reform in Changing America* (Philadelphia: Temple University Press, 1976), which provides valuable background and additional bibliography. For a typical free-seating debate, see *Congregationalist* 78 (1893): 245, 255–256, 848–849. On the Social Gospel and the Jews, see Egal Feldman, "The Social Gospel and the Jews," *American Jewish Historical Quarterly* 58 (March 1969): 308–322; Leonard J. Mervis, "The Social Justice and the American Reform Movement," *American Jewish Archives* 7 (June 1955): 171–230; Bernard Martin, "The Social Philosophy of Emil G. Hirsch," *American Jewish Archives* 6 (June 1954): 151–166; and John F. Sutherland, "Rabbi Joseph Krauskopf of Philadelphia: The Urban Reformer Returns to the Land," *American Jewish History* 67 (June 1978): 342–362.

21. Hopkins, *Rise of the Social Gospel*, 154–156; William S. Rainsford, *Let Us Anchor Our Churches and Make Them Free* (New York, 1890); and Myer Stern, *The Rise and Progress of Reform Judaism* (New York, 1895), 77–78.

22. Jacob R. Marcus, ed., *The American Jewish Woman: A Documentary History* (New York: Ktav, 1981), 383; on Frank, see Simon Litman, *Ray Frank Litman: A Memoir* (New York: American Jewish Historical Society, 1957); and Reva Clar and William M. Kramer, "The Girl Rabbi of the Golden West," *Western States Jewish History* 18 (1986): 99–111, 223–236, 336–351.

23. *Reform Advocate*, 20 June 1896, pp. 359–360; *American Hebrew*, 28 August 1896, p. 414.

24. William Rosenau, "The Attitude of the Congregation to the Non Member," *Central Conference of American Rabbis Yearbook* 8 (1898): 65.

25. *A History of Congregation Beth El, Detroit, Michigan, Volume 2, 1900–1910* (Detroit: Winn & Hammond, 1910), 35–40, 80; Minutes, 5 April 1904, Temple Beth El Minute Book, Box X-6, American Jewish Archives, Cincinnati, Ohio. For other brief accounts, see Irving I. Katz, *The Beth El Story* (Detroit: Wayne University Press, 1955), 99–101; Robert Rockaway, "The Progress of Reform Judaism in Late 19th and Early 20th Century Detroit," *Michigan Jewish History* (January 1974), 17; and idem, *The Jews of Detroit* (Detroit: Wayne State University Press, 1986), 124.

26. *Constitution and By-Laws of Congregation Beth El* (Detroit: 1892), 7, 11–12; Minutes, 8 September 1903–27 April 1904, Beth El Minute Book; *History of Beth El* 2: 38.

27. Leo Franklin, "A New Congregational Policy," Beth El Scrapbook, Box X-201, American Jewish Archives. See also *American Israelite* 17 (November 1904): 4.

28. Franklin, "A New Congregational Policy"; Minutes, 11 May 1904, Beth El Minute Book.

29. Minutes, 11 May 1904, 8 November 1904, Beth El Minute Book; newspaper clipping, 15 February 1905, Beth El Scrapbook.

30. Ibid., and Minutes, 18 September 1905, Beth El Minute Book.

31. Gordon S. Wood, *The Creation of the American Republic* (New York: W. W. Norton, 1969), 70–75, traces the origin of this tension. See also Martin Diamond, "The American Idea of Equality: The View From the Founding," *Review of Politics* 38 (July 1976): 313–331; and David M. Potter, *People of Plenty* (Chicago: University of Chicago Press, 1954), 91–110.

32. Franklin, "A New Congregational Policy."

33. Minutes, 7 December 1905, Beth El Minute Book.

34. Ibid., 31 October 1904; and Franklin, "A New Congregational Policy," *History of Beth El* 2: 39.

35. Franklin, "A New Congregational Policy"; Melvin Urofsky, *A Voice That Spoke for Justice: The Life and Times of Stephen S. Wise* (Albany: State University of Albany Press, 1982), 34–38; Julius J. Nodel, *The Ties Between* (Portland: Temple Beth Israel, 1959), 89–98; and White and Hopkins, *The Social Gospel*, 232. Leo Franklin subsequently proposed abolishing stratified dues, but his board ignored him; see Minutes, 18 September 1905, Beth El Minute Book.

36. Stephen S. Wise, "What Is A Free Synagogue?" in *Free Synagogue Pulpit* (New York: Bloch, 1908), 1:10–15.

37. Cyrus Adler to Solomon Schechter, 28 December 1910, Solomon Schechter Papers, Jewish Theological Seminary of America, New York; Rubin, *Third To None*, 253. Interestingly, Mordecai Kaplan, who also sought to "break down the social barriers which prevent Jews of different economic status from sharing their spiritual interests," did not advocate a free synagogue, but rather one maintained jointly by the Jewish community and the beneficiaries; see *Judaism As A Civilization* (1934, rpt. New York: Schocken, 1967), 427.

38 Louis Witt, "The Basis of Membership in the American Synagogue," *Central Conference of American Rabbis Yearbook*, 21 (1911), 195–212; Ernest Lee, *Temple Israel: Our First Century 1854–1954* (Memphis, Tenn.: 1954), 38; Marcus L. Aaron, *One Hundred Twenty Years: Rodef Shalom Congregation* [pamphlet] (Pittsburgh, Pa.: Rodef Shalom, 1976), 8; Arthur Mann, ed., *Growth and Achievement: Temple Israel 1854–1954* (Cambridge: Riverside Press, 1954), 36; Anne Nathan Cohen, *The Centenary History: Congregation Beth Israel of Houston Texas, 1854–1954* (Houston, Tex.: The Congregation, 1954), 50; Leo M. Franklin, *An Outline History of Congregation Beth El* (Detroit: Beth El, 1940), 27; Frank J. Adler, *Roots in a Moving Stream* (Kansas City: Congregation B'nai Jehudah, 1972), 192; Marjorie Hornbein, *Temple Emanuel of Denver: A Centennial History* (Denver: Congregation Emanuel, 1974), 128–129; and Ethel and David Rosenberg, *To 120 Years!* (Indianapolis: Indianapolis Hebrew Congregation, 1979), 99. See also Leon Jick, "The Reform Synagogue," in Wertheimer, *The American Synagogue*, 99. The venerable Temple Emanu-El of San Francisco maintained "sixteen different categories of seats . . . which precisely reflected the socioeconomic stratification of the membership" into the late 1950s; democratization and the "fair share" plan were only fully implemented in the 1960s. See Fred Rosenbaum, *Architects of Reform* (Berkeley, Cal.: Judah L. Magnes Museum, 1980), 91–92, 167.

39. Heilman, *Synagogue Life*, 36–39.

40. See also my introduction to Alexandra S. Korros and Jonathan D. Sarna, *American Synagogue History: A Bibliography and State-of-the-Field Survey* (New York: Markus Wiener, 1988). Discussions regarding whether to introduce a "democratized" synagogue polity and a "progressive" income-based dues structure seem to me to fall into the same structural category of reforms; the subject requires further investigation.

41. Nathan Glazer, *American Judaism*, 2d ed. (Chicago: University of Chicago Press, 1972), 138; cf. White and Hopkins, *The Social Gospel*, xii, 230, and items cited in note 20.

42. Murray Friedman, *The Utopian Dilemma* (Bryn Mawr, Pa.: Seth Press, 1985), 89–92.

CHAPTER
21

The Unspeakable Relationship: Religion and Bigotry in America

Bigotry rooted in religion is one of the most difficult topics in the history of American religion, and aside from the burning of the Ursuline convent in Boston in 1834, many books, including textbooks, give it little attention. One has the feeling that historians often find it too difficult, and sometimes too sensitive, to discuss.

In fact, hatred of religions, from traditional American Indian religion to Catholicism, Mormonism, and Judaism, has proven to be distressingly persistent in American history. Often, it has manifested explicitly religious roots. Its most recent manifestations have centered on a dislike of Islam, especially during the brief Gulf War of 1990, which produced a typically wide range of ugly incidents, from vandalism of Muslim property to denying building permits for Muslim temples.

This excerpt from Leonard Dinnerstein's wide-ranging history of anti-Semitism in America describes the extraordinary range of anti-Semitism that flourished during the Great Depression of the 1930s. Dinnerstein evokes the explicitly religious origins of this anti-Semitism, not only in such infamous anti-Semites like the Protestant fundamentalists William Dudley Pelley and Gerald Winrod and the Catholic priest Father Charles Coughlin, but more devastatingly in the casual prejudice of respected magazines like the *Christian Century* and the bigoted comments of well-known clergymen.

What constituted the specifically religious origins of American anti-Semitism? How did religious organizations and individuals support and spread anti-Semitism? Was this support direct, indirect, or both? Does anything specifically religious account for the apparent substantial decline of anti-Semitism since the late 1940s? Is there something in religious experience or belief itself, or something specifically in Christianity, that stimulates or subtly supports religious bigotry in the absence of impediments to the contrary? What similarities and differences might one see in historically common religious support for prejudice against African Americans in the nineteenth and twentieth centuries?

Additional Reading: In addition to Dinnerstein's *Antisemitism in America,* one also should see Jules Isaac, *The Teaching of Contempt: Christian Roots of Anti-Semitism*

(New York, 1964). Deborah E. Lipstadt, *Denying the Holocaust: The Growing Assault on Truth and Memory* (New York, 1993) discusses recent attempts to downplay or deny the existence of the Holocaust that reflect new expressions of anti-Semitism. Leo P. Ribuffo, *The Old Christian Right: The Protestant Far Right from the Great Depression to the Cold War* (Philadelphia, 1983) discusses both anti-Semitism and anti-Catholicism. Ray A. Billington, *The Protestant Crusade, 1800–1860* (New York, 1938) and D. L. Kinzer, *An Episode in Anti-Catholicism: The American Protective Association* (Seattle, 1964) outline different aspects of nineteenth-century American anti-Catholicism. Many varieties of American bigotry, rooted in equally wide-ranging conspiracy theories, are digested in David Brion Davis, ed., *The Fear of Conspiracy: Images of Un-American Subversion from the Revolution to the Present* (Ithaca, 1971).

Leonard Dinnerstein
Antisemitism in the Depression Era (1933–1939)

Initially, antisemitic displays in the United States did not increase with the onset of the Great Depression.[1] But after 1933, when a Nazi-led government came to power in Germany and Franklin D. Roosevelt inaugurated a New Deal at home, the deepening economic crisis contributed to an explosion of unprecedented antisemitic fervor. Fueled also by the rise of Protestant and Catholic demagogues, deeply entrenched Protestant fundamentalism, and the widespread expression of antisemitic attitudes by respectable social and religious leaders, they illustrated how centuries of denigrating Jews culminated in the most savage accusations, and in some urban areas—especially New York and Boston—violent physical attacks. In the 1930s American antisemitism was "more virulent and more vicious than at any time before or since"[2] as rabid antisemites, almost without exception, envisioned an international Jewish conspiracy aimed at controlling the government of the United States. They believed that unless maximum vigilance was exercised, Christian America would be lost.[3]

The ingrained prejudices of respectable people, an attitude confirmed as proper in the 1920s, contributed to the escalated ferocity. Their beliefs and behavior set the tone that allowed for the excesses of the more frustrated and demonstrative Americans. A vignette of how futile it was to try to alter entrenched views occurred in 1931 when one man complained that he had been hearing for years how "the Jews were steadily driving the Gentiles out of business" from people who were doing quite well economically. In his attempt to convince friends and

From Leonard Dinnerstein, *Antisemitism in America* (Oxford University Press, 1994). Reprinted by permission of Oxford University Press.

relatives of the inappropriateness of antisemitism he came up against a brick wall. One woman told him that the strength of his argument only fortified existing beliefs:

> John, you mean well and I love to hear you talk, but you have unwittingly re-
> inforced every feeling we have about the Jews and you have splendidly shown
> up the very thing which makes them so dangerous, and that is that every now
> and then they are able to fool some good man like you. That is what makes it
> all so hopeless.[4]

"Nordic" Americans held deeply rooted stereotypes of most minorities in the United States, and Jews were hardly alone as victims of discrimination. But unlike African Americans, no legal segregation kept Jews in an inferior position, they were not banished from communities like Mexicans and their American-born children who were rounded up and sent to Mexico involuntarily, nor were they interned as Japanese Americans on the West Coast would be during World War II. Since the beginning of the twentieth century Jews adjusted to existing discriminatory conditions by establishing their own businesses, working in civil service or for coreligionists, attending less prestigious schools, and living mostly in neighborhoods with people of their own background. Although Jews were socially and culturally marginalized by the prejudices of the dominant society, for the most part they maintained a higher standard of living than either WASPs or members of other ethnic groups. Moreover, even during the 1930s American-born children of east European Jewish immigrants continued to move upward much faster than children of other immigrants who arrived in the United States in the late nineteenth and early twentieth centuries.[5] Nonetheless, in the 1930s a majority of American Jews probably lived close to what we now call "the poverty line," victims of both the depression and also a pervasive intolerance. After the stock market crashed in October 1929, the depressed economy hurt the poorest Jews but all of them suffered from apprehensions steadily reinforced by antisemitic rumblings in the non-Jewish world.[6]

In the United States, as in Europe, antisemitism had been growing for at least two generations but political antisemitism was acceptable in the European nations to an extent that it never was, or would be, across the Atlantic. It spread rapidly after the breakup of the German and Austro-Hungarian empires, and throughout the 1920s riots, pogroms, and indiscriminate assaults on Jews occurred in the new states of eastern and central Europe. Jews came under attack by classmates at universities in the Ukraine, Latvia, Poland, Hungary, Romania, Austria, Greece, and Germany while in England antisemitism seemed rife immediately after the end of World War I. Its societal manifestations diminished by 1926 but it remained strong in the universities.[7]

After 1929, coincident with worldwide depression, conditions worsened for Jews throughout Europe. Nazism gained strength in Germany and German Jews visiting the United States reported that the growth of a Nazi party "had been stimulated, to a great extent, by the anti-Jewish publications which had been sponsored by Henry Ford in the United States."[8] In eastern Europe governments began to bar Jews from employment, small cooperatives eliminated Jewish shopkeepers and artisans, and universities restricted Jewish admissions. The precarious situation of the Jews in Romania may be seen from the fact that some Romanians wore swastikas even before July 11, 1930, when every Jewish home in the village of Balaceano was smashed after the signal for the attack came from the church steeple. A year later 54 Jewish families had their homes burned down in Salonika, Greece.[9] As outbursts continued, a British publication stated in July, 1932, that

> a crusade of anti-Semitism has been raging from the Rhine to the Vistula, and from the Baltic to the Aegean Sea, during the past six months, with a vindictiveness that almost surpasses all previous manifestations of anti-Jewish hatred since the end of the war.[10]

Six months later Adolf Hitler was sworn in as Chancellor of Germany.

As the depression worsened in the United States, Hitler's attacks on Jews as the root causes of the world's economic and social problems no longer seemed so outrageous to genteel bigots. As frustrations intensified, people eagerly blamed Jewish businessmen, who allegedly controlled the money supply, for the economic crisis. Throughout the country, those who had easily accepted myths about the nefarious qualities of Jews and who had imbibed the Populist ethos about the malevolence of "Wall Street" bankers and international financiers had no difficulty in believing the carelessly hurled economic charges.[11]

Jew hatred permeated the United States. Hostility pulsated in small towns and large cities, in fashionable social circles and exclusive boardrooms, and even on the floor of Congress.[12] A Mount Vernon, New York, man wrote in 1933:

> before we see this Hitler flareup end, it would not surprise me to have it reach America and have the blessing of the very men who have been damning Hitler now. Because when the Jew finally reaches that point when he will be satisfied at nothing but complete control of money, business. society, and government, well, goodbye Jew. And it is only a question of time until the ever-recurring pogrom becomes necessary.[13]

Maud Nathan, a New York Jewish social reformer and socialite, complained that "the prejudice against Jews, of which one was not conscious fifty years ago, has become so serious that today it is a burning question and is frankly spoken of as 'The Jewish Porblem.'"[14] A Pennsylvania Congressman declared that the Jews have all the gold and money while the Gentiles have only "the little slips of paper," and financier Jack Morgan, son of J. P. Morgan, told a friend that he did not like Hitler "except for his attitude toward the Jews, which I consider wholesome." Author Laura Z. Hobson recalled being at a dinner party where the discussion turned toward Hitler and Germany. One of the guests remarked:

> "The chosen people ask for it, wherever they are."
> "Oh, come on," another man said. "Some of my best friends are Jews."
> "Some of mine are, too," Hobson heard herself saying, slowly.
> "Including my mother and father."[15]

It is not clear from Hobson's description of the event whether other guests sympathized with her or the bigot.

The types of people with whom Hobson dined also abhorred many of Franklin D. Roosevelt's closest advisors and the programs they devised to pull the nation out of the depression. New agencies were created that gave the federal government unprecedented authority to regulate and control business and agriculture while providing direct relief to individuals throughout the nation. To facilitate the implementation of a massive reform agenda the President ordered subordinates to find the most talented people available, recommended to Cabinet officials that Felix Frankfurter, Dean of the Harvard Law School, be used as a source for lawyers, and reached out to individuals and groups not heretofore well represented in the government to help propel his New Deal.[16] As a result of the President's actions more minorities and women achieved responsible positions in the federal government than ever before.

Of all these groups, Jews, both relatively and absolutely, benefitted the most.[17] As Governor of New York, Roosevelt worked comfortably with Jews and as an administrator sought to bring talented people into his political orbit.[18] After he moved to the White House, Felix Frankfurter and Supreme Court Justice Louis D. Brandeis stood out among his closest advisors on governmental policies. Within his administrative circle, the President felt extremely comfortable with Sam Rosenman, his former chief assistant as Governor of New York, whom he finally brought to Washington in 1937. And at different periods Ben Cohen and David Niles were also highly regarded subordinates. Some agencies, like the Securities and Exchange Commission and the Departments of Agriculture, Labor, and Interior, had many Jews in high positions.[19] For the first time in American history, therefore, the federal government provided significant numbers of opportunities for Jews.

Within months of Roosevelt's taking office in March 1933 rumors spread that Jews were running the government. During the summer inquiries poured into the *Kiplinger Washington Newsletter* about how many Jews were employed by the new administration and what influence they possessed. Anti-Roosevelt Americans frequently blamed Jewish advisors for New Deal policy failings and antisemitic verbiage became both common and obsessive. In October 1934 a New York woman wrote to the President:

> On all sides is heard the cry that you have sold out the country to the Jews, and that the Jews are responsible for the continued depression, as they are determined to starve the Christians into submission and slavery. You have over two hundred Jews, they say, in executive offices in Washington, and Jew bankers run the government and [Bernard] Baruch is the real President. This is the talk that is heard everywhere.[20]

Many Washington politicians as well as some of the nation's wealthiest people had already expressed similar views.[21] In June that year, *Boston Herald* editor Frank Buxton confided to former Secretary of State Bainbridge Colby, "I was amazed at the intensity with which highly intelligent men argued that Jews were controlling the President."[22] Eight years later journalist W. M. Kiplinger specifically rejected that perception when he wrote that while "men who are Jews occupy very influential positions, there is no such thing as a 'Jewish influence' in Washington."[23]

Nevertheless, for the first time in American history the religious heritage of the President and some of his advisors became an issue of public discussion. Millions of Americans believed that Jewish influence over Roosevelt was responsible for the administration's "Jew Deal."[24] Thus, so long as Roosevelt occupied the White House, tales circulated that he not only favored Jews in making appointments but that he, too, was of Jewish ancestry. An extensive amount of antisemitic literature flooded the 1936 presidential campaign including an essay by the Reverend Gerald Winrod of Kansas, one of the better known fundamentalist Protestants who had started the Defenders of the Christian Faith, stating that the President was descended from Rosenbergs, Rosenbaums, Roosenvelts, Rosenblums, and Rosenthals.[25] (The litany was reminiscent of the *Katholische Volkszeitung*'s description of about 40 people with the name of Rosenfeld attending William McKinley's second inauguration in 1901.) A doggerel also circulated at that time informing readers that President Roosevelt allegedly told his wife:

> You kiss the niggers,
> I'll kiss the Jews,
> We'll stay in the White House
> As long as we choose.[26]

Christian religious groups and publications also contributed to the growing critiques of Jews. *The Christian Century*, "the nation's most prominent liberal Protestant weekly magazine,"[27] had long been analyzing "The Jewish Problem." In the 1930s it published more than twenty articles and editorials apparently sympathetic to the plight of the Jews yet at the same time urging them to assimilate and become "real" Americans.[28] The editors acknowledged in May 1933 that

> the Christian mind has never allowed itself to feel the same human concern for Jewish sufferings that it has felt for the cruelties visited upon Armenians, the Boers, the people of India, American slaves, or the Congo blacks under the Leopold imperialism. Christian indifference to Jewish suffering has for centuries been rationalized by the terrible belief that such sufferings were the judgment of God upon the Jewish people for their rejection of Jesus. If it is God's judgment, why should Christians interfere, and why should they sympathize?

Yet *The Christian Century* itself assumed the same stance. It urged Jews to convert because "Israel needs Jesus to complete its own life."[29]

In April 1936 the magazine intensified its efforts and began publishing a series of pieces virtually demanding conversion of the Jews to Protestantism, blaming them for their sorry predicament in the United States, and warning, in veiled terms, of dire consequences should they refuse to comply. While continually attacking antisemitism per se, *The Christian Century* reinforced the views of respectable bigots who thought of themselvs as tolerant. The Magazine argued that in a dynamic society it was difficult for two religions to be mutually tolerant. A May 13 editorial told every Jew he

> will never command the respect of the non-Jewish culture in which he lives so long as he huddles by himself, nursing his own "uniqueness," cherishing his tradition as something which is precious to *him* but in the nature of things cannot be conveyed to others, nor participated in by others.

On June 9 another editorial proclaimed:

> The simple and naked fact is that Judaism rests upon an impossible basis. It is trying to pluck the fruits of democracy without yielding itself to the processes of democracy. In a dynamic society a national culture cannot help seeking the unity of all its component elements.

Then, on July 1, came the denouement. While denying any antisemitic feelings, the editors of *The Christian Century* concluded that Jews "must be brought to repentance—with all the tenderness, in view of their agelong affliction, but with austere realism, in view of their sinful share in their own tragedy."[30]

Such pronouncements from one of the nation's premier Christian journals alarmed a great many Jews. Sober-minded and intelligent individuals ran *The Christian Century;* nontheless, these responsible Christian liberals were committed to bringing nonbelievers into the fold. Their views could not be dismissed as the rantings of the lunatic or fundamentalist fringe. *The Christian Century* did not speak for Protestant America but it reflected what millions of ordinary middle-class Protestants thought—and for that reason its comments were frightening to Jews.

Fundamentalist Protestants also thought that Jews should convert to Christianity. More so than in the 1920s, fundamentalists were increasingly alarmed about the effects of modernism, evolution, and the spread of communism. At a 1931 Atlantic City conference, evangelical Christians considered the question "The Christian Approach to the Jew—especially in North America." Speakers agreed that mistreatment of Jews by Christians in the past had prevented Jews from knowing "Jesus in His true character, mission and power," but they argued that Christianity was the fulfillment of Judaism and that Jews "must be brought back to faith in God. . . . All sinners need slavation."[31] Many fundamentalists could not understand the reluctance of Jews to embrace Christ. As Dr. Louis Evans of Pittsburgh told a 1935 audience in Princeton, "Christ is the universal need. He is no more sectarian than sunshine or rain."[32]

Fundamentalists also beleived deeply that America must continue as a "Christian nation founded on God's word" and that communism threatened that position.[33] Their perspectives on communism and Jews allowed them to see Hitler and his policies in a different light. A later day assessor of articles in *The Alabama Baptist* in the 1930s concluded that the editors saw Jews as a deicide people, interested only in material gain, greedy and hypocritical, and sympathetic to, if not actually members of, the Communist Party. This observer wrote that from the point of view of Alabama Baptists, "a man, even Hitler, cannot be all bad if he does not drink, smoke, or allow women to use cosmetics." Many fundamentalists also interpreted Hitler's actions toward Jews as God's "rod of correction" for "Jewish sin and unbelief."[34] After *Kristallnacht* in 1938, when Germans went on a rampage against Jews in their country, *The Alabama Baptist* opined, "While we are not party to Jewish persecutions, we believe this era of persecution can be used as an opportunity to preach repentance to Israel."[35]

William Dudley Pelley, the son of a Protestant minister, stood out as the most prominent fundamentalist antisemite, a man convinced that he was divinely inspired to lead a mass movement against the anti-Christian conspirators in America. In 1932 he had a vision that something important would occur on January 30, 1933, and after Hitler became Chancellor of Germany that day Pelley interpreted the accession as a God-given sign. He then began to think of himself as the American Hitler. In February 1933 Pelley founded the Silver Legion, generally known as the Silver Shirts, which offered the same venomous message in the United States as did the leader of Germany. Like Hitler, Pelley used materials from Henry Ford's "International Jew" and *The Protocols of the Elders of Zion* in many of his various publications, including *Liberation*.[36]

Several of Pelley's views perplexed rational people. He claimed to have spent seven minutes in Heaven during which he allegedly conversed with God. Pelley also described an international conspiracy with 300,000 to 400,000 European Jews coming to the United States to spearhead an assault on the American government.[37] And he also stated that he had "proof—pressed down and overflowing— that the New Deal from its inception has been naught but the political penetration of a predominantly Christian country and Christian government, by predatory, megalomaniacal Israelites and their agents."[38] Pelley's assertions provided the raison d'etre for his group, the Silver Shirts, which one 1933 observer dubbed "the most important native anti-Semitic organization in the United States."[39] During the 1930s the Silver Shirts enjoyed especially strong support in the South, the Pacific Northwest, and California.[40]

Other antisemitic groups in the 1930s, several of which were also headed by fundamentalists, included the Friends of New Germany that became the German-American Bund, the Defenders of the Christian Faith, the Knights of the White Camelia ("We're for Christ and the Constitution"), the Industrial Defense Association, the American Nationalist Confederation, the James True Association, and the National Union for Social Justice. In fact, from 1933 through 1941, over 100 antisemitic organizations were created, as contrasted with perhaps a total of five in all previous American history.[41] The men who headed the most important of these new organizations included Pelley, the somewhat deranged son of a Christian minister, the Reverend Gerald Winrod, who spearheaded the Defenders of the Christian Faith and who praised Hitler for saving Germany from "Jewish communism,"[42] and Father Charles Coughlin of the National Union for Social Justice, the only Catholic but the most notable hate monger of the decade. These zealots cloaked their views with religious imageries, defended the anticommunist (thus antisemitic) policies of Adolf Hitler, and charged that the New Deal programs of Franklin D. Roosevelt emanated from the Jewish conspiracy fantasized in *The Pro-*

tocols of the Elders of Zion.[43] Pelley, who issued a stream of antisemitic pamphlets under a variety of titles from his headquarters in Asheville, North Carolina, told a House of Representatives Committee in 1940:

> I don't hold any hatred toward any Jew in the United States. I feel exactly as the Nazi Party in Germany felt in regard to Germany, regarding the Jewish element in our population, yes sir.[44]

During World War II rabble rousers like Pelley, Winrod, and Coughlin would be deemed fascist extremists by the American government and silenced under the provisions of the 1917 Sedition Act that prohibited speech aiding the enemy. Yet in the 1930s they received support not only from religious people who accepted the truthfulness of Jewish responsibility for a communist conspiracy to undermine the government of the United States[45] but also from fearful men and women suffering from and frustrated by the depression. The rantings of the demagogues resembled medieval accusations against the Jews as well as views popularized earlier in the twentieth century by men like Burton Hendrick, Madison Grant, and E. A. Ross. In later years, Protestant religious journals, and the fundamentalist press in particular, reported Hitler's persecution of the Jews but they generally failed to convey the horror of Nazi pogroms, were indifferent to the plight of the Jews, believed that the Jews were partly responsible for Nazi attacks, or saw the tragedy as the fulfillment of God's judgment. Many of their readers subscribed to all of the above views.[46]

Catholic, as well as Protestant, hostility toward Jews also intensified in the 1930s. Fears of communist subversion, the rise of Hitler, and the depression in the United States did not create Catholic antisemitism but exacerbated existing prejudices and led to vituperative expressions of antipathy toward Jews. Catholics and Jews differed on a wide variety of domestic issues as Catholics generally favored, and Jews opposed, state aid to parochial schools, religious instruction in public schools, censorship, and bans against divorce and birth control. In New York City politics, Irish Catholics and Jews differed over the election of liberal-progressive Fiorello La Guardia as Mayor in 1933. Nationally both groups backed Roosevelt but many members of the Catholic hierarchy pulled away from the President in the middle of the decade because they thought his New Deal "communistic." Father Charles Coughlin was among the leaders of those who sought to thwart Roosevelt's reelection in 1936 when Jews embraced the President.[47] Catholics in general, and the church in particular, favored order, authority, and conservatism while the more liberal Jews valued intellectual exploration, socialism, and even communism.[48] In response to a 1939 nationwide poll question, "If you had to choose between Fascism and Communism, which would you choose?" 66 percent of Catholics chose fascism, 67 percent of Jews chose communism.[49] Moreover, a tradition of hostility toward Jews existed in Catholic America that for decades had led to assaults on Jewish children and adults by Irish youth in New York, Boston, Pittsburgh, Jersey City, Philadelphia, and other cities.[50]

The American government's international policies widened the rift between Catholics and Jews. Catholics opposed Roosevelt's recognition of the Soviet

Union in 1934, criticized the administration and non-Catholic Americans for their apparent indifference to outrages against Catholics in Mexico, and expressed relatively little opposition to Hitler's policies. Jews, on the other hand, generally supported Roosevelt's positions in foreign policy and saw Hitler as the devil incarnate. A small minority even believed that Stalin, who before the Nazi-Soviet pact of 1939 was the only European head of state to denounce Hitler's Germany and antisemitism, would lead the world to a socialist nirvana.[51]

But it was the Spanish Civil War that had the most profound effect on Catholic-Jewish relations. The war began in July 1936 when a military coup, led by General Francisco Franco, attempted to overthrow the popularly elected, left-wing Spanish government. Civil war ensued, with the Soviet Union aiding the established government and the Catholic Church, along with Nazi Germany and fascist Italy, backing the rebels. To American Catholics who supported church positions it seemed obvious that the anti-Franco movement was "dominated by Jews."[52] The Brooklyn *Tablet*, the official archdiocesan newspaper, observed in March 1937, "It is rather galling to find vociferous and misrepresentative Hebrews championing Stalin and Caballero while they denounce Hitler."[53] When a few Catholic periodicals like *Commonweal*, the *New World*, and the *Catholic Worker* tried to give some perspective to the Franco-Loyalist conflict they "were doomed to failure from the start. There is no parallel in all our history," a Catholic scholar later wrote, "for the rabid abuse [these publications] brought down on themselves."[54]

The war brought smoldering Catholic-Jewish animosities into the open, as both Catholic periodicals and priests forcefully expressed antisemitism. Two leading diocesan newspapers, *The Boston Pilot* and the Brooklyn *Tablet*, were especially strong in their opposition to Jews, and Catholics were advised to read only their own publications and shun those published or dominated by Jews.[55] In 1937, the *Catholic Transcript* of Hartford informed readers that "the Jews . . . are hated because they are too prosperous, too successfully grasping. . . . They are the richest men in the world."[56] In Cincinnati, the editor of the diocesan *Catholic Telegraph-Register* repeated much of what appeared in other Catholic periodicals but in a more venomous fashion. Over a period of eight years, from 1936 through 1943, he accused Jews of being pagans, asserted that the Soviet government was predominantly Jewish and that the leader of Loyalist Spain was also a Jew, accused many Jews of being communists and atheists, and claimed that antisemitism was a result of the immoral business ethics of Jews. After World War II began in Europe, and many Americans feared that the United States might be dragged into the conflagration, the *Telegraph-Register* editorialized in August 1941:

> Today there is a highly organized minority of the war party in our country. It is vocal, it is tyrannical in smearing patriotic Americans who disagree with its program. Jewry in certain aspects is a very highly organized minority. It possesses great wealth and extraordinary influence. . . .
>
> Jewry seems committed to a war program for our country. Jewry seems concerned with the things of a passing day. Yet, if this country goes to war, we predict that opposition to Jews will gain uncontrollable momentum. They will be blamed, in large measure, for influencing the officials and agencies favoring war.[57]

Catholic hatred of Jews was later commented on by a woman who received a parochial school education in the New Deal era. Abigail McCarthy, former wife of the unsuccessful 1968 aspirant to the Democratic presidential nomination, Eugene McCarthy, recalled that she was taught that the Jews had rejected Jesus and they in turn were the rejected people. The students did not genuflect during the prayer for "the perfidious Jews" on Good Friday, either. She asserted that whole immigrant groups arrived in the United States with the same smoldering and venomous antisemitism that flourished in the nations that they left behind. McCarthy also characterized her fellow Catholics as "racists," who have been that way "throughout our history in this country—and there are anti-Semites among us. If truth were known there are probably more anti-Semites than there are racists. Some of us are Klansmen at heart."[58]

By 1938 conditions were ripe for a charismatic Catholic to vocalize these views to the general public. A Detroit priest, Father Charles Coughlin, seized the opportunity and in articulating positions favored by many in the Catholic hierarchy, he became one of the most controversial and revered figures of his time. As one of his biographers put it: "He was Christ; he was Hitler; he was savior . . . he was demagogue."[59] Coughlin had already established a reputation as a national critic of malevolent and predatory economic forces and his mellifluous and appealing radio voice won him millions of followers in 1933 and 1934. During the early years of the New Deal he also made references to money lenders and international financiers who kept Americans in the throes of depression and in 1935 he complained about "the Tugwells, the Frankfurters, and the rest of the Jews who surround" the president. By 1936 this pastor of the Little Flower Church in Royal Oak, a Detroit suburb that had earlier been a bastion of the Ku Klux Klan, was friendly with prominent antisemites like Henry Ford and Joseph P. Kennedy. He then joined, and became a leader of, the unsuccessful campaign to prevent Franklin D. Roosevelt's reelection.[60]

In 1937 Detroit's newly appointed Edward Cardinal Mooney tried to curtail Coughlin's public activities but the Vatican intervened on his behalf. A few months later the charismatic priest turned his criticism sharply against the Jews, and developed the largest national following of any demagogue in American history. Coughlin's emergence as the United States' most prominent and vocal Jew-hater coincided with the German *anschluss* of Austria in March 1938. Capitalizing on known Catholic animosities and the growing reluctance of western European and North American countries to welcome Jewish refugees, Coughlin sensed that attacking Jews would enhance his status among Catholics and those who sought easy explanations for their woes. He received copies of the fraudulent *Protocols of the Elders of Zion* from the men who had supplied them to Henry Ford some years earlier, and in July Coughlin's newspaper, *Social Justice*, began reprinting selections of the forgery.[61] In early November 1938 *The New Republic* charged the priest with being "cynically aware that he is peddling falsehood," and asserted that there was "almost no editorial difference between the Nazi weeklies and Coughlin's *Social Justice*."[62]

But criticism from the liberal press hardly bothered Father Coughlin and both American and European events may have spurred his activities. Observers sensed much greater antisemitic fervor in 1938 on both continents. During the fall, Americans read about the worst antisemitic political campaign in Minnesota history as Jews, while being labeled Communists were also accused of gangsterism, radicalism, and controlling the state government. Farmer-Labor Party Governor Elmer Benson had appointed the first Jewish regent in state history which upset many voters, while rumors also spread that the state's first lady and most of the governor's aides were also Jewish. Campaign rhetoric obviously impressed the voters as all but one member of the Farmer-Labor Party, including the governor, lost on election day.[63]

A much more shattering event occurred the following week in Germany. On the night of November 9–10, 1938, *Kristallnacht*, Germans brutally attacked Jews throughout the nation, burned their synagogues and destroyed their businesses, invaded their old-age homes and children's schools. German police also arrested at least 20,000 of the victims. Never before had there been a pogrom of that magnitude and the civilized world reacted with revulsion. Over 90 percent of Americans who knew of the event disapproved of German actions. President Roosevelt declared, "I myself could scarcely believe that such things could occur in a twentieth-century civilization."[64]

Only ten days later, on the night of November 20, Father Coughlin gave the most incredible radio address of his career. Coughlin minimized German barbarities on *Kristallnacht* as he launched into an expansive antisemitic diatribe. He blamed Jews for imposing communism on Russia, and noted that Germans correctly believed that Jews were responsible for the economic and social sufferings of the Fatherland ever since the signing of the Treaty of Versailles. "Nazism," Father Coughlin told listeners, "was conceived as a political defense mechanism against Communism and was ushered into existence as a result of Communism."[65]

To support his contentions Coughlin used counterfeit documents disseminated by the Nazis. Twenty-four of twenty-five "quasi-Cabinet members" of the Soviet Union, and 56 of the 59 members of the Communist Party in Russia in 1935 were alleged to be Jewish. The radio priest also claimed to have before him a quotation from the September 10, 1920, issue of *The American Hebrew* in which the editors allegedly claimed that the Bolshevik revolution of 1917 "was largely the outcome of Jewish thinking, of Jewish discontent, of Jewish effort to reconstruct." Coughlin expressed some sympathy for the 600,000 German Jews persecuted by the Nazis but immediately followed that observation with his opinion that Nazism could not be eradicated until Jewish leaders in synagogues, finance, radio, and the press, attacked communism and coreligionists who showed any sympathy for it.[66] Coughlin also complained that the American press and the American government were more upset about the treatment of Jews in Germany than they were about the attacks on Catholics and their property in Mexico and Spain. The radio priest accused the American press of "muzzling the truth" about the horrors in these countries where Catholics were the victims, especially Spain which was the world's "battleground of Communism versus Christianity." Coughlin began his peroration with the observation that "Thanks be to God, both the radio and the press at length have become attuned to the wails of sorrow arising from Jewish persecution." He then advised his audience that "Gentiles must repudiate the excesses of Nazism. But Jews and gentiles must repudiate the existence of Communism from which Nazism springs."[67]

Officials at New York City radio station that carried the talk, WMCA, were incensed by the speech. They had screened the presentation earlier and had pointed out several errors of fact that needed correction. Spokesmen for the priest assured officials that the changes would be made but they were not. Coughlin submitted this, and subsequent, radio presentations to the archdiocese for prior censorship and he received permission to deliver his talks; he may have thought that the objectionable passages had been eliminated. A half century later a Catholic theologian observed:

> the astounding fact of the matter is that ecclesiastical censors named by [his supervisor, Cardinal] Mooney had previewed and passed Coughlin's anti-Semitic broadcasts as not offending against Catholic faith or morals. It was a pre-Vatican II Catholicism in which anti-Semitism did not arouse moral outrage and institutional considerations outweighed virtually all else.[68]

But at station WMCA antisemitism and erroneous dissemination of information did arouse moral outrage. Immediately after Coughlin finished his talk an announcer came on the air and stated: "Unfortunately, Father Coughlin has uttered certain mistakes of fact,"[69] and then proceeded to enumerate them. In contrast to what Coughlin had said, the Bolshevik Central Committee was not dominated by Jews, Jewish bankers had not financed the Bolshevik Revolution, no British white paper had ever accused the American Jewish banking firm of Kuhn, Loeb of having aided the Communists, *The American Hebrew* had never stated that the Jews were responsible for the Bolshevik Revolution, and so forth. It later turned out that most of Coughlin's "facts" came from Nazi publications like *World Service*.[70]

A few prominent Catholics and periodicals took exception to the distortions in Coughlin's presentation. They included the *Michigan Catholic, Commonweal,* and George Cardinal Mundelein of Chicago who announced that Coughlin spoke for himself and not the church. Monsignor John Ryan accused Coughlin of being guilty of great distortions of fact, and of promoting antisemitism in the United States,[71] while an editorial in *Commonweal* denounced Coughlin's "tendentious radio talk of November 20," which "gained him . . . accolades from the inspired German Nazi press." The editorial condemned Coughlin's

> cavalier disregard for pertinent historical testimony, his insensitivity to the consequences of his acts on German and Italian Jews, his all too pious acceptance of propaganda from a party whose Fuhrer proudly boasts his machine is based on huge lies.[72]

Catholic World scolded Coughlin, though not by name, in an editorial undermining the thrust of his speech while reinforcing many Catholic beliefs that laid the groundwork for the charges. These words, in turn, made the radio priest's accusations more palatable:

Anti-semitism is unjust, brutal and opposed to the teachings of Christ. If simple-minded people have sometimes thought that they needed to avenge our Savior for the treatment He received from His own people, they are very badly mistaken.

Of course, it is true that the Jews were rejected by God as the nation through which salvation was to come to the world, when they called down upon themselves and their children the blood of Christ. It is probably true that many of the hardships that have befallen God's chosen people are the punishment of the Heavenly Father, who wants to bring them back to Him whenever they "grow fat and kick." But neither Hitler nor Mussolini or any other individual has a special mandate from God to carry out this punishment.[73]

Despite the mild chastisement of the *Catholic World*, Coughlin's views apparently touched the right chord among millions of Americans discontented with their own lives, fearful of communism, and frustrated by the enduring depression and the failure of Roosevelt to turn the economy around. No American Catholic had ever before achieved such commanding attention and approval in the United States.[74] A Roseford, Illinois, priest voiced an opinion undoubtedly shared by millions of others: "If Father Coughlin be not the most useful citizen in America, he is among the first in that distinguished category."[75] In December 1938, 45 radio stations carried his weekly address that 3.5 million Americans listened to regularly; another 15 million had heard him at least once. Two-thirds of his loyal followers and more than half of those who tuned in occasionally subscribed to his views while polls showed that the lower the economic class, the larger the percentage of people who approved the radio priest's views. Among the lowest classes of Irish Catholics, and in the Irish middle classes, Coughlin had enormous support. His office received approximaely 80,000 letters a week, 70 percent of which came from Protestants, and it took 105 staff members to read them.[76]

Perhaps because of Coughlin's exhortations, perhaps because of another downturn in the economy in 1938, perhaps because of the increased and cumulative effect of Nazi policies that led to an augmented number of German Jews trying to get into the United States, or perhaps because of a combination of factors, observers throughout the United States sensed an increased ardor in both antisemitic feelings and expressions. According to George N. Shuster, a prominent Catholic layman who deplored the bigotry of so many of his coreligionists and who would later become president of New York City's Hunter College, Coughlin's

utterances stiffened the backs of all those who in one way or another were friendly to Hitler and Mussolini. It gave anti-Semitism the same religious inlay which played so great a role in the Austria whence Hitler came; it raised the issue of fascism vs. democracy; and it carried the virus of race hatred to regions where it had never previously been known.[77]

Thus, as Shuster pointed out, not only were Catholics aroused by Coughlin but his continuing attacks in print and on the air reflected sentiments heard throughout the United States. A Chicago businessman with "a reputation for liberalism" indicated that "the Jews are the cause of all our troubles in this country and I wish that every one of them could be deported."[78] In Minneapolis, a street-car conductor obviously believed the same thing. Forced to move a stalled auto off the track so that his trolley could proceed, and wihout knowing who the driver was, he muttered, "That dirty Jew, we ought to have a Hitler here."[79] One Catholic priest in Akron, Ohio, claimed, "The Jews here are at the bottom of most of our troubles and will someday suffer for it." A 68-year-old rubber plant worker in the same city told an interviewer, "I don't know what's the matter with me, but I hate the sight of a Jew. They control the money of the United States." He then added, "I'm like Hitler when it comes to the Jews. They would all leave the country if I had the power. I get mad when I start talking about them."[80] And in St. Louis, where the local chapter of the Friends of New Germany was generally known as the "Hitler Club," antisemitic slogans proliferated. Some parks and pools displayed signs readings: "Restricted to members and Gentiles only."[81]

Prominent officials throughout the country received letters from citizens reflecting this intense animosity toward Jews. On November 18, 1938, only eight days after *Kristallnacht* and two days before Father Coughlin's sensational radio address attacking Jews, Idaho Senator William Borah spoke out against relaxing our immigration laws to increase the number of refugees admitted to the United States.[82] As a result of the talk hundreds, perhaps even thousands, of Americans inundated his office with messages of congratulations and appreciation. This mail not only supported Borah's stance regarding refugees but also included ferocious attacks on Jews.

The letters may have repeated tired shibboleths yet they mirrored the bigotry so many Americans had already revealed to pollsters in 1938. (At least half of all respondents that year thought Jews were partially or entirely responsible for Hitler's treatment of them while four separate inquiries resulted in anywhere from 71 to 85 percent stating that they opposed increasing immigration quotas for refugees.[83]) With great self-assurance correspondents mentioned a variety of inaccuracies including the "fact" that the President's family had been known as "Rosenfelt" in Holland, that Jews controlled the economy, that they prospered while others starved, that they were "the scum of Europe," and that millions of Americans were "put off their farms" and "lost their homes during the Jewish New Deal depression." A man from Fond du Lac, Wisconsin, praised Borah's "stand regarding the Jew. We don't want any part of them in this country, at least no more of them. There are far too many of them now." A New Yorker wrote, "Please Senator Borah dont allow anymore jews to come into the U.S.A. We have enough trouble here without bringing in the greatest trouble making race in the history of the world." Another New Yorker claimed that

> the Jewish problem has been with us for over 2000 years since the time of Pontius Pilate. The Jews have been ejected from and are a problem to any nation they inhabit. The Jews themselves are a very large measure responsible for this. Why don't they ask themselves why they are anathema all over the world? Germany is not the first nation nor shall it be the last confronted with this dilemma.

A resident of Washington, D.C., complained that he

> had twenty-five years experience with the Jew and have yet to find a good one. You probably know more about them than I do. If there is to be a comparison between the German and the Jew, there is not a good quality possessed by the German that is in a like manner possessed by the Jew. The German is clean, law-abiding, ethical in business, patriotic, and American. The Jew is dirty, lawless, unethical, unpatriotic and un-American.[84]

"There must be some reason for all this dislike of the Jews," another of Borah's correspondents speculated.[85]

The harsh antisemitic sentiments expressed in Nomember and December 1938 escalated during the winter. As part of his crusade to eliminate communism Coughlin called for the establishment of a united Christian Front in the May 23, 1938, issue of his newspaper, *Social Justice*.[86] His call met with an enthusiastic response from his Irish Catholic admirers in some of the largest cities in the United States. Embittered and unnerved by the depression and its downward turn again in 1938, displaced from seats of political influence and power in New York City, and upset by the apparent potency of militant elements in the labor movement and elsewhere who championed radical changes in society as well as the Loyalist cause in the Spanish Civil War, Irish Catholics were ripe for the demagogic appeals made by men like Coughlin. They provided the backbone for Christian Front chapters in the sections and cities where more than 85 percent of all American Jews lived: Brooklyn, New York, Boston, Philadelphia, Baltimore, St. Paul, Minneapolis, Chicago, St. Louis, Detroit, Pittsburgh, Cleveland.[87] In all of these places Christian Fronters "were likely to be anti-Semitic, bellicose and vulgar."[88] Christian Fronters who received the most attention resided in Boston and Brooklyn where about 90 percent of the participants were Irish Catholics. In both areas the local diocesan newspapers, *The Boston Pilot* and the Brooklyn *Tablet*, staunchly supported Father Coughlin. Christian Front meetings were not exclusive, and members of the German American Bund, Protestant War Veterans, Christian Labor Front, Christian Order of Coughlinites, Crusaders for Social Justice, Crusaders for Americanism, American Nationalists, and the Christian American League often appeared at gatherings, many of which ended with the Nazi salute.[89]

At these rallies Christian Fronters were called on to "liquidate the Jews in America." Copies of *Social Justice* and the Brooklyn *Tablet* were sold, Coughlin was celebrated, and Jews were assailed as communists, international bankers, and war mongers. Speakers referred to the President of the United States as "Rosenfelt" or "Rosenvelt" or some similar sounding Jewish name, praised Franco as "that great Christian general who drove the reds out of Spain," and championed Hitler as "the savior of Europe." One critic assailed most Christian Front speeches as "plain, unvarnished incitements to murder," while another described the organization as a "savage anti-Semitic movement."[90]

From 1939 through 1942 roving gangs of Christian Fronters picketed, and placarded obscene stickers on, Jewish-owned retail establishments, desecrated synagogues, and indiscriminately attacked Jewish children and adults on the streets of cities like New York and Boston where sympathetic policemen of Irish background allowed the outrages to continue. In New York City more than 400 members of the police force also belonged to the Christian Front. On one occasion a Jew passed by an antisemitic rally where the speaker of the moment proclaimed that the only good Jews were in a cemetery. The passerby retorted that he was a good Jew and very much alive. Immediately a policeman on duty arrested the Jew for disturbing the peace. An incredulous judge could not believe what the patrolman had done but the officer explained that he arrested the "culprit" on specific orders from his captain, Michael McCarron.[91]

The Christian Fronters were variously assailed as storm troopers for Coughlin, young thugs, and neo-Nazis but they were hailed in working-class Irish Catholic neighborhoods for helping thwart the spread of communism. Leaders of the group included priests like Thomas E. Malloy, called the "Bishop of the Christian Front," and other prominent clerics and Catholic laymen who admired Father Coughlin. These men commanded respect from fellow Irish Catholics, especially since neither the archbishops of Brooklyn, New York, or Boston publicly criticized the radio priest or his followers. Church leaders even failed to endorse the newly formed Christian Committee Against Anti-Semitism in April 1939 on the ground that it would divide loyal Catholics.[92] The Brooklyn *Tablet* acknowledged that some members of the Christian Front were "anti-Semitic. Well what of it? Just what law was violated?"[93] One student later wrote that

> the Irish character of the Front seems . . . to have been due to the well known loyalty of the Irish to the Catholic Church. The devout and even militant Catholicism of the Front organization's leaders, and the support given the Frontists by *The Tablet* all testify to the fact that the Front was primarily a Catholic movement.[94]

The activities of the Christian Fronters and Coughlin's continuing attacks on Jews, both on the radio and in print, also triggered a noticeable upsurge in antisemitism in the New York area.

Christian Fronters and their cohorts also provided most of the audience for a spectacular display of antisemitic fervor that the German American Bund put on at New York City's Madison Square Garden on February 20, 1939. Ostensibly a celebration of George Washington's brithday, the arena was filled with 19,000 animated people, hundreds of Nazi flags, 400 men who looked like storm troopers in their Nazi uniforms, and 1,745 New York City policemen. Throughout the arena massive banners proclaimed: "Stop Jewish Domination of Christian America!" and "Wake Up America! Smash Jewish Communism." Mention of Father Coughlin's name resulted in prolonged cheers and applause while shouts of "Heil Hitler" punctuated the evening.[95]

The combination of Coughlinites, Christian Fronters, and Nazi sympathizers celebrating in unison alarmed concerned Americans. A *Nation* reporter wrote on April 1, 1939,

> this account of anti-Semitism in New York City today could not have been written a year ago. These things now in abundant open manifestation were not

happening then. But in 1939 anti-Semitism in New York has ceased to be whis-
pered and has become an open instrument of demagoguery, a vast outlet for
idle energies.[96]

Journalist James Wechsler attributed the rise of this antisemitic furor to "Coughlin's personality, Coughlin's speeches, and Coughlin's propaganda." The Christian Front, he added, provided "the dynamic core of the movement. It calls the
mass meetings, floods the city with leaflets, and rallies the crowds under its own
signature." *The Christian Century* added, "Father Coughlin . . . is thoroughly
Hitlerish in outlook, in method and in the effect he produces."[97]

A spate of other articles in 1939 reinforced the impression of rising hostility
toward Jews. In June, historian Henry Pratt Fairchild observed that in this country
"some degree of hostility or dislike of Jews in general is very widespread, even
among the most broad-minded and kindly disposed of his associates." The
Catholic *Interracial Review* noted in July that "the rapid spread of anti-Semitism
has caused well-justified concern." And in November, a man with a Jewish wife,
living in the suburbs of an eastern city, admitted:

> my work has taken me into about every large city in the United States and into
> many small cities, too. My face and name bring me into contact with Christians
> at their clubs, bars, and homes. And each time I travel I grow more conscious
> of the rising tide of anti-Semitism that is moving across the country.

A New England Episcopalian minister added that he had lived "over forty years
in a country where 'something would have to be done about the Jews.' I've been
surrounded by and part of a passive anti-Semitic multitude of Christians." But
there had been "no concerted effort. No *active* desire to do something." Yet in
1939, he emphasized, there were leaders. There were active and organized efforts
to do something about the Jews and it frightened him.[98]

As anguished as the New England minister was, his apprehensions did not
compare with the fears and anxieties of American Jews who desperately wanted
to reverse what appeared to be the unrelenting growth of antisemitism in the
United States. A 1940 article in the American Jewish *Congress Bulletin* noted that
"at no time in American history has anti-Semitism been as strong as it is today."[99]
To be sure, American animosity did not compare in severity with what was happening to Jews in Europe, but American Jews did not know what calamity might
next occur in the United States. Psychologist Kurt Lewin advised American Jews
how and when to inform their children of the situations that they might encounter. "The basic fact is that [your] child is going to be a member of a less privileged minority group, and he will have to face this fact." Do not try to avoid a discussion of the subject of antisemitism because "the problem is bound to arise at
some time, and the sooner it is faced, the better." The child might not be called a
"dirty Jew," Lewin wrote, until about the fourth grade, he or she could be expected to be invited to parties of their Gentile peers until adolescence when the in-
vitations would cease, and both boys and girls would not have to face the existence of discrimination in colleges and jobs until the end of their high school
years.[100]

Jewish community leaders admonished coreligionists to remain circumspect in their public behavior, to draw no attention to themselves as Jews, and to disassociate themselves from any group considered foreign to American society.[101] "Conservative Jews," a 1938 article in *The Nation* indicated,

> faced with the insanity of anti-Semitism, are tempted to abandon rationality themselves and accept as their own criteria of behavior the prejudices that operate against them. A radical Jewish labor leader or public official is looked upon not merely as a wrong-headed fellow, but as a menace to the race; a Jew who militantly espouses even the cause of free speech is considered a person of dubious judgment.[102]

The hostile attitudes exhibited toward Jews by so many Americans had devastating psychological effects on individuals who could not bear their minority status. "The fact is," Lewis Browne wrote in 1939, "we Jews as Jews can't do anything. Working by ourselves, we are utterly impotent. For, being a minority, we cannot act; we can only react. All of which means simply this: if the Jewish problem is ever to be solved, it will have to be done by the Gentiles." One Jewish writer even claimed that "the vast majority of Jews do not remain Jews by choice. Basically, the Jew hates his Jewishness, and bewails his fate."[103]

Thousands of Jews abandoned their heritage. A man who chose to remain anonymous indicated that he found it impossible to be both a Jew and an American. He therefore converted and claimed that he enjoyed being a Christian.

> I am now raising children who need never learn to endure snubs, who will never be tempted to retaliate against cruel discrimination. From this pleasant sunshine, I look back with horror at the somber world in which my race-proud kin persist on their ancient and unhappy courses. Life is good. I never regret my step.[104]

That same author wrote how embarrassed he had been by other Jews who spoke English badly, who used gestures to emphasize their points, and who interspersed Yiddish words or expressions in their speech.[105]

The vast majority of Jews, however, suffered silently or bewailed their fate. Untold numbers modified or altered their names and several reporters at *The New York Times* believed that publishers Adolph Ochs and Arthur Hays Sulzberger were so sensitive to antisemitism that they encouraged newcomers to use initials instead of their given name of Abraham in bylines. Thus readers noted stories by A. H. Raskin, and in later years by A. H. Weiler and A. M. Rosenthal, without becoming aware of their Jewish-sounding given names. (New York *Tribune* editor William O. McGeehan had tried to influence one of his sportswriters to do the same thing in the 1920s but Jesse Abrahamson refused to become A. Bramson.) In the 1930s many Jews changed their names to increase their economic opportunities and comfort levels. Milton Levine became Milton Lewis in the hopes that it would advance his journalistic career and the young Mel Israel gladly accepted the advice of CBS radio officials who told him that keeping his name would hinder professional advancement. Israel then changed his surname to Allen and went on to a lengthy career broadcasting New York Yankees baseball games.[106]

In the 1930s a Jewish name was not only a hardship for those people trying to move into mainstream America but was also a vestige of Old World and immigrant origins from which they wanted to distance themselves. Many Jewish college students changed their names just before they graduated; some people waited a bit longer. A study of name alterations in Los Angeles in the 1930s indicated that the largest number of people who applied for changes were married and prosperous Jewish males who lived in mixed Jewish and Christian neighborhoods. The study provided no analysis or explanation as to why this particular group stood out, but a safe assumption is that being identified as Jewish narrowed their social and economic opportunities. People in Hollywood, for example, often changed their names for business reasons.[107] One Hollywood writer/director, Abraham Polansky, admitted:

> when I arrived at Paramount as a contract writer, another Jewish writer told me to change my name. He told me it sounded Jewish and that movies were seen all over America. I didn't change my name and nothing happened. But many actors did. Americans wanted to see Americans.[108]

During World War II the National Jewish Welfare Board surveyed Jews in the armed services and found that over 50 percent of the returned questionnaires came from people with generalized American surnames like "Smith" and "Brown," who presumably wanted to hide their backgrounds or avoid discrimination. By the late 1940s 46 percent of those people who sought name changes in Los Angeles were Jewish although Jews constituted only 6 percent of the city's population.[109]

Other Jewish responses to the antisemitism of the 1930s were reflected by the reaction of some high-status Jews after the death of Justice Benjamin Cardozo of the U.S. Supreme Court in July 1938. Secretary of the Treasury Henry Morgenthau, publisher Arthur Hays Sulzberger of *The New York Times,* and other well-connected Jews urged Roosevelt not to appoint Felix Frankfurter as Cardozo's replacement because his name, *Time* magazine asserted, had "come to symbolize Jewish radicalism in the New Deal." They feared that with Brandeis still serving, "putting a second Jew on the Court would play into the hands of anti-Semites at home and abroad."[110] On this occasion, however, the President chose to take a symbolic stand and wrote to Judge Julian W. Mack:

> I feel it is peculiarly important—just because of the waves of persecution and discrimination which are mounting in other parts of the world—that we in this country make it clear that citizens of the United States are elected or selected for positions of responsibility solely because of their qualifications, experience, and character, and without regard to their religious faith.[111]

Frankfurter had been a valued advisor to the President for several years and although Roosevelt waited until January 1939 before selecting him, the nomination sailed through the Senate with little difficulty. During Frankfurter's confirmation hearings, however, Senator Patrick McCarran of Nevada asked him "Are you a Communist?" and then followed up with "Do you believe the doctrines of Karl Marx?" After Frankfurter indicated that he was neither a communist nor a sympathizer with Marxist thoughts, the Senate Judiciary Committee unanimously recommended his approval. Significantly, many Senators preferred not having their stance recorded and floor confirmation came on a voice vote.[112]

Members of the public showed less hesitancy in expressing their views of the appointment. Letters came into Senator William Borah's office accusing Frankfurter of being "a dangerous radical" and "a Jew of frankly Communistic activities." One writer wanted "a person, who first of all is a native born American of pioneer stock—and a devout Christian," another indicated that "a Jew has no right in our courts. We want white men there," and a third claimed that his "objection to Jews in our government is . . . based . . . upon moral grounds, which were established by the Bible, and the teachings of Jesus Christ."[113] William Pelley of the Silver Shirts claimed that the appointment of Frankfurter to the Court doubled his business and George Shuster wrote that "the remarks of various editors" of Catholic journals "on the appointment of Felix Frankfurter to the Supreme Court would make up a rather harrowing little anthology."[114]

Thus, as the decade ended, Jews were more uneasy about the future than they had been ten years earlier. *Fortune* magazine reported in February 1936 that incidents and expressions in the 1920s had aroused concerns but in the 1930s made important Jewish leaders, "men who had previously looked to the future with complete confidence," fearful. "The apprehensiveness of American Jews has become one of the important influences in the social life of our time." *Fortune*'s concern with the rumors led it to examine Jewish power in the business world. Its investigation found that a majority of Jews were poor or living on the margin of poverty in the 1930s but they had to endure accusations that they controlled the banks and monopolized economic opportunity in America. The journal's lengthy analysis of American Jewish business interests led to the conclusion that there was absolutely "no basis whatsoever for the suggestion that Jews monopolize U.S. business and industry." typically, those who held such beliefs refused to relinquish them.[115]

American Jews knew of existing antisemitism but before 1933 it had been mainly religious, intellectual, verbal, social, and economic. There had also been sporadic attacks on children and adults in a number of cities in this country. But in the 1930s the intensity of antisemitism, the appeal of hate organizations, and the popularity of demagogues combined with an escalation of serious physical abuse, especially in the cities of the northeast and midwest where more than 85 percent of all American Jews dwelled, to have an absolutely chilling effect. And the worst thing was that the hatred seemed to be accelerating. For the first time in American history Jews feared that their attackers might acquire the kind of political influence and respectability that antisemites had in Europe and achieve similarly devastating results. "There is no method by which the present gravity of anti-Semitism may be measured," one Jew wrote just before the United States entered World War II, "the present virulence of anti-Semitism is undefinable, its future unpredictable."[116]

Public opinion polls came into vogue toward the end of the 1930s and their assessments, however crude, reinforced the sense of Jewish insecurity in America. In 1938 at least 50 percent of Americans had a low opinion of Jews, 45 percent thought that they were less honest than Gentiles in business, 24 percent thought that they held too many government jobs, and 35 percent believed that the Jews in Europe were largely responsible for the oppression that had been heaped on them. To the question "Should we allow a larger number of Jewish exiles from Germany come to the United States to live?" 77 percent of the respondents said no. In sum, about 60 percent of those polled had negative impressions of Jews, most finding them greedy, dishonest, and aggressive.[117]

Looking back decades later to assess the status of the Jews in the 1930s provides one with a distorted picture. On a per capita basis, although Jews ranked among the more prosperous Americans economically, the majority of them were poor. It was evident that the second generation of east European immigrants had advanced in status from that of their childhood years but they faced an antisemitism among Gentiles that was deep seated, more unpleasant than a serious threat. Yet American Jews, seeing what Hitler had done in Germany and now personally experiencing the impact of discrimination and racial rhetoric in the United States, seemed more fearful about the future than ever before. For many, there was no light at the end of the tunnel. In both Protestant and Catholic periodicals their faith had been attacked and their raison d'etre questioned. The President of the United States may have brought many Jews into the federal government but he seemed unwilling or unable to cope with the rising tide of antisemitism that Jews saw all about them. A quiet sense of desperation engulfed American Jews who had witnessed several decades of increasing attacks on them from almost every major segment of society. Ironically, although the depression led to increased manifestations of antisemitism, the return of prosperity during World War II did not mitigate its effects. Polls and other measuring rods used to deduce the quantity and intensity of antisemitism during the war suggested that the situation of the Jews in the United States continued to be precarious. It seemed that the very accomplishments of the Jewish Americans were hindrances to their being fully accepted, or at least comfortably tolerated. A sense of foreboding continued to spread among Jews in the United States as their country itself entered an era of maximum mortal danger.

NOTES

1. Arthur Liebman, *Jews and the Left* (New York: John Wiley, 1979), p. 425; Nearptint File—Special Topics, Anti-Semitism (1921–1959), folder, "Anti-Semitism, 1921–1929," box 1 (1921–1938, AJA.

2. Robert T. Handy, *A Christian America: Protestant Hopes and Historical Realities* (New York: Oxford University Press, 1971), p. 66.

3. George Wolfskill and John A. Hudson, *All But the People: Franklin D. Roosevelt and His Critics, 1933–1939* (New York: The Macmillan Co., 1969), pp. 66, 72; Egal Feldman, *Dual Destinies: The Jewish Encounter with Protestant America* (Urbana: University of Illinois Press, 1990), p. 244; George M. Marsden, *Fundamentalism and American Culture: The Shaping*

of Twentieth-Century Evangelism, 1870–1925 (New York: Oxford University Press, 1980), pp. 207, 210.

4. John Sheridan Zelie, "Why Do The Gentiles Rage?" CC, 48 (October 7, 1931), 1239, 1241.

5. Nathan Glazer, "Social Characteristics of American Jews, 1654–1954," AJYB, 56 (1955), 20 ff.; Deborah Dash Moore, *At Home in America: Second Generation New York Jews* (New York: Columbia University Press, 1981), passim; Lawrence H. Fuchs, "American Jews and the Presidential Vote," *The American Political Science Quarterly*, 49 (July, 1955), 385.

6. Henry L. Feingold, *A Time for Searching: Entering the Mainstream* (Baltimore: The Johns Hopkins University Press, 1992), pp. 148–149.

7. Leo P. Ribuffo, "Henry Ford and *The Inernational Jew*," AJH, 69 (June, 1980), 440; M. Ginsberg, "Anti-Semitism," *The Sociological Review*, 35 (January–April, 1943), 7; X, "The Jew and the Club," *The Atlantic*, 134 (October, 1924), 451; Ralph Philip Boas, "Jew-Baiting in America," *The Atlantic*, 127 (May, 1921), 659; "Anti-Semitism Is Here," *The Nation*, 147 (August 25, 1938), 167; Minutes, V (January 13, 1929–February 14, 1932), passim, VI (March 13, 1932–December 23, 1933), 66; Isabel Cohen, "The Reign of Anti-Semitism," *New Statesman and Nation*, 4 (July 23, 1932), 97; Subject File: "Anti-Semitism," reel 77, Felix Frankfurter mss., LC; Conrad Hoffmann, "Modern Jewry and the Christian Church," *International Review of Missions*, 12 (April, 1934), 189; Aaron Goldman, "The Resurgence of Antisemitism in Britain during World War II," JSS, 46 (Winter, 1984), 37–38.

8. Minutes, V (January 13, 1929–February 14, 1932), 1497.

9. Minutes, V (January 13, 1929–February 14, 1932), 1454, "Memorandum on Conference with Charles A. Davila, Romanian Minister to the United States, December 18, 1929," and "Abstract of Statement of Dr. Bernhard Kahn at Meeting of the Executive Committee, December 14, 1930"; Philip S. Bernstein, "Unchristian Christianity and the Jew," *Harper's Magazine*, 162 (May, 1931), 660, 665; William Zuckerman, "The Jews—A Nation Trapped," *The Nation*, 131 (August 20, 1930), 200–201; "Miscellaneous, 1911–1939," folder, 6, box 6, of A. J. Sabath mss. Collection #43, AJA: Cohen, "Reign of Anti-Semitism," p. 97.

10. Cohen, "Reign of Anti-Semitism," p. 96.

11. Max Vorspan and Lloyd P. Gartner, *History of the Jews of Los Angeles* (Philadelphia: JPS, 1970), p. 206.

12. William Manchester, *The Glory and the Dream* (Boston: Little, Brown, 1974), p. 8; Thomas Karfunkel and Thomas W. Ryley, *The Jewish Seat: Anti-Semitism and the Appointment of Jews to the Supreme Court* (Hicksville: Exposition Press, 1978), p. 61; Johan J. Smertenko, "Hitlerism Comes to America," *Harper's Magazine*, 167 (November, 1933), p. 660; Donald S. Strong, *Oranized Anti-Semitism in America: The Rise of Group Prejudice During the Decade, 1930–1940* (Washington: American Council on Public Affairs, 1941), p. 174; John F. Stack, Jr., *International Conflict in an American City: Boston's Irish, Italians, and Jews, 1935–1944* (Westport, Conn.: Greenwood Press, 1979), p. 92; AJYB, 37 (September 28, 1935–September 16, 1936), p. 156; Paul S. Holbo, "Wheat or What? Populism and American Fascism," *Western Political Quarterly*, 14 (September, 1961), 735; Leo P. Ribuffo, *The Old Christian Right* (Philadelphia: Temple University Press, 1983), p. 18; J. A. Rogers, "Negroes Suffer More in U. S. Than Jews in Germany," *The Philadelphia Tribune*, September 21, 1933, p. 3.

13. Richard F. Nelson, "Nothing Will Save Us but a Pogrom!" CC, 50 (June 28, 1933), 850.

14. Maud Nathan, *Once Upon a Time and Today* (New York: G. P. Putnam's Sons, 1933), p. 275.

15. Minutes, VI (1932–1938), 178; Ron Chernow, *The House of Morgan: An American Banking Dynasty and the Rise of Modern Finance* (New York: Atlantic Monthly Press, 1990), p. 394; Laura Z. Hobson, *Laura Z.: A Life* (New York: Arbor House, 1983), p. 115.

16. Leonard Dinnerstein, "Jews and the New Deal," AJH, 72 (June, 1983), 463ff.

17. Jerold S. Auerbach, *Unequal Justice: Lawyers and Social Change in Modern America* (New York: Oxford University Press, 1976), pp. 187–188.

18. Dinnerstein, "Jews and the New Deal," p. 463.

19. W. M. Kiplinger, "The Facts About Jews in Washington," *Reader's Digest*, 41 (September, 1942), 3; *The New Dealers*, by Unofficial Observer (New York: The Literary Guild, 1934), p. 322.

20. [signature illegible] to FDR, October 21, 1934, OF 76C, FDR mss.

21. AJYB, 37 (1935–1936), 153–154; Wolfskill and Hudson, *All But the People*, p. 86; newspaper clipping, May 20, 1934, box 160, Raymond Clapper mss., LC; Zosa Szajkowski, "The Attitude of American Jews to Refugees from Germany in the 1930's," AJHQ, 61 (December, 1971), 106; *The New Dealers*, p. 332; Myron Scholnick, "The New Deal and Anti-Semitism in America" (unpublished Ph.D., Department of History, University of Maryland, 1971), pp. 33, 76–77; "Washington Notes," *The New Republic*, 77 (January 10, 1934), 250.

22. Quoted in Scholnick, "The New Deal," p. 77; see also Richard Yaffe, "The Roosevelt Magic," *The National Jewish Monthly*, 87 (October, 1972), 31; Bruce Allen Murphy, *The Brandeis/Frankfurter Connection* (New York: Oxford University Press, 1982), pp. 133, 288; Marquis W. Childs, "They Still Hate Roosevelt," *The New Republic*, 96 (September 14, 1938), 148; T. R. B., "Washington Notes," *The New Republic*, 77 (January 10, 1934), 250; "Anti-Semitism Is Here," p. 167; Wolfskill and Hudson, *All But the People*, 65ff; E. Digby Baltzell, *The Protestant Establishment* (New York: Random House, 1964), p. 248.

23. W. M. Kiplinger, "The Facts About Jews in Washington," *Reader's Digest*, 41 (September, 1942), 2ff; see also, Frank Freidel, *Franklin D. Roosevelt: Launching the New Deal* (Boston: Little, Brown & Co., 1973), p. 393.

24. Wolfskill and Hudson, *All But the People*, p. 66; see also Franklin Thompson, *America's Ju-Deal* (Woodhaven, N.Y.: Community Press, 1935).

25. Scholnick, "The New Deal," p. 79; Michael Gerald Rapp, "An Historical Overview of Anti-Semitism In Minnesota, 1920–1960—With Particular Emphasis on Minneapolis and St. Paul" (unpublished Ph.D., Department of History, University of Minnesota, 1977), p. 61; Wolfskill and Hudson, *All But the People*, pp. 66–67, 70; Paul W. Ward, "Washington Weekly," *The Nation*, 143 (November 7, 1936), 540; copy of Winrod's article, "Roosevelt's Jewish Ancestry," *The Review*, October 15, 1936, in folder, "Edmundsen Service [NYC]," PPF #1632, FDR mss.

26. Quoted in Wolfskill and Hudson, *All But the People*, p. 87.

27. Feldman, *Dual Destinies*, p. 201.

28. Franklin H. Littell, "American Protestantism and Antisemitism," in Naomi W. Cohen, ed., *Essential Papers on Jewish-Christian Relations in the United States* (New York: NYU Press, 1990), p. 184.

29. "Jews and Jesus," CC, 50 (May 3, 1933), 582.

30. "The Jewish Problem," CC, 53 (April 29, 1936), 625; "Jews, Christians and Democracy," CC, 53 (May 13, 1936), 697; "Jews and Democracy," CC, 53 (June 9, 1937), 734–735; "Tolerance Is Not Enough!" CC, 53 (July 1, 1936), 928.

31. "Shall Christians Let the Jews Alone?" *Missionary Review of the World*, 54 (July, 1931), 517.

32. "The Jewish Question in America," *Missionary Review of the World*, 58 (September, 1935), 388.

33. Marsden, *Fundamentalism and American Culture*, p. 207.

34. William R. Glass, "Fundamentalism's Prophetic Vision of the Jews: The 1930s," JSS, 47 (Winter, 1985), 67, 69; Jimmy Harper, "Alabama Baptists and the Rise of Hitler and Fascism, 1930–1938," *Journal of Reform Judaism*, 32 (Spring, 1985), 7, 8, 9 (quote on page 8).

35. The Alabama Baptist, December 15, 1938, p. 4.

36. Ribuffo, *Old Christian*, pp. 56–57; Strong, *Organized Anti-Semitism*, pp. 40, 46.

37. Wolfskill and Hudson, *All But the People*, pp. 68, 72.

38. Quoted in ibid., p. 72.

39. Smertenko, "Hitlerism," p. 663.

40. Stanley High, "Star Spangled Fascists," *The Saturday Evening Post*, 211 (May 27, 1939), 7.

41. Ibid., pp. 5, 6, 70: Strong, *Organized Anti-Semitism*, pp. 16, 146; Alvin Johnson, "The Rising Tide of Anti-Semitism," *Survey Graphic*, 28 (February, 1939), 115; Norton Belth, "Problems of Anti-Semitism in the United States," *Contemporary Jewish Record*, 2 (May–June, 1939), 6ff.

42. Quoted in David J. Jacobson, *The Affairs of Dame Rumor* (New York: Rinehart & Co., 1948), pp. 316–317.

43. Ribuffo, *Old Christian*, pp. 17, 73, 104, 117; David H. Bennett, *Demagogues in the Depression* (New Brunswick: Rutgers University Press, 1969), p. 279; Stack, *International Conflict*, p. 53; William C, Kernan, "Coughlin, the Jews, and Communism," *The Nation*, 147 (December 17, 1938), 655.

44. Quoted in Walter Goodman, *The Committee* (New York: Farrar, Straus and Giroux, 1968), p. 94; see also David S. Wyman, *Paper Walls: America and the Refugee Crisis, 1938–1941* (University of Massachusetts Press, 1968), pp. 15–17.

45. Wolfskill and Hudson, *All But the People*, pp. 66, 72; Glass, "Fundamentalism's Prophetic Vision," p. 69; Marsden, *Fundamentalism and American Culture*, p. 207.

46. Robert W. Ross, *So It Was True: The American Protestant Press and the Nazi Persecution of the Jews* (Minneapolis: University of Minnesota Press, 1980), pp. 40, 45, 57, and passim; Chuck Badger, "The Response of Christian Fundamentalists to the Holocaust, 1933–1945" (unpublished seminar paper, Department of History, University of Arizona, December, 1987), p. 12ff., copy in possession of the author; Glass, "Fundamentalism's Prophetic Vision," pp. 67, 69; Gerhard Falk, "The Reaction of the German-American Press to Nazi Persecutions, 1933–1941," *Journal of Reform Judaism*, 32 (Spring, 1985), 22. See also Deborah E. Lipstadt, *Beyond Belief: The American Press and the Coming of the Holocaust, 1933–1935* (New York: The Free Press, 1986).

47. Edward C. McCarthy, "The Christian Front Movement in New York City, 1938–1940" (unpublished M. A. thesis, Department of History, Columbia University, 1965), pp. 171, 177; Feingold, *A Time for Searching*, p. 198ff.; William C. Kernan, "Coughlin, the Jews, and Communism," *The Nation*, 147 (December 17, 1938), 655; Stack, *International Conflict*, p. 101; Ronald H. Bayor, *Neighbors in Conflict: The Irish, Germans, Jews, and Italians of New York City, 1929–1941* (2nd edition; University of Illinois Press, 1988), pp. 90, 148–149.

48. *A Time for Searching*, pp. 193 and 221.

49. John P. Diggins, *Mussolini and Fascism: The View from America* (Princeton: Princeton University Press, 1972), pp. 336–337.

50. Budd Schulberg, *Moving Pictures: Memories of a Hollywood Prince* (New York: Stein and Day, 1981), p. 5; Kirk Douglas, *The Ragman's Son* (London: Pan Books, 1988), p. 21; Ann Birstein, *The Rabbi on Forty-Seventh Street: The Story of Her Father* (New York: Dial Press, 1982), p. 88; Diggins, *Mussolini and Fascism*, pp. 185, 192; William Foote Whyte, "Race Conflicts in the North End of Boston," *New England Quarterly*, 12 (December, 1939), 642; Bayor, *Neighbors in Conflict*, p. 94ff; Ron Avery, "From A to 'Zink': Philadelphia Jews in Sports," in Murray Friedman, ed., *Philadelphia Jewish Life, 1940–1985* (Ardmore, Penn.: Seth Press, 1986), p. 295; Charles I. Cooper, "The Jews of Minneapolis and their Christian Neighbors," JSS, 8 (1946), 36; *New Republic*, 95 (May 25, 1938), 66–67; Carolyn F. Ware, *Greenwich Village, 1920–1930* (Boston: Houghton Mifflin Co., 1935), pp. 139, 140.

51. McCarthy, "The Christian Front," pp. 161, 170; Arthur Liebman, "The Ties That Bind: The Jewish Support for the Left in the United States," AJHQ, 66 (December, 1976), 305; Vorspan and Gartner, *History of the Jews of Los Angeles*, p. 202; Neal Gabler, *An Empire of*

their Own: How The Jews Invented Hollywood (New York: Crown Publishers, Inc., 1988), pp. 330–331.

52. McCarthy, "The Christian Front," p. 161.

53. Quoted in J. David Valaik, "In the Days Before Ecumenism," *Journal of Church and State,* 13 (Autumn, 1971), 469.

54. George N. Shuster, "The Conflict Among Catholics," *American Scholar,* 10 (Winter, 1940–1941), 11.

55. Valaik, "In The Days Before," p. 468.

56. Quoted in Oswald Garrison Villard, "Issues and Men," *The Nation,* 148 (April 22, 1939), 470.

57. Catholic Telegraph-Register clippings, June 4, 1936, September 17, 1936, March 25, 1937, June 5, 1937, June 26, 1937 in folder 12, *"Catholic Telegraph-Register,* 1936–1966," box 42 JCRC mss., collection #202, AJA.

58. Abigail McCarthy, "An Ugly Resurgence," *Commonweal,* 109 (December 17, 1982), 679; see also John T. Pawlikowski, *Catechetics and Prejudice: How Catholic Teaching Materials View Jews, Protestants, and Racial Minorities* (New York: Paulist Press, 1973), pp. 8, 13; James O'Gara, "Christian Anti-Semitism," *Commonweal,* 80 (May 22, 1964), 252; James O'Gara, "Catholics and Jews," *Commonweal,* 80 (May 29, 1964), 286.

59. Sheldon Marcus, *Father Coughlin: The Tumultuous Life of the Priest of the Little Flower* (Boston: Little, Brown & Co., 1973), p. 11.

60. Handy, *Christian America,* p. 78; Stack, *International Conflict,* p. 53; George N. Shuster, "The Conflict Among Catholics," *Contemporary Jewish Record,* 4 (February, 1941), 48; John Cooney, *The American Pope: The Life and Times of Francis Cardinal Spellman* (New York: Dell Books, 1986), pp. 100–101.

61. Shuster, "Conflict," *Contemporary Jewish Record,* p. 48; Ronald Modras, "Father Coughlin and Anti-Semitism: Fifty Years Later," *Journal of Church and State,* 31 (Spring, 1989), 234; Alan Brinkley, *Voices of Protest: Huey Long, Father Coughlin and the Great Depression* (New York: Alfred A. Knopf, 1982), pp. 266, 269ff.

62. George Seldes, "Father Coughlin: Anti-Semite," *The New Republic,* 96 (November 2, 1938), 353.

63. Hyman Berman, "Political Antisemitism in Minnesota During the Great Depression," JSS, 38 (Summer/Fall, 1976), 261, 263.

64. Quoted in Wyman, *Paper Walls,* p. 73.

65. Charles J. Tull, *Father Coughlin and the New Deal* (Syracuse, N.Y.: Syracuse University Press, 1965), p. 197; "Persecution—Jewish and Christian," in Charles E. Coughlin, "Am I an Anti-Semite?" *Anti-Semitism In America, 1878–1939* (New York: Arno Press, 1977), 36–37. This essay is the text of the radio address that he made on November 20, 1938.

66. Kernan, "Coughlin, the Jews, and Communism," p. 658; Coughlin, "Am I an Anti-Semite?" pp. 37–38, 41, 42.

67. Coughlin, "Am I an Anti-Semite?" pp. 44, 46.

68. "Slap," *Life,* 32 (November 28, 1938), 65; Modras, "Father Coughlin," p. 246.

69. Ibid.

70. T, November 21, 1938, p. 7; Kernan, "Coughlin, the Jews, and Communism," p. 655ff.; Alan Brinkley, *Voices of Protest: Huey Long, Father Coughlin and the Great Depression* (New York: Vintage, 1983), p. 266.

71. Francis L. Broderick, *Right Reverend New Dealer: John A. Ryan* (New York: The Macmillan Co., 1963), p. 253; John A. Ryan, "Anti-Semitism in the Air," *Commonweal,* 29 (December 30, 1938), 260, 261.

72. "Week by Week," *Commonweal*, 29 (December 9, 1938), 169.

73. Hans Ascar, "Catholics and Anti-Semitism," *Catholic World*, 150 (November, 1939), 175–176.

74. Arnold Benson, "The Catholic Church and the Jews," *The American Jewish Chronicle*, 1 (February 15, 1940), 7.

75. Quoted in Ralph L. Kolodny, "Catholics and Father Coughlin: Misremembering the Past," *Patterns of Prejudice*, 19 (October, 1985), 19.

76. Wyman, *Paper Walls*, p. 17; Bayor, *Neighbors in Conflict*, p. 88; High, "Star-Spangled Fascists," p. 72; Kolodny, "Catholics and Father Coughlin," p. 18; Morris L. Ernst to FDR, May 14, 1942, in subject file, "Ernst, Morris L., 1940–1942," PSF, box 132, FDR Library.

77. Shuster, "The Conflict Among Catholics," *American Scholar*, p. 12.

78. Quoted in "Anti-Semitism Is Here," p. 167.

79. Quoted in Herbert Samuel Rutman, "Defense and Development: A History of Minneapolis Jewry, 1930–1950" (unpublished Ph.D., University of Minnesota, 1970), p. 120.

80. Both quotes in Alfred Winslow Jones, *Life, Liberty, and Property* (Philadelphia: J. B. Lippincott Co., 1941), pp. 216, 274.

81. Burton Alan Boxerman, "Reaction of the St. Louis Jewish Community to Anti-Semitism, 1933–1945" (unpublished Ph.D., St. Louis University, 1967), p. 64; Burton Alan Boxerman, "Rise of Anti-Semitism in St. Louis, 1933–1945," *YIVO Annual of Jewish Social Science*, 14 (1969), 252.

82. Wyman, *Paper Walls*, pp. 71–72.

83. David S. Wyman, *The Abandonment of the Jews* (New York: Pantheon Books, 1984), p. 8; Charles H. Stember, *Jews in the Mind of America* (New York: Basic Books, 1966), p. 138.

84. These are quotes randomly selected from hundreds of letters in four folders marked, "Jewish Refugees and Immigration Laws, November, 1938," "Jewish Refugees and Immigration Laws, 1938," box 766, folder, "Jewish Refugees and Immigration Laws, Dec, 1938," box 767, and folder, "Nomination of Felix Frankfurter, 1939, Jan. I," box 774, William E. Borah mss., LC.

85. Mrs. Wm. Schweigert (city illegible) to W. E. Borah, December 28, 1938, folder "Jewish Refugees and Immigration Laws, Nov., 1938," box 766, Borah mss.

86. John Roy Carlson, *Under Cover* (New York: E. P. Dutton & Co., 1943), p. 54; Martin E. Marty, *Pilgrims in Their Own Land: 500 Years of Religion in America* (Boston: Little, Brown & Co., 1984), p. 399.

87. Marcus, *Father Coughlin*, p. 156; Stack, *International Conflict*, pp. 129, 142; McCarthy, "The Christian Front," pp. 158, 177, 182, 192; Alson J. Smith, "The Christian Terror," CC, 56 (August 23, 1939), 1017; Gordon W. Allport and Bernard M. Kramer, "Some Roots of Prejudice," *The Journal of Psychology*, 22 (1946), 28; Carlson, *Under Cover*, p. 56; Theodore Irwin, "Inside the 'Christian Front,'" *The Forum*, 103 (March, 1940), 103–104; "Letters to the Editors," *The Nation*, 149 (August 12, 1939), 180; Stanley Feldstein, *The Land That I Show You* (Garden City, NY: Anchor Press/Doubleday, 1978), p. 346; Wallace Stegner, "Who Persecutes Boston?" *The Atlantic Monthly*, 174 (July, 1944), 48; Holbo, "Wheat or What?" p. 735; Tull, *Father Coughlin*, pp. 207–208, 244; Wyman, *Paper Walls*, p. 18. For a succinct discussion of the Christian Front in New York City, see Bayor, *Neighbors in Conflict*, p. 97ff.

88. McCarthy, "Christian Front," p. 76.

89. McCarthy, "Christian Front," p. 90; Irwin, "Inside the 'Christian Front,'" pp. 106, 107; James Wechsler, "The Coughlin Terror," *The Nation*, 149 (September 22, 1939), 96; Smith, "The Christian Terror," p. 1017.

90. Smith, "The Christian Terror," pp. 1017, 1018; McCarthy, "Christian Front," p. 43; Selden Menefee, *Assignment: U.S.A.* (New York: Reynal and Hitchcock, Inc., 1943), p. 11;

Irwin, "Inside the 'Christian Front,'" pp. 102, 107; Feldstein, *The Land That I Show You,* p. 346; Marcus, *Father Coughlin,* p. 156.

91. Jay Dolan, *The American Catholic Experience: A History from Colonial Times to the Present* (Garden City, NY: Doubleday & Co., Inc., 1985), p. 404; "Letters to the Editors," p. 180; Stack, *International Conflict,* p. 128; David H. Bennett, *Demagogues in the Depression* (New Brunswick: Rutgers University Press, 1969), p. 280; Smith, "Christian Terror," p. 1017; Wechsler, "The Coughlin Terror," p. 96; Stegner, "Who Persecutes Boston?" p. 50; McCarthy, "Christian Front," p. 36; Irwin, "Inside the 'Christian Front,'" pp. 103, 108; Tull, *Father Coughlin,* pp. 207–208; Marcus, *Father Coughlin,* p. 156; Naomi W. Cohen, *Not Free To Desist: The American Jewish Committee, 1906–1966* (Philadelphia: JPS, 1972), p. 217; Thomas Kessner, *Fiorello H. LaGuardia and the Making of Modern New York* (New York: McGraw-Hill Publishing Co., 1989), p. 523.

92. Stack, *International Conflict,* pp. 58, 98; George Britt, "Poison in the Melting Pot," *The Nation,* 148 (April 1, 1939), 374; Cooney, *American Pope,* p. 101; Jonathan Daneils, *White House Witness, 1942–1945* (Garden City, NY: Doubleday & Co., Inc., 1975), p. 80; McCarthy, "Christian Front," pp. 13, 45, 78, 90, 95, 96, 116, 119–120.

93. Quoted in Kessner, *Fiorello,* p. 523.

94. McCarthy, "Christian Front," p. 100.

95. High, "Star-Spangled Fascists," pp. 7, 72–73; Britt, "Poison in the Melting Pot," p. 374; "The Nazis Are Here," *The Nation,* 148 (March 4, 1939), 253.

96. Britt, "Poison in the Melting Pot," 376.

97. Wechsler, "The Coughlin Terror," p. 96; "Century Marks," CC, 106 (May 3, 1989), 462.

98. Henry Pratt Fairchild, "New Burdens for America," *The Forum,* 101 (June, 1939), 317; "The American Pattern for Anti-Semitism," *Interracial Review,* July, 1939, p. 99; "The Shadow of Anti-Semitism," *The American Magazine,* 128 (November, 1939), 91, 92.

99. Quoted in David Brody, "American Jewry, The Refugees and Immigration Restriction (1932–1942)," in Abraham J. Karp, ed., *The Jewish Experience In America: Selected Studies From The Publication of the American Jewish Historical Society* (5 volumes: New York: KTAV Publishing House, Inc., 1969), V, 336.

100. Kurt Lewin, "Bringing Up the Child," *Menorah Journal,* 28 (Winter, 1940), 29–30, 43–44.

101. "Current Proceedings of Anti-Semitism," pp. 14–15, in folder 4a, box 50, JCRC mss.; "Harvest of Violence," *The Economist,* 189 (October 25, 1958), 324; Arnold M. Eisen, *The Chosen People in America: A Study in Jewish Religious Ideology* (Bloomington: Indiana University Press, 1983), 70; Helga Eugenie Kaplan, "Century of Adjustment: A History of the Akron Jewish Community" (unpublished Ph.D., Department of History, Kent State University, 1978), pp. 437, 441–442; Cohen, *Not Free To Desist,* p. 203; Judith E. Endelman, *The Jewish Community of Indianapolis: 1849–to the Present* (Bloomington: Indiana University Press, 1984), pp. 122, 177; Philip Rosen, Robert Tabak, David Gross, "Philadelphia Jewry, the Holocaust, and the Birth of the Jewish State," in Friedman, ed., *Philadelphia Jewish Life,* p. 31; Brody, "American Jewry," p. 344; see also Solomon Lowenstein, "The American Principle of Tolerance," *Proceedings of the National Conference of Social Work,* 66th Annual Conference, Buffalo, New York, June 18–24, 1939 (New York: Published for the National Conference of Social Work by Columbia University Press, 1939), p. 36.

102. "Anti-Semitism Is Here," p. 168.

103. Lewis Browne, "What Can the Jews Do?" *Virginia Quarterly Review,* 15 (Spring, 1939), 225; Albert Levitan, "Leave the Jewish Problem Alone!" CC, 51 (April 25, 1934), 555.

104. Anonymous, "I Was a Jew," *The Forum,* 103 (March, 1940), 10.

105. Ibid., p. 8; see also "I Married a Jew," *The Atlantic Monthly,* 163 (January, 1939), 38–46; "I Married a Gentile," *The Atlantic Monthly,* 163 (March, 1939), 321–326.

106. Gay Talese, *The Kingdom and the Power* (New York: World Publishing Co., 1969), p. 59;

Edward S. Shapiro, *A Time for Healing: American Jewry Since World War II* (Baltimore: The Johns Hopkins University Press, 1992), p. 109; Richard Kluger, *The Paper: The Life and Death of the New York Herald Tribune* (New York: Alfred A. Knopf, 1986), p. 386; David Halberstam, *Summer of '49* (New York: William Morrow and Co., Inc., 1989), p. 151.

107. Morris Freedman, "The Jewish College Student: 1951 Model," *Commentary*, 12 (October, 1951), 311–312; Nitza Rosovsky, *The Jewish Experience at Harvard and Radcliffe* (Cambridge: Harvard University Press, 1986), p. 31; Jean Baer, *The Self-Chosen: "Our Crowd" Is Dead; Long Live Our Crowd* (New York: Arbor House, 1982), p. 254; Natalie Gittelson, "AS: It's Still Around," *Harper's Bazaar,* 105 (February, 1972), 134; Leonard Room, Helen P. Beem, Virginia Harris, "Characteristics of 1,107 Petitioners for Change of Name," *American Sociological Review,* 20 (February, 1955), 34–35; Neil C. Sandberg, *Jewish Life in Los Angeles* (New York: University Press of America, 1986), p. 37; see also Hershel Shanks, "Irving Shapiro: 'You'll Never Build a Career with a Name like Shapiro,'" *Moment,* 13 (September, 1988), 33ff.

108. James Greenberg, "Our Crowd," *American Film,* 13 (July–August, 1988), 42.

109. Abraham G. Duker, "Emerging Cultural Patterns In American Jewish Life," PAJHS, 39 (June, 1950), 386; Vamberto Morais, *A Short History of Anti-Semitism* (New York: W. W. Norton & Co., 1976), pp. 64 and 262n.

110. "Anti-Semitism Is Here," p. 167; Joseph P. Lash, *Dealers and Dreamers* (New York: Doubleday, 1988), p. 386; Michael E. Parrish, *Felix Frankfurter and His Times: The Reform Years* (New York: The Free Press, 1982), p. 276; Ferdinand M. Isserman, "FDR & Felix Frankfurter," *The National Jewish Monthly,* 80 (November, 1965), 16; *Diaries of Harold Ickes,* pp. 2967–2968, LC; Max Freedman, ed., *Roosevelt and Frankfurter: Their Correspondence— 1928–1945* (Boston: Little Brown, 1967), pp. 481–482.

111. Quoted in Scholnick, "The New Deal," p. 160.

112. Karfunkel and Ryley, *The Jewish Seat,* pp. 93, 96.

113. Letters in folder, "Nomination of Felix Frankfurter, 1939, Jan. I," box 774, Borah mss.

114. High, "Star-Spangled Fascists," p. 70; Shuster, "The Conflict Among Catholics," *American Scholar,* p. 6.

115. "Jews in America," *Fortune,* February, 1936, in Leonard Dinnerstein and Frederic Cople Jaher, eds., *The Aliens: A History of Ethnic Minorities in America* (New York: Appleton-Century-Crofts, 1970), p. 230.

116. Milton Steinberg, "First Principles for American Jews," *Contemporary Jewish Journal,* 4 (December, 1941), 587, 588.

117. "Confidential Report on Investigation of Anti-Semitism in the United States in the Spring of 1938," pp. 12, 38; Blaustein, *Public Opinion, 1935–1946,* under the direction of Hadley Cantril (Princeton: Princeton University Press, 1951), p. 385; Wyman, *Paper Walls,* p. 22.

CHAPTER
22

Catholicism, Gender, and Modern Miracles

Belief in miracles, meaning events that defy the "laws of nature" and appear to have supernatural origin, is one of the oldest traditions in many, if not all, religions, and in the Judeo-Christian tradition specifically; Moses parted the Red Sea to allow the Israelites escape from Egypt, and Christ raised Lazarus from the dead, then rose from the dead himself.

Robert Orsi's article demonstrates how the veneration of a little known saint, Jude Thaddeus, emerged in twentieth-century Chicago to become perhaps the single most widespread devotion to a saint in modern American Catholicism. The story is remarkable for several reasons. Many devotions to saints have clearly ethnic patterns in both Europe and America, while the devotion to St. Jude is distinguished by its nonethnic appeal to women. The stories told by the patrons of St. Jude openly express strong belief in divine intervention despite (or because of?) the apparent secularism of the culture around them. Finally, the transmission of the devotion from one patron to another through letters and classified newspaper advertisements demonstrates how the individuality of the religious experience survives and prospers in an urban industrial society.

Additional Reading: Morton T. Kelsey, *Healing and Christianity in Ancient Thought and Modern Times* (New York, 1971) and Ronald L. Numbers and Darrel W. Amundsen, *Caring and Curing: Health and Medicine in the Western Religious Traditions* (New York, 1986) outline the general history of religion and medicine. Robert E. Curran, "'The Finger of God is Here': The Advent of the Miraculous in the Nineteenth-Century American Catholic Community," *Catholic Historical Review*, 73 (1987): 41–61, describes the earliest episodes of reported miracles among American Catholics, and Ann Taves, *The Household of Faith* (Notre Dame, 1986) describes the rising importance of devotions to saints in nineteenth-century America. The rising importance of miracles among evangelical Protestants is described in David E. Harrell, Jr., *All Things are Possible: The Healing and Charismatic Revivals in Modern America* (Bloomington, 1975).

Robert A. Orsi

"He Keeps Me Going": Women's Devotion to Saint Jude Thaddeus and the Dialectics of Gender in American Catholicism, 1929–1965

Devotion to Saint Jude Thaddeus, patron saint of hopeless cases, began in an incident at Our Lady of Guadalupe Church, a Mexican national parish in South Chicago, in the spring of 1929. Our Lady of Guadalupe was a new church, built in 1928 by Claretian missionaries, a Spanish order of men who had assumed as one of their concerns the care of Spanish-speaking migrants in North American cities. The church was located in an ethnically mixed neighborhood, and representatives of the community's many different Catholic cultures had participated in its dedication ceremonies. South Chicago was dominated in these years by slaughter-houses and steel mills, and crisscrossed by train tracks. In prosperous times, a gritty cloud of cinders and dust darkened the streets even in the middle of the afternoon. These were not prosperous times, however, so the air was clearer, but the neighborhood was shadowed by economic crisis. Shrine historians emphasize the grim mood in South Chicago in the early months of 1929.[1]

Visitors to the church in these hard times could bring their prayers and petitions to two saints whose statues stood on a small side altar to the right of the central image of *Nuestra Señora de Guadalupe*. Saint Thérèse of Liseux, the Little Flower, occupied the place of prominence above this side altar, and off to one side on a detached pedestal stood a large statue of Saint Jude Thaddeus, who was at this time virtually unknown in American Catholicism.[2]

Most of the people kneeling before the two statues were women, although the story of the Shrine's origins does not make this explicit. Popular piety in American Catholic culture has largely been the pratice and experience of women, just as it has always been publicly dominated by male religious authorities.[3] As the devotion to Saint Jude eventually took shape in Chicago, it too became women's practice. Jude is identified by his devout with particular women in their lives. The minority of men who participate in the cult point back to their mothers, wives, or sisters when they talk about the first times they prayed to the saint. As one man told me, "I lived on Ashland Avenue [in Chicago]. My mother lived on Ashland Avenue for forty-five years. She called on Saint Jude whenever she had a problem, and I have followed in her footsteps."[4] Women have characteristically assumed special responsibilities in the pratice of the cult; they were thought to be in a particularly close relationship with Jude not accessible to men, and as a result their prayers were believed to be more powerful and efficacious.

The clergy at various American Catholic shrines, well aware of this feature of the devotions over which they presided, have often seemed embarrassed by it; and they have sometimes worried that they were exploiting women to raise funds for clerical projects.[5] During the 1930s, the founder of Chicago's enormously popular Sorrowful Mother novena tried to goad men into attending services in greater numbers by offering then a reward of cigarettes, and the director of Jude's shrine warned in 1958 that prayer is "not only the practice of pious women and innocent children but a deadly earnest necessity for all equally."[6] But it is mainly women who appear in a pictorial essay on the shrine prepared in 1954.[7] However unacknowledged this participation is officially, the legend of the founding of Jude's shrine takes on new meaning, and raises new questions, when it is glossed with the fact of women's central role in the cult.

Thérèse was a celebrated figure, beloved for her "little way" of sancitity, the path of submission, humility, and silence. Contemporary authors have discovered another Thérèse, fiercely independent and spiritually innovative, but this was not the figure of the Catholic popular imagination in 1929. "Thérèse of Lisieux," writes Monica Furlong, "sweet, childlike, obedient, tragic, has been until recent times a cherished icon of Catholic womanhood," cast in "one of the favorite moulds of traditional female sanctity, the mould of virginity, of suffering, of drastic self-abnegation."[8] It is more difficult to determine how people understood Saint Jude, but I have asked his contemporary devout, many of whom have participated in his cult since its early years, and they most often emphasize his manly qualities. I was told that Jude "is tall, handsome, with a cleft in his chin"; "looks like Saint Joseph"; "[looks like] a very loving big brother or father"; "is quiet, soft-spoken, sure of himself"; "is very handsome—he looks like Jesus." One woman described him as "a great man, who is close to God and has a pull with him." Another said the saint is "a powerful healer. He looks like Christ. He looks like a man who wants you to test him on whatever the petitions may be." A sixty-eight-year-old woman whose devotion to Jude began twenty-five years ago gave me a longer description:

> I picture St Jude as a man to be of 5 feet and between 9 to 11 inches in height with a good and average build. He gives the appearance of a very kindly, loving, and caring person with a Big Heart. He looks like a very humble and courageous man, with a very Fatherly disposition, and compassion for all mankind particularly those who are desperate for help. His very close resemblance to his Cousin Jesus is simply outstanding and beautiful.[9]

The statue of Jude in Chicago, consistent with an older iconographical tradition, shows the saint holding in his arms a small image of Jesus' face, so that when the devout look at Jude they are looking into the faces of two men, a transposition of the familiar depiction of the Madonna and Child. The belief that Jude was an Apostle further identifies him with the church and its male authorities. One of my sources made this identification explicit: "Sometimes when I pray to him for something I need desperately it seems like he is standing right next to me in Mass vestments."[10]

Legends about the origins of devotions to particular saints, in Western and Eastern cultures, point to the supernatural influences determining the site of the devotion, and this is true of the account preserved at the shrine in Chicago as well. During Holy Week of 1929, the story goes, visitors to the church began gathering at the base of Jude's statue in ever greater numbers. So insistent was their devotion to the unknown Apostle that the clergy finally decided, on Holy Saturday, to reverse the two statues, giving Jude the place of prominence over the side altar, where he remains today. The cult of Saint Jude begins in this reversal. According to shrine chroniclers, this spontaneous expression of devotion to Jude was a sign that the saint himself had willed Chicago, an industrial city of immigrants in the middle of the United States, as the location of the modern revival of his cult.

The clergy had less supernatural reasons for preferring Jude to the Little Flower. Jude's cult was founded by Father James Tort, an ambitious and savvy young priest from Barcelona who is described in an early profile as a "little high-pressure" man.[11] The Claretians needed some means of supporting their various enterprises in the United States, and Tort must have realized that only limited help would come from Chicago's formidable Cardinal, George Mundelein, who believed that priests should finance and support their own endeavors.[12] Although there is no evidence of this, Tort surely knew that popular devotions were a well-tried and promising source of funds, but at the same time he also must have been aware that there was already a local cult of the Little Flower at a nearby Carmelite parish in Chicago, as well as a thriving national devotion based in Oklahoma City.[13] Jude, on the other hand, had the singular advantage of truly being the "unknown saint," as he is identified in the early years at the shrine.

Devotion to Saint Jude took shape then somewhere between the desires of the devout and the ambitions of the clergy. For our purposes it is not important whether or not this legend it true: this is how the shrine imagines its founding. The story of the switched statues, however, does raise the two interconnected sets of questions with which this essay is concerned, one having to do with the language and structures of gender in religious traditions and the other with the nature and practice of popular religion. But before I outline these issues, we need to look at how women think about this saint's place in their lives.

"AN ONGOING RELATIONSHIP"

The most obvious characteristic of devotion to Saint Jude is the impulse of the devout toward narrative. Because Jude is the "hidden saint," as the shrine presents him, obscured in history by the unfortunate popular misidentification of him with Judas, the devout promise that they will make his actions in their lives public so that others will learn of him. This is the reason for all the discursive practices associated with the cult, from the long letters women write to the shrine to the simple thank-you notices that appear in the classified sections of local newspapers around the country. Women entered the world of the cult knowing that their connection with Jude would sooner or later give them the chance to describe in some public forum the most awful experience of their lives.

This transformation of experience into narrative took (and still takes) many forms. Women told their stories to other women, to strangers in hospitals, to family members, to needy colleagues at work. Jude's older devout, the women whose devotion dates to the early years of the cult's history, structure their autobiographies with reference to the saint's place in their lives; Jude has been their constant and trusted companion, they believe, every day, and at every major crisis or turning point in their experience. They reconstruct their lives with reference to Jude, imagining themselves in relation to this Other. Hagiography here takes on a new connotation: these women do not write and talk *about* the saint but about themselves and the saint together.

The following narrative was prepared in response to a request I made through the shrine's mailing list for stories of women's devotion to Jude. The woman writing is sixty-two years old, married, and the mother of two adult children who live close to her in a small New England town.

"I am writing," she begins, "because Saint Jude has been sharing all of my burdens, giving me peace of mind and generally being with me for more than 30 years." She first encountered the devotion in 1954, when "a crippled man" appeared at her door selling religious articles. "At that time I was 29 years old, newly married, pregnant, and living in my husband's family's house with my mother-in-law," a situation that was causing her some unhappiness. Jude's devout typically can remember the circumstances of their initial meeting with the saint, and they privilege this moment in their autobiographies: after encountering Jude, things change; something new happens. As another woman wrote to the shrine about her first meeting with Jude in 1941, "I never heard of this wonderful Saint, and it makes me feel like a different person since I know about him."[14]

Saint Jude intervened in the tense situation developing between the young woman and her mother-in-law. The couple was able to find their own home, and shortly afterwards their child, a boy, was born. "From that time on, I very seldom made a decision or took any action in my life without asking Saint Jude for his guidance."

"How has he helped my family?" she asks. She has been married for thirty-four years, and even though "our life together was not perfect, all problems were minor and handled quickly by prayer to Saint Jude." Jude helped her raise her son and daughter, "particularly when [they] were teenagers and out on their own . . . I would ask Saint Jude to care for them while I could not, and he always did!" Although her husband is "not as verbal or demonstrative in his devotion to Saint Jude as I am," he has seen what the saint has done for them and "I feel he also trusts Saint Jude for our future and is thankful for our past."

Jude helped her advance over the years from her first job as a "typist" to the position of managing executive of a town, the post from which she has recently retired. "I could not have accomplished this had Saint Jude not been with me all the way, putting the correct words and actions into my head when I required assistance." She has always told her friends and co-workers about Jude, and she kept shrine prayer cards in her desk to give to people who needed them. She has a statue of Jude on her bedroom dresser, and "in times of great stress I light a vigil light in front of this statue. . . . I feel my prayers are always answered, altho' my requests are not always granted." She closes her story, "I feel I have been very privileged to have Saint Jude with me always to help carry my burdens and share my joys."

The sense here at the end is of a partnership between Jude and this woman: Jude has helped her bear her own burdens, he has not miraculously taken them away. As another woman wrote me, "I am sure I pester Saint Jude too much, but he keeps me going and he never fails, although I try to help myself first."[15]

There was a postscript to the letter of the New England mother, appended three months later. "Before I completed this correspondence last June, my husband was diagnosed as having bladder cancer! I will not go into detail, but with the constant help of Saint Jude we have had the best summer I can remember." Although the future is uncertain, she says at the end, "I have complete confidence that Saint Jude will care for us both."[16]

Since the founding of the devotion in Chicago in 1929, many thousands of American Catholic women have lived in what another correspondent called "an ongoing relationship" with the saint.[17] They have carried his picture in their purses, set his statue up in their homes in places where, as they say, they can look into his "soft, sympathetic," "penetrating," "compassionate" eyes when they need to and have talked to him as they go about their days.[18]

These older women encountered Jude during the "heyday of devotionalism" in American Catholic culture, in Jay Dolan's phrase, from the 1920s to the 1960s, an extraordinarily creative period in the history of American Catholic popular piety when women and clergy, sometimes together, frequently at odds with each other, experimented with devotional forms and sturctures in response to the community's changing needs and perceptions.[19] Jude's cult grew rapidly in these years, moving along dispersed tracks of narrative exchange in neighborhoods and across the country. The devotion existed primarily in women's conversations with each other. As one woman explained to me:

> I share my devotion to Saint Jude with all [the] members in my family and try to promote devotion to [among?] my friends and have succeeded. I have a friend who was terrified because the doctor discovered a lump on her breast and she came to me because I just had my right breast removed and I gave her the [Saint Jude] prayerbook and told her she must have faith in Saint Jude and she will come thru.[20]

Jude here is the medium for the exchange of confidences, shared fear and discomfort, and the occasion for the expression of support; and through conversations like this the devotion to Saint Jude became one of American Catholicism's most important and visible popular cults.

HOPELESS CASES

The women who entered the world of Jude's devotion, seeking his face on medals and prayer cards, addressing his statue on their night tables, were impelled by fear and need. Jude was called upon only when all other help, divine and human, had failed. But what constitutes "hopelessness"? What kind of social or cultural experience is a crisis defined as "desperate"?

The hagiographical autobiography cited above offers some indication of what women meant by a hopeless situation: Jude helped in times of personal transition (from single to married, at the threat of impending widowhood), cultural change (during adolescence in the difficult 1960s), sickness, uncertainty, and when a beloved significant other turned away either in sickness, death, incapacity, powerlessness, or rejection. These were not "private" (as opposed to "public") occasions: Jude was called upon at just those moments when the effects and implications of changing historical circumstances (economic distress, the evolution of new medical models and authorities, and war, to cite just three of the recurring situations described by the devout) were directly and unavoidably experienced within the self and family.

"Crisis"—these situations of hopelessness—always has specific historical coordinates. There has been a tendency in discussions of the cult of saints to construe the entreaties of the devout as perennial: people have always gotten sick, this argument goes, and sick people always desire to be better, and this is why they pray to saints. But "crisis" itself is a cultural construction: people construe their unhappiness, experience their pains, talk about their sicknesses, and search for the appropriate intellectual, moral, and emotional responses to their dilemmas in socially and culturally bound ways. Because Jude stands at the intersection of the "private" and "public," praying to him became the way women encountered, endured, imagined, thought about, and learned the appropriate responses to "crisis." The cult offered women a critical catechesis in ways of living.

Women came to Jude as sisters, daughters, mothers, aunts—in other words, as figures in socially constructed and maintained kinship roles. The women who first turned to the saint in the late 1920s and 1930s belonged to an important transitional generation in American Catholic history. Historians have noted the beginnings of the dissolution in these years of the immigrant enclaves, the intricately constructed honeycombs of mutual responsibility and support in urban Catholic neighborhoods. Once the immigrant family had been the primary source of economic stability and social security, shaping an individual's fundamental choice of job, spouse, and residence; now the children of immigrant parents were confronted with new challenges and possibilities in a changing social and economic world.[21]

This new generation of American-born or raised Southern and Eastern Europeans had also begun to entertain new kinds of ambitions: the power and authority of immigrant parents, often not explicitly denied, had begun to wane as their children entered a work world in which their parents could be of limited support and assistance. The woman whose autobiography we have studied began her work life as a typist, a position which required skills lacking in the immigrant generation. The period was marked by conflict between the generations in these

Catholic ethnic communities as younger people sought greater autonomy in choosing companions, work, spouses, residence. In southern and eastern European immigrant communities, tension and anger over changing roles and expectations and distress over the loosening of traditional authority would be most sharply focused on young women.[22]

The letters written by women to the Chicago shrine over the years reflect these particular conflicts and special pressures. Jude was called upon when women were unable successfully to negotiate among contradictory cultural assignments and responsibilities: to help resolve conflict over the choice of a spouse, for example, or to assist young women in their efforts to live their married lives in a newer, more American idiom as their husbands' partners, to aid them in finding and keeping jobs, and in securing adequate childcare while they worked.[23]

The devotion began in the experience of the Depression, flourished during the Second World War, and continued to grow in the post-war years; this is the public chronology of the cult. But these historical periods were experienced by the devout in particular ways, and the letters of need and gratitude written by women to the shrine and published in the *Voice of Saint Jude* constitute a running gloss on the recent past, disclosing the inner history of these years. During the Depression women wrote about their grief at their husbands' unemployment and their own dismay at not being able adequately to meet the household responsibilities they believed were theirs.[24] Women took their husbands to the shrine and prayed there with them, reestablishing through Jude a bond that was otherwise threatened. "We are praying," one woman wrote, "that my husband will hold his job and make good."[25]

In the late 1940s and throughout the 1950s, women brought to Jude their fears of the pain of childbirth or their terrible unhappiness at not being able to have children. A woman confided to the readers of the letters page of the *Voice of Saint Jude* in April 1952:

> During my pregnancy I was quite ill; and I was in such great fear of the pain I would have to endure when the baby would arrive. Yet with Jude's help I had the strength to see my illness through, and at the actual birth I suffered so little that I could hardly believe it was all over and I was the mother of a beautiful child.[26]

Another woman wrote that she had become "obsessed with fear" before her daughter's birth, but that she "wore [Jude's] medal (even on the delivery table) and put my fear and anguish in his hands."[27] Many women named their children Jude or Judith in gratitude for the saint's help.[28]

During the 1950s, when married women began looking for work outside the home again in greater numbers, the devout turned to Jude for assistance in dealing with the new problems they were facing. This is how one woman understood this particular moment in her life:

> I applied for a secretarial position [after being away from this work for five years] and while on the way to this job I prayed to Saint Jude who granted me this job. To this day and forever I shall thank him. Also granted was the guid-

ance he gave me to get my boy started in kindergarten. For three weeks my boy cried when I took him and attempted to leave him in the room. The teachers and I had given up. One day as I was taking him home a stranger saw me crying and taking my boy home. She told me to pray to Saint Jude for help which I did and on the second day my boy went to class without a fear. I shall always be grateful and say a prayer for this stranger and Saint Jude.[29]

Single women turned to Jude for help in finding good husbands and then for assistance in dealing with the inevitable family tension that erupted over their choices. Younger women wrote that Jude helps "through all the frustrations and problems of being a teenager."[30] Mothers asked him to guide them in responding to the needs and values of their maturing children: "show me the right way to help my son" one woman prayed to the Saint during a family crisis.[31] Older women sought Jude's assistance in caring for dying parents, living with the loneliness of widowhood, and facing the problems of aging.

Women understood themselves to be accomplishing something when they turned to Saint Jude: in partnership with him, they changed things, found work, settled problems.[32] The least helpful way of reading this devotion would be to try to account for what happens after prayer in the way that last century's scientists "explained" the cures at Lourdes. More important is to consider how these women created and sustained a world in relation to Jude, how they imagined reality and its alternatives, and how they constructed this world in their devotions. The stories women told about themselves and Saint Jude were not static recapitulations of experience, explained by referring to the economic crisis of the Depression or the physical threats of the social pressure to have children after the war. The narrative process is central here: the letters do not represent the recasting of experience in another, "symbolic," key, but the reexperiencing of experience in a new way.

We have seen that the women believed themselves to be "different persons" after encountering Jude. Without Jude's help, one woman wrote me, "I don't think I would be as a good a person."[33] The world and the self are remade in relation to Jude, but what is the world and who is the self so constituted?

NEW AND BETTER PERSONS: QUESTIONS OF GENDER IN THE DEVOTION TO SAINT JUDE

Women who say that they became new persons in their encounters with Jude at the most desperate moment in their lives are alerting us to a central feature of devotionalism studied specifically as women's practice. Feminist historians for the last two decades have been struggling with fundamental issues of the study of women's history: Is this the history of domination? resistance? of women's culture or women's sphere, as an earlier division had it? Joan Scott has recently suggested that a new approach to women's history entails a new understanding of politics and subjectivity as well as a new analysis of gender. Drawing on poststructuralist understandings of subjectivity, Scott writes that "identities and experiences are variable phenomena . . . discursively organized in particular contexts or configurations." From this perspective gender is defined as culturally sanctioned and maintained "knowledge about gender differences."[34]

Religious traditons, with their considerable institutional and psychological authority, are highly privileged expressions of what is considered true and real (at least to certain segments of modern society), and devotionalism, which was the way most Catholics engaged their tradition in the mid-twentieth century, served as the site of particularly compelling discursive organizations of truth about gender. Religious sanctions were applied and divine approbation given to specific presentations of "maleness" and "femaleness" in the various media, official and popular, of American Catholicism. Women were positioned in a certain way in relation to the sacred, and this position was said to reflect and reveal women's fundamental identity.

What world of meaning, then, did women enter when they turned to Jude and imagined him looking at them with sympathy and understanding? The first task here will be to indicate some of the characteristic patterns of behavior, clusters of symbols, and affective responses (Geertz's "moods and motivations") that comprised American Catholic devotionalism in the middle years of this century. "Woman" was constructed in the tropes and metaphors of devotional culture in specific ways. When women prayed to the saint, practiced the cult, and discovered or created new selves in the process, they were learning by an intimate pedagogy the religiously consecrated cultural grammar of gender, and they were taking shape as selves within the gendered forms and structures with which reality is constituted by religious traditions.

Women entered the world of Jude's devotion at particularly difficult times, as we have seen: in their own perceptions, the world had become unhinged, everything was upside down, and they were feeling desperate, hopeless, and abandoned. Once we have identified some of the levels of meaning in the devotional construction of "woman," can we go on to say that at such desperate moments women were located in (and even located themselves in) a particular ordering of the world? To borrow a term from the structuralist study of ideology, are women "interpellated" here into the organization of gender characteristic of devotional culture?

The second part of the discussion that follows suggests another more dialectical possibility for understanding women and popular religion. Gender is not a static social category into which people are *fitted*. As Scott notes, constructions of gender emerge out of highly conflictual and open-ended cultural processes and so bear the marks of contradiction, dissent, resistance, repression. We will have to consider whether or not devotional culture is marked in this way as well, opening the way for creativity amid its fissures. But we need to begin with the world that women entered through Jude's eyes.

"WHY SHOULD A VOICE LIKE MINE BE HEARD?" WOMEN IN AMERICAN CATHOLIC DEVOTIONAL CULTURE

The devotion to Saint Jude does seem to have reproduced in another register the characteristic structures of male-female relations during the Depression. Susan

Ware observes that there was a clear division of men and women's roles in the United States in this period, with women assigned primary responsibility for the maintenance, economic and moral, of the home. "Women had complete responsibility for the domestic sphere and played a crucial role in holding families together against the disintegrating forces of the Depression."[35] Threatened by their increasing inability to fulfill this sustaining role in hard times, women turned to religion for "consolation," as Ware puts it, and church attendance rose. William Chafe suggests that this inward turning and search for religious consolation and security reinforced women's traditional roles.[36] A number of studies of American working people have shown that workers tend to hold themselves responsible for losing their jobs, even in periods of manifest economic crisis, and evidence from the Depression suggests that women blamed their men for their inadequate support. One man remembers his feelings in Bethlehem, Pennsylvania, in the 1930s: "I think Roosevelt's program saved the self-respect and the sanity of a lot of men.[37]

Seen against this background, Jude appears to be a further expression of the resentment and disorientation women experienced when their husbands lost their jobs, on the one hand, as well as another way of saving male sanity and self-respect, on the other. Nowhere in the published letters (or in my conversations with the devout about these times) is there any expression of anger against an economic system that could make families feel hungry and threatened. Instead, women prayed to Jude for his help in finding work for their husbands; and when at last, often after long, sustained periods of searching, the latter did find jobs, their wives explicitly attributed their success to Jude, not to the men's skill, diligence, or dedication, or to changes in the economy. "I started a Novena on Easter Sunday so my husband would find work," one woman informed the shrine. "I am so happy to say that he went to work the other day. I am sure that without Saint Jude's help he would have failed to secure employment."[38] This is the characteristic structure of Depression narrratives: they open with an incomprehensible event (unemployment), describe the woman's turning to Saint Jude, and end in an incomprehensible event (finding work), reinforcing—by finding religious meaning in—an alienated understanding of the social process. There is a pervasive sense of passivity throughout: men are fired, men are hired. "Some time ago," another woman wrote the shrine in 1935, "I asked you to remember my husband in your prayers for the novena [sic] that he might secure work. At the same time I prayed hard and placed Saint Jude's picture in my front window and asked him to call my husband to work. A few days later he was called to work."[39]

Women were turning here to a male to help men, so that the devotion reproduced and confirmed female dependence on, and silent, unobtrusive support of, men. The public life of Jude's cult was male dominated. The Claretian rationale for the devotion was to provide financial support for young boys attending the order's seminary in Momence, Illinois. Pictures of seminarians regularly appeared in the *Voice of Saint Jude,* along with photographs of clergy and the other major group of males publicly identified with the cult, the Chicago Police. Tort founded the Police Branch of the Saint Jude's League in 1932 both to secure Jude's protection for the police and to involve the latter in his various fundraising efforts.

Several times a year the Chicago Police marched in full dress uniform around the shrine, or, after 1948 when a special meeting hall was opened for the fraternal organization in the Claretian building in the Loop, around the Claretians' downtown church. One thousand policemen received communion together at the shrine in 1936, five thousand on October 27, 1946. Pictures of these events routinely appeared in the *Voice*.[40]

Women were participating then in a devotion to a male saint, officially understood to derive his power from his kinship relationship with Jesus, a devotion that was publicly represented, not by women (with the unintentional exception of the pictorial history cited earlier), but by priests, boys destined for the clergy, and armed adult men.[41] The devout supported this structure out of a strong sense of duty: once Jude had acted for them, they understood themselves to have acquired a lifelong debt. One man told me that his mother sent a donation to the shrine even during the most difficult days of the Depression in thanksgiving for something Jude had done for her and in support of the boys in the seminary.[42]

American-born or raised women, the daughters of the immigrants, were thus initiated into understandings of themselves as women, common in Irish and southern and eastern European Catholic cultures: bound by duty and need to a male religious figure who was thought to be particularly responsive to their prayers, women acted in the cult as the strong, quiet, invisible centers of emotional, moral, and practical order and stability in their homes.[43] One way of understanding devotionalism in this period is as the disciplining of a new generation of Catholic women. As a preist writing in another popular devotional perodical, *Little Flower Magazine*, warned: "How much then there is for the [Catholic] women of America to do in their own gentle, womanly way. They must be the custodians of modern society to drive from it all sham and sin and falsehood; to scorn evil and love good; women of good lives, of intelligence, of tender feeling; women with pity and mercy, the living images of God's tenderness; an unsparing devotion to the happiness of others."[44]

There was a great deal of uneasiness in devotional culture that young Catholic women "in these days of movies, automobiles, trolleys, golf, sensational magazines, woman suffrage and women in business, sport, etc." (as these days were defined by Martin Scott, S.J., writing in the influential devotional journal *Ave Maria*) were not living up to the ideal of "the Catholic woman." The intensity and venom with which young women were imagined and criticized in devotional culture during these transitional years reflects this fear. "The ranks of the Magdalens will be recruited by numbers all too great," the editors of *Ave Maria* feared in 1927, because of the atmosphere in "stores and shops and factories and offices," and against this they they urged "early training and parental control."[45] If women fall, according to Msgr. Thomas Riley, so does culture, because conscience is but "everyman's nagging wife."[46]

The discipline of economic hardship during the Depression was welcomed by some Catholic writers as an antidote to the dreams of young women. Mothers, wrote Nellie Ivancovich in *Ave Maria*, who are responsible for "building that citadel of the Church and of society, the Christian home," have been threatened of late by their own ambitions in "pagan and materialistic culture." But this is changing: "The many reasons that drew a large number of women away from the home—money, pleasure, prosperity—have failed in these days of depression, and people are learning that in the search for advantages something of much greater value has been lost—the proper care and training of the children." Fortunately, although mothers have been failing, the "ideal of perfect motherhood, a memory or a vision of 'Mother' as she was or might have been," has persisted.[47]

There were two categories of women in devotional culture: old women who had been broken by time and labor and young women who needed to be broken by time and labor. Older mothers are always tired, beaten, sad, and silent; young women are always rebellious, dangerous, wild. Rosie, a young bride in "Jim Graney's Wife," a short story published in *Ave Maria* in 1920 by Helen Moriarity, is an idle, rebellious red-haired beauty, "intoxicated with life, vain of the beauty which had captivated sober Jim Graney, selfish with youth's supreme and thoughtless egotism." She is contrasted in the story with Jim's mother, whose life is characterized by "self-sacrifice." One afternoon, Jim comes home and finds Rosie out with friends and his mother lying in a heap on the floor, crushed by overwork. When Rosie comes home, Jim exiles her forever from his house.

Rosie responds by indenturing herself as a servant to her own mother's family, and the transformation of the young woman by suffering begins. "Time . . . laid a devastating hand on her bright hair, ruthlessly took the lilt out of the gay voice, and set the giddy feet on duty's rugged path." She slaves for her family, converting their slovenly home into the cleanest dwelling in the neighborhood, but "in the process she herself became little more than an indistinguishable blur. A bent, pale little drudge, with red work-worn hands, the hair that was once her pride drawn back into a dull knot at the back of her head, she bore slight resemblance to the radiant, round-cheeked beauty that had charmed the heart out of sober Jim Graney."

As it turns out, Jim prefers red hands to red hair. His mother dies, and Jim, wounded in a railroad accident, is lying on his bed when he hears a "timid voice" asking him if he wants supper. At first he cannot recognize his wife, but when he does, he yields to the "tender touch of Rosie's toughened but capable hand." They reunite, raise many children together, and at the end of the story, gay young Rosie has become a "popular and beloved matron."[48]

Rosie and her sisters were treated harshly in devotional culture in these years. Inevitably wild and dangerous, they were frequently shown luring their "sober" men into danger. "Let's live on thrills," a young woman cries in a short story in the *Voice*, taunting her man on to drive recklessly, an adventure which ends with her in the hospital after the car crashes. "Freddy sustained only a broken collar bone. It was Barbara who paid the severe penalty with a crushed chest."[49] Young women are defined by their discontent and ambitions.[50]

They are punished for these things: the stories always end with the young women chastened by grief, pain, sickness—which they admit they have brought on themselves—alone in squalid rooms, abandoned by everyone except the saints and the Virgin, resigned to their new lives. Stories that played with this theme were published regularly in the *Voice*, a striking counterpoint to the expressions of suffering and grief in the letters columns. The plot is always the same: a successful young woman abandons the friends of her childhood in her lust for fame and glory, which she achieves very briefly before disaster strikes, after which she learns the true meaning of life. Susan Grayson, in Anne Tansey's "Will-o-the-Wisp," was the pet of her teachers and the darling of a fast crowd of friends. After graduation, she seeks glory on the stage (indeed, she changes her name to "Gloria"), which she finds, although "success went to Susan's head." Suddenly, inexplicably, Susan breaks down and is confined to a hospital for three years—"careless and extravagant living exacted its toll." Alone, abandoned by the friends of her days of triumph, humiliated, Susan comes to her senses. She turns to the saints for help, but even here Tansey cannot refrain from ridicule, depicting the sad woman as "rushing" frantically "from saint to saint for succor." Susan finally finds Jude and accepts her lot in life: at the end she is living in a "shabby house in a poor section" but she is "placidly happy" and content with the "companionship of no one" other than Jude.[51] Not even young nuns are exempt from this treatment: in another story, when a novice's mother objects to the harsh discipline her daughter is undergoing at the hands of her novice mistress, the young religious replies, "Mother darling! It is only what I deserve, and you know it!"[52]

Women were warned in devotional culture that to make choices for themselves was to risk the certain destruction of their families. Their desires are always corrosive.[53] So dangerous were these women that at times their ambitions are treated as capital offenses: one young woman's murder in a story published in the *Voice* is called "retributive justice" for her having abandoned the "simple shepherd" who loved her as a girl.[54]

But the favorite gender trope of devotional culture was the woman in pain: suffering was understood to be women's true destiny and vocation, and the source of their access to power in the sacred world.[55] Suffering defined the vocation of motherhood. "We are 'two in one flesh,' with [mother] by a far more intimate physical union than she can possibly achieve with her husband," according to a priest writing in *Sign*, allowing the oedipal subtext of offical devotionalism perilously close to the surface. This is because "she suffers for us as she suffers for no other."

> In a sense, she dies for us that we might live, for it is of her substance, by the destruction of part of her, that our physical substance grows, differentiates, matures, and is delivered. Of all this, father is a silent spectator, quite helpless to do anything for this child.[56]

Mothers, who are always contrasted in devotional culture with wild young women, suffer with and for their children, and in this way redeem them.

The Christological undercurrents in this portrayal of mothers dying, children (sons) rising, is made explicit in the devotional treatment of Mary, who is described as "co-operatrix" in Jesus' work.[57] Mary alone can avert the disaster that God intends for humankind, becoming in this way the model woman standing loyally beside her fallen, depraved children. In a favorite imaginative exercise of devotional literature, a clerical writer asks, "How would your mother feel if she were to meet you on the way to the electric chair or the gallows?" Any good mother would behave in this situation like Mary. "She approaches Him and kneels, wipes the sweat and blood and spit from His face, throws her arms about Him. True mother even in this anguish, she seeks to console, rather than be consoled, to lift Him up rather than be lifted up, to encourage Him rather than be encouraged."[58]

Women are not just called to suffering in devotional culture, however; they are also taught how to suffer as women: cheerfully, resignedly, and above all, silently. A young, very sick female character in a story published in the *Voice* silences herself so as not to ruin "the little haven to which Jimmy [her brother] might come to the rest he had earned by honest toil."[59] When women complain, they bring down spiritual and physical disaster on their families.[60] Instead, they are called upon to imitate Mary, who is held up as the model of silent and resigned suffering. "Be brave then," a priest writing in *St. Anthony's Messenger* urges his women readers, "whoever you are, be silent, in imitation of her whose heart held the sorrows of the world."[61] "Why were you silent?" a character asks Mary in a poem published in *Ave Maria*; the Virgin modestly replies, "Why should a voice like mine be heard?"[62] Injunctions to silence seem particularly perverse in the devotional press because it was precisely here, in their letters of thanksgiving and request, that women broke their silence.

On May 30, 1920, a poor Roman matron, Anna Maria Taigi, was beatified by Benedict XV. She was quickly taken up by American Catholic devotional writers and offered as a model to mothrs and wives. Taigi had been a "gay bride," according to Florence Gilmore in a sketch published in *Ave Maria*, until "the grace of God touched her soul." Seeing her "frivolity" now in a new light, Taigi began to wear "the commonest and coarsest clothes," under which she hid a hairshirt. She endured a life of terrible sufferings, which included a violently abusive husband, "cheerfully and smilingly" and sought ways to increase her discomforts. "Hot as Rome often is and hard as she worked, Anna Maria often passed several days without a drink of water." She was "unfailingly patient" with her abusive husband, "silent when he was angry, eager to please him in every way." God rewarded Taigi for her silent and willing suffering with the grace of healing: "the mere touch of her toil-roughened hands cured the sick."[63]

Women's pain/women's power; women in pain/women healers; female silence/male violence—this is the grammar of gender in American Catholic devotionalism in the crucial years after the end of immigration. The path marked out for women was clear: rebellion yielded crushing pain, while suffering and sickness made women powerful matrons, able to heal. All women had to do was keep silent. Broken, they were strong; through their own pain they secured the power to heal others.

This seems to be the logic of Jude's devotion as well. Women assumed all the responsibilities for their families in times of distress. They called on the saint, often in grueling prayer marathons that lasted all night or for days; as one woman put it, she prayed "until my throat ached" for a cure for a relative.[64] When a couple was in trouble, for example, or a man's business failing, it was always the responsibility to the women involved to pray and to make whatever sacrifices were thought necessary to propitiate the sacred. The devout believed that to some extent Jude's response to them was dependent on the quality of their prayer: it must be strong, intense, self-sacrificial.[65] It was women's task to negotiate with the sacred, bartering their own sacrifice and devotion for the welfare of their families. Women also assumed the duty of acknowledging and remembering the saint's intervention: years after a crisis, the women of a family continued to write to the shrine, recalling the moment of Jude's intervention.[66]

Women acted as the centers of prayer, domestic unity and order, success, and health, through their special alliance with Saint Jude: they prayed to Jude constantly, monitored his responses, assumed all responsibilities toward the sacred, wrote the narratives of distress and gratitude, and served as their families' memories. True to the warning against complaint in the devotional image of woman, the devout never expressed anger or resentment in their narratives at the husbands who left them, the doctors who failed to comfort them, or the children who rejected them. Participation in the devotion sealed women's sense of obligation: they were responsible for everything. They were also uniquely positioned to suffering—in some sense, identified with it, responsible for it. Like Mary in the devotional literature, they had assumed responsibility for averting disaster and had devoted themselves to others in need. A new generation of Catholic women seemed trapped in the consequences of devotional fantasies: they have been cast as the hidden figures responsible for holding up the world by the powers that are theirs through suffering, brokenness, and self-sacrifice.

WHOSE VOICE? THE DIALECTICS OF POPULAR RELIGION

This is as far as a historian can go with the structural study of culture, which fails the social historian when he or she comes to the question of how people live in, with, and against, the discourses which they inherit. Göran Therborn has pointed out that ideology is always dialectical: people are both located in and empowered by particular arrangements of reality.[67] Gianna Pomata has criticized Donzelot's *The Policing of Families* in a way that is useful here. She writes,

> The tutelary 'police' is here reconstructed and analyzed through its 'knowledge,' that is to say, the texts of doctors and philanthropists; but the book lacks, by contrast, a reconstruction of the other 'knowledges' which this police encountered and with which it came into conflict, above all the knowledge of popular traditions. In this manner the book privileges the image of social processes and relations of power which emerges from texts linked to the 'police,' in relation to other possible images, other points of view.[68]

I would prefer to focus not on other knowledges but on the seams, disjunctures, and alternative possibilities within popular Catholicism itself. "The point of the new historical investigation," Joan Scott argues, "is to disrupt the notion of fixity, to discover the nature of the debate or repression that leads to the appearance of timeless permanence in binary gender representation."[69] Our task now is to uncover the polysemy of devotional culture, ritual, and belief.

Consider, as a way of beginning this discussion, whose "voice" was heard at the shrine. According to the official understanding, by narrating his intervention in their lives, women were giving Jude back his voice, which had been muted in history because of his identification with Judas. But the "voice" heard at the shrine was always double: by talking about Jude's actions in their lives, women were also speaking their own experience, finding a voice for themselves. Jude could not speak apart from the devout; his voice could be heard only in theirs. Indeed, the devout treated this as a bond of reciprocity or mutuality between heaven and earth: Jude needed them as much as they needed him. Women were thus enabled through this devotional ventriloquism to articulate aspects of their experience which they might otherwise have been unable to speak. The reciprocity between heaven and earth found its ultimate expression in this identity of voices.

Women did not only inherit Jude; they also invented him out of their needs and desires, and continued to invent him throughout their lives as they faced the successive crises and dliemmas of their experience. Jude's followers believed that when they wrote about the saint they were presenting him to the world for the first time. In this way Jude resembles the nameless spirits Gananath Obeyesekere has studied in the religious imaginations of Sri Lankan Buddhists. Obeyesekere writes that in distinction to the formalized, highly delineated dieties of the official pantheon,

> Spirits, by contrast, are a known *category*, but they are not known beings. . . . [T]he individual exercises an option or choice in selecting a spirit from a known cultural category; and he manipulates the spirit. When these conditions obtain . . . the symbol or ideational set is used by the individual to express his personal needs.[70]

Although Jude was certainly in the recognizable and highly valued category of saint, he had had only the most modest prior tradition of popular devotion and the Chicago shrine claimed with some justice to have discovered this hidden figure. Like the spirits Obeyesekere studied, Jude was available for psycho-social improvisation: the blankness of Jude in the tradition became the space for the imaginative work of the devout.

Women imagined Jude as a sympathetic, caring, engaged man, who understood their needs and desires, a figure bound to them by various ties of reciprocity and mutual need and so both constrained and inclined to act on their behalf. Women claimed Jude by imagining him looking at them—in this way they took him away from the shrine and brought him into the centers of their experience. When I asked one woman what Jude looked like, she began by saying that of course he resembled the statue at the shrine, and then went on to offer a powerful, personal, alternative imagining of him.[71] Another woman pointed out that "in enjoying friendship with Saint Jude you feel an intimate personal feeling, almost like you are the only one praying to him."[72]

I have argued that it was a new generation of women who turned to Jude, imagining him into being as much as encountering him in the official cult, when the saints of their various immigrant communities no longer seemed adequate to their needs. The saint that was invented between Chicago and the personal experience of the devout was imagined to have a particular understanding of the special problems of women. He is compassionate and sympathetic, one woman wrote me, and has an "awareness of how we feel when we are going through a desperate situation."[73] Saint Jude, another woman told me simply, "sees us for what we are."[74]

The intensity with which Jude was imagined, of course, reflected the dire circumstances of need and distress that motivated this imagining. "I was twenty years old, single, and very ill, and scared," a woman described the time of her first meeting with the saint, and went on to picture him as "kind, personable, and loving. I always relate to the picture on my prayercard."[75] Jude appeared then as the object of desire, his image constructed of many different sources, and the intensity of this desire threatened the closure of the discourse of woman and gender in devotional culture.

The initial deep connection between Jude and the devout was most often established through an imagining of his eyes, which one woman described as "penetrating," and more generally of his smiling, attentive, and compassionate face. His eyes are "compassionate and loving," "kind and sad," "soft and pleasing."[76] Jude's face is always turned toward his followers in gentle consideration. The devout say that Jude is: "a gentle, kind, loving person who you would like to embrace"; "kind, generous, and helpful"; and "someone to lean on."[77] Above all, Jude is a powerful friend who is sincerely interested in helping and understanding his devout. The saint, according to one woman, is "a compassionate person that would listen to your problems and intercede for you." Jude is "capable of handling the most serious problems in life." Unlike the living persons in their lives, finally, Jude never "turn[s] his head when I ask him for help."[78]

The conversations women had with this figure, who they imagined in this way, were private and complex, often kept secret from husbands and children, and understood to be distinct from saying the official prayers published at the shrine.[79] "Oftentimes I carry on a full conversation" with Jude, one woman explained, and added that "periodically I plead and become angry." Women say that they came away from these conversations "full of hope."[80]

The material culture of devotionalism facilitated this process of personal appropriation. Women could send away to the shrine for various objects—statues, medals, prayer cards, oils, car ornaments—which they could then use and manipulate as they wanted, often to the consternation of the shrine clergy. This extensive or detachable quality of shrine culture was an important source both of women's power and improvisatory creativity in the practice of the cult. Women painted Jude's statue in bright colors, hid it in secret places in their homes or displayed it in elaborate home shrines; they sewed his medals into their husbands' and children's clothing and wore them on their underclothes when they went for radiation therapy. Unitl the early 1960s, when it was discontinued at the shrine, women used holy oil blessed with Jude's relic to heal themselves and their families and friends. The oil became the instrument of their power: they administered it on the bodies of sick kin and passed it on to friends with careful instructions about its proper use. When healings occurred, these women expected to be included in the thanksgiving for Jude's intervention.[81] (Older devout still manage to obtain oil for themselves, mainly from a rival shrine of Saint Jude in Baltimore.)

Women used the objects available at the shrine to create networks of support and assistance among their female relatives and friends similar to those their mothers and grandmothers had relied on in the transition from the old world to the new.[82] As they exchanged prayer cards of Saint Jude with each other in times of trouble, women also shared their stories, perceptions, and problems, and the saint became the privileged medium of communication between mothers and daughters, sisters, and friends. As one woman described this interweaving of voices, "A young lady friend of mine sent me the picture of Saint Jude with [the] prayer on the back. When we write to each other she would tell me her troubles, and I mine."[83] The exchange between women involving Jude was always an exchange of feelings, confidence, trust; it was also an exchange of information, one piece of which was about Jude, but included folk remedies, self-healing practices, advice on dealing with troubled husbands and children, recommendations of doctors, and life stories.

Acting within this network and in relationship with the gentle, powerful, attentive companion saint, women felt themselves to be empowered in new ways. They broke off relationships with "mean" boyfriends, rejected unwanted medical treatments, passed difficult qualifying exams of different sorts, and confronted family crises with newfound confidence.[84] Throughout the 1940s and 1950s, for example, when the official voices of devotional culture were decrying women's return to work, the devout found in their relationship with Jude the strength and confidence to look for, secure, and keep their new jobs.[85] Women have always written to describe problems they are having at work, their hopes of finding better employment, and their struggles with management. They have used prayer cards and medals to create networks of support with other women at work.[86] So central has Jude been to the working lives of women in these years that a contemporary devout has come to believe that the saint is particularly interested in the concerns of working women: "it has been my experience . . . that [Saint Jude] is especially good with finding employment and in solving problems related to employment."[87]

Finally, women resisted through various devotional practices, especially the construction of narratives of crisis, the silence imposed by Catholic devotional culture on women in the "Catholic home." The contrast between the male-articulated culture of innocence, as this has been well described by William Halsey in *The Survival of American Innocence*,[88] and the picture that takes shape in the letters' pages is striking: the narratives written to the shrine recount tales of alcoholic husbands, financial struggles that are not glossed by sentimental celebrations of Christian poverty, women's fears of having more babies, and so on. Women found their own sources of power and support and their own ways of speaking amid the complex possibilities of devotional culture.

"DEVOTIONAL LIFE CAN BECOME EXUBERANT"

In 1943, Joseph Donovan reflected on one of his colleague's scruples about a new devotional practice in his monthly column of advice for parish clergy in *The*

Homiletic and Pastoral Review. Some Irish-American women had taken to eating prayer cards of the Virgin Mary in the hope that this would secure their petitions. Donovan warned his clerical colleague not to be too fussy about such practices. After all, he points out, "devotional life can become exuberant."[89]

Although the clergy were often uneasy with this exuberance, as Donovan's comments suggest they also contributed in these years to an atmosphere of devotional experimentation and creativity. Many voices could be heard in the devotional world, speaking often against each other or from different perspectives, for different audiences. As one woman put it, writing to the shrine in 1949 about her trouble in finding adequate day care for her daughter while she worked, "This may not sound like a difficult problem to you, but. . . ."[90] She seems to be writing past the shrine clergy here to the other women who read and wrote for these pages.

This leads to a new understanding of devotionalism, not only as the place of gender construction, but as the privileged site of gender contestation in American Catholic culture. Devotional culture was polysemous and polyvalent. Women not only "discovered" who they were in the dense devotional world that developed through much of this century in the United States, but created and imagined themselves, manipulating and altering the available grammar of gender. Religous traditions must be understood as zones of improvisation and conflict. The idea of a "tradition" itself is the site of struggle, and historically situated men and women build the traditions and counter-traditions they need or want as they live. Finding meaning in a tradition is a dialectical process: women worked with the forms and structures available to them, and their imaginings were inevitably constrained by the materials they were working with. Still, through the power of their desire and need, and within the flexible perimeters of devotional practice, they were able to do much with what they inherited.

Women believed that they became agents in a new way with Jude's help. Their prayers made things happen in their lives. Then they sat down and wrote out accounts of their experience for publication at the shrine. These narratives must not be understood to provide "closure" to painful experiences in any simple sense. Rather, the narrative process, occurring within the complex world of devotional culture, was a zone of reimagination, a privileged exercise in which frightening experiences were engaged, struggled with, shared, endured, remembered, and in some sense healed. Women used the resources of devotional culture to recreate their world.

Again, the analysis here must always be dialectical. Women did not directly challenge the family arrangements which they experienced as oppressive, more often finding new ways of coordinating their lives within these structures with Jude's help; and I have discussed in this essay some of the ways that Jude's devotion recreated normative structures of gender relations. But these dimensions of the devotion must be read from the perspective of women's own appropriations, manipulations, and recreations of the forms and structures of devotionalism.

Finally, popular religion can now be seen as one of the central intersections of "public" events and "private" experience. Jude appeared as a figure in the space between prayer, desire, and need, on the one hand, and social and cultural structures, authorities, and norms, on the other. Although the devout do not recognize the disciplinary distinction between inner and outer, Jude was both a "public" symbol encountered by women in the language and structures of a particular religious tradition at a particular moment in their social experiences and the creation of private desire and imagination. The saint is a kind of boundary crossing figure for the devout, serving as a special kind of emissary between levels of their experience. History is always the story of this conjuncture of inner and outer.

THE STORY OF THE SWITCHED STATUES AGAIN

Why did the daughters of immigrants turn to Saint Jude in the difficult days of 1929? We know how they went on to imagine Jude, and what their lives with this saint looked like. Perhaps they were dissatisfied with the holy figures that their parents prayed to, suspecting that these saints could not understand their new experiences and feelings. Perhaps they were frightened by their fathers' and husbands' difficulties at finding and keeping work, and in response they created a powerful, sympathetic man for themselves who could help them but who was also dependent on them for his own voice.

But I have begun to wonder whether this generation of Catholic women may also have been turning away, perhaps unconsciously, from the model of the Christian woman offered in Thérèse—the saint of "suffering" and "self-abnegation"—in favor of a saint whose existence was rooted in their needs and who would not only understand and comfort them, but empower them as well.

Power in what sense though? Freedom, Sartre said in an interview late in his life, is what a person can make of what has been made of him or herself. This is the dialectic of devotionalism.

NOTES

1. This paper has benefitted from the close scrutiny and generous criticism of two of my friends and colleagues at Indiana University, Jeff Isaac and Rich Miller. I am grateful to both of them for their help.
   The history of the founding of the Church of Our Lady of Guadalupe is based on *Dedication of Our Lady of Guadalupe Church*, September 30, 1928. Chicago: John H. Hannigan Publisher; "Necrology: Father James Tort, C.M.F.," a privately printed biographical sketch, 1955; *Our Lady of Guadalupe Church: 50th Anniversary Bulletin, 1924–1974*, privately printed by the Claretian Fathers, 1974; Joachim DePrada, C.M.F., "Our Founder Is Dead," *Voice of Saint Jude* (hereafter cited as *Voice*), June 1955, p. 34; Frank Smith, "Load of Bricks Stumps Priest Who Fled Bullets," *Voice*, February 1935, p. 18; James Tort, C.M.F., "Dedication Anniversary of the National Shrine of Saint Jude," *Voice*, February 1935, pp. 12–13; George Hull, "Life Begins at Forty," *Voice*, June 1935, pp. 7–10; John Schneider, C.M.F., "Tenth Anniversary," *Voice*, April 1942, pp. 12–17. The history of the shrine is told in comic-book from in "Jude the Forgetten Saint," published in 1954 by the Catechetical Guild Educational Society.

2. Mary Lee Nolan and Sidney Nolan, in their comprehensive survey of contemporary shrine culture in Western Europe, note that Jude ranked third among the Apostles as a "pilgrimage saint," with at least none European shrines dedicated to him. They go on to say,

however, that "the cult of this apostle, who replaced Judas Iscariot among the original group, developed slowly and became important only in the Twentieth Century." Nolan and Nolan, *Christian Pilgrimage in Modern Western Europe* (Chapel Hill, N.C., and London: 1989), p. 137.

3. For women's central place in nineteenth-century popular piety see Ann Taves, *The Household of Faith* (Notre Dame, Ind., 1986).

4. Interview with Frank K, sixty-six years old, Los Angeles, California.

5. J. P. Donovan, C.M., takes up the question of clerical scruples on this matter in "Is the Perpetual Novena a Parish Need?" *Homiletic and Pastoral Review* 56, no 4 (January 1946): 252–57. Donovan, who wrote a regular advice column for his clerical colleagues, says that some clergy had concluded that devotional practices like the perpetual novena were either "rackets" or "sentimentality." For a rather bitter clerical admission of the predominance of women in devotional culture see Francis W. Grey, "The Devout Female Sex," *Ave Maria* 26, no. 20 (November 12, 1927): 609–12.

6. John M. Huels, O.S.M., "The Friday Night Novena: The Growth and Decline of the Sorrowful Mother Novena," privately printed by the Eastern Province of Servites, Berwyn, Illinois, 1977, pp. 21–23; and Joachim DePrada, C.M.F., "To Whom Shall We Turn?" *Voice*, December 1958. In several different gatherings of clergy I have heard it dryly observed that the problem with the ordination of women is that if women take over clerical duties there would be no one left in the pews.

7. "We Visit a Solemn Novena," *Voice*, October 1954, pp. 14–17.

8. Monica Furlong, *Thérèse of Lisieux* (New York, 1987), p. 1. For an excellent review of the "posthumous history" of the Little Flower, her changing image over time, see Barbara Corrado Pope, "A Heroine without Heroics: The Little Flower of Jesus and Her Times," *Church History* 57 (March 1986): 46–60.

9. Personal communications: FG-F-49-Chicago-M; AC-F-70-Chicago-W; MPD-F-75-So. Chicago-W; MTD-F-27-Haiti-M; AI-F-55-Chicago-D; AG-F-55-Chicago-S; DD-F-62-Whiting, Ind.-M; FA-F-68-Indiana-S. I distinguish in the notes between two kinds of direct communications to me. "Personal communication" refers to women's written responses to twenty very general questions about their devotions to Saint Jude which I distributed at the shrine in Chicago during a novena in the summer of 1987. Seventy women responded. (I did not ask that only women participate, nor do the questions imply that I think men would not pray to Saint Jude, but only five men wrote to me.) Most of the women who responded to my questons did so at length, adding sheets of paper to the form I had distributed. "Personal correspondence" refers to letters sent me about Saint Jude; I received forty of these. I also conducted about thirty-five interviews with the devout, and these are cited in the text as well. These three sources are intended to supplement the letters written to the shrine over the last fifty years.

I will identify my sources by a consistent designation, beginning with fictitious initials, followed by gender, age, residence, and marital status. In the latter category, M=married, S=single, W=widowed, D=divorced.

10. Personal correspondence: MMc-F-89-LaCrosse, Wisc.-W.

11. George Hull, "Life Begins at Forty," *Voice*, June 1935, pp. 8–9.

12. On Mundelein, see Edward R. Kantowicz, *Corporation Sole: Cardinal Mundelein and Chicago Catholicism* (Notre Dame, Ind., 1983), and Charles Shanabruch, *Chicago's Catholics: The Evolution of an American Identity* (Notre Dame, Ind., 1981). According to shrine accounts, Mundelein was an enthusiastic supporter of the cult in its early years, Hull, "Life," p. 8.

13. Information on this important popular devotion is in *Little Flower Magazine*, published monthly until the mid-1970s by the Carmelite Fathers of Oklahoma City. There is a historical sketch of the origins of the devotion to the Little Flower in Chicago in *The Sword*, May 1948, pp. 106–16.

14. *Voice*, February 1941, p. 18, Mrs. EF, Detroit.

15. Personal correspondence: MCM-F-89-LaCrosse, Wisc.-W.

16. Personal correspondence: RA-F-62-Dracut, Mass.-M.

17. Personal correspondence: AM-F-65+-Carol Stream, Ill.-M.

18. Personal communication: JF-F-49-Chicago-M; BE-F-66-Chicago-M; CD-F-75-Milwaukee-M.

19. There is unfortunately no comprehensive history of this period. Jay Dolan has a short and helpful chapter on the subject in *The American Catholic Experience: A History From Colonial Times to the Present* (Garden City, N.Y., 1985), "The Catholic Ethos," pp. 221–41. The best study of American Catholic popular religion in the nineteenth century is Ann Taves's *Household*, cited earlier. Joseph Chinnici's recent history of piety in the United States, *Living Stones: The History and Structure of Catholic Spiritual Life in the United States* (New York, 1988), is unfortunately not concerned with popular religion.

20. Personal communication: CD-F-75-Milwaukee-M. Another woman wrote me: "I give these prayer cards out all over the U.S. My friends and people are scattered from Cleveland, Ohio, Minnesota, Illinois, Louisiana, Kentucky, Florida, Nevada, Newportnews, Taft, Scranton. I sent for 1000 [prayer cards]. All I can say Where I go my Patron Saint Jude goes with me." Personal correspondence: CG-F-75-Richmond, Va.-W.

21. This sketch of the changing history of immigrant communities is based on a number of studies both of particular ethnic communities as well as of immigration more generally. I owe a great deal to John Bodnar's *Workers' World: Kinship, Community, and Protest in an Industrial Society, 1900–1940* (Baltimore and London, 1982), and *The Transplanted: A History of Immigrants in Urban America* (Bloomington, Ind., 1985). These transitions are helpfully discussed in Shanabruch, *Chicago's Catholics*, pp. 155–87. For studies of particular communities see Judith E. Smith, *Family Connections: A History of Italian and Jewish Immigrant Lives in Providence, Rhode Island, 1900–1940* (Albany, N.Y., 1985); Humbert Nelli, *Italians in Chicago, 1880–1930: A Study in Ethnic Mobility* (Oxford, 1970); Dino Cinel, *From Italy to San Francisco: The Immigrant Experience* (Stanford, Calif., 1982); Virginia Yans-McLaughlin, *Family and Community: Italian Immigrants in Buffalo, 1880–1930* (Ithaca and London, 1971); Samuel L. Baily, "The Adjustment of Italian Immigrants in Buenos Aires and New York, 1870–1914," *American Historical Review* 88 (April 1983); Joseph John Parot, *Polish Catholics in Chicago, 1850–1920; A Religious History* (DeKalb, Ill., 1981); Paul Wrobel, *Our Way: Family, Parish, and Neighborhood in a Polish American Community* (Notre Dame, Ind., 1979); Dennis Clark, *The Irish in Philadelphia: Ten Generations of Urban Experience* (Philadelphia, 1973); Lawrence McCaffrey, Ellen Skerret, Michael F. Funchion, and Charles Fanning, *The Irish in Chicago* (Urbana and Chicago, 1987); Peter d'A. Jones and Melvin G. Holli, *Ethnic Chicago* (Grand Rapids, Mich., 1981); Audrey S. Olson, *St. Louis Germans: The Nature of an Immigrant Community and Its Relation to the Assimilation Process* (New York, 1980); Josef J. Barton, "Religion and Cultural Change in Czech Immigrant Communities, 1850–1920," pp. 3–24, in Randall M. Miller and Thomas D. Marzik, eds., *Immigrants and Religion in Urban America* (Philadelphia, 1977); William J. Galush, "Faith and Fatherland: Dimensions of Polish-American Ethnoreligion, 1875–1975," pp. 84–102, in Miller and Marzik, *Immigrants and Religion;* and M. Mark Stolarik, "Immigration, Education, and the Social Mobility of Slovaks, 1870–1930," pp. 103–16 in Miller and Marzik, *Immigrants and Religion.*

22. As Linda Gordon has observed of this period in her study of family violence in Boston, although "parental violence against adolescents of both sexes" in immigrant communities which were just experiencing the loss of the "family economy," was "particularly intense," it was "more so with grils." Linda Gordon, *Heroes of Their Own Lives: The Politics and History of Family Violence, Boston, 1880–1960* (New York, 1988), p. 188.

23. *Catholic Women's World*, a "new type of Catholic magazine," according to its editors, "designed for the modern woman," began publication in June 1939. Although intended for a college-educated, middle-class audience, the magazine is a useful guide to the changing

concerns and needs of young Catholic women in these years. Of particular interest here is the treatment of married life in the magazine: the women in *Catholic Women's World's* fiction, advice columns, and true stories all seem to feel that they must work carefully and conscientiously to make their marriages successful, to the extent even of taking classes to learn how to do special things in the kitchen and around the house. (Adele de Leeuw, "Bookcases and Broccoli," *Catholic Women's World* 1, no. 5, [November 1939].) There are beauty hints each month and pages of recipes, as well as highly ambivalent advice about love and work from Jane Frances Downey. Although Jude's devout came from all social classes, *Catholic Women's World* points to a broader shift in social mores among younger Catholic women. The entry of these women into the culture of expertise, their need for advice on everything from buying towels to changing diapers, suggests that they had begun to feel that their mothers' counsel was of limited usefulness to them.

24. "My husband and I were married less than two months," a woman wrote the shrine in October 1936, "when he lost his position. Needless to say, it brought about a great deal of worry and shattered our dreams for the future." *Voice*, October 1936, Mr. and Mrs. MJB, Chicago.

25. *Voice*, September 1936, p. 15, Mrs. MCG, Chicago. For relations between men and women in this period see Susan Ware, *Holding Their Own: American Women in the 1930s* (Boston, 1982), pp. 8–18, and William Chafe, *The American Woman: Her Changing Social, Economic, and Political Roles* (Oxford, 1972), pp. 135f.

26. *Voice*, April 1952, p. 32, DD, Detroit.

27. *Voice*, July 1950, p. 7, PR, Saint Louis.

28. Personal communication: ER-F-74-Chicago-M.

29. *Voice*, July 1953, Mrs. GH, Chicago.

30. *Saint Jude's Journal*, January 1967, p. 4, Miss JF, Baltimore. The *Journal*, a small, four-page, simply printed devotional newsletter, began publication in 1960. At the same time, the *Voice of Saint Jude* was renamed *U.S. Catholic*, and all devotional material was shifted out of that periodical and into the newsletter. The *Voice* had been evolving over the years into a more general Catholic family magazine, which had long been the ambition of its clerical and lay editors and publishers. But the devotional material had fit quite well into this evolving format through the 1940s and 1950s, and indeed there were important connections between the devotional features of the periodical and the more sophisticated political and social commentry that had begun to appear: Jude, for example, was as stalwart an anti-Communist as any Catholic editor. Something else was happening, though, in Chicago and elsewhere at the end of the fifties: devotionalism, which had flourished in the postwar years, had come under sharp criticism from liturgical reformers, parish clergy, and a new generation of Catholic laity. The repositioning of the devotional material at the shrine reflects this new sensibility.

31. *Voice*, April 1958, DSS, Rosindale, Mass.

32. I discuss this aspect of the devouts' understanding of themselves in "What Did Women Think They Were Doing When They Prayed to Saint Jude," *U.S. Catholic Historian* 8, nos. 1–2, (winter/spring 1989): 67–79.

33. Personal correspondence: AS-F-65+-Carol Stream, Ill.-M.

34. Joan Scott, *Gender and the Politics of History* (New York, 1988) p. 24.

35. Ware, *Holding Their Own*, pp. 2–24.

36. Chafe, *The American Woman*, p. 135.

37. Bodnar, *Workers' World*, p. 116.

38. *Voice*, June 1935, p. 16, SMT, Chicago.

39. *Voice*, January 1935, p. 16, Mrs. ME, Chicago.

40. On the Police Branch of the Saint Jude's League see: Frank Smith, "Load of Bricks

Stumps Priest Who Fled Bullets," *Voice*, February 1935, p. 18; Father Anthony, C.M.F., "The St. Jude Novena," *Voice*, March 1938, p. 10; John Schneider, C.M.F., "Tenth Anniversary," *Voice*, April 1942, pp. 12–18; Joseph M. Puigvi, C.M.F., "Jottings on Devotion to Saint Jude," *Voice*, December 1946, p. 7; "Police Overflow Church for Annual Communion," *Voice*, June 1948, p. 7; "19th Annual Police Mass," *Voice*, June 1951, p. 19; Joachim DePrada, "Our Founder Is Dead," *Voice*, June 1955, p. 34; "Guns and Missals," *Voice*, October 1954, pp. 28–29.

41. A recent shrine director suggested to a reporter from a local Chicago paper that, in the reporter's words, "policemen are logically clients of Saint Jude . . . in that they carry clubs." Peter Schwendener, "The Patron Saint of Hopeless Cases," *Reader*, May 27, 1983, p. 34. Jude is usually shown holding a thick wooden shaft, the implement of his martyrdom.

42. BC-M-55-Queens, N.Y.-M.

43. As John Bodnar writes, "in nearly every immigrant household economy, the central manager of financial resources, children's socialization, and the entire operation, was the married female." *Transplanted*, pp. 81–82.

44. Father Marrison, O.C.D., "The Woman in Social Life," *Little Flower Magazine* 15, no. 9 (December 1934): 5.

45. "The Discipline of Girls," *Ave Maria* 25, no. 26 (June 25, 1927): 821.

46. Joseph McClellan, "Everyman's Nagging Wife," *Ave Maria* 90, no. 13 (September 26, 1959): 5–9.

47. Nellie R. Ivancovich, "Motherhood," *Ave Maria* 35, no. 11 (March 12, 1932): 338–40.

48. Helen Moriarity, "Jim Graney's Wife," *Ave Maria* 12, no. 15 (October 9, 1920): 463–66, and 12, no. 16 (October 16, 1920): 494–98. See also: E. M. Walker, "East End Granny," *Ave Maria* 25, no. 25 (June 18, 1927): 781–83; James A. Dunn, "The Picture," *Sign* 28, no. 8 (March 1949): 20–23; Constance Edgerton, "Desert Love," *Voice*, April 1938, pp. 17–18; Anne Tansey, "Receive This Word," *Voice*, June 1944, pp. 14, 16–17; Pauline Marie Cloton, "Larry's Wife," *Sacred Heart Messenger*, 56, no. 6 (June 1921): 325–32.

49. Tansey, "Receive This Word," p. 14.

50. P.J.C., "Contentment," *Ave Maria* 35, no. 14 (April 2, 1932): 437.

51. Anne Tansey, "Will-o-the-Wisp," *Voice*, July 1944, pp. 10, 17.

52. Sister M. Marguerite, R.S.M., "Barter and Exchange: For Fathers Only," *Voice*, May 1947, pp. 4, 19, 24.

53. Ben Hurst, "Sibyl's Awakening," *Ave Maria* 26, no. 22 (November 26, 1927): 688–91; Ann Tansey, "Going Home," *Voice*, September 1944, pp. 10, 16.

54. Edgerton, "Desert Love," p. 18.

55. For a good discussion of the history of women's identification with suffering in the Catholic tradition, and the special place in this story of Augustine's suffering mother, Monica, see Clarissa W. Atkinson, "'Your Servant, My Mother': The Figure of Saint Monica in the Ideology of Christian Motherhood," pp. 139–72 in Atkinson, Constance H. Buchana, and Margaret R. Miles, eds., *Immaculate and Powerful: The Female in Sacred Image and Social Reality* (Boston, 1985).

56. Hilary Sweeney, C.P., "When Ignorance is Bliss," *Sign* 28, no. 11 (June 1949): 39–40.

57. "The Union of Jesus and Mary," *Ave Maria* 12, no. 26 (December 25, 1920): 820–21. This theme is most strongly articulated in the widely read work of Don Sharkey. See for example *The Woman Shall Conquer* (New York, 1954), which is a celebration both of Mary's (and in general, women's) powers and of women's suffering.

58. Arthur Tonne, O.F.M., "Swords of Sorrow," *St Anthony's Messenger* 48, no. 8 (January 1941): 25, 47.

59. Maude Gardner, "The Undaunted Christmas Spirit," *Voice*, December 1937, pp. 15–17.

60. Sister M. Adelaide, R.S.M., "Short Wave to Saint Jude," *Voice,* April 1950, p. 4.

61. Tonne, "Swords," p. 31.

62. Alice Pauline Clark, "The Silent Saint," *Ave Maria* 35, no. 12 (March 19, 1932): 353.

63. Florence Gilmore, "Wife, Mother, and Saint," *Ave Maria* 35, no. 8 (February 20, 1932): 240–43; also Countess de Courson, "A New Beata. Anna Maria Taigi," *Ave Maria* 11, no. 25 (June 19, 1920): 782–87.

64. *Voice,* December 1950, p. 5, MC, Chicago. One female correspondent reports that she made a fifty-four day "rosary novena" while she and her husband were looking for a home. *Voice,* September 1958, ARS, Chicago.

65. *Voice,* May 1955, p. 34, Mrs. CEN, Bay City, Michigan; ibid., June 1951, p. 32, RM, St. Louis; personal communication: DH-F-67-Indiana-M.

66. *Voice,* January 1935, Mrs. MB, Chicago; ibid., March 1935, p. 15, Mrs. EH, Hasbrouck Heights, N.J.; ibid., December 1950, p. 5, IB, Kent, Conn.; ibid., April 1955, p. 34, Miss CM, Chicago.

67. Göran Therborn, *The Ideology of Power and the Power of Ideology* (London, 1980), pp. 16–18.

68. Quoted in Peter Dews, *Logics of Disintegration: Post-Structuralist Thought and the Claims of Critical Theory* (London and New York, 1987), p. 188.

69. Scott, *Gender,* p. 43.

70. Gananath Obeyesekere, *Medusa's Hair: An Essay on Personal Symbols and Religious Experience* (Chicago, 1984), pp. 115–22.

71. Personal communication: DA-F-54-Chicago-W.

72. Personal communication: EA-F-59-Chicago-M.

73. Personal communication: BC-F-36-Joliet, Ill.-S.

74. Personal communication: BF-F-75-So. Chicago-W.

75. Personal communication: GG-F-55-Chicago-M.

76. Personal communications: BB-F-48-Chicago-S; HH-F-33-Chicago-M; CD-F-75-Milwaukee-M; CH-F-69-Chicago-W.

77. Personal communications: DG-F-76-Chicago-M; AH-F-58-Chicago-M; BE-F-66-Chicago-M.

78. Personal communications: CD-F-67-Chicago-M; EF-F-63-Chicago-W; *Journal,* April 1967, p. 4, OJB, Forest Park, Ga.

79. Personal communication: BG-F-63-Chicago-M. She writes, "Somehow I would much rather talk [to] him than say the Journal prayers."

80. Personal communications: BD-F-46-Chicago-M; AH-F-58-Chicago-M.

81. See, for example, *Voice,* January 1935, p. 17, Mrs. CGF, Chicago; ibid., May 1935, p. 16, Mrs. MHF, Chicago, and Mrs. MK, Chicago; ibid., March 1950, p. 6, AS, Wyoming, Ohio; ibid., April 1950, p. 5, LW, Malden, Mass.; ibid., March 1951, p. 29, DR, Santa Clara, Calif.; ibid., March 1958, Mrs. ERP, Lawrence, Mass.; *Journal,* August 1966, p. 4, Mrs. PS; ibid., April/May 1964, p. 4, Mrs. MS.

82. See Bodnar, *Workers World,* p. 173.

83. Personal communication: US-F-65+-Michigan-M. On the importance of women's networks see Ellen Ross, "Survival Networks: Women's Neighborhood Sharing in London Before World War I," *History Workshop* 15 (Spring 1983): 4–27; Mary P. Ryan, "The Power of Women's Networks: A Case Study of Female Moral Reform in Antebellum America," *Feminist Studies* 5, no. 1 (Spring 1979): 66–86; and Temma Kaplan, "Female Consciousness and Collective Action: The Case of Barcelona, 1910–1918," *Signs* 7 (1982): 545–66.

84. Personal correspondence: MF-F-60(?)-Yarmouth, England-S; *Voice,* April 1941, p. 18, Mrs. AG, Chicago; ibid., May 1953, p. 33, Mrs. PK, Louisville, Ky. "When I have a prob-

lem," a correspondent wrote in 1967, "I always say a prayer to Saint Jude and it seems I can face that problem with more courage." *Journal,* August 1967, Miss MP, no location cited.

85. On the consensus in the devotional press against women's working see Joseph McShane, S.J., "And They Lived Catholicly Ever After: A Study of Catholic Periodical Fiction between 1930 and 1950," unpublished paper; on the general social disapproval of this, see Chafe, *American Woman,* pp. 174–89.

86. *Voice,* July 1955, Mrs. MF, Cincinnati.

87. Personal communication: BC-F-36-Joliet, Ill.-S.

88. William Halsey, *The Survival of American Innocence* (Notre Dame, Ind., 1980).

89. Joseph P. Donovan, C.M., "Novenas and Devotional Tastes," *Homiletic and Pastoral Review* 43, no. 7 (April 1943): 643–44.

90. *Voice,* June 1949, p. 4, MC, Providence, R.I.

CHAPTER

23

Martin Luther King and the Secular Power of Religious Rhetoric

The most significant social reform movement of the twentieth century has been the Civil Rights movement. Although "secular" in its goals, the Civil Rights movement was very much a product of the African-American church tradition, and nowhere was this more clearly reflected than in the life of Reverend Martin Luther King, Jr. King's rhetoric, as the following essay by Hortense J. Spillers makes clear, was a preacher's rhetoric, and the summons to America to wake up to the sin of racism was a sermonic summons in the tradition of prophetic preaching from Augustine to Frederick Douglass. Thus, where many biographies of Reverend King focus on secular political issues, Spillers's analysis makes it clear that from the Montgomery bus boycott of 1955–1956 to his assassination in Memphis in 1968, King himself understood his mission in the prophetic Christian message of love, reconciliation, nonviolent protest, and, ultimately, redemption.

In what ways did King's values and style affirm and depart from the style of the African-American preachers described in Montgomery's essay earlier in this volume or from the style of Frederick Douglass's 1847 Syracuse, New York, speech? Listen to a recording of King's great "I Have a Dream" speech at the 1963 march on Washington and use Spillers's suggestions to dissect King's style, his weaving together of religious and secular themes, and his stress on redemption for America.

Additional Reading: On African-American preaching and social reform see Charles V. Hamilton, *The Black Preacher in America* (New York, 1972); Martin Luther King, Jr., *Stride Toward Freedom* (New York, 1958); *Strength to Love* (New York, 1963), and *The Trumpet of Conscience* (New York, 1967). On the rhetoric of African-American preaching see Gerald L. Davis, *I Got the Word in Me and I can Sing It, You Know: A Study of the Performed African-American Sermon* (Philadelphia, 1985). On African-American religion see Charles Long, *Significations: Experience and Images in Black American Religion* (Philadelphia, 1986); Cornell West, *Prophesy Deliverance!* (Philadelphia, 1982). Important primary source documents are reprinted in Milton C. Sernett, ed., *Afro-American Religious History: A Documentary Witness* (Durham, 1985). On African-American religious thought see James H. Cone, *For My People: Black Theology and the Black Church* (Maryknoll, 1984) and Peter J. Paris, *The Social Teaching of the Black Churches* (Philadelphia, 1985).

Hortense J. Spillers[1]

Martin Luther King and the Style of the Black Sermon

A description and evaluation of the political career of Dr. Martin Luther King, Jr., will, of necessity, include an account of the southern Baptist Church in its historic influence on the life and mind of black people in this country, especially the South. Without such understanding, the moral and political lessons of the King era will be missed. To my mind, the power of his delivery, the magnificence of his pulpit style, were accountable, in large measure, for his overwhelming popularity in the South and throughout much of the nation.

The ground-swell of his movement, then, was of a southern soil: highly religious and traditional in its use of a style and manner that are endemic to the black religious experience; this brings the emphasis where I want it—an exploration of King's pulpit style, poetic in texture and traditional in delivery.

The old-fashioned black preacher of the South, unlike King, rarely went to school to learn or adorn his trade. He imitated the preaching elders of his community in the selection of subject matter and content. For example, "The Eagle Stirs His Nest" is a favorite sermon of black ministers of the South. I have no clues to the age of the sermon nor where it first appeared, but I remember it from my childhood (at least twenty years ago) and would suggest that my minister heard it first from someone else. Though each minister brings to the sermon his own individuality, the material of the sermon is universal in its accessibility and appeal. The genius of sermons like "The Eagle" and "Dry Bones" lay in their technique of delivery. The minister weaves analogy and allegory into the sermon, comparing and juxtaposing contemporary problems in morality with and alongside ancient problems in morality. These build toward an emotional pitch and climax that are made possible by the minister's sense of timing and dynamics. The delivery of the message is best described by what the minister woes with his voice: intonation and pitch, dynamics and rhythm, movement and timing.

These features of speech are briefly, but saliently, described by Mike Thelwell, who considers them problems in paralinguistic techniques.[2] Thelwell differentiates between two languages that the African slave adopted, after being stripped of his tribal identity and indigenous language: 1) the language that he adopted for the white overseer and slave master (Thelwell calls this the "Sambo" dialect

From *Black Scholar* 3 (1971). Reprinted by permission of the author.

which often appears as parody in the works of southern white humorists) and 2) the real language (the essential, "unwigged" language) of the slave which was close to the poetry of the sermon and spiritual, "language produced by oppression, but one whose central impulse is survival and resistance."[3] Forced to adopt the language and religion of a foreign, imposed master, the slave minister found his particular historic moment under the conditions of a captured and historically-amnesiac person who would be free. The disparity between the reality and the dream molded the emotional pith of the sermon as it operated on minister and hearer.

Without the vocabulary of his white counterpart, the black minister had "to get over," so to speak, to communicate, with his power to act, to dramatize the sermon, since its ultimate effectiveness lay in his "tone of voice" rather than in his vocabulary and power of analysis. With the King James Bible as the woof of the sermon, the technique of delivery was the warp, weaving the moral lesson, spinning the emotional moment. The technique impresses me as an invariable of the black sermon, linking men as wide apart in age and temperament as the Rev. C. L. Franklin and Dr. King. That this process or technique has been passed down from generation of preachers to the next, places the black sermon in the oral tradition, distinguishing it from the historical tradition where the mentifacts and ideas are enclosed in and circumscribed by the written word.

Dr. King knew the oral tradition intimately, being himself a son of a preaching father. Though he was trained in the universities and academies, his sermons were infused and enlightened by the interpretation of the gospel message as he heard it while young and growing in the southern hill-soil of Georgia. That basic and shared experience fired the response of black people by the thousands who heard him. The audience may have understood the historical-political analyses, but to be sure, the heart will long remember and take joy in the emotional achievement of the Word as King delivered it.

The most effective observer of King's style is the human ear. The recordings of his sermons, widely accessible now, will demonstrate more effectively than the pen the "how" of the process. Many of the sermons and speeches in the King Collection[4] are handwritten drafts which were later printed. This makes it possible to compare and examine the texts. King always preached a sermon; even his political speeches in their poetic detail and structure were sermons. These may be called political sermons with King James replaced by current political idealogues, interspersed and peppered with Biblical allegory. The appeal, right along, was made to the emotions—one's love of inspiration, one's sense of triumph over disaster. The belief was that the inspired person, sharing a particular ethnic journey with others, will join hands with his fellows in the reaching of a common goal; for King, that goal was the full integration of black people into the American thing.

King, on his later political career, 1965–68, was apparently turning a corner—beginning to assess the national black struggle in terms of the globe. But the early King, the King of the Montgomery Bus Boycott and the voter registration campaigns of the South, was the basic and fundamental King who believed that the idiom of non-violence would not only work as a political tact, but also as a moral purgative, cleansing the death-rot of a racist mad-land. It was from the King of these years, 1954–64, that this analysis comes. I have concentrated on two of his early sermons and one of his addresses.

An explication of text is possible because King was a meticulous writer. Being an experienced preacher before he became a political leader, he knew what his audiences would like, but he did not leave the organization of his ideas to chance. The text was there as skeletal guide and outline, delineating carefully certain details of the moral and religious lesson, which to King, was one and the same. In this sense, he was part of the growing tradition of young, university-trained black preachers, who combine analysis with the manner and style of the elders. The combination is formidable, melding the traditions of the folk and the scholar. These processes, if not antagonistic to one another, are, at least, contrasting modes of expression. With the folk, the expression arises in spontaneity, springing from the emotions. Though the expression may be learned and transmitted, its impulse is emotional and its rhythms joyful, festive, and triumphant; with the scholar, the expression is cerebral, prejudged, so to speak, springing from the intellect. The intellectual statement informs and clarifies, whereas the emotional statement, which may inform and clarify as well, certainly inspires and invigorates.

A figure would simplify the distinction: the intellectual statement is like a scythe, cutting through weeds of chaos, making them a plain path, while the emotional statement is like a balm, flowing over troubled waters. It is the distinction that is made between rhetoric and poetics.[5] In the former, the speaker or writer is about the effective organization of material in a presentation of truth, appealing to the intellect. In the latter, the speaker or writer is about the presentation of ideas in an emotional and imaginative way. The emotional statement may represent the poetic mode and the rhetorical statement the intellectual mode. Both are orally rendered, both tend to persuade, in King's case, to politicize and educate in a certain way, but the difference lies in their mode of appeal and operation. Though these refer to elements in a vacuum and do not ultimately account for the chemistry and dynamics that operate between speaker and hearer, I think that they will be sufficient as operational terms. In King, the rhetorical style as he learned it in the academies met the poetic style of his fathers as he experienced it in the South. In his case, the poetry, basic and inviolable to his message, was that of the black sermon. His oratory carried the emotional stuff, while his analysis carried the moral message. In King, the two were complements.

A reading of the sermons reveals two important features: nominality[6] and metaphoricality. The prominent linguistic feature of the sermons is their nominality where a greater number of nouns, adjectives, and adjectival clauses abound than verbs and verb forms. Though verbal and nominal refer to written texts, I suggest that the reference works with King, since for him the text was hand-delivered first. Modification (adjectiveness) and nominality in King combine to create a picturesqueness and grandness of speeech that were his hallmark. This particular feature (adjectiveness and nouness) in all its variations is at the heart of King's metaphors—the dominant poetic quality of his message.[7] The moral lesson, the political idealogues, were informed by and structured in terms of the metaphor which usually presented a picture of contrasts or opposites. The argument, then, proceeded by way of the figure which always gave rise to a mental picture or image.

This clothing of the argument in figurative dress is one of the basic differences that I perceive between poetry and prose; the poet relies on images to carry the subject, stripping his line clean and bare of certain syntactical intrusions, i.e., furthermore, consequently, therefore, however, etc. There are fewer words per idea with the poet, whereas the prose writer relies on fewer pictures and images and more words and concepts. King, while working in the conceptual and ideological, knew that the Word came alive in a figure, and he was a man of the living Word with his sights fixed clearly on this earth.

On May 17, 1956, King preached at the Service of Prayer and Thanksgiving in the the Cathedral of St. John the Divine, New York City. The title of the sermon, "The Death of Evil Upon the Shore," gives a clue to the intent and form of the sermon. Right away, evil is given a persona, which becomes, in the context, a dramatic function. Evil represents the death of the spirit in the traditional scheme of religious thinking, but it connotes, as well, war and destruction. In King's sermon, evil specifically stands for political oppression in the name of the Egyptian pharoahs, who were eventually put to rout by Moses and the sons of Israel. By broad analogy and principle, the American scene is here transformed into a modern-day Egypt with its appropriate pharoahs who are holding in bondage and thrall some 30 million blacks. King perceived a basic division of people along racial and historic lines, representing conflicting destinies and motives, one oppressing, the other resisting. The sons of Israel would advance the good—the Word of God—whereas the Pharoahs would impede the good, becoming themselves the *dramatis personae* of evil.

The modern-day pharoahs, in their moral perfidy, would as oppressors hold back the light, while black men as the oppressed would advance the light by forcing a moral awareness upon the conscience of the pharoahs. King's implicit message is that oppression and resistance must run parallel and contiguous until they converge with resistance cancelling out oppression. Explicitly, his statement is: History records Israel's struggle with every Egypt. In other words, oppression and resistance are invariable rhythms in the historical process. He is saying emphatically that "Every Israel" must keep on keeping on until victory is theirs. King was a persistent symbolist, seeing the struggle of his own people in terms of Israel's liberation struggle against Egypt.

The evil that will die upon the shore is pictured as the "nagging tares disrupting the orderly growth of stately wheat." In the metaphor, an image-making term is substituted for a concept, and the writer-speaker relies on the associations of the words to carry the impact. The tare is the unwanted growth, the bother, the worry, the unfaithful. In the Day of Judgment, I am told that God himself will separate the tares (the unfaithful) from the wheat (the faithful). The terms of King's metaphor, then, present a contrast, with tares representing oppression and humiliation and wheat representing order and a Christian ethic. Tares, as the disrupting, inharmonious evil, are clothed in "the garments of calamitous wars which left battlefields painted with blood, filled nations with widows and orphans, sent men home physically handicapped and psychologically wrecked." The vision is one of destruction, made vivid by the phrase: "battlefields painted with blood," as though someone had indeed, taken the energy and time to paint the earth in blood. The image betokens the extent of calamity.

King defines the struggle between good and evil in terms of religious war: "All great religions have realized that in the upward climb of goodness, there is the down pull of evil." "Upward climb" and "downward pull" sum up the contrast and carry the picture of resistance and oppression, which is a recurring motif in King's sermons. Said another way:

> A mythical Satan, though the work of a conniving serpent, may gain the allegiance of man for a period, but ultimately he must give way to the magnetic, redemptive power of a humble servant on an uplifted cross. . . .

King's ear for rhythm was sure and unfailing. The cadence is strong and emphatic when he comes to: "magnetic redemptive power of a humble servant on an uplifted cross." The staccato, martial beating of "magnetic redemptive power," (all words capitalized and emphasized in their rhythmic thrust), gives way to the alternate beats of a "humble servant on an uplifted cross," where humble and uplifted are the stress words. He continues:

> Evil may so shape events that Caesar will occupy a palace and Christ a cross, but one day that same Christ will rise up and split history into A.D. and B.C., so that even the life of Caesar must be dated by his name. . . .

The triumph of evil, represented in the palatial wealth of Caesar, is only temporary, for the cross of sacrifice and moral redemption, the sign of Christ, will launch a new phase of moral and imaginative awareness of men. The picture of the rising Christ, splitting history into A.D. and B.C., is an exciting and vivid picture-idea, appealing to the hearer's sense of triumph—good dramatically overcoming evil. The advent of Christ so historically significant that the dating of time started anew.

In the poetry of the black sermon, "that same Christ" and "one day" are recurrences. In their nature, they are like refrains. "This same Jesus who walked beside the sea; this same Jesus, the man of Galilee . . . this same Jesus will save your soul" are three lines from a gospel favorite that is often sung during Easter Services in the Baptist Church. The song-writer takes his cue from the sermon where the preacher, in recounting the miracle and mystery of Christ, assures the hearer that Christ is a personal, subjective savior who is concerned about the daily welfare of each individual believer. A hypothetical construction may be this:

> This same man who sits high and looks low, who rounded the world in the middle of his hands; this same man who fed five thousand and still had food left over; this same man who raised the dead, who walked the waters and calmed the sea—this same man is looking out for you and me.

By repetition and amplification, the passage builds and spins out. In many cases, the preachers' own words are echoed and verified by his audience, thus making the Word more emphatic. For example, the passage above may be interspersed thusly:

> This same man (*same* man!) who sits high and looks low, who rounded the world in the middle of his hands (the *middle* of his hands!), this same man who fed five thousand and still had food left over, (Yessuh! Had some left). This same man who raised the dead, who walked the waters and calmed the sea, (Let's hold him up, church!) this *same* man is looking out for you and me.

The phenomenon is referred to as the "Amen Corner" where the believers support and sustain the preacher by repeating certain of his own words or their own exclamations. The phenomenon was never absent when King spoke. Readers may recall King's Montgomery speech, "We're On the Move," and the unidentified man who stood at his side. ("Montgomery to Memphis" documentary.) After picking up the tenor of King's rhythm the man began to repeat the key words: "Yessuh, we're on the move!" Soon thereafter, the audience had been transformed into a vast echo chamber with King giving out the mainline, i.e., "We can't be dissuaded now . . . and no wave of racism can stop us," and the audience saying with him: "We're on the move!" This process, spontaneous in its thrust, is highly technical and consistent; the speaker, with his innate sense of timing and rhythm, knows exactly which words will be prominent and what phrases an audience will respond to because he has seen the technique work for his elders time and again.

With King, the success of the technique was more attributable to his sense of euphony[8] and resonance than to gesture and movement. King often brought together words that ended in the same sound to create a kind of rhythm and cadence. In the Thanksgiving Sermon, he refers to the "humiliating oppression, the ungodly exploitation, the crushing domination" of the Egyptian pharaohs. The combining of words that have an equal number of syllables which rhyme (same vowel and consonant sounds) creates a rhythm. This is not strictly metrical, because the speaker does not intend to make verse and meters, but the effect, the texture, is certainly rhythmical, lending itself to memory. King often referred to southern legislators as oppressive forces with their "lips dripping in interposition and nullification." This is similar in its structure to the three phrases that speak of the pharaohs. This particular device has the effect of "setting the scene" before the hearer. The picture or image, then, is often marked by rhythm and tempo as well as contrast and opposition: "It was a frightful period in their history. It was a joyous daybreak that had come to end the long night of their captivity." The difference between night and day is the difference between oppression and liberation. In the metaphor, the concept is enlightened and clarified; identification of the problem or concept in terms of a visual image is a teaching device, for it makes the idea concrete and vivid. At the same time, the metaphor creates the poetic moment—the heightened, elevated language is most characteristic of Biblical language which certainly influenced King's style.

When King's imagination set to work on an old familiar story, the story itself was enlivened to the extent of becoming life and blood, experience and option with the hearer. On November 4, 1956, King preached before his own congregation at Dexter Avenue Baptist Church in Montgomery. He updated the message of Paul to the early churches around the Roman empire by creating "Paul's Letter to American Christians." This is a contrivance which summons the hearer's "poetic faith"—"the willing suspension of disbelief"—but the device works well, with King making explanations as he goes along: It is miraculous, he begins, that Paul should be writing 1900 years after his last letter appeared in the New Testament; "how this is possible is something of an enigma wrapped in mystery."

The Churchillian comment used here notes the "mystery" at the same time that it dismisses it. In other words, the hearer is ready now to accept the miracle of Paul's letter to Americans. The fact that Paul, the main epistleist of the early church, is "writing" this letter says something about the emergency King felt in his own message. He goes on: "May I hasten to say that if in presenting this letter the contents sound strangely Kingian instead of Paulinian, attribute it to my lack of complete objectivity rather than Paul's lack of clarity."

King was apparently fond of ringing, resounding statements; these are earmarks of his style: "Kingian" and "Paulinian" match in tone the phrases: "my lack of complete objectivity" and "Paul's lack of clarity." Part of the hearer's joy lies in his knowing that the preacher can play with words and make beautiful, pleasing combinations of sound out of them. Paul, speaking through King, goes on to say:

> I have heard so much about you; I wish I could visit . . . I have heard of the *fascinating* and *astounding* advances that you have made in the scientific realm. I have heard of your *dashing subways* and *flashing airplanes* . . . Through your scientific genius, you have been able to *dwarf distance* and *place time in chains*. You have been able to *carve highways* through the stratosphere . . . I have also heard of your *skyscraping buildings* with their *prodigious* towers sweeping skyward. . . . That is wonderful. . . . [Italics mine]

The words and passages that appear in italics are the stress words, to my mind. These were probably emphasized in the delivery and apparently selected for their pleasant sound. "Dashing subways and flashing airplanes" (all words of equal syllables, suggesting a trochaic rhythm) are onomatopoeic in their matching of the sound of the sense. "Carved highways through the stratosphere" brings the idea of civil engineering (earth-building) heavenward, preparing the hearer for "skyscraping buildings with their prodigious towers sweeping heavenward."

The imagery captures the marvel of America's technological genius which is further contrasted with her moral and spiritual failure. The nation that has been able to "dwarf distance and place time in chains," thus making the world a neighborhood, has not been able to make of that neighborhood a brotherhood:

> You have allowed the material means by which you live to outdistance the
> spiritual ends for which you live. You have allowed your mentality to outrun
> your morality . . . Your civilization to out-distance your culture . . .

By building up the contrasts, King introduces one of the recurring motifs of his
sermons—the passage of time and its meaning in the life of man. Though men
live on earth, in a state of generation, their ultimate allegiance must go to God:
"This means that although you live in the colony of time, your ultimate allegiance
is to the empire of eternity. You have a dual citizenry . . . You must never allow
the transitory evanescent demands of man-made institutions to take precedence
over the eternal demands of the almighty God . . ."

In King's last sermon, delivered in Memphis, April 1968, he said that he had been
to the mountaintop and viewed the Promised Land but probably would not go to
the Promised Land with his followers. He felt then that his life would not be a
long one, but the point, he said, was not the longevity of a man's years, but in the
quality of his life. Therefore, time for him was an instrument of the eternal will,
measuring and manifesting itself in the life of the ethical man. Even if denied the
opportunity to live the long life, King felt satisfied at that moment that his life had
been spent in the attempt to make the ethic of non-violence a reality.

His persisting concern was with the mess that men had made of materialism
and technology; the mess is betokened in the values and preferences of the society. In making the idea definite and vivid, King relied on objects close-at-hand:

> I am afraid that many among you are more concerned about making a living
> than making a life. You are prone to judge the success of your profession by the
> index of your salary and the size of the wheel-base on your automobile, rather
> than the quality of your service to humanity.

In the mad and violent rush for the acquisition of luxury-goods, decision makers
have often abused their power: "Oh, America, how often have you taken necessities from the masses to give luxuries to the classes. . . ." Though capitalism is exploitive in its practices, King did not feel that communism was an answer, and to
his mind communism was the opposite of Christianity, not capitalism. In King,
the communist analysis is general and incomplete: ". . . Communism is based
on an ethical relativism and a metaphysical materialism that no Christian can accept." The structure of the phrases: "ethical relativism" and "a metaphysical materialism" is similar to "necessities from the masses" and "luxuries to the classes."
There is a feeling of finality in the phrasing; cryptic and summary-like, these are
similar to a slogan or catch-word, and for that reason can be misleading.

A structure very similar to the foregoing quotations is used again and again
in this sermon where King comes to question not only the abuses of capitalism
and secular authority, but also those of clerical authority: "A divided Protestantism and an infallible Roman Catholicism . . . a segregator and a segregated,
disrupting the "I thou" making it an "I-it." In this instance, the key words are the
modifiers, "divided" and "infallible," and the key concept that of disruption and

division. In Buber's philosophy, one person's preponderance over another destroys the human relationship between the two, making it one of a master to an object or thing.

In King's estimation, segregated institutions of the South, of which the Church was the most pre-eminent example, summed up the ultimate badness of America's institutional immorality: "The underlying philosophy of Christianity is diametrically opposed to the underlying philosophy of segregation, and all the dialectics of the logician cannot make them lie down together." Just as the tares and wheat do not belong together, nor the sheep lie down with the lion, segregation and Christianity are also opposed. Dichotomies in King were not only at the heart of his metaphors, but also at the core of his reality—one was either in the camp of the ethical or among the troops of the unenlightened, and his figures ranged according to the variation on that particular theme.

King's "finest hour," perhaps, in terms of his political and oratorical achievement came in the summer of 1963 when on August 28, he delivered the now-famous "I Have a Dream" sermon in the shadows of the Lincoln Memorial. The choice of that particular sight was fraught with historic symbolism, for after one hundred years of "no win," the black man of America returned in person and spirit to the original place of the issuance of the Emancipation Proclamation to write it again in his own terms. Historians will long argue the value of "The March on Washington," which Malcolm X referred to in one of his speeches as "The Farce on Washington." To argue cause and effect in the chain of human events is the province and mandate of the historian, and King's cause, like others, will be examined in the beam-eye of history. It is important that the historical judgment, however, be made in light of the cast of things at the time—where men's heads were—where they perceived they would go at that moment. Many blacks across the country then felt that a remarkable "stride toward freedom" had been made within the decade. For them, King, on that sweltering August day wore a crown and his sermon was that of a great coronation that many thousands had come to in order to wash their robes in the sweet springs of renewal.

An understanding of the scene is important to an understanding of the sermon itself. The black preacher has always been, historically, a beacon-spirit to his people; he was the one who was most in touch with God, assuring his listeners that even though the business of life was a cross to bear, God himself was waiting in the wings of history to secure the safe passage of those who loved Him and did His will. This simplistic and uncomplicated faith in an ultimate and final good stirred the spirit and the protest of black people long before and after the Emancipation. It was the faith that motivated and inspired the lives of agrarian blacks of the South who had known the plow before and after the whip. When their sons fanned out through the American North and Midwest, that faith was tempered and deflected by the hard circumstances of urban reality; but even here there were the "storefronts" which in strange-name places like Harlem and the So'Side carried still, the ritual and poetry of home. "The Dream Deferred," the cruel paradox of a "Native Son," who was an alien son after all, the hoax of the "Promised

Land" all stung and confused the imagination of the urban dweller, who had fled the southern backfields looking for glory.

The post-emancipation "Black Codes" of the southern legislators had locked the southern black man in an apartheid so consistently vicious that it was perhaps, unrivalled anywhere on earth, and the Church, itself segregated, was silent in the face of the K.K.K. The North had not legislated against blacks, but it had circumscribed them by custom and practice which made it possible for them to ride in the *front* of the bus to the program. The northern and southern experience had been different for the black man only in degree, not in kind which North and South was co-terminous, co-existent and co-operative. In neither place was it intended that the black man be a governor of self and kind. The Garvey Movement was little known in the South, having had brief and partial success in the North and Midwest. The Bolshevik Revolution and its early impact on that thinking of black people in America had not touched the South either and apparently affected an elite-intelligentsia of the North. Here, briefly, was the black man's legacy in 1963; the feeling was: Now or Never, and the sectors of the nation each had their solution. King apparently spoke for the South and the black man's "deferred dream" of civil and human rights.

His sermon took place at a time when sense of impending triumph was at its peak, perhaps unmatched by anything in the recent past with the probable exception of the Reconstruction Era and its promises of equality and universal manhood suffrage. The sense of racial solidarity was strong and the feeling of unity pervasive. It seemed, indeed, that the long night of captivity was surely breaking now into the joyful daybreak of liberation. King, as minister and leader was the apotheosis, the living embodiment of that promise. His sermon was the emotional catharsis which, in a sense, washed away the tears from the tired and fevered spirit of his followers.

The language of the opening paragraph of the sermon is reminiscent of Lincolnian language; in his address at the battleground of Gettysburg, Lincoln had said: "Fourscore and seven years ago, our fathers brought forth upon this continent, a new nation, conceived in liberty and dedicated to the proposition that all men are created equal. . . ." By reminding the nation of its political legacy, King re-echoed Lincoln: "Five score years ago a great American, in whose symbolic shadow we stand, signed the Emancipation Proclamation." Briefly and straightaway King was into the heart of things—no long prelude, no long introduction. This is very close in spirit to the "in medias res" (into the heart of things) beginning of the ballad. This feeling of immediacy invests the entire sermon. "This momentous decree came as a great beacon light of hope to millions of Negro slaves who had been seared in the flames of withering injustice. It came as a joyous daybreak to end the long night of captivity . . ." Darkness and light, daybreak and night, are seminal in King, capturing in a picturesque manner the idea of dichotomy.

Many of the motifs and images of King's earlier sermons appear in "I Have a Dream." For example, in "A Knock at Midnight," which appears in the small volume of sermons entitled "Shattered Dreams," King talks about midnight at a time of day: a state of the individual psyche and the status of institutional morality. It was midnight all over America, and the danger zone was everywhere. The night of captivity was at its most frightful point at midnight. In "Shattered Dreams," the sermon that gives its title to the volume, King talks of how men must behave when their dreams have been shattered and their hopes blasted, when they, like the Apostle Paul, have their vision of going to Spain and Rome in triumph transformed into the reality of a narrow jail cell. The destructibility of the dream is constant, but one must meet it with a fiery hope just as constant, which says after all: "I still have a dream."

Even after the promise of the Emancipation, the black man's dream has still been put off time and time again:

> One hundred years later, the life of the Negro is still sadly crippled by the manacles of segregation and the chains of discrimination. One hundred years later, the Negro lives on a lonely island of poverty in the midst of a vast ocean of material prosperity. One hundred years later, the Negro is still languished in the corners of American society and finds himself an exile in his own land. . . .

The repetition of "one hundred years," each time amplifying the argument, heightens the feeling; the images are those of stasis, paralysis, and captivity; manacles and chains, lonely island of poverty, languishing exile all image forth the plight of the black man in America.

The marching to Washington is the same as the cashing of a check against America's justice bank. All the terms of the metaphor refer to banking and money, highlighting the disparity between the nation's wealth and the black man's poverty:

> When the architects of our republic wrote the magnificent words of the Constitution and the Declaration of Independence, they were signing a promissory note to which every American was to fall heir. This note was a promise that all men would be guaranteed their inalienable rights . . . It is obvious today that America has defaulted on this promissory note insofar as her citizens of color are concerned. Instead of honoring this sacred obligation, America has given the Negro people a bad check, a check which has come back marked "insufficient funds." But we refuse to believe that the Bank of Justice is bankrupt. . . .

The idea of justice being a bank against which funds are drawn is a very successful and clever idea, reminiscent of other preachers' talk about "heaven's savings bank," where the earthbound Christian stores up his treasures. King's idea speaks of the quantity of the default in materialistic terms:

> We refuse to believe that there are insufficient funds in the great vault of opportunity of this nation. So we have come to cash this check—a check that will give us upon demand the riches of freedom and the security of justice . . .

The urgency of the demand is capitalized:

> Now is the time to make real the promises of democracy. Now is the time to rise from the dark and desolate valley of segregation to the sunlit path of racial justice. Now is the time to open the doors of opportunity to all of God's children. Now is the time to lift our nation from the quicksands of racial injustice to the solid rock of brotherhood . . .

The saint's cry to the Lord to plant his feet on "higher ground," Owen Dodson's black mother praying that one day she with her sons will be able to strike her feet on freedom's "solid rock," are ancient themes in the Baptist Church; there are associations that may be made with King images. Implicit in the imagery is the idea of journey—long, trying and apparently endless. But in complement to that idea is one of perseverance and courage: Like the old woman who tells her story in the poem, "My Life Ain't Been No Crystal Stair," the young person is emboldened to keep on keeping on because the way is steep for all who would walk the straight and narrow path of moral and ethical commitment. In terms of the Baptist Church, the "straight and narrow" is usually a visual reference to the Christian life of obedience, patience and humility. In King, the base of the vision is broadened, though still maintaining an overlay of religiosity.

Just as the Christian maintains his allegiance to the Kingdom of God, the black man must also maintain his allegiance to the idea of passive resistance to racial injustice: "This sweltering summer of the Negro's legitimate discontent will not pass until there is an invigorating autumn of freedom and equality. . . ." King makes an interesting switch here in the symbolic meaning of the seasons. Usually summer is a fair time. In Shakespeare, winter, not summer, is the time of discontent and fall and winter represent death. In Shakespeare's *Richard III*, Gloucester says in opening soliloquy: "Now is the winter of our discontent / Made glorious summer by this sun of York. . . ."[9] King no doubt drew his structure from the Shakespearean mold, though the valence or weight of the images is shifted. Elsewhere in King, autumn is associated with the "Alpine November of the soul." Though autumn is harvest-time, its perennial association is not usually one of invigoration and renewal, but in this context autumn presents an interesting contrast to the terrible and paralyzing heat of summer.

King continues: "The whirlwinds of revolt will continue to shake the foundations of our nation until the bright day of justice emerges. . . ." The thrust of King's message was especially significant at this time since the nation was only two summers away from the Watts Rebellion. King read the winds and America could choose to make the check good by securing the full citizenship rights of all its citizens or not. If not, then Watts would say, in effect, that there would be no justice banks for anyone. Many of King's young followers were getting tired of trying to force America into the dawn of moral consciousness by singing and praying to her shrines, memorials and billy clubs. They further believed that the March would have assumed quite another character had the force of the original "steam roller" that Malcolm X speaks of been allowed to roll the banks of the placid Potomac. If there were clouds of doubt hanging over the Civil Rights Movement that day, that hour, those were they, and King implied as much: In protesting, the Negro must not allow his "thirst for freedom" have him "drink from the cup of bitterness and hatred . . . again and again we must rise the the majestic heights of meeting physical force with soul force. . . ."

King did not advocate the condemnation of the white race but the condemnation of its deeds; he felt that the distinction was real and important since many white individuals had grasped the reality that their destiny was the black man's and his freedom mightily bound to their own:

> We cannot walk alone . . . We cannot turn back . . . We cannot be satisfied as long as the Negro is the victim of unspeakable horrors of police brutality. We can never be satisfied as long as our bodies, heavy with the fatigue of travel, cannot gain lodging in the motels of the highways and the hotels of the cities. We cannot be satisfied as long as a Negro in Mississippi cannot vote and a Negro in New York believes that he has nothing for which to vote. We cannot be satisfied as long as the Negro's basic mobility is from a smaller ghetto to a larger one. No, no we are not satisfied, and we will not be satisfied until *justice rolls down like water and righteousness like a mighty stream.* . . . [Italics mine]

The italicized passage comes from the Prophet, Amos. It runs throughout King's philosophy and sermons, vividly depicting the pregnancy and fullness of justice and righteousness unimpeded. The figure portrays the opening of the floodgates; when applied to the concepts of justice and righteousness, the feeling is one of overwhelming power. The sentiment of the passage carries the idea of racial justice and the mandate for it both North and South. It comes to the conclusion that blacks throughout the country are reduced to a single, minimal plane because of their color, and the upshot of color prejudice manifests itself in different ways—in many places of the South, blacks have been robbed of suffrage—in the North, their voting rights turned no real political gain and capital. It is significant that King was beginning to understand the intricate involvement of color and class in the national arena. Blacks being relegated to a "lonely island of poverty" in a sea of opulence was no mere accident.

King recognized that the manhood struggle of his people, though manifesting itself differently in the different parts, demanded the energies of all the people. There was nothing especially romantic about the fight, though its language as he delivered it was intended to be a balm: "I am not unmindful that some of you have come here out of great trials and tribulations." The Scriptures speak of the great multitudes, coming up from every nation. Mahalia Jackson, great songster of gospels, sings a song familiar to the ear and spirit: "These are they from every nation on their way to the great coronation, coming up through great tribulations, on their way to the crown in glory." Behind this notion is a psalm of thanksgiving: "My soul looks back in wonder at how we made it over." King quoted from biographers, historians, and poets, but more often than not, the spirituals fired his vision.

Headlines became in King's mouth events of epic proportion: "Some of you have come fresh from narrow jail cells. Some of you have come from areas where your quest for freedom left you battered by the storms of persecution and staggered by the winds of police brutality. . . ." The language matched the importance and dignity of the subject. It was like the red-light of his message:

> You have been the veterans of creative suffering . . . Go back to Mississippi, go back to Alabama, go back to South Carolina, go back to Georgia, go back to Louisiana, go back to the slums and ghettoes of our northern cities, knowing that somehow this situation can and will be changed . . .

A charge to keep the multitudes had, a creed and God to glorify. Here King is ardent, passionate, and burning in his desire that others see as he had seen, live as he had lived, and accept the charge of Christ to love and keep on working: "Let us not wallow in the valley of despair." Psalmist David's "valley of the shadow of death," John Bunyan's "slough of despond" are images of the Christian allegory of fall and experience. In King, the valley is also the test and trail. The captivated moved from the valley to the mountaintop, from the low palces to the "rock that is higher than I." In order to lead the captivated, the leader of the captivated must move from the mountaintop (the vision) into the low and crooked places (the pit of experience). The allegory of the Christian journey, the model and vision of the suffering Christ were constants in King's terminology and concepts. He understood and interpreted the moral struggle exactly in its terms and images.

The last part of Kings's August sermon vividly summed up what the non-violent struggle had been about during the decade. I quote it to demonstrate its imaginative use of metaphors, its repetitive devices, and the way that it builds toward an emotional climax:

> I have a dream that one day this nation will rise up and live out the true meaning of its creed: 'We hold these truths to be self evident. . . .' I have a dream that one day on the red hills of Georgia the sons of former slaves and the sons of former slave-owners will be able to sit down together at the table of brotherhood. I have a dream that even the state of Mississippi, a desert state sweltering with the heat of injustice and oppression, will be transformed into an oasis of freedom and justice. I have a dream today that my four children will one day live in a nation where they will not be judged by the color of their skin but by the content of their character. I have a dream today . . . that one day every valley shall be exalted, every hill and mountain shall be made low, the rough places will be made plains, and the crooked places will be made straight, and the glory of the Lord shall be revealed, and all flesh shall see it together. . . .

The passage moves in contrasts, a kaleidoscope of lightness and darkness, betokening the disparity between the two by placing them side by side.

> This is the faith with which I return to the South. With this faith we will be able to hew out of the mountains of despair a stone of hope. With this faith we will be able to transform the jangling discords of our nation into a beautiful symphony of brotherhood. With this faith, we will be able to work together, to pray

together, to struggle together, to go to jail together, to stand up for freedom together, knowing that we will be free one day. . . .

The thronging multitudes were with him as he went on up a little higher:

. . . So let freedom ring from the prodigious hilltops of New Hampshire, let freedom ring. Let freedom ring from the mighty mountains of New York. Let freedom ring from the heightening Alleghenies of Pennsylvania; let freedom ring from the sonw-capped Rockies of Colorado! Let freedom ring from the curvaceous peaks of Colorado! Let freedom ring! But not only that: Let freedom ring from Stone Mountain of Georgia. Let freedom ring from Lookout Mountain of Tennessee! Let freedom ring from every hill and mole-hill of Mississippi. From every mountainside, let freedom ring . . .

And when freedom is ringing from everywhere and within the earshot of every man, the entire brotherhood of man, united under the eternal fatherhood of God can in a gesture of Thanksgiving, join hands and shout it out: "Free at last! Free at last! Thank God almighty, we are free at last!" The cycle of the imagery is brought full circle, having begun in reference to the Emancipation Proclamation and ending in what was probably the former slave's psalm of emanicipation, "Free at last!"

King had moved cryptically and effectively from one phase of the sermon to the next, with the last turned into a powerful, evocative, and dramatic poem. By using a repetitive device, "let freedom ring" which unites the whole in resounding song, King heightens and sustains the passage. The audience echoed and kept pace, like in Montgomery when King asked: "How long?" the audience returned with : "Not long!" The crowd returned to him here, like the southern congregations of old, as a powerful sea-wind, resounding and chanting the words of triumph and overcoming. Mrs. King observes that in those final moments of the sermon, King stopped reading from the text, being lifted and carried himself in the overflow of powerful feeling.[10] The technique requires a co-operative, concerted effort in order to be successful.

Often when audiences are slow responding to the message, the preacher will chide: "You don't have to witness! or "I know I'm right about it!" This usually brought about the desired result. The technique was the instrument and generator of the emotional moment, and though the preacher was in charge of the technique, he was not outside or above it. His own word operated upon him as he brought the message to his followers. In that sense, he was one with his followers in a quickened response to the marvel and mystery of God through the Word.

One of the interesting typographical features of the "let freedom ring" passage is its being set out in verse form. This was perhaps a cue to King about the cadence to be adopted for those particular lines. Prodigious, mighty, heightening, snowcapped, and curvaceous are stress words in the passage, conveying the notions of majesty and remoteness. Stone Mountain, Lookout Mountain, hill and mole-hill of Mississippi are symbolic of the South, and in King's view at the time the most recalcitrant, stubborn places in the nation, for they summed up the atrociously immoral condition of institutional life in the deep South. The refrain as King delivered it did not conform exactly to the written document. For example, the phrase, "let freedom ring" often framed a passage, appearing at the beginning and at the end where it sometimes began another passage simultaneously: "Let freedom ring from the mighty mountains of New York, let freedom ring . . . from the heightening Alleghenies of Pennsylvania, let freedom ring from the snow-capped Rockies of Colorado. . . ." This structuring gives the passage the feeling of continuity and unity, where one phrase is not distinct from the others except for its images and colors. In that manner, the protest of blacks was a continuum and a continuity.

It seems only natural that when freedom is ringing from all the high places of the nation, men will sing: "Free at Last!" It is significant that King ended many of his sermons with quotations from gospels and spirituals; in his mouth, the sentiments came alive, perhaps more so than they'd been in some time. It was his way of summing up, for in the words of the spirituals, intellectual and peasant kinds would not only understand, but also feel together. The impulse of pity, the sense of joy, were endemic to King's message just as they had always been to the message of the black sermon, whose poetry was a poetry of triumph and overcoming.

NOTES

1. Hortense J. Spillers is a member of the Department of English at Cornell University.

2. Mike Thelwell, "Back With the Wind: Mr. Styron and the Reverend Turner," *William Styron's Nat Turner: Ten Black Writers Respond*, Boston: 1968, p. 80. The phenomenon of paralanguage was given the name by Henry Lee Smith and George L. Traeger; the problem of paralanguage is the problem of phonetic transcriptions: silence, pitch, stress, accent, terminal, and juncture. Morton W. Bloomfield and Leonard Newmark, *A Linguistic Introduction to the History of English*, New York: 1965, pp. 82–83.

3. *Ibid.*

4. The King Collection of correspondence, sermons, addresses and business transactions is presently available at the Mugar Library, Boston University; grateful acknowledgment is due Dr. Gottlieb of the Library's Special Collections for permitting me access to the papers.

5. A short description of the origin and history of rhetoric, as a classical device of argument, is given in the Thrall and Hibbard edition: *A Handbook to Literature*, New York: 1963, p. 415. The distinction that is made between rhetoric and poetics conforms here to the old Aristotelian concept. Poetics also refer to the criticism of poetic practice: " A system or body of theory concerning the nature of poetry. The principles and rules of poetic composition. . . . *Ibid.*, p. 361.

6. This concept is borrowed from Rulon Wells, who makes an interesting description and evaluation of the verbal vs. nominal style: ed. J. V. Cunningham, *The Problem of Style*, New York: 1966, pp. 253–259.

7. A metaphor is a figure of speech that expresses an idea or concept in terms of an image; the metaphor is an implied comparison between one or more things. One of the items in the analogy takes on the qualities of another; for example, the concept of old age may be figuratively expressed as the coming of winter, where the frost or snow or winter bespeaks the grey hair of the old man. In Thrall and Hibbard, an interesting discussion of metaphor is given by way of I. A. Richards' definition. He suggests that there is a tenor of the figure

which is the idea being expressed or the subject of the comparison; the vehicle is the image by which the idea is conveyed. Thrall and Hibbard, pp. 281–282.

8. Euphony and resonance refer to pleasant sound, the pleasing combination of vowels and consonants.

9. G. B. Harrison, ed. "The Tragedy of King Richard the Third." *Shakespeare: The Complete Works,* New York: 1948, I, i, 1.1, p. 226.

10. Coretta Scott King, *My Life With Martin Luther King, Jr.,* New York: 1969, p. 239.

CHAPTER
24

Debate and Documents: Religion, Society, and Politics in Modern Times

We conclude our Reader with three documents from modern America. Each represents a different vein of activism by religious leaders in the 1960s, 1970s, and 1980s.

The essay by Reverend Joseph J. Johnson, Presiding Bishop of the Christian Methodist Episcopal Church in Shreveport, Louisiana (a small African-American denomination when he published this essay in 1970), exemplifies the turn to "liberation theology" by African-American ministers in the 1960s and 1970s. The essay is all the more interesting because Johnson is at pains to bring the full array of theological exegesis to bear on his argument, ranging from work by Rudolph Bultmann and Emil Brunner to the great nineteenth-century Danish theologian, Sören Kierkegaard. Yet Johnson also forcefully criticizes "white theologians" for ignoring the black religious experience. In doing so, and by concentrating on the "comfortable," Johnson believes that too many preachers and theologians missed the essence of Christ's mission—to liberate men and women from "their most distressing problems," which the African-American experience in America exemplified in abundance. As Johnson writes, "The church building must be a point of departure, a departure into the world, into the dirty here and now."

The statement by the U.S. Catholic bishops on religion and economic policy represents the high point of liberal social activism within the twentieth-century U.S. Catholic Church. Like Johnson's essay, the statement is careful to place its principles about the morality of economic life in the context of Catholic teaching generally, including "traditional" teaching about family, morality, and the sanctity of society. The statement came at a unique time in the history of the American bishops, who exhibited more conservative viewpoints in previous decades and who returned to them as Pope John Paul XXIII appointed more conservative bishops in the next decade.

Finally, the excerpt from Jerry Falwell's *Listen America!* captures the emergence of conservative Protestant evangelical activism in the aftermath of liberal activism in the 1960s. Falwell was the leader of the "Moral Majority" movement of the 1970s and 1980s, a movement that exerted its principal political influence within the Republican Party and that helped elect Ronald Reagan President in 1980 and 1984 and George Bush in 1988 (a decline in evangelical support led to Bush's defeat by Bill Clinton in 1992). In *Listen America!* Falwell offers an intriguing rationale for political activity by religious conservatives. Like the essays by Johnson and the U.S. Catholic bishops, Falwell lodges that rationale within a broader understanding of religion's purposes, but one that offers a far different vision of religion, politics, and America.

What assumptions do these religious leaders share about relations between religion, society, and politics? What role do they believe government should play, if any, amidst public conflicts over religious, moral, and secular values? Using the analytical and methodological tools you have learned from this Reader, construct an essay highlighting one, or more than one, in the form of a debate.

Additional Reading: Hans A. Baer and Merrill Singer, *African-American Religion in the Twentieth Century: Varieties of Protest and Accommodation* (Knoxville, 1992), Randall Burkett, *Black Apostles: Afro-American Clergy Confront the Twentieth Century,* edited by Richard Newman (Boston, 1978), and James H. Cone and Gayraud S. Wilmore (eds.), *Black Theology: A Documentary History* (Maryknoll, 1993) describe varieties of African-American religious activism. Patrick Allitt, *Catholic Intellectuals and Conservative Politics in America, 1950–1985* (Ithaca, 1994), John T. McGreevy, *Parish Boundaries: The Catholic Encounter with Race in the Twentieth-Century Urban North* (Chicago, 1996), Mel Piehl, *Breaking Bread: The Catholic Worker and the Origin of Catholic Radicalism in America* (Philadelphia, 1982), and Mary Jo Weaver, "Feminists and Patriarchs in the Catholic Church: Orthodoxy and Its Discontents," *South Atlantic Quarterly,* 93 (1994): 675–692, describe the wide range of twentieth-century Catholic activism in America. Michael Barkun, *Religion and the Racist Right: The Origins of the Christian Identity Movement* (Chapel Hill, 1994), two books by Steve Bruce, *Pray TV: Televangelism in America* (New York, 1990) and *The Rise and Fall of the New Christian Right: Conservative Protestant Politics in America, 1978–1988* (Oxford, 1988), and Alan Peshkin, *God's Choice: The Total World of a Fundamentalist Christian School* (Chicago, 1986) describe conservative Christian activism in the late twentieth century.

Joseph A. Johnson, Jr. Jesus: The Liberator

Paul, in I Cor. 1: 18–24, speaks about the doctrine of the cross. To some, this doctrine is sheer folly; to others, it is the power of God. Some thought the doctrine of the cross was weakness, but to the believers it is a revelation of the power of God,

From *Andover Newton Quarterly Review* 10 (1970), 85–96. Reprinted with permission of The Pilgrim Press, Cleveland, Ohio.

the wisdom of God and the love of God. Jesus Christ is the subject of the gospel. Paul writes:

> This doctrine of the cross is sheer folly to those on their way to ruin, but to us who are on the way to salvation it is the power of God. Scripture says, 'I will destroy the wisdom of the wise, and bring to nothing the cleverness of the clever.' Where is your wise man now, your man of learning, or your subtle debater—limited, all of them, to this passing age? God has made the wisdom of this world look foolish. As God in his wisdom ordained, the world failed to find him by its wisdom, and he chose to save those who have faith by the folly of the Gospel. Jews call for miracles, Greeks look for wisdom; but we proclaim Christ—yes, Christ nailed to the cross; and though this is a stumbling-block to Jews and folly to Greeks, yet to those who have heard his call, Jews and Greeks alike, he is the power of God and the wisdom of God.
>
> I Cor. 1: 18–24 N.E.B.

Jesus, the Liberator, is the power of God, the wisdom of God and the love of God. Paul knew first hand of the operation of these qualities, wisdom, power and love. He could never quite understand this new wisdom, this new power and this new love which he had experienced in Jesus, the Liberator. It was a queer kind of wisdom and love that had chosen him, one who had been a persecutor of the Church and now summoned to be a messenger of the crucified-risen Lord. He could never comprehend this kind of love that had permitted Jesus, God's only son, to die on the cross for the salvation of men. Paul is astonished and amazed at this new revelation of love:

> While we were yet helpless, at the right time Christ died for the ungodly. Why, one will hardly die for a righteous man—though perhaps for a good man one will dare even to die. But God shows his love for us in that while we were yet sinners Christ died for us.   Romans 5: 6–8

Paul's new life had been determined by this encounter with Jesus, the Liberator. This new life which was God given was the life of grace and he shouts "By the grace of God, I am what I am." The experience of this wisdom, power and love, Paul defines as "the power of God unto salvation." It was a new kind of power, a power that had granted him freedom to life, righteousness, peace and joy, and also freedom from sin, from the law and from death. The liberating power of Jesus had emancipated him and set him free. He exhorts his fellow Christians: "For freedom Christ has set us free; stand fast therefore, and do not submit again to a yoke of slavery." Galatians 5: 1

Jesus, the Liberator, had given to Paul not only freedom but also a new self-understanding. This new self-understanding, according to Bultmann, is bestowed with faith and it is freedom through which the believer gains life and thereby his own self.[1] Paul discovered that he who belongs to Jesus, the Liberator, and thus to God has become master of everything. He declares to the Christians at Corinth that this grace-freedom event which they had experienced in Jesus, the Liberator, placed the whole world at their disposal:

So let no one boast of men. For all things are yours, whether Paul or Apollos or Cephas or the world or life or death or the present or the future, all are yours; and you are Christ's; and Christ is God's.   I Cor. 3: 21–23.

Jesus is the Liberator. He is the revelation of the wisdom, the power and the love of God. This was the message which the early Christian preachers were commissioned to proclaim. This message was called the Kerygma. We preach Christ, Paul shouts. At the heart of the Kerygma lies this fundamental Christological affirmation: Jesus is the Liberator! Jesus is the Emancipator!

Nineteen hundred years have passed since these stirring words were written by Paul and various interpretations of Jesus the Liberator have been presented. These interpretations range all the way from Jesus as the Son of God, of Paul, the writers of the Synoptic Gospels, John and Hebrews to the Jesus of Barth, Brunner, Bonhoeffer, Tillich and S. Kierkegaard.

The tragedy of the interpretations of Jesus by the white American theologians during the last three hundred years is that Jesus has been too often identified with the oppressive structures and forces of the prevailing society. His teachings have been used to justify wars, exploitation of the poor and oppressed peoples of the world. In His name the most vicious form of racism has been condoned and advocated. In a more tragic sense this Jesus of the white church establishment has been white, straight haired, blue eyed, Anglo-Saxon, that is, presented in the image of the oppressor. This "whiteness" has prevailed to the extent that the black, brown, or red peoples of the world, who had accepted Jesus as Lord and Savior, were denied full Christian fellowship in His church and were not accepted as brothers for whom Jesus died.

I am aware of the fact that this lecture is being delivered at one of the oldest Theological Schools in this country. I have been asked to address myself to the theme, "The Christian Faith in a Revolutionary Age" and to indicate the techniques by which this faith may be communicated.

You should expect that we would first critically evaluate the existing understanding of the Christian faith as interpreted and presented by white theologians and as a Black American reveal to you the thinking concerning this interpretation of the Christian faith in the black community. We begin with the premise that white Theology is severely limited in its interpretation of the Christian faith in so far as the non-white peoples of the world are concerned. This limitation is one of the causes for the quest for a Black Messiah.

THE LIMITATIONS OF WHITE THEOLOGY

To be sure, during the past fifteen years we have entered, in so far as the black community is concerned, into one of the most exciting periods in the life of the black people of this country. For more than one hundred years black students have studied in predominantly white seminaries and have been served a theological diet, created, mixed and dosed out by white theological technicians. The black seminarians took both the theological milk and meat and even when they had consumed these, their souls were still empty. Those of us who went through the white seminaries did not understand why then. We had passed the courses in the four major fields of studies; we knew our Barth, Brunner and Niebuhr. We had entered deeply into a serious study of Bonhoeffer and Tillich, but we discovered that these white theologians had described the substance and had elucidated a contemporary faith for the white man. These white scholars knew nothing about the black experience, and to many of them this black experience was illegitimate and unauthentic.

The black man's religious style was considered sub-human by many of the white theological seminaries of this Nation and the emotional nature of his religious experience was termed primitive. For the black seminary student to become a great preacher really meant that he had to *whitenize* himself. He had to suppress his naturalness and re-make himself in the image of a Sockman, Fosdick or Buttrick. You see, insofar as the white seminaries were concerned there were no great black preachers, and if a black preacher was fortunate to be called great by the white community, it meant that he was merely a pale reflection of the white ideal.

The young black seminary student today has been introduced into a whole new experience—one fashioned by the late Martin Luther King, Jr. but clarified and profoundly interpreted by Frantz Fannon, Malcolm X, Stokely Carmichael and Ron Karenga. The young black seminary student today has been tried by every conceivable ordeal that sadistic racial minds can devise; from the fire hoses to vicious dogs, from tear gas to electric animal prods. They have matched wits with the white racist of the power structure and are helping to pull down the system of segregation and discrimination. They have no objection to the combination of such words "black and power," "black and theology," "black and church," "black and Christ," "black and God." They believe Du Bois who wrote, "This assumption that of all the hues of God, whiteness is inherently and obviously better than brownness or tan leads to curious acts. . . ." They are not shocked nor are they discouraged if the term "black power" seems to offend or frighten white or black Americans. To these young blacks, "black power" means consciousness and solidarity. It means the amassing by black people of the economic, political, and judicial control necessary to define their own goals and share in the decisions that determine their faith. Fannon, Malcolm X, Carmichael and Karenga forced the black seminary students to ask these questions: What do these white American and European theologians of a white racist dominated religious establishment know about the soul of black folks? What do Barth, Brunner and Tillich know about the realities of the black ghettos or the fate of black sharecroppers' families whose souls are crushed by the powerful forces of a society that considers everything black as evil? Could these white theologians see the image of the crucified Jesus in the mutilated face of a rat-bitten child, or a drug addict, bleeding to death in a stinking alley?

We have learned that the interpretation of Christian Theology and of Jesus expounded by white American theologians is severely limited. This is due to the simple reason that these white scholars have never been lowered into the murky depth of the black experience of reality. They never conceived the black Jesus walking the dark streets of the ghettos of the north and the sharecropper's farm in the deep south without a job, busted, and emasculated. These white theologians could never hear the voice of Jesus speaking in the dialect of blacks from the southern farms, or in the idiom of the blacks of the ghetto. This severe limitation of the white theologians' inability to articulate the full meaning of the Christian faith has given rise to the development of Black Theology.

The Commission on Theology of the National Committee of Black Churchmen has issued a statement on Black Theology. In this document Black Theology is defined:

> For us, Black theology is the theology of black liberation. It seeks to plumb the black condition in the light of God's revelation in Jesus Christ, so that the black community can see the gospel is commensurate with the achievement of black humanity. Black Theology is a theology of "blackness." It is the affirmation of black humanity that emancipates black people from white racism thus providing authentic freedom for both white and black people. It affirms the humanity of white people in that it says "No" to the encroachment of white oppression.

The black scholars are indebted in a measure to white theologians. We have learned much from them. However, the white theologians in their interpretation of the Christian faith have ignored the black Christian experience. Many have felt that this black Christian experience was devoid of meaning and therefore could be omitted in their exposition and interpretation of the Christian faith. To be sure, this was a grievous error. The omission of the black Christian experience by white interpreters of the Christian faith meant that the message of the Christian faith thus interpreted was oriented toward the white community. Therefore this message had nothing significant to say to the black man who is now struggling for identity and dignity. The black theologians were forced to look at the black Christian experience and interpret this experience so as to ascertain what the black Christian experience has to say to the black man concerning the vital matters of the Christian faith. Black Theology is a product of black Christian experience and reflection. It comes out of the past. It is strong in the present and we believe it is redemptive for the future.

THE QUEST FOR THE BLACK JESUS

The reason for the quest for the black Jesus is deeply embedded in the black man's experience in this country. The black man's introduction to the white Jesus was a catastrophe! Vincent Harding reminds us that the blacks encountered the American white Christ first on the slave ships that brought us to these shores. The blacks on the slave ship heard His name sung in hymns of praise while they died chained in stinky holes beneath the decks locked in terror and disease. When the blacks leaped from the decks of the slave ships they saw His name carved on the side of the ship. When the black women were raped in the cabin by the white racists, they must have noticed the Holy Bible on the shelves. Vincent Harding declares,

The horrors continued on American soil. So all through the nation's history many black men have rejected this Christ—indeed the miracle is that so many accepted him. In past times our disdain often had to be stifled and sullen, our angers silent and self destructive. But now we speak out.[2]

One white perceptive theologian, Kyle Haselden, has observed that

The white man cleaves Christian piety into two parts: the strong, virile virtues he applies exclusively to himself; the apparently weak, passive virtues he endorses especially for the negro. "Whatsoever things are true, honest, just, pure, lovely" belong to the white man; "whatsoever things are of good report" belong to the Negro. The white man takes the active and positive Christian adjectives for himself: noble, manly, wise, strong, courageous; he recommends the passive and negative Christian adjectives to the Negro: patient, long-suffering, humble, self-effacing, considerate, submissive, childlike, meek.[3]

White theology has not presented us with good theological reasons why we should not speak out against this gross perversion of the Christian faith. White theology has not been able to re-shape the life of the white church so as to cleanse it of its racism and to liberate it from the iron claws of the white racist establishment of this nation. White theology has presented the blacks a religion of contentment in the state of life in which they find themselves. Such an interpretation of the Christian faith avoided questions about personal dignity, collective power, freedom, equality and self-determination. The white church establishment presented to the black people a religion carefully tailored to fit the purposes of the white oppressors, corrupted in language, interpretation and application by the conscious and unconscious racism of white Christians from the first plantation missionary down to Billy Graham.

The white Christ of the white church establishment is the enemy of the black man. The teachings of this white Christ are used to justify wars, exploitation, segregation, discrimination, prejudice, and racism. This white Christ is the oppressor of the black man and the black preacher and scholar were compelled to discover a Christ in his image of blackness. He was forced to look at the teachings of Jesus in the light of his own black experience and discover what this black Jesus said about the realities of his own life. The black preacher, seminary student, and scholar had their work cut out for them. If Bultmann's task was to demythologize the New Testament, the black preacher and scholar had to detheologize his mind of the racist ideas which had crept into interpretations of Jesus and to see Him in the depth of His full humanity.

We remind you, we were asked to address ourselves "in the general area of understanding and communicating the Christian faith into today's revolutionary society." The first requirement is one of admitting the inadequacies of an understanding of the Christian faith which is used to support our contemporary racist society. Black and white scholars must read again the scriptures with new eyes and minds so as to hear the words of Jesus in their disturbing clarity.

The subject of all preaching is Jesus Christ. As Paul says, "We proclaim Christ—yes, Christ nailed to the cross and though this is a stumbling block to

Jews and folly to the Greeks, yet to those who have heard His call, Jews and Greeks alike, He is the power of God and the wisdom of God."

A RECOVERY OF THE HUMANITY OF JESUS

Detheologizing demands that we recover the humanity of Jesus in all of its depth, length, breadth, and height. Jesus was born in a barn, wrapped in a blanket used for sick cattle, and placed in a stall. He died on a city dump outside Jerusalem.

The New Testament presents with disturbing clarity its record of the birth, ministry and death of Jesus. There is no attempt to hide the stark realities which confronted Jesus from the barn of Bethlehem to the city dump of Jerusalem. The realism is naked and stark. Jesus was born in a barn. He died on a city dump. Even the place of the birth of Jesus is identified with the needs and the conditions of people. Where the need is the deepest, the situation most desperate and the pain the sharpest, that is precisely where Jesus is. We repeat, even in the birth of Jesus, the gospels of Matthew and Luke identify him with the needs, the suffering, the pain and the anxieties of the world. You see most of the world's babies are not born in the palaces of kings or the government houses of prime ministers, or the manses of Bishops. Most of the world's babies are born in the ghettos of corrupt cities, in mud houses, in disintegrated cottages with cracked floors and stuffed walls where the muffled cries of unattended mothers mingle with the screams of newborn infants.

Bultmann writes about the offense of the incarnation of the word.[4] He contends that the revealer appears not as man in general, that is not simply as a barrier of human nature but as a definite human being in history—Jesus of Nazareth—a Jew. The humanity of Jesus is genuine humanity. The writer of the Gospel of John has no theory about the pre-existent miraculous entrance into the world nor of the legend of the Virgin Birth. You know this legend or myth is presented to us in the Gospels of St. Matthew and St. Luke. The writer of the Gospel of Mark, the Evangelist of the Fourth Gospel and Paul teach a high Christology without reference to the Virgin Birth.

Permit us to make this suggestion: Suppose we would omit the phrase "of the Holy Spirit" from Matthew 1: 18 where it is recorded that "Mary had been betrothed to Joseph, before they came together she was found to be with a child," what would this teach us about the humanity of Jesus? The reaction of many would be instantaneous and we would be accused of teaching "a doctrine of the illegitimate birth of Jesus." These objectors would insist that the birth of Jesus was due to a special act of God in and through humanity and that since Jesus is who He is and has done what He has done, this requires that His entrance into the world through humanity must be unique. Those who advocate this position forget the teachings of Jesus in particular and the New Testament writers in general concerning all life. Jesus taught that all life comes from God and that the birth of every child embodies and expresses a unique act of God.

Who Jesus was, was determined not necessarily by the manner of His birth but rather by what He did. John Knox states that the first form of the Christological question was, "What had God done through Jesus?"[5] The New Testament writers go to great length in presenting and discussing the saving deed of God through Jesus.

It was the belief of most writers of the New Testament that God was at work in the life and deeds of Jesus and that what God was doing in Jesus had both soteriological and eschatological significance. The conviction shared by most New Testament writers was to the effect that the last days had finally dawned and that God was acting decisively for man's salvation, renewal and liberation. Again John Knox notes that the supreme importance of Jesus was determined more by his role and function than by his nature and further, "the Christological question, which was originally a question about the eschatological and soteriological significance of an event, has become a question about the metaphysical nature of a person."[6] What must be done, therefore, if we are to understand the meaning and significance of Jesus, the Liberator, is to go behind the metaphysical speculation concerning Him and ascertain and study those events which were foundational and believed by writers of the New Testament to possess saving and liberating significance. Men knew Jesus in terms of what he had done for them. J. K. Mozley states, "There is in the New Testament no speculative Christology divorced from the gospel of the Savior and the salvation he brings."[7] The early Christians were not seeking abstract definitions concerning the person of Jesus. The language of the early Christians was experimental, functional and confessional. The foundation for the theology of St. Paul is the experience of what God had done for him in his own conversion, and he is basically interested in Jesus and the Redeemer, Revealer and Liberator.

Brunner has argued that the titles given to Jesus in the New Testament are verbal in nature and character. They all describe an event, a work of God, or what God has done through Jesus in and for mankind. Further, Brunner writes, "Who and what Jesus is can only be stated at first at any rate by what God does and gives in him."[8]

Brunner insists that all Christological titles must be understood not in terms of their substantive implications but in terms of their verbal functions. The term *Christos* may be interpreted as the one in whom and through who God is to establish his sovereignty. The title *Son of God* is functional and it suggests an office and *the work* of the Liberator rather that a description of his metaphysical nature. Even the title *Immanuel* is defined in terms of its functional implications because this title means "God is with us." The title *Kyrios* describes the one who rules over the church. And finally, the title *Savior* points to the one who is to bring the healing, salvation and liberation for which mankind yearns.[9]

The significance of Jesus for religious living is determined by what Jesus has done for mankind and all of the Christological titles applied to Jesus emphasize His gift of Liberation to and for men.[10]

The divinity of Jesus is a divinity of service. His humanity was stretched in service so as to include the whole world of man in its miseries, slavery, frustration, and hopelessness. The New Testament word used to express this deep concern for men is *splagchnizesthai*. This word means to be moved with compassion and it is used to describe an emotion which moved Jesus, the Liberator, at the very depth of His being. This word also indicates the depth of Jesus' concern and identification with others. Whenever the Gospel writers use this word *splagchnizesthai* in reference to Jesus they were attempting to describe the manner and the way in which Jesus identified Himself completely with others and how He entered into the world of their misery and suffering, their slavery and hopelessness, and provided the means for liberation and renewal.

The men and women of the New Testament period who witness this ministry of service, love, and liberation reach the astounding conclusion that Jesus is the Revelation of a new kind of freedom and has made available to men the liberating power of God's love. Jesus is God acting in the service of men, thereby enabling them to realize their God-given potentials as human beings and as sons of God.

The Christians of the first century saw in Jesus the Liberator the answer to their most distressing problems. Jesus, in His ministry, identifies Himself with all men. The early Christian believed that He provided the answer to their most distrubing problems and whatever they needed He was sufficient. The writers of the Four Gospels interpreted Jesus in the light of what they considered to be the greatest need of mankind. For the writer of the Gospel of Matthew, Jesus is the new Rabbi; for Luke, He is the great Physician; for Mark, He is the Stranger satisfying the deepest needs of men; and for John, Jesus is the Revealer.

The people of all races, because of His service, are able to identify with Him and to see in His humanity a reflection of their own images. Today the black man looks at Jesus—observes His ministry of love and liberation and considers Him the black Messiah who fights oppression and sets the captive free.

COMMITTED TO THE MESSAGE AND MISSION OF JESUS

The radicalness of the humanity of Jesus is not only expressed in His service but also in His speech. We must permit His speech to address, probe, disturb and challenge us. Professor Ernst Fuchs has called the rise of the gospel a speech event—an opening of a new dimension of man's awareness, a new break-through in language and symbolization. Professor Fuchs writes:

> The early Church is itself a language phenomenon. It is precisely for this reason that it has created for itself a memorial in the new stylistic form of the Gospel. Even the Apocalypse of John, and more than ever the apostolic epistles, are creations of a new language that transforms everything with which it comes into contact.[11]

The words of Jesus have the rugged fibre of a cypress tree and the jagged edge of the cross-cut saw. His language is extreme, extravagant, explosive as hand grenades which are tossed into the crowds that listened to Him. A tremendous vigor and vitality surges through his words. In Jesus' words, "A man with a log in his eye tries to pick a cinder out of his brother's eye." In the words of Jesus "a giant hand hangs a millstone around the neck of one who exploits a little child and hurls the sinner into the midst of the sea." In the words of Jesus—"a man asks for bread and is given a stone, another asks for fish and is given a snake." In the words of Jesus, "men strain at the little gnats and gulp down the camels." In the words of Jesus, "a mountain develops feet and casts itself into the sea." He attacks the religious establishment of his day—the religious leaders, the ordained ministers with such phrases as "you hypocrites," "you blind guides," "you blind Pharisees," "you brood of snakes," "you serpents," "you murderers."

Jesus spoke with authority and with power!

In the city of Nazareth where he was reared, this dark long haired, bearded ghetto lad of Nazareth took over the synagogue service and read his universal Manifesto of Liberation:

> The spirit of the Lord is upon me because he has anointed me; He has sent me to announce good news to the poor, to proclaim release for prisoners and recovery of sight for the blind; to let the broken vicitims go free, to proclaim the year of the Lord's favour.   Luke 4: 18–19 (NEB)

The reading of this liberation Manifesto caused debates, rebuttals, accusations, counter rebuttals, wrath, anger and hate. The Gospel of St. Luke is explicit in describing the reaction of the religious establishment to the manifesto of liberation of Jesus. "When they heard this, all in the synagogue were filled with wrath, and they rose up and put him out of the city, and led him to the brow of the hill on which their city was built, that they might throw him down headlong. But passing through the midst of them he went away."   Luke 4: 28–30

Liberation was the aim and the goal of the life of Jesus in the world. Liberation expresses the essential thrust of his ministry. The stage of his ministry was the streets. His congregation consisted of those who were written-off by the established church and the state. He ministered to those who needed him, "the nobodies of the world," the sick, the blind, the lame and the demon possessed. He invaded the chambers of sickness and death and hallowed these with the healing words of health and life. He invaded the minds of the demon possessed and in those dark chambers of night he brought light, sanity and order. Jesus ministered to men in their sorrow, sin and degradation and offered them hope and light and courage and strength. He offered comfort to the poor who did not fit into the structure of the world. Jesus comforted the mourner and offered hope to the humble. He had a message for the men and women who had been pushed to the limits of human existence and on these he pronounced his blessedness.

The people who received help from Jesus are throughout the Gospels on the fringe of society—men who because of fate, guilt and prejudices were considered marked men; *sick people*, who must bear their disease as punishment for crime or for some sin committed; *demoniacs,* that is those possessed of demons; *the lepers,* the first born of death to whom fellowship was denied; *Gentiles*, women and children who did not count for anything in the community and *the really bad people*, the prostitutes, the thieves, the murderers, the robbers. When Jesus was pressed for an explanation of the radicalness of the thrust of his ministry his answer was simple and direct. "Those who are well have no need for a physician but those who are sick. I came not to call the righteous, but sinners."

The greatness of Jesus is to be found precisely in the way in which he makes himself accessible to those who need him, ignoring conventional limitations and issuing that grand and glorious welcome—"Come unto me all ye that labor and are heavy laden and I will give you rest."

The Gospel of St. Mark records the healing of Peter's mother-in-law. Please listen to this passage. "And immediately he left the synagogue and entered the house of Simon and Andrew, with James and John. Simon's mother-in-law lay sick with a fever, and immediately they told him of her." Now, verse 31 tells us what Jesus did: "And he came and took her by the hand and lifted her up, and the fever left her, and she served them."   Mark 1: 30–31

Jesus is saying to his disciples the only way to lift is to touch. You cannot lift men without touching them. Jesus is saying to the church—the people of God— the church must not be locked in its stained glass fortress with its multicolored windows, red cushioned seats, crimson carpets and temperature controlled auditorium where according to Kierkegaard, "An anemic preacher, preaches anemic gospel about an anemic Christ to an anemic congregation."[12]

The church building must be a point of departure, a departure into the world, into the dirty here and now.

We are challenged to continue in our world Jesus' ministry of love and liberation. We must recognize that to be a Christian is to be contemporaneous with Jesus, the Liberator. To be sure, to be a Christian is not to hold views about Jesus but rather to become a contemporary with Jesus in His ministry of suffering and humiliation and of love and liberation. To be a Christian is to be committed to the man Jesus in spite of the world's rejection of Him, in spite of Christendom's betrayal of Him, and in spite of the social and intellectual stigma involved in accepting and following Him. To be a Christian is to stand with Jesus and participate in His ministry of love and liberation at the crossways of the world where men are crucified on the crosses of poverty, racism, war and exploitation. To be a Christian is to try again to introduce Christianity into Christendom and to set free again the powers of the love and liberating ministry of Jesus, the Liberator.

NOTES

1. Rudolph Bultmann, *Theology of the New Testament*, tr. Kendrick Grobel, Vol. I (London, 1952), pp. 330–331.

2. "Black Power and the American Christ," in *The Black Power Revolt*, ed. Floyd B. Barbour (Boston: F. Porter Sargent, 1968), p. 86.

3. Kyle Haselden, *The Racial Problem in Christian Perspective* (New York: Harper and Brothers, 1959), pp. 42–43.

4. Rudolph Bultmann, *op. cit.*, Vol. II, 1955, pp. 40–41.

5. John Knox, *On the Meaning of Christ* (New York: Charles Scribner & Sons, 1947), p. 49.

6. *Ibid.*, pp. 55–56.

7. "Jesus in Relation to Believing Man," *Interpretation, A Journal of Bible and Theology* (January, 1958), p.11.

8. Emil Brunner, *The Christian Doctrine of Creation and Redemption* (London: Lutterworth Press, 1952), p. 272.

9. *Ibid.*, p. 273.

10. Ferdinand Hahn, *The Titles of Jesus in Christology* (New York: World Publishing Co., 1969), pp. 347–350; Oscar Cullmann, *The Christology of the New Testament* (London: *SCM* Press LTD, 1959), pp. 3–6.

11. Ernst Fuchs, *Studies of the Historical Jesus* (Napierville, Ill.: Alec R. Allenson, Inc., 1960), p. 68.

12. Sören Kierkegaard, *Attack Upon Christendom*, tr. by Walter Lowrie (Princeton: Princeton University Press, 1946), p. 30.

U.S. Catholic Bishops   A Pastoral Message: Economic Justice for All

Brothers and Sisters in Christ:

1. We are believers called to follow Our Lord Jesus Christ and proclaim his Gospel in the midst of a complex and powerful economy. This reality poses both opportunities and responsibilities for Catholics in the United States. Our faith calls us to measure this economy, not only by what it produces, but also by how it touches human life and whether it protects or undermines the dignity of the human person. Economic decisions have human consequences and moral content; they help or hurt people, strengthen or weaken family life, advance or diminish the quality of justice in our land.

2. This is why we have written *Economic Justice for All: A Pastoral Letter on Catholic Social Teaching and the U.S. Economy.* This letter is a personal invitation to Catholics to use the resources of our faith, the strength of our economy, and the opportunities of our democracy to shape a society that better protects the dignity and basic rights of our sisters and brothers, both in this land and around the world.

3. The pastoral letter has been a work of careful inquiry, wide consultation, and prayerful discernment. The letter has been greatly enriched by this process of listening and refinement. We offer this introductory pastoral message to Catholics in the United States seeking to live their faith in the marketplace—in homes, offices, factories, and schools; on farms and ranches; in boardrooms and union halls; in service agencies and legislative chambers. We seek to explain why we wrote the pastoral letter, to introduce its major themes, and to share our hopes for the dialogue and action it might generate.

WHY WE WRITE

4. We write to share our teaching, to raise questions, to challenge one another to live our faith in the world. We write as heirs of the biblical prophets who summon us "to do the right, and to love goodness, and to walk humbly with your God" (Mi 6:8). We write as followers of Jesus who told us in the Sermon on the Mount: "Blessed are the poor in spirit. . . . Blessed are the meek. . . . Blessed are they who hunger and thirst for righteousness. . . . Your are the salt of the earth. . . . You are the light of the world" (Mt 5:1–6, 13–14). These words challenge us not only as believers but also as consumers, citizens, workers, and owners. In the parable of the Last Judgment, Jesus said, "For I was hungry and you gave me food, I was thirsty and you gave me drink. . . . As often as you did it for one of my least brothers, you did it for me" (Mt 25:35–40). The challenge for us is to discover in our own place and time what it means to be "poor in spirit" and "the salt of the earth" and what it means to serve "the least among us" and to "hunger and thirst for righteousness."

5. Followers of Christ must avoid a tragic separation between faith and everyday life. They can neither shirk their earthly duties nor, as the Second Vatican Council declared, "immerse [them]selves in earthly activities as if these latter were utterly foreign to religion, and religion were nothing more than the fulfillment of acts of worship and the observance of a few moral obligations" (*Pastoral Constitution on the Church in the Modern World,* no. 43).

6. Economic life raises important social and moral questions for each of us and for society as a whole. Like family life, economic life is one of the chief areas where we live out our faith, love our neighbor, confront temptation, fulfill God's creative design, and achieve our holiness. Our economic activity in factory, field, office, or shop feeds our families—or feeds our anxieties. It exercises our talents—or wastes them. It raises our hopes—or crushes them. It brings us into cooperation with others—or sets us at odds. The Second Vatican Council instructs us "to preach the message of Christ in such a way that the light of the Gospel will shine on all activities of the faithful" (*Pastoral Constitution,* no. 43). In this case, we are trying to look at economic life through the eyes of faith, applying traditional church teaching to the U.S. economy.

7. In our letter, we write as pastors, not public officials. We speak as moral teachers, not economic technicians. We seek not to make some political or ideological point but to lift up the human and ethical dimensions of economic life, aspects too often neglected in public discussion. We bring to this task a dual heritage of Catholic social teaching and traditional American values.

8. As *Catholics,* we are heirs of a long tradition of thought and action on the moral dimensions of economic activity. The life and words of Jesus and the teaching of his Church call us to serve those in need and to work actively for social and economic justice. As a community of believers, we know that our faith is tested by the quality of justice among us, that we can best measure our life together by how the poor and the vulnerable are treated. This in not a new concern for us. It is as old as the Hebrew prophets, as compelling as the Sermon on the Mount, and as

current as the powerful voice of Pope John Paul II defending the dignity of the human person.

9. As *Americans*, we are grateful for the gift of freedom and committed to the dream of "liberty and justice for all." This nation, blessed with extraordinary resources, has provided an unprecedented standard of living for millions of people. We are proud of the strength, productivity, and creativity of our economy, but we also remember those who have been left behind in our progress. We believe that we honor our history best by working for the day when all our sisters and brothers share adequately in the American dream.

10. As bishops, in proclaiming the Gospel for these times we also manage institutions, balance budgets, meet payrolls. In this we see the human face of our economy. We feel the hurts and hopes of our people. We feel the pain of our sisters and brothers who are poor, unemployed, homeless, living on the edge. The poor and vulnerable are on our doorsteps, in our parishes, in our service agencies, and in our shelters. We see too much hunger and injustice, too much suffering and despair, both in our own country and around the world.

11. As pastors, we also see the decency, generosity, and vulnerability of our people. We see the struggles of ordinary families to make ends meet and to provide a better future for their children. We know the desire of managers, professionals, and business people to shape what they do by what they believe. It is the faith, good will, and generosity of our people that gives us hope as we write this letter.

PRINCIPAL THEMES OF THE PASTORAL LETTER

12. The pastoral letter is not a blueprint for the American economy. It does not embrace any particular theory of how the economy works, nor does it attempt to resolve the disputes between different schools of economic thought. Instead, our letter turns to Scripture and to the social teachings of the Church. There, we discover what our economic life must serve, what standards it must meet. Let us examine some of these basic moral principles.

13. *Every economic decision and institution must be judged in light of whether it protects or undermines the dignity of the human person.* The pastoral letter begins with the human person. We believe the person is sacred—the clearest reflection of God among us. Human dignity comes from God, not from nationality, race, sex, economic status, or any human accomplishment. We judge any economic system by what it does *for* and *to* people and by how it permits all to *participate* in it. The economy should serve people, not the other way around.

14. *Human dignity can be realized and protected only in community.* In our teaching, the human person is not only sacred but also social. How we organize our society—in economics and politics, in law and policy—directly affects human dignity and the capacity of individuals to grow in community. The obligation to "love our neighbor" has an individual dimension, but it also requires a broader social commitment to the common good. We have many partial ways to measure and debate the health of our economy: Gross National Product, per capita income,

stock market prices, and so forth. The Christian vision of economic life looks beyond them all and asks, Does economic life enhance or threaten our life together as a community?

15. *All people have a right to participate in the economic life of society.* Basic justice demands that people be assured a minimum level of participation in the economy. It is wrong for a person or group to be excluded unfairly or to be unable to participate or contribute to the economy. For example, people who are both able and willing but cannot get a job are deprived of the participation that is so vital to human development. For, it is through employment that most individuals and families meet their material needs, exercise their talents, and have an opportunity to contribute to the larger community. Such participation has a special significance in our tradition because we believe that it is a means by which we join in carrying forward God's creative activity.

16. *All members of society have a special obligation to the poor and vulnerable.* From the Scriptures and church teaching, we learn that the justice of a society is tested by the treatment of the poor. The justice that was the sign of God's covenant with Israel was measured by how the poor and unprotected—the widow, the orphan, and the stranger—were treated. The kingdom that Jesus proclaimed in his word and ministry excludes no one. Throughout Israel's history and in early Christianity, the poor are agents of God's transforming power. "The Spirit of the Lord is upon me, therefore he has anointed me. He has sent me to bring glad tidings to the poor" (Lk 4:18). This was Jesus' first public utterance. Jesus takes the side of those most in need. In the Last Judgment, so dramatically described in St. Matthew's Gospel, we are told that we will be judged according to how we respond to the hungry, the thirsty, the naked, the stranger. As followers of Christ, we are challenged to make a fundamental "option for the poor"—to speak for the voiceless, to defend the defenseless, to assess life styles, policies, and social institutions in terms of their impact on the poor. This "option for the poor" does not mean pitting one group against another, but rather, strengthening the whole community by assisting those who are most vulnerable. As Christians, we are called to respond to the needs of *all* our brothers and sisters, but those with the greatest needs require the greatest response.

17. *Human rights are the minimum conditions for life in community.* In Catholic teaching, human rights include not only civil and political rights but also economic rights. As Pope John XXIII declared, "all people have a right to life, food, clothing, shelter, rest, medical care, education, and employment." This means that when people are without a chance to earn a living, and must go hungry and homeless, they are being denied basic rights. Society must ensure that these rights are protected. In this way, we will ensure that the minimum conditions of economic justice are met for all our sisters and brothers.

18. *Society as a whole, acting through public and private institutions, has the moral responsibility to enhance human dignity and protect human rights.* In addition to the clear responsibility of private institutions, government has an essential responsibility in this area. This does not mean that government has the primary or exclusive role, but it does have a positive moral responsibility in safeguarding human rights and ensuring that the minimum conditions of human dignity are met for

all. In a democracy, government is a means by which we can act together to protect what is important to us and to promote our common values.

19. These six moral principles are not the only ones presented in the pastoral letter, but they give an overview of the moral vision that we are trying to share. This vision of economic life cannot exist in a vacuum; it must be translated into concrete measures. Our pastoral letter spells out some specific applications of Catholic moral principles. We call for a new national commitment to full employment. We say it is a social and moral scandal that one of every seven Americans is poor, and we call for concerted efforts to eradicate poverty. The fulfillment of the basic needs of the poor is of the highest priority. We urge that all economic policies be evaluated in light of their impact on the life and stability of the family. We support measures to halt the loss of family farms and to resist the growing concentration in the ownership of agricultural resources. We specify ways in which the United States can do far more to relieve the plight of poor nations and assist in their development. We also reaffirm church teaching on the rights of workers, collective bargaining, private property, subsidiarity, and equal opportunity.

20. We believe that the recommendations in our letter are reasonable and balanced. In analyzing the economy, we reject ideological extremes and start from the fact that ours is a "mixed" economy, the product of a long history of reform and adjustment. We know that some of our specific recommendations are controversial. As bishops, we do not claim to make these prudential judgments with the same kind of authority that marks our declarations of principle. But, we feel obliged to teach by example how Christians can undertake concrete analysis and make specific judgments on economic issues. The Church's teachings cannot be left at the level of appealing generalities.

21. In the pastoral letter, we suggest that the time has come for a "New American Experiment"—to implement economic rights, to broaden the sharing of economic power, and to make economic decisions more accountable to the common good. This experiment can create new structures of economic partnership and participation within firms at the regional level, for the whole nation, and across borders.

22. Of course, there are many aspects of the economy the letter does not touch, and there are basic questions it leaves to further exploration. There are also many specific points on which men and women of good will may disagree. We look for a fruitful exchange among differing viewpoints. We pray only that all will take to heart the urgency of our concerns; that together we will test our views by the Gospel and the Church's teaching; and that we will listen to other voices in a spirit of mutual respect and open dialogue.

A CALL TO CONVERSION AND ACTION

23. We should not be surprised if we find Catholic social teaching to be demanding. The Gospel is demanding. We are always in need of conversion, of a change of heart. We are richly blessed, and as St. Paul assures us, we are destined for glory. Yet, it is also true that we are sinners; that we are not always wise or loving

or just; that, for all our amazing possibilities, we are incompletely born, wary of life, and hemmed in by fears and empty routines. We are unable to entrust ourselves fully to the living God, and so we seek substitute forms of security in material things, in power, in indifference, in popularity, in pleasure. The Scriptures warn us that these things can become forms of idolatry. We know that, at times, in order to remain truly a community of Jesus' disciples, we will have to say "no" to certain aspects in our culture, to certain trends and ways of acting that are opposed to a life of faith, love, and justice. Changes in our hearts lead naturally to a desire to change how we act. With what care, human kindness, and justice do I conduct myself at work? How will my economic decisions to buy, sell, invest, divest, hire, or fire serve human dignity and the common good? In what career can I best exercise my talents so as to fill the world with the Spirit of Christ? How do my economic choices contribute to the strength of my family and community, to the values of my children, to a sensitivity to those in need? In this consumer society, how can I develop a healthy detachment from things and avoid the temptation to assess who I am by what I have? How do I strike a balance between labor and leisure that enlarges my capacity for friendships, for family life, for community? What government policies should I support to attain the well-being of all, especially the poor and vulnerable?

24. The answers to such questions are not always clear—or easy to live out. But, conversion is a lifelong process. And, it is not undertaken alone. It occurs with the support of the whole believing community, through baptism, common prayer, and our daily efforts, large and small, on behalf of justice. As a Church, we must be people after God's own heart, bonded by the Spirit, sustaining one another in love, setting our hearts on God's kingdom, committing ourselves to solidarity with those who suffer, working for peace and justice, acting as a sign of Christ's love and justice in the world. The Church cannot redeem the world from the deadening effects of sin and injustice unless it is working to remove sin and injustice in its own life and institutions. All of us must help the Church to practice in its own life what it preaches to others about economic justice and cooperation.

25. The challenge of this pastoral letter is not merely to think differently, but also to act differently. A renewal of economic life depends on the conscious choices and commitments of individual believers who practice their faith in the world. The road to holiness for most of us lies in our secular vocations. We need a spirituality that calls forth and supports lay initiative and witness not just in our churches but also in business, in the labor movement, in the professions, in education, and in public life. Our faith is not just a weekend obligation, a mystery to be celebrated around the altar on Sunday. It is a pervasive reality to be practiced every day in homes, offices, factories, schools, and businesses across our land. We cannot separate what we believe from how we act in the marketplace and the broader community, for this is where we make our primary contribution to the pursuit of economic justice.

26. We ask each of you to read the pastoral letter, to study it, to pray about it, and match it with your own experience. We ask you to join with us in service to those in need. Let us reach out personally to the hungry and the homeless, to the poor and the powerless, and to the troubled and the vulnerable. In serving them,

we serve Christ. Our service efforts cannot substitute for just and compassionate public policies, but they can help us practice what we preach about human life and human dignity.

27. The pursuit of economic justice takes believers into the public arena, testing the policies of government by the principles of our teaching. We ask you to become more informed and active citizens, using your voices and votes to speak for the voiceless, to defend the poor and the vulnerable and to advance the common good. We are called to shape a constituency of conscience, measuring every policy by how it touches the least, the lost, and the left-out among us. This letter calls us to conversion and common action, to new forms of stewardship, service, and citizenship.

28. The completion of a letter such as this is but the beginning of a long process of education, discussion, and action. By faith and baptism, we are fashioned into new creatures, filled with the Holy Spirit and with a love that compels us to seek out a new profound relationship with God, with the human family, and with all created things. Jesus has entered our history as God's anointed son who announces the coming of God's kingdom, a kingdom of justice and peace and freedom. And, what Jesus proclaims, he embodies in his actions. His ministry reveals that the reign of God is something more powerful than evil, injustice, and the hardness of hearts. Through his crucifixion and resurrection, he reveals that God's love is ultimately victorious over all suffering, all horror, all meaninglessness, and even over the mystery of death. Thus, we proclaim words of hope and assurance to all who suffer and are in need.

29. We believe that the Christian view of life, including economic life, can transform the lives of individuals, families, schools, and our whole culture. We believe that with your prayers, reflection, service, and action, our economy can be shaped so that human dignity prospers and the human person is served. This is the unfinished work of our nation. This is the challenge of our faith.

Jerry Falwell

The Imperative of Moral Involvement

Bible-believing Christians and concerned moral Americans are determined to do something about the problems that we are facing as a nation. In our family we were recently sitting in the family room having a time of Bible study and devotions and discussing some of these crucial issues. One of my children asked, "Dad, will I ever grow up to be as old as you are in a free America?" Another one of my children asked, "Will I ever get to go to college?" and "Will I ever get married?" Speaking about the vital issues is not just a question of dealing with our generation but with the generations to come. Our children and our grand children must forever be the recipients or the victims of our moral decisions today.

My responsibility as a parent-pastor is more than just concern. The issue of convenience is not even up for discussion. If the moral issues are really matters of conviction that are worth living for, then they are worth fighting for. In discussing these matters further with other pastors and concerned Christian leaders, I have become convinced of the need to have a coalition of God-fearing, moral Americans to represent our convictions of our government. I realize that there would be those pastors who misunderstand our intentions. I know that some object that we are compromising in our involvement with people of different doctrinal and theological beliefs. As a fundamental, independent, separatist Baptist, I am well aware of the crucial issues of personal and ecclesiastical separation that divide fundamentalists philosophically from evangelicals and liberals. I do not believe that it is ever right to compromise the truth in order to gain an opportunity to do right. In doctrinal and spiritual matters, there is no real harmony between light and darkness.

I am convinced of two very significant factors. First, our very moral existence as a nation is at stake. There are many moral Americans who do not share our theological beliefs but who do share our moral concerns. Second, we must face the fact that it will take the greatest possible number of concerned citizens to reverse the politicization of immorality in our society. Doctrinal difference is a distinctive feature of a democracy. Our freedoms have given us the privilege and the luxury of theological disagreement. I would not for a moment encourage anyone to water down his distinctive beliefs. But we must face realistically the fact that there are Christians in the world today who have lost the luxury of disagreement. When the entire issue of Christian survival is at stake, we must be willing to band together on at least the major moral issues of the day.

One only needs to travel to Rhodesia, as I was privileged to do earlier this year, to realize that the Christians there have lost their opportunity to argue with one another. The recent election of Comrade Mugabe, the new Marxist dictator of that country, may well have ended any opportunity of genuine Christian witness there. Petty theological differences do not mean a whole lot today to Christians living in Russia, China, Cambodia, Mozambique, or Rhodesia! Undoubtedly, the next target of communist conquest will be the Republic of South Africa. The many Christian believers of that great nation need our prayers that their doors remain open to the Gospel. If we are not careful the United States will be next. We may not have the luxury of theological disagreement much longer. The time may soon come when claiming to be any kind of Christian may cost you your life!

Our ministry is as committed as it ever has been to the basic truths of Scripture, to essential and fundamental Christian doctrines. But we are not willing to isolate ourselves in seclusion while we sit back and watch this nation plunge headlong toward hell.

Moral Americans can make the difference in America if we are willing to exert the effort to make our feelings known and if we are willing to make the necessary sacrifices to get the job done. In October 1978, our church entered what seemed at the time to be a losing battle. Pre-election polls in September 1978 in the state of Virginia indicated that there was general apathy regarding pari-mutuel betting. Those in favor of pari-mutuel betting expected it to win approval easily. Convinced that gambling is typical of a nation losing its moral values and that it is a sin based upon a lust for things, we took a strong stand against it. While some of our politicians argue that gambling would increase revenue in the state, I knew that it would ultimately cost taxpayers in increased welfare costs or destroy families and increase police protection in prison costs. Gambling is supported by men who are dominated by greed, and who do not consider the havoc that gambling causes to the home.

Our church took a stand against pari-mutuel betting and rallied other good people in the state of Virginia against it also. On November 7, 1978, pari-mutuel betting was rejected by the voters in the state of Virginia. Virginia newspapers stated, "Both the winners and the losers credited an aggressive campaign by the religious leader as bringing about the betting proposal's demise." Those newspapers went on to quote my comment: "The vote is an indication of what the Christian people in Virginia have been able to do by simply uniting their efforts. This is the first time that six thousand Virginia churches of all denominations have joined hands in a moral campaign, and this should be, as I see it, a forecast of future endeavors together."

To change America we must be involved, and this includes three areas of political action:

1. REGISTRATION

A recent national poll indicated that eight million American evangelicals are not registered to vote. I am convinced that this is one of the major sins of the church today. Until concerned Christian citizens become registered voters there is very little that we can do to change the tide of political influence on the social issues in our nation. Those who object to Christians being involved in the political process are ultimately objecting to Christians being involved in the social process. The political process is really nothing more than a realization of the social process. For us to divorce ourselves from society would be to run into the kind of isolationism and monasticism that characterized the medieval hermits. Many Christians are not even aware of the importance of registering to vote. It is perfectly legal, for example, for a deputy registrar to come right to your local church at a designated time and register the entire congregation. I am convinced that those of us who are pastors have an obligation to urge our people to register to vote. I am more concerned that people exercise their freedom to vote than I am concerned for whom they vote.

2. INFORMATION

Many moral Americans are unaware of the real issues affecting them today. Many people do not know the voting record of their congressman and have no idea how he is representing them on political issues that have moral implications. This is one of the major reasons why we have established the Moral Majority organization. We want to keep the public informed on the vital moral issues. The Moral Majority, Inc., is a nonprofit organization, with headquarters in Washington, D.C. Our goal is to exert a significant influence on the spiritual and moral direction of our nation by: (a) mobilizing the grassroots of moral Americans in one clear and effective voice; (b) informing the moral majority what is going on behind their backs in Washington and in state legislatures across the country; (c) lobbying intensely in Congress to defeat left-wing, social-welfare bills that will further erode our precious freedom; (d) pushing for positive legislation such as that to establish the Family Protection Agency, which will ensure a strong, enduring America; and (e) helping the moral majority in local communities to fight pornography, homosexuality, the advocacy of immorality in school textbooks, and other issues facing each and every one of us.

Christians must keep America great by being willing to go into the halls of Congress, by getting laws passed that will protect the freedom and liberty of her citizens. The Moral Majority, Inc., was formed to acquaint Americans everywhere with the tragic decline in our nation's morals and to provide leadership in establishing an effective coalition of morally active citizens who are (a) prolife, (b) profamily, (c) promoral, and (d) pro-American. If the vast majority of Americans (84 per cent, according to George Gallup) still believe the Ten Commandments are valid today, why are we permitting a few leading amoral humanists and naturalists to take over the most influential positions in this nation?

Tim LaHaye has formed a code of minimum moral standards dictated by the Bible; his code would be used to evaluate the stand of candidates on moral issues. These minimum standards are:

a. Do you agree that this country was founded on a belief in God and the moral principles of the Bible? Do you concur that this country has been departing from those principles and needs to return to them?
b. Would you favor stricter laws relating to the sale of pornography?
c. Do you favor stronger laws against the use and sale of hard drugs?
d. Are you in favor of legalizing marijuana?
e. Would you favor legalizing prostitution?
f. Do you approve of abortions on demand when the life of the mother is not in danger?
g. Do you favor laws that would increase homosexual rights?
h. Would you vote to prevent known homosexuals to teach in schools?
i. Do you favor capital punishment for capital offenses?
j. Do you favor the right of parents to send their children to private schools?
k. Do you favor voluntary prayer in the public schools?
l. Do you favor removal of the tax-exempt status of churches?
m. Do you favor removal of the tax-exempt status of church-related schools?
n. Do you believe that government should remove children from their parents' home except in cases of physical abuse?

o. Do you favor sex education, contraceptives, or abortions for minors without parental consent?
p. Except in wartime or dire emergency, would you vote for government
   spending that exceeds revenue?
q. Do you favor a reduction in taxes to allow families more spendable income?
r. Do you favor a reduction in government?
s. Do you favor passage of the Equal Rights Amendment?
t. Do you favor busing schoolchildren out of their neighborhood to achieve
   racial integration?
u. Do you favor more federal involvement in education?

The answers to these questions would be evaluated in the light of scriptural principles.

If you were to ask the average Christian who his congressmen and senators are, there is a good possibility that he could not tell you. Some congressmen have gone so far as to brag that their constituents back home have no idea what their real voting record is. In order to affect our nation's moral future we must become informed about the issue. Dwight Eisenhower once stated: "Our American heritage is threatened as much by our own indifference as it is by the most unscrupulous office seeker or by the most sinister foreign threat. The destiny of this republic is in the hands of its voters."

3. MOBILIZATION

The history of the church includes the history of *Christian involvement in social issues*. The preaching of John Wesley and George Whitefield led to great revival movements in England and America. The great awakening in colonial America prepared the way for the proper application of freedom stemming from the Revolutionary War. In England, William Wilberforce crusaded against slavery in the British Empire, while Robert Raikes established the Sunday school movement to give children religious training and elementary training in reading and writing. In the meantime, Lord Shaftesbury lobbied for child-labor laws and protection of the insane. At the same time, John Howard, influenced by the Wesleyan revival, devoted his life and fortune to prison reform in England. William Booth, a Methodist minister, organized the Salvation Army to carry out open-air evangelism and social work. In 1844, George Williams founded the YMCA, to meet the needs of young men in the cities of England and America. Evangelist Dwight L. Moody raised thousands of dollars for the support of the YMCA and other youth movements. During the same period of time the great missionary movement exploded worldwide. William Carey, a Baptist, went to India not only to evangelize but also to organize the people on a self-supporting industrial level. David Livingstone, the great Congregationalist missionary to Africa, not only proclaimed the Gospel but also openly opposed the Arabian slave trade and exploitation of the African natives. Robert Morrison translated the Bible into Chinese and established vocational industrial training schools to help the people. In America, out-standing evangelical preachers such as Charles G. Finney, Albert Barnes, and Lyman Beecher called on Christians to feed the poor, educate the unlearned, re-form the prisons, humanize treatment for the mentally ill, establish orphanages, and abolish slavery. Led by the work of Jerry McCalley, there were eventually seventy-six rescue missions opened in New York City alone in the nineteenth century.

The turning point in Christian involvement in social action seems to have been the repeal of prohibition in 1933. A wide variety of Christians and moral Americans were united in the crusade against alcohol for nearly twenty years. Led by the preaching of evangelist Billy Sunday, prohibition finally became law in 1919. Its eventual repeal caused many Christians to conclude that we have no business trying to legislate Christian morality on a non-Christian society. The Depression and World War II followed shortly thereafter, and Christian concern about social issues hit rock bottom during the fifties and sixties. We have tended to develop the attitude that our only obligation is to preach the gospel and pre-pare men for heaven. We have forgotten that we are still our brother's keeper and that the same spiritual truths that prepare us to live in eternity are also essential in preparing us to live on this earth. We dare not advocate our responsibility to the society of which we are so very much a vital part. If we as moral Americans do not speak up on these essential moral issues, who then will? As Christians we need to exert our influence not only in the church but also in our business life, home life, and social and community life as well.

Since government has the power to control various areas and activities of our lives, it is vital that we as concerned Americans understand the importance of our involvement in the political process. Everett Hale, author of *The Man Without a Country*, once said: "I'm only one—but I am one. I cannot do everything—but I can do something. What I can do, I should do, and what I should do, by the grace of God, I will do." In order to make your influence felt, the first thing you must do is to know who to contact in positions of authority. Elected officials depend upon the voice of the people, and elected officials are willing to listen to those groups who will speak out on the issues. It is important for you to know who your elected officials are: your senators, congressmen, governor, state attorney general, state senator, state representative, county officials, etc. One of your important obligations is to write or call your elected officials and express your opinions on moral issues and legislation. In order to support good candidates you need to become familiar with their campaign issues. To do this it would be well to attend your political party's precinct and committee meetings. Don't be afraid to go, and don't be afraid to speak out. At these meetings people are selected as delegates for county and state meetings. In most states the county and state meetings will adopt a party platform. In some states they will elect delegates to the national conventions, which will eventually select the party candidates for President and Vice President.

Another area of involvement is to join with other concerned citizens in your region to promote godly morality. Recently in Virginia, profamily citizens united and showed up in force at the Virginia Conference on Families. Because of this they carried the day, for their view on the family rooted firmly in the tradition of the Bible. They were able to gain a majority representation on the Virginia committee. Not only is it important to vote, but it is important to encourage others to do so as well. Never underestimate the power of your vote in a given election. In 1948 Lyndon Johnson was elected to the U. S. Senate from Texas by less than one hundred votes. Edmund Burke once said: "All that is necessary for the triumph of evil is that good men do nothing."

America was born in her churches, and she must be reborn there as well. The time has come for pastors and church leaders to clearly and boldly proclaim the Gospel of regeneration in Christ Jesus. We need a return to God and to the Bible as never before in the history of America. Undoubtedly we are at the edge of eternity. Some are already referring to us as "post-Christian America." We have stretched the rubber band of morality too far already. A few more stretches and it will undoubtedly snap forever. When that happens we will become like all the other nations preceding us who've fallen under the judgment of God. I love America not because of her pride, her wealth, or her prestige; I love America because she, above all the nations of the world, has honored the principles of the Bible. America has been great because she has been good. We have been the breadbasket of the world, we have fed our enemies and canceled their national debts against us while maintaining an exorbitant debt of our own. We have bound up the wounds of a dying and hurting world. We have rushed to nearly every international disaster in the twentieth century to provide comfort and financial aid. In spite of all of this, we have been cursed and belittled by our friends and foes alike. All too often we have been looked upon as "ugly Americans." Instead of closing our hearts to the needs of the world, we have opened our doors to its peoples. Instead of only exporting the products of our commercial expertise, we have imported the goods of nearly every country in the world. In many ways we have been our brother's keeper. But good deeds alone will not save a nation, nor an individual.

Salvation is of God. Regeneration is the theological term for the new birth. Jesus said to Nicodemus nearly two thousand years ago: "Except a man be born again, he shall not see the kingdom of Heaven." (Jn. 3:5) The Apostle Paul stated: "For whosoever shall call upon the name of the Lord shall be saved." (Rm. 10:13) Regeneration is not based upon moral goodness alone. If our morality could make us acceptable in the sight of God, we could literally work our way to heaven and brag about ourselves. Christians are concerned about moral issues not because they want to brag about themselves but because they have experienced the reality of the life-changing power of God. The Bible clearly states: "For by grace are ye saved through faith; and that not of yourselves; it is the gift of God, not of works, lest any man should boast." (Ep. 2:8–9) Salvation is a gift from God. It is a gift that you need to receive personally by faith. Romans 6:23 says, "For the wages of sin is death, but the gift of God is eternal life through Jesus Christ our Lord." If you have never received Christ as your personal Savior, I would urge you to do so. Acknowledge your sin, accept His forgiveness and the gift of life that He offers.

I am convinced that we need a spiritual and moral revival in America if America is to survive the twentieth century. The time for action is now; we dare not wait for someone else to take up the banner of righteousness in our generation. We have already waited too long. The great American Senator Jesse Helms said: "Each of us has a part to play in bringing about the great spiritual awakening that must come upon this land before we are brought to our knees by the chastisements of God. Each of us must place our hope and reliance in God, and in that hope and reliance turn our energies to restoring a government and society that serves us as sons of God. . . . Faith and courage are not dispensed by civil governments or revolutions, but by the spirit of God. Americans as a people must once again rise up and reclaim their nation from the slothful, divisive, prodigal, and treacherous individuals who have bartered away our freedoms for a mess of pottage . . . we must return to the author of liberty to enjoy again what once we had so abundantly."

We should thank God every day that we were born in a free land. We must pray that God will help us to assume the obligation to guarantee that freedom to the generations that will follow. In a time when freedom is becoming less and less a privilege to the peoples of the world, we cannot value our American citizenship too highly. No one in the world knows the freedoms that Americans know. Those who so often criticize our country with their anti-American, antimilitary, anticapitalist attitudes must forever realize that the very freedom that allows them to do this is the freedom they are trying to destroy. Let them take anti-Soviet slogans and march up and down the streets of Moscow; they would swiftly disappear.

Right living must be re-established as an American way of life. We as American citizens must recommit ourselves to the faith of our fathers and to the premises and moral foundations upon which this country was established. Now is the time to begin calling America back to God, back to the Bible, back to morality! We must be willing to live by the moral convictions that we claim to believe. There is no way that we will ever be willing to die for something for which we are not willing to live. The authority of Bible morality must once again be recognized as the legitimate guiding principle of our nation. Our love for our fellow man must ever be grounded in the truth and never be allowed to blind us from the truth that is the basis of our love for our fellow man.

As a pastor and as a parent I am calling my fellow American citizens to unite in a moral crusade for righteousness in our generation. It is time to call America back to her moral roots. It is time to call America back to God. We need a revival of righteous living based on a proper confession of sin and repentance of heart if we are to remain the land of the free and the home of the brave! I am convinced that God is calling millions of Americans in the so-often silent majority to join in the moral-majority crusade to turn America around in our lifetime. Won't you begin now to pray with us for revival in America? Let us unite our hearts and lives together for the cause of a new America . . . a moral America in which righteousness will exalt this nation. Only as we do this can we exempt ourselves from one day having to look our children in the eyes and answer this searching question: "Mom and Dad, where were you the day freedom died in America?"

The choice is now ours.

Index

Index

Index

Ward, Nathaniel, 30
Washington, Booker T., 298, 309
Weber, Max, 335, 336, 339, 341, 343–44
Wheaton, Samuel, 131
Whitefield, George, 89, 90, 93–94, 111–15, 117, 118, 120–23, 131, 132, 135, 345, 508
Wigglesworth, Michael, 29
Williams, Roger, 30, 39, 63
Winrod, Gerald, 412, 417, 419–20

Winthrop, John, 29, 31–33, 35–40, 193, 239
Witchcraft, 239, 240, 247–51,
    Z. Budapest, 241, 248, 249; *see also* Occultism
Woman's Rights Movement, 166; *see also* Feminism
Wycliffe, John, 61

Yale University, 115, 131, 205
Young, Brigham, 179; *see also* Mormons